ANARCHIST VOICES

WITHDRAWN

ANARCHIST VOICES

· An Oral History of Anarchism in America ·

PAUL AVRICH

PRINCETON UNIVERSITY PRESS · PRINCETON, NEW JERSEY

Library of Congress Cataloging-in-Publication Data

Avrich, Paul.
Anarchist voices: an oral history of anarchism
in America / Paul Avrich.
p.   cm.
Includes bibliographical references and index.
ISBN 0-691-03412-5 (cloth: acid-free paper)
1. Anarchism—United States—History.
2. Anarchists—United States—Interviews. I. Title.
HX843.A98   1994 1995
320.5′7′0973—dc20   94-16620 CIP

This book has been composed in Electra

Printed in the United States of America

10   8   6   4   2   1   3   5   7   9

Contents

PART FOUR: SCHOOLS AND COLONIES

PART FIVE: *ETHNIC ANARCHISTS*

PART SIX: *THE 1920s AND AFTER*

List of Illustrations

Preface and Acknowledgments

OVER A PERIOD of nearly thirty years, between 1963 and 1991, I conducted more than two hundred interviews with anarchists throughout the United States. The majority of the interviewees were of European birth (Jews and Italians being the most heavily represented) and had been active during the heyday of their movement between the 1880s and 1930s. Nearly all of the interviews were conducted in English, although a few were in other languages, or in a mixture of languages, since the interviewees, as they spoke, sometimes lapsed into their native tongues. The interviews varied greatly both in quality and length; some, indeed, were scarcely more than fragments and have not been included in this volume. Nor have I included informal conversations (which numbered in the thousands) or, with two exceptions (Mark Schmidt and Esther Walters), interviews conducted on the telephone. Regrettably, I came too late to interview the major figures of the movement (Emma Goldman, Benjamin Tucker, and the like), all of whom had long since passed away. I made no effort, moreover, to interview anarchists outside the United States, although I encountered more than a few during trips abroad and benefited from what they told me.

In all, there are 180 interviews in this collection, 5 of which have been previously published (details are provided in the notes). All schools of anarchism are represented, not excluding the terrorists, and there is a wide range of ethnic groups: Spanish, French, German, Russian, and Chinese, in addition to Italians and Jews. A number of individuals were interviewed more than once, some as many as four or five times. In such cases, I have combined the interviews into a single account for the sake of coherence and readability.

It should be noted that not all the interviewees were themselves anarchists. Leon Shapiro, for example, was a Menshevik, but he had been acquainted with a number of Russian anarchists (including Nestor Makhno and Alexander Schapiro), about whom he had interesting recollections. Similarly, Clara Halpern belonged to the Socialist Revolutionary Maximalists, an ultramilitant group that in some ways resembled the anarchists yet shrank from embracing the abolition of government. The rest include an attorney of Emma Goldman (Arthur Leonard Ross), two of her secretaries (Millie Grobstein and Pauline Turkel), two witnesses in the Sacco-Vanzetti case (Beltrando Brini and Lefevre Brini Wager), and a large number of relatives, friends, and associates of anarchists, among them sons of Johann Most, Rudolf Rocker, and Joseph Labadie, daughters of Peter Kropotkin, Benjamin Tucker, and Gustav Landauer, and a grandson of Nicola Sacco.

Of all the major movements of social reform, anarchism has been subject to the grossest misunderstandings of its nature and objectives. No group has been more maligned and misrepresented by the authorities or more feared and detested by the public. But who in fact were the anarchists? What kind of people were they? Why did they become anarchists? In what activities did they engage? How did they cope with popular abuse and official persecution and harassment? What did they want and what did they achieve? Did their views on anarchism change over the years? Did they have any regrets or disappointments?

Such are the questions addressed by the interviewees, and their observations and recollections shed interesting light on a range of subjects, from immigration, revolutionary agitation, and political repression to economics, education, and the arts. They differ, as will be seen, on many points, particularly on the questions of property, organization, and violence. Communists and individualists, revolutionaries and pacifists, they encompass a fascinating and sometimes contradictory variety of temperaments and beliefs. For all their differences, however, they are united in their rejection of the state, their opposition to coercion and exploitation, their hatred of injustice and tyranny, and their faith that people will live in harmony once the restraints imposed by government have been removed.

In bringing together these interviews, my object has been to make them available to students and scholars in an accurate and readable form. Editing has been kept to a minimum. All words are those of the interviewees. Nothing has been added or invented, though some repetition has been eliminated and the word order occasionally rearranged for the sake of clarity. To enhance the usefulness of the text, I have added headnotes, explanatory notes, and illustrations, as well as a detailed index that will allow readers with an interest in a particular individual, theme, or event—Emma Goldman, anarchist schools, the Sacco-Vanzetti case, for example—easy access to relevant material. In addition, a bibliography and a list of periodicals have been appended to supplement the index and notes.

In many ways I consider this work the most important that I have ever undertaken. For the interviews, taken together, comprise a unique oral history of the anarchist movement, preserving for posterity the story of the anarchists as they themselves have recalled it. As such, they add a human dimension often lacking in scholarly monographs, not to mention the accounts of journalists, policemen, and officials, and of other, for the most part hostile, observers.

This volume, I believe, will provide an invaluable source for all future students of anarchism. No one has previously embarked on a comparable venture, nor could such be undertaken in the years ahead. Most of the interviewees had already reached an advanced age when I interviewed them (they were born typically in the 1880s and 1890s; the oldest, Lena Shlakman, was born in 1872) and have since passed away. Oral history, however, is not a substitute for conventional history, which is based on documentary evidence. At best it constitutes a supplement, adding data and impressions recalled long after the event. Memory is often defective, and errors are bound to occur. Wherever possible, then, the testimony in this book should be checked against the available printed and manuscript sources, which are indicated in the notes and bibliography.

Apart from the interviewees and their families, I am indebted to a number of friends and colleagues who assisted in the preparation of this volume. I am particularly obliged to Richard Drinnon, biographer of Emma Goldman and Professor Emeritus at Bucknell University, and to Professor George Esenwein of the University of Florida, America's leading authority on Spanish anarchism, for reading the entire manuscript and offering invaluable suggestions. My thanks are also due to Bill Laznovsky of Princeton University Press for his expert editorial assistance. Others who have aided me in important ways are Professor Pei-yi Wu of Queens College, Professor Richard Polenberg of Cornell University, Professor Abraham Ascher of the Graduate School of the City University of New York, and Professor Nunzio Pernicone of Drexel University, the foremost American authority on Italian anarchism. I am exceedingly grateful, in addition, to Queens College for granting me a Presidential Research Award for the Spring 1992 semester, which facilitated the completion of the book. The responsibility for its contents, however, remains my own.

New York City
May 1, 1993

PART ONE

Pioneers

• ORIOLE TUCKER RICHÉ •

BEATRICE FETZ • HELENA BAILIE

• LAURANCE LABADIE •

ALEXANDRA KROPOTKIN • JOHN J. MOST, JR.

• MARY SCHWAB • HENRY R. SCHNAUBELT •

MILTON W. THORPE • GRACE UMRATH

• ELMER B. ISAAK •

MARION BELL • BRIGITTE HAUSBERGER

• FERMIN ROCKER •

1. "The Anarchists of Chicago," memorial drawing by Walter Crane
(*Liberty*, London, November 1894)

INTRODUCTION

By the early 1960s, when I began to interview the anarchists, the classical phase of the movement, bounded by the Paris Commune of 1871 and the Spanish Revolution of the 1930s, had long since drawn to a close. Though soon to experience a revival, anarchism seemed a moribund phenomenon, its adherents dwindling and ineffectual, its literature rapidly drying up. Without exception, moreover, its major spokesmen had passed from the scene. Among the most notable, Peter Kropotkin had died in 1921, Errico Malatesta in 1932, Benjamin Tucker in 1939, and Emma Goldman in 1940. Rudolf Rocker, the last of the great anarchists, passed away in 1958, and there was no one of comparable stature to take his place.

Rocker's son, however, was still alive, and he readily consented to be interviewed. Also alive were the daughters of Tucker, Kropotkin, and Gustav Landauer, as well as the elder son of Johann Most, all of whom likewise submitted to interviews and provided valuable recollections. With the exception of Fermin Rocker, now in his eighty-sixth year, these offspring of pioneer anarchists have since expired, as have the son of Joseph A. Labadie (1850–1933) and the daughter of Thomas H. Bell (1867–1942), whose interviews appear below along with the rest. Beyond this there are interviews with several other individuals who could recall the earlier days of the movement: children of associates of Tucker, who assisted him on his magazine *Liberty*; grandchildren of Abe and Mary Isaak, publishers of the journal *Free Society*; and relatives of the Chicago anarchists implicated in the Haymarket bombing of the 1880s, the major anarchist episode of the period.

All in all a wide range of views is represented: individualist anarchism, mutualist anarchism, collectivist anarchism, communist anarchism, and syndicalist anarchism, to mention only the most conspicuous. Johann Most, for one, adhered to the collectivist persuasion associated with the Russian anarchist Bakunin, according to which private property must be abolished and individuals rewarded in proportion to their labor. In the spirit of Bakunin, moreover, Most disdained conciliatory tactics as well as piecemeal measures of reform. Achieving limited improvements, as he saw it, would blunt the revolutionary ardor of the workers, weaken their will to resist, and delay the final destruction of capitalism. Again and again he underscored the futility of compromise and the need for popular insurrection to overthrow the established order. An ardent proponent of direct action, he argued that violent revolution was the only means of resolving the social question. He repeatedly urged the workers to arm themselves in order to exterminate the "reptile brood," the "race of parasites," as he branded all capitalists and rulers; and in his handbook *Revolutionary War*

Science, published a year before the Haymarket incident, he furnished detailed instructions on the manufacture of explosives and the uses to which they could be put in the war of the poor against the rich.

Most's flaming rhetoric roused his followers to a high pitch of enthusiasm. Not only was he one of the greatest radical orators of his time, but his newspaper, the *Freiheit*, which he edited for twenty-seven years, acquired a place in the front ranks of German revolutionary literature; and decades after his death in 1906 his powerful "Hymn of the Proletariat" continued to be sung by German-speaking workers of every radical denomination, in Europe as well as in America.

By the 1890s, however, Most was toning down his appeals to revolutionary violence, and especially to individual acts of terrorism. At the same time, he was evolving from Bakunin's collectivist anarchism to the doctrine of anarchist communism, of which Kropotkin was the leading exponent. According to Kropotkin, any system of rewards based on an individual's capacity to produce was merely another form of wage slavery as under capitalism. By drawing a distinction between what is mine and what is yours, he maintained, a collectivist economy rendered itself incompatible with the true ideals of anarchism. Collectivism, moreover, necessitated some central authority to measure individual performance and to supervise the distribution of goods accordingly, so that the collectivist order contained the seeds of inequality and domination.

Kropotkin regarded his own theory of communist anarchism as the antithesis of the wage system in all its forms. For the principle of productivity he substituted the principle of need: members of the community would be the judge of their own requirements and would take from the common storehouse whatever they deemed necessary, whether or not they contributed a share of the labor. Kropotkin's benign optimism led him to assume that once political oppression and economic exploitation had been eliminated, all, or nearly all, would work of their own free will, without any compulsion whatever, and take no more than they needed for a comfortable existence. Anarchist communism, he believed, would put an end at last to every manner of coercion and privilege and usher in a golden age of liberty, without government or property, without hunger or want, a shining era of freedom in which people would live in harmony and direct their own affairs unimpeded by any authority.

In common with Most, it might be noted, Kropotkin was active in the protests against the trial of the Haymarket anarchists. Describing the Chicago affair as "a retaliation upon prisoners taken in the virtual civil war that was going on between the two classes," he wrote to the American press objecting to the death sentences imposed on the defendants and, together with William Morris and George Bernard Shaw, addressed a mass rally in London against their impending execution. A year after the hanging he declared that "the commemoration of the Chicago martyrs has almost acquired the same importance as the commemoration of the Paris Commune." The integrity and courage of the hanged men, he said a decade later, "remain a lesson for the old, an inspiration for the young."[1] And in 1901, during a visit to the United States, he placed flowers at the tomb of the men whose cause he had championed from the time of their arrest fifteen years before.

Deeply moved by the Haymarket tragedy, Kropotkin followed the development of American anarchism with special interest. Long before he visited the United States, he was corresponding with American anarchists, reading their books and periodicals, and sending them messages of support. He was familiar with the writings of both the individualist and collectivist schools, citing Tucker as well as Most in his *Encyclopaedia Britannica* article on anarchism. For his own part, Kropotkin exerted an increasing influence on American anarchists, as well as on socialists and other reformers. Starting in the 1880s, his articles appeared in all the leading anarchist journals, including Tucker's *Liberty*, Most's *Freiheit*, Abe Isaak's *Free Society*, and Emma Goldman's *Mother Earth*. By the turn of the century, the anarchist movement in America had become predominantly anarchist communist in orientation, owing to Kropotkin's influence. "He was a prominent figure in the realm of learning," wrote Goldman, "recognized as such by the foremost men of the world. But to us he meant much more than that. We saw in him the father of modern anarchism, its revolutionary spokesman and brilliant exponent of its relation to science, philosophy, and progressive thought."[2]

Not everyone accepted this appraisal. Rejecting both Most's collectivism and Kropotkin's communism, the individualist anarchists, among whom Tucker was the foremost representative, exalted personal freedom over any cooperative arrangements and distrusted all organizations, economic or otherwise, that might harden into bureaucratic form. The individualists, moreover, opposed the revolutionary methods preached alike by Most and Kropotkin, favoring education and propaganda to achieve their libertarian goals. Influenced by the German philosopher Max Stirner, whose book *The Ego and His Own* was their testament, they resisted the claims of collective entities and demanded the total liberation of the human personality from the fetters of organized society.

For Most and his incendiary rhetoric the individualists had particular disdain. Indeed Tucker, for whom Most's collectivism "logically leads to and rests upon authority," went so far as to excommunicate him from the movement, repudiating "man, principles, and methods," and denying him "even the name of Anarchist."[3] Towards Kropotkin Tucker's attitude was more charitable. In spite of their philosophical differences, he counted the Russian prince "among the most prominent anarchists in Europe" and translated some of his essays for *Liberty*. He also had praise for Bakunin, placing him in "the very front ranks of the world's great social saviors."[4] In 1885 he translated *God and the State*, Bakunin's most celebrated work. The book sold well, becoming the most widely read and frequently quoted of all Bakunin's writings, a distinction which, more than a century later, it still enjoys.

Tucker himself, by contrast, had no great book smoldering inside him. Nor, in contrast to Most or Emma Goldman, did he acquire a reputation as a speaker, being reserved and ill-at-ease before the podium. He was, however, an accomplished translator—of Proudhon as of Bakunin and Kropotkin. More than that, he was a first-rate editor and writer, one of the finest journalists American radicalism has produced. Of *Liberty* he had particular cause to be proud. It was meticulously designed and edited, with a brilliant galaxy of contributors, not least among them Tucker himself. Its debut in 1881 was a milestone in the history of the anarchist movement, and it won an audience wherever English was read. As a publisher, moreover, Tucker issued a steady stream of books and pamphlets on anarchism and related subjects over a period of nearly thirty years.

By the turn of the century, however, the heyday of individualist anarchism had passed. And in 1908, his storehouse of books and papers destroyed in a fire, Tucker departed for Europe, never to return. From that moment, Tucker abandoned his role as a purveyor of anarchist ideas. Although he retained the anarchist label, he had come to believe that free banking and similar measures, even if inaugurated, were no longer adequate to break the monopoly of capitalism or weaken the authority of the state.

With the passage of time, as his daughter relates, Tucker grew increasingly pessimistic. The "monster, Mechanism," he wrote in 1930, "is devouring mankind."[5] By then he had outlived his reputation as a social thinker. His retirement, in Monaco, was virtually complete. Few people knew who he was or were acquainted with his work, and his death in 1939 passed almost unnoticed. He had lived to be eighty-five, and the global war that he had feared and predicted was looming on the horizon.

Apart from the collectivists, communists, and individualists, three additional groups deserve notice: the mutualist anarchists, who, influenced principally by the French anarchist Proudhon, hovered between individualism and collectivism; the anarcho-syndicalists, who, emerging at the turn of the century, pinned their hopes on the labor movement and called for workers' self-management of the factories; and the pacifist anarchists (including Tolstoyans), who, while differing among themselves on economic issues, spurned all revolutionary activity as a breeder of hatred and violence.

Whatever their disagreements, these groups, along with the others, shared a common determination to make a clean sweep of entrenched institutions and to inaugurate a stateless society based on the voluntary cooperation of free individuals. All, moreover, foresaw the consequences of the Marxian brand of socialism and offered a continual and fundamental criticism of all forms of centralized authority. They warned that political power is intrinsically evil, that it corrupts all who wield it, that government of any kind stifles the creative spirit of the people and robs them of their freedom.

A final group, which bears mention if only because it is so often neglected, consisted of eclectic anarchists who drew on all schools of economic thought and refused to attach a prefix—individualist, collectivist, communist, syndicalist—to their anarchist label. Troubled by the bitter debates among their comrades, they called for greater tolerance within the movement, for an "anarchism without adjectives," as some of them termed it. The rejection of all dogma, they insisted, was the very essence of the libertarian spirit. They held, as Rudolf Rocker put it, that individualism, communism, and the rest represented "only different methods of economy, the practical possibilities of which have yet to be tested, and that the first objective is to secure the personal and social freedom of men no matter upon which economic basis this is to be accomplished."[6]

Rocker himself adhered to this position, as did his compatriot Gustav Landauer, whose daughter (Brigitte Hausberger) is interviewed in this section. Both men preached an undogmatic brand of anarchism that encompassed a range of theoretical elements. Landauer, whom Rocker called a "spiritual giant,"[7] was at once an individualist and a socialist, a romantic and a mystic, a militant and an advocate of passive resistance. He was also the most influential German anarchist of the twentieth century, with the possible exception of Rocker himself. Journalist and philosopher, novelist and critic, Landauer was a versatile figure. He was in close touch with writers of the Expressionist movement, above all Ernst Toller and Georg Kaiser, and he played an active part in the avant-garde theater, being affiliated with the Neue Freie Volksbühne from 1892 until his murder by right-wing soldiers in 1919. Beyond all this, he made his mark as a translator of both anarchist and non-anarchist writers, including Kropotkin, Proudhon, and Walt Whitman, of whom he was a lifelong admirer. His tragic and brutal death, poignantly recalled by his daughter, made him the principal anarchist martyr of the Bavarian revolution.

With Landauer's removal from the scene, Rocker took his place as the foremost German anarchist. Friend of Kropotkin and biographer of Most, he edited a succession of periodicals, published a stream of books and pamphlets on diverse subjects, and emerged as one of the greatest orators of the movement, alongside Most and Emma Goldman. Rocker, although a gentile, became the apostle of anarchism to the Jewish workers of London in the years before the First World War. The story of how he came to Whitechapel and became a Yiddish writer and editor is one of the most fascinating of that period. A German by birth and upbringing, he had not so much as met a Jew until he was eighteen. Yet he settled among the Jews, took one of their daughters for his wife, learned how to speak, read, and write their language, and shared in their poverty and suffering. Alexander Berkman thought him "one of our very finest men and comrades." His companion, Milly Witkop, was also "a beautiful character," said Berkman,[8] and their deep and abiding affection was one of the great love stories in the history of the anarchist movement.

Rocker spent the war years in a British prison camp, having been interned as an "enemy alien," despite his opposition to German authoritarianism and regimentation. After the war he returned to his native country, accompanied by his wife and son. There he became the driving force of the German anarchist movement and the principal founder of the International Working Men's Association, the so-called Berlin or Anarcho-Syndicalist International, established in 1922. When Hitler came to power in 1933, Rocker and his wife had to flee for their lives (Fermin had meanwhile left for the United States). Escaping to Switzerland on the last train out of Berlin, they became part of the great wave of refugees from Nazi oppression that enriched American life over the next generation.

Rocker spent the last twenty-five years of his life in the United States, speaking and writing for libertarian causes. Arriving in New York in September 1933, he undertook a number of coast-to-coast lecture tours, contributed countless articles to anarchist publications in several languages, and produced a series of books that made a permanent contribution to anarchist philosophy and history. His *Nationalism and Culture*, a powerful indictment of the state, was hailed by Albert Einstein as an "extraordinarily original and illuminating work," while Bertrand Russell called it "an important contribution to political philosophy, both on account of its penetrating and widely informative analysis of famous writers, and on account of the brilliant criticism of state-worship, the prevailing and most noxious superstition of our time."[9]

In 1937 Rocker settled at the Mohegan Colony in Westchester County, New York, renting a cottage from the anarchist bookseller Leon Kramer. He was later given his own house by the anarchists of the colony, to whom he was a venerable figure (see Part Four). While he took little part in the social or administrative life of the community, he was its dominant intellectual leader for the next twenty years. His death in 1958 marked not only the passing of the last great anarchist with an international reputation. It also sounded the death knell of the Mohegan experiment, the last of the major anarchist colonies in the United States.

• ORIOLE TUCKER RICHÉ •

Ossining, New York, January 21, 1973[10]

Oriole Riché, born in 1908, was the only child of the individualist anarchist Benjamin R. Tucker (1854–1939) and his wife and fellow anarchist Pearl Johnson. Oriole, the wife of Jean Riché, a French-born chef, taught French at the Dobbs Ferry Middle School and lived on the site of Stillwater, a School of Living colony established in 1939 by Ralph Borsodi,[11] similar to the one at Suffern, New York, in which Laurance Labadie (q.v.) lived. Across the road from Oriole lived Beatrice Fetz (q.v.), the daughter of Tucker's associates George and Emma Schumm, while at the bottom of the hill stood the house of Margaret Noyes Goldsmith, a granddaughter of John Humphrey Noyes, the celebrated founder of the Oneida community. Oriole was a fine-looking woman with a youthful appearance and vivid memory, particularly where her parents were concerned. I looked forward to coming back at a later date in order to talk to her again about her father. But she died suddenly in June 1974, at the age of sixty-five, so that our conversation was never completed.

I WAS BORN in New York City on November 9, 1908, delivered by Dr. E. B. Foote,[12] Father's friend and fellow libertarian. I was named after J. William Lloyd's[13] daughter, Oriole Lloyd. My parents had been hoping I would arrive on November 11, the anniversary of the Haymarket executions. After the disastrous fire in January 1908,[14] Father had decided to move to France. He didn't want to start all over again. Besides, he loved France and always said he wanted to die in France.

He and Mother went to Paris in the summer of 1908 and rented a house in the suburb of Le Vésinet, near Saint-Germain. They came back to the U.S. to have me born here (Mother was expecting a difficult birth and wanted the family on hand). But by Christmas I was in France, aged six weeks old. And there I stayed. When I was three and a half, Mother and I did come to the States for a few months to see her family. After the war, though, we never came back as a family. In 1936, I came by myself for three months. America had been as far away to me as the moon. It was a fairyland to me: Mother kept talking about it, tried to keep it alive, but to me all the names I heard seemed like people stepping out of mythology.

Mother—Pearl Johnson—was the daughter of a New England couple, Horace Johnson and Florence Hull, one of four daughters of Moses Hull, a minister of advanced views who became a well-known spiritualist. Pearl went to the Sunrise Club in New York and knew Bea Schumm. It was George Schumm[15] who suggested her to Father to work in his bookshop a few years before I was born. One of Mother's sisters was Dr. Bertha Johnson. Fred Schulder,[16] who worked as a salesman for *Liberty*, was Aunty Bertha's boyfriend. His son with Adeline Champney, Horace Champney, was the Quaker who sailed a boat to Vietnam a few years ago to protest against the war.

When Father's mother died, she left him a nice sum of money. He put it in an annuity and had a comfortable income thereafter of $1,650 a year. In New York he lived pleasantly, though not lavishly, in a two-room hotel suite. Another reason he decided to go to France was that he and the family could live rather well there on his income. My parents, incidentally, were never legally married. Yet they were the most monogamistic couple I ever saw, absolutely devoted to each other until the end. Oddly enough, they believed in having separate rooms and, if one had the means, even separate houses, coming together when you wanted to. They couldn't afford that though! I always liked the idea of my husband coming home at night and not having to plan and make a date to see him!

We lived in Le Vésinet the first six years, traveling a good deal. The winter following the outbreak of the war we stayed with Henry Bool in England,[17] and when we returned to France we moved into an apartment in Nice. We stayed there eleven years. But taxes were rising sharply in France, so we moved to Monaco, where we rented a nice house for thirteen years, and where Father died in 1939.

During the war Father was anti-German from the start. The German government, German militarism, German regimentation—he hated them with a passion. And he loved France. France was the only thing that counted—French food, French wine, French newspapers and books. He wanted to be buried there. He never came back to the United States, and never wished to. He didn't speak French very well, but he read it easily. He had a great admiration for Clemenceau,[18] to whom he bore a close physical resemblance.

After the war, Father was afraid of trouble. He was afraid, as a foreigner, of being disturbed. He wanted to be left alone. There was no contact with Emma Goldman or Alexander Berkman, who were living in southern France. Father disliked both of them. Mother had been friends with Emma Goldman in New York, and once she saw them on the street in Nice but decided not to approach them. John Henry Mackay[19] used to come down, and George Bernard Shaw came once for afternoon tea.[20] When I was eighteen I gave French lessons to Henry Cohen's[21] sister. Pryns Hopkins,[22] who was living in Nice, came over to visit, and some nephew of Tolstoy's, but otherwise not many of Father's old friends.

In France the whole family lived an anarchistic life. When I asked a question—like how in the world would we get along without police—Father would say look it up on page so and so of *Instead of a Book*.[23] Mother, by contrast, would explain carefully. She was a born teacher and psychologist. But Father was a born non-teacher. He couldn't speak to a young person. Mother always gave me sensible answers. He had it all worked out—it was very discouraging to talk with him—he always had irrefutable arguments, he always seemed right. And that turned me off. He made no allowance for human feelings and frailties. Just hew to the line and let the chips fall where they may. Mother, too, said he had no psychological understanding of people. He had great affection and respect for me, but we couldn't discuss anything.

Father, incidentally, believed in contracts. We had written contractual arrangements around the house. When I was eighteen, he wrote a whole contract about my paying a share of what I made from giving piano lessons. That might seem cold and calculating, yet it made everything clear and simple. He never would have entered my room without knocking, even when I was a little girl. He was old-fashioned in many ways. He rode in a car two or three times in Paris. But he was scared stiff of them. He thought they were dangerous. As a result, I disliked them too and didn't go in them for a long time.

Sometime during the 1920s Victor Yarros wrote an article on anarchism, virtually repudiating his whole connection with it, his whole past.[24] This made Father furious. He wrote to him, and there was a bitter controversy. Around that same time, the Sacco-Vanzetti affair took place. That was the first blow to my good feeling about America. Father wrote a letter to an American paper blasting the travesty of justice that had taken place.

The Spanish Civil War came during the last years of his life. He was certainly against Franco, but he didn't seem to get excited about it. He worried a great deal about the approaching world war, though. He thought we should escape to Denmark, where it was safe! We were scared stiff by Munich. Things got worse and worse. We didn't know what to do—to uproot him and come to America and go to live at Aunty Bertha's? It was really a blessing that he died when he did, you know. The very next day we packed up his books and papers.

We came to New York on October 5, 1939. Mother went to Aunty Bertha's farm, and I stayed with George Macdonald,[25] a miserable isolationist to the nth degree!

In 1940 we took an apartment on Amsterdam Avenue. Mother died there in 1948. I had married meanwhile. Mother died when my first daughter was six or eight months old. We came up here in 1948. My older daughter Marianne has a brain like her grandfather, yet with such sympathy and understanding for everyone. Now she is twenty-five and getting an M.A. in social work in Baltimore. Her sister, twenty-three, is studying dance in Toronto.

Father's attitude towards communism never changed one whit, nor about religion. He was very consistent all his life. In his last months he called in the French housekeeper. "I want her," he said, "to be witness that on my deathbed I'm not recanting. I do *not* believe in God!" I was interested, even sympathetic, in his ideas. But I was never really an anarchist. I don't think it would ever work. Neither did Father at the end. He was very pessimistic about the world and in his political outlook. But he was always optimistic about himself, always cheerful, happy; he never sat and brooded, but was content to look out at the view and at his books. He sang hymns from Sunday School—the "Rock of Ages" and that sort of thing—and couldn't keep a tune. He had a reputation as a cold person. But how he loved Mother! And he cried easily at anything noble.

• BEATRICE FETZ •

Ossining, New York, January 21, 1973

Beatrice Fetz was the daughter of George Schumm (1856–1941) and Emma Heller Schumm (1856–1940), longtime associates of Benjamin Tucker, the foremost propagator of individualist anarchism in the United States. For twenty years George Schumm was proofreader and assistant editor of Tucker's journal *Liberty*. He was also the translator of John Henry Mackay's *The Anarchists: A Picture of Civilization at the Close of the Nineteenth Century*, published by Tucker in Boston. He and his wife, moreover, did many other translations for Tucker and in 1888 brought out a German-language version of *Liberty* under the title of *Libertas*. After *Liberty* expired in 1908, Schumm worked on *The New York Post* and then as chief proofreader for *The Nation*, until his retirement in 1930. His daughter Beatrice, eighty-eight when I interviewed her, a wonderful woman with an excellent memory and sharp wit, lived across the road from Tucker's daughter Oriole (Riché, q.v.), on the site of the Stillwater Colony founded by Ralph Borsodi in 1939. She died in 1980 at the age of ninety-five.

FATHER WAS BORN of German parents in Galena, Illinois, on January 26, 1856, and died here around September 15, 1941. His father had gone to California in the gold rush but didn't get much gold. Mother was born in Sauk City, Wisconsin, on October 1, 1856, also of German parents; her father was a Forty-Eighter. She died here on March 29 or 30, 1941. Father went to work at thirteen as a printer's devil, then became a compositor. He went to San Francisco at seventeen and worked as a printer. He published a little German paper, *Der Wächter*. He met mother in Chicago. She had graduated from the University of Wisconsin, Madison, in 1879 or 1880, where she roomed with Belle Case, the future Mrs. Robert La Follette.[26] Father enrolled at Cornell around 1875, worked his way through, majored in philosophy. He became very interested in Karl Heinzen's *Pionier*.[27] One summer, while a student, he went to Boston and worked as a typesetter for the *Pionier* and became very good friends with Heinzen, whose granddaughter Rose, about my age, is still alive in Lewiston, Maine.

After Cornell, Father and Mother, who taught in Chicago, got together. They were married there and remained absolutely devoted to each other all their lives. William Salter[28] said that father knew more about Nietzsche than anyone else in the world. Father and Mother established the *Radical Review*, which lasted about two years (1884–1885). I was born in Chicago in 1884. Father went up to St. Paul, Minnesota, to teach German in public school for a while. He could recite German poetry endlessly, from memory. With the Forty-Eighters and the Freie Gemeinde he was in a liberal milieu and evolved towards anarchism.

When I was three we went to Boston, drawn by Benjamin Tucker, to work for his *Liberty*. Tucker owned two crummy little houses in the Crescent Beach section. In one of them he published *Liberty* and *Libertas*. He lived upstairs. Victor Yarros also lived there. In the other house lived Sarah Holmes,[29] and my parents and I lived upstairs. We lived there about three years, and I went to nursery school in Roxbury with Rose Heinzen. Tucker had a bellowing laugh, and we had to run away lest he laugh again. On the boat to Europe he was known as *"l'homme qui rit,"* after Victor Hugo's novel of that title. Yet he was a terribly proper person. He wouldn't be seen in his shirtsleeves for anything.

I was only a small child then, but I can remember a tremendous amount of talk about Haymarket. Father knew August Spies[30] from Chicago. He had a very beautiful voice, and when taken to the gallows sang "Annie Laurie."[31] Father went to see him in jail and he said, "We had nothing to do with the bomb." My impression is that they disliked Johann Most, but we never saw him.

Sarah Holmes was a clam. She stuck to our family. She lived in our house in a room in the attic. She and Tucker were sweethearts. She had been a telegrapher. She had met a Dr. Dyer, gone with him to Europe, had a child (Vega), and come back to Boston. She was gung-ho for women's rights and didn't do any housework. So Dyer went off with the child, and she cried her eyes out. She was an exceedingly self-centered person. She was a sponge. She did the dishes sometimes as a help to my mother. She'd dust a leg of the piano, go out and read some Browning, then dust the other.

Victor Yarros lived with a young lady named Rachelle Slobodinsky,[32] who had come over with him from Russia. I was a girl of three, with a little white dress and a sash, and she objected to my mother that she overdressed me! She studied medicine and became a specialist in venereal diseases in Chicago. She and her husband lived in Hull House with Jane Addams,[33] and she lectured there on venereal disease to groups of men whom they brought in off the street, as far as I can remember. We never saw them after they left the east. He died in California not very long ago, in the fifties perhaps.

We moved to New York in 1899 or 1900. J. William Lloyd was the father of my best friend Oriole. They lived in Westfield, New Jersey, in a house with three or four acres of land. He wrote poetry, but didn't do anything for a living, as far as I know. His wife had died. Oriole, I think, was born in Florida. His sister took care of her. Leonard Abbott[34] built a little house on Lloyd's property in Westfield. His son Morris came to my summer camp in Woodstock in the early twenties.

Max Baginski's[35] wife Millie was Father's sister. They lived in the Bronx for many years, but he spent his last years on a farm in Towanda, Pennsylvania. He considered me a conservative creep, associated with the Tucker school. He and Father never had much to talk about, though we were very good friends with Millie. In Chicago Baginski had been a member of Die Feuchte Ecke [The Damp Corner], a beer-drinking club. My father thought a great deal of Robert Reitzel,[36] one of the names of my childhood, and we always got the *Arme Teufel*. Voltairine de Cleyre,[37] whom my parents respected, was never very well because she had inherited syphilis from her father. Father and Rudolf Rocker visited each other often in Croton (we lived on Mount Airy) and Mohegan, and had wonderful long discussions.

There were no real activities among the Tuckerites after 1908, no groups, no journals worth speaking of. Friends got together and talked but there was no movement. Father was a proofreader for the *New York Post*, then worked for *The Nation* as a makeup man for the last years of his life. My brother, incidentally, bought the small house in Ossining that Bolton Hall[38] had given Emma Goldman. He sold it, and now it is part of an estate.

I was disgusted that my family hadn't told me about the English cooperative movement. We got a cooperative going in Croton, and that seemed to me a good way of coping with the economic question, yet they never said anything about it. All that talk I heard, it seemed long involved sentences that led nowhere. I never thought that all those things they were talking about could ever work.

• HELENA BAILIE •

Freeport, New York, March 26, 1973

Helena Tufts Bailie, Professor of Sociology, Emerita, at Nassau Community College on Long Island, is the daughter of William Bailie (1866–1957), the biographer of the pioneer American anarchist Josiah Warren (1798–1874)[39] and an associate of Benjamin R. Tucker, America's leading apostle of individualist anarchism. Her mother, Helen Tufts Bailie (1874–1963), was likewise an anarchist, though not as individualistic as her husband, being a friend of Emma Goldman and involved in the Modern School movement inspired by the execution of Francisco Ferrer in 1909 (see Part Four). Professor Bailie, as she notes in her interview, was named after the anarchist poet Helena Born, a close friend of her parents and frequent contributor to Tucker's journal *Liberty*.

I WAS BORN in 1914 and am a professor of sociology at Nassau Community College, with an A.B. from Radcliffe and a Ph.D. from Columbia. My parents were William Bailie, a member of Benjamin Tucker's circle in Boston, and Helen Tufts Bailie, also a member of Tucker's circle but a friend and admirer of Emma Goldman's as well. Father was born in Belfast in November 1866, the son of a carpenter. His father died in an accident when father was eleven. So he had to go to work. He was apprenticed to a basket weaver. He left Belfast at eighteen for Manchester, where he married his landlady's daughter and had children. He became interested in William Morris[40] and Edward Carpenter,[41] as well as Kropotkin. He was an avid reader, self-educated, and learned to read French and German. He was an early member of the American Economic Association. He came to Boston and established a wicker-basket firm. He met Tucker through *Liberty*. His lover, Helena Born, was close to Miriam Daniell, both from Bristol, both contributors to *Liberty*. Helena (I'm named after her) died of cancer in 1901, having turned Father over to Helen Tufts. Father was later active in the Ethical Society. He was basically a pragmatist and saw himself in the tradition of Jefferson. He opposed socialism because he thought it would lead to bureaucracy.

Mother was from an old New England family. She was a secretary in Louis Brandeis's law office in Boston and later a proofreader for Houghton Mifflin. In 1928 she was expelled from the DAR[42] chapter in Somerville, Massachusetts, for criticizing its Red-baiting activities (the chapter was named after her ancestor, Anne Adams Tufts). A typescript of her diary is in the Smith College Women's Collection.

Father had respect for his workers as men and as craftsmen. He allowed them to decide their wages, according to the individual's skills and experience. He himself had started his apprenticeship in Manchester by reading to the men and going out for beer. He kept his business records in code. There was nothing shady about that, but part of his "Mind your own business" philosophy. Father's interests were much broader than anarchism, where Tucker was more concentrated on anarchism. Mother, like Pearl Johnson Tucker, had strong sympathies for Emma Goldman and the anarchist-communists.

One of my first memories of my parents was of their soapboxing in the street for women's suffrage. Their friend, Adeline Champney, taught me to read by the Montessori method.[43] I remember playing with those cut-out alphabetical letters. Letters and words became my friends. I still love to do word puzzles. Father died in 1957 or 1958, mother around 1963. (She was born January 9, 1874.) Mother was neurotic and unhappy. When mad she wouldn't speak to us for weeks. My younger brother died at three of pneumonia he had caught from me, and she never forgave me.

• LAURANCE LABADIE •

Suffern, New York, March 22, 1975

Laurance Labadie, born on June 4, 1898, was the son of Joseph A. Labadie (1850–1933), the well-known anarchist printer and founder of the Labadie Collection of radical and labor literature at the University of Michigan, Ann Arbor. Laurance, a tool maker and automobile worker in Detroit, learned to operate the small hand press that he inherited from his father, on which he printed his own essays and poems. He also inherited his father's political views, being a great admirer of Josiah Warren, Pierre-Joseph Proudhon, Lysander Spooner, and Benjamin Tucker, of whom Jo Labadie had been a longtime associate. "To me," wrote Laurance in 1935, "Tucker has done more practical work for the advancement of liberty than any other man, living or dead, with the possible exception of Proudhon."[44]

When I visited him in 1975, Laurance lived in a little stone house in the woods, once part of a School of Living colony founded by Ralph Borsodi, a single-taxer who preached a back-to-nature philosophy. The house was filthy and had no source of heat except for a small potbellied stove. It was cluttered with books and journals, including an original set of Tucker's *Liberty*. In addition, there were letters and photographs from Tucker and other anarchists, as well as Tucker's big mahogany desk, complete with pigeon-holes and roll-top cover, given to Laurance by Tucker's daughter (Oriole Tucker Riché, q.v.). Ill and alone—a "recluse," he called himself—Laurance was a small, bearded man of seventy-six, agitated, cantankerous, and out of sorts. His mind wandered, at times he was incoherent, and he seemed to be anxious for rest. He died five months later, on August 12, 1975, one of the last of the old guard of individualist anarchism. His books and papers were deposited in the Labadie Collection by his niece, Carlotta Anderson.[45]

MY FATHER, as you know, was an anarchist in Detroit. Mother was a devout Catholic, but gentle and undomineering. Neither of them told me what to do or how to behave. They never said, "Don't do this" or "Don't do that," but let me develop in my own way. Father never even spoke to me about anarchism; he thought it was not his business to indoctrinate me in anything. Around our house they were always talking about anarchism, Father with his visitors and friends. That was their life, their overriding interest. They talked about it all the time.

Father met Peter Kropotkin in Detroit in 1901 [actually 1897], in the engineering room of the waterworks. Kropotkin and Elisée Reclus,[46] as I recall it, were building a papier-maché model of the world. Father wrote a note about Kropotkin and inserted it in a bound volume of the journal *Truth*, at a page with a drawing of Kropotkin [in the August 1884 number]: "Kropotkine was a small man, with a large head, bushy hair and whiskers, talked English very well, and his movements were quick, as tho surprised."

James Martin wrote a good book about individualist anarchism,[47] but it leaves out the human element; you don't get the feeling that these people knew each other.

I can see Mussolini being a Stirnerite: Every man for himself. Stirner didn't preach any morality. So Father was right in not taking a stand with Benjamin Tucker [in favor of Stirner's individualism] rather than with Kropotkin's communist anarchism, and that made Tucker angry.

The communistic principle is inherent in the very life process. A new-born child must be given according to his needs; the problem is to wean the child towards self-sufficiency.

What would you think if I told you that anarchism is a pipe-dream? But that's exactly what I've come to believe.

Agnes Inglis[48] was a "beautiful person," to use the current language.

John Scott[49] and Jo Ann Wheeler [Burbank, q.v.] sent me the mimeograph machine from their *Mother Earth*. I repaired it and printed my paper *Discussion* on it.

Steven T. Byington's[50] translation of the Bible, *The Bible in Living English*, was published in 1972 by the Watchtower Society in New York, who bought the rights from his estate.

• ALEXANDRA KROPOTKIN •

New York City, March 10, 1965

Alexandra Kropotkin (known as "Sasha") was born in Bromley, England, on April 15, 1887, the only child of Peter Kropotkin (1842–1921), one of the preeminent figures in the history of anarchism. She was named after Kropotkin's brother

Alexander, who had committed suicide in Siberian exile the year before her birth. When the tsarist order crumbled in 1917, Sasha accompanied her parents to their homeland, but she left after her father's death in 1921, repelled by the Bolshevik dictatorship. Settling in New York, she supported herself by writing magazine articles as well as a Russian cookbook. Though not herself an anarchist, she cherished her father's memory, lectured on him at the Libertarian Book Club (see Part Six), and kept in touch with his former comrades. She died on July 4, 1966, at the age of seventy-nine.

You're writing a history of Russian anarchism? What are you trying to prove? There's only one important thing: the Commie sons-of-bitches wanted power! And I'll tell you something else: there were a lot of funny bastards among the anarchists too!

Father refused to see only one man during all our years in England. He would see everyone, from the Emperor of Japan to the most raggedy anarchist. That man was Lenin, who was in London for a conference during the early part of the century. The Bolsheviks took away everything, including our 90,000-*desiatin* estate in Tambov province [nearly 250,000 acres]. I hate politics and power-seekers!

My name, Sasha, was unpronounceable to the English. I was called "Miss Satchel." I drank cow's milk as a baby, and the cow was also called "Satchel." I can dimly remember looking out the window from my crib and seeing the leaves on the trees. My English nurse, Nellie, a Salvation Army member, was shocked that I didn't say prayers at night. She taught me, and Father did not object. Since then I have never lost my belief in a supreme wisdom.

Father taught me to fence with sticks. He believed that women should know how to defend themselves. I knew all the curse words, and Father relied on me for such information. We had a steady stream of visitors, including strangers as well as close friends, like Cherkezov.[51] *Diadia* (Uncle) Cherkezov is what I called him, and soon all the anarchists called him *Diadia*.

Cherkezov and Father and Rocker spoke often at the Berner Street and Jubilee Street Clubs. Did you know that on his trip to America Father induced Booker T. Washington to write his memoirs?[52] Or that when I grew up they tried to marry me off to a Bakunin?

When the First World War broke out, Father was mad that he was too old to enlist in the French Army. When he returned to Russia in 1917, Kerensky[53] offered him a government post as Minister of Education. Father replied indignantly, "Don't you know that I am an anarchist?" Father later met Lenin (whom he wouldn't see in England) at the apartment of Bonch-Bruevich.[54]

Emma Goldman visited Father at Dmitrov.[55] She was a frightful person! When Father died, Lenin offered a state funeral for him, with burial in the Kremlin wall. But I refused, and he was buried, with religious hymns, with his ancestors in the Novodevichii Monastery. The funeral procession passed the Butyrki prison, where the inmates shook the bars on their windows and sang an anarchist funeral anthem.

Did you know that an anarchist named Rubinchik organized the Kronstadt rebellion?[56] I hid him out after it was over.

The Goldwater defeat[57] made me sick. I haven't yet gotten over it. Fanny Schapiro[58] is very ill, but you ought to see her. She has a box or two of her husband's papers in her closet. You ought also to see Mark Mratchny [q.v.]. He's a psychoanalyst on Gramercy Park. I'll call him up for you. You know, psychoanalysis is shit!

• JOHN J. MOST, JR. •

Boston, October 28, 1979

John J. Most, Jr., was the elder of two sons of Johann Most (1846–1906), the leading German anarchist in America. A retired dentist, he lived alone in a small apartment in a Boston senior citizens' project. I telephoned and wrote him a number of times in an effort to arrange an interview, but Dr. Most adamantly refused. In October 1979, after participating in a Sacco-Vanzetti conference at the Boston Public Library, I went to his apartment uninvited and knocked on the door. Presently Dr. Most appeared. He told me to go away; he was sick, needed rest, and had to take his pills. After a moment's hesitation I walked inside, made him a cup of tea (which he drank with his pills), and stayed and talked for three hours. I parted as a friend. Over the next few years we exchanged a number of letters, and he repeatedly invited me to visit him. He was lonely, he said, and unwell. But I, to my shame, never went. He died of pneumonia on January 30, 1987, at the age of ninety-two.

I WAS BORN in New York on May 19, 1894, the son of Johann Most and Helene (with an "e" at the end) Minkin. I had a younger brother, Lucifer, who died at the age of fifty-four. I was eleven when Father died. I loved and admired him. He was a thousand years before his time, morally, mentally, and intellectually. But I hardly ever saw him, as he lectured and traveled all over and was very busy with his paper, *Freiheit*, which he edited on Pearl Street in lower Manhattan, not far from the Brooklyn Bridge. So I hardly knew him. Yet I had great respect for him and his ideals. He was a very brave man, always being persecuted by the police. He was the most hated man in America.

We were very poor and lived in a series of basement apartments on the Lower East Side. The neighbors threw insults—and sometimes rocks—at us: "There go the filthy anarchists!" "There's that anarchist rat family!" We were abused continually. Even now, in my old age, I'm occasionally accosted; once this happened in a neighborhood supermarket, where someone called me a "dirty anarchist."

Once when Father was imprisoned on Blackwell's Island, the police came and ripped up our whole apartment. And after the Haymarket incident they tried to kidnap him and take him to Chicago to be tried along with the others as an accessory. Teddy Roosevelt, too, was always denouncing the anarchists, and especially my father. Once in St. Louis Roosevelt was publicly criticizing Father, who happened to be in the audience. Father hollered out, *"Halt Maul, Heisser Luft!"* (Shut your mouth, Hot Air!) He was arrested on the spot and kept in jail for five days until Teddy had left town.

Father felt that even his own anarchist friends had betrayed him—Justus Schwab,[59] Max Baginski, and the rest. August Lott[60] had an affair with my mother while Father was alive. Alexander Berkman was as phony as a three-dollar bill. Father thought him a hypocrite; he called Berkman and Emma Goldman "financial anarchists," who made a living off the movement. He strongly disapproved of the three of them—Berkman, Goldman, and their artist friend [Modest Stein]—living together as a threesome. "Degenerates," he called them. Emma had guts and brains but was lacking in character, he thought. He never forgave her.

Even Father's death is an example of how his comrades let him down. He was lecturing in Cincinnati and staying with Genosse [Comrade] Weiss. He had a severe cold, probably pneumonia, yet he had to go outside to use the privy, a block away from the house. Maybe Weiss didn't realize how sick he was. In his last years Father was very unhappy about his comrades and the way the world was going. But he never doubted his anarchism. That was his religion.

At home Father spoke to us in English, but with a heavy accent, though he knew English well. He didn't believe in circumcision, but I had an infection at the age of three and a half and had to be circumcised. It's still an unpleasant memory. There were so many tragedies in our life. And my parents did not get along. (They were never, of course, formally married.) Mother was too young for him; she was nineteen and he forty-six or forty-seven when they got together. She was a midwife by profession, an intelligent woman who later wrote her memoirs in the *Forverts*. Though Jewish, she came to believe in the divinity of Jesus and thought that Moses was a tyrant. She died at the age of eighty, about twenty-five years ago. In Father's last years things became worse and worse between them. He was growing old and getting impatient. They quarreled and threw pots and pans at each other when my brother and I were babies. Mother, I think, was unfair to him. She should have been more tolerant.

So you can see how sad our lives were and why I did not want to talk to you. I still share my father's ideas. My son, Johnny Most the sportscaster,[61] has no interest in anarchism whatever. But my grandchildren are interested, very much so. Your visit was an historic occasion for me. It was an honor and a pleasure to meet you. God bless you—to use a crude expression!

• MARY SCHWAB •

Walnut Creek, California, September 26, 1981

Born in Russia in 1884, Mary Schwab emigrated with her family at the age of five and sold newspapers on the streets of Philadelphia. Moving to Peoria, Illinois, where her father had found work in a brewery, Mary left school at fifteen to become a factory worker. In 1911 she moved to San Francisco and the following year married Rudolph Schwab, the son of a defendant (Michael Schwab) in the Haymarket trial. Although she never completed high school, Mary enrolled in night classes at San Francisco Law School and graduated at the top of her class. She was also an accomplished artist and, during the Depression of the 1930s, organized an art class that became the center for Bay Area artists involved in the WPA. I interviewed Mary in the company of her sister Berta Rantz, a former teacher and an impressive personality in her own right. Mary died on March 30, 1983, at the age of ninety-nine.

I WAS BORN Manya Charsky on March 10, 1884, in Labinsk in southern Russia. My father, Leon Charsky, later took his wife's name, Rantz, and was known as Louis Rantz. He was a distiller and the overseer of an estate, a very capable man who could do anything with his hands. He was born in 1831 or 1832 and had a liberal father who took him around the country when practicing his trade—a glazier, I think. Father became a socialist early in life and remained a humanitarian until he died.

We left Russia when I was five years old. I was a talkative, serious child, always asking questions, and they had to tape my mouth when we sneaked across the border to Tarnopol. We traveled steerage from Hamburg and it was awful—crowded, people relieving themselves where they slept, and so on. I went up on deck once by myself and found a bathroom—the first indoor toilet I ever saw—and got locked in. I had to shout until they came and got me out.

We lived in Philadelphia for a few years, in poverty. Father got a job in a brewery in Peoria, Illinois, supervising the yeast department, at twenty-five dollars a week, a very good salary in those days (the 1890s). When we went out there to join him he took us to a nice house he had rented. We opened the door and there was a rush of warm air—it had a furnace, the first we ever had. In Philadelphia we froze during the winter. We remained in Peoria for quite a few years. I went to school there and learned shorthand but never finished high school. Father meanwhile was kicked out of his job when someone left a valve open at the brewery and he was held responsible. He was reduced to night watchman at a salary of nine dollars a week.

I came to San Francisco in December 1911, when I was twenty-seven. In Philadelphia, where we had returned from Peoria, I had joined the Socialist Labor Party and read the *Weekly People*. I particularly admired the articles by an "Alexander Ralph" of San Francisco, and now I met him. He turned out to be Rudolph Schwab, son of the Haymarket anarchist Michael Schwab, a tall, handsome young man and fellow member of the SLP. We fell in love at first sight and were inseparable until his death. The whole family loved me, despite my being Jewish, and took me in, especially Mother Schwab—all except Rudolph's sister Ida, who was not very friendly.

Rudolph and I got married. We took part in the Portland free-speech fight of 1913 (I have a whole valise of material about it). Girls picking berries were striking for higher wages, and we went up there to help them. We made speeches, were arrested, spoke again, raised money, and gave it all to the strikers. C.E.S. Wood[62] gave us his support and encouragement. It was an independent strike, not sponsored by the SLP, and we were kicked out of the party for it.

During the strike Lucy Parsons[63] came to Portland and met us. She said to Rudolph, "You remind me of Michael and Maria." Maria, Rudolph's mother, was a lovely woman, also a member of the SLP in San Francisco and warm and friendly to me. Around 1915 she went to South America to see her brother Rudolph Schnaubelt, who had fled there after the Haymarket incident and set up a metals shop, I think, and did very well. He raised a family, which Mother Schwab met. She corresponded with them until Rudolph's death, around 1927 or 1928. He never came back to the U.S. or we would certainly have known about it. Mother Schwab told us that they did not know who threw the bomb. She talked about the rigged trial and false testimony and how her husband was unjustly convicted and how she loved him. The case left him a broken man.

My husband Rudolph was a passionate reader, and he wrote articles and poetry. When we read Frank Harris's *The Bomb*,[64] an awful book, we decided to go to Chicago to do research on the case and write our own history. But we never did. Rudolph organized a jitney union in San Francisco (Alex Horr[65] was a member), and he was on a police list of sixty men to be arrested after the Mooney-Billings affair.[66] He went to Los Angeles to organize a jitney union there. I saw him off at the station. A few days later I got word that he had fallen ill with the flu—the great epidemic had broken out. I went down immediately and found him in the hospital. He was dying. His beard and mustache had begun to grow again, since he was unable to shave. "Beard and mustache returned"—those were his last words to me, spoken with a faint smile. That was in May 1917.

I was devastated by his death. It was as though I myself had died. At loose ends, I enrolled in the San Francisco Law School in 1917, though I had no high school diploma. The professor who interviewed me was impressed by my knowledge of economics, sociology, and the like, gleaned largely from SLP schools. I was graduated in 1921 and afterwards became the first woman assistant district attorney in San Francisco's history.

• HENRY R. SCHNAUBELT •

Stockton, California, September 24, 1981

Henry R. Schnaubelt was seventy-nine years old when I interviewed him in 1981. A retired baker, he lived alone in a small house in Stockton, California. In appearance he was tall and sturdy, with clear blue eyes and florid complexion. The Schnaubelt clan—Edward, Henry, Rudolph, Ida, and Maria (wife of the Haymarket defendant Michael Schwab), as well as their mother Rebecca—played an active role in the anarchist movement in Chicago during the 1880s. Rudolph, indeed, was (falsely) accused of throwing the Haymarket bomb. Fleeing Chicago, he made his way to England and from there to Argentina, where he prospered, raised a family, and lived out his life in peace. I asked Henry (son of Edward and nephew of Rudolph) if he had any documentary materials. "Well," he replied, "I still have the old family picture book." The words were music to the historian's ears. Opening the album, he drew out a beautiful photograph of Rudolph Schnaubelt and his family in Buenos Aires, taken about ten years after the Haymarket incident. Henry Schnaubelt died on June 16, 1992, two weeks before his ninetieth birthday.

MY UNCLE RUDOLPH went to Buenos Aires and, as far as I know, he never came back to the U.S. He never got in touch with the family if he did, and that would have been very unlikely. I heard that he was raising cattle in Argentina and making a good living at it.

My Uncle Henry changed his name to Snowbelt. He became a deputy sheriff in San Francisco and was killed in a shoot-out with bandits. He's buried in San Francisco.

My father, Edward Schnaubelt, came to California after the Haymarket affair. When I was a boy, he staked a claim in Trinidad, just north of Eureka, but was done out of it by an unscrupulous partner, a land speculator who hired armed guards to kick us off the land. We were gathering up our gardening tools—my father, my brother, and I—when the guards began shooting. My brother and I ran and got away, but Father was killed. That was in 1913, when I was twelve. Father is buried in Trinidad. His gravestone reads, "Murdered by Capitalism."

• MILTON W. THORPE •

Hayward, California, September 26, 1981

Dr. Thorpe, a physician, was the husband of Johanna Altgeld Thorpe, named after Governor John P. Altgeld of Illinois. Altgeld, in 1893, pardoned her father, Michael Schwab, a defendant in the Haymarket case, who had been serving a life sentence in prison. Johanna Thorpe grew up in San Francisco, where she became a doctor and a noted humanitarian, assisting in the rescue of Jews during Hitler's persecutions. She died in 1972.

I WAS BORN in San Jose on January 6, 1901, and attended medical school at Berkeley, as did my wife Jennie. Her name was Johanna Altgeld Schwab, after the governor who had pardoned her father. We were married in 1927. Her mother, Maria Schwab, died soon afterwards, in the same year I think. She had come to San Francisco not long after her husband died. In Chicago she had remarried—a barber—and they all came out here. They were here when the earthquake and fire took place, in 1906.

My wife was a great philanthropist. She gave to the NAACP[67] and other causes. She belonged to the Socialist Labor Party in San Francisco—the whole family did—and was a member of the Communist Party for a short time. She tried to save Jews from the Nazis during the Second World War.

Rudolph Schnaubelt was Maria Schwab's older brother. He went to South America and made a lot of money down there. As far as I know, he never came back to the United States. He married down there and had children. My wife corresponded with them, but I no longer have the letters.

• GRACE UMRATH •

New York City, September 24, 1974; October 27, 1975

Grace Umrath is the granddaughter of Abe and Mary Isaak, pacifist Mennonites from Russia who became revolutionary anarchists in the United States, editing *The Firebrand* and *Free Society* and founding the Aurora Colony in California. Grace was a dancer in New York and then a librarian in California before marrying Heinz Umrath, a Dutch official at the United Nations, who died in 1987. I interviewed her in the New York apartment of her cousin Elmer Isaak (q.v.).

THE MENNONITES, as you know, originated in Holland and moved to Germany in the sixteenth or seventeenth century. In the late eighteenth century they were invited by Catherine the Great to colonize the Ukraine. They were good farmers and were granted freedom from military service in exchange for two years of forestry service. They never swore on the Bible. They spoke a low German dialect, a Plattdeutsch that resembled modern Dutch.

My grandparents, Abe and Mary Isaak, were born in the Mennonite village of Rosenthal, near Ekaterinoslav. Grandfather was born on October 4, 1856, and died at Lincoln, California, on December 10, 1937. Grandmother was born April 5, 1861, and died in 1934. Grandmother's father was the religious leader of the community. My grandparents were married according to the Mennonite rites, but their first child, Peter, had been conceived two months before, and when he was born seven months after their wedding Grandmother's father, as religious leader of the sect, threatened to excommunicate them. Grandpa said that if you excommunicate me I'll never come back, so Grandma's father relented.

But Grandpa and Grandma left the colony for Odessa anyway. There he got a job in a bookstore and began reading revolutionary literature. He became an anarchist and never went back to the colony. When the tsarist police were about to arrest him, he sent his wife and three children to the colony and fled to Rio de Janeiro. He wrote to his family and told them to join him, but Grandmother's father, who had promised to pay their fare to America, said no and insisted on the United States or he would not give them the money. So Grandpa went to Oregon, and his family sailed for New York and went right on to Portland to join him.

That was in 1889. They both went to work, and for a year left their children with an old Russian farmer with a homestead out in the woods, where they practically starved. By 1895 they had earned a little money and knew enough English to start *The Firebrand*. Grandma helped support the paper, and *Free Society* after it, by taking in wash. Then Grandpa bought an old farm outside Portland and published the paper there. They raised their own food, had a cow, lived on very little, and put all their money into the paper, which they edited with Henry Addis and A. J. Pope until 1897. That was when Grandpa and the other editors were arrested for publishing an "obscene poem" by Walt Whitman in the paper and sending it in the mail.[68] One old fellow was not there when the police came and was so insulted at not being arrested that he turned himself in!

After Grandpa's release, he moved his family to San Francisco and started the paper going again under the new name *Free Society*, as *The Firebrand* had been banned from the mails. They remained in San Francisco from 1897 to the end of 1900, and then moved to Chicago. (Pete, the oldest child, stayed in San Francisco.) They bought an old house and resumed publication of *Free Society*. Everyone who came through Chicago—Abner Pope, Emma Goldman, Voltairine de Cleyre—stayed in the house, though Voltairine moved in with Jake and Annie Livshis, who had a small dry goods store near the Loop and eked out a shabby existence. Mother said that Voltairine was very beautiful.

When Kropotkin visited Chicago in 1901, my grandparents and their children took the train to a station outside the city to meet him and have a chance to talk to him before he was swamped by an admiring crowd in the city. Mother worked for Clarence Darrow[69] for a while, then enrolled in medical school. When my grandparents left Chicago for New York after the McKinley assassination,[70] Mother wanted to stay, but Grandpa said she was too young and insisted that she go with them.

That year, 1901, Leon Czolgosz had come to see Grandpa and said he was going to kill McKinley and wanted to join the anarchist organization. Grandpa said we have no organization to kill anybody. He thought the fellow was an *agent provocateur* and published a warning in *Free Society*. Governor Warren's report on the Kennedy assassination[71] mentions Czolgosz and *Free Society* but not Grandfather, and has the facts all wrong.

What happened was that after McKinley was shot the police came to the house to arrest my grandparents. Not long before, when a group of anarchists had tried to free Alexander Berkman from prison, they had corresponded with my Uncle Abe and he had kept all the letters. Now, when the police arrived, Grandma ran upstairs to get them and rolled them up into her skirt. As she went to the basement door a policeman tried to stop her but Mother grabbed him by the collar and started to talk to him quickly, long enough to allow Grandmother time to put the letters in the furnace. The police knew she had done something and ran downstairs and searched and searched but couldn't find anything. The letters weren't burned but only mixed up with the rest of the trash in the furnace.

The police took them all to prison. Mother and Grandmother were released after one night, and Grandpa and Uncle Abe several days later. Mother was put in a cell with drunks and prostitutes, and it was quite a traumatic experience in her life. She always thought it made her timid—afterwards she would always lock up the house when she was alone, and so on. Grandpa was very proud of the incident and loved to tell the story. Darrow offered to defend him, but he and his son were released.

They moved to New York after the affair and kept the paper going till 1904 in a house Grandpa bought on Teller Avenue in the Bronx. He worked at Maisel's bookstore[72] to make ends meet. Around 1908 they sold the house to Saul Yanovsky[73] and went to California to start the Aurora Colony. My grandparents were never at Home Colony [near Tacoma, Washington], but Mother went up there a few years later and married Franz Erkelens. (He had formerly been married to Grace Allen, the schoolteacher and a daughter of George Allen.) I lived there for a while. You ought to see Sonya Keene in Seattle. She was Sadie Edelstadt, and her parents, like her Uncle David,[74] died of tuberculosis, so she was brought up in Chicago and Montana by her Uncle Abe and his wife. Abe was a shoemaker, then a shoe store proprietor, who sold boots to miners. They moved with Sonya to Home Colony. Mother, who had known them all in Chicago, went to visit, met Erkelens, and married him.

I met Alexander Berkman in San Francisco when he was publishing *The Blast* with Fitzi.[75] It was shortly before the Preparedness Day bomb went off. I had read his *Prison Memoirs of an Anarchist* and idolized him. He was very nice and dignified but no longer young. I once asked "Zully"—Ben Zuller—if it was possible that Mooney and Billings were guilty of the bombing, and he said, "There's a small possibility that they were innocent!" He advised me to ask Uncle Pete about it—Pete was also on the Mooney-Billings defense committee. I believe that Mooney and Billings *were* framed but that they were also guilty. The prosecutor knew they did it but, not having sufficient evidence to convict them, purchased false testimony and other fraudulent evidence.

I used to take piano lessons from Rena Mooney. She had a large copy of that photograph—with the clock—on the piano leaning against the wall. It was a phony picture, you know, a composite with the clock superimposed.[76] The defense could never produce the negative in court. Berkman may also have been in on the scheme, but I have no precise knowledge about that. What happened, as I heard it, was that Billings had a suitcase rigged with dynamite, intended for a plant being struck. It was a Sunday—the day was chosen so that no one would be killed as in the Los Angeles Times explosion of 1910.[77] Because of the parade, however, he was unable to cross Market Street. With the time bomb going, he panicked, put down the suitcase, and ran. Someone who knew him saw him and reported it to the police, who afterwards arrested him. Many of the comrades thought it a mistake to have used Billings, who had a previous record with dynamite. As for the photograph with the clock, it was never, as I said, produced at the trial by the defense, and everybody used to look at the picture and laugh at it. They all knew it was a fake.

I don't know if Eric Morton[78] was involved. He later became a heavy drinker, and after his young daughter—she was about seventeen—died of Hodgkin's disease, his wife Anna (a sister of Esther Abramowitz Fox Foster) left him. He died, an impoverished alcoholic, in the County Hospital in San Francisco around 1930.

Grandpa, as I said, went out to California and bought this big piece of land near Lincoln, partly with money that Grandma inherited from her family in Russia and partly from subscriptions by prospective colonists. It had a big house and fine orchards. But the members came mostly from New York, Chicago, and other cities, they had no farming experience, and their idea of an anarchist colony was sitting under a tree with fruit dropping into your mouth. A few were Jewish doctors and dentists, and some accused Grandfather of being high-handed and anti-Semitic—which he wasn't—during the bitterness of the breakup. Grandpa was the only real farmer, and he and Grandma did a lot of work on the place. Grandpa, by the way, preached and also practiced free love. He had affairs with all those names you mentioned. As a young man in Russia he was called "the kissing bug," and only when a baby was on the way did he get married. He practiced free love except one time when a man looked fondly at Grandma, and then he didn't practice it. In fact, he sent her on a trip to Europe with Emma Goldman to break it up. That was around 1900, and Grandma went on to Russia to visit her family.

At any rate, the colony broke up. The land was divided up, with those who had paid in large amounts of money getting twelve acres and smaller amounts six. The members drew lots after making a numerical grid of the land, and Grandpa drew a number for a good plot with the big house—called the Colony House—on it. But fearing accusations of shenanigans, he put it back, then picked a number with a plot of unimproved land. There were about thirty families in the colony, including a Frenchman with a motorcycle named Bouquet. Grandpa cleared his plot, built a house, and lived there for the rest of his life. By the First World War his anarchist activity was largely over. He corresponded with many people but was no longer active in the movement.

But he retained his anarchist philosophy to the end. Pete had become a Communist, and when he came on visits they had violent arguments deep into the night, so that people on the next farm could hear them. When Abe Junior's son became a Communist in the 1930s, Grandpa broke off his correspondence with them. Grandpa was not even a state socialist, let alone a Communist. He wanted a society with no government, no state.

• ELMER B. ISAAK •

New York City, February 12, 1974

Elmer B. Isaak, an engineer who worked with Robert Moses, the New York urban planner, is the grandson of Abe and Mary Isaak, Mennonite immigrants from southern Russia, who were among the most active anarchists in the United States between the 1890s and 1920s, publishing the journal *Free Society* and founding the Aurora Colony in California (see interview with Elmer's cousin, Grace Umrath).

I WAS BORN in 1912 and am a civil engineer by profession. My father was Abe Isaak, Jr., and my mother, Rose, who is Jewish, is ninety-one and still lives in Mount Vernon, New York, where my father died in 1953. My Aunt Mary, Father's sister, is still alive at eighty-eight in Santa Cruz, California. She had lived in Home Colony for several years during the 1940s and 1950s, as well as some thirty or forty years before that, when she married Franz Erkelens, a fellow colonist. Her daughter Dorothy lives in Berkeley, California, and her other daughter, Grace [Umrath, q.v.], in Amsterdam. Pete Isaak, Mary's older brother, died in California in the 1940s; he had a daughter, Mildred, who died of cancer in her forties. Dad had me and my brother Harvey.

Abe and Maria (Mary) Isaak married in 1879 in a Mennonite colony near Odessa. Their three children were born there: Pete (1880), Abe Junior (1883), and Mary (1885). The family moved to Odessa, where Abe Senior became active in the anti-tsarist movement. He was about to be arrested in 1889 but was warned and left for America. He sent for his family the following year. They stayed in New York for a couple of years and then went to Portland, Oregon.

Father went to school in Portland. Their language, of course, was German. In school the teacher called the roll, and each student raised his hand and said "Present." Father didn't understand this, and when his name was called he held up his hand with a pencil and said "Pencil." Another story that Father used to tell of Portland was that Grandfather went to take the trolley to work but forgot his fare and had to go home for it and caught a later car. The earlier one, it turned out, plunged over a bridge and many people were killed. The whole family helped publish *The Firebrand* and later *Free Society*. That's how Father learned the trade of printer, which he was to practice for most of his life.

My grandparents were naturalized in San Francisco in 1899. The family founded *Free Society* there and moved it to Chicago and then New York, where they lived in the Bronx. Father remained in New York when the family went west to start Aurora Colony in Lincoln, California. He married Mother in 1911, which caused a furor among the anarchists. He worked as a compositor, then as a linotype operator, for the *New York Sun* and became chairman of his union chapel. He was always proud of that. He later went into business but paid his union dues till the day he died, and they, the typographical union, buried him.

By the 1930s Father had ceased to believe in anarchism. He never talked anarchism to me. He read *The Nation* and *New Republic* and became a good New Deal Democrat. He kept some of his contacts with the anarchists, though, and we used to visit Stelton and spent a few summers at Mohegan Colony in the 1920s. He was also deeply influenced by Henry George and the single tax and got me to read *Progress and Poverty*.[79] And he and Mother, and especially my grandparents, spoke often of the Haymarket affair. Haymarket, with the big monument near Chicago, became real to me, and I had an emotional feeling about it.

Grandfather, by contrast, never abandoned his anarchism. He was always talking to me about it, from the first time we visited him at Lincoln, California, in 1920. The Aurora Colony had broken up by then, but some of the oldtimers were still there. It was a fruit farm, with peaches, pears, and marvelous figs. Grandfather clung to anarchism to the end. But he wasn't dogmatic about it. For him anarchism was not just "no government," but society would be organized into committees to produce goods and services. Anarchism did not mean disorganization; it meant simply no formal government. But he never convinced me that it would work. As an old man he still believed that there would be a social revolution some day. He died at the farm of rectal cancer in November 1937, an anarchist to the end. I was there when he died.

Grandmother, who died at the farm around 1934, used to call him "Isaak." Once a month he got all dressed up in rural splendor, with a wide hat and a good coat, to attend meetings of the local irrigation board of the Nevada irrigation district in California, of which he was chairman. Then he would come home and mutter about the "damned fools" on the committee. So much for his future society of local committees!

• MARION BELL •

Los Angeles, California, June 21, 1974

Marion Bell (known as "Maisie") was the daughter of the tall, red-bearded, Scottish-born anarchist Thomas Hastie Bell (1867–1942), praised by Emma Goldman for his "propagandistic zeal and daring" and by Kropotkin as "a thoroughly honest and fully reliable man."[80] Bell's wife Lizzie, a "lovely girl," in Goldman's description, was a sister of the well-known English anarchist John Turner, the first to be deported from the United States under the anti-anarchist law of 1903, adopted in the wake of President William McKinley's assassination. Thomas Bell's sister, Jessie Bell Westwater, was yet another member of the anarchist clan, as indeed was Maisie, though Maisie was never active in the organized movement. She did, however, have interesting recollections of such important figures as Emma Goldman, Alexander Berkman, and Voltairine de Cleyre. In frail health when I interviewed her, Maisie died of heart failure in 1979.

MY FATHER, Thomas Bell, became an anarchist as a young man in Scotland. He was later secretary to Frank Harris, the writer. He knew several languages well—but I believe you know this already. Mother, who had five sisters and six brothers, came from the Turner family of Bardfield, England. Her older brother John[81] had a small grocery on Red Lion Street in London. He also worked as an insurance agent and organized the Shop Assistants' Union. Mother worked in his store during the 1880s, met his friends, and became an anarchist. She got together with Father, and they were active in the London movement. They knew Louise Michel,[82] Errico Malatesta,[83] Peter Kropotkin (here's a letter from Kropotkin, dated 1900, testifying to Father's character), Cherkezov, Chaikovsky,[84] Stepniak,[85] Nettlau,[86] and William Morris. They visited Louise Michel in Paris. She kept dozens of stray cats. She gave Mother her photo [Maisie shows it to me]. They lived not far from Kropotkin, and they lived in Whiteway colony[87] for a while, where they were friendly with Rachelle Edelmann[88] and liked her enormously. They knew Harry Kelly[89] during his London years, and his wife, Mary Krimont, had lived with them in London. Mother—Lizzie Turner Bell—was a lovely person and far ahead of her times. She and Father never got married, yet her mother was very puritanical.

Uncle Jack (John Turner) came to the U.S. on a lecture tour in 1896. He got as far west as Denver. He met Voltairine de Cleyre in Philadelphia and was deeply impressed by her. He told Mother about her, and they were excited at the news that she was coming for a visit to England [in 1897]. When she arrived she and Mother became good friends. Mother fixed her hair with a little curl for the photographer [Maisie shows me a picture]. When she went to lecture in Scotland Mother went with her. Mother said she had such fun with

her. After her return to America she wrote Mother [Maisie shows me the letter—it reflects the warm, humorous side of Voltairine].

Father came to New York in 1904, a year after Uncle Jack had been expelled
from the U.S. in the wake of the McKinley assassination. Mother and I came in
1905 (Mother was then pregnant with my brother Tom). Father was living in
Emma Goldman's apartment when we arrived, and we stayed there too. I was
two years old then. Mother thought Emma a good cook and a very accomplished person. Mother had been sick on the boat coming across and said that
there was nobody like Emma, who took care of her and me. Stella Ballantine
[Emma's niece] helped too. That was around September 1905.

When I was three I had a birthday party—I was born on April 2, 1903, in
Nice, where Father was working for Frank Harris—and they used it as an occasion to raise money for *Mother Earth*, which Emma was about to launch. Father worked as a translator for Cook and Bernheimer. Between 1906 and 1910,
when we left for Arizona, I remember Voltairine de Cleyre visiting us quite
often, and how my parents looked forward to her visits. We all did, in fact,
because she was interested in us children—and she gave us cookies. I don't
have the same memory of Emma Goldman when she came to visit. In fact, she
thought that Mother was crazy for having another baby after myself and Tom
Junior. Mother said that for such an intelligent person Emma didn't show such
good judgment in picking men. But Emma felt the same way about Mother:
she believed that Father, with his severe asthma, was not going to live very
long.

I have no recollections of Alexander Berkman in New York, but we visited
him in San Francisco in 1916, and though he was so busy with his paper [*The
Blast*] and with the Mooney-Billings case he was extremely friendly and did
everything to make us feel at home. We just had a wonderful time staying with
Berkman and Fitzi. I was thirteen then, and I listened but didn't do any talking.
Berkman came in every now and then to chat with Mother. Oh, I was so impressed with him. Such a beautiful character! And Fitzi too—she was so lovely!
When we got back to Arizona they had trouble mailing *The Blast* from San
Francisco, so they sent them to us. We kids went around on bicycles mailing
batches in different post boxes. The papers went to Argentina and many other
places. I remember thinking how they were being sent all over the world, to
people that Mom and Dad knew, like Netlow [the spelling that Nettlau used in
England] and Malatesta in London.

Father talked a lot about Eric B. Morton, who also worked on *The Blast*, and
especially about how Morton had tried to tunnel Berkman to freedom from
prison. We visited Morton in San Francisco in 1925. He had a beautiful daughter. I thought she was the most beautiful girl I had ever seen. She died—I think
of cancer of the throat. Then his wife left him.

We had moved from New York to Arizona in 1910. We got a homestead and
went on the land. Uncle Bert (Albert Turner) had settled in Colorado after
living for a while in Canada. He had had a ranch and a mine, had been very

wealthy, a speculator making money, losing money. We were supposed to go to Florida to a warm climate for Father's asthma. The men in his office gave him hip boots for Florida as a going-away present. But Uncle Bert wrote and said come west. Father had been a sheep rancher in Texas when he was twenty-one years old, so he knew something about the country. So we all got together and settled on a homestead between Phoenix and Buckeye, where alfalfa was grown. The Roosevelt dam had just been built and that gave the prospect of plentiful water. Uncles Bert and Charlie met us at the station. But after getting horses from an Indian reservation and going around the area, they decided not to stay there. So the men drove the wagon over towards Phoenix, Dad with all his books and papers. They put up a tent on our homestead and slept through a rainstorm. There was just nothing there—no house, no other place to live. But we stayed there till 1921, when we came to live in Los Angeles. We were still on the farm near Phoenix when we got word of Kropotkin's death [February 8, 1921]. I remember all three—Mom, Dad, and Uncle Bert—sitting there with tears rolling down their faces, all broken up about it. They sent a telegram of condolence to Sophie Kropotkin in Moscow.

After visiting Berkman in San Francisco, we came down by boat to Los Angeles. We met William C. Owen[90] there. He had written a long letter to Father about the Magón brothers. Owen was feeling sick and was a bit crotchety, but I was very much impressed with his writing. He had edited the English page of Magón's newspaper, *Regeneración*. In Arizona and California the people used and insulted the Mexicans so terribly, you know! Father would get Mexicans out of all kinds of trouble when we lived in Phoenix. One was put in a mental institution for talking back to the boss's wife, and Father got him out. I saw Enrique Flores Magón many times after we moved to Los Angeles. He had married a widow with five or six children. He was a very nice person and talked quite a lot, but Father always said that Ricardo Flores Magón was the driving force of the movement. Enrique was cheerful, charming, and pleasant, when you'd think he'd be so bitter at the way they were treated. César Chavez and his farm workers are like another Magón movement.

I have another letter from Owen to Charles B. Cooper,[91] an oldtime anarchist in Los Angeles. Father had lived with Cooper in New York in 1904, before we arrived from Scotland. In Los Angeles Cooper visited us often. He was well-read and played the piano. He used to tell me not to read only anarchist propaganda but good literature too. The first time he came to visit us in Los Angeles he brought a list of names and questions to ask Father about, and I thought that was so amusing, his catching up on old friends and what had happened to them.

My parents knew the Isaaks in New York. Dad really admired old man Isaak. For years I had been hearing about "old man Isaak, old man Isaak," so when I went to visit the Isaaks in Lincoln in 1925 (I went with Augustin and Clementine Laforge, a French anarchist couple) I got such a surprise! He was way up in years, but he looked so straight and healthy! He had a nice place and even grew oranges up there. Isaak and Laforge were active in forming producers' cooperatives. I enjoyed the evening with them, and when I went down to Berkeley I met the daughter, Mary.

We knew all the anarchists in Los Angeles—the Kropotkin Group, C. V. Cook, Sprading, Swartz, Henry Cohen, Hans Rossner, Walter Holloway, Scarceriaux, Sanftleben.[92] Dad corresponded with Sadakichi Hartmann,[93] who lived on an Indian reservation east of Los Angeles and whom Mom and Dad had known in New York. He was a heavy drinker, quite an entertainer, a very odd sort of person. Scarceriaux was very dedicated and dependable, a stocky man and a nice, pleasant person. He translated part of Father's Oscar Wilde book[94] into French, but it was much too flowery and not at all like Father.

C. V. Cook was raised in Iowa, went to Chicago, then came west. Sadie and C. V. were just precious. Henry Cohen's wife was twenty years older than he was, and I once made a great faux pas when I referred to her as his mother. Hans Rossner came from Chicago, where he'd been an anarchist since the Haymarket days. By the time we knew him he was bitter and pessimistic, but Father respected his opinion. One day Ollie Rossner (Hans's wife) said, "I'm going to have a cousin visiting from Chicago, Lillian Harman."[95] Mother was astonished: "Lillian Harman? I took her around a bit in London!" [in 1898]. Mother told me that Lillian was a nice person, "but of course she wasn't like Voltairine!" Lillian came, and we had a wonderful time. Her daughter Verna Johnston came out here to live, and my brother Tom used to visit her son George when he lived in Los Angeles.

Sprading had a good forum before we got here. He used to blame the IWWs[96] for breaking up the meetings. Cooper and Sprading were on the outs when we got here. And I didn't care much for Sprading. He was an affected speaker, not natural. He, Rossner, and Cook all used the word "libertarian" rather than "anarchist," while C. L. Swartz used the word "mutualist." Rudolf and Milly Rocker were here in 1926. Rebecca August's [q.v.] husband drove them down from San Francisco. There was an anarchist couple in Los Angeles with two daughters, named Emma and Voltairine.

We got acquainted with many of the anarchists at the Walt Whitman School.[97] It was kind of falling apart when we got here. They still ran the day school and had lectures, but it was dwindling. The Communists were taking over and there was terrible quarreling. The same thing happened later in Mohegan. The school was near beautiful Hollenbeck Park. It had so many interesting people. William Thurston Brown[98] had already left, and a man named Levine, a Communist, was director. At the meetings Father used to get up and ask, "Don't you believe in free speech?"

Pryns Hopkins was lecturing at Claremont College during his later years. They brought much of his stuff from the Santa Barbara school [Boy Land] to the Walt Whitman School to use—books, specimens, scientific equipment. We met quite a few people in L.A. from Home Colony. Robert Turner, one of Mother's brothers, had lived there, as had C. V. Cook's daughter, Evadna, and

Radium LaVene [q.v.]. But Mother always said, "I never met anybody like our friends in New York or London or Whiteway." I think she was right. The anarchists were a special kind of people.

• BRIGITTE HAUSBERGER •

Philadelphia, October 28, 1976

Brigitte Hausberger was the youngest of three daughters of the noted German anarchist Gustav Landauer (1870–1919). Born near Berlin in 1906, she was educated mostly at home by tutors. Her mother, the poet and translator Hedwig Lachmann, died of influenza in February 1918, and her father was murdered by soldiers in Munich on May 2, 1919, during the Bavarian Revolution. Brigitte married a Dr. Peschkowsky in the late 1920s (he later changed his name to Nichols, after his father, Nicolai), and they had two sons, Mike Nichols, the theater and film director, and a physician. Brigitte left Germany in 1940 and settled in New York. After Dr. Peschkowsky died, she married Dr. Franz Hausberger, who had come to the United States after the war and was a research physician in Philadelphia, where Brigitte, who had a Ph.D., assisted him in his laboratory. She was tall, thin, and fine-looking, like her father. In her house hung beautiful portraits of her father and mother, painted from life in the early part of the century. Brigitte also had some books and photographs, but she had sold her father's library. His correspondence and papers are housed in the International Institute of Social History in Amsterdam and in the Buber Archive at Hebrew University in Jerusalem.

I WAS BORN in Hermsdorf, a suburb of Berlin, in 1906. My mother, Hedwig Lachmann, was Father's second wife and the daughter of a cantor; that's why he calls her "Jüdin" in some of his letters. My sister Gudula was born in 1902. Charlotte ("Lotte"), Father's daughter by his first wife, also lived with us. Father dominated our home both spiritually and physically. He was six feet five inches tall and Mother five feet two. What a sight! When they walked together, people would turn and look. Then there was his fur hat, which made him even taller. But apart from his height, it was his constant seriousness that made me, as a child, regard him with awe. He was very strict, and his height made him all the more forbidding.

Father slapped me three times during my childhood. The first time was when I yelled *"scheisse"* [shit] at a playmate, a boy, who had spat at me. Father was on the balcony and heard me. He ran down and slapped me, then gave the little spitter quite a scolding. I got the second slap when we were having red-beet soup for dinner. I didn't like it and said, "It tastes like sand mixed with soap." Father did not allow any criticism of food. Food that was prepared had to be eaten. We had to finish it all. Gudula and I were not even allowed to take the film off boiled milk, but we found a way to do it without his knowing.

The third slap occurred somewhat later. In the meantime another lesson in behavior took place in Krumbach, where we spent the summers. It was in 1918, the year my mother died. A man used to come to the house selling mushrooms. He had a terrible stammer: "P-p-p-pilze," he would say. When he left, I mimicked him and said that it took him half an hour to say *Pilze*. Father was greatly annoyed. Instead of laughing at my talent for mimicry, he put me on his knee, took his watch from his vest pocket, and told me to repeat *Pilze* with a stutter for half an hour. I kept it up for ten minutes before I had to stop. I then burst into tears. Father let me down from his knee, patted my head, and said nothing. But the lesson has remained with me to this day. Whenever I hear or read of an exaggeration, I recall the word *Pilze*.

But Father did not slap me that time. The third slap came when I was amusing my sister Gudula by imitating the Catholic prayers that I heard people recite in the street over their rosaries. I copied their sing-song intonation. Father came in and slapped me for making fun of these simple, pious people. Such punishments do not conform with present-day pedagogy, but they did teach me not to use vulgar language, not to refuse any dish at table, and not to make fun of any religion.

In our own house we celebrated Christmas every year and had a large tree, the biggest that Father could find, decorated with shiny ornaments. Father played Santa Claus and would read us a *Märchen* of Brentano. And Easter was also a big event. We would go to the woods and hide Easter eggs, and afterwards would all go on an egg hunt. Once I found a golden necklace in an egg left in our house. There was a note with it: "Dear child, Give this to your mother. The Easter Bunny." I still have that necklace!

Those were the things he did, thoughtful things. We lived in a Jewish neighborhood in Hermsdorf, and I played with Jewish children, but we were the only ones who celebrated Christmas and Easter. We were known as *freireligiöse* or "dissident." At school I was the only child who sat alone while the others studied religion and recited their prayers. But I attended school only briefly, and Gudula had no formal schooling at all. Instead, Father hired private tutors for us and also taught us a lot himself.

In our home, as a rule, silence reigned. Mother, a poet and translator, was occupied with her writing, and we had to be quiet because she was at work. Yet I can recall how much I enjoyed cuddling against her arms, which were so soft. She was a very quiet person, and it was Father who helped us with our education. Father worked very late at night, but before he went to bed he would come into my room, put me on the "potty," then back to sleep. He did that, not Mother. I was at that time no more than three years old, yet how vividly I can recall every sweet moment of motherly and fatherly affection.

There wasn't the family "togetherness" that one finds so often today. We met at meals, but otherwise did little together as a family. Father and Mother were working, and we had to be quiet. Our main meal was at midday, with a light supper in the evening: blueberries and milk I especially liked! Father, by the way, was a good swimmer and an even better ice skater. In winter we went ice-skating on Sunday mornings, which we all liked very much. He smoked a lot—cigarettes, Russian cigarettes, with large mouthpieces. In the attic in Krumbach where he worked we found a large trunk filled with these mouthpieces.

Every Sunday we had guests, such as the Bubers, Richard and Paula Dehmel, Julius Bab and his family, and other literary and artistic friends.[99] We would play with their children and dance and laugh together. The evenings would often become musicales, with Mother at the piano. But we had no anarchist guests. Father met his anarchist friends away from home, which was far from downtown Berlin, and he spoke very little to us children about anarchism, though once he painted for us a picture of an ideal socialist village, founded on mutual aid, without money but with comradely affection, and where each would work freely and peacefully at his own preferred craft.

Father revered Kropotkin and called him "my great friend." And one day a man in a tattered suit came to our house, and the maid told father that a "beggar" was at the door. Father came down and exclaimed, *"Aber, es ist der Mühsam!"* It was the anarchist writer Erich Mühsam,[100] whom I liked very much. That was around 1915. One time when Father visited Willy Spohr[101] he took me along, in 1912 or 1913. We went for a rowboat ride, and they argued about the coming war, so much so that they didn't see a big boat in our path until I warned them, and we got out of the way at the last moment.

Speaking of the war, Bernhard Meyer, a wealthy furrier, told me that Father often said to him, "Herr Meyer, war is coming. Leave Germany." So they went to Switzerland and missed the horrors of the war. Herr Meyer said, "He had the foresight to send us out of Germany."

We ourselves were on a train when the war broke out, coming back from our summer vacation. During the summer we used to visit both my grandmothers, at Karlsruhe and at Krumbach. Now we were returning from Krumbach to Berlin. In the same car were some English tourists. Mother, who spoke and translated a number of foreign languages, conversed with these tourists in English. The train was stopped in Weimar. Mobilization had begun. I remember the hostility of the other passengers towards the English, who had suddenly become our "enemies," and towards my mother who was speaking affably with them. Mother began to weep quietly.

That year we stopped exchanging gifts for Christmas. We still had a tree and candles and spent time together. But no gifts. Father didn't want to celebrate in wartime, when people were suffering and dying. A nephew of Father's, Walter Landauer, had been mobilized into the army. When he came home on furlough we went to meet him at the station. His train was late by several hours. It was cold and drafty in the station. Mother began to cough. That was the year of the great influenza epidemic, and Mother became very ill. Father did not leave her bedside through the whole week that she was sick. She died in our home in February 1918.

Father did not allow me to look at my mother's body. "I want you," he said, "to remember your mother just as you remember her now." Many people came to pay their last respects. I overheard Father telling one of the mourners that I was his "only sunshine in those dark days." I took that literally and would not allow myself to show my grief. I was what he wanted me to be—sunshine. I tried so hard to be gay that my aunt scolded me: "Your mother just died, yet you are laughing." I bottled up my grief, and did so forever after. Nor did Father take me to the funeral. Gudula went—she was sixteen—but I stayed home alone.

Mother's death was a severe blow to my father. For he was bound to her in spirit, as he so eloquently expressed it in a famous letter to her. I recall how in 1915, in the very midst of the war, my mother composed an anti-militarist poem called "With the Defeated," some lines and phrases of which Father helped her to polish. Father was so inspired by this poem that in a letter to her he wrote, "I thank you, Hedwig, you Jewish daughter and my dear wife." That poem appeared later in the German paper *Der Jude*, and I learned to recite it by heart and remember it to this day.

I recall, too, how the First World War ended. My father plunged himself at once into the thick of the revolution in Germany, especially in Berlin. In those stormy days and nights he was seldom at home. Yet however busy or far away he was, in his letters he never ceased to concern himself with his children, and especially with me, his beloved youngest daughter. In his letters he would remind me to get plenty of fresh air, not to neglect my arithmetic and French, of which he himself supplied readings and examples in his letters.

That summer, the summer of 1918, Kurt Eisner's[102] children were with us in Krumbach. Father, who was then in Munich, sent us a telegram instructing us to take our valuables and go to Uncle Hugo in Merseburg, on Lake Constance. That was our last communication from him. Uncle Hugo (Father's brother) owned a chain of department stores and had a big house there, at the village of Deisendorf above Merseburg. He picked us up in a horse and buggy and brought us to the house. There I had a traumatic experience which has remained with me all my life. Hugo's wife was standing at the top of the stairs. "My God," she said. "So much luggage! How long are you going to stay?" Even now I prefer to stay in a motel when visiting my son.

Not long after that, Uncle Hugo gave us a task. He had an old vineyard on a hill that was full of stones. He gave us—myself, his children, and the Eisner children—the job of picking up the stones and carting them away. I still remember how much it hurt to go barefoot on the freshly cut grass. While we were doing this, Uncle Hugo called me aside and quietly told me that German soldiers in Munich had murdered my father. I stood there bewildered. After standing there for a few minutes, I returned to gather stones with the other children. I did not tell them anything. Only at noon, during lunch, did Uncle Hugo tell the other children about my father's death. I suppressed my feelings. Later I found an abandoned corner in the woods where no one could see me, and there, hidden from everybody, I made two small graves [she begins to cry, then says, "Well, I didn't suppress them completely, obviously."], two mounds of earth such as I had seen in the Catholic cemetery in Hermsdorf. On the two graves I put flowers and made a cross from branches for each grave. No one knew anything of this. But for several days I stole away to my secret graves and placed fresh flowers there.

That fall the Eisner children went back to their mother, and we three Landauer children went to our grandmother in Karlsruhe. Life for the first time became a little normal. Lotte went to the conservatory, met Dr. Max Kronstein, and married him. They had a daughter. Lotte became pregnant again and quite ill. A doctor in Karlsruhe operated on her gall bladder in her apartment, then he and Max Kronstein drank to the successful operation—from which she never woke up. That was around 1926. Gudula, who became a professional musician, survived Hitler and the Holocaust and came to New York after the war. She was killed by a bus on Central Park West in 1948.

• FERMIN ROCKER •

New York City, January 26, 1972

Fermin Rocker, named after the Spanish anarchist martyr Fermín Salvochea, is the son of the great German anarchist Rudolf Rocker (1873–1958), biographer of Johann Most and author (among many other works) of *Nationalism and Culture* (1937), *Anarcho-Syndicalism* (1938), and *Pioneers of American Freedom* (1949). Fermin, a professional artist, studied at the Berlin School of Arts and Crafts and served his apprenticeship as a lithographer. For many years he lived in New York, painting, sketching, making prints, illustrating books, and working at an animated cartoon studio. In 1973 he returned to London, where he had been born in 1907 and about which he wrote a fascinating memoir of his childhood.[103]

WHEN MY PARENTS came to the United States in 1933, they lived in the Amalgamated Houses on Grand Street on the Lower East Side. Father hated it: it was dreary, with few trees or parks. They spent the summer of 1936 on Mount Airy in Croton-on-Hudson. A few anarchist families lived there, but it was a development rather than a colony. There was no school but there were some cultural activities. George Schumm, Benjamin Tucker's printer, lived there with his wife and daughter [Beatrice Fetz, q.v.], and Tucker's wife Pearl and daughter Oriole [Riché, q.v.] used to visit them. Schumm was related to Max Baginski: Baginski was married to Schumm's sister.

My parents moved to Mohegan the following summer and decided to stay all year round. They rented the cottage of Leon Kramer, the bookseller, and his wife Celia. By that time the school was already on its last legs. It was run by Robert Bek-Gran,[104] a German, who gave fencing lessons. He was a very hearty chap and had affairs with the colonists' wives.

By that time the anarchists at the colony were in a minority; the Communists and Zionists were much stronger and more effective. There were constant clashes. There were quarrels even among the anarchists themselves, between the hards (strong anti-Communists) and the softs. The hards included Joe and Eva Brandes [q.v.] and their in-laws, Pat and Sophie Bannister, who were uncompromising in their anti-Communism. Bannister was a dour, cranky Englishman.

The colony had no working-class base. The inhabitants were largely middle-class, mostly faddists and eccentrics. Many of the women were health and food faddists, devotees of Dr. E. K. Stretch, an advocate of health foods. When Hitler's troops were invading all over Europe, Lydia Gordon[105] made up a jingle: "The soldiers march, because of starch." (Starch was taboo among the Stretchites.)

I can't think of one normal one among the bunch. All had some kind of quirk. There was an Englishman named Bill Stevens (like Bannister, he had a Jewish wife), a real crank, dour and taciturn. He'd meet you on a rainy day and gloat, "Lovely weather." He had lived at the Whiteway Colony in England. He was a handy carpenter and a good farmer.

The nationalities at Mohegan were fully integrated. Most of the gentiles had Jewish wives. The French contingent, partly stemming from the Ferrer Center in New York, included André Miroy (he took his last name from his wife Anita Spiegel, meaning "mirror" in German; his real name was Herrault), a translator in New York, who avoided and scorned Romanic words in English, preferring pure American words, like "fuck" and "shit." This was not for shock effect but for purity of language. André had a brother, Milo Herrault, a garage mechanic. The others were André Longchamp, also a translator; Jacques Dubois, a simple worker—his was the only full French family—his wife was French too; and Henri Dupré, a chef.

Many Moheganites came from the Ferrer Center or Stelton. The bulk were Russian Jews, with mixed occupations. The Russians of gentile background included Samusin, a dental technician, and Dodokin, who made orgone boxes for Wilhelm Reich,[106] the psychoanalyst.

The colony was a very fertile place to raise funds—for the Spanish Civil War, for World War II refugees, and so on. Many musicians lived there and gave frequent concerts, especially during the summer, when cultural events—balls, concerts, lectures—were held every weekend, usually in connection with fundraising. The Spanish Civil War and Nazi-Soviet Pact had a shattering effect on the colonists. Moyshe Morris was a diehard anarchist and his wife a diehard Communist, though the family was somehow a going concern. But after the Hitler-Stalin Pact she left the Communist Party.

I myself was born in London on December 22, 1907. I had a half-brother, Rudolf, who was fourteen years older. Anarchism was not as central for me as for my parents, yet I considered myself very much an anarchist. I found Kropotkin the most appealing figure, though I adhered to the anarcho-syndicalist organization in Berlin during the 1920s.

I came to the U.S by way of Canada in 1929. By then I was no longer an anarchist, indeed no "ist" of any kind. Where "isms" make their mistake, especially the radical ones, is that society, with all its evils and injustices, has evolved very gradually over a long period of time and still has a great many virtues, so that to make a clean sweep and start all over again is merely a delusion. You would end up worse than before. Only gradual improvements are possible.

Another fact the anarchists must face is that the Communists at least have a workable program: to seize power and establish a dictatorship. They are not bound by any scruples. Here is where the anarchists fall on their faces. On the one hand they are committed to revolution, but on the other they have done nothing to prepare for it. As a result, the Communists took over. Yet admittedly the anarchists could not have established their own dictatorship. What then was to be done? A dilemma. I can only point out to you what's wrong. What's right is a different matter.

But I do have more faith in gradual than in revolutionary methods. Look at Britain: no revolutionary panaceas but much better than in my day. Contrast it with France, darling of Kropotkin, classic land of the revolution. True, it is one of the more inhabitable countries, but Britain is ahead in tolerance, humanitarianism, and social concerns. Britain has avoided falling into the downright reaction that has overtaken France from time to time.

But if I cannot accept the anarchist credo there are many wholesome things about it that have strong appeal—for instance that the emancipation of the working class must be accomplished by the workers themselves. That's very sound. We must get away from expecting everything to happen from the top. There is more than a little truth in Kropotkin's faith in small self-supporting regions, rather than immense industrial entities with intricate specialization and division of labor. Yet how far one can decentralize in a complex, modern society I simply don't know.

The anarchist movement had its heyday prior to the First World War and the Russian Revolution. Basically there were two kinds of anarchists: the less intellectual kind, who were wedded to the idea of revolution for its own sake and who therefore found the successful revolution in Russia irresistible and became Communists, and those who were more thoughtful, who probed deeper—Kropotkin, Malatesta, Rocker—and saw the dangers of revolution. But the latter, after the Russian Revolution, were unable to make new converts. All through the 1920s anarchists were at best fighting a rear guard action against the spread of communism and fascism. Only in Spain did they increase in power, but that was the exception. In the United States, after Emma Goldman and Alexander Berkman were deported, the movement had few if any inspiring leaders. The old generation gradually died out, without a new generation to take its place. And so the movement itself died out.

From the 1920s onward the anarchist movement was already a relic, largely a leftover from the past, an immigrant movement that could not last beyond another generation. There was no indigenous movement left in the U.S., save for a few isolated figures like Leonard Abbott and Harry Kelly. Emma Goldman had been more successful in attracting native Americans to the libertarian cause than anyone else. In my father's words, "Emma Goldman was made for anarchism," at least for the period up to 1920. She had a particular blend of heartiness and aggressiveness that fit the American temper. She loved America and was never able to adjust after her expulsion. Then again, had she been allowed to return permanently during the 1930s, she might not have been able to adjust either, for the country was changing so quickly and so profoundly.

There are many individuals in the movement that I recall quite vividly. Hippolyte Havel[107] had a good mind but was not very deep. He was incapable of any sustained intellectual effort. Modest Stein (the "Fedya" of Berkman's and Goldman's autobiographies) was a remarkable person, very independent and full of vitality to the last. He was a successful commercial artist who did illustrations for slick magazines. After the Russian Revolution he gravitated towards the Communist orbit. His daughter [Luba Stein Benenson, q.v.] married a staunch Republican, Park Avenue people, friends of Thomas Dewey.[108]

I first met Max Baginski in the early 1920s in Berlin. He was one of those who were never really able to adjust to America. My father had an extremely high opinion of him and liked him very much as a human being. Baginski was able, articulate, and intelligent. Once a German judge had given him the maximum sentence because of his brilliance, on the grounds that he should have known better. He was a reticent person, a Silesian, like Augustin Souchy,[109] and a good friend of the playwright Gerhart Hauptmann. He filled him in when he wrote The Weavers, as he knew the milieu very well. He had gone to Germany in the 1920s but could no longer adjust there either and so returned to the U.S. and lived in the Bronx. He was a man without a country, a frustrated person, in contrast to Father's buoyant optimism.

Father hated Marcus Graham's[110] guts. Father had a vast number of devoted friends with whom he kept up a voluminous correspondence and close friendship even after their departure from the movement, when some had turned "bourgeois" and conservative. They were friends by moral rather than intellectual qualities; he brought out the best in them. He was tolerant and flexible in attitude towards non-anarchists, especially liberals and democratic socialists. Of all American cities New York was the one he liked least. He had a soft spot for Los Angeles, Philadelphia, Chicago, and in Canada for Winnipeg and Toronto. In Los Angeles one of the most active anarchists (of a very active group) was Bessie Kimmelman. They all used to congregate at her place. Hers was another case of a devout anarchist married happily to a devout Communist.

I always liked Alexander Schapiro,[111] even as a child in London, and he was always kind to me. He was well-educated, intelligent, with a good scientific mind. He was close to the Kropotkin family. But he was flawed by a dogmatic streak and was rather intolerant, especially in comparison with my father. He did not suffer fools gladly. Father, by contrast, associated with intellectuals yet never lost his way back to simple, ordinary people if he felt they were honest and sincere. He was not at all a snob. Malatesta and Kropotkin were that way too, also Nettlau and probably Nieuwenhuis.[112] But figures of the second rank—Schapiro or Mratchny [q.v.], for example—were far more self-important, far more decisive and overbearing, and would antagonize people needlessly. Nor was Schapiro averse to getting rich. After World War II he got involved with sending relief packages to Europe—as a business venture. The aggravations and complications that arose may have hastened his death.

For many anarchists America was still the land of opportunity, the place to get rich. How shocked I was when I came to the U.S. to find so many anarchists talking about their Wall Street holdings. Many were hurt by the stock-market crash. Linder, Cohen, and Cohn[113] lost their shirts. Schapiro had worked with the Bolsheviks for several years, long after others had broken with them, yet during the Spanish Civil War he was one of the sharpest critics of anarchists who joined the government.

I met Durruti when he came to our house in Berlin in the mid-twenties.[114] He was a very nice, warm person, not at all the gangster type portrayed by James Joll in *The Anarchists*.[115] I forged the passport that enabled him to live in Germany—the one thing I did for the anarchist movement. Once in Souchy's apartment, Souchy's companion Thérèse, a small, attractive French woman prone to hysteria, threatened to throw herself out of the window, and Souchy was wringing his hands when Durruti opened the French windows for her and said, "*s'il vous plaît*." Of course nothing happened, and she calmed down.

· PART TWO ·

Emma Goldman

FREDA DIAMOND · LUBA STEIN BENENSON

· JEANNE LEVEY ·

PAULINE H. TURKEL · HILDA ADEL

· ROGER N. BALDWIN ·

ALBERT BONI · GABRIEL JAVSICAS

· IDA GERSHOY ·

ARTHUR LEONARD ROSS · KATE WOLFSON

· ORA ROBBINS ·

MILLIE GROBSTEIN · AHRNE THORNE

2. Emma Goldman, St. Louis, 1912 (Paul Avrich Collection)

INTRODUCTION

FROM THE END of the nineteenth century until her deportation to Russia in 1919, Emma Goldman was one of America's most celebrated women radicals. A born propagandist and organizer, she championed a wide range of unorthodox causes, from women's equality, sexual liberation, and birth control to labor activism, libertarian education, and artistic freedom. Strong in her opinions, hot in her sympathies, she was a powerful orator who toured the country restlessly, incessantly, selling vast quantities of radical literature and raising funds for the anarchist movement, of which she was a leading representative. "She always spoke with great inner conviction," her comrade Rudolf Rocker remarked, "and one felt that she really meant what she said."[116] Her function, said the writer Floyd Dell, was that of "holding before our eyes the ideal of freedom. She is licensed to taunt us with our moral cowardice, to plant in our soul the nettles of remorse at having acquiesced so tamely in the brutal artifice of present day society."[117]

Her passionate espousal of radical causes made Goldman the target of persecution. She lived from day to day in the steady glare of notoriety. Her defense of Leon Czolgosz, the assassin of President McKinley, brought down on her the hatred of the authorities. Feared as a sponsor of anarchy, of violence, free love, and revolution, she was vilified in the press as "Red Emma," "Queen of the Anarchists," "the most dangerous woman in America."

Yet Goldman refused to desist. Maligned, abused, imprisoned, she continued to challenge accepted values and to defy conventional social and political standards. As her reputation increased, she became an international figure, known to governments and radicals throughout the world. With her exuberant and overpowering vitality, her audacity and physical courage, and her dauntless advocacy of unpopular causes, she emerged as one of the most influential women of her time. Her name appeared on lists of the world's greatest women, beside those of Jane Addams, Annie Besant, Helen Keller, and Madame Curie.[118] Anarchists and other dissenters named their daughters after her (among them Emma Gilbert, interviewed in this volume). Her life, said the novelist Theodore Dreiser, "is the richest of any woman's of our century." Frank Harris, the English writer, went even further. Her idealism and courage, he said, her integrity and love of truth, placed her "among the heroic leaders and guides of humanity for ever."[119]

Goldman began life in 1869, the daughter of middle-class Jewish parents in Kovno, Lithuania, then part of the Russian empire. In December 1885 she emigrated to the United States, settling in Rochester, New York, where she worked in a clothing factory and attended meetings of a German socialist group. In May 1886 a bomb was thrown during a workers' meeting near Haymarket Square in Chicago, killing and injuring a number of policemen. Although the bombthrower was never identified, eight anarchists were brought to trial and convicted of the crime, despite a lack of evidence against them. In November 1887 four of the defendants were hanged and a fifth committed suicide in his cell, while the others were sent to prison. The trial of the Chicago anarchists, prominently reported in the press, kindled widespread interest in anarchist personalities and ideas. The unfairness of the proceedings, the savagery of the sentences, the character and bearing of the defendants fired the imagination of young idealists, Goldman among them, and made numerous converts to their cause. The Haymarket trial, said Goldman, was "the decisive influence in my life." It was the death of the Chicago anarchists "which brought me to life and helped to make me what I am."[120]

In 1889, after an unhappy marriage to a fellow worker, Goldman moved to New York City and threw herself into radical activities. Almost at once she met Alexander Berkman, known as "Sasha," her first real love, with whom she would remain associated for half a century. Through Berkman she became acquainted with Johann Most, editor of the anarchist journal *Freiheit*, "the man of magic tongue and powerful pen," as she describes him,[121] who became her ideological mentor. It was Berkman and Most who had the strongest influence on Goldman during her initial years in the anarchist movement. In 1892, indeed, Goldman conspired with Berkman and other comrades to assassinate Henry Clay Frick, the union-busting manager of the Carnegie steel mills in Homestead, Pennsylvania. The conspirators, however, failed in their purpose. Though wounded by pistol and dagger, Frick made a quick recovery, while Berkman, his assailant, spent fourteen years behind bars, an experience hauntingly described in his *Prison Memoirs of an Anarchist*, published six years after his release.

While Berkman languished in prison, Goldman emerged as the foremost anarchist in America, eclipsing even her mentor Johann Most. She too had a taste of incarceration, although brief in comparison with Berkman's. In 1893 and 1894 she spent a year on Blackwell's Island in New York for telling an audience of unemployed workers that it was their "sacred right" to take bread by force if their demands for jobs and sustenance went unanswered. Her prison work as a practical nurse led Goldman to arrange a lecture tour in 1895 that took her to England (where she met such famous anarchists as Peter Kropotkin, Errico Malatesta, and Louise Michel) and to Austria, where she studied nursing and midwifery at the Allgemeines Krankenhaus in Vienna. On her return to the United States, where she began to earn a living as a nurse, she plunged herself anew into radical activity, beginning a series of cross-country speaking engagements that won her a national reputation. In 1899 she made a second European tour, returning the following year to her nursing and propaganda work in America.

In 1901 Goldman's agitational efforts were interrupted by President McKinley's assassination by Leon Czolgosz, a self-proclaimed anarchist who had attended one of her lectures. The authorities endeavored to establish her complicity, and though not a shred of evidence was found to connect her with the attack, she was hounded, mistreated, and briefly imprisoned. On her release, she adopted the pseudonym "E. G. Smith" and went into temporary seclusion.

By 1906, however, Goldman was back in the public eye, speaking and working for anarchism as before. Over the next dozen years she campaigned vigorously for free speech, birth control (which brought her a fifteen-day jail sentence), and libertarian education, among a variety of political and social causes. Her lectures on modern drama were especially well-attended, introducing such playwrights as Ibsen, Strindberg, and Hauptmann to American audiences. "No one did more," said Van Wyck Brooks of Goldman's efforts, "to spread the new ideas of literary Europe that influenced so many young people."[122] Nor was this all. In addition to pamphlets and books, including her own *Anarchism and Other Essays* (1910) and *The Social Significance of the Modern Drama* (1914), she published a handsome monthly journal, *Mother Earth*. Edited by Alexander Berkman, released from prison in 1906, it became the outstanding anarchist periodical in the country.

In 1917, when America entered the First World War, Goldman's fortunes took a turn for the worse. As outspoken critics of the war, she and Berkman were arrested and charged with conspiracy to interfere with the draft. Tried in federal court, they were speedily convicted and sentenced to two years' imprisonment and a ten thousand dollar fine each. Goldman's *Mother Earth*, along with Berkman's new paper *The Blast*, was shut down by the authorities. On completion of their terms in prison (Goldman in Jefferson City, Berkman in Atlanta), they were held for deportation proceedings. In December 1919, at the height of the Red Scare, they were put aboard a military transport and shipped back to their native Russia.

Like radicals throughout the world, Goldman and Berkman had, from its inception, been enthusiastic supporters of the Russian Revolution, joining the chorus of praise not only for the overthrow of the tsarist order but also for the accession to power of the Bolsheviks. In 1918 Goldman had hailed "Lenin, Trotsky, and the other heroic figures who hold the world in awe by their personality, their prophetic vision and their intense revolutionary spirit." The Bolsheviks, she had declared, "are translating into reality the very things many people have been dreaming about, hoping for, planning and discussing in private and public. They are building a new social order which is to come out of the chaos and conflicts now confronting them."[123]

Once in Russia, however, their enthusiasm rapidly cooled. They were stunned by the suppression of dissent, the wholesale arrests of Russian anarchists, the dispersal of Makhno's guerrilla army in the Ukraine, and the conversion of the local soviets into instruments of party dictatorship, rubber stamps for a new bureaucracy. The Bolsheviks, they complained, while ruling in the name of the workers, were in fact destroying the popular initiative and self-reliance on which the success of the revolution depended (see interview with Roger Baldwin). The final blow came in March 1921 with the crushing of the Kronstadt rising, during which workers and sailors demanded freely elected soviets and free speech for all left-wing groups. Kronstadt's suppression, lamented Berkman, marked "the beginning of a new tyranny."[124]

In December 1921, their illusions shattered, Goldman and Berkman left Russia. After a brief stay in Stockholm, they moved to Berlin, from which they lashed out at Lenin's dictatorship in a stream of pamphlets and articles, and especially in Goldman's *My Disillusionment in Russia* (1923) and Berkman's *The Bolshevik Myth* (1925), the first book-length denunciations of Bolshevik tyranny by revolutionaries of international renown. Granted a British visa in 1924, Goldman moved to London and labored to mobilize public opinion against emerging Soviet totalitarianism (see interview with Gabriel Javsicas). The following year she took up residence in France, first in Paris and afterwards in St. Tropez, where, assisted by Berkman, she worked on her great autobiography, *Living My Life*, published in 1931. Her only visit to the United States following her deportation occurred in 1934, when she received permission from Franklin Roosevelt's labor secretary, Frances Perkins, to conduct a ninety-day lecture tour.

Berkman, meanwhile, had settled in Nice, where he was having a difficult time. Under constant threat of expulsion by the French government, he earned a precarious living by translating, editing, and occasional ghost-writing, which had to be supplemented by gifts from comrades and friends. By the early 1930s his health had begun to fail. In 1936 he underwent two operations for a prostate condition, which left him in chronic pain. Finally, in June of that year, suffering from his illness and unwilling to exist on the generosity of others, he shot himself to death in his Nice apartment. He died just three weeks before the outbreak of the Spanish Revolution, which, as Goldman suggested, might have revived his spirits and given him a new lease on life.[125]

Goldman herself, crushed by Sasha's death, had only four more years to live. What saved her from utter despair was a call from Barcelona to come and help combat General Franco and advance the revolutionary cause. Placing herself at the disposal of her comrades, Goldman made three trips to Spain between 1936 and 1939, returning each time to London or Paris to act as a publicist and fundraiser for the CNT-FAI (Confederación Nacional del Trabajo-Federación Anarquista Iberica).

The victory of Franco in 1939 came as a staggering blow. Goldman, then seventy years old, went to Canada to raise money for the Spanish refugees. Living with friends in Toronto, she also launched a campaign to save four Italian anarchists from deportation (see interview with Attilio Bortolotti). It was her last battle against the state, and she won. In February 1940, however, Goldman suffered a paralytic stroke, from which she never recovered. She died three months later, on May 14, six weeks before her seventy-first birthday. Her body was removed to Chicago and buried in the Waldheim Cemetery, near the graves of the Haymarket anarchists, whose martyrdom had inspired her life.

For a quarter-century after her death, Goldman was a largely forgotten figure. Since the 1960s, however, she has had a remarkable revival, which shows no sign of petering out. Not only has her face adorned T-shirts, posters, and mailing cards, but she appeared as a character in E. L. Doctorow's novel *Ragtime* and in Warren Beatty's movie *Reds*, for which the actress who played her, Maureen Stapleton, won an academy award. Her story, moreover, has inspired a spate of plays, poems, and songs, to say nothing of biographies and documentaries, while student circles, book stores, feminist groups, and birth-control centers have adopted her name, such as the Emma Goldman Women's Health Clinic of Iowa City.

Goldman, it might be added, has come to figure in textbooks on American history and literature. Her own writings, above all *Living My Life*, have been widely reprinted and translated, and a veritable army of scholars, most of them women, have been delving into her life and career. In 1982 a writer in the *New York Times*, a paper that had maligned her repeatedly during her lifetime, referred to Goldman as "the great American anarchist and anti-war activist." And in 1990 the fiftieth anniversary of her death was commemorated by her anarchist comrades in New York, a number of whom are interviewed in this volume.

The interviews which follow vary considerably both in content and scope. For the most part, however, they emphasize the personal side of Emma Goldman, her faults as well as her talents, her weaknesses as well as her strengths. Several dwell on her physical appearance and her powerful appetite for sex. "Emma was more than a little vain," her friend Freda Diamond observes. "She thought she was the Queen of Sheba. She thought she was a very attractive, beautiful woman. She held herself that way. She dressed well. But in fact she was far from beautiful." Millie Grobstein agrees: "She impressed me as an ordinary woman—short, heavy, and stocky." This was especially the case after Goldman reached middle age, when she grew increasingly dumpy and unappealing. Yet she seldom lacked for lovers, often men considerably younger than herself. "Emma was always sexually inclined," Julius Seltzer recalls, "always hugging and squeezing me." "Emma loved young men," echoes Gabriel Javsicas, himself an object of her affections. "At one point she suggested that we sleep together, but I demurred." To her Chicago comrade Jeanne Levey, she was "an oversexed personality, and she made all sorts of advances to men. In fact, many men—including my own husband—would say, 'Save me!' She would devour them." "She liked men," remarks Ida Gershoy, "especially young men. She really liked the boys! She was very fond of my husband, and also of my older brother, who once came to visit."

Goldman's pleasures were by no means limited to sex. She smoked, drank, cooked, danced, and frequented the theater and opera. "Emma always liked the good things in life," says Kate Wolfson, "and she had wealthy friends who supplied them. But that didn't detract from her sincerity as an anarchist. She was a very physical woman; she enjoyed food, dancing, sex, and all the things that people *should* enjoy." She was particularly fond of dancing, even in her later years. "She was very funny to watch," recalls Ida Gershoy, "so short and squat and having such a time of it." She was also an "excellent cook" (Millie Grobstein), a talent of which she was justly proud. "Have some of E. G.'s coffee," she would say. "Have some of E. G.'s pudding" (Ida Gershoy).

Goldman's greatest talent, however, was public speaking. "She had an odd voice with a peculiar accent," Freda Diamond recalls. "But she was a good speaker and made an impression." Roger Baldwin remembers her as one of the finest speakers he ever heard. "Her lectures," he says, "which I began to attend in 1911 while in St. Louis, opened up all kinds of new literature to me—Ibsen, Schopenhauer, the Russians. She introduced many people to a whole literature of protest." She was also "very good at repartée" (Ahrne Thorne) and knew how to handle hecklers. And yet, for all her oratorical gifts, she suffered from stage fright. "She was extremely nervous before the lecture," Millie Grobstein remembers, "ate very little, and before mounting the platform took a drink of whiskey and paced up and down. Yet the minute she got on the platform she was herself, in full command. She was at home. All her fears and anxieties seemed to disappear."

In her relations with friends and comrades, Goldman receives a mixed appraisal. More than a few complain of her self-centeredness, her vanity, her obstinacy and domineering nature. The publisher Albert Boni found her "hardboiled and too damn cocksure of everything she had to say." "Emma was an awful person to live with, you know," Ida Gershoy remarks. "She could be quite captivating, but also difficult—the worst bitch in the world!" For some she had an abrasive quality that Berkman, for instance, lacked: "I liked Berkman better than Emma. She was too self-centered" (Gussie Denenberg). "Emma was hard to warm up to personally" (Eva Brandes). "Though she cared about her family and friends, she was very self-centered—too self-centered for an anarchist" (Ahrne Thorne). "I didn't like Emma Goldman as much as Berkman. She was too much I, I, I" (Sarah Taback).

Goldman's secretaries, by the same token, found her often demanding and inconsiderate. "Emma was difficult to work with," Pauline Turkel recalls, "impatient and strict." "She would pile on the work so much," says Millie Grobstein, "and the deadline was always so short!" To children at the New York Ferrer School (see Part Four) she seemed impatient and aloof. When classes let out, they would sometimes walk over to the offices of *Mother Earth*, a few blocks away, where Berkman always gave them a warm welcome. "Sasha was nice to us," Magda Schoenwetter recalls, "but Emma was a pain in the ass. I couldn't stand her red face and dumpy figure. She was busy and would chase us out." "I detested Emma Goldman," says Emma Gilbert, her namesake. "She was so repulsive and extremely domineering, extremely self-centered. There are people you meet whose eye engages you and you feel they are interested in you. Sasha was like that, but not Emma. She was completely egotistical. Of course, she had great capacity, but not on a personal level."

Even Goldman's most faithful admirers would admit to these defects in her behavior. And yet, whatever her faults and inconsistencies, they weighed little in the scale against her idealism and courage, her crusading spirit and devotion to her cause. "Emma had a strong character," Lena Shlakman remarks, "too strong for some, but she was honest and fine, and I liked her." "Emma was very vain," says Jeanne Levey, "yet she was the greatest person that I have ever met in my lifetime."

If at times she could be imperious and insensitive to the feelings of others, Goldman's generosity and essential humanity shone through. She had an extraordinary capacity for establishing lifelong friendships and was always ready to offer assistance. "I once needed a doctor," Ahrne Thorne recalls. "She recommended someone, and she asked me about it later. If a friend needed help, she would do everything she could, mobilize all available forces, go out of her way for you." Thus when Millie Grobstein's father fell ill with rheumatic fever, Goldman was the first to help. "She would come to the house every day—it was a three-story house—and trudge up those two flights of stairs, bringing him medicine, feeding him lunch, all to relieve my mother of part of the burden. She was so compassionate! It's incredible that people thought the opposite of her." Another case was that of Hilda Adel, for whom Goldman helped to arrange an abortion. "She told me what was to be done, whom to see, everything I needed to know," Adel recalls. "She didn't know me that intimately, yet she was concerned about me and determined to help—on the very day that she was thrown out of the country! So those who call her harsh or selfish can't convince me!"

Few who remember Goldman can forget such examples of kindness, many more of which could easily be cited. Nor can they forget her other qualities— her unflagging energy, her indomitable spirit, her tenacity in the face of persecution. But above all, perhaps, they recall her sincerity and eloquence in promoting her ideas—on anarchism, feminism, and the rest. "She opened your mind and made you think about things you never thought about before," says Freda Diamond. "That was her outstanding characteristic. *She made people think!*"

• FREDA DIAMOND •

New York City, May 13, 1983

Freda Diamond, an attractive and dynamic personality, is a successful designer of lamps and home furnishings. For many years she was an intimate friend of the black actor and singer Paul Robeson.[126] During the early decades of the century

Freda's mother, Ida Diamond, was a close friend of Emma Goldman, whose brother Morris became her lover and Freda's surrogate father. Freda has vivid recollections not only of Emma and her brother but also of Alexander Berkman ("Sasha") and Ben Reitman, Emma's longtime lover.

I WAS BORN in New York City on April 11, 1905. My parents were both born in Russia. My mother Ida was a successful dress designer, and we lived on Madison Avenue. She was also an anarchist, a reader of the *Fraye Arbeter Shtime*, and a friend of Emma Goldman. Emma loved Mother. It was hard not to love her. She didn't belong to any groups or organizations, but she was a real anarchist. My father left when I was three. We never heard from him again. He simply disappeared, leaving my mother and us children (I had a sister and a brother) to fend for ourselves. Moe Goldman, Emma's younger brother, moved in not long after—we were then living in the Bronx, on Vise Avenue—and was my mother's lover all the years that I and my sister and brother were growing up. Moe became our substitute father, especially to my kid brother. He was warm and sweet and very affectionate. He helped us with our homework, took us on outings, and we all loved him.

Emma was often at our place to see her brother and visit with us. Once when I was a little girl she and Ben Reitman[127] took me to see Maude Adams in *Peter Pan*. I thought Reitman very handsome. He was tall, dark, attractive. He looked like a he-man, you know. He wore a black fedora hat, a bow tie, and carried a cane so big that it looked like the trunk of a tree. He was cutting a figure, and he knew it.

Occasionally Mother took us to Emma's lectures. I once heard her talk on Ibsen. She spoke well. She had an odd voice with a peculiar accent. But she was a good speaker and made an impression. Emma was more than a bit vain. She thought she was the Queen of Sheba. She thought she was a very attractive, beautiful woman. She held herself that way. She dressed well. But in fact she was far from beautiful. She had a very bad figure, as I remember it. She didn't have time for small talk. And yet she wasn't pompous. We soon became friends, young as I was, though at first she was a little frightening. Not that she actually was. But she looked important, she acted important. She was an imposing figure.

It was easier to like Sasha than Emma. Emma treated us as people, not as children. Berkman was gentler. He had a sweet smile. What a wonderful man he was! He treated us with more tenderness. One incident with Berkman I'll never forget. It was just before Thanksgiving when we were very little. It was not many years after Berkman got out of jail. He came to our house in the Bronx and brought a box of candy. On it was a chocolate turkey. "What's that?" we asked. "It's a bird," answered Sasha. "Oh, what a funny looking bird," I said. Then Sasha said, in a soft, tender voice, as if telling us a story: "I had a friend who was a bird. He was my best friend when I was all alone and had no friend. I would save part of my roll every day and put it on the window sill and share breakfast. And one day a very bad man came along and killed the bird." We all cried. Much later I read the story in Berkman's *Prison Memoirs of an Anarchist*. It was the warden who had killed the bird and, Sasha later told us, he hit the warden with a stool.[128]

I'll tell you another story about Berkman. It was during my first trip to Europe. I was very young, a student at Cooper Union, majoring in design. (I am now an industrial designer, mainly of lamps and furniture.) I went to Paris—my aunt was living there. She took me to the home of the violinist Jan Hambourg.[129] They were giving a party for Yehudi Menuhin—a hot chocolate party—who was about nine years old, a child prodigy.[130] After a while I said I had to leave. Mrs. Hambourg asked me indignantly where I had to go. I said I had to have tea with Alexander Berkman. She turned white and said, "My father was the judge that sent him to prison!"[131]

When Sasha and Emma were released from prison [in 1919] they returned to New York. Just before they were deported they took my mother and Leonard Abbott to a matinee to hear the first performance by Jascha Heifetz. Then everybody came back to our house. Before they departed for Russia, Emma left all her books in our apartment. They were stacked up in high piles. My sister and I, without Mother's knowledge, packed them in boxes and brought them to Geffen's Book Store near Cooper Union. One book, I remember, was *The Great French Revolution*, inscribed by Kropotkin to Emma. Another book, which we left in the apartment, was Emma's copy of *Prison Memoirs of an Anarchist*, inscribed by Sasha: "First copy off the press. To Emma, who helped to live my life and write it."[132] Geffen gave us twenty dollars. On the way home we met Mother on the street and proudly handed her the money. "Where did you get that?" she asked. We told her, and she cried. But she never reprimanded us. Some of the books remained in the apartment. I still have *The Evolution of Sex* by Patrick Geddes, with Emma's signature in it [she shows it to me], and I have some of Emma's and Sasha's later works, including *Living My Life* (inscribed "Freda Diamond, Affectionately, Emma Goldman") and *What Is Communist Anarchism?* ("Freda Diamond, Emma Goldman"). And I have a photograph of Sasha taken in Nice in 1935 [she gives this to me to keep].

It was through Moe and Emma that I got to know the Cominsky family—Saxe Commins,[133] Stella Ballantine, "Beenie" (Louis), and especially Ruthie, who was my good friend. She was homely and unattractive, but later married and had a child, followed by a nervous breakdown. They were the children of Emma's sister Lena, who lived in Rochester. Lena was cool to Emma, just the opposite of Helena, who always gave her support and affection. Not that Lena didn't care for Emma. She was ashamed of her radical and sensational ways. *Es past nit* [it won't do]—especially in Rochester—to have a sister like that! In addition to Moe, Emma had a brother Herman, who I think was in men's clothing and remained in Rochester like Lena and Helena. (I had a good friend, Nan Lyons—Nettie Levy—who could have told you all about them—she came from Rochester—but she just died.)

Saxe's real name was Isidore Cominsky. He had completed dental school but gave it up to become an editor. Saxe had charm, but was an opportunist. He used Emma and used Fitzi [M. Eleanor Fitzgerald]—that's how he came to the Provincetown Players and got to know Eugene O'Neill.[134] Through O'Neill he got a job at Covici-Friede, O'Neill's publisher, before moving to Random House.

Moe, you may know, had studied to be a doctor, but I don't know if he ever passed his boards. He never actually practiced medicine. For a long time he didn't do much of anything, and Mother supported him. Then he met Isidore Landsman, who was in the X-ray business. Moe got interested and went to work for him. Eventually he got a job as a radiologist at the Seaview Hospital on Staten Island, the largest tuberculosis hospital in the United States. He used X-rays to treat the patients.

One day, without any warning, Moe called from the hospital. He had married a nurse, an Irish girl named Daisy. He left our house and never came back, just like my father when I was a child. Stella and Saxe begged Mother not to make trouble, and she didn't. Of course she would not have in any case. Moe worked later in the Veterans' Hospital in Northport. But he fell ill with cancer and had to have his leg amputated. When Mother heard about this, she called Saxe and Stella and suggested starting a family fund. They refused. They never gave a penny for his support. So Mother called on me and my sister to help out—we were working by then—and we raised a fund for him. Mother went to his apartment for a week to shop and cook and do everything for him. Daisy seemed helpless and couldn't cope. We supported them to the day he died. I would have nothing to do with Saxe after that. When Moe died, Saxe cabled and asked about the funeral. I told him to go to hell! Once I was walking on Fifth Avenue and passed him. He was with Bennett Cerf[135] and said hello. I refused to recognize him and called him a skunk. And I haven't changed my mind. Emma, by the way, sent Moe a little money when she could and left him six hundred dollars when she died.

Let's return to Emma. I was visiting her in Toronto, along with Ruthie Commins, when Sacco and Vanzetti were executed. That night I shall never forget. Emma was staying with a Jewish anarchist family.[136] She had a phone in her room and it rang all evening long. There were calls from all over the world, but especially from Boston, pleading with her to do something. But there was nothing she could do, and she knew it. For someone as positive as Emma, she was quite modest, not at all like the commander-in-chief many took her to be. "What can I do, what can I do," she murmured very quietly, anxiously. Then came the call that they had been electrocuted. We were devastated.

I saw Emma again a few years later, when she was allowed to visit the States. I heard her speak—on birth control, I think it was. It sounded like the same old stuff she had been saying when I was a child, and I told her so. She was furious—she could get mad very easily. But she loved me just the same.

Emma had a powerful impact on my life. She opened so many horizons. She was a unique force—different from anyone else, not like any other person you met. She opened your mind and made you think about things you never thought about before. That was her outstanding characteristic. *She made people think!*

• LUBA STEIN BENENSON •

New York City, December 4, 1973; March 22, 1990

Luba Benenson is the daughter (and only child) of Modest Aronstam (later Stein), a well-known American illustrator and the "Fedya" of Alexander Berkman's *Prison Memoirs of an Anarchist* and Emma Goldman's *Living My Life*. In 1892 Aronstam conspired with Berkman and Goldman to assassinate Henry Clay Frick during the Homestead steel strike near Pittsburgh. The attempt, however, was unsuccessful. Frick, though seriously wounded, quickly recovered, while Berkman, who committed the deed, spent fourteen years in prison. The episode is recounted in the memoirs of Berkman and Goldman, but they omit any reference to Aronstam's role. He died in New York in 1958.

MY FATHER was born Modest Aronstam in Kovno, Russia, on February 22, 1871. He died in New York City at eighty-seven, on February 26, 1958. He and Alexander Berkman were cousins: I believe that Berkman's mother was my father's aunt. Father's father, Lazar Aronstam, had come to Kovno from Vilna. He was a pharmacist by profession and had two sons and a daughter. My father went to the *gymnasium* with Berkman. Like Berkman, he emigrated to America, while his brother remained in Kovno (as did his sister) and took over the pharmacy when Grandfather died. The sister married and had a son, Roma, who became a movie director. I saw my grandparents in 1904, when I was two years old and we visited them in Russia. It was during the summer and we went to the beach. I have no personal recollection of this, but I saw my grandmother again, in Bad Kissingen, in 1913 when I was eleven. By then Grandfather was dead.

Father came here when he was seventeen, in 1888, and ran into Berkman almost as soon as he arrived. Berkman introduced him to Emma Goldman. Father said that, except for my mother, he never met a more attractive woman than Emma. I knew her, and she was quite good looking, and Berkman was a lovely man. Did you know that after Sasha's unsuccessful attempt on Frick Father went to Pittsburgh to finish the job? The pockets of his trousers were filled with dynamite. He intended to blow up Frick's house. When he got off the train he passed a newspaper stand and his eyes fell on a headline: "AARON STAMM HERE TO KILL FRICK." So he dumped the dynamite in an outhouse and left on the next train. Father told me, by the way, that he was present when Emma Goldman horsewhipped Johann Most; and he recounted the incident when Berkman got angry at him for lavishing twenty-five cents on a meal. He also told me that Berkman, although he had failed to kill Frick, killed other people and could have been executed, but I can't remember the details.

During the later 1890s, before photography came in, Father worked as a pen-and-ink artist for the New York *World* and the *Sun*. After that he became popular as an illustrator for magazines, doing covers for *Love Story*, *Adventure*,

Argosy, and other leading periodicals. He married my mother, Marcia Mishkin, on June 18, 1899, and I was born on September 10, 1902. Mother was a professional photographer, a sister of the well-known photographer Herman Mishkin, who had the concession to photograph the singers of the Metropolitan Opera. As he became increasingly successful, Father drifted away from the anarchist movement, though he continued to see Sasha, Emma, and other old comrades and contributed money regularly. He changed his name to Stein sometime after I was born. Sasha and Emma used the name "Fedya" to protect his identity. I was four when Berkman was released from prison. He often came to our apartment in New York, a sweet and charming man. Father remained good friends with Sasha and Emma till their deportation.

Hippolyte Havel also came to our house, and Harry Kelly, but I have only vague recollections of them. Claus Timmermann[137] also remained close to Father. He became an alcoholic. He was my babysitter. He worked as a dishwasher in my husband's parents' boarding house in Ellenville, New York. Then he became a handyman at Camp Greylock in Massachusetts. He was a fine carpenter. They were really a foursome, though he wasn't amorously involved with Emma, as were Father and Berkman. Though Claus earned very little, every time he got paid he sent some money to Emma and Sasha in France. He died at Camp Greylock around 1940. Once, when I was seventeen or eighteen, Father was called to Bellevue because Claus was there. He had drunk wood alcohol, and they said he was dying. But right after the call, Claus arrived. He had made a quick recovery!

Father was strongly sympathetic to the Bolshevik Revolution and remained pro-Bolshevik until the thirties. He made a trip to Russia in 1931, then visited Emma and Sasha at Bon Esprit. He told me that Berkman had cancer of the prostate when he shot himself. Father did the relief of Emma Goldman on her tombstone, which is signed by him.[138] Father liked women and they liked him. He did not save his correspondence, but I have a few pictures of him and a letter to him from Emma.

• JEANNE LEVEY •

Miami, Florida, December 19, 1972

Born into an immigrant family in Chicago, Jeanne Levey frequented Jane Addams's Hull House, joined the anarchist movement, and came to know such figures as Emma Goldman, Alexander Berkman, Ben Reitman, and Rudolf Rocker. After her marriage, Mrs. Levey rose from poverty to riches and founded the Parkinson's Disease Hospital in Miami (her husband died from the illness). She became a friend of Congressman Claude Pepper and through him of Eleanor Roosevelt. But she never lost her affection for the anarchists. When I interviewed her in her Miami apartment, she showed me a portrait on the wall of Sadakichi Hartmann, painted from life in California. In 1977, while visiting Miami, I telephoned Mrs. Levey in the hope of paying her a visit. Unfortunately it could not be arranged. She was bedridden, she told me, having suffered a stroke earlier that year. She spoke of her love for Rudolf Rocker and the other old comrades, all long since dead. She herself died around 1980.

I WAS BORN in Chicago in 1888, a year after the Haymarket executions. We were a very poor family, and I saw great poverty all around us. When I was fifteen or sixteen years old, I already thought that there was great injustice and that poverty was a prevalent thing in this country, and that basic social reform was necessary. I had—and still have—a complete identification with the have-nots and the suffering. I went to Hull House and was one of Jane Addams's pets. I studied Esperanto because I thought that if there was one language there would be more understanding and less conflict among people.

Emma Goldman was an oversexed personality, and she made all sorts of advances to men. In fact, many men—including my own husband—would say, "Save me!" She would devour them. Emma was very vain, yet she was the greatest person that I have met in my lifetime. She was far greater than Alexander Berkman, who was conceited and opinionated. Eleanor Roosevelt once told me, at our ADA[139] luncheon, that *Living My Life* is one of the great books of our time.

Paul Robeson came to Emma when she was publishing *Mother Earth*, and she helped him finance his education.[140] She loved America with a strong passion. Berkman did not have as much of America as she did, as his young manhood was spent in prison. Emma was a wonderful person. Ben Reitman loved her very much. He was an unusual personality in his own right and is not to be dismissed.

As for other women in the movement whom I met or saw in Chicago, Lucy Parsons didn't amount to very much. In fact she was a rather ordinary person, quite ugly and a rather distasteful personality. It was through her association with her husband that she became famous. I heard Voltairine de Cleyre speak in Chicago. She was beautiful, she was poetic, there was something mellifluous about her voice. Emma was jealous of all the pretty women, all the attractive ones, including Voltairine, who came into her path. Yet she was big enough to love them nonetheless. Annie Livshis, at whose house in Chicago Voltairine stayed, was the epitome of everything magnificent in the human spirit: gentle, soft-spoken, devoted to her cause.

Abe Isaak was another remarkable figure. His daughter Mary lives in Santa Cruz. She had two beautiful daughters. One of them [Grace Umrath, q.v.] danced in the New York City Ballet. Ben Capes[141] was close to Matthew Schmidt. I used to visit Caplan and Schmidt in prison.[142] Caplan was a free spirit but not a great personality. Schmidty was extraordinary, an unusual man and quite a philosopher. After his release from prison, he directed a labor radio station in Chicago. He died about fifteen years ago.

Sadakichi Hartmann had the most beautiful hands I ever saw. During the First World War his wife had him arrested for lack of support. The judge told him to go work in the shipyards, so he did. But they found him sleeping in a corner and he was arrested again. He was a derelict, but with a most magnificent ability to use his hands; I heard him recite "The Raven," and it was unforgettable. I once arranged a lecture for him in Hollywood. He had two protruding front teeth. He never had a dollar and he really exploited all of us. Yes, I knew Gregory Maximoff[143] well in Chicago. He was a thoughtful man. There was nothing vulgar or uncouth about him.

I never lost touch with the anarchists and have always felt that theirs was the world I was brought up in. I don't care what you call it, but all the things that the anarchists said sixty or seventy years ago have taken on respectability. If anarchism did nothing else but serve that purpose, it was worth it. But unfortunately it has been so distorted, so misunderstood. Otherwise it might have been a great force for educating people, for liberating them.

• PAULINE H. TURKEL •

New York City, January 21, 1972

During 1917 and 1918 Pauline Turkel, a half-sister of Henry Fruchter (q.v.), was Emma Goldman's secretary at the offices of *Mother Earth* in New York and, with Hilda Adel (q.v.) and M. Eleanor Fitzgerald ("Fitzi"), worked for the release of political prisoners during the Red Scare that followed. She visited Emma Goldman in Munich in 1923 and saw her again in Paris the following year, when Emma was en route from Germany to England.[144] In after years Pauline served in the American consulate in Rome and was associated with the Provincetown Players in Greenwich Village (of which Fitzi was the manager), where she was a friend of Eugene O'Neill, Hart Crane, Djuna Barnes, and other writers. From 1937 until her retirement in 1964 she was managing editor of *The Psychoanalytical Quarterly* in New York. In Lucy Robins Lang's description, Pauline had "the face of Da Vinci's Madonna . . . surveying the world with a faint, sad apprehension."[145] She died on April 5, 1987.

I WAS BORN in New York on February 21, 1899, of Jewish immigrant parents from Galicia. I became an anarchist through my half-brother, Henry Fruchter [q.v.], who later turned to socialism. I attended lectures at the Ferrer Center on East 107 Street and met Emma Goldman at the offices of *Mother Earth*. I became her secretary in 1916 or 1917. I helped organize the 1917 rally for Mooney and Billings in Madison Square Garden and was active with Emma Goldman, Alexander Berkman, and M. Eleanor Fitzgerald ("Fitzi") in the No-Conscription effort that year.

Fitzi and I became intimate friends. We lived together in Greenwich Village from 1918 to 1923 and afterwards had a house in Sherman, Connecticut, where Fitzi died in 1955. In 1918 the police raided our apartment and seized our correspondence. I went to the office of Attorney General Palmer's chief New York agent to get them back. While he was on the telephone, his secretary put a legal-sized yellow sheet on his desk. I took a peek and saw that it had a transcript of a phone conversation between me and Fitzi that morning. I demanded—and got—my letters back and added, "I don't like my phone tapped." The agent turned green with embarrassment. During that time, Ben Capes used to write letters to me and called me "Bluebird," from Maeterlinck's play. Detectives tried to find "Bluebird" and questioned me in the office of the League for the Amnesty of Political Prisoners, where I worked, about who "Bluebird" was.

Emma was difficult to work with, impatient and strict. Sasha was nicer. I loved him very much. In 1923 Fitzi and I visited Sasha and Emma in Munich. The police arrested us—except Sasha, who managed to slip away—and they had a full dossier on Emma, with pictures going back to her childhood. We later visited them in France. Emma was very jealous of Fitzi, whom Sasha adored. Later on, Emmy Eckstein[146] was jealous of both Fitzi and Emma. Fitzi had visited Sasha in Altanta prison before he was deported. Fitzi, a beautiful redhead, was very good to me— actually brought me up, like a mother (she had no children of her own). She loved and helped people who were creative, for example, Djuna Barnes[147] and Hart Crane.[148] Crane lived at our house in Connecticut for a time. He drank a lot and became difficult. Fitzi was generous to everybody but herself. She even helped Mike Gold,[149] already a Communist, with his plays when she managed the Provincetown Playhouse. When I got encephalitis in our New York apartment, she cared for me selflessly. Bob Minor[150] tried to get her to join the Communist movement, but she refused. I inherited the Connecticut house in 1955 and sold it in 1964 to Professor Charles Issawi of Columbia.

While on the way with me to the Provincetown Playhouse, Hippolyte Havel once spread his coat over a puddle, like Sir Walter Raleigh, to let me pass. "Fedya" was Modest Stein, who became a successful artist, drawing covers for popular magazines. I was told by a very reliable source that the 1916 bombing in San Francisco[151] was done by Mexican revolutionaries. Becky Edelsohn committed suicide in California about four months ago.[152] I gave my Emma Goldman letters to Jeanne Levey [q.v.], who recently gave them to the Tamiment Library.

• HILDA ADEL •

Croton-on-Hudson, New York, April 14, 1973; September 18, 1979

Hilda Kovner Adel and her companion Sam Adel were young anarchists in New York City in 1917, when the United States entered the First World War. Opponents of the war, they frequented the offices of *Mother Earth*, published by Emma Goldman and Alexander Berkman, and attended their trial for obstructing the draft, for which Emma and Sasha (as Berkman was called) were sentenced to two years in prison plus a ten thousand dollar fine each. In 1918 Hilda and Sam joined the Frayhayt Group, a circle of Jewish anarchists who distributed leaflets denouncing American military intervention in Soviet Russia. In a celebrated case, Jacob Abrams, Mollie Steimer, and two other members of the group were imprisoned under the Sedition Act and subsequently deported. To assist them, Hilda and Sam helped organize the Political Prisoners Defense and Relief Committee, to which Emma Goldman refers in her autobiography.[153] In 1927 Hilda and Sam settled in the Mount Airy Colony at Croton, New York, where Sam died around 1960 and Hilda in 1984, at the age of ninety-two. Sam, it might be mentioned, was an uncle of Leon Edel, the noted literary historian and biographer of Henry James.

I WAS BORN Hilda Kovner in Chernigov, Russia, eighty-one years ago and emigrated to the United States in 1906. I lived with an uncle in Etna, Pennsylvania (near Pittsburgh), until 1912. That year I went to Boston and through my sister entered radical circles. I sold anarchist literature and in 1917 engaged in anti-draft resistance. In 1917 I got together with Sam Adel, a fellow anarchist, and we moved to New York. On the night of our arrival, our comrades Jacob Schwartz and Jacob and Mary Abrams took us to an anarchist meeting on the Lower East Side. At first we had no place to stay, but Fitzi [M. Eleanor Fitzgerald], whom we met at the offices of *Mother Earth*, put us up in Sasha's room until he came back from jail a few days later. He was being held on extradition charges in connection with the Mooney-Billings case. Fitzi was tall, red-haired, and handsome. And she had soul! She was a wonderful person. I later worked for her at the Provincetown Players. She and Sasha were lovers, but they never had children. "We can't have children," Sasha told her. "The revolution is too important."

In June 1917 Sasha and Emma Goldman were indicted for interfering with the draft. Sam and I went to court on the last day of the trial. Harry Weinberger[154] had given us a pass, but they wouldn't let us in because Sam had long hair. So we stood outside the courtroom in the hall. At one point the door opened and I could see Emma and hear her speaking, sarcastically: "Thank you judge for the justice you have given us."[155]

Sam was a cabinetmaker by trade and an individualist by conviction, influenced by Stirner and Nietzsche, but we mingled with anarchists of different types, including Fitzi, Harry Kelly, and Leonard Abbott at *Mother Earth*. We also attended *Fraye Arbeter Shtime* gatherings but found Joseph Cohen, who presided, an autocrat in the way he conducted meetings, cold and inflexible.

In early 1918 a small group was formed in New York: Sam, myself, Jack Abrams, Mollie Steimer, Jacob Schwartz, Hyman Lachowsky, Rose Mirsky, Sam Lipman, and a few others. We published a Yiddish anarchist paper called *Frayhayt*, which defended the Russian Revolution and opposed American intervention in the Civil War. In August 1918 we printed anti-intervention leaflets on our press and took them to a factory downtown. Mollie went into a washroom and threw them out the window. But police arrested a newcomer to our group [Hyman Rosansky] and he informed on us. Mollie, Jack Abrams, Lachowsky, Schwartz, and Lipman were arrested. Most of the group, by the way, lived together in an apartment on East 104 Street. Schwartz died in Bellevue Hospital after being beaten by the police. The rest were tried and given long sentences and heavy fines. We organized a Political Prisoners Defense Committee to try to secure their release, even if this meant deportation, and to aid other political prisoners. We finally succeeded, and the four [Abrams, Steimer, Lipman, and Lachowsky] were deported to Russia in November 1921.[156]

In December 1919 Sasha and Emma had also been expelled. Emma spoke to me personally the day she was deported. I needed an abortion. We were poor; Sam was out of work; we had no money. I was working at the time at the Bureau of Legal Advice (Mr. Witherspoon was its secretary) and was typing a letter when Emma called on the telephone. She told me what was to be done, whom to see, everything I needed to know. She didn't know me that intimately, yet she was concerned about me and determined to help—on the very day that she was thrown out of the country! So those who call her harsh and selfish can't convince me!

During the early 1920s Sam, I, and the other members of the prisoners' committee published a bulletin for political prisoners, *The American Political Prisoner*. In 1924 Sam and I went to the West Coast. We visited Home Colony in Washington and lived in California for a while. Meanwhile, in 1925, George Seldes[157] and Harry Kelly had founded Belle Terre, a summer colony in Croton with houses and cabins. In 1926 Kelly began the Mount Airy colony, and we came here in 1927. Each house was on a quarter-acre plot, and five-and-a-half acres were set aside for a school but it was never built. I still live in the same house built by Sam, called "Samilda Cottage," after Sam and Hilda.

• ROGER N. BALDWIN •

New York City, January 29, 1974

Roger Baldwin (1884–1981), founder of the American Civil Liberties Union and a lifelong champion of individual freedom and human rights, was employed in 1911 as a probation officer in St. Louis when he attended a lecture by Emma Goldman. "I was electrified the moment she opened her mouth," he recalled. "She was a great speaker—passionate, intellectual, and witty. I'd never heard such a direct attack on the foundations of society. I became a revolutionist, though I continued to work at practical reforms."[158] A short while later, Baldwin proclaimed himself a philosophical anarchist, a follower of Thoreau as well as of Goldman, whom he regarded as a major influence on his life, though they were to disagree sharply in their assessment of Lenin and the Bolsheviks.

Baldwin also came to know Alexander Berkman, Carlo Tresca, and other leading anarchists and worked to save Sacco and Vanzetti from execution. In addition, he visited Peter Kropotkin's widow in Moscow, edited a volume of Kropotkin's writings,[159] and spoke on Kropotkin at the Libertarian Book Club of New York on the fortieth anniversary of his death. (The title of his address was "Kropotkin's Teachings for the World of Today.") On the eve of his own death, in 1981, Baldwin harked back to Emma Goldman: "In the years since I met Miss Goldman, I have never departed from the general philosophy represented in libertarian literature—that is, in the goal of a society with a minimum of compulsion, a maximum of individual freedom and of voluntary association, and the abolition of exploitation and poverty."[160]

THE ANARCHISTS, as I knew them, were always right and always ineffective. They never resigned themselves to making compromises, which are necessary in any struggle. Emma Goldman did somewhat better than most, however. She was interested in immediate issues as well as in her philosophy. She was extraordinarily motherly in her relations with other people, partly because her motherhood had been frustrated by her not being able to have children. She was an extremely literate person, who lived in books as well as in history. Her lectures, which I began to attend in 1911 while in St. Louis, opened up all kinds of new literature to me—Ibsen, Schopenhauer, the Russians. She introduced many people to a whole literature of protest.

Berkman? What a strange man! He, unlike Emma, was just full of despair. He never gave up completely his belief in violence, to which desperate men are prone. He took his own life, finally. While he held anarchist views and professed to be an idealist, and therefore an optimist, he really at heart had no faith in himself. That's why he had all those mistresses. He couldn't be faithful. He had a very disorderly life. But he was a very nice person. His *Prison Memoirs* showed the same contradictions as his life: compassion for his fellow inmates combined with fatalism and cynicism. He never had the affirmation of life that Emma had. I knew her well, and I saw considerable of Berkman in Paris in 1926–27, when I spent a whole year there. He did some translations for me, for which I paid him. He and Emma treated me—and I think now that they were right—as very naive. I didn't see in the proletarian dictatorship what they did. They sensed the inherent drive for domination in the Bolsheviks, while I accepted, like a damned fool, their professed belief in the withering away of the state. I thought that they were at least aiming in the right direction, while Emma and Sasha knew that they were aiming the opposite way. I thought that by education and trade unions they would evolve along the right lines, but I was wrong. It took me a long time to find out that the state is irresistible, and that once power is seized and exercised you don't give it up.

I spent a good deal of time in Russia in 1927 and 1928, and visited many prisons—in Tiflis, Yaroslavl, Leningrad, Moscow, three in Moscow—and talked with numerous political prisoners, anarchists among them. All the while I was in Moscow I stayed at Madame Kropotkin's home—the Kropotkin Museum—in a guest room upstairs. She was living outside the city, in Dmitrov, where he had died. She was a very sentimental old lady and kept all the flowers from his funeral, with all the streamers and banners that had been carried with them, downstairs in a room of the Moscow house. She took me out to his grave, which had a picture of him on the tombstone. She had great reverence for him, though I don't think she ever understood his ideas. It was a kind of pilgrimage for me.

I met many anarchists through her. They were all very quiet about their attitude towards the government, not so much out of fear, I think, as through a sense of futility. Few visitors came to the museum, but there was an anarcho-syndicalist bookstore opposite the university downtown and quite a few people went there. I arrived in June and left in September of 1927, just before Trotsky's exile, and things were all in ferment. I saw both Kropotkinite and Tolstoyan anarchists, because I had a foot in both camps. I carried a letter from the American Quakers to the Russian Quakers and Tolstoyans. I went to a number of meetings that the Tolstoyans held quite openly, though their people were still being arrested for refusing conscription. I even addressed one meeting on conscientious objection, and over three hundred people attended. I went to the trials of Tolstoyan C.O.'s. They were very outspoken about their attitude towards the state, and were eager to hear about my own experiences as a C.O. during the war.[161]

I never met Voltairine de Cleyre, but I liked what she wrote in *Mother Earth*. Emma was always talking to me about her, and she admired her enormously. Emma may have had a certain self-importance, but her spirit was very generous. My experience with her was one of affection and friendship up to the time she died. The individualist anarchists, like Benjamin Tucker, never inspired me, despite the fact that they claimed Thoreau and Emerson, whom I claimed too. They always struck me as isolated. They never engaged in any social movement, never took part in the popular struggle. The Tolstoyans were also likely to remain apart from mass movements, but they had great compassion for the common people.

I went to the Ferrer School in New Jersey when I first came to New York in 1917 or 1918. Harry Kelly, my old friend from St. Louis, brought me, and I even spoke there once or twice. The school was run by saints. Alexis and Elizabeth Ferm[162] were so dedicated, so self-sacrificing, that no setback or discouragement—and there were many—could stop them from carrying out their mission. The colony itself had a very pleasant community atmosphere. There was nothing particularly striking about their educational theories, except that they gave the children great freedom and had no obligatory curriculum. Emma knew John Dewey[163] quite well, by the way, and had a high regard for his educational ideas. I shared a platform with Dewey and John Haynes Holmes[164] in Town Hall when Emma came back in 1934.

Harry Kelly was the quietest and most nonresistant anarchist you could ever dream of, and his talk about anarchism was the mildest recital of principles that you might read in a book. I never heard him get excited or even be severely critical of anyone. He had a nice, pleasant manner, calm and cool. He and I were both from St. Louis and both admired Kropotkin, and when we both took part in founding the League for Mutual Aid,[165] we got its name from Kropotkin's "mutual aid," a fundamental ethical principle. Leonard Abbott was a literary man, on the staff of several magazines. We all went very often to Romany Marie's restaurant, around the corner from here,[166] a very good place to eat.

I knew both Sacco and Vanzetti and visited them in prison, especially Vanzetti, very often. I was one of the trustees of Sacco's estate, money given him by radical French trade-unionists for his family. Sacco was very difficult to deal with, not communicative and very suspicious of everyone. But Vanzetti trusted you and was almost childlike in his confidences. I got to know him rather well, and he maintained his innocence to the end. Both of them wrote me farewell letters, which I unfortunately gave to the son of Tolstoy's executor to put up on a bulletin board in Moscow and never saw again. I am sure that Vanzetti was innocent of the first crime. And in the second case I'm quite sure that neither of them fired any shots, but not at all sure that the gang was unknown to them.

Who killed Carlo Tresca?[167] Yes, I'm sure who killed him. He was about to expose some dirt on the Generoso Pope family, and they rubbed him out. It was an inside job among the Italians, without any political implications, either Communist or fascist.

I've entertained many social theories which have a liberating effect on the restrictions that people have been living under. But I've never embraced any of them. I never could accept a doctrine that has definite boundaries to it. I just have to keep my mind free. The anarchists of all of them come closest to removing these restraints. In all our peace and civil liberties work, even today, the power of the state has always been the main opponent. Anarchism is based on the philosophy that an increase in individual choice and freedom is the road to a better society, and all libertarians share that view. The Communists have the same ultimate goal, but believe that a temporary dictatorship is necessary before we can get to it. I still think that it may be necessary. I have never considered anarchism as a philosophy that has guided me but as a philosophy that has elements which appeal to me, above all liberty and voluntary association. I think that anarchism is a bad word. It is open to too many misinterpretations and has generally been associated with violence and assassination, rather than with any creative ideas. There never was an anarchist movement. There were isolated sects and groups that often quarreled with each other, each one going its own way. It is a philosophy taking many different forms. But they all agree on freedom of expression and resistance to controls by one person over another. It never was born and never will die. For it springs from the human soul and will last as long as man lasts.

• ALBERT BONI •

New York City, January 24, 1974

Boni, eighty-one years old when I interviewed him, was head of the Readex Microprint Company. In 1915, with Lawrence Langner, he founded the Washington Square Players and was also associated with the Theater Guild. During the 1920s, with Horace Liveright, he published the Modern Library, before selling it to Bennett Cerf, publishing works by Theodore Dreiser, Thornton Wilder, and Ford Madox Ford. With his brother Charles he published *Letters from Russian Prisoners*, edited by Alexander Berkman (1925), and with Liveright published Berkman's *The Bolshevik Myth* (1925). Boni was later one of the pioneers in the paperback book club field. He lived in the Free Acres colony in Berkeley Heights, New Jersey, and was a friend of Joseph Ishill, the anarchist printer. He died in Florida in 1981, at the age of eighty-eight.

I WAS NOT an anarchist but a socialist. I didn't like Emma Goldman. She was pretty hard-boiled and too damn cocksure of everything she had to say. Berkman, though, was a lovable person, despite his attempt to kill Frick. I read *Mother Earth* and may have gone to the Ferrer Center.[168] But I was never close to either one until I met them both in Russia, which I visited in 1920–1921. When they arrived in Moscow I was already there. They were disillusioned because they found that anarchists had been imprisoned by the Bolshevik regime. I went with Henry Alsberg[169] to visit them. They were very excited because they had just received a letter from Lenin offering them a special train to travel around Russia and gather material for the Museum of the Revolution. We encouraged them to do it.

I later was arrested on suspicion of being a spy for the American government and because I disagreed with some of the Bolshevik policies. I was in a prison camp for a while, and then deported on a train with an armed guard. In the Petrograd station I saw another train with a banner "Museum of the Revolution." So I jumped off and ran to it, with my guard chasing after me. Berkman calmed him down, then we talked. He told me that the previous night someone reached into the window of his sleeping car and stole his best trousers. I said, "Sasha, don't worry," and ran back to my own train and brought an officer's uniform that I'd bought from an English colonel in prison camp. I gave it to Berkman. I never saw a man squirm as much as he, for a military uniform, complete with braiding, represented everything he detested. But he accepted it. He and Emma left Russia not long afterwards. She later wrote, in *Living My Life*, that they had met me and Alsberg and liked him better. [Boni was still visibly irritated by this.]

I was a member of the Free Acres Colony[170] for many years. Bolton Hall was a fine person. I knew Joseph Ishill[171] well—also a loveable man, but his wife was a damn nuisance. I arranged with the University of Florida for them to go there, but she made all kinds of demands and they left after a few months. I gave my Ishill collection to the Tamiment Library.

• GABRIEL JAVSICAS •

New York City, May 27, 1980

Gabriel Javsicas, born in Russia in 1906, met Emma Goldman in 1924 while a student at the London School of Economics. They quickly became good friends. Afterwards Javsicas (originally Jawschitz) studied economics at Columbia University, visited Emma in France, and traveled with her to Spain in 1928. At the time of the Spanish Civil War he served as an economics advisor to the CNT-FAI in Barcelona, where he saw Emma once again. During this period he wrote on Spain for *The Nation*, the *Atlantic Monthly*, *Harper's*, and other magazines. He later served on the board of Spanish Refugee Aid, was a supporter of Amnesty International, and was an editor, with Abe Bluestein (q.v.), Murray Bookchin, and Sam Dolgoff (q.v.) of *News from Libertarian Spain*. He died of a heart attack on January 14, 1982, while at the wheel of his car in New York.

I CAME to London in November 1924, at the age of eighteen, after graduating from high school in Frankfurt-am-Main. My father owned a lumber factory in Memel, and he wanted me to join the business, a very prosperous one. But I was bent on studying at the London School of Economics, and he finally agreed. My cousin Sasha and I got lodgings in London through a student organization. We were sent to a Mrs. Zhook, Doris Zhook, who had rooms to let at 3 Titchfield Terrace. We knocked at the door. It was opened by a woman who spoke excellent German, a very forceful personality. She told us that Mrs.

Zhook was away and that she too was a lodger in the building. She showed us our rooms, and we took them.

This woman became our great friend. She cooked us breakfast—an excellent breakfast. We began to discuss things: politics, art, and the like. I said I had read about the Soviet regime; it was a book in German, possibly by Kurt Tucholsky.[172] Tucholsky said that he had watched the November 7 demonstration on Red Square and that it had reminded him of an Easter procession in Rome, a kind of state religion in which a humanitarian ideal had been turned into a new tyranny. She said that this was quite right, that she had seen it all herself.

Can you imagine my surprise when, about three weeks after taking my lodgings at Titchfield Terrace, I opened the newspaper and saw a picture of my new friend. "Red Emma," it was captioned, "Living in London." I knew very little about anarchism, but I knew that she was a remarkable woman, and I liked her! The article was about a speech she had made at a meeting organized by Rebecca West,[173] with Josiah Wedgwood[174] in the chair. Everybody had been invited. Bertrand Russell was there, and so was Harold Laski, my teacher at the London School of Economics. George Bernard Shaw and H. G. Wells, however, declined to come.

When Emma got up to speak, the article said, she was wildly applauded. When she sat down there was absolute silence. She had criticized the regime in Soviet Russia as a dictatorship not *of* the proletariat but *over* the proletariat, a very unpopular stand to take at that time among liberals and socialists. I heard her speak soon afterwards in a hall in the East End. Someone in the audience asked her about the mutiny of the Kronstadt sailors. She told of how a sailor from Kronstadt had come to Petrograd during the revolt and reminded Zinoviev[175] how he and his comrades had saved the revolution in 1917. A Communist in the hall got up and shouted, "You're lying!" But she wasn't. Her words had the ring of truth. She was a forceful, convincing speaker. I was deeply impressed. She repeated what she said at the previous meeting: that the Bolsheviks had betrayed the revolution and established a dictatorship over the proletariat. I accepted this implicitly.

Emma and I became close friends. We talked a lot, went places together, and afterwards wrote to one another. I took her often to the theater—she especially loved that! Emma loved young men. At one point she suggested that we sleep together, but I demurred.

During my Christmas vacation in 1924 I went to Berlin, and there I met Alexander Berkman. Emma had given me his address. I told him how much I admired his book, *Prison Memoirs of an Anarchist*, and he was pleased. I fell in love with both of them instantly. Berkman had a sharp wit, a kind of graveyard humor. Just before he was deported from America he learned that Frick had died, and he said: "I'm glad he left the country before me."[176]

After leaving Berlin, Berkman rented a house in St. Cloud, a suburb of Paris. Soon afterward, Emmy [Eckstein], his companion, joined him—a package of poison if there ever was one, an absolute disaster. She came from the lowest kind of middle-class bourgeoisie in Hungary. Her dream was to be Frau Berkman, and she nagged him day and night to marry her. One couldn't simply drop in for a visit, as I liked to do. She got terribly upset. She was a fool and a hypochondriac. She later found a quack in Nice who tried to cure her stomach trouble by shortening her intestine. Instead, he shortened her life.

Berkman's political philosophy was very simplistic, and there was a strong Marxist element in it: the economic basis of history, the role of the working class in overthrowing capitalism, the primacy of the economic factor—hence his *economic* deed was superior to Czolgosz's *political* deed. He believed that the revolution had a right to defend itself by all and any means, including imprisonment and execution.

In 1928 Emma and I traveled from France to Spain. I was there only a week; she stayed a bit longer. We went to a café together, and she was the only woman in the place. There was great excitement. Everyone craned his neck to see her. She went to see Federico Urales—the anarchist Juan Montseny, Federica's father.[177] She asked him about the anarchist movement in Spain. He said there wasn't any movement because the young people had no ideals but were interested only in dancing and going to the movies. How wrong he was! Just a few years later there were millions of anarchists in Spain.

Fedya, their old comrade, turned up in St. Tropez in 1930 or 1931. He had become a successful artist and had long since abandoned anarchism. He had an apartment on Gramercy Park, a very exclusive neighborhood. But he was lonely. He wanted to look up his old friends, the friends of his youth.

Not long afterwards Berkman developed prostate trouble. In 1936 he had an operation, which transformed him from a powerful individual into a doddering old man. He had unbearable pains after the operation. He was convinced that he had cancer. There wasn't any sense in living any longer.

During the Spanish Civil War I saw Emma in Paris. She seemed very subdued. She was getting old and was mellowing. She favored the anarchists' joining the Spanish government. Alexander Schapiro and I strongly opposed it. Schapiro was one of the most intelligent of the anarchists I knew. Rocker, too, was a truly thinking person. I loved him. He had a Germanic admiration for learning. He had read a great deal and knew a great deal. A very charming man.

• IDA GERSHOY •

New York City, June 8, 1983

Ida Gershoy, born about 1903, was the wife of Leo Gershoy, the well-known historian of modern France. Their dentist at Rochester, New York, where Gershoy was teaching in the late 1920s, was Emma Goldman's nephew, Saxe Commins, the future editor at Random House. It was through him that the Gershoys got to

know Goldman and Alexander Berkman, whom they visited in France. The birthday party to which Ida refers in the interview took place on June 27, 1928, not
1929, and celebrated Goldman's fifty-ninth, not sixtieth, year. In a letter to Berkman, dated June 29, 1928, Goldman describes the occasion: "What looked to be
a dreary and lonesome birthday turned out to be a gay affair. All thanks to my
thoughtful secretary [Emily Holmes Coleman, known as "Demi"]. She had quite
a conspiracy, invited the Gershoys, Saxe's friends, bought three bottles of champagne and some delicious cakes, and marched everything up to our terrace, ice
and all. I had suspected that Demi is up to something; she is a poor conspirator.
But I did not expect champagne. Well, we drank until eleven and then went down
to the village to dance. We came back at two in the morning. I got up a bit tired
yesterday, but I wrote all afternoon [she was working on her autobiography, *Living My Life*]. So you see the champagne must have been good, it had no after
effects. I enjoyed the party immensely but even more so Demi's fine spirit, her
thoughtfulness."[178] Ida Gershoy died in New York on November 27, 1991.

MY HUSBAND, Leo Gershoy, was teaching at the University of Rochester, and
Saxe Commins was our dentist there. We met him just by going to him for
dental work. We started as patients but became intimate friends. That was in
the 1920s. Emma Goldman and Alexander Berkman were both living in France
at that time. Emma, you know, knew all the rich people in Rochester. In fact,
a group of them bought her the house she had in St. Tropez. Stein of Stein &
Bloch [the clothing manufacturers] was one of them, if I'm not mistaken.

Leo and I were going to go to Europe for an extended trip. Saxe said, "You
must look up *Tante* Emma." She was living in a hotel in Paris. Our hotel was
not far away, and we went over to see her. She made a tremendous impression.
She was a very powerful woman with an overwhelming personality. She was not
at all good-looking, but in a curious way was rather handsome, with her big
blue eyes and overpowering personality. She was getting ready to leave for her
house in St. Tropez. We knew nothing about St. Tropez and had never been
there. "You must come and visit me," she said. She liked both of us very much.

That's how we got to St. Tropez—through Emma. It was not a very fashionable place at that time. It was a charming town then; it's changed a good deal
for the worse since. A number of artists lived there, and when you bought fish
or vegetables the shopkeeper would ask, "Is it for eating or painting?" We spent
six months in St. Tropez that year and came back the following year for another six months. We found a charming villa that we were able to rent for only
a hundred dollars for the entire six months.

We would walk over to Emma's house three or four times a week. It was a
small but very pleasant house, with a nice garden. The gardener, a handsome
Frenchman, was very devoted to Emma. She was writing her autobiography at
the time, but had a steady stream of visitors and quite a few dinners and parties. Emma was fond of drinking—especially wine—and was very proud of her
cooking. "Have some of E. G.'s coffee," she would say. "Have some of E. G.'s

pudding"—or whatever she was making that day. Emma was an awful person to live with, you know. She could be quite captivating, but also very difficult—the worst bitch in the world!

We also saw Berkman quite often. Sasha was living in Nice with his companion Emmy Eckstein. He was a really wonderful man. We didn't think we would like him, but developed a great affection for him—and we weren't anarchists and weren't accustomed to such people. Leo found him fascinating and talked with him all the time. Sasha had a perfect command of English, of course, but spoke with a noticeable accent, Russian or Jewish I would call it. (Emma's, by contrast, was very slight.) He also knew French very well, but his accent was quite appalling! His Emmy was a very uninteresting girl. She was sort of pretty in a way, but never said very much and was very much under Sasha's thumb. She had no personality. Emma was rather nice to Emmy, and she never said anything unpleasant about her, at least when I was around. And she always invited her to come to visit with Sasha. They almost always came together—to our dismay, since we didn't find her very enthralling.

Emma, who bossed everyone in sight, always was very meek when Sasha was there. All he had to do was give her a look and she acquiesced. He was the only one who could intimidate her. I think it was because of his act—his attempt on Frick—and her role in it. That was their great bond. She was intensely devoted to Sasha, I think because of her feeling of guilt over the Frick affair and Sasha's long imprisonment. They had a deep understanding of one another, a strong rapport. They were constantly in communication, and every little thing that happened to Sasha was very important to Emma.

Sasha and Leo often talked about anarchism and about history. Sasha said that his next book would be called "I Have to Leave"—he was always being harassed and driven out of places! He was very fond of Leo, and was fond of me too. He liked girls, and I was very young then. He wasn't at all good-looking. Not that he was terribly homely. He looked very Jewish. He had a long nose and a loose lip. I was quite appalled when I first saw him, he looked so unattractive. But he was intelligent, he was kind, and he was sweet; and after a while I came to love him; and Leo did too. He never said anything nasty about anybody, where Emma constantly did.

But she too could be sweet and charming, and often was. And she liked men, especially young men. She really liked the boys! She was very fond of my husband, and also of my older brother, who once came to visit. One time one of her old flames from America came to visit—I can't remember his name—one of her "great loves," she said. I had pictured him as tall and handsome, but he turned out to be short and homely, with a crossed eye. Another visitor was Gabriel Jawschitz [later Javsicas, q.v.], an extremely odd-looking young man. But she was very fond of him. I think they had been lovers.

Emma was lots of fun, but not Berkman. He couldn't relax enough to be fun. He laughed, of course, and told amusing stories, but deep down he was very serious, maybe because of his years in prison. Sasha never talked about his experience in prison. Emma, though, talked often about her youth in America, about Rochester, about how she became an anarchist and how she became a nurse and how she hid from the police; and when she did so she was very charming. She and Sasha talked about the *Buford*[179] and their experiences in Russia, which they were dead set against.

In June of 1929, I think it was, there was a party on Emma's sixtieth birthday. Leo and I and my brother were invited. We couldn't afford champagne, so we brought a bottle of Asti Spumante. It was supposed to be a surprise party, but Emma knew all about it. She was all spiffed up, ready for the "surprise"! Afterwards, when we all got a little drunk, we drove to town and went dancing. Emma loved to dance! She was very funny to watch, so short and squat and having such a time of it. There was another party somewhat later, when Frank Harris, Bernard Shaw, and I forget who else, had a party for her in Nice. After that she gave a party for them at her house in St. Tropez. Shaw, though, didn't come, and I was terribly disappointed. Frank Harris was there, and he tried his best to seduce me and all the other girls.

We also knew Demi—Emma's secretary, Emily Holmes Coleman—very well. She was a friend of Saxe Commins's and was living in Paris. She looked us up when we arrived, and we became fast friends. She was a very strange girl—she'd been in several institutions—absolutely beautiful, charming, witty, but always on the verge of having a fit. And I think she had plenty of set-tos with Emma. She wrote a very interesting book, *The Shutter of Snow*, a novel about her first stay in a mental hospital.[180] She was always slightly crazy, but had her good periods and bad periods. Demi was married and had a son. Her husband was an extremely nice man, and their little boy looked like an angel, though was anything but. She and her husband were divorced, and he went to Australia, I think, and remarried, but died long ago. I don't know what became of Demi.

After our second year in St. Tropez we continued to keep in touch with Emma. Leo had quite a few letters from her and some pictures, but I haven't been able to find them. (He died eight years ago.) Our friendship with her extended over a period of several years. When she came back to America in the 1930s, she called us up. Someone had a party for her, and we were invited. Fitzi was there; Emma was very fond of Fitzi, and Fitzi was of her.

The next time I saw Emma was in England a few years later. By then Sasha was dead. He had shot himself, you know. He was fascinated by guns and always wanted to have them. I think he felt guilty that he wasn't able to kill Frick. And when he committed suicide he was still a bad shot! He was in agony before he died. I believe he'd been suffering from cancer and wanted to make an end of it. Emma was speaking in London when I saw her. It was during the Spanish Civil War. She spoke very well, by the way, as she did also in private company. She was putting on quite a show. Next to her hung a huge flag with the letters "CNT/FAI" and a big "EG" underneath. That was the last time I saw her, in all her glory, speaking before a big London crowd.

• ARTHUR LEONARD ROSS •

New York City, February 3, 1974

Arthur Leonard Ross, a New York attorney, met Emma Goldman in Paris in 1924 and became her legal representative in the United States, from which she had been deported in December 1919. He helped raise money for the purchase of her cottage in St. Tropez, sent books to her for her preparation of lectures in Toronto, negotiated with Alfred Knopf for the publication of her autobiography, and helped arrange her visit to the United States in 1934. "Arthur Leonard Ross, kindest and most lavish of men," she wrote in St. Tropez in 1931, "gave me his untiring efforts as legal representative and adviser. . . . He was the rare type that one gets to consider in a short time as a good friend."[181] Ross died in New York in the spring of 1975.

I FIRST BECAME acquainted with the anarchists through my friends Roger Baldwin [q.v.], Harry Weinberger, and Frank Harris. I'm now eighty-eight, and Harry especially was an old friend of mine—we were kids together in New York. My practice was largely with authors, so I never made much money. But I was able to help Fitzi [M. Eleanor Fitzgerald] meet the payroll of the Provincetown Players by lending or giving her money; and I gave Emma Goldman five hundred dollars to help her buy her house in France, "Bon Esprit." I was also Frank Harris's executor, drew up Fitzi's will, and was attorney for the Provincetown Players for a while, after Harry Weinberger. I gave all my correspondence and papers to the Tamiment Library of New York University.

Before I ever knew Emma and Sasha, I attended their trial before Judge Mayer. He was a Jewish judge, and, like the judge in the Rosenberg case, had to prove his loyalty to America. So he gave them no quarter. He wouldn't allow Harry Weinberger even a day or two to prepare his case. So they represented themselves. I gave the full record of the case to the Tamiment Library, and you can read it there. Every time I read it it hurt my heart to see what a terrible beating they got. That's the way they treated anarchists in those days.

I met Emma in Paris during the 1920s, when my friend Frank Harris and his wife introduced me to her. A few years later I helped her publish her autobiography, *Living My Life*. Then, on December 13, 1933, I got a telegram from her asking for help to visit America. Roger Baldwin went to see Frances Perkins,[182] while I dealt with the government lawyers. I personally vouched that Emma would make no political speeches during her stay here. And the first thing she did was to make a political speech! It was about Kropotkin, and it was quite an occasion, as it was her first—and only—return to America after her Russian experience. Town Hall was packed, and people were hanging from the chandeliers. I thought the upper gallery would collapse, it was so heavy with people.

The hall—in fact the entire block—was surrounded by police, and I had trouble getting in. I was on the platform and made a sketch of Emma as she spoke [he shows it to me].

Afterwards I went to see Emma in Toronto. Most people would find it hard to believe, but she loved America deeply, in spite of what it did to her. She could talk and breathe relatively freely here, where in Russia they pent her up. Yet the only way she could return permanently was in a coffin. The Roosevelt administration allowed her to be buried in Waldheim, next to the Haymarket anarchists, and that was a great event for America. I wouldn't expect a Nixon to give permission like that. But when Roosevelt was in office, we were a bit freer and more tolerant than we are now.

It was through Emma that I got to know Joseph Ishill, a fine printer and craftsman. I have his *Free Vistas, Bibliography, Peter Kropotkin,* and other beautiful works. His daughter Crystal just wrote me a nice six-page letter from Ohio, where she lives with her mother, Rose Freeman.

I represented Walter Starrett (Van Valkenburgh),[183] also through Emma's request. He had inherited some real estate upstate and was having trouble collecting, but I got his money for him. He had worked for the railroad as a young man and lost a leg in an accident. He was a good bookkeeper but was fired from his job when his anarchist activities became known. He never got over that. He took to drink and fell heavily into debt and finally separated from his wife. When we collected the real estate money I paid off his debts, and he came to me for the rest of the money. He went to a saloon on the Bowery and all the money was stolen. Then he went home and committed suicide. His wife died a few years ago, and a daughter, a teacher out west, just died recently. Her son was a lawyer out there. Another daughter, Mrs. Edna Holden, lost her husband not long ago. I spent all my time on those poor people. I never got a nickel—and they didn't have a nickel to give me to begin with.

• KATE WOLFSON •

New York City, October 16, 1972

Kate Wolfson, an immigrant from Odessa, joined the anarchist movement in New York, where she was acquainted with Emma Goldman and Alexander Berkman. Moving to Philadelphia, she attended the Sunday School of the Radical Library, started by Joseph Cohen and Abe Grosner (see Part Four). She afterwards resided in Stelton, where her daughter attended the Modern School. During the early 1930s, Kate visited Emma Goldman in St. Tropez and in Berlin. She saw her for the last time in 1934, when Emma was allowed to conduct a three-month lecture tour in the United States. Kate died in New York in 1977.

I WAS BORN Katya Blackman in 1895 and came to New York from Odessa in 1907, at the age of twelve. My sixteen-year-old sister had become an anarchist in the 1905 Revolution; she returned to Russia in 1917 and is still alive in Odessa, where I've visited her several times. My fourteen-year-old sister Bertha also became an active anarchist towards the end of the revolution, in 1906 and 1907. She became Hugo Rolland's [q.v.] wife in the U.S. and the mother of his son Siegfried [q.v.]; Siphra is the second wife and mother of their daughter Sandra.

I was introduced to the anarchist movement by my sisters in New York. We went to Emma Goldman's lectures on drama and birth control, which we regarded as secondary issues. We were fiery young militants and more concerned with economic and labor issues, and we resented her dwelling on such things as theater. Once we walked into her lecture and refused to pay the fifty cents admission, saying to her that "if you were concerned about workers you wouldn't charge fifty cents and would talk about basic questions like food and jobs." As Sasha said, Emma always liked the good things of life, and she had wealthy friends who supplied them. But that didn't detract from her sincerity as an anarchist. She was a very physical woman; she enjoyed food, dancing, sex, and all the things that people *should* enjoy. Ben Reitman was an example of her physical desires. He looked coarse and gross, and we got the impression that he was not genuinely interested in anarchist ideals.

We moved to Philadelphia in 1916. I attended the Radical Library Sunday School, where I met Ray Miller [Shedlovsky, q.v.] and where Abe Grosner was in charge. In the evening there were lectures by Joseph Cohen, Will Durant,[184] and others. We read the *Fraye Arbeter Shtime*, but we were more in the Russian movement than in the Yiddish. We wore black anarchist ribbons with the slogan *Khleba golodnym, volia ugnetennym* [Bread to the Hungry, Freedom to the Oppressed]. Some of the young men collected guns and dynamite to take to Russia and the revolution. My oldest sister went back in 1917 to take part in the revolution. Her husband was purged by Stalin in the 1930s.

I married, moved to New York, and had a daughter. When Irene was three we went to Stelton because of the school. I didn't want her in public school, with its regimentation and under teachers who had little respect for children. And I wasn't disappointed in the Ferrer School. Aunty Ferm had good ideas about education. We lived there for six years, and both our daughters went to the school and were very happy there. The school gave them an opportunity to do creative work (see Irene Blackman's art work in the *Voice of the Children*). Hugo Gellert [q.v.] was very good with the children. "God damn it, those kids can paint better than I can," he said. Bill Pogrebysky had been a pupil in the school and became Gellert's assistant. He went back to Russia in the late 1920s and died in the Red Army in World War II.

We parents used to go into the circle in the morning assembly and participate with the kids. Dora Keyser's [q.v.] little round blond-haired boy kept to himself, and Dora asked Aunty, "Why do you let him waste his time like that?" Aunty replied, "He's learning how to evaluate space, by himself. Children never waste their time if you leave them alone—they are learning very important things."

Aunty had a basic respect for the innate instinct of children to learn, unless you stop them, and stopping them is what creates so much trouble in our schools. She never interfered with children when they were learning. She was a true educator. I used her book and her methods at the Grand Street Settlement, where I directed the child care center for nineteen years. Once I weighed my daughter Irene at Stelton when she was a small child. Aunty said, "Do you think she's a piece of meat?" To her children weren't so many pounds of flesh and bone, but spiritual beings. I didn't get to know Uncle as well—he worked mostly with the older children, and I was with the little ones, as was Aunty.

There were many interesting people at Stelton. Joseph Cohen was a bright and knowledgeable man. Hippolyte Havel walked up to me one day while I was mowing the lawn. "Kate, you got a penny?" he said in his European accent. "Sure, but what do you want a penny for?" "I want to go down the road and when people say 'there goes Hippolyte without a penny in his pocket' they'll be wrong." Sherwood Trask[185] had a more formal approach to teaching than the others. He had classes in history and geography, and he often took the kids on overnight hikes. He had a good sense of humor and was a very able teacher. Mary Hansen[186] had a quiet way of talking that was very impressive. She was very contained within herself, a fine person. April Farm was founded by Charles Garland in Pennsylvania in the late 1920s. A few people from Stelton went there, but it didn't last long, two or three years at most. One of our kids, Anita Alvarez, became a Broadway dancer and starred in *Finian's Rainbow*. Every child at Stelton was sensitive to beautiful things. They've retained that to this day, whatever their politics might be. The colony was poor, but it was a happy place.

In 1931 the kids and I left Stelton to visit my oldest sister in Archangel, where she and her husband were high-ranking Communist officials in charge of the lumber industry. On the way, we went to France and decided to spend some time on the Riviera. At St. Tropez a real estate agent told us about "Madame Colton," that is, Emma Goldman.[187] We left our name and address, and in the evening Emma came to visit with homemade gefilte fish. She was warm, friendly, unassuming. We stayed in St. Tropez for six months, and Emma's house became our second home. We talked about everything—art, literature, anarchism—and became close friends. She always had interesting visitors.

After three months in Russia, we returned to the U.S. via Berlin, where Emma was then living in a pension. We stayed there six weeks. I had left Moscow enthusiastic for Russia and the Communist idea. Emma didn't get angry or even try to convince me otherwise, but only said, "You have a right to your views, but some day you'll change your mind." Despite her fame, she retained all her human qualities; she had concern for ordinary people and their ordinary, everyday affairs, and she didn't put me down when I became sympathetic with the Communists.

I saw Emma again when she came to the U.S. in 1934, and she had lost none of her fire and none of her humanity. We also saw Alexander Berkman in Nice in 1932 or 1933. He was a gentle, sensitive human being, very soft, very sentimental. I loved him dearly. He loved my little girls. When we were waving goodbye through the train window he had tears in his eyes. In Berlin I met Augustin Souchy, Rudolf Rocker, Erich Mühsam (who took me to dinner), and Senya Fleshin and Mollie Steimer.[188] They are still in Mexico, where I have visited them. Her sister lives in Miami. I'm seventy-seven now and still an anarchist. Unlike other political groups, their honor, their integrity are still intact.

• ORA ROBBINS •

Flushing, New York, December 5, 1985

Ora Robbins is the daughter of Esther Laddon, an anarchist in Toronto, with whom Emma Goldman stayed while on a lecture tour in 1927 and 1928. "The dear woman, Esther Laddon," writes Goldman in her memoirs, "was about my own age, but she mothered me as if I were her child. She fretted about my health and worried about my meals, and buttonholed everybody to warn them not to dare miss hearing the great orator E. G."[189]

MY MOTHER, Esther Laddon, came to New York from Russia in 1889 and eventually settled in Toronto, where she raised my two brothers and myself. Mother had already been an anarchist as a girl and fell in with the anarchist circles in Toronto. When Emma Goldman came to Toronto in 1927, she and Mother, both anarchists, both born in Russia in 1869, both former seamstresses, became good friends. Emma stayed at our house at 132 Lytton Boulevard, a large Victorian house with a garden. Emma took over the house, dominated the place. She stayed up all night talking on the phone. She drank a good deal of whiskey. And she woke up late in the morning. Comrades from the U.S. came in droves to visit her, as she was not allowed to cross the border.

I thought Emma was wonderful. She was a brilliant woman and a marvelous speaker, full of original ideas. She was so liberal in her views about young people. She talked to me about companionate marriage, without any official sanction. She gave me letters of introduction to the theater people in Greenwich Village—including Fitzi [M. Eleanor Fitzgerald] at the Provincetown Playhouse—as I wanted to become an actress. Fitzi took me under her wing when I arrived in New York in 1928. I acted in a play by e. e. cummings that year.

In 1927 Emma organized a big protest meeting against the execution of Sacco and Vanzetti. She handed me a long poem to read at the meeting. That same year I was on the back porch of our house with Emma when news came that Isadora Duncan had been killed in an accident,[190] and Emma was deeply moved.

• MILLIE GROBSTEIN •

Brooklyn, New York, April 20, 1975

Millie Grobstein is the older of two daughters of Joseph and Sophie Desser, whose home in Toronto was a center of the Jewish anarchist movement between the wars. As a high-school senior in 1934 and 1935, Millie acted as secretary to Emma Goldman, who was then living and lecturing in Canada. Millie performed the same function during 1939 and early 1940, taking dictation and typing Goldman's letters. In February 1940 Goldman suffered a stroke and died in Toronto in May.

MY FATHER, Joseph Desser, was born in Lask, Poland, on March 18, 1885. He was a young boy when his parents died and lived with his father's brother or sister. He had a religious upbringing and attended the yeshiva. In 1902, when called to serve in the Polish army, he went to London, where his older brother lived. It was there that he met Langbord, Simkin, and nearly all of the later Toronto group—and, of course, Rudolf Rocker. He stayed in London six years. He learned the craft of tailor there, gave up religion, and joined the Arbeter Fraynd Group. He was always in awe of Rocker, praising him in the highest terms. He just loved him! And his wife Milly too.

Father emigrated to Toronto around 1908, again following his older brother. He took up tailoring and became a founder of the Fraye Gezelshaft Branch 339 of the Workmen's Circle,[191] which was also the main anarchist group in Toronto. He was constantly going to meetings, was rarely home, got up early, went to work, then to meetings, and came home late. Every Saturday and Sunday he peddled the *Fraye Arbeter Shtime* at the Workmen's Circle and the Labor Lyceum. Outside work, our house at 759 Bathurst Street became the center of the anarchist movement in Toronto. Everybody in the movement who lived in Toronto or was just passing through knew that house! Father was also fond of theater and opera and went when he had a chance, though that wasn't very often.

Emma Goldman came to Toronto in 1934 and stayed in our house till she could find an apartment. She impressed me as an ordinary woman—short, heavy, stocky. From newspaper accounts I expected a fiery, domineering woman, yet she was very gentle, kind, motherly. That's the way she seemed to me, anyhow. During the time I spent with her in Montreal, from December 1934 to March 1935, she was just like a mother to me and did everything a mother would do. When she first came to Toronto, in 1926, I was eleven or twelve years old. Father was very ill with rheumatic fever, and she would come to the house every day—it was a three-story house—and trudge up those two flights of stairs, bringing him medicine, feeding him lunch, all to relieve my mother of part of the burden. She was so compassionate! It's incredible that people thought the opposite of her.

After her first visit, Emma went back to France for a while, and then returned to Toronto. It was then, in 1934, that I became her secretary. I could type and take dictation, and Father suggested that I help her after school. I was in my last year in high school then. I took dictation and typed her letters. I was very nervous the first time I worked for her. She wrote an enormous number of letters all over the world, to friends, relatives, comrades. Sometimes she made notes first, sometimes she dictated right out. Her mind was very keen. She was able to think very quickly.

That was the greatest period of my life. Just knowing her and being with her is something I'll never forget. I'll cherish it forever. Her ability to do the things she did, her clear mind and strong intellect, her determination to fight the ills of society—I often wish I could have done all that. I wish I had the strength of character, the ability. She was a very strong personality. She was also a good housekeeper and an excellent cook.

Emma never offended me in any way. The only thing I resented once in a while was that she would pile the work on so much, and the deadline was always so short! Yes, she had a fine sense of humor. She was jovial. You never felt depressed when you were with her, even with all the great problems of the world in those days, which disturbed her very much, though she maintained her spirits. Her eyesight was very poor, and her handwriting was awful. I had a hard time deciphering it at first.

Emma never delivered a lecture spontaneously, off the cuff, but would always prepare them carefully in advance. She would write her notes and I would type them verbatim, triple-spaced, in capitals. But you would never know that she was reading. She would master her notes so well, almost memorize them. But she had to have those notes in front of her. She was extremely nervous before the lecture, ate very little, and before mounting the platform took a drink of whiskey and paced up and down. Yet the minute she got on the platform she was herself, in full command. She was at home. All her fears and anxieties seemed to disappear. She was a forceful and engaging lecturer, with a good, clear voice. She had a European accent, but it was nothing strong, and she had a perfect command of the language. She spoke mostly on drama— Russian, German, English (George Bernard Shaw, for example). She wasn't allowed to speak on political subjects, yet she managed to bring them in very subtly.

Emma talked about Alexander Berkman constantly. She was heartbroken by his death and always spoke of him with affection and love. Yes, she did mention Voltairine de Cleyre, more than once. I'm sure of that. But I don't recall specifically what she said, except that she admired Voltairine's work. We had her collected writings. Father sent a stack of *Mother Earths* to Agnes Inglis, and we sent more after he died. Ben Reitman came to Toronto in the 1920s, when I was a kid, wearing a cowboy hat and cowboy boots. He walked into the house and you knew he was there!

Apart from my parents, the Jewish anarchists in Toronto included Julius Seltzer [q.v.], Julius Schiff, Sasha Gurian, Morris and Becky Langbord, Mr. and Mrs. Simkin, Mr. and Mrs. Steinberg, Louis Judkin, and others. Julius Seltzer had a knit-goods factory in Toronto. A number of the comrades, including Ahrne Thorne [q.v.], used to work for him. Yet he firmly opposed the organization of a trade union in the factory, and there were even strikes because of that. Emma was shocked that an anarchist would behave in that manner.

Spain was Emma's main preoccupation before the war. She did a great deal in Toronto, making speeches and collecting money for the anarchists in Spain and for the refugees after the crushing of the Spanish Revolution. It was during that time that the Libertarian Group was organized. It was an offshoot of the Jewish group, but with some non-Jewish members like Dorothy Rogers,[192] Attilio Bortolotti [q.v.], and a Swede named Carl [Newlander].[193] Father, Thorne, and other Jewish anarchists were active. The idea was to carry on propaganda in English. They sold literature, held forums, organized lectures, including lectures by Emma, and their meetings were held in our house.

Emma never lost her strength. She was vigorous, vital to the end. As a matter of fact, I had been working with her the day that she suffered her stroke. I took dictation that afternoon and, as usual, went home to type it up. I left her at about five o'clock. It was a lovely day in early spring. I had just walked in the door when our phone rang. It was Tom Meelis, the Dutch anarchist, where Emma had her rooms. He told us the shocking news: she had had a paralytic stroke and was taken to the hospital. I went to visit her every day. Her speech was gone, yet her mental faculties were all there. She patted me, pointed for something, the flowers on the dresser, wanting me to read the card, pointing with her eyes. To see such a vital woman one minute immobilized the next was profoundly disturbing. It was very painful every time I went to visit. I would come home all broken up. Yet she was still communicating. She was ill for about six weeks. She didn't recover; she died in May of that year, 1940.

I didn't know Rudolf Rocker as well as I did Emma. He and Milly visited our home several times. He was a very lovable person. Whenever he came back from a lecture tour in Canada, he would pat me on the head and say, "How you've grown!"

In 1939, after the war started, there was a burning session in our basement to get rid of the "seditious literature." I remember that furnace going in August! All the archives and papers were burned. They were not lost in any flood. The police were barging in on all known anarchists. They raided Bortolotti's house. They never did get to us, though Dad was expecting them. Father died on June 8, 1941, of a lumbar embolism, just a year after Emma.

• AHRNE THORNE •

Bronx, New York, October 2, 1979

Ahrne Thorne (real name Thorenberg) was born on December 26, 1904, of a Hasidic family in Łódź, Poland. In his teens he broke with tradition and worked his way to Paris, where he was converted to anarchism during the agitation for Sacco and Vanzetti. He emigrated to Toronto in 1930, became an associate of Emma Goldman, and began to write for the *Fraye Arbeter Shtime*, a Jewish anarchist journal in New York. From 1940, when Ahrne and his wife Paula moved to New York, he worked as a printer for Yiddish publications before assuming the editorship of the *Fraye Arbeter Shtime*. Under his supervision, the paper occupied a distinctive niche in the Yiddish intellectual and cultural world. It closed its doors in 1977, after eighty-seven years of publication. Ahrne himself passed away on December 13, 1985, in his eighty-first year. With characteristic modesty, Ahrne preferred not to be interviewed about his own life and career. He consented, however, to offer reminiscences of Emma Goldman in Toronto.[194]

I ARRIVED in Toronto from Paris in 1931 and got a job at Julius Seltzer's [q.v.] clothing factory. He admired my designs of sweaters, but the Depression was in full swing, so I worked as a machine operator. One day Seltzer came over to me and began to discuss politics and the world situation—whether Hitler would come to power, and so on. Among the writers I referred to was Rudolf Rocker. "Rocker?" asked Seltzer, astounded. "How do you know about Rocker? Why, he comes here to Toronto! He stays at my place!" So we found out—boss and worker—that we were both anarchists!

My first meeting with Emma Goldman took place in 1932. I was introduced to her at a gathering in a comrade's home. I think it was Morris Langbord's house, where she was staying. About twenty people attended. But this first encounter with her was a disappointment. All the others had known her before and wanted to know about mutual friends and acquaintances: How is this one? What is that one doing? Where is so-and-so? I wanted to hear about world issues. So, at this meeting at any rate, there was a conflict of interests.

But as I got to know her I was deeply impressed. I was both an anarchist and a member of the IWW in Toronto. I distributed announcements of her lectures, attended them all myself, and found her a great speaker. Her lectures were bitterly anti-Bolshevik—the "red fascists," she called them, destroyers of the revolution. The Communists and Trotskyites in the audience were violently opposed to her. During the speech itself there was constant heckling. This she didn't mind; she was very good at repartée and knew how to handle them. (Rocker, by the way, hated heckling; he hated to be interrupted and wanted to be left alone to finish his speech.) But during the question-and-answer period there was frequent tumult and uproar, particularly when she denounced Lenin and Stalin, and some meetings were broken up as a result.

Emma was always terribly serious. Do you notice any humor in her writing? Very little. The same with her speeches. When I would make a joke she didn't like it. "This is a serious matter," she would say, "so let's discuss it seriously." She avoided small talk. But she had a deep personal warmth. I once needed a doctor. She recommended someone, and she asked me about it later. If a friend needed help, she would do everything she could, mobilize all available forces, go out of her way for you.

A good example was when the three Italian anarchists got arrested in 1939. After the defeat of the Spanish Revolution, a number of Spanish anarchists fled to France and then Canada. In September 1939 the Second World War broke out. All letters were stopped and censored. The authorities found a letter from Italian anarchists in Toronto advising their Spanish comrades to come to Canada, an easy country to get into in those difficult days. The police raided Ruggero's home, found a large quantity of anarchist literature and a rusty revolver. Ruggero [Benvenuti], Bortolotti [q.v.], and a third Italian named Vic [Vittorio Valopi] were arrested. They were in danger of deportation to fascist Italy. They needed a lawyer and money for their defense. Emma plunged into action. She got a lawyer and raised funds. Money was collected in New York and other cities, as well as in Canada, after she appealed to her comrades in America.

I was once in the lawyer's office and asked to see the penal code under which our comrades were being prosecuted. He gave it to me and I read it. It said "dissemination" of revolutionary literature. I pointed this out to the lawyer—Cohen, I think his name was[195]—"dissemination," not "possession," whereas they had been arrested for mere possession. He opened his eyes. He asked me if I had ever had any legal training, which of course I hadn't. Emma told me later that he was impressed. He used the argument in his defense.

Paula and I went to visit the three Italians in jail. Two of them, Ruggero and Bortolotti, are still alive (Vic died a couple of years ago). We spoke to them through a barred window, with a guard listening to every word. In court they were found not guilty and were immediately released. Emma had worked hard to achieve that result. She made speeches, wrote letters, organized teas and gatherings to raise money. Emma was a woman of action. She was not a theorist, not a deep thinker. And though she cared about her family and friends, she was very self-centered—too self-centered for an anarchist.

When I first met Emma she was very depressed about Living My Life, which had just come out the previous year. It was a big book and too expensive, and in the Depression it didn't sell. I had begun to read it, not in English but in Yiddish, in the Forverts, beautifully translated by M. Osherowitz. It had been appearing daily, but it stopped abruptly. An editorial note said that the rest of the book consisted of internal anarchist bickerings and was without general interest. In reality, the sex parts had largely stopped!

While in Toronto, Emma was visited by a young man from Chicago named Frank [Dr. Frank Heiner], who lived with her for stretches at a time up there.

He was strong-looking and handsome, but blind. I didn't like him very much. I asked him how he became an anarchist. He said he had become an anarchist through reading *Living My Life*. I didn't like such quick decisions. But Emma liked him very much. He was probably her last lover—a blind fellow who couldn't see how old she was!

The comrades were always inviting Emma to their homes. But Paula and I never invited her. We were very poor. We had only one room with little furniture. It was on the top floor, too high up for Emma to walk. She was puzzled. One day Tom Meelis, a Dutch anarchist (his first name was actually Anthony, and he was a printer by trade), simply brought her over in his car without warning us. She told me straight out: "You know why I came to see you here—I wanted to find out why you didn't invite me!"

Emma celebrated her seventieth birthday in 1939. The three Italians were out of jail. There was a banquet in Pythian Castle. A Spanish anarchist who had recently fled to Canada greeted her in the name of the CNT. He spoke in French, a very bad French, and I translated it into English. There were other speeches in her honor, and lots of flowers. Her answer was a very pessimistic one. "It's a beautiful party," she said. "I should be glad to see so many friends. And I *am* glad. But after the defeat of the Spanish Revolution and the outbreak of a new world war I feel very sad." She was depressed, and I went home depressed.

At seventy Emma was still in good health. She had been having trouble with her feet for a number of years. In 1934, when she visited America, an Italian comrade made her a pair of comfortable shoes, and when she put them on she cried and kissed him.[196] But otherwise she had much of her old vitality and spirit. On New Year's Eve of 1939–1940 we went to a party at her home. Dorothy Rogers was there, the Meelises, Bortolotti, and a few others. She was again in a pessimistic mood. She reminisced about New Year's parties of the past, including one in Spain, when she was working for the CNT in Barcelona. She told us that when she was in the CNT headquarters an air-raid alert was sounded. Everyone rushed downstairs to the shelter. But she refused to go. "It was not heroism," she told us. "If a bomb hit me, I didn't care. I was ready to die." Then she spoke about Alexander Berkman's death—the call she got from Emmy early in the morning to come at once, that a tragedy had happened. When she arrived, the police were accusing Emmy of killing him, and she had a job trying to convince them that it was suicide.

One evening not long afterward, I had just come home from work when I got a call from Tilio Bortolotti: Emma had a stroke at the Meelises' home. Come as quickly as possible. I grabbed a streetcar. When I got there, she was lying on a couch with her eyes closed. They had been playing bridge—Emma, the Meelises, and a neighbor. Suddenly they noticed that she was bending over on her side. They thought she had dropped a card. But she remained like that. She didn't get up. They saw that she was ill. When she didn't respond, they called an ambulance. The ambulance arrived shortly after I did. By then she was again conscious. As the attendants lifted her onto a stretcher, her dress rolled up over her knees, and with one hand she pulled it down to cover her exposed knees.

Emma stayed in the hospital for a few weeks. I visited her often and tried to cheer her up. She was fully conscious. She could hear and understand. But she couldn't talk. What worse punishment for Emma could there be? I thought. Speaking was her life. She was always talking. But there she lay, unable to utter a word. She never recovered the power of speech. The hospital could do nothing more for her, so she went to the Meelises' place to live. In America a committee was organized—John Haynes Holmes was a member—to raise funds for her medical bills. I suggested to Tom Meelis getting a set of moveable letters for Emma to enable her to form words. They got it but she refused to use it. And she couldn't write because her right hand was paralyzed from the stroke. She wanted to die. After Spain and the outbreak of the war she had grown increasingly pessimistic. She had said that if the First World War had been a "war to end all wars," this was a war to end the world. She had lost her will to live. I saw her the day before she died. She was a pitiful sight, speechless and forlorn. It was a tragic end.

There was a funeral ceremony for Emma in the Labor Lyceum on Spadina Avenue. But she was not to be buried in Toronto. Her body was to be taken by train to Chicago and interred in the Waldheim Cemetery, near the Haymarket martyrs and Voltairine de Cleyre. So she finally got back to America. She had loved America. She considered it her country. She had been born there spiritually and intellectually, as she told me. The greatest moments of her life had been spent there. Outside America she felt without a home. How she wanted to return! She always blamed J. Edgar Hoover[197] for keeping her out. He had won his spurs in her deportation case, she said. And now he was blocking her from coming home.

· PART THREE ·

Sacco and Vanzetti

SPENCER SACCO • GEMMA DIOTALEVI • JENNIE PAGLIA

• RALPH PIESCO • GEORGE T. KELLEY •

BELTRANDO BRINI • LEFEVRE BRINI WAGER

• CONCETTA SILVESTRI • JENNY SALEMME •

CATINA WILLMAN • JOSEPH MORO

• BARTOLOMEO PROVO • VINCENZO FARULLA •

SEBASTIANO MAGLIOCCA • SARA R. EHRMANN

• ART SHIELDS • FRED J. COOK • GEORGE VAUX •

HARRY RICHAL • LOUIS TARABELLI • CHARLES POGGI

• FEBO POMILIA • FLORENCE ROSSI •

GALILEO TOBIA • ELIDE SANCHINI • ORESTE FABRIZI

• ALBERICO PIRANI • VALERIO ISCA •

JOHN VATTUONE • WILLIAM GALLO • GUY LIBERTI

• HUGO ROLLAND • ESTHER TRAVAGLIO •

VINCENZO FERRERO • DOMINICK SALLITTO • LINO MOLIN

• MARK LUCA • FRANK BRAND •

ATTILIO BORTOLOTTI

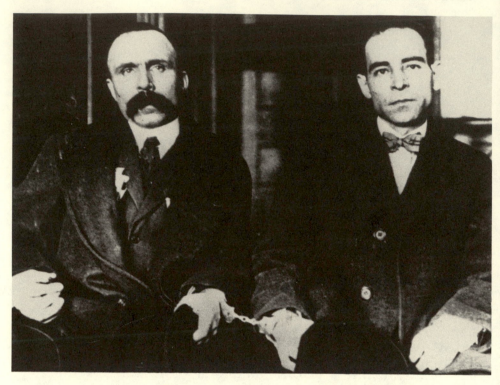

3. Bartolomeo Vanzetti and Nicola Sacco, 1923 (Boston Public Library)

INTRODUCTION

MORE THAN seventy years have passed since the arrest of Nicola Sacco and Bartolomeo Vanzetti, sparking one of the most controversial episodes in American history. On the morning of December 24, 1919, four men made a bungled attempt to rob the payroll of the L. Q. White Shoe Company in Bridgewater, Massachusetts. One of the men—the "shotgun bandit," he was called—fired at the moving payroll truck. The driver, swerving around a streetcar, managed to escape, whereupon the bandits jumped into an automobile, which sped down a side street and got away. No one was injured, and the $30,000 payroll remained intact.

On April 15, 1920, another holdup, this one successful, occurred in the town of South Braintree. Shortly after 3 P.M. Frederick Parmenter and Alessandro Berardelli, employees of the Slater & Morrill Shoe Company, were shot to death and robbed of the company payroll. Two men armed with handguns did the shooting. A car carrying other men then appeared, picked up the killers, and carried them to a safe getaway. The money, nearly $16,000, was never recovered.

Three weeks later, on May 5, Sacco, a shoe worker, and Vanzetti, a fish peddler, both Italian immigrants and anarchists, were arrested as participants in the South Braintree crime. Vanzetti, in addition, on the flimsiest of evidence, was indicted for the Bridgewater holdup. Accused of being the "shotgun bandit," he was swiftly brought to trial and convicted. Judge Webster Thayer, who presided, meted out the maximum sentence of twelve to fifteen years' imprisonment to a defendant with no previous criminal record and for a crime in which no one had been hurt and nothing stolen.

Sacco was more fortunate. Found to have been at work on the date of the Bridgewater holdup, he could not be indicted for that crime. Records showed, however, that he had not worked on April 15, when the South Braintree murders took place. Vanzetti, being a fish vendor, had no factory alibi at all. In September 1920 indictments were returned against both men. The following year they were brought to trial.

According to the prosecution, Sacco took part in the actual shooting and Vanzetti was one of four accomplices. The evidence against them was contradictory. On the one hand, a number of witnesses identified them as members of the holdup gang. Both were armed on the night of their arrest, Sacco with a .32-caliber automatic, Vanzetti with a .38-caliber revolver. Both told lies when questioned by the police. Their weapons, moreover, seemed to fit the circumstances of the crime, and this weighed heavily against them with the jury. On the other hand, both men had substantial alibis, neither had been convicted of any previous crime, and witnesses for the prosecution altered the stories they had told the police and private investigators after the holdup. Furthermore, no information was presented to the jury about the other bandits, who were never apprehended, and the authorities were unable to connect the stolen money with the defendants or their associates.

The trial, occurring in the wake of the Red Scare, took place in an atmosphere of intense hostility towards the defendants. The district attorney, Frederick G. Katzmann, conducted a highly unscrupulous prosecution, coaching and badgering witnesses, withholding exculpatory evidence from the defense, and perhaps even tampering with physical evidence. A skillful and ruthless cross-examiner, he played on the emotions of the jurors, arousing their deepest prejudices against the accused. Sacco and Vanzetti were armed; they were foreigners, atheists, anarchists. This overclouded all judgment. Judge Thayer, who once again presided, likewise revealed his bias. Outside the courtroom, during the trial and the appeals which followed, he made remarks that bristled with animosity towards the defendants ("Did you see what I did with those anarchistic bastards the other day? I guess that will hold them for a while."). When a verdict of guilty was returned, many believed that the men had been convicted because of their foreign birth and radical beliefs, not on solid evidence of criminal guilt.

In the aftermath of the trial, as legal appeals delayed sentencing, a mounting body of evidence indicated that the wrong men had been apprehended. Key prosecution testimony was retracted and new evidence produced that was favorable to the defendants. Herbert Ehrmann, a junior defense attorney, built a strong case against the Morelli gang of Providence, which specialized in stealing shipments from shoe manufacturers (see interview with Sara Ehrmann).

All this, however, availed nothing. For the attitude of the authorities had become so rigidly set against the defendants that they turned a deaf ear to contrary views. As a result, a growing number of observers, many of whom abhorred anarchism and had no sympathy with radical propaganda of any kind, concluded that the defendants had not received a fair trial. The judge's bias against the defendants, their conviction on inconclusive evidence, their dignified behavior while their lives hung in the balance—all this attracted supporters, who labored to secure a new trial. At the eleventh hour, Governor Alvan T. Fuller conducted a review of the case, appointing an advisory committee, headed by President A. Lawrence Lowell of Harvard, to assist him. The Lowell Committee, as it became known, though finding Judge Thayer guilty of a "grave breach of official decorum"[198] in his derogatory references to the defendants, nevertheless concluded that justice had been done.

As events moved towards a climax, the case assumed international proportions, engaging the passions of men and women around the globe. Anatole France, in one of his last public utterances, pleaded with America to save Sacco and Vanzetti: "Save them for your honor, for the honor of your children and for the generations yet unborn."[199] In vain. On August 23, 1927, the men were electrocuted in defiance of worldwide protests and appeals. By then, millions were convinced of their innocence, and millions more were convinced that, guilty or innocent, they had not received impartial justice.

This then was no ordinary case of robbery and murder. Other factors, as yet imperfectly understood, propelled it into international prominence. Set against the background of the Red Scare and its aftermath, it highlighted some of the major issues of the day: mass immigration, labor militancy, repression of radicals. Like the Haymarket affair of the 1880s, it was an episode that divided the nation, arousing deep-seated emotions, defining loyalties, and spawning a literature of criticism and protest. No other case of the period attracted more widespread attention, for it had a significance that made it symbolic of its time and place, elevating it to the level of tragedy and uncovering an aspect of American society that would not otherwise have been so nakedly exposed. "It revealed," wrote Edmund Wilson in 1928, "the whole anatomy of American life, with all its classes, professions, and points of view and all their relations, and it raised almost every fundamental question of our political and social system."[200]

Not surprisingly, then, it is a case that refuses to die. So many forces were at work, so many issues and principles at stake, that for more than six decades it has remained the subject of controversy. In 1947, twenty years after the executions, a group of prominent citizens, including Eleanor Roosevelt, Albert Einstein, and Herbert Lehman, offered the state of Massachusetts a bas-relief plaque of Sacco and Vanzetti by the sculptor of Mount Rushmore, Gutzon Borglum, only to have it rejected by the governor. In 1959 a resolution in the state legislature to exonerate the defendants failed of adoption. More recently, Governor Michael S. Dukakis marked the fiftieth anniversary of the executions by proclaiming August 23, 1977, "Nicola Sacco and Bartolomeo Vanzetti Day." Dukakis, while sidestepping the issue of innocence or guilt, declared that "the atmosphere of their trial and appeals was permeated by prejudice against foreigners and hostility toward unorthodox political views."[201]

The interviews that follow shed considerable light on Sacco and Vanzetti and on the movement of which they were a part. As with the interviews about Emma Goldman, the emphasis is on the human dimension, on Sacco and Vanzetti as people rather than as social or political symbols. What sort of men were they? What kind of lives did they lead? In what activities did they engage as immigrants, workingmen, and anarchists?

From the recollections of his friends and neighbors in Milford, Massachusetts, Sacco emerges as a young man of exemplary character, modest in both manner and speech. "He didn't say much," Ralph Piesco recalls. "He didn't drink. He was a very clean man in language as well as in his person. You never heard any vulgarity from him." He was always courteous and polite, Gemma Diotalevi remembers, and he "never spoke out of line." "He was very romantic, loved his wife, the two of them like sweethearts," says Joseph Moro, a fellow anarchist and shoe worker. "Sacco was a genius at his work, that machine running so fast, sharp like a razor; you miss by a thousandth of an inch and you ruin the shoe. He was quick, precise, a wonderful worker." To this day, Sacco is remembered with affection by the older residents of Milford, for whom he was a hardworking young man of regular habits and a credit to the community, incapable of committing the crimes with which he was charged. "I don't know anybody who said anything against Sacco," says Gemma Diotalevi. "He was a wonderful fellow, a gentleman in every sense of the word."

Vanzetti, a bachelor, had a more difficult time adjusting to the hardships of immigrant life. In contrast to Sacco, the skilled worker and settled family man, Vanzetti belonged to the class of common laborers who washed dishes, dug ditches, pushed wheelbarrows, and wielded shovels, the most overworked and underpaid workers in America. He shared the lot of many Italian-born immigrants: the crowded rooming houses, the loneliness, the back-breaking toil, the scornful epithets of "guinea" and "wop." He had become a "foreigner," an intruder, the object of jibes and insults from men whom, he wrote, "I would have left in the dust had my English been a tenth as good as my Italian."[202]

Matters improved in 1913, when Vanzetti found a home with the Brini family of Plymouth, with whom he lived for four years. "He was not a drinking man and didn't play cards," recalls Lefevre Wager, the oldest of the Brini children. "He was a studious man. At home he liked to sit and read. But he also loved the outdoors. He liked to walk. We went with him to gather mayflowers and violets, blackberries and redberries on Castle Hill, or walked with him on the beach or along the railroad tracks picking up pieces of coal. He was a gentle soul. There was not a bit of meanness in him. I never saw him angry. That man didn't know how to be mean." "He was like a child," says Joseph Moro. "He wrote me beautiful letters. Talking to him you could fall in love with him. He talked like a poet—he was born to be a poet—and he knew what he was talking about."

Vanzetti's poetic bent and sweetness of nature must not, however, obscure the fact that he was a dedicated revolutionary militant, for whom the state was an evil, tyrannical power of enslavement, oppression, and destructiveness. "Vanzetti was anarchism personified," recalls Beltrando Brini, Lefevre Wager's younger brother. "He didn't want to be restricted or to acknowledge any boss. He believed in the perfectibility of human nature, something that does not in fact exist. That was his blind spot." The same was also true of his comrade Sacco. From 1912 on, anarchism was their strongest passion, the guiding beacon of their lives, the focus of their daily activities. "Both Nick and I are anarchists," declared Vanzetti, "the radical of the radical—the black cats, the terrors of many, of all the bigots, exploitators [sic], charlatans, fakers and oppressors."[203]

The image of Sacco and Vanzetti as a "good shoemaker" and "poor fish peddler" tends to obscure their actual character. Far from being the innocuous dreamers so often depicted by their supporters, they belonged, as the interviews show, to a branch of the anarchist movement which preached insurrectionary violence and armed retaliation, including the use of dynamite and assassination. Such activities, they believed, were replies to the monstrous violence of the state. The greatest bombthrowers and murderers were not the isolated rebels driven to desperation, but the military resources of every government—the army, militia, police, firing squad, hangman. Such was their position, as it was of their mentor Luigi Galleani, who showered praise on every rebellious deed and glorified the perpetrators as heroes and martyrs, sacrificing their lives for the oppressed.

Nor was this all. Between 1917 and 1920, during a period of intense antiradical persecution, Sacco and Vanzetti were themselves part of a dynamite conspiracy of which Attorney General A. Mitchell Palmer and other high officials were the targets. Men of determination, they would not stand idly by while their comrades were being deported, their printing presses silenced, their meetings disrupted and dispersed. Their code of honor, on the contrary, taught that revolutionaries should retaliate against the repressive use of force, that submission to the state was cowardly and unworthy of a true anarchist.

Were they also involved in holdups? That some Italian anarchists engaged in theft, counterfeiting, and other illegal activities is evident from testimony in the interviews. With regard to holdups, however, no definitive answers are provided, only hearsay, rumor, and speculation. Most of those with whom I have spoken remain unshakably convinced of the defendants' innocence: "I believe that Sacco and Vanzetti were not guilty of the holdups" (Sebastiano Magliocca). "I have no reason to believe that either of them was guilty" (Vincenzo Farulla). "Everyone in the defense committee said they were innocent" (Bartolomeo Provo). "All the comrades felt that they were innocent. Anybody who knew them knew that they had nothing to do with it" (Harry Richal). "When Vanzetti was arrested we were stupefied. What was this? It can't be. We couldn't believe that the man did what they said he did. He was so gentle, so good. He helped people, not hurt them" (Lefevre Wager).

A few, however, take a different view, at least as far as Sacco is concerned: "I traveled on the same boat as Riccardo Orciani, who told me that Sacco was guilty of the robbery but Vanzetti was not, though he knew about it and was part of the same group. Even Felicani [founder of the defense committee] intimated as much to me many years later" (Hugo Rolland). "I am sure that Vanzetti was innocent of the first crime. And in the second case I'm quite sure that neither of them fired any shots, but not at all sure that the gang was unknown to them" (Roger Baldwin). "Buda told me that Sacco took part in the Braintree holdup. 'Sacco was there,' he said. I remember it distinctly. I felt sure that he was telling the truth" (Charles Poggi).

Yet Sacco has his staunch defenders: "We all thought that Sacco was not the type of person to commit that kind of crime" (Gemma Diotalevi). "Grandmother was extremely fond of him. She always stood up for him and couldn't believe that he could do those nefarious things" (George T. Kelley). "He never spoke of holdups or anything like that. I'm convinced he could never have committed such a crime. Yes, he carried a gun, but so did I in those bad times" (Joseph Moro).

Suggestive though these statements may be, they do not settle the issue of whether Sacco and Vanzetti were guilty of the crimes for which they were executed. More than seventy years after the trial, the case against them remains unproved. Nor, on the other hand, can their innocence be established beyond any shadow of doubt. In coming years, one hopes, new evidence will be discovered and deeper understanding obtained. In the end, however, we may never succeed in resolving the controversy.

• SPENCER SACCO •

Cambridge, Massachusetts, January 8, 1987

Spencer Sacco is the grandson of Nicola (real name Ferdinando) and Rosina Sacco. Spencer taught music at Salve Maria College in Providence, Rhode Island, before becoming an antiques dealer. He is the only one of three sons of Dante Sacco to interest himself actively in the Sacco-Vanzetti case.

MY GRANDMOTHER, Rosina Sacco, is now in her early nineties. She was born into the Zambelli family of Lonato, in Lombardy. Their roots went way back, and her grandparents and great-grandparents had land there and, I think, a grocery store. They were a prosperous family, but her father drank and lost his money. Around the turn of the century, he emigrated to America with his wife and son, leaving my grandmother in a convent in Lonato. She liked the convent, liked the sisters, and remained there a few years. When she was twelve or thirteen, around 1906 or 1907, her family sent for her and she came over alone. Her mother, by the way, was a seamstress, and Grandma also sewed and knitted very well and made all her own clothes.

I'm not sure how Grandma met my grandfather, Ferdinando Sacco. She was about sixteen or seventeen when they got married. It was in 1909, I think; Daddy was born in 1910.[204] I don't know how she became an anarchist. Probably she got it from my grandfather: Italian women of that generation often adopted the views of their husbands. But she was an anarchist and an atheist— a real atheist, too! She and her second husband, Ermanno Bianchini, refused to go to Aunt Ines's church wedding, though they did go to the reception. And they wouldn't go to Daddy's funeral.

Grandma, as I said, was an anarchist. She called Carlo Valdinoci,[205] who blew himself up in front of Palmer's house, *"un grande anarchico,"* and she admired his brother, Giuseppe I think his name was, who was responsible for the Wall Street bombing[206] and was never seen again. Yes, he definitely did it, just as Carlo was definitely the man at Palmer's house. By the way, the Valdinocis and the Saccos were very close, and after the executions the sister, Assunta Valdinoci, lived with Grandma, Daddy, and Ines.

At home they never talked about the case. The first time I heard of it I was about nine years old and my assistant cub-scout master said to me, "Did you know that your grandfather was electrocuted?" A year or two later, when I was ten or eleven and we were living in a two-family house in Norwood, the landlord's eighteen-year-old son went into the cellar, where my brother Steven, then fourteen or fifteen, was making a model airplane, and started pushing him around. "Your grandfather was a murderer! Your grandfather was a murderer!" I heard the shouting and called the school, where my parents were attending a PTA[207] meeting. They came right home. Dad talked to the landlord. Then he sat us down in the living room and told us the story of his father.

Otherwise he didn't talk about it a lot. When the Chessman case[208] was compared with the Sacco-Vanzetti case he was disturbed. Daddy couldn't conceive of the possibility of their guilt. He was certain that, unlike Chessman, they were innocent. He told me that he visited his father in Dedham jail: "Father threw a ball to me over the jail wall, and I threw it back." That was the way they played.

After the execution, Grandma, Dinny (my father Dante), and Ines moved to Millis, near Ermanno Bianchini, an ardent anarchist. The ashes were divided: part went to Torremaggiore, part to Cuneo,[209] some to the Defense Committee (they're now in the Boston Public Library), and some to Grandma, which she kept, I think, in a canister in a dome-topped trunk. Once, as a child, I was playing hide-and-seek and hid in the trunk, and Grandma got upset and spanked me—the only time in my life.

Grandma and Manno began to live together, though they didn't get married till many years later, when they were concerned about their social security. From Millis they moved to Watertown, directly across from my parents. Bianchini was a cement-finisher by trade. From there they moved to a rundown farm in Eastondale, near Bridgewater, and raised chickens. That was in the late forties, after World War II.

Manno was a real anarchist, a Darwinist to the nth degree. Both were devoted anarchists and were devoted to each other. They lived an anarchist life together, self-sufficient, buying little, saving what they had. Manno sheltered Grandma from outsiders. He felt that people wanted to see her only to make money from the case. For years she never spoke to anybody except family and close friends. She had a difficult time. Her own sister Adele and her husband Joseph Tedeschi stopped talking to her after my grandfather's arrest.

But there were some friends, some from the "best" Boston families. Grandma and the kids stayed at Leon Henderson's farm on occasion. I still remember their daughter, Teddie Henderson Snelling, who lives in Winchester, I think. And there was Edward Holton James—I knew his daughters Elizabeth and Victoria; Vicki married Alexander Calder, the sculptor, who died not long ago.[210] James, a nephew of Henry James, married money and had money of his own. He lived in Concord, and I fished in his trout stream there as a child. He also had a house on the Cape, in East Ham, and we summered there.

It was James who bailed out the protestors who were arrested on the Boston Common. After the execution, he convinced Grandma to let Daddy go with him to Europe, to Geneva, to study medicine. After a year in Switzerland, James went to Italy to see Mario Buda, and Daddy came home. He never continued his medical studies. Instead, he became a truck driver for Woodland Dairy in Watertown. My mother was a bookkeeper there, and that's how they met. Then he became a driver for Filene's,[211] and Mister Filene, who had sympathized with Sacco and Vanzetti, sent him to truck mechanics' school. While there he picked up airplane mechanics. Afterwards he worked for Wiggins Airways as parts manager. He was a good father and a good provider. But the case would never let him alone, much as he wanted it to. When Felicani[212] died in 1967, we all went to the wake. But people pestered us—"That's Sacco's son," and the like—so Daddy got disgusted and left. He died four years later, in 1971, on August 22, ironically, the date of the executions.

The first time Grandma mentioned the case to me was in 1965, when I was a sophomore at Boston University. I had been mugged on Boston Common and punched in the eye while wearing glasses and got bits of glass in my eye. Grandma and Manno came to the house that evening. I mentioned that I had to go to the police station to look at mug shots. Grandma said, "Don't go. They'll never find them. They haven't found the Braintree robbers. They never find them!"

A few months ago, in 1986, I asked Grandma for the first time whether Sacco and Vanzetti were guilty. "Did they do it?" She said, "What for? We were going back to Italy." I asked, "Why do you think they were convicted?" "Oh, that Katzmann, he was a bastard!" I had never heard her swear before in my life. She also had no use for newspaper reporters. "That's newspaper talk," she would say. She gave no credence to newspapers.

In 1977 I showed Grandma Dukakis's proclamation. "I'm glad," she said, and thanked me for my part in it. I went to Italy and gave a copy to Vincenzina Vanzetti. She was delighted. Did you know, by the way, that Mussolini was two-faced about the case? He sent a cipher to President Coolidge to this effect: "As regards Sacco and Vanzetti, we are not anxious to have them back here." And Coolidge answered: "Don't worry, I have a good man in Alvan Fuller." Robert D'Attilio[213] told me this. Grandma, incidentally, remembers Upton Sinclair's visit[214] after the executions. She said she was petrified of him, a tall— to her, she was tiny—American man asking a lot of questions.

Grandma never went back to Italy, not even for a visit. She remained here with Bianchini until the end. He died inch by inch with arthritis and angina. You've never seen anybody so in love as Manno and my grandmother—it was unholy! He finally went to the hospital, but she went too, suffering from severe diabetes. He died in January 1985. She's now in a nursing home. She wears glasses and is legally blind. I see her from time to time. Her memory fades in and out. She once asked me what music I was playing in. I simply said, "an opera," thinking what could she know about it. She asked what opera. I replied, *Le Nozze di Figaro*, and she launched into an enthusiastic discussion of a scene in the second act. She knew it by heart! And she has a passion for Pavarotti.[215]

There are no photographs or letters, as far as I know. Grandma had a letter from Sacco to Ines,[216] but we haven't been able to find it. I doubt that you can learn anything from my mother or Aunt Ines. Whatever my grandfather did, I'm proud of him. He ought to have done even more!

• GEMMA DIOTALEVI •

Milford, Massachusetts, September 19, 1987

Gemma Diotalevi, a native of Milford, Massachusetts, was a friend of Nicola Sacco and his wife Rosina, who lived in Milford during their early years in the United States. Gemma was also acquainted with the Kelley family, in whose shoe factory Sacco was later employed (see interview with George T. Kelley). Gemma died in Milford in November 1989 at the age of ninety-two.

I WAS BORN in Milford on July 17, 1897. I was four years old when, in 1901, we moved to this house at 28 Cedar Street (now 26 Cedar Street), in the Plains section, the Italian quarter of Milford. The streets here have names like Columbus Avenue, Naples Street, Genoa Street. My father, Antonio DePasquale, was the local funeral director. He owned the house and the smaller house next door. He was born in the village of San Marco la Catola, province of Foggia.

I don't know anybody in Milford who said anything against Sacco. He was a wonderful fellow, a gentleman in every sense of the word. The Zambellis lived next door in the downstairs apartment of the other house owned by my father. They came from Lombardia in the northern part of Italy. I was friendly with Rosina. She was small and pretty, with a little round face, rather quiet and shy. She was a doll. Her mother was a good woman, a religious woman. The father worked, but I don't recall what he did.

I don't remember their getting married, Sacco and Rosina. Her father may have objected—maybe he didn't like Sacco's ideas. Sacco didn't go to church. He didn't have any religion. If they did marry, I doubt that it was in a church. After they got together, they lived at 11 East Main Street, next to the Sacred Heart of Jesus church. The house was torn down long ago when the church rebuilt and expanded. It was the Italian Catholic church in town. There was another Catholic church attended by the Irish and a Congregational church for the Yankees. They didn't like the Italians—the Irish or the Yankees. The Irish used to stone the Italians in those days. But later we got friendlier and everything straightened out. The Kelleys[217] were always friendly with our family in the early years. We went to their house to play croquet on the lawn. They were very nice people.

Every so often my sister Eva and I would visit Sacco and Rosina on Main Street. He was a small, nice-looking boy. They were very nice to us. Sacco never spoke out of line or out of turn. Rosina would give us cookies and soda. We spoke in Italian, though Sacco did know some English—my sister Mary was his teacher. Mary was six years older than me, born in 1891. She graduated from Milford High School in three years, and then from Framingham State Teachers' College. At twenty she was already a teacher, the first Italian schoolteacher in Milford. She taught second grade at the Plains School and also taught night school. She thought the world of Sacco. He was cute and bright, an intelligent person in his way.

We all thought that Sacco was not the type of person to commit that kind of crime. The Italians in Milford followed the case and were all loyal to Sacco. Father, a strict disciplinarian, would never have let us go to Sacco's house if he knew anything bad about him. When he was arrested we were all very surprised. We couldn't believe it. Nobody in Milford believed that he was guilty. Father, a conservative, was ready to go to Dedham to testify for Sacco, but he was never called.

• JENNIE PAGLIA •

Needham, Massachusetts, August 10, 1988;
Hollywood, Florida, December 10, 1988

Jennie Paglia was born of Italian immigrants in Milford, Massachusetts, where she was acquainted with Nicola and Rosina Sacco. Jennie's husband, Pasquale Paglia, was an anarchist of the Luigi Galleani school,[218] as was her brother-in-law, Ralph Piesco (q.v.). Jennie died in Hollywood, Florida, in May 1991.

I WAS BORN Jennie Calitri in Milford, Massachusetts, on May 24, 1904. We lived at 56 East Main Street. My father, Lorenzo Calitri, was a stonecutter from Panni, a town in Foggia province, who came to the United States with my mother Carmela Paglia (my husband's cousin), also from Panni, in 1900, settling in Milford. When I was a child, about five or six years old, Sacco was boarding with people who lived downstairs in my father's house on East Main Street. When he met Rosina, she was living with her family on Meade Street in the Plains section. Sacco was called Ferdinando, or "Freddy." Rosina was about nine years older than me and went to school with my brother Costanzo. I went to school with her sister, Adelina I think. Their father, Zambelli, shot a peeping Tom, who was looking in their window, with a rifle and wounded him in the knee. His leg had to be amputated up to the thigh. That was around 1910, when I was six.

Nick Sacco, Ferdinando's cousin, came over from Torremaggiore around 1913, together with Aquafresca, with whom he opened a bakery in Milford. During the trial he didn't want anything to do with Sacco, partly because he had the same name. Rosina Sacco, by the way, began her affair with Ermanno

Bianchini while Sacco was in prison. Someone told him about it. That's why he went on a hunger strike and was taken to a mental hospital.

Leo De Filippis was a socialist in Milford. The radicals—mostly socialists and IWWs—had a club on East Main Street, directly across from our house (probably 55 East Main Street). All the radicals met there and called themselves socialists; there were no anarchists in Milford then. Saverio Piesco was a leader of the club. He acted in many plays and wrote a play that was performed in Milford, *Il Monaco Nero: Rasputin*. The Piescos, the Calzones, and some of the other Foggian families in Milford were "Gheghers," who spoke an Albanian dialect. Other Foggian families in Milford were the Berardis and the Lanzettis, who had a daughter Ribelle.

I remember the Hopedale strike of 1913.[219] Ettor and Giovannitti came to speak. A policeman was shot to death. A young woman, Palmira Mirolini, who lived across the street from us, was called "the lady in red," a firebrand who led the children (including me) up the street singing "La Bandiera Rossa." That was during the strike. She later married a man named Boni and had a restaurant in the North End of Boston.

In 1919, when I was fifteen, I went to New London, Connecticut, with my future husband, Pasquale Paglia. (My mother and his father were brother and sister.) We married there a year later and remained until 1922. My husband was an anarchist and had not registered for the draft in 1917 and spent a night in jail. There was a big anarchist group in New London. I met Riccardo Orciani[220] there—he came to our house—tall, nice-looking. That was in 1921. He came on a motorcycle to see Gemma and Milly Mello (who were cousins). Gemma[221] had come from Paterson to work in the silk mills in New London. She was about eight years older than me, not pretty, but intelligent. She went to the group, to the men, crossed her legs and smoked—not my type. She later moved to Brooklyn. We also went to Brooklyn and lived there till 1928, when we moved to Needham. My husband died in 1966. I moved in with Maria Mogliani in Braintree for ten years and lived with her in Miami during the winter.

A week before the Franklin explosion,[222] in February 1919, the men came to visit my husband in Milford. They played *bocce* and cards. I read about the explosion in the paper and went across the street to show it to my husband and Saverio Piesco. Silverio De Chellis left a son, Vero. Eustachio De Chellis left six children. Another man killed was called Palumbo.

I met Ella Antolini[223] during the Second World War. She worked as a seamstress at Priscilla Wedding Gowns in Boston. She was not my type. She was blonde, of medium height, and capable at her work. But she ran away to Florida with Nick Piesco[224]—who had a wife, Alba—and had a hot and heavy affair. Ella has a son Febo in Hollywood, Florida, and a daughter there, Linda, who is an alcoholic and killed a man there not long ago.

I knew John Scussel[225] in Needham. He was blondish, quiet. His son Nino lives in Ohio, I think. Emilio Coda[226] had a son in Needham; and the woman Coda was living with is still alive. Two of Luigi Falsini's[227] daughters live in

Needham (one died). Two of Adelfo Sanchioni's[228] children were killed in a sailboat accident at Cape Cod in 1952, along with five others. It was a terrible tragedy.

What is my creed? I am an atheist. I believe in nature. I try to do good for people. I love my family, and my family loves me. That is my creed.

• RALPH PIESCO •

Brockton, Massachusetts, October 9, 1987

Ralph Piesco, brother-in-law of Jennie Paglia (q.v.), came from the same province in Italy (Foggia) as Nicola Sacco. Like Sacco, he settled in Milford, Massachusetts, and became a shoe worker. Ralph (Raffaele) and his brothers Saverio and Nicola were all active in the anarchist movement and friends of Sacco and his wife Rosina.

I CAME to Milford from Italy in 1916, when I was fifteen years old. I was born in the town of Casalvecchio, twenty-six kilometers from Torremaggiore, where Sacco came from. The Calzones also came from Casalvecchio, and others came from Casalnuovo, Castelnuovo, Pietroconne, Sansevero, and other Foggian towns. Foggiani had been emigrating to Milford for a long time. Most left for economic reasons. It was a poor province with a history of strikes and peasant disturbances. During one strike, around 1908, Filomena Rubini was shot to death by soldiers. My father and two brothers, Saverio and Nicola, were already here when I arrived. Many of our *paesani* lived on Mount Pleasant Street (where we and the Calzones lived), Beech Street, and East Main Street.

My father had been a shoe worker in Italy and he was a shoe worker here. He worked for Regal Shoe. I worked there too. My brothers were also shoe workers, a common occupation for Italian immigrants. Saverio died in Brockton three years ago at the age of ninety-five. He had been a soldier for six months in Italy. He had a wife and child. He liked to dress up. He acted in plays and played the mandolin—he had taken lessons in Italy for three years and played it well. We put on plays in Milford, like *Rasputin* and *Tempeste Sociali*,[229] and organized picnics to raise money for the movement.

Sacco and Rosina took part in the plays along with me and my brother. I was only fifteen or sixteen then. The Saccos lived around the corner from us, on Hayward Street. He was the quiet type, an ordinary person. He didn't say much. He didn't drink. He was a very clean young man, in language as well as in his person. You never heard any vulgarity from him. Rosa was an intelligent young woman. She dressed carefully. You couldn't help liking her. Sacco worked as an edge-trimmer. I wanted to be an edge-trimmer when I came to Milford, but I wasn't good enough. It was the best job in the factory, skilled work that paid the best money. Sacco was very good at it. Michael Kelley was a very nice man—a foreman at Milford Shoe.

Sacco never lived with the Iannetellis; they lived on Central Street, not East Main. He may have lived with another Foggian family there, the Consolettis. Sacco had a cousin named Nick Sacco, who lived on East Main Street. He ran a bakery with another Foggian named Aquafresca. He was not an anarchist.

There were two radical circles in Milford, an IWW group on East Main Street and an anarchist group on Plains Street. Each had about twenty-five members, all Italians. Saverio went to the IWW one. Some of its members had been involved in the 1913 strike in Hopedale, when the IWW tried to organize the workers and a striker, Maccrocobi, was killed. Sacco also took part in it. In 1916 Sacco, my brother Saverio, and Luigi Paradiso were speaking at a meeting and were arrested by the Milford police chief, Murphy. Orciani, by the way, did not live in Milford, but he did come here for picnics.

Saverio moved to Brockton not long after the First World War, and I moved to Westfield, New Jersey. I came here many years later. I knew William Callahan[230] here—a good lawyer, a nice person, a bachelor.

• GEORGE T. KELLEY •

Worcester, Massachusetts, January 9, 1987

George T. Kelley, a professor of economics at Worcester State College, is the grandson of Michael F. Kelley, proprietor of the shoe factory in Stoughton, Massachusetts, in which Nicola Sacco was employed. Sacco and his family, moreover, rented a house owned by Kelley behind his own house, and the Saccos and Kelleys were on friendly terms. Kelley always retained his faith in Sacco's good character. He said: "A man who is in his garden at 4 o'clock in the morning and at the factory at 7 o'clock, and in his garden again after supper and until nine and ten at night, carrying water and raising vegetables beyond his own needs which he would bring to me to give to the poor—that man is not a 'holdup man.'"[231]

THE Three-K shoe factory was started by my grandfather, Michael F. Kelley. The three K's were Michael and his two sons, George T. and Leon (my father). The emblem on the shoe box had three faces, Michael, George, and Leon. I was named after Uncle George, who died in the late 1920s, before the execution of Sacco and Vanzetti.

Sacco was a skillful and reliable worker. One time, however, he distributed radical literature in the factory, and they cautioned him against it. Not only, as the owners, did they want peace in the factory, but there was an element of concern for Sacco as well. He was like part of the family. The Saccos lived in a small house behind the family house and owned by them. Besides working in the factory, Sacco repaired things in the Kelley homestead and was a watchman at the factory. Grandmother was extremely fond of him. She always stood up for him and couldn't believe that he could do those nefarious things. She was taken with the whole family and assisted at Ines's birth.

They were aware of his radicalism but didn't know what to make of it. They saw him as a good worker, a family man, a kind person. Grandmother asked him to kill a chicken now and then, and he was very squeamish about it. He didn't like killing chickens. It was an odd relationship between an Irish business family and an Italian worker. "Give up the radical crap. Be an American," Grandfather would tell him. Dad said that, apart from everything else that was said against them, Italian immigrants were regarded as bomb-throwers. That was the stereotype. You might want to talk to my aunt in New Hampshire, Ann Riordan, a sister of my father and uncle. There were six children, three boys (Leon, George, and Arthur) and three girls, including Ann. When the events began to occur in 1920, the girls were sent away to camp in Milford for the summer.

• BELTRANDO BRINI •

Fort Lauderdale, Florida, March 14, 1987

Beltrando Brini was a child of six when, in 1913, Bartolomeo Vanzetti came to live with his family in Plymouth, Massachusetts. Seven years later, at the age of thirteen, he was the star defense witness at Vanzetti's first trial, testifying that he was delivering eels with Vanzetti on the day of the Bridgewater holdup, in which Vanzetti was accused of taking part. Encouraged by Vanzetti, who considered him his "spiritual son," Brini attended Boston University and went on to become an elementary school principal, a member of several chamber music groups, and the conductor of the Brockton Symphony Orchestra, a position that he held for ten years. His recollections of Vanzetti, whom he idolized and loved, provide a vivid insight into the man who, together with his comrade Nicola Sacco, was executed in 1927.

I WAS BORN in Plymouth, Massachusetts, in 1907. My father was a great reader—he read his books in Italian—and gave his children literary names: Lefevre (called Faye) [Lefevre Brini Wager, q.v.], after a character, I think, in Dumas; Zora, after a character in Tolstoy, I believe; and Bertrando, after the Italian writer Bertrando Spada. When I started school, my name was incorrectly recorded as Beltrando, and so it remained. My friends have always called me "Bel." At home I was called "Dolly," never "Trando," as Upton Sinclair has it in his novel *Boston*, which is about 60 percent fiction and 40 percent truth. Faye is two years older than I, and Zora four years younger.

Both my parents came from the Bologna region and spoke the Bolognese dialect. They met in Italy but married after they emigrated (separately) to America. Father (Vincenzo) was born in 1870, Mother (Alfonsina) in 1879. He died in 1935, Mother in the 1970s. Father worked at the Plymouth Cordage Company until he retired in 1934, a year before his death. His job—very heavy work—was to take the bales of sisal and feed them into a machine. Mother worked as a "specker"—she picked out threads—at Puritan Mills. She was a devout Catholic, while father was an anarchist and atheist of the Galleani school. I think Galleani once stayed at our house in Suosso's Lane in North Plymouth, the Italian and Portuguese quarter of Plymouth, where the Cordage was located. The Italians were despised by the Yankees, who treated them as second-rate citizens, as the Negroes were treated in the South. Galleani was always being quoted in our house. Father subscribed to the *Cronaca Sovversiva*, and there was a Club Sovversiva in North Plymouth on Court Street, near the railroad station. There was also a social hall on Suosso's Lane, the Amerigo Vespucci Hall, but that was for the general Italian community, not the anarchists.

Our house was open to wayfarers, and there was a constant flow of Italian immigrants in and out. When anybody needed a room people would say, "Go to the Brinis." That's how Vanzetti came to us—not because father was an anarchist, but because we were known to take in transients. He came only for a day, but he stayed for two, he stayed for three, and he stayed for four years. That was from 1913, when I was six, until 1917, when he went to Mexico.[232]

Vanzetti was anarchism personified. He didn't want to be restricted or to acknowledge any boss. He believed in the perfectibility of human nature, something that does not in fact exist. That was his blind spot. He treated us with love and respect. And he treated animals the same way. Once he found a sick kitten in the street, an infection all over its face; he brought it home, kept it in a box on the porch, washed its eyes with boric acid and nursed it back to health. He loved nature, flowers, the sea with the same unadulterated love. As we walked in the woods and on the beach he established in my mind, with his conversation and his actions, values and virtues that have remained with me ever since. They have lasted my entire life, and my memory of him is still fresh sixty years after his execution.

Vanzetti made me feel useful by sending me on little errands—once he asked me to get a money-order for him and I walked all the way to the Plymouth post office—and made me feel proud of myself, something my father never did. He talked to me and spent time with me. Father, though he loved to read, spent a good deal of time in the club playing cards. Yet both he and Vanzetti were anarchists, and they spent many nights debating the issues that anarchists debated, such as the relative merits of syndicalism, individualism, and communism. My bedroom was next to the kitchen, where they talked, and I still can recall their conversations. Vanzetti made me feel very proud of my ability to do anything. He would sit by me when I played the violin and tell me when the notes were wrong—in "Old Black Joe," for instance, one of his favorite songs. He had a good ear for music, as well as a rich baritone voice, when he spoke or sang. I enjoyed listening to him. I spent a lot of time with Vanzetti. He taught me Italian—at home we spoke the Bolognese dialect—and was a good teacher.

Our neighbor Cristofori played the violin—his sister played the piano—and that's how I first became interested. Vanzetti encouraged me. He was also very nice to my sister Faye, who joined us in the Italian lessons. She too had great affection for him, but he was not as close to her as he was to me. Vanzetti, by the way, had no love affairs, no women friends, to my knowledge, or at least I never saw or heard of any. He was a slender man—he never had any excess weight—of average height and always well-groomed, though I didn't care for his big mustache. He had deep-set eyes and a sonorous voice. I spoke to him in English, and he spoke it well. To my parents he spoke Italian, though he could get along in the Bolognese dialect.

Vanzetti was like a father to me. He was around more than my own father, as he didn't keep factory hours. He took an interest in everything I did. We walked on the beach together, in the woods, along the railroad tracks. Once we met a group of children in the woods who were selling mayflowers that they had picked. Instead of buying one or two, Vanzetti bought them all. When I asked him why, he said that the children had spent all day picking the flowers and deserved to be rewarded for their effort. Another time, on Halloween, I had a jack-o'lantern without a candle. I had no money for one. So Vanzetti gave me two pennies. When I looked in my hand I saw that he had made a mistake and had given me a penny and a dime. I returned nine cents to him, though he didn't want to take it. He had no sense of money, no interest in it.

The last time I saw Vanzetti as a free man was an embarrassing experience. I was playing baseball near Suosso's Lane. In the adjoining street was a vegetable garden enclosed by a fence. Our ball sailed into the garden and I went to retrieve it, stepping on the vegetables. When the owner came out I didn't excuse myself and was probably a bit rude. Vanzetti was coming down the street and saw it all. He came up to me, got down on one knee so that his face was close to mine, and told me in a quiet way that I had done the wrong thing. He asked me to apologize. I vowed that I would never do it again. That was shortly before he was arrested, in the spring of 1920.

Vanzetti lived with us for four years, beginning around 1913. Then, in 1917, he left for Mexico. I was too young to understand any of it. While he was away, government agents came to our house. We had gotten a letter from Vanzetti and they were interested in seeing it. It was resting on a shelf in the kitchen. While they were looking around, Faye removed it and hid it. When Vanzetti came back to Plymouth the following year, my sisters and I were growing up and there was no place for him to live with us. So he took a room with Mary Fortini at 35 Cherry Street, a few blocks away, coming to visit us two or three times a week. I remember the day of his return. I was on my way home and from a distance caught a glimpse of his head through the window. I was over-

joyed to see him! He gave me confidence and self-esteem. He made me feel like
something.

Sometime after his return Vanzetti began to sell fish. Sometimes he himself
caught the fish—he had a small rowboat—but usually he ordered the fish from
the markets in Boston. He talked of going into partnership with Frank Jesse, a
fisherman who testified at his trial. Every so often Vanzetti went away from
home—occasionally for a few days at a time—to meet with his pals and help
with the cause, raising money and the like. But I never heard him mention the
name of Sacco. Sacco was a complete mystery to me. The first time I heard of
him was when he and Vanzetti were arrested. I saw him, of course, at the
Dedham trial, but he had never been to our house, as far as I know, and I had
never laid eyes on him before. And I never saw Vanzetti with a gun. There were
certainly no guns in our house. I can't see him with a gun at all. Would he have
been capable of using one in connection with his theories? Possibly. But I have
no knowledge that he did, or even that he knew how to use one. That he had
a gun when he was arrested is something I could never understand. He certainly didn't use it for protection when selling fish. He never had enough cash
for that; and what money he had he left lying around the house and my mother
had to take care of it for him. And I never heard of dynamite in connection with
Vanzetti. His room was an open book. There was no paraphernalia or equipment for carrying out violent deeds. I never saw him perform any act other than
what I would describe as gentle and considerate. I cannot even *conceive* of his
doing anything violent.

Yes, I was with Vanzetti on the day of the Bridgewater crime. Of that I am
certain. I was not coached by anybody and did not memorize a fake story. I was
of course disappointed not to drive the horse and wagon, but that didn't matter
much because I was so happy to be making the rounds with Vanzetti. And
there's absolutely no question about the date. There were numerous other
witnesses to corroborate it. It could not have been December 23d because I
had to go to school that day. But the 24th was a holiday, so I was able to
accompany Vanzetti. It's impossible that I mistook the date. After we finished,
Vanzetti paid me for my help at the corner of Cherry Street and Court Street,
and I used the money to go to the movies. The other witnesses, by the way,
were not anarchists but ordinary Italians and mostly devout Catholics. They
had no sympathy with Vanzetti's views, but they knew he was an honest man.
Yet my mother and father had to do a lot of coaxing to get them to come to
court. They were embarrassed to be associated with Vanzetti. But they had
bought eels from him that day and knew that he was innocent. Afterwards,
many people in Plymouth shunned me because of my connection with Vanzetti. Anarchism was not a popular cause.

The trial was a difficult experience. I had watched Katzmann in action before I was called to the stand. He terrified me. I was very uneasy after seeing
how he bullied and shouted at the others. But I think I didn't show it. I braced
myself. Judge Thayer seemed a passive figure. He allowed lots of things to

continue that he shouldn't have. So I was very surprised when he spoke kindly to me during a recess. I had associated him with the camp of Katzmann and the prosecution.

In the years after their conviction I did what I could to assist the Defense Committee. Felicani, a fine man, spoke slowly, deliberately, in measured tones. I had a great deal of respect for him. He was calm, never excited, always reassuring. As with Vanzetti, I loved to hear him speak. Felix Frankfurter questioned me in regard to the case, I suppose when he was working on his article for the *Atlantic Monthly*.[233] I was also questioned by John Dos Passos[234] and by Upton Sinclair; and I remember walking Dos Passos to the North Plymouth station to catch the train to Boston. In my sophomore year at college (Boston University) Elizabeth Glendower Evans[235] let me stay at her house in Brookline for the whole year (1926–1927). And I used to go around New England and New York and play the violin and speak of my acquaintance with Vanzetti to raise money for the defense. Often Edward Holton James accompanied me on those trips. He had an apartment on Beacon Hill and a house at Cotuit, on the cape, which I visited during the summer. He had a beautiful violin and invented a little disc to put on the Victrola.

In the weeks before the execution I was interviewed by Governor Fuller. He seemed friendly, he took me to lunch, and he said, "If you have anything else to say don't hesitate to get in touch with me." Afterwards I went to see him, along with other witnesses, and demanded, since he did not believe us, to be arrested for perjury. And on the day of the executions, August 22, I tried to get to see him, but his secretary Herman MacDonald wouldn't let me in.

I still look back with emotion to those days and years with Vanzetti. He was my ideal. For some boys it was Ty Cobb, but for me it was Bartolomeo Vanzetti!

• LEFEVRE BRINI WAGER •

Plymouth, Massachusetts, April 12, 1987

From 1913 to 1917, when he went to Mexico to avoid conscription, Bartolomeo Vanzetti lived with the family of Vincenzo Brini in Plymouth, Massachusetts (see interview with Beltrando Brini). Lefevre (known as "Faye"), the oldest of the three Brini children, appeared as a witness for Vanzetti at the Sacco-Vanzetti trial in Dedham.

I CAN REMEMBER the day that Vanzetti arrived. He had stopped at the club on Suosso's Lane—the Amerigo Vespucci Club—and asked for lodgings. Somebody told him to come to our house. He arrived with two big suitcases. We kids saw the suitcases and thought he might have some goodies! He had a mustache and a Van Dyke beard. He looked kind. He was neat. He spoke Italian, not the Bolognese dialect that we spoke at home. He didn't know much English. Mama showed him the room, and he was pleased with it.

My parents came from Bologna. Father came here first, then sent for Mama. They were married in Plymouth. I was born here in 1905, not in the house at Suosso's Lane, which Father bought a few years later, but in a rented apartment. Beltrando [Brini, q.v.] (I called him "Dolly") was born a year and a half later, and Zora a couple of years after that. Father had a job at the Cordage. It was very dusty work, no good for him. His overalls were so oily. I hated that job. I think that it shortened his life. Mother didn't work then, but later worked at Puritan Mills as a "specker." The Cordage was a very big factory. At six o'clock in the evening the whistle blew and people filled the road. Peanut vendors would be there to meet them with hot peanuts on Wednesday payday.

Vanzetti was usually out—working or looking for work. He had different jobs. He worked for the Cordage for a while, he dug clams, and so on. He didn't go to the club with Dad much. He was not a drinking man and didn't play cards. He was a studious man. At home he liked to sit and read. But he also loved the outdoors. He liked to walk. We went with him to gather mayflowers and violets, blackberries and redberries on Castle Hill, or walked with him on the beach or along the railroad tracks picking up pieces of coal. He was a gentle soul. There was not a bit of meanness in him. I never saw him angry. That man didn't know how to be mean. He brought a sick kitten to the house and nursed it back to health. Every day he fed it milk and washed its eyes. Once he gave his boots to a man who didn't have any and had a family. And when he lost his pocketbook and it was found, he didn't believe it was his because it had too much money in it; even though Mother recognized it and said it was his, he refused to take it. He liked us kids. He was very affectionate to all of us, played with us. He wanted to learn English, so I taught him English while he taught me Italian. He did very well. And I learned the Italian too. When I got married, in 1924, he sent me a lovely gift, made by the prisoners in Charlestown.

Father was an anarchist, a subscriber to *Cronaca Sovversiva*. Mother had more faith and remained a Catholic. She was a darling—and a very hard worker. Dad talked loud with his friends—including Vanzetti—about politics. We kids didn't understand any of that—we just went out and played. Dad loved gardening, and Vanzetti helped in the garden. I never heard him talk of violence or guns. There were no guns in our house. The neighbors, mostly devout, conservative people, thought a lot of Vanzetti. He was good to all of them. When the Cordage went on strike, Vanzetti was there every day until it was over. I don't know what he did, but he was active for the cause, even though he didn't work there any more.

The following year, 1917, Vanzetti went to Mexico. I didn't know what for. I missed him, of course. I missed him at table. I missed making his bed and taking care of his clothes. We heard later that he didn't want to be drafted, didn't want to fight in the war. Every once in a while we got a letter from him. One time two men came to the house from the government. I knew they could hurt him. There was a letter from him on the kitchen shelf over the sink. I went and hid it under my clothes. My parents were at work, and I was the only one at home. When Vanzetti came back, Father got him a place with Mary Fortini on Cherry Street. Mother had a full-time job and couldn't take in boarders. Mary Fortini was not an anarchist. The Fortinis were lower-class people, uneducated, but good, hardworking people. Oh, the day Vanzetti took off his beard—were we surprised! But he always kept his mustache.

When Vanzetti was arrested we were stupefied. What was this? It can't be. We couldn't believe that the man did what they said he did. He was so gentle, so good. He helped people, not hurt them. Never! Besides, he was in Plymouth. We KNEW he didn't do it. I said to Mother, "It can't be. There's a mistake." But we didn't get alarmed. We thought it would be rectified. As time passed, though, we *did* get alarmed. We went to visit Vanzetti almost every day in Plymouth jail. We brought him violets—and cookies. I used to walk there—it was good weather, spring. We brought him newspapers and books. He didn't seem upset. He always had faith that he would be liberated.

My poor brother! They put him through hell in court. Mother told him to tell the truth. And Bel was smart. There was no coaching or rehearsing. Just tell the truth. I attended the trial in Plymouth. Judge Thayer was a gaunt man with grey hair. He always had a stern look. The alibi witnesses were not anarchists. Politics were not in their line. All they cared about was the family, the church. Some of them couldn't even read and write. They testified for Vanzetti because they knew he was innocent. Bel told the truth. He hadn't memorized a story. That was his day with his friend Vanzetti. He knew what he had done, where he had gone, even better than Vanzetti.

I testified at the Dedham trial. That Katzmann—I hated him! Was he fresh! The night before, I ran a temperature for fear of that man. I was so glad when I heard he died—and the same for that whole bunch: Thayer, Fuller, all those who framed the two men. I had never seen Sacco, by the way, before the trial. And I didn't speak to him even then. My heart was full of Vanzetti. Katzmann bullied me, and I got upset. I also got kind of fresh. He was a man of medium height, with greying hair, a good talker. My mother was convalescing from an operation, and I stayed home from work to take care of her. That's how I met the peddler [Joseph Rosen].[236] A beautiful day it was, I remember so well. Vanzetti was selling fish. He met the peddler on the street. He took him to Mamma to look at the cloth. And he had an order of fish for us—it was a Friday.

Vanzetti's sister, Luigina, came to our house before the execution. Poor thing, what a tragedy for her. She and Mamma went to jail in Charlestown to see him. It still hurts, sixty years later. I loved him, you know. He was good to all of us. And Sacco, too. I felt bad for him. He had a wife and two kids. I felt very sorry for him. I get mad sometimes when I think of it. Poor Vanzetti! To know him was to love him.

• CONCETTA SILVESTRI •

Malden, Massachusetts, February 13, 1988

I first met Concetta Silvestri in 1979 at a Sacco-Vanzetti conference in the Boston Public Library. Then eighty-four, she was a small woman with white hair, blue eyes, fair complexion, and a lively, sparkling personality. Sixty years earlier she had been an anarchist in Franklin, Massachusetts, a disciple of Luigi Galleani and comrade of Sacco and Vanzetti, whom she visited in prison after their arrest. In early 1990 Concetta moved to a nursing home in Malden, where she died three years later at the age of ninety-seven.

I WAS BORN in 1895 in the town of Langiano, province of Chieti, on the Adriatic coast of the Abruzzi. I was fifteen years old when I came to the United States in 1910 (I'll be ninety-three this year). My father sent for us. He had already gone to America and had a job in a rubber factory in Franklin, Massachusetts. When we arrived I went to work right away, in a factory making horse blankets, operating a sewing machine. I had no regular school, only evening classes for a little while. I had been raised a Catholic, but at sixteen or seventeen I opened my eyes more and more.

I met my husband, Silverio De Chellis, in Franklin and became an anarchist like him. We met Sacco during a strike in Hopedale in 1913, when some of us went over to support the pickets. We also saw him in a performance of a play in Milford, where he lived, and met Rosina too. She followed his ideas. We went to Milford quite often—it is not far from Franklin—for picnics and plays. We also visited Luigi Galleani in Wrentham, another nearby town. There were picnics there too, and songs. [She sings Pietro Gori's "Canto di Maggio" in a lovely, clear voice.] Galleani was a very severe man: whatever he says goes. But he had a fine character, and you hung on every word when he spoke.

In February 1919 there was a strike in Franklin, in the factory where my husband worked. He and three other men decided to put a bomb in the factory. They were determined to shut it down. I was at home and heard the explosion (we lived quite near to the factory). All the dishes fell from the cupboard and broke. The bomb had gone off prematurely. All four men were killed: my husband, his older brother, and two comrades, all young men in their twenties. In no time the town was filled with police. Everywhere you saw police—policemen hanging from trees. Soon after the explosion they came and arrested me. I was his wife and they wanted information. They held me for three or four months. They questioned me and questioned me, but I told them nothing. "If you don't talk we will deport you," they said. "Do you want me to tell lies?" I asked. "Yes," they said, "tell us lies and we will repeat them after you!" They began deportation proceedings. "Well, you are going back to Italy," one of them said. But they had no evidence against me. So here I am!

Were Sacco and Vanzetti involved with dynamite? Well, they were both in Mexico; they were all activists there. They were both very strong with the Idea. They didn't stop to think what might happen to them. "If I die, I die, but that's what I wanted to do." That was the way they felt. They were different types: Sacco was excitable; Vanzetti was calm, thoughtful, and explained everything (*Sacco era riottoso; Vanzetti era calmo, pensava, spiegava tutte le cose*). But both of them were militants and were ready to do whatever was necessary to achieve their Idea.

Were they involved in holdups? I don't know. Sacco was a very, very active man. He would do anything for the cause. Sacco knew what he wanted. And he could fight. We often visited Sacco in Dedham prison, and we also visited Vanzetti in Charlestown. He was a quieter man, slow-talking. He knew what he was saying.

By then I was living in Malden, only a twenty-minute drive from Charlestown. When my husband was killed, my son Vero was seven months old. I didn't want to live in Franklin anymore. The police were watching me all the time. They used to follow me around. They waited at the train to see what was in my bag. And people would point at me and say, "That's the one." So I moved to Malden, where I wasn't known, and lived with my brother-in-law and sister. That was later in 1919, about six months after the explosion. Rosina Sacco moved here after the trial, and Assunta Valdinoci[237] lived with her and the children [she points to the house from the kitchen window].

You know that the comrades sent Vanzetti to New York after Salsedo and Elia were arrested.[238] I also went to New York—not with Vanzetti—to try to see Salsedo, but they wouldn't let me in. He was kept in a tall building on Park Row. I had already been in New York a few months earlier to hear Emma Goldman speak. It was not long before she was deported. She was a woman who made you think. Her words went into your brain and you couldn't forget them.

Many of the Italian women kept to their old beliefs even when their husbands were anarchists. But there were some that were active in the movement: Giannetti (I can't recall her first name) in Franklin; Lucia Mancini in Needham (she died in Florida), who was with Tugardo Montanari until he was deported, and they had a daughter. I later saw Montanari in Paris—a very spunky man. There was also Ella Antolini, as well as a few others. Ella was a strong character. She was in jail with Emma Goldman and was close to Carlo Valdinoci before her arrest for carrying dynamite. Ella and I later worked together for Priscilla Wedding Gowns in Boston (we made Grace Kelly's wedding gown in the 1950s[239]). I worked on a machine and she gave out the work as a supervisor. She died in Florida a few years ago.

Luigi Falsini was a Toscano from Carrara. Adelfo Sanchioni ran a shoe factory, in Lynn, I think. His boy and girl drowned in a boating accident off Cape Cod with five other children. Luigi Vella, in Westfield, New Jersey, was my first husband's brother-in-law (my husband's sister's husband). I later got together with Alfonso Silvestri ("Giambon"), who died in Florida.

• JENNY SALEMME •

Malden, Massachusetts, February 13, 1988

Jenny Salemme and her husband Joe, a tailor, were anarchists in East Boston and took part in amateur theatrical performances in their club on Maverick Square. Joe often visited Vanzetti in Charlestown prison before his execution in 1927.

I WAS BORN in Naples on December 24, 1900. My father, Giuseppe, was from Pescara, in the Abruzzi. His mother had a little inn, and her husband was a butcher who provided meat for the hunters—noblemen from Naples—who came to the inn, which was in Catignano, in the hills near Pescara. Grandfather prepared their game and Grandma did the cooking. The hunters fell in love with their little boy (my father), who brought wine to the table and did other errands. They asked my grandparents to let them take him to Naples.

It was there, some years later, that he met my mother. Mother, Giulietta, was from Modena and was a designer of hats. "Giulietta can even make the legs for the flies," her sister said. A countess in Naples heard of her and invited her to come down from Modena to design for her. She met Father, who had become the major-domo of the castle, and they got married.

Father had a sister in the North End of Boston, who wrote about the great America, the "land of gold." Father, Mother, and I went in 1902. We lived in a dingy little place with a kerosene lamp on the wall. Mother couldn't take it. Modena had been so much more beautiful and elegant, and she had a middle-class upbringing and a good education. So, while Father stayed in Boston, Mother and I went back to live with my grandparents. We remained until I was ten. Father wrote that we should come back: America had changed, everything was beautiful. Grandma urged us to return. "That child doesn't have a father anymore," she said. "She needs her father."

So we returned to America in June 1910. But Mother still didn't like it, and she returned again to Modena. Father wouldn't let me go. He worked for a wholesale liquor business in the North End. We moved to the owner's house in Belmont, where I went to school. The kids mocked my language and my pierced ears and earrings ("Look at the guinea!") But I stuck it out and graduated from Belmont High School.

There was terrible feeling against Italians in Massachusetts at that time. Italians were confined to certain neighborhoods, and so on. When I was eighteen, Father took me to my aunt in East Boston. She persuaded him to let me stay with her. She was an actress and took me to the club on Maverick Square for rehearsals of the *filodrammatica* [theater group]. They put on *Primo Maggio, Tempeste Sociali*, and other radical plays.

It was there that I met my husband, Joseph Salemme, who acted in the plays. He came from Gaeta and was a tailor by occupation. He had run away from

Italy at seventeen, around 1912. He had belonged to the Young Socialist group in Gaeta. His father had gambled away all his money. So my husband always said, "No guns and no cards in this house!" I too began to act in the plays. We went all over—New London and other cities. Joe was an anarchist, a disciple of Galleani, but not as dogmatic as some of the others. He belonged to the Amalgamated Clothing Workers and later voted for Henry Wallace.[240] When that happened, *L'Adunata* considered him a traitor and stopped sending him the paper. He died of a ruptured appendix thirty-five years ago at the age of fifty-six. Our son Hugo is an ornamental iron craftsman who did some of the fixtures on Copley Square.

My husband loved Vanzetti and visited him often in Charlestown prison. He cried every time he came home from the jail. Some comrades said that Sacco was in fact involved in the holdup, but my husband was not one of them, and he wouldn't have said it if he knew. Rosina, by the way, had a lot of resentment and bitterness against the movement after the execution, and she largely isolated herself from it.

Adelfo Sanchioni and his brother Renato both went to Mexico in 1917. They had lived in Lynn before going to Mexico and afterwards in East Boston. Both were shoe workers and they came from the Marche. Adelfo was a good character actor in the plays at Maverick Square. Luigi Falsini was Adelfo's brother-in-law; his sister Vilma was Adelfo's wife. She also acted in the plays. Falsini was a marble setter from Carrara who brought the trade over with him. Vincenzo Colarossi was a bachelor who lived in rooming houses in and around Boston, a tailor like my husband, who was his close friend. His cousin Umberto lived in Jamaica Plain, I think, and had a daughter, but I don't know what became of her. Vincenzo finally married but died young soon afterwards.

Mario Buda[241] was in the plays with us. He was bald and small, but not too small, with a large nose. Gambera[242] was an eccentric in every way. He was a Sicilian, sort of the Mafia type. I think he lived in Roxbury. Joe once went there to pick him up to go to the club in East Boston and found his wife chained to the stove. From then on he couldn't stand Gambera. Cesarini was also from Roxbury, I think. Alessi was from Sardinia, a mason, I believe. Fernando Tarabelli built houses and was a man of good, strong character. Sam Farulla took care of the library in East Boston and filled orders for literature. Felice Guadagni was an intellectual, well-educated, and wrote and lectured a lot. Joe Amari always wore the anarchist black tie and hat. Amleto Fabbri was tops, a type like Vanzetti. To know him was to love him, a gentle, kind person. He came down with angina and died a long time ago. He had gone back to Italy but returned to the U.S. and died in the 1940s, I think. He was the idea of the movement.[243]

Aldino Felicani had a dictatorial attitude. He felt he knew everything. When he took the floor you couldn't contradict him. After Galleani left, Felicani became the head man in the movement. Everyone looked up to him. And he knew what was happening in the movement. It was a small movement, but a very convinced and solid movement. Most of the group in Roxbury were Romagnoli and Marchigiani. Ella Antolini worked in a factory with Concetta [Silvestri, q.v.] and later went to Florida. She was good-looking—rather tall, slim, fair—like Greta Garbo.

• CATINA WILLMAN •

Fort Lee, New Jersey, March 2, 1989

Catina Willman, born in Sicily in 1899, was an anarchist in Brooklyn from the 1920s to the 1940s. She visited Sacco and Vanzetti in prison and testified for Calogero Greco and Donato Carillo, acquitted in 1927 of murdering two Italian fascists in New York. For many years she was the companion of Armando Borghi (1882–1962), who returned to Italy from the U.S. at the end of the Second World War. She died on November 13, 1991, at the age of ninety-two.[244]

I WAS BORN Caterina D'Amico in Sicily on April 26, 1899. We emigrated to the United States and lived in Brooklyn. I heard Galleani speak at an open-air meeting when I was a teenager, and I liked what he had to say and the way he said it. He spoke directly to my heart. I became an anarchist and took part in picnics, amateur theatricals, and other activities. At that time there were two Italian anarchist groups in Brooklyn: the Circolo Volontà, a Galleanist group with Joe Parisi as the most active figure, and the Anarchist Group of South Brooklyn, with a mixed membership.

I visited Sacco and Vanzetti in prison after their conviction at Dedham. Sacco was a very nice boy, like an angel. Vanzetti was very smart, smarter than Sacco. Both were very nice, but Vanzetti was more intelligent. In Brooklyn we had recitals and picnics to raise money for their defense. We did the same later for Greco and Carillo, who were accused of killing fascists in New York. I testified for them at their trial. Clarence Darrow was the defense lawyer and got them off.

Vincenzo Capuana was a gentle and intelligent man. He had spent eight years in prison in Boston. In New York he wanted to blow up *Il Progresso* (the pro-fascist paper of Generoso Pope) at Elm and Worth Streets in lower Manhattan. But he saw children playing ball there and didn't want them to get hurt. So he began to leave when he was arrested and put in jail. In 1938 he was deported to Italy, where he was immediately imprisoned by Mussolini. He died before the war was over.

• JOSEPH MORO •

Haverhill, Massachusetts, April 13, 1987

From 1926 to 1928 Joseph Moro, a shoe worker, served as the last secretary of the Sacco-Vanzetti Defense Committee, founded by Aldino Felicani in 1920. A friend and comrade of Sacco and Vanzetti, he visited both men in prison and worked in vain to save them from execution. They were electrocuted in Boston on August 23, 1927.

I WAS BORN on September 13, 1894, in Ortona, province of Aquila, in the Abruzzi. Ortona was a town of about five thousand people, near Pescara on the Adriatic. My parents were devout Catholics, very religious. As a child, I myself was a mystic and believed in resurrection. Father was a merchant, a traveling salesman, selling dry goods and cloth. He had a cart pulled by a horse or a mule. Angelo Moro was his name. He had to talk, make jokes, in order to attract customers. When he met my mother, her father did not approve, did not want his daughter to marry a peddler. But Father threatened to elope, so Grandfather consented.

Within a few years Father accumulated wealth by selling material to carpenters, shoemakers, and the like. From peasants he gathered fruit, nuts, almonds, and shipped them to Rome, making a good deal of money. We lived in a house on the square and had a comfortable life, when suddenly Father was unjustly accused of dealing in stolen goods. He was arrested and spent six months in jail in Pescara. Ultimately he was proven innocent, but the damage had been done. He had lost everything. He emigrated to the United States, to Lawrence, Massachusetts, with my two older brothers. He worked in a textile mill for three dollars a week. He came back to Italy when I was eight or nine, after four or five years in America, but he died only a few months later.

Meanwhile Mother had opened a little store in San Sebastiano, selling novelties and dry goods. I was a sickly child, born with a rash on my head, and didn't walk till I was five. The teachers didn't want me in school. Outside of the town there was a fountain in honor of Santa Lucia. Following Mother's advice, I dipped my head in it about a dozen times. In two or three days a crust started to form. It fell off and the rash disappeared, and after that my hair grew in. From then on we went to the fountain every year on the feast day of Santa Lucia, December 13. I believed then that a miracle had occurred, that Santa Lucia had cured me. (I later understood that it was some mineral in the water that produced the effect.) My mother, religious as she was, also believed it.

I came to America with my mother in 1911, when I was sixteen years old. We settled in Haverhill, where Mother spent the rest of her life. I got a job in a shoe factory in Stoneham, where my older brother lived. I was still religious in those days, still a mystic. I preached the gospel every Sunday to the Italian immigrants. I felt it in my heart. While I was working in Stoneham, an anarchist from Lynn named Giovanni Eramo[245] came to work in the factory. I started to talk religion to him, but he was way above me, much stronger. His arguments persuaded me. He later left the shoe trade and bought a linotype machine. He became the printer of *Cronaca Sovversiva* after it moved to Lynn in 1912.

One Sunday, in 1912 I think, the Lynn anarchists had a picnic near Wakefield. I found the place just in time to see a play by Pietro Gori, *Calendimaggio*. I was deeply moved. It inspired me so much that in twenty-four hours I gave up all my religion, all my former beliefs, and started to read anarchist literature, including *Cronaca Sovversiva*. Galleani, the editor, was a little deep for a man like me without an education, but I tried to make the best of it. Every Saturday I went to Boston and got *Cronaca*, *Il Proletario*, and other radical papers. That's all that I was reading—it kept me going all week long.

I also attended Galleani's lectures. I heard him speak many times, many times, a great speaker. Galleani had lots of friends and lots of enemies, because he was too honest, too strict in his beliefs. To him *Cronaca Sovversiva* was his soul, his life. He sacrificed his whole being for anarchism. Anarchism for him, and for us, meant to be active, to be strong, to do not only mentally but also physically if necessary.

In May 1917 Galleani published his article "Matricolati!," indirectly advising his followers to avoid registering for the draft, even if that meant leaving the country. Some, like Sacco and Vanzetti, went to Mexico, where things were rough and they ran out of money. Others changed jobs and worked where they weren't known. I didn't register for the draft, so I couldn't remain in Stoneham, where people knew me. I went to Taunton and got a job in a factory making kitchen stoves, working in the stockroom. Galleani lived not far away in a barn in the woods. A lot of comrades, refusing to register and out of work, lived there with him and killed time by fixing up the barn.

Galleani was a real man, a born rebel. He would never give in. He published a few more issues of *Cronaca Sovversiva*, reading every word before it was printed, very fussy about it. Practically every Sunday I went to see him at the barn. In February 1919 I invited him to Taunton together with his family to attend a party, a kind of *ballo in maschera*. He was going to be deported anyway, so he accepted. Word spread that he was coming to Taunton to speak. A huge crowd gathered from all over, and we had an all-night party and dance. Galleani spoke against war and for social revolution.

A day or two afterwards there was an explosion in nearby Franklin. Two [actually four] comrades were killed while placing a bomb in a factory. The police blamed it on Galleani; they said it was a consequence of the meeting in Taunton. They began to look for me too. I had been fired from my job in Taunton for talking against religion but soon found work in a shoe factory in Brockton.

The following Saturday half a dozen federal agents came looking for me; they thought the Taunton "conference" was about making bombs and that the explosion in Franklin was "circumstantial evidence." They came two or three times but didn't find me, as I had moved to a shoe factory in South Braintree. There I was soon fired for talking about starting a strike after a comrade had been dismissed. I went back to Brockton and then returned to live with my mother in Haverhill. That night agents came looking for me in Brockton, but I was gone. They never caught up with me.

I joined the Sacco-Vanzetti Defense Committee in 1926 at the request of Amleto Fabbri. Fabbri, like myself, was a shoe worker, a fine man, active, honest. After Galleani was deported, he went back to Italy with his family to take part in the revolution. Augusto Rossi and his family also went. Rossi had been a building contractor in Needham; he was the father of Bruno's[246] wife, Fiorina [Florence Rossi, q.v.]. He made money and gave money for the propaganda. Galleani was certain that the revolution would break out in Italy any day, and they followed him. But they did not stay more than two or three years, returning to the U.S. shortly before Mussolini took power.

Fabbri became the secretary of the Sacco-Vanzetti Defense Committee while his wife was still in Italy. William G. Thompson, the defense attorney, told him that if he wanted his wife to come back to the States he would have to quit the committee. So Fabbri asked me to take his place and to take care of the Italian propaganda. (In English we had several good men, including Louis Bernheimer and especially Gardner Jackson.[247]) At that time I was working in a shoe factory, Heiss & Son in Cambridge, making about sixty or seventy dollars a week. I took a 50 percent cut in pay to work for the Defense Committee, receiving thirty-five dollars a week and writing my own check.

So that's how I took the job, though it was dangerous to be associated with the case. Once a federal agent tried to worm his way into the committee. He was nice-looking and friendly. He hired a taxi for me to bring leaflets to a protest meeting. When we got there, a comrade recognized him and told me that he worked for the government.

Fabbri was a sincere man and had faith in me. I accepted and stayed to the last. I'm the only one still alive from the committee. Giovanni Gambera was one of the original members, but he was never important. I wonder how much he really told his son and how much the son made up—and with a name like Ideale![248]

When I joined the committee I became friendly with Aldino Felicani, a very intelligent man even though he never went to college or had much of an education. Yes, he believed that Sacco and Vanzetti were innocent, just as I did. He had a job at *La Notizia*, and every day he got something into the paper about the case. He reported how Judge Thayer, at the Plymouth trial, disbelieved the Italian witnesses and told the jury that Vanzetti's ideas were "cognate with the crime." That got the readers angry, so that in a sense it was Thayer himself who built up the case. Contributions began to come in, and picnics were held for the benefit of the defense.

I knew both Sacco and Vanzetti. Sacco, like myself, was a shoe worker, but his was a more skilled craft, an edge-trimmer. (I was a wood-heel nailer.) Sacco was a genius at his work, that machine running so fast, sharp like a razor; you miss by a thousandth of an inch and you ruin the shoe. He was quick, precise, a wonderful worker. I was working in Taunton after the war, and Sacco was in Stoughton. I went to see him quite often. He was very romantic, loved his wife, the two of them like sweethearts. He never spoke of holdups or anything like that. I'm convinced he could never have committed such a crime. Yes, he carried a gun, but so did I during those bad times.

I also knew Vanzetti pretty well. Around 1919 he came up here to Haverhill two or three times to speak at meetings. He was a good speaker, so attractive to listen to. One time he came to our house. He had hurt his forehead at work and wore his cap over the bruise. My mother asked, Who is he? But once we sat down to eat and talk we all loved him. He was like a child. He wrote me beautiful letters. Talking to him you could fall in love with him. He talked like a poet—he was born to be a poet—and he knew what he was talking about.

After the execution I thought, "Two more victims of the capitalist system." William G. Thompson was another. Before he came to us he was a leading Boston attorney. Afterwards every door was shut with a padlock. The case shortened his life. I'm sure of it. Now, to tell the truth, I am even more convinced of the injustice around us than before. People have to improve themselves. I am filled with ideas about this.

• BARTOLOMEO PROVO •

Los Gatos, California, November 11, 1989

Bartolomeo Provo (known as Bartolo, like Vanzetti, whom he knew) became an anarchist in Massachusetts on the eve of the First World War, a disciple of Luigi Galleani. Like Sacco and Vanzetti, he refused to register for the draft and went into hiding until hostilities concluded. With Sebastiano Magliocca (q.v.) and other comrades, he attended the trial of Sacco and Vanzetti in Dedham and worked to prevent their execution. A carpenter by trade, Bartolo rode the rails from coast to coast, settling at last in California. An amateur artist, he made drawings for the anarchist press, including a sketch of Galleani. He died in Los Gatos in 1993.

I WAS BORN on January 22, 1898, in a small mining town near Du Bois, Pennsylvania, about sixty miles northeast of Pittsburgh. My father, Giacomo (Jim), was working in a coal mine, mining soft coal. I was born near the entrance to the mine, so to speak, and knew the hard conditions of life there. Both my parents (my mother's name was Catrina) were born in Ferrara di Montetaldo, a mile from the Austrian border, in the province of Verona. Father came to the United States in 1880. Before that he had been in Argentina. From the United States he went back to Italy, married my mother, and returned to the United

States a year or two before I was born. Both Father and Mother were illiterate but taught themselves to read and write.

I lived in the mining camp for seven or eight years and attended first grade. In 1906 we all returned to Italy, to the town of Caprino in Verona province, not far from Lake Garda. I was eight years old. After completing the seventh grade I went on to a technical high school. I wanted to be an architect. I used to draw and got praise for it. My teacher encouraged me. I spent half a day in school and half a day apprenticed to a carpenter.

My father owned a farm in Caprino. It was very different from America. My impressions of Italy were something out of this world. In America I saw woods, rivers, and dirty faces, the dirty faces of miners. When we docked in Genoa I saw all those farms so beautifully cultivated. I got so enthusiastic, you have no idea. My uncle also had a farm in Caprino. The vines were so loaded with grapes it seemed like paradise. We went swimming in Lake Garda every Sunday. I spent my last day in Italy swimming in the lake.

In Caprino I joined the Circle of Socialist Youth. The biggest baker in town was a socialist, and I hung around with his son. My older brother Francesco (born in Italy) and I became members of the group and attended all its meetings. To undermine the group, the church officials in town provided a meeting place for young people, with food, an orchestra, and dancing. One by one our members drifted away, and that was a great disappointment to me.

Our family returned to America in 1913. Father did not want his children to work in the mines; there were eleven altogether, and I was the second oldest, after my brother Francesco. So he did not go back to Pennsylvania but to Springfield, Massachusetts, instead. He had worked there in 1880 as a stone cutter, as he had done in Argentina. At that time the contractor had lost his money and could not pay Father his wages. In 1916 Father met him on a road in Springfield. The contractor greeted him and said, "Don't you know me?" Father did not recognize him. "Remember when we worked on that wall?" said the man, and gave Father fifty dollars.

In Springfield I went to high school for a while, a trade school, for seven or eight months. Then I started to work in a shop that made tweezers. I earned ten cents an hour and worked twelve hours a day, a total of $1.20. It was a small factory with about twenty-five or thirty men. I did that pretty close to a year. It was not interesting work, but I didn't mind. I always liked to work. But I loved carpentry.

I left the tweezer shop to work on a tobacco farm in Connecticut. I had a cousin working there, in Torrington. I stayed there a couple of years, until 1916. There was a man doing carpentry work, and I worked with him for a few months. Then I got a job in a skate shop. That was still in 1916. I was a rebel. We were poorly paid, and the workers said they would back me up if I asked for a raise. I went to the superintendent and asked for a raise for all the workers. He answered by laying me off. "You're a good worker," he said, "but you have too much faith in others." He was right. The other workers were a bunch of hypocrites. They said they would strike but they didn't. They were afraid of losing their jobs. I was very disillusioned—but not disillusioned enough, because I remained a rebel.

Then America entered the war. It was in April 1917. I took off and went to the woods with a few other comrades. I was an anarchist by then. Some of the comrades went to Mexico, including Secondo Vitale, a barber from Springfield, one of my very best friends. We became wood-choppers in the Springfield area. We did that till the war ended in November 1918. We lived in a shanty that we had built. One day a doctor drove by in a horse and buggy and shouted, "The war is over!" So we gathered up our things and went to Northampton, the nearest town, and celebrated by drinking beer. We had a wonderful time that night.

How did I become an anarchist? It happened in Torrington, when I was working in the skate shop. Since I had a nice handwriting, one of my jobs was to copy orders from slips into a book. One night a man there started to talk against the social system and also against me, because I seemed to be an official doing office work. I agreed with him about the capitalist system and said I was ready to tear it down anytime. He asked me to subscribe to *Il Proletario*, the IWW paper. I did not join the IWW, but I liked their spirit very much. After the superintendent laid me off, I went to Springfield and saw a leaflet announcing that Costantino Zonchello[249] was going to speak on "The Italians in America." I attended the lecture and was very enthusiastic about it. I went over to talk to him, and he asked me if I subscribed to any paper. I said, "*Il Proletario*, but I don't like it very much." He suggested that I subscribe to *Cronaca Sovversiva*, so I did. That was in 1915. I was not even eighteen years old. And since then that was it—up until now anyway.

I liked *Cronaca Sovversiva* very much. Young people want literature that stirs your rebellious spirit, and that the *Cronaca* did. I like Galleani's writing so much you have no idea! He was honest and also humorous and had great knowledge. He was also a great orator, the greatest in the anarchist movement at that time. By 1916 I considered myself an anarchist. I attended the plays and picnics as well as the lectures. Galleani came often to lecture in Springfield. I once acted as chairman and introduced him.

My younger brother and I went to all the meetings. I would never miss a lecture or recital, even if an atomic bomb fell down! I had a good friend in Springfield named Armando Del Moro who also attended the different gatherings. Later I lived with him in Los Gatos for twenty years until his death. He was a good friend of Bruno [Raffaele Schiavina], whom I had met a couple of years before he was deported. He was living in New Britain at the time. It was around 1916, and he came to Springfield to speak. I liked him very much—he was better even than Postiglione.[250] He was a serious speaker and knew what he was talking about. But he could never match Galleani. Galleani had guts. Bruno did not rise even to the knees of Galleani. Galleani had courage!

After the war I left for Baltimore, where my brother Francesco lived. I stayed there about four years, going back and forth to Massachusetts. In 1920, shortly after the arrest of Sacco and Vanzetti, I happened to be in Springfield, where my parents still lived. One of the comrades asked me if I knew them. I said I didn't think so. Another said, "When you spoke against the Bolsheviks in Russia, Vanzetti was against you. He was in favor of the Communists at that time." I was always against the Communists, as was Galleani, and Vanzetti thought I was merely echoing Galleani's ideas without thinking for myself. So I then recalled who he was.

Later in 1920 I went to Boston and was asked to help with the defense. I asked the comrades at Maverick Square, "Do you think Sacco and Vanzetti are guilty?" Before I start to defend anybody I like to know who they are. "No, they are absolutely innocent," came the reply. "They are as guilty as I am." I asked others. Not one said they were guilty. I was invited to the Defense Committee, and one comrade told them, "Bartolo has doubts about their innocence." I denied it. Everyone at the committee said the men were innocent.

I was then working for a contractor and living in Boston. I met Felice Guadagni and other members of the Defense Committee and liked them very much. Guadagni once invited me to dinner. He knew a great deal and wrote for several newspapers, including *La Notizia*, for which Felicani worked as a printer. Felicani and Guagdagni were heavy drinkers; in fact the whole Defense Committee drank heavily. Guadagni spoke on Sacco and Vanzetti in Springfield and ate at my parents' house. Guadagni's wife, from an aristocratic family, later left him and returned to Italy. After that he moved to New York.

I also knew Emilio Coda, another member of the committee. I met him at the club on Maverick Square in East Boston. I was there with Amari, a wonderful comrade. Around midnight we heard a knock at the door. It was Coda. He said the place was "a pigsty" (*un porcile*). I didn't like him much. He was too rude, too arrogant. Yet he did dedicate his life to the movement.

During 1921 I went to the trial in Dedham about half a dozen times with comrades from Boston, including Sebastiano Magliocca [q.v.]. Judge Thayer had a long face, like a Puritan, hard and cold. Fred Moore[251] was then searching for the real criminals and got almost to know who did it. I was there when Moore announced this to the Defense Committee. He said that Sacco and Vanzetti objected to his searching for the guilty party. "We don't pay a man to go looking for criminals," they told him. "What do you want me to do?" Moore asked the committee. "I spent thousands of dollars and am close to finding them." Felicani got up and said, "It is not our business to pay detectives to find lawbreakers," and told Moore to give it up.

A year or two later, a meeting was held in Springfield to discuss the rescue of Sacco and Vanzetti. The idea was to free them when they were on a train from the prison to the courthouse, when they were guarded by only two detectives. Cesare Stami and his gang were there. They wanted five thousand dollars to do the job. They should have done it, you know, but we didn't have the five thousand dollars. Stami was involved in several holdups. He would stop at nothing. He held up a bank in Detroit—his men were shooting everywhere. That was around 1924. Later that year they held up a train in Pennsylvania that was carrying a shipment of gold. But one of the men was a stool pigeon and tipped off the police. The train was surrounded by detectives, and Stami was killed with three or four others. I was told this in Old Forge, a mining town in eastern Pennsylvania where a number of Galleanisti lived and worked. I never agreed with those methods. They said we are exploited so we take back, but most of what they stole was for themselves and not for the Ideal.

One more thing about Sacco and Vanzetti. A comrade from Phoenix, now dead, told me that there was a priest in Youngstown, Ohio, where he had lived before moving to Arizona, who was always preaching against the anarchists. Vanzetti, he said, made a bomb and placed it at the front door of his church, but a dog sniffed it out and it was discovered before it could go off. The comrade who told me this was Andrea Di Toffolo [actually De Toffol], a bricklayer from Udine in the Friuli, a big, powerful man weighing 250 pounds, who built a motel in Phoenix. He's no longer alive. He told me this a few years ago at a picnic in Theresa Park here in Los Gatos. He said that Vanzetti lived in his house in Youngstown at the time, during the war.[252] I didn't know that Vanzetti was ever in Youngstown, and I was very surprised to hear it. Until now I never repeated this story to anybody because I thought it might hurt Vanzetti and be used against him.

Starting in 1924 I became a hobo. I traveled on freight trains and met all the hoboes in the country. I did this for two years and learned more in that time than I had in my whole life before. But one of the old-time hoboes told me that it was not for me, that I was not a real hobo. And he was right. I quit it in 1926. But I continued to move from place to place—Cleveland, Chicago, St. Louis, Detroit. I spent many years in Detroit and knew all the anarchists there—Italian, Russian, Spanish, Jewish, and others. I was a soap-boxer in all those cities and knew Sam Dolgoff [q.v.] and other speakers. I always worked as a carpenter and mingled among the anarchists. In one year I worked in five different states.

I moved to Los Gatos in 1960 and have been here ever since. I continued working as a carpenter and retired at sixty-five. I never married or had children—I never wanted to marry—but I had plenty of girl friends, always anarchists, nearly always Jewish. And I always remained a rebel. Not long ago two FBI men came to Los Gatos and began to question me. I had been an agitator on all my jobs here. I interrupted and said, "I've been an anarchist since 1916, and now I'm a better anarchist than I was then!" They left. Were they surprised!

What do I think of anarchism now? I think it's the most beautiful idea in the world. And what the anarchists predicted came true. Anybody who takes power, however good they may seem, becomes worse once corrupted. I never regretted being an anarchist. I was always an anarchist, since the age of sixteen. When I look back on my life—I am now ninety-two—I am glad that I have always been an anarchist. I have never seen a better or nobler idea.

• VINCENZO FARULLA •

Somerville, Massachusetts, February 12, 1988

A native of Sicily, Vincenzo ("Jimmy") Farulla emigrated to the United Sates with his brother Sam on the eve of the First World War and settled in the Boston area. Sam became a member of the original Sacco-Vanzetti Defense Committee, founded by Aldino Felicani in 1920. The following year both Sam and Jimmy attended the trial in Dedham, which ended in Sacco and Vanzetti's conviction for murder. Despite a worldwide campaign of protest, they were executed in 1927.

I WAS BORN in 1895 in Pietraperzia, province of Caltansotta (now Enna), Sicily. My brother Salvatore (Sam) was born in 1898. We came together to the U.S. in 1914 for economic reasons, as work was hard to get in Sicily. Our older brother Lawrence had come before us—in 1911 or 1912—and settled in Lynn, where we had friends from our home town. When Sam and I arrived we lived in East Boston. I worked in a tin factory for eighteen years. In 1932 I left the tin factory and went to work for Keystone Camera, doing precision work until 1948. That year I went back to Sicily to see my family, and when I came back Keystone was on strike. I got a new job as an upholstery cleaner. Then I went into business for myself—cleaning upholstery—till 1961. My wife—from Castelnuovo della Daunia, Foggia province—and I got married in 1939, and we have a daughter.

My brother Sam at first worked together with me in the tin factory for several years. Then, in 1921 or 1922, he became a builder of houses in Newtonville. He was a member of the original Sacco-Vanzetti Defense Committee, formed in 1920. The stock market crash wrecked his business. He went to New York and became a leather worker. After that he went to work in the same doll factory as Mike and Sebastiano Magliocca [q.v.]. He organized a union and became its president for a year. Then he started his own doll's clothing business. Mike and Bastiano worked for him. They also made toys for children. Sam got lung cancer, probably from the plastic he used in the factory (he was not a smoker), sold the place, and died on January 18, 1971.

As I said, we lived at first in East Boston, in an Italian neighborhood. Non-Italians called us "guineas," "wops," "macaroni stranglers"; kids threw snowballs at us, and so on. Sam got acquainted with a barber in East Boston, a socialist. He introduced Sam to the Italian Naturalization Club on Maverick Square, which included socialists, anarchists, syndicalists, and other Italians. They worked to help you out to become a citizen, but the socialists, anarchists, and syndicalists couldn't get along. Sam was the librarian of the club and sold books through the mail.

I heard Luigi Galleani speak a few times, on Richmond Street in the North End. He expressed what I wanted to say but couldn't because I didn't have the words. I did not know Sacco and Vanzetti. But during their trial in Dedham I went with some friends and waited in the street to see them taken from the jail to the courthouse, and they greeted us as they passed. I have no reason to believe that either of them was guilty.

Eduardo Alessi and Luigi Falsini were both marble setters, both from Carrara. They were good people, unable to hurt anybody. Antonio Cesarini painted churches—he was a house painter by trade. Adelfo Sanchioni was an intelligent man, a shoe worker who became the superintendent of a shoe factory. Vincenzo Colarossi was a tailor, Angelo Monello a tile setter. Domenico Scarinci worked for Augusto Rossi, the builder.

• SEBASTIANO MAGLIOCCA •

Brooklyn, New York, July 18, 1987

An immigrant from Sicily, Sebastiano Magliocca was an anarchist in Boston during the 1920s and afterwards in New York. His brother Mike (Michele) was secretary of *L'Adunata dei Refrattari* (1922–1971) during its final years. Sebastiano died in his sleep on March 16, 1990, at the age of ninety-two.

I WAS BORN in Sicily on January 21, 1898, and became a socialist as a young man. I emigrated to the United States in 1921 to escape the fascists, who were already on the rise in Sicily. My father was heartbroken when I left. My older brother Michele, who also became an anarchist in Boston, emigrated later. I landed in Boston and got a job in Watertown in a shoe factory, making shoes with rubber soles. Later, in New York, I worked for thirty-two years in a doll factory, making shoes for dolls. In Boston I was attracted to anarchism and joined the Gruppo Autonomo di East Boston, where I lived. We worked to raise funds for the Sacco-Vanzetti defense. Amleto Fabbri, a member of the Defense Committee, was a shoemaker, a fine, intelligent man. We all loved him.

There were a lot of people making bombs in those days just after the war. Nicola Recchi[253] was one of them. I met him in Rome after the Second World War. He was missing a hand and couldn't work and had to rely on friends in the movement for support. His hand was blown off while he was making bombs in Luigi Falsini's house in East Boston, in 1919, I think. Augusto Rossi was active in the group, a builder in Needham and the father of Bruno's wife, Fiorina [Florence Rossi, q.v.]. He was not involved with bombs, though, nor were Sacco and Vanzetti, as far as I know. I believe that Salsedo was pushed from the window by federal agents. I don't know if the Wall Street explosion was the work of anarchists.

Johnny Gambera was on the Defense Committee at the beginning, but he didn't do anything and was not much to talk about. He didn't work, never had a job, and his wife supported him and the family. His wife's uncle, Angelo

Monello, was also a member of the original Defense Committee. Sam Farulla was another member, a very nice guy and good friend. His brother Jimmy [Vincenzo Farulla, q.v.] is still living near Boston, and the Sanchinis' daughter [Elide Sanchini, q.v.] is living in Connecticut. Felice Guadagni, though he was called "Professor," did not teach but gave lectures and wrote for *La Notizia* and other papers. He was a nice guy but didn't like to work.

Bruno returned to the United States in 1928 and became the editor of *L'Adunata*. The Communists raised half a million dollars for Sacco and Vanzetti but kept it for their own purposes and gave nothing to the Defense Committee. Tresca, too, kept some money raised at a lecture for Sacco and Vanzetti and used it for his paper, *Il Martello*. I believe that Sacco and Vanzetti were not guilty of the holdups and had nothing to do with explosives. Fred Moore spent too much money and was the wrong attorney for the case. If they had Thompson from the beginning they would never have been convicted.

• SARA R. EHRMANN •

Brookline, Massachusetts, January 7, 1987

Sara Ehrmann was born in 1895 into a prosperous German-Jewish family in Kentucky and grew up in Rochester, New York. During the 1920s her husband, Herbert B. Ehrmann, served as junior defense counsel under William G. Thompson in an effort to obtain a new trial for Sacco and Vanzetti, convicted of robbery and murder in Massachusetts. In the course of his investigations, Ehrmann built a strong case against the Morelli gang of Providence, but all legal appeals were rejected and on August 23, 1927, Sacco and Vanzetti were electrocuted. After the executions, Sara Ehrmann, who had assisted her husband in his investigation of the Morellis and had visited Sacco and Vanzetti in prison, became active in the movement to abolish capital punishment. She died in Brookline in 1993.

MY HUSBAND, Herbert Ehrmann, who died in 1970, was a graduate of the Harvard Law School. We moved into this house in 1920. Together with his former roommate Reg Smith, he had run the Boston Legal Aid Society. Then, at the request of the Cleveland Foundation, he made a survey of the criminal justice system, with particular emphasis on the courts. We went to Cleveland in 1921 and returned here in 1922. By then everybody was talking about the two "wops" convicted of murder in Dedham. In 1924 Fred Moore was dismissed as defense attorney and William G. Thompson took over the case. Mr. Thompson was very reserved, an Episcopalian, a lovely person, tall, bright, and kind; and he had a charming wife. He told friends at the Harvard Law School that he needed a young man to help him, and Herbert was recommended.

I attended the sentencing in Dedham in April 1927. Judge Thayer was a little man with a wrinkled face, his robes flowing all over him. I sat on the bench next to Gardner Jackson. Thayer sentenced them to die "with a current of electricity passing through them until dead." Then he took his robes majestically around him, rose from the bench and walked up the steps. Newspaper men gathered. Thayer put his hand out and said, "Well, boys, how did I do?" Nobody answered, nobody took his hand. "Come on, boys," he said, "I've always been good to you, you know."

The older ladies had been lovely to Rose Sacco. I visited her house with Elizabeth Glendower Evans. They had nothing but bare floors, a table, some chairs, nothing more. Mrs. Evans supplied clothing for the children. Justice Brandeis let the Sacco family live in his home at Dedham one summer. I visited Sacco in the Dedham jail. Mrs. Evans took me and introduced me to him. He was a jolly little fellow with nice twinkly eyes. I brought my two little boys to the prison yard and he threw them a bag of candy. Later, I saw both Sacco and Vanzetti in Charlestown prison. Towards the end, Mr. Thompson and Herbert went to see them and asked them to appeal to Governor Fuller for clemency. Vanzetti agreed, saying that if he was alive he could prove his innocence. Sacco refused. Two days later, Herbert and Mr. Thompson asked me to go see him and plead with him for the sake of his family. They took me to the prison. Sacco greeted me with a smile, the same twinkle in his eyes. I told him why I had come. He put his hand on my arm and said, "Mrs. Ehrmann, dear, I am innocent. I cannot, even for the sake of my family, say that I am guilty. I cannot beg for mercy."

After the execution Mrs. Sacco cut herself off from the world. She couldn't bear it any more, and that frightful thing just ruined their lives. She forbade her children from talking about it at all. As a result of the case, I myself became involved in prison reform, and especially in the effort to abolish capital punishment. Professor Chafee[254] called me to work with him, and I was active in the Massachusetts Council for the Abolition of the Death Penalty and in the American League to Abolish Capital Punishment.

• ART SHIELDS •

New York City, December 23, 1986

Art Shields, a well-known labor reporter, worked as a publicist for the Sacco-Vanzetti Defense Committee in Boston. He visited Sacco and Vanzetti in prison and wrote an important early pamphlet on the case, *Are They Doomed?*[255] Shields died in New York in February 1988 at the age of ninety-nine.

I AM NINETY-EIGHT years old, born in 1888. My father was a minister of the Moravian church, which traced its origins to John Huss and Comenius, and I went to a Moravian college, Bethlehem College. My actual name is Thomas Arthur Shields, but my father's name was also Thomas, so at home I was always

Arthur. I was called Art by my friends, and that name stuck when I became a writer and reporter.

After college I worked in machine shops and on a dam in southeastern Ohio, very heavy work. I was an IWW by the time of the Sacco-Vanzetti case and was working on a paper called *Financial America*, a rival of the *Wall Street Journal*, but not as important. During the trial I became editor of *Industrial Solidarity*, an IWW paper. I was not yet a Communist, but was leaning that way.

I came to the Sacco-Vanzetti case through Elizabeth Gurley Flynn.[256] I was a great admirer of hers. I met her in 1919 when I came back to New York from Seattle, where I was during the general strike. I wrote press releases for the Workers Defense Union, of which she was a founder. It formed a bridge between the IWW, left socialists, and trade unionists. She asked me to go to Boston to do a pamphlet on the Sacco-Vanzetti case. There was practically no publicity at that time, the fall of 1920. So I went to Boston, spent two months there working on a pamphlet and doing releases for the Defense Committee. I wrote an article in *The Liberator* in late 1920. My pamphlet, *Are They Doomed?*, came out in early 1921. I returned to Boston several times between 1920 and 1927 to do publicity work.

My successors were Eugene Lyons and then John Nicholas Beffel. Lyons afterwards got a job for United Press and served as a correspondent in the Soviet Union.[257] When I went there later I was told that he had smuggled valuable art objects out of the country. Beffel was a better man than I for the job. He had more experience, and he was left, but not as left as I, so he could get into publications that I couldn't, *The New Republic*, for example.[258]

The Sacco-Vanzetti Defense Committee was ideologically opposed to Communism, but in practice they were glad to get help from all radicals. Sacco and Vanzetti wrote letters to *The Labor Defender* greeting them as comrades. The International Labor Defense sent them money and wrote them letters to keep up their spirits. Sacco and Vanzetti welcomed it. Aldino Felicani was a modest person, a man of few words who spoke to the point, a very devoted man. I was especially fond of Emilio Coda, a coal miner from West Virginia who had taken part in a bloody gun battle during a 1922 strike, which I wrote about in *The Labor Defender* and the *Daily Worker*. He was extremely anti-Communist, though. (I was not yet a party member, but a pretty active sympathizer.) Nevertheless, he was gold in his sincerity.

In 1920 and on my later trips, I visited Sacco and Vanzetti in prison—Vanzetti a number of times and Sacco a few times. Sacco was very intense. He could communicate in English, but with some difficulty. He would get an idea and repeat it: "I want to finish my case! I want to finish my case!" Vanzetti was calmer, more philosophical. He looked at things in a broader way—an extraordinary person. He was eloquent in English, speaking with Italian nuances. My first visit to him was in 1920. He had been convicted in the Bridgewater case, but it was before the trial at Dedham. I saw them last in 1927, when I came to Boston for about three weeks to help in the effort to get the Department of Justice to open its files. Sacco-Vanzetti was a bigger case than Haymarket, partly because of the larger prestige of the people who were ready to protest. I think it was largely the personality of Vanzetti that did it. He spoke like a prophet.

I played another role in the case near the end. It was I who raised the question among a group of defense lawyers of going after the receipt for Vanzetti's eels. Their answer was that it could not possibly be kept all these years. But I insisted. I pressed the issue very strongly. So they decided to go. Four of us went: Ehrmann, Felicani, Musmanno, and myself.[259] We went to the fish market. Place after place said they didn't keep receipts so long. Finally, we went to one of the biggest. They kept receipts upstairs and we were welcome to look. The receipts were in bags. We spilled them out onto a big table into four piles, one for each of us to go through. I think it was Felicani who found it.

Musmanno's motives for entering the case, by the way, were tinged with Italian nationalism and an element of opportunism. A year before, in 1926, he wrote a letter to the Pittsburgh press praising the fascists in Rome. Soon after that he ran for office—the Pennsylvania legislature—and was defeated. The next year he came out for Sacco and Vanzetti, got a lot of publicity, and was elected. After he published his book on the case, he became a rip-roaring anti-Communist screaming in the courtroom.

Fred Moore, the defense counsel, had a good and a bad side. The good side is that he was a tireless worker and investigator. But he didn't work closely enough with the Defense Committee. Factions developed in the committee, not among the anarchists but among some of the liberals and others who became members, including Mary Donovan, a socialist and strong anti-Communist. Moore, in his IWW cases, mysteriously disappeared on several occasions. When fired by the Defense Committee he was very bitter. He began to tell people that Sacco may have been guilty, if not Vanzetti. I can't enter into his mind to say whether he believed it or not, but I completely rejected it. The evidence of a frame-up against them was too strong. There was nothing linking them to bombing or violence. As for Sacco's guilt, that's the damnable work of Moore. He came to the IWW from ideological motives. He had been a young lawyer in Spokane for the railroads. He dealt with injury cases and tried to get the victims the lowest possible settlement. But one case was so raw that it swung him in the other direction. He worked with Clarence Darrow in the McNamara case[260] and began representing the IWW in cases.

A man named Rohmann, a writer for the socialist *Call* who had been publicity agent for the Amalgamated Clothing Workers, a very reputable journalist, told me that he went to Park Row to find out about Salsedo. Salsedo was screaming—they were apparently beating him. Agents spotted Rohmann, who gave his feelings away, and they chased him. He ran down the stairs and got away. He wrote a story about it for the *Call*, but it appeared in the late edition and is not in the paper's official file.

I heard Emma Goldman speak. She was a good speaker, but I didn't like her. She was not based primarily on the working class. Berkman was a dedicated person, but he did a lot of harm: at Homestead he made a hero out of Frick.

Before Berkman's attempt, Frick had lost a lot of prestige, the strike was going strong, and even with his own class he came under criticism. Berkman's act changed all that. After eleven days in the hospital, Frick came back as a hero. On the other hand, Berkman worked very hard in the Mooney affair. He was forever in the struggle to free Mooney and Billings.

• FRED J. COOK •

Interlaken, New Jersey, August 7, 1989

Fred Cook, a veteran investigative reporter, is a longtime contributor to *The Nation*, in which he published several pieces on the Sacco-Vanzetti case, most notably "The Missing Fingerprints" (December 22, 1962). His books include *The Warfare State* (1962), *The FBI Nobody Knows* (1964), *The Corrupted Land* (1966), and *Maverick* (1984).

IN 1962 Carey McWilliams asked me to review Francis Russell's *Tragedy in Dedham*[261] for the *Nation*. I read the book and found it peculiar. The first three-quarters leads me to believe in the innocence of Sacco and Vanzetti; then, suddenly, towards the end, Sacco becomes guilty. I told McWilliams that something more than a mere review of Russell's book was needed, and he suggested that I get in touch with Tom O'Connor[262] in Massachusetts, whom he knew. I called O'Connor and told him my reaction to Russell, and especially how he slides over the fingerprint evidence. He thoroughly agreed with what I said. A few days later a small man appeared at my door in Interlaken with a bundle in his arms. It was O'Connor. He had taken a bus down from Massachusetts and a taxi from Asbury Park to my house. The bundle contained the transcript of the trial and xerox copies of clippings from local Massachusetts papers on the fingerprint evidence. These were solid, carefully written articles, nothing sensational about them. All of a sudden the fingerprint evidence disappeared. Nothing more was heard of it. Russell later said there was no fingerprint evidence. But there had been, as the newspaper articles showed, and evidently they were not the right fingerprints for the prosecutor's version of the case.

O'Connor came down a few more times, and we talked about the case. He was a very dedicated man, but frustrated because nothing ever came of the criticisms and new evidence that he and others put forward. He was skeptical, though, of Ehrmann's Morelli thesis. I thought it was persuasive—I reviewed Ehrmann's book in the *Nation* in 1969.

I wrote a piece for the *Nation* on the FBI and later published a book on the FBI. When my *Nation* piece appeared I got a call from a man named Rohmann, a reporter for the old New York *Graphic* or *Call*. He told me that he was in the Department of Justice office on Park Row when they were questioning Salsedo. He heard the interrogation—the beating—going on. The next morning Salsedo was out the window on the sidewalk. Rohmann said his paper ran an account of what he heard, but I went to the files and never found it.

• GEORGE VAUX •

Bryn Mawr, Pennsylvania, July 21, 1987

George Vaux is the nephew of Edward Holton James, himself the nephew of Henry and William James. Convinced of the innocence of Sacco and Vanzetti, James, a wealthy Bostonian, threw himself into the campaign to secure a new trial for the two men, or at least to save them from execution. The campaign failed. Sacco and Vanzetti were electrocuted in Charlestown prison on August 23, 1927.[263]

UNCLE NED was a James, and all the Jameses are screwballs. Just too much temperament. Actually he was quite sane, if somewhat eccentric. I found him charming. I spent a whole summer with him in Geneva in the 1930s. He had a flat there and went every summer to watch the League of Nations. He always talked with a grin, as though he were a huge joke. He deprecated himself, you know, and that was very charming. He was of average height, with the distinctive James physiognomy. He wore a beard during the 1920s but gave that up later. His father, Robertson James, worked for a railroad company in Milwaukee. He had an alcohol problem and was never successful. But he married into the Holton family, who were very wealthy. And Edward married Louisa Cushing, immensely wealthy. He had graduated from Harvard and read law in a law firm in Madison, Wisconsin. He practiced in Fargo, North Dakota, and then in Seattle, where he tried to shut down the saloons.

Uncle Ned went to Europe, helped publish *The Liberator* with E. F. Mylius,[264] and got into trouble for slandering King George V. He was kicked out of England and went to Berlin. He was a socialist by then and got mixed up with Rosa Luxemburg[265] and her crowd. He was arrested by the Berlin police and deported to Holland, but he recrossed the border, was arrested again, and was locked up in Moabit prison. He was released in November 1918 and returned to his mother in Concord. In 1919 he enlisted as a private in the army. He washed cars for officers at Fort Devens and served in the military police during the Boston police strike.

Uncle Ned became interested in the Sacco-Vanzetti case. He always believed in their innocence. He said there was insufficient evidence to establish their guilt. He measured the shed and showed that a larger car could not fit. In 1928 he sailed to Genoa. From there he went to Rome and saw Mussolini, who arranged for him to see Mario Buda on Lipari. Many years later I met Dante Sacco at the Calder house in Connecticut.[266]

After his return to Italy in 1932, he went to India to study the Gandhi movement and wrote a pamphlet about it. He played the violin very badly and invented a new system of playing it. In his later years, from the late 1930s on, he got mixed up with the Silver Shirts, believed in America for the Americans, and criticized Franklin Delano Roosevelt for getting the country into war, for which the American Legion in Concord attacked his sanity. During the early 1950s he and the Duke of Bedford published *The Word* in Glasgow, edited by Guy A. Aldred.[267]

• HARRY RICHAL •

Needham, Massachusetts, March 11, 1988

Harry Richal was born Evaristo Ricciardelli in Italy in 1898 and emigrated to the United States in 1913. Settling in Needham, Massachusetts, where he worked as a carpenter and builder, he became an anarchist of the militant school of which Luigi Galleani was the prophet and Sacco and Vanzetti fellow disciples. In 1921 he attended the trial of Sacco and Vanzetti and later visited them in prison. He is the only surviving member of the Gruppo Libertà di Needham, founded in 1925.

I WAS BORN near Fano, in the Marche, on May 3, 1898, a small, pleasant city. The last time I went back there was in 1968, and it had grown quite a bit. My original name was Evaristo Ricciardelli. My father, Giacomo, was a worker on the farm where I was born. We were poor and he couldn't afford to feed the family—there were six boys, and a girl, who died. In 1902 Father left the farm and went to the United States. He went all over—Albany, Pawtucket, all over—working on the railroad. He came to the U.S. three times. After two years he returned to Italy for four or five months, then came back to America. Finally he made enough money to bring the family over. The first time he had my eldest brother with him, seventeen years old. The third time he brought the rest of us. We landed in East Boston in 1913 and came straight to Needham.

The population in Needham was then about seven thousand; now it's five times that size. We all stayed in the same neighborhood and raised families. I've been here for seventy-five years. We chose Needham because my oldest brother was living here; he worked in the plastering business. There were only a few Italian families here when we arrived. I went to school for eight months in 1913–1914, and the kids teased us and called us "guinea wops." But the Italian population kept growing and all that changed. In Italy I had gone to school up to fourth grade and could read and write. Here I had to quit school to go to work. My brothers were all plasterers, but not me. In Italy I had been a carpenter and cabinetmaker since I was twelve years old, so I continued the carpentry work here.

In Needham there were a number of people who were associated with *Cronaca Sovversiva*—Augusto Rossi, Giobbe Sanchini, and others. I used to listen to them talk and found it interesting. I liked the way they were talking and I liked the way they were acting. I liked the Idea. I began to read *Cronaca Sovversiva*, but was too young to understand it, being seventeen or eighteen at the time. I used to go to hear Luigi Galleani speak in Boston and other towns; we all did. He was a real professor, a good speaker; he was the best! The comrades, myself among them, built a little stone house on his farm in Wrentham for him to use as a study.

I met Bruno [Raffaele Schiavina] in 1918 or 1919, before he was deported to Italy. He was a great friend of the Rossis and came to their house in Newton. He was deported in 1919, along with Galleani and the Sanchinis (who were then living in Needham), because they were making propaganda, because they were anarchists. Some had gone to Mexico in 1917, like the Sanchioni brothers. Renato married a Mexican girl and brought her here; they lived in Lynn. Adelfo owned a small shoe factory in Nashua, New Hampshire, but lived in Needham. I built two houses for him, one here and one on the Cape.

Some of the fellows broke into freight cars and took shoes and clothing. Mario Buda took the stuff and disposed of it, peddling it as a sideline. Buda lived in Wellesley; they called him *Nasone*, big nose. He had shoes in his car before Sacco and Vanzetti were arrested. But he had nothing to do with any holdups. Neither did Sacco or Vanzetti, or Riccardo Orciani. Orciani, who lived in Needham and worked in a foundry, came from the same village near Fano as I did. His family had horses and went up the mountain to pick up charcoal. He went back there after the trial. I think Moore told him to go home. He was accused of being an accomplice, but I never heard anything like that. All the comrades felt that they were innocent. Anybody who knew them knew they had nothing to do with it. I went to the trial in Dedham every Saturday, and I also visited Vanzetti in prison. He was a good person.

Augusto Rossi took his family back to Italy in 1919. During 1919 and 1920 there were disturbances in Italy and many thought the workers were taking over. But that didn't happen, and some, including Rossi, came back here, in 1921 or 1922, I think. He still had land in Newton, and in 1923 he said to me why don't we build houses on it. So we did—and we did pretty well until the Depression, when it all went sour. By then Gus had died; he died young, in 1926. He was a fine man, a contractor, very intelligent. I worked for him and built a house for him in Needham.

In 1925 the Gruppo Libertà di Needham was founded, and we built a clubhouse on Sachem Street. It had about thirty members then, and I am the only one left. Comrades came to Needham from Chicago, Detroit, Pennsylvania to find jobs, and Rossi gave them work. John Scussel was one of them. He lived in Detroit before he came to Needham, a bricklayer by trade. He died of tuberculosis a long time ago. He and Luigi Bacchetti came here from Detroit around 1925 and went to work for Rossi. They helped build our clubhouse too. Comrades from all over came to the club—Moro [q.v.] from Haverhill, Falsini from East Boston—for the meetings, plays, and picnics.

Dominick Scarinci was a cement worker. He worked for me and for Rossi. He was a nice, intelligent boy, very quiet and studious. He read French. He spent all his spare time in the library, although he was just a laborer. Bruno liked him, and whenever he needed facts and dates he asked him. Cesarini was a house painter who lived in Winthrop, next to East Boston. Gambera was a windbag, who liked to talk. Ella Antolini lived with Vincenzo Venchierutti here in Needham. Emilio Coda lived here too. He may have been involved in the Thayer bombing.[268] He was the one who got Bruno back here from Europe. I gave him fifty dollars to help arrange it. He died here in the 1950s [1946]—hit by a car.

• LOUIS TARABELLI •

Needham, Massachusetts, March 11, 1988

Louis Tarabelli, a building contractor in Needham, Massachusetts, is the son of Fernando Tarabelli, an Italian-born carpenter, disciple of Luigi Galleani, and comrade of Sacco and Vanzetti.

MY FATHER, Fernando Tarabelli, was the finest man I ever knew in my life. He was born around 1885 in Iesi, in the Marche, and came to Boston in 1905 to find work. He and my mother and older brother lived on North Street in the North End. He was a carpenter by trade, a very good carpenter, and in Italy had made caskets. Here he went to work in a shoe factory in Lynn but got into trouble during a strike when he broke a scab's hand with a hammer, and the police told him to get out of town. He moved to Old Mystic and worked as a boat builder.

Father was a born craftsman and a born rebel, a great admirer of Luigi Galleani. He said that Galleani spoke so well that the ordinary guy in the street didn't understand him. Galleani's daughter Ilya, a doctor, brought me into the world. Father lived with Galleani in Wrentham for six months and helped build the stone house that Galleani used as his library. For a time Father also lived in Quincy, where Ferruccio Coacci,[269] a fellow Marchigiano, once stayed with him. Father hid him for two or three months in the attic.

Father also lived in Somerville and was part of a group of militants there that included Nicola Recchi. Father thought Recchi was a great man. He was later tortured horribly in Argentina—I heard that a pair of pliers was used on his balls. We used to raise money for him at picnics, and I would send it to him in Buenos Aires. He wrote me some letters to thank me and sent me his picture, sitting in the sun in front of his house, his left hand covered with a handkerchief. I gave it to Bob D'Attilio. It was in Somerville, I think, that Recchi lost his hand while making bombs—or in the Boston area at any rate.

Father was close-mouthed and didn't say much about his activities, but Bruno [Raffaele Schiavina] once told me that he once beat up a cop during a disturbance in Boston. At a picnic Ralph Piesco [q.v.] told me that Sacco could have been involved in the South Braintree holdup but not Vanzetti. Father said it was not true. Some anarchists, though, robbed freight cars in Framingham and other towns. I knew the guys who did it. They're all dead now.

The biggest groups at that time were in East Boston and Needham, though there were smaller but active groups in Milford, Roxbury, Lynn, and other towns. The Needham group had about thirty or forty members. During the Dedham trial, the comrades made soup and pasta for Sacco and Vanzetti and delivered it to the jail every Sunday.

Some of the Needham anarchists had previously lived in Boston and other towns. Luigi Falsini came from East Boston. He was a little fellow, very small, a marble setter from Carrara. His son had a grocery store in East Boston. Ella Antolini moved here from Boston in the early 1940s. She was a beautiful woman and a real fighter. She later moved to Florida, where she died. John Scussel also lived here, in the house next door to Ella's. He died about forty years ago. Emilio Coda lived here too, until he was run over by a car and killed. He had a fiery temper, a very bad temper. He once drew a pistol on my father, and my mother had to calm him down. Coda also had dynamite. When Nalo bought his house he found dynamite hidden under the stoop. Another of the old militants who lived here was Dominick Ricci. He tied a weight around his neck and jumped into the river. That was around 1960.

Ernesto Bonomini once stayed in our house in Needham. He had been an expert tailor. He later learned upholstery in California and worked for Twentieth Century Fox. When I asked him about his killing Bonservizi, he said, "That pleasure had to be mine."[270] The clubhouse on Sachem Street is still intact but hasn't been used by the anarchists for some time. The club on Maverick Square in East Boston was torn down during the 1950s, and the few remaining comrades met in a small place across the street until the early sixties. Rosina Sacco came to my father's and brother's wakes in the mid-1960s, around 1966 or 1967, but I haven't seen her since.

• CHARLES POGGI •

Flushing, New York, September 30, 1987

Born in Boston in 1912, Charles Poggi returned to Italy with his parents and grew up in the Romagna town of Savignano, where he came to know Mario Buda. Buda, a disciple of Luigi Galleani and comrade of Sacco and Vanzetti, told Poggi many interesting things about the Italian anarchist movement in America, particularly as it relates to the Sacco-Vanzetti case. Poggi, who returned to the United States in 1930 and became a waiter in some of New York's most elegant restaurants, visited Buda in Savignano during the 1950s and corresponded with him until his death in 1963.[271]

My PARENTS came from Fiumicino, a town in the Romagna region of Italy. My father, Giovanni Poggi, was born in 1884 and came to America in 1905. He worked in a coal yard in Roxbury, a section of Boston, where I was born on November 4, 1912. I attended elementary school in West Groton.

My parents decided to return to Italy in 1920, when I was eight years old. In 1921 we moved from Fiumicino to the nearby town of Savignano, on the Rubicon River, where my father and his brother opened a little café. Mario Buda, who had known my father in Roxbury, frequented the café. He was a short man with a little mustache, nicely trimmed, and wore an anarchist tie. I got to know him well—in fact, he introduced me to anarchism. He would recite the poems of Pietro Gori and tell me about anarchist ideas. I found it all fascinating. He and Father hid the anarchist literature when fascist raids were expected.

Buda didn't have a job, but he must have had some money, as he came to the café every day. According to some rumors, Buda was a spy for Mussolini and went to France and reported on the Italian anarchists there. My father too once told me, "They say he was a spy." Maybe this was later, after his release from prison. He was arrested in 1927. I saw him in handcuffs at the railroad station, a *carabiniere* on either side, half a Toscano (cigar) in his mouth, calm, cool, and collected. He came back to Savignano in 1932, but by then I had gone to America. In later years I worked as a waiter for several New York restaurants and was a captain at Toots Shor's for twenty years.

I left Italy in 1930, when I was eighteen years old, and returned to Roxbury where I was born. There were still quite a few old comrades in the area (about ten or so in Roxbury itself) who had been close to Sacco and Vanzetti. The rumor among them was that Sacco was involved in the South Braintree holdup but not Vanzetti. I can see him in that role, Buda and Vanzetti as well, all of them sons of Galleani. Buda's younger brother Carlo, who was not a radical, once said to me, "You heard Galleani speak and you were ready to shoot the first policeman you saw."

When I visited Savignano in 1955, I talked to Buda about the movement. He was happy to see me and asked about his old friends. He said, "Come see me and have a glass of wine." We sat down in his house on the Via Castelvecchio. He told me how he escaped from Massachusetts to Italy in 1920. He was having breakfast when he saw Chief Stewart[272] coming towards the house. He skiddooed out the back door. Before going to see someone in Chicago, he left seven hundred dollars with his brother. When he returned to Boston, his brother, in tears, told him that the bank had failed and the money was lost. Buda went to Providence with what little he had, got a visa, and sailed back to Italy. He never saw his brother or heard from him again: all relations between them were broken.

Buda also told me that Sacco took part in the Braintree hold-up. "Sacco was there" (*Sacco c'era*), he said. I remember it distinctly. I felt sure that he was telling the truth. I didn't ask him who else was involved, but he didn't mention Vanzetti, and I assumed that he was not. I had a strong feeling that Buda himself was one of the robbers, though I didn't ask him and he didn't say. He did say, though, "Money we used to go and get where it was (*andavamo a prenderli dove c'erano*)"—meaning factories and banks.

I once told Bruno [Raffaele Schiavina] what Buda said to me—'*Sacco c'era*' and the rest. It was during the early eighties. I saw Bruno often in those days. I was visiting his house in Brooklyn. We were in the attic on the third floor, where Bruno was showing me his books. He had a complete set of *Cronaca Sovversiva*, bound and in good condition, and he showed me his first article, published in 1915. It was then that I told him what Buda said. Bruno did not reply. He looked past me out the window. Then he said, "*Andiamo di sotto*" (Let's go downstairs).

Buda was a real militant, capable of anything. In 1933 I drove to New York with Buda's nephew, Frank Maffi. We stayed with friends on Sixty-Second Street. Frank said, "Let's drive downtown and see my uncle's bomb," and he took me to Wall Street, where the big explosion took place in September 1920,[273] just before Buda sailed for Italy. You could still see the holes in the Morgan building across the street. I didn't ask Buda about this during our 1955 encounter.

In 1931 I attended a Sacco-Vanzetti memorial meeting in Boston's Old South Church. Felix Frankfurter was there, seated directly in front of me. William G. Thompson spoke, followed by Arturo Giovannitti. Thompson said, "I will die happy if I know that Sacco and Vanzetti held me in the same high esteem that I held them," or words to that effect.

Andrea Ciofalo[274] and Buda were buddies. Mario always sent regards to him from Italy. Ciofalo was still collecting money at meetings in Brooklyn in the 1950s and 1960s. I knew Aldino Felicani well. He had nerves of steel. He never got excited. He was, in his quiet way, a man of action. Yes, he may have been involved with bombs. Amleto Fabbri was a fellow Romagnolo; he came from Santarcangelo, about three miles from Savignano. In the U.S. he lived in Revere, Massachusetts. He was a shoemaker by trade and an anarchist of the old school. Everybody loved him.

• FEBO POMILIA •

Miami, Florida, December 8, 1988

Febo Pomilia is the son of Gabriella (Ella) Antolini, a member of the I Liberi Group in New Britain, Connecticut, at the time of the First World War. At the age of eighteen, in January 1918, Ella was arrested while transporting dynamite to Chicago and spent a year and a half in prison at Jefferson City, Missouri, where Emma Goldman was her fellow inmate. After her release, Ella returned to New England and worked as a seamstress. She remained a devoted anarchist until her death in Miami in January 1984. Febo died of cancer in 1993.

MY MOTHER, Ella Antolini Pomilia, was born into a peasant family in Ferrara province in 1899. Her father, Santo Antolini, was a wheelwright. The family came to the United States when Mother was about ten years old. An employment agent had gone to their town and talked them and other families into coming to America to work as contract laborers in Louisiana. They lived in a shack and life was very hard. Grandfather worked as a wheelwright for a lumber company; the rest, including Mother, worked in the fields, picking cotton and harvesting sugar cane. They replaced the black slaves who had left after the Civil War. They got along well with the Negro population in Louisiana. They too were in effect indentured laborers, tied to a system of peonage. They were paid very little monetary compensation, but they had a little garden in which they grew their own vegetables. They went to the company store for flour and sugar, but just about everything else they grew in their garden, and two of my uncles (Mother's brothers Luigi and Alberto) went hunting for game. Grandfather and my uncles were all anarchists; it was an anarchist family.

At some point the family went back to Italy, but returned to Louisiana in less than a year. Luigi and Alberto soon went north and got jobs in a factory in New Britain, Connecticut, becoming wage slaves instead of indentured slaves. A third brother, Renato, became a farmer in Vineland, New Jersey. He got sick—with leukemia, I think—and his wife, an Italian peasant, ran the farm.

When Luigi and Alberto got settled up north, they wrote to Grandfather and said that we've got to get you out of there; soon afterwards they went down to Louisiana and helped them run away from their employer, the Maxwells of Maxwell House Coffee. They all hopped on a train and rode north in a cattle car, making their way to New Britain.

Mother was about thirteen when she arrived in New Britain. Grandfather worked, and his sons worked as bricklayers. Grandfather was a strong character. No, I didn't know that Mother had married there at sixteen or why she became an anarchist, except that it was in the family. I know that she was sent to

Jefferson City penitentiary in 1918 for carrying dynamite, but I don't know the details.

After prison Mother lived in Detroit, where she met my father, Jerome Pomilia, born in Trapani, Sicily, where he was apprenticed to a fine-man's tailor. He emigrated to New York and moved to Detroit, where he met Mother in 1920 or 1921. I was born there on February 2, 1922. She knew Agnes Inglis in Detroit, as well as John Scussel.

From Detroit we moved in 1927 to New Britain, then to Hartford and to Boston, where Mother worked as a seamstress and fitter, while Grandma (in New Britain) took care of me. Father opened a tailor shop in Boston. I lived with the Grassos, anarchists in Hartford, for six months so I could finish high school. Mr. Grasso [Girolamo Grasso] was a wonderful person. He once ran over a dog with his car and vowed never to drive again—a vow he kept. Mother and Father divorced in the late thirties or early forties, and Mother soon moved to Needham.

Mother loved to read and to visit art museums in Boston. She was hungry for culture. Scussel lived in a house next to Mother's, and Emilio Coda lived in a shack in back of Scussel's property. Mother delivered the eulogy at Coda's funeral in the 1940s. Scussel died of tuberculosis soon after.

We went to see Mrs. Galleani in Needham. We heard that Galleani snuck back into the country one time during the late 1920s to see his family. (We were living in Hartford when we went to see Mrs. Galleani.) No one ever said that Sacco and Vanzetti were guilty of the holdup, certainly not Mother. While living in Needham, Mother worked as a fitter in Boston. She moved to Florida with Vincenzo Venchierutti in the 1950s. She worked as a fitter for Judi Leslie, a dress shop at Bal Harbour, and also did work on the side. She was an excellent seamstress.

In 1982 Mother suffered a stroke, which left her partly paralyzed. But she still got around and was active till she came down with cancer a year later. Twice a week she drove to the library, and she attended the anarchist picnics at Crandon Park. She died of cancer in Hialeah Hospital in January 1984. She was cremated and I took my boat and scattered her ashes in a canal in Everglades Park. My sister Linda (there were no other siblings) was an alcoholic, a troubled person, who committed suicide three years ago [she had stabbed a man to death before that].

• FLORENCE ROSSI •

Needham, Massachusetts, February 14, 1988

Florence ("Fiorina") Rossi is the daughter of Augusto Rossi, a building contractor in Massachusetts and comrade of Sacco and Vanzetti. For nearly sixty years she was the companion of Raffaele Schiavina (known as "Bruno" and "Max Sartin"), editor of *L'Adunata dei Refrattari*, the principal Italian anarchist paper in the United States from the 1920s through the 1960s.

I WAS BORN in Pesaro, in the Marche, in 1906, and came with my parents to America when I was two months old. There were nine more children, all born in the United States. My father, Augusto Rossi, was a builder, and we lived in Newton, on Adams Street. We moved to Needham in 1919, then followed Galleani back to Italy to help the cause. When Mussolini came to power we returned to the U.S. and lived again in Needham, where Father resumed his work as a builder. He died in 1926 at the age of forty-six.

Ella Antolini was a beautiful lady, slender and intelligent. All the young fellows were crazy about her. I think her husband was a Sicilian. She came to Needham from Boston around 1940. I also knew Carlo Valdinoci. I was in love with him when I was twelve years old. He lived in our house in Newton in 1918 or 1919. He was a handsome fellow with dark hair. We had three vacant rooms in front, and he and his brother and sister came to live there.

Luigi Galleani was sober all the time. He talked to me and was nice. He had met his wife Maria on Pantelleria, when he was a prisoner there. She already had a son, Salvatore, and they had four more children together.

Dominick Ricci was a carpenter and lived in Bridgewater with Giovanni Fruzzetti before Fruzzetti was deported. Then he came to Needham. He never lived with us, as far as I can recall. He went to Italy, got married, and came back to Needham.

Yes, of course I knew Gemma Mello, but that wasn't her real name. Her companion in Brooklyn was Frank Di Pietro. Before that she may have been a silk worker in Paterson.

Amleto Fabbri lived with us for a while, beloved by all the comrades.

I first met Bruno in 1917 when I was ten years old. He was the administrator of *Cronaca Sovversiva*. One day he brought the subscription list to our house on Adams Street to hide. After that he came every Saturday and made up the lists for distributing the paper. I don't know what became of it. One day two government agents came to the house and asked Father if he knew Raffaele Schiavina. Bruno was right there on the front lawn. Father said, "No, I don't know anybody by that name."

Bruno loved the opera, and he acted in plays (including *Senza Patria* by Pietro Gori), though he was not a great actor. We got together in 1931, after he returned to America from Europe. Clemente Duval[275] lived with us for a while before his death. He had been living with a shoemaker in Brooklyn named Olivieri, but his house was next to the subway and Nonno—that's what we called Duval—couldn't sleep. So we moved to Brooklyn from New Jersey, and he moved in with us. He was small, old, and disfigured from arthritis. But he exercised every morning, and a French comrade, Dr. Guilhempe, used to come to examine him. The neighbors thought he was Bruno's father. He lived with us for a few months. He felt he was going to die and didn't want to cause us any trouble, so he returned to Olivieri, where he died two days later.

After Father and our family returned from Italy, in 1922 I think it was, we visited Sacco and Vanzetti in prison a number of times. Once, when we visited Sacco in Dedham jail, the radio was playing a song, "Memories, memories, days of long ago," and the tears flowed down Sacco's cheeks. He was a very sentimental man. For his ideal he was tough, but he was a gentle soul.

• GALILEO TOBIA •

New York City, March 9, 1989

Born in New York's Little Italy section, Galileo Tobia grew up in the same Sicilian town as Valerio Isca (q.v.) and Dominick Sallitto (q.v.). In 1926 he returned to the United States and joined the anarchist movement. A tile setter by trade, he was a close friend of Raffaele Schiavina, editor of *L'Adunata dei Refrattari*. He died in Rensselaer, New York, in 1993.

I WAS BORN in 1909 in Manhattan, on Prince Street in Little Italy. My father was an anarchist of the Galleani type, a member of the Bresci Group in East Harlem. He came from Calatafimi in Sicily, the same town where Valerio Isca [q.v.] and Domenico Sallitto [q.v.] were born. In 1913, when I was three, we returned to Calatafimi. I came back to the United States in 1926, a year before Sacco and Vanzetti were executed. Everyone was talking about the case. I never heard any comrade say that they were guilty. There was no doubt in anyone's mind about their innocence. That Gambera story cannot be believed. Yes, Gambera was on the Defense Committee, but only for a few days. Besides, the story comes from his son and is third-hand.[276]

Galleani was a great writer and speaker. He was a master of anarchism. He really put anarchism on the map. Salsedo was so badly beaten that they threw him out of the window to cover up their brutality. Andrea Ciofalo I knew very well. I lived in the Bronx after returning to the U.S., and then in Brooklyn. I knew all the comrades. Ciofalo was arrested in the Bronx in 1919, but he jumped into a construction pit and got away. He went to Italy, expecting the revolution to break out, but came back illegally in 1921, I think, and worked in his brother Ottavio's tile shop. Ottavio did beautiful mosaic work. (I too am a lifelong tile setter.) Federal agents arrested a cousin of Ciofalo's who had the same name, Andrea Ciofalo, but when they found out they had made a mistake they gave up the search.

Ella Antolini married a Sicilian in Detroit. They came to Connecticut. I met her in Hartford in 1927. She had two children. I also knew Emilio Coda. They say that he did some of the work that other people got credit for, such as shooting a fascist in New York. John Scussel lived in Needham, a tall man, very sincere in his belief in his ideas. Gemma Mello died in Harlem in the 1950s. Bruno [Raffaele Schiavina] was stern in his ideas. We used to argue quite a bit, but we never held a grudge. We once traveled across the country to California together.

• ELIDE SANCHINI •

Manchester, Connecticut, March 12, 1988

Elide Sanchini, a factory worker in New Britain, Connecticut, is the daughter of Giobbe and Irma Sanchini, deported with their mentor Luigi Galleani during the Red Scare of 1919. The Sanchinis had been active in the Italian anarchist movement in New England and were comrades of Sacco and Vanzetti.

MY FATHER, Giobbe Sanchini, was born on October 8, 1887, in Pesaro province in the Marche. He went to Switzerland as a boy to find work. He returned to Italy and served in the army for one and a half years. Then he emigrated to America. That was around 1910. He stayed in New York for a while, then moved to New Britain, Connecticut, where he worked as a bricklayer. It was there that he met my mother, Irma Cassolino, who had been born in Tonco in Piemonte (Cuneo province, I think) on December 18, 1893. They were married in New Britain on December 27, 1913.

Father had anarchist sympathies already in Italy and Switzerland, and he became a follower of Galleani in America. He told me that Galleani was a great speaker, *"molto impressivo, molto forte."* Mother followed Father's political ideas, becoming a staunch anarchist. There was a group of Galleanisti in New Britain, including their close friend Ella Antolini. They all took part in the meetings, the lectures, and the *filodrammatica* both in Connecticut and Massachusetts. When Ella was arrested in 1918, Father wrote a poem to her and sent it to her in prison. I met Ella in Needham during the 1960s. She was a very lovely girl and was a militant anarchist when young, a propagandist. Was she involved with dynamite? Possibly. The anarchists were brutally treated in those days, and dynamite had its uses. It depended on where you put it. They had good reason to use it. Violence is a bad thing, but sometimes it is necessary— against fascism, for example.

Father did not go to Mexico in 1917. Sacco and Vanzetti went—Father knew them both; they were friends and believed in the same things. And the Sanchioni brothers went, Adelfo and Renato. Renato married a Mexican girl there and brought her back to Massachusetts.

My parents moved to Needham before their arrest in 1919. They had two daughters, and one on the way, when they were deported with Galleani. The ship landed in Genoa. From there they went to Naples, where Father was arrested, but he was released because Mother was about to have a baby. They returned to Father's native town near Pesaro. I was born there in 1925. Mother died in childbirth, so I never knew her. Father then started a pasta factory near Fano. On April 1, 1933, he married a woman from an anarchist family whose father named her sister Anarchia, though they stopped calling her that after Mussolini came to power.

During the years before Mussolini, Father continued his anarchist propaganda and helped to organize meetings. Schiavina came to speak in those days, before he fled to Paris. Father remained in Italy and became a public works supervisor. But he always believed in anarchism. He loved the Idea. He died on December 24, 1951. I came to America in 1961 to live with my brother and sister. I worked as a sewing-machine operator here in Manchester, and I now work in New Britain, where I commute every morning by bus, two hours each way. I will stop next year and then return to Italy.

Nicola Recchi used to visit us at our home in Italy. That was after the Second World War. He had suffered very much and had been tortured in Argentina. He talked about the old days in America, about bombs. His left hand was missing. I have some letters from him and a picture that he sent me from Buenos Aires. The picture is inscribed to me "with great memories and affection," and the last letter, dated October 13, 1971, ends: "Sixty-two years ago on October 13 Francisco Ferrer was shot by reactionaries in Barcelona."

• ORESTE FABRIZI •

Watertown, Massachusetts, January 2, 1988

Oreste Fabrizi, a small, neat man of ninety-one, with grey hair and glasses, had been a socialist in Italy but converted to anarchism in the United States after the execution of Sacco and Vanzetti. He became an associate of Aldino Felicani, founder of the Sacco-Vanzetti Defense Committee, and contributed to Felicani's journal *Controcorrente*.

I WAS BORN on March 1, 1897, in San Donato, province of Caserta. Luigi Quintiliano[277] was my cousin. I have written my memoirs and have a scrapbook on the Sacco-Vanzetti case, as well as some printed material. I left Italy for America in 1923, after Mussolini came to power. I was a member of the socialist party and vice-mayor of my town, which had a socialist mayor and administration. I landed in Quincy on July 15, 1923, and stayed with relatives for three and a half years. I worked as a stonecutter and then as a plasterer. I still work at my old trade by designing tombstones, but my eyes are failing and I'm hard of hearing. I had left my wife and two children in Italy and returned there in December 1926. But I was warned by friends that I would be arrested on charges of plotting against the life of Mussolini, so I returned to the United States. That was in October 1927, just after the execution of Sacco and Vanzetti. I lived with my unmarried sister in Watertown and worked as a plasterer. In 1932 I broke my arm while on the job and was permanently disabled. I opened a bar and restaurant in Watertown in 1935 and brought my family over from Italy. I ran the restaurant for twenty-three years.

My politics changed during my years in America. I met anarchists and syndicalists as well as socialists and became associated with *Il Proletario*, a syndicalist paper in New York. I was a member of the executive board and wrote a column, "Con la Lenza." We also had an *Il Proletario* in Somerville for two years; then it went back to New York and soon ceased publication. In Somerville we had a Filodrammatica di Circolo di Cultura Operaia, in the Casa del Popolo at 26 Mansfield Street. Fiorina Rossi [q.v.] acted in the group. And we had lectures and picnics for *la stampa nostra*.

I met Aldino Felicani at the end of 1927, after my return from Italy. A friend took me to his printing shop on Portland Street in Boston and introduced me to him. We became very close friends. I helped him get out *Controcorrente* and wrote a column for it, "A Piombo." Felicani was not dogmatic. He talked to everybody, listened to everybody, learned from everybody. He was not like the anarchists from *L'Adunata*. They were too rigid, too inflexible. We had nothing against them personally, but every time we got together there was an argument. We had different conceptions of socialism. The worst of the lot was Giovanni Gambera. He was absolutely insufferable [*insupportabile*]. He agreed with no one and argued with everybody. He believed that only he knew what was right. He was very contentious and was always arguing with Felicani.

I personally never met Sacco or Vanzetti. But Felicani was their best supporter. He was a 100 percent Sacco-Vanzetti man. And he loved *Controcorrente*. He worked very hard on it. He wanted to be in touch with people, all kinds of people. Towards the end of his life I begged him to stop *Controcorrente*. He was tired and didn't look well. He said, "As long as I have a pencil in my hand and ink in the machine we'll keep it going. It's our mission." He died in 1967; I delivered a eulogy at his funeral.

• ALBERICO PIRANI •

New York City, March 20, 1975

Alberico Pirani, who emigrated from Italy in 1907, was active in the anarchist movement in Chicago. In 1917, like Sacco and Vanzetti, he went to Mexico to avoid registering for the draft. From Mexico he went to Venezuela, where he met his wife Maxima in Caracas. She returned with him to the United States, where he found work as a hatmaker in New York. A warm, emotional man, with white hair and florid complexion, Pirani was easily stirred to wrath against oppression and exploitation. He was also possessed of an insatiable thirst for knowledge. An avid reader of anarchist literature, he never missed a lecture or luncheon at which books or ideas were discussed. At the 1977 banquet of the *Fraye Arbeter Shtime*, commemorating the fiftieth anniversary of Sacco and Vanzetti's execution, he was interviewed by Israel Shenker, a reporter for the *New York Times*. "I'm international," Pirani said. "I ain't got no country. When you mention country and religion, wash your mouth. That's the way you kill millions of people, for God and country and flag. Look at America—seventy-three Gods, two hundred twenty-six religions."[278] Pirani died in Brooklyn, New York, on January 23, 1985. His wife Maxima died in 1993 at the age of 104.

I WAS BORN in the village of Ostra, near Ancona, on August 24, 1888. August 24 is the worst day in history. Mount Vesuvius exploded on that day in A.D. 79, and that was the day of St. Bartholomew's Massacre in 1572, when twenty thousand Huguenots were killed. My father was five years old when his father died. The family had nothing to eat, so his mother sent him to a farm where he worked to help support them. When he was fifteen he walked all the way to Rome, carrying wine to earn some money. Then he had a little farm near Ancona and raised a family. My parents came to America in 1912 but went back to Italy in 1920.

I began to work in a saloon in Ancona when I was ten, in 1898. That year I took part in protest marches against government tyranny, the *fatti di maggio*, for which Bresci returned from America to kill the king.[279] I had no laces on my shoes so I could slip them off quickly if I had to run from the police. A king— horrible! When Bresci killed Umberto we had a breath of freedom. I knew Bresci's wife—she was Irish—and two daughters in Chicago from about 1909 to 1912. One of the daughters married an Italian comrade. The Italian anarchists sent both girls to college, and then they went to California.

I emigrated from Italy when I was eighteen, in 1907, and came to Chicago, where my brother was living. I was already a socialist through my brother-in-law, who organized farm workers in Italy. Chicago! That was the day! Now look at the world! I helped organize strikes, took part in demonstrations, distributed literature, resisted the war, and became an anarchist. We had a group of thirteen IWWs that met every Sunday in Chicago Heights. Some of them were steel workers, and I delivered radical papers to every nationality.

There was also a larger Italian group of seventy-two comrades, and I am the only survivor. Olivieri, a steel worker from Gary, died in January of this year; he had put up a thousand dollars to translate Kropotkin's *Ethics* into Italian. What wonderful men: Raffaele Bello, Umberto Postiglione (he published *L'Allarme*); what marvelous comrades they were!

Though we believed in organizing the workers, we also loved Galleani and read his paper religiously. Postiglione edited it for a while, I think. We collected money for it and for his speaking tours. He came to Chicago in 1912 or 1913, one of the best speakers I ever heard. He took a revolver from his pocket and showed it to me. He always carried it with him. "If the police try to corner me, they will have to watch out," he said. They were really true people, true men! Malatesta may have been more popular than Galleani, and his language more easy to understand, but Galleani was deeper, a philosopher. A lot of people didn't understand Galleani, but they loved him anyway. Galleani was the top anarchist. Malatesta was closer to the people, spoke their language, took part in their strikes and demonstrations.

In those Chicago days I would put aside five or six dollars every week from my twelve or thirteen dollars' pay for the propaganda. My father was a liberal and freethinker, and after he came to America the comrades often came to our house. I would go to the railroad to take coal for the furnace. But I never sell myself! One time I met Voltairine de Cleyre on the street when she was on her way to give a lecture. I heard Emma Goldman several times. I once joked to her, saying, "You are not a real anarchist," and she said, "Pirani, don't say that!"

Around 1915 or 1916 an anarchist named Crones poisoned the Chicago bankers.[280] He put poison in their soup—turtle soup it was—at a banquet for 260 people. He used to come to our meetings, a short fellow, and once he got up and said, "What kind of anarchists are you? Why don't you do something?" Then he poisoned the soup. And they never caught him. He once called the police and said "I'm here." But he wasn't. Ten thousand policemen were after him. He hid out with the anarchists in Massachusetts [actually in Middletown, Connecticut] and died there many years later. It was after the Crones affair that the Bresci daughters went to Seattle and then California. One of them is still there, in Los Angeles I think, but she's been out of contact with the comrades for many years.

I was young then; I had guts. I wasn't afraid of anything. We went to Gary and plastered the walls with posters against the war. We circulated petitions for Mooney and Billings. We resisted conscription. The Chicago Coliseum was filled with antiwar protestors. To escape the draft I fled to Laredo, Texas, where a Mexican Indian comrade, Miguel Calvo, helped me across the border. I went to Monterrey. There were eighteen comrades in our group there, including Sacco. He was very serious, had a very deep mind. He didn't talk much. From there I went to Mexico City and got a job with an oil company.

I came to New York in 1919 and got a job as a machine-operator making ladies' hats, my trade until I retired. I worked for one place on Thirty-Seventh

Street for eleven years. My wife, Maxima, also operated a sewing machine, and we have one in our house. We'd be lost without it. I met my wife in Venezuela, where I went after Mexico. We have no children. We had a baby son, but he died of pneumonia in 1922, when he was eighteen months old.

I reentered the United States on a false Venezuelan passport. Brand [q.v.] and Borghi[281] both used it later to get into the country. My wife speaks Italian as well as her Spanish, and I speak Spanish, Slovenian, and some French, in addition to Italian and English. I also learned a little Esperanto after the war. We had a club on Twenty-Third Street. In 1919 and 1920 we used to go down to Stelton every weekend to help build the school. At the club we put on dramas and had lectures in Spanish as well as Italian. I wrote hundreds of poems and still have many of them at home in our Brooklyn apartment.[282] But the movement wasn't the same as it had been before 1917. The Third International[283] spoiled the whole revolutionary movement. We organized protests for Francesco Ghezzi[284] and other Italian comrades imprisoned in Russia.

Ludovico Caminita[285] was a short man with a big mouth, a politician. I didn't trust him. Pedro Esteve[286] was an outstanding comrade. In Tampa he was a reader in a cigar factory. He spoke good Italian, and every Sunday we got together at his house in Weehawken, New Jersey. He came to Stelton many times and spoke in Spanish and Italian. In 1925 he spoke for the first time in English. A week later he died. Carlo Tresca was a friend to everybody, he talked to everybody, and was not a bad fellow, but he was not in the same class as Galleani or Malatesta. Borghi lived with me in Brooklyn before the Cooper Union business and wrote his book on Mussolini in our apartment.[287] Boy, we used to argue! He always wanted to be right 100 percent.

After the Second World War I went back to Mexico City and visited the comrades there: Proudhon Carbó, Mollie Steimer, Senya Fleshin. I saw Simon Radowitzky[288] in Cuernavaca and embraced him warmly. We had protested here for his release from prison.

Anarchism is a part of me. You take away my anarchist idea and you take away my life! Oh, yes, I still feel that way. As much as ever! I hate the state! I hate religion! I want to be cremated when I die. Meanwhile I go to lectures and send money to the anarchist papers. Here is twenty-five dollars for *Freedom*.

• VALERIO ISCA •

New York, November 25, 1972; Miami Beach, Florida, March 16, 1988

From the 1920s on, Valerio Isca, a machinist by trade, was active in both the Italian and English-speaking anarchist movements in New York. He also had a house in the Mohegan Colony with his wife and fellow-anarchist Ida Pilat, a professional translator, who died in 1980.[289] For more than three decades Valerio and Ida were devoted members of the Libertarian Book Club, founded in 1945 (see Part Six). Valerio's chief ideological mentors were Peter Kropotkin, Errico Malatesta, and Rudolf Rocker, whom he knew at Mohegan and came to venerate. (Valerio wrote a preface to the Italian edition of Rocker's *Nationalism and Culture*, published in 1960.) Valerio is also a great admirer of Henry David Thoreau, whose portrait hung on the wall of his Mohegan cottage, with an open copy of *Walden* on the desk beneath.

MY FATHER was Giuseppe Isca (1857–1911), born in Monte Erice, an old Greek town in Sicily situated on a mountain and so isolated and easily defensible that it was never conquered. My father was a forester, employed by the Italian government. He moved to the town of Calatafimi, in Trapani province, about forty miles from the city of Palermo, in connection with his work and had a couple of men under his supervision. It was there that I was born, on December 22, 1900. My father, a conservative, named me Valerio Umberto Isca, after King Umberto, whom Bresci had assassinated earlier that year, but I got rid of that middle name soon enough!

My mother, Elvira Bandiera, came from Naples. Her father (1820–1905) was from a town near Venice, then under Austrian jurisdiction. To avoid military service, he went to Siena, in Tuscany. He had been a gunsmith in Venice but now worked as a mechanic in a silk factory. In Siena he met a beautiful girl named Rosa Di Bartolo. They had nine children, five boys and four girls, two of them born in Siena and the rest in Naples, where he moved and took care of the steam engines in a powerhouse. He got a better job in Trapani, in Sicily, also in charge of a powerhouse, and moved there with his family, though some of the children remained in Naples.

My mother was thirteen when she came to Sicily. After her father retired, he returned to Naples, where he died in 1905. Mother had meanwhile met my father in Trapani. He was a very tall man, 6'6" in height, and blond, not dark like me. I resembled my mother, who was 5'6" tall, with dark hair and complexion. She was a loving and affectionate person. She died in 1946. My parents were married in Trapani, but soon moved to Calatafimi (population twelve thousand) because of Father's job. All six of their children were born in Calatafimi. One boy died at the age of five. I was the third child. I attended elementary school for five years, from the age of six to eleven. The best time in Calatafimi was during the summer, when we went to the neighboring forest, where father was in charge, and we lived in a house there. There I was free. I was running around the whole forest. I must have known every tree there. That's when my love of nature and the woods began.

Father died in 1911. I finished the school year, then went to work to help support the family. I was ten and a half years old. I worked in a wheat-processing mill for two years, a hard and brutal job, from six in the morning to late in the evening. I helped start the engine, cleaned up the factory, and did other odd jobs. Then I worked in another mill for four years, from 6 A.M. to 6 P.M. That was better—I could see my friends and go to evening school—so my life became easier, though it was still brutal work and we were extremely poor.

War came to Italy in 1915, when I was fourteen years old. My uncle in a nearby town needed men for his mill—also a wheat-processing mill—since his workers went into the army. So he came to our house and took me to work in his mill, of which he was a part owner. In 1918 I myself was drafted into the army and served nine months. I was sent to aviation school to learn about motors in airplanes. That's when I got my first real skills as a mechanic. After I was released from the army I went back home. I no longer had the job with my uncle, who had rehired his old workers and had no place for me. I worked as an assistant in an ornamental iron shop for about nine months; then my uncle took me back in his mill. Incidentally, Domenico Sallitto [q.v.] comes from the same town, Calatafimi, where he managed his father's coffee shop. He was a socialist then, and I became one too.

In 1922 my older sister Josephine went to America with her child Frank—he now lives in Brooklyn—to join her husband in Jersey City, where he worked for the A&P. I decided to go with her. Jobs were scarce in Sicily, and our family was very poor. On the ship I saw a man repairing machinery. I told him he was doing it wrong. He took me to the chief engineer, who asked me to work for him and paid me 150 lire. Mussolini came to power soon after I arrived here. I had intended to return to Italy, but now I decided to stay.

At first I lived in my sister's home in Jersey City. My brother-in-law had a friend who was a partner in an automobile repair shop. I went to work for him, repairing cars for eighteen dollars a week. After a few months I got a job making sidewalks, pushing a wheelbarrow for thirty dollars a week. But winter came and there was no more work until spring, so I found a job with Union Carbide, manufacturing dry-cell batteries. I operated a lathe at twenty-three dollars a week. I worked there for three years. Then I moved to Brooklyn with my sister's family (by then she had two sons). I lived with them for seven years—till I got together with Ida—commuting to Union Carbide in Jersey City.

In Brooklyn we lived on Suydam Street and Central Avenue. One day I met on the street the brother of the ironmonger for whom I had worked in Calatafimi. He worked for a hospital equipment company in Brooklyn and got me a job there. So I quit Union Carbide and for the next two years I made stretchers, desks, operating tables—all metal work—for hospitals. The company moved to Johnstown, Pennsylvania, and asked me to come along, but I was going with Ida by then, and she wouldn't leave New York, so I refused. Instead, I went to work for Studebaker, repairing cars. The factory was at 101 Dean Street in Brooklyn, and I worked there about a year. Then, in July 1929, I went to work making sterilizers for the Hospital Supply Company in Manhattan, where I remained until 1943.

When I came to America in 1922 I was a socialist sympathizer, though not a member of any party. It was the Sacco-Vanzetti case that drew me to anarchism. The same goes for Ida and many other young radicals of that period. The motivating force was a search for justice for these two innocent men. We were firmly convinced—and remain so today—that it was a frame-up.

In Brooklyn, where I lived with my sister, there was a mutual aid society composed of people from our town in Sicily. I was asked to join. I attended one of its meetings, but it was terrible. They argued among themselves over petty matters. So I refused to join. A neighbor suggested that I go with him to the Circolo Volontà, a storefront club on Central Avenue with about a dozen members. They were an anarchist group, read *L'Adunata dei Refrattari*, and were mostly Sicilians. Education and propaganda was their main concern. Joe Parisi, the organizer, had come from my hometown years before and spoke excellent English. That was in 1923, in the midst of the Sacco-Vanzetti appeals. We collected money to send to Aldino Felicani in Boston for the defense. We held outdoor meetings on street corners to protest against the treatment of the two men. We invited Luigi Quintiliano, a friend of Sacco and Vanzetti, to speak at our club. During this agitation we merged with another Brooklyn group called Germinal, and our membership rose to about twenty-five. There was also a third Italian group, the South Brooklyn Anarchist Group, which joined the campaign for Sacco and Vanzetti. The Bresci Group in East Harlem had dissolved following the Red Scare, before I came to America.

During this time I began to read anarchist literature. Of all the anarchist writers Kropotkin had the greatest influence on me, especially his *Conquest of Bread*, though I was also deeply moved by the poems and plays of Pietro Gori. I also, of course, read *L'Adunata*, but I have never favored terrorism or individual action, and I have always believed in the necessity of organization, so I never agreed with Luigi Galleani or participated in his groups. I once spoke at a meeting of the Spanish Group in Manhattan, and Frank Mandese[290] was there. "Valerio," he said, "why don't you preach violence to this group?" Of course, I refused.

But I never took part in Carlo Tresca's groups either, though I had a certain sympathy for his ideas. I am not an individualist or a syndicalist, but rather an anarchist of the Malatesta type, an anarchist without labels or prefixes. In fact, more than an anarchist I prefer to be called a libertarian. "Anarchist" frightens people, drives them away, destroys our potential following.

During the 1920s and 1930s there were still many Italian anarchists in America. In Barre they were mostly quarry workers, in Lynn they worked in shoe factories, in New York as waiters, barbers, plumbers, garment workers, construction workers. Westfield, New Jersey, had an active Italian group, mostly of the Tresca variety, but only one member is still alive, Charles (Carmelo) Briguglio.

Armando Borghi played only a small role in the American movement. Borghi came to America through Canada in the 1920s, after Mussolini's rise to power. He went to see Sacco and Vanzetti in prison. The South Brooklyn Group paid his passage, and his companion, Virgilia D'Andrea,[291] came later to join him. A comrade from New Jersey went to Paris and married her so she could come as an American citizen.

At first, when he was here legally, Borghi lectured and wrote and built up a following. But the Italian consul in Boston managed to seize his passport, and when his visa expired he was unable to renew it, so he was arrested and taken to Ellis Island for deportation. That was in 1930. His bond of $2,500 was collected by comrades and Borghi jumped bail. He hid out in my apartment. Ida and I were living on West Thirteenth Street in Brooklyn (Gravesend Bay), and he stayed with us for a month. Virgilia, who was in California at the time, rushed to our house and stayed for about a week. Then things cooled off. Borghi and Virgilia went to live with John Vattuone [q.v.], also in Brooklyn, before renting an apartment for themselves. It was there that Virgilia died of cancer in 1933, a tragedy for the movement.

After Borghi went underground, his influence began to fade. Though primarily a syndicalist, he also wrote for L'Adunata under pseudonyms (Etimo Vero, Girarrosto, etc.). He was deported in 1947 and became editor of Umanità Nova in Italy. Borghi was an anarchist first and a syndicalist second, while Tresca was a syndicalist first and an anarchist second. But neither Borghi nor Tresca was on the same level as Malatesta or Rudolf Rocker. Borghi was a good speaker and a good actor on the stage, but he did not have their bearing or charm. He was not as great a man as they. But wherever he went he resuscitated activity. He had no respect for books, by the way. If he needed a page, he tore it out and put it in his pocket. He did that even with our books when he lived in our apartment. Virgilia, though, was a marvelous person—so gentle, a fine speaker. Her speeches, which she wrote out and read (she was a former schoolteacher), were masterpieces of eloquence. She went to evening school to learn English. She wrote beautiful poems, every one of them.

The Italian movement in America was always dominated by personalities. Tresca had his groups and L'Adunata had its, and there was no cooperation between them. Borghi remarked of the Galleanists that "the so-called anti-organizationists were the best organized group." Tresca and Bruno [Raffaele Schiavina] never got along. Borghi called Osvaldo Maraviglia, manager of L'Adunata, "un gesuitello," a hypocrite. Both groups denounced fascism, but here I would give more credit to Tresca. As long as he was alive, there was continuous antifascist agitation—on the streets, in the squares, at the meetings—while Bruno could not come out and address meetings, being an illegal resident. On the surface Tresca had the larger following, yet actually there were just as many Galleanists, but they never went out into the streets after the Palmer raids and the dissolution of the Bresci Group. They were less visible than the Tresca group but still quite numerous. Tresca tried to attract radicals from outside the anarchist movement, which Bruno never did.

During the 1930s the government tried to deport Sallitto [q.v.] and Ferrero [q.v.], who had a little restaurant in Oakland, California. After they were arrested, Sallitto, who comes from the same town as I do, wrote to me asking for help. I went to Isaac Shorr, a lawyer and anarchist sympathizer who specialized in deportation cases. He told me that the first thing to be done was to bring the case to New York. On the day they were to surrender for deportation, he said, they should do it on Ellis Island instead of in California. He would accompany them and request a bail of a thousand dollars each.

In order to raise the money, I called a meeting of comrades and friends at the Stuyvesant Casino on Second Avenue and Ninth Street. I explained the situation and a collection was made. But all I got was seventeen dollars (it was during the Depression). I emerged from the meeting broken-hearted. I must have looked very dejected, because a block away I met Rose Pesotta[292] and she asked me what was the matter. I told her, and she said, "Come with me." We crossed the street and went to a candy store that had a telephone booth. She called Philip Kapp, treasurer of the Joint Board of the ILGWU, and told him to send a messenger to Ellis Island the following morning with two thousand dollars for Ferrero and Sallitto's bail. She hung up and told me to go home and not to worry.

The next day Ferrero and Sallitto were released on bail. Sallitto went to Brooklyn to stay with his aunt, and Ferrero came to live with us. Then we started the agitation, organizing a defense committee. At this point the Committee for the Protection of the Foreign-Born, a Communist outfit, stepped in and offered its services. Sallitto accepted their intervention and their lawyer, a lady named King.

We were getting nowhere until we learned that Frances Perkins, the Secretary of Labor, was coming to New York to attend a dinner in honor of the twenty-fifth anniversary of Mary Simkhovitch as the director of the Village Settlement House. A small group, including myself and Bill Taback,[293] went to Mrs. Simkhovitch and begged her to let us see Mrs. Perkins. She led us into a room and told us to wait. A few minutes later Mrs. Perkins came in, and we got up from our chairs to greet her. She said, "I know why you came, and I know about the case. As far as Sallitto is concerned, we have no proof that he is an anarchist, so he will be released and his bail returned. As for Ferrero, we have ample proof that he is an anarchist—he was the editor of an anarchist paper, and so on. My advice is to have him disappear, and we will not look for him. You will lose a thousand dollars, but it can't be helped." We thanked her and left. The next day Ferrero said good-bye to us. Then, as Mrs. Perkins recommended, he jumped bail and disappeared, living underground in California, though we didn't know where he went until many years later.

Besides my association with the Italian comrades, I began, in 1925, to attend meetings of the Road to Freedom Group, also known as the International Group because it had members of different nationalities. It met in the hall of the Spanish Group (Cultura Obrera, later Cultura Proletaria), which had a center on East Twenty-Third Street near Third Avenue. In those days the Spanish Group was the largest in New York, containing maybe two hundred members, some of whom went back to Spain during the Civil War. Unlike the Italian anarchists, the Spaniards had a powerful influence within the Spanish community at large, joining many of its social clubs, mixing with other Spaniards, and spreading libertarian ideas. This was something the Galleanists refused to do. Under Galleani's influence they were determined to remain "pure" and anti-organizationist, and as a result they isolated themselves from potential recruits. The Spanish comrades, by contrast, had a motto: "Everything within the organization. Nothing outside the organization." Their model was the CNT-FAI in Spain.

I used to go to the Spanish Group all the time, even until the 1960s. I met Pedro Esteve there a few times shortly before his death. He once told a story about Malatesta. He and Malatesta had been together in Spain and later in London. Malatesta never refused a beggar a coin. Esteve once said, "Why did you give the man money? He'll only buy liquor with it." Malatesta replied, "Of course. What do you expect him to do—buy an automobile?"

The Road to Freedom Group consisted of the English-speaking element within the International Group. Its members included Rose Pesotta, Walter Starrett (his real name was Van Valkenburgh), his wife Sadie Robinson (secretary of the group), Lisa Brilliant, and others. They published a journal, *The Road to Freedom*. The young people also had a group, called The Rising Youth, which published a short-lived paper of that name. It was founded by twin daughters of a Jewish watchmaker comrade named Goodman, but they left it for the Spinoza Society. Another member was Benny Frumkin [q.v.], son of Leibush Frumkin of the *Fraye Arbeter Shtime*. He had been brought up in Stelton.

All the anarchists—American, Spanish, Italian—worked together to support the Sacco-Vanzetti defense. In 1927 I attended a meeting for Sacco and Vanzetti at the International Group, then on Twenty-Third Street. It was there that I met my companion Ida, who happened to be sitting next to me. My English was very bad then. She lived on West Eleventh Street and Second Avenue with Clara Larsen [q.v.]. She worked as a translator for Keystone Driller Company, an oil-well drilling firm. We went to dances and meetings together and began to live with each other two years later, in April 1929. She told me she was born in Odessa in 1900, the same year as I was, but I found out later that she was really four years older, born in 1896. On the night of Sacco and Vanzetti's execution, by the way, I attended a rally in Union Square with an Italian comrade. When the news of the execution was announced we cried uncontrollably. The crowd broke up and we went home to Brooklyn on the subway. When we emerged at the Montrose Street station we were still crying. A policeman saw us and said, "So they've been executed." He realized why we were crying. He wasn't bragging about it either.

The Road to Freedom Group held a summer camp at Croton and then Lake Mohegan, from about 1928 to 1931. Ida used to go there on weekends (she worked during the week) and I went up to visit her. We lived in a tent, and in later years we pitched a tent during the summer at the home of Dr. Domenico Cascio in Highlands, New Jersey. Ida loved the outdoors and was a devoted hiker, in spite of her physical frailty—she was five feet tall and weighed only eighty-five pounds. Ida got pregnant in 1931, but the doctor said she was too weak to bear a child and would die. So he gave her some pills and that was the end of it.

When Keystone Driller went bankrupt in 1932, owing to the Depression, Ida worked as secretary of the Pioneer Youth Camp for a few years, under Alexis Ferm. We visited Arden Colony[294] in Delaware and met Frank Stephens, a friend of Emma Goldman. Ida became a translator and office manager of an export firm until she retired in the 1960s. Every year we went on a trip—to Italy, to Maine, to upstate New York. From 1931 on we sometimes rented a house in Stelton for our summer vacation. Ida and I got married in 1939, soon after the war had broken out in Europe. She was very happy about that.

In 1955 we bought a house in Mohegan. Milly Rocker died there in November of that year, and Ida translated Rudolf's tribute to her into English, which Joseph Ishill published as a pamphlet. Ishill was a member of the Thoreau Fellowship, like myself. Mohegan was much more beautiful than Stelton, but Stelton had a Ferrer School and a wonderful social life. Every Saturday night they had something going for the school, and every Sunday for *The Road to Freedom* or *Fraye Arbeter Shtime*. I was very close to Rudolf Rocker, whom I first met in 1934 at the Amalgamated Coop's, where he lived after coming to America. He lived there a couple of years before moving to Mohegan. His house was bought for him by the *Fraye Arbeter Shtime*, which had established a fund for him. When Rudolf died, the house went to his son Fermin [q.v.]. I was impressed by the humility of Rocker. He never boasted, never looked down on anyone. But he was proud of having been a friend of Malatesta. When he talked about Malatesta his eyes sparkled. He had a wonderful memory and could speak for two or three hours without losing his train of thought or the audience's attention.

I myself am proud that I was instrumental in having Rocker's *Nationalism and Culture* published in the Italian language. I made the arrangements, collected the money, and persuaded Rocker to add a new chapter to bring it up to date. He wrote it in English, and Ida fixed it up. The book was published in two volumes, volume one in Naples and volume two in Pistoia. The leftover copies were sent at my expense to anarchist groups all over Italy to be sold for their benefit. Later, also at my expense, Rocker's *Pioneers of American Freedom* was published in Italian by Antistato of Milan.

In 1938 I was diagnosed as having Parkinson's disease. But I was able to continue working, and I worked for Berger Industries in Maspeth as a machinist and foreman from 1943 till my retirement in 1970. During this period I spent summers and weekends at Mohegan, wrote for Felicani's *Controcorrente*, and was active in the Libertarian Book Club, as was Ida. Ida died in 1980, and I have been alone ever since.

My ideas on anarchism have not changed very much. For me anarchism is mainly a question of education. Anarchism at bottom is an ethical philosophy. When a man realizes that it is immoral to exploit another man and immoral to oppress another man, and when he refuses to do so, that man has become an anarchist, as far as I am concerned.

• JOHN VATTUONE •

Santa Rosa, California, November 12, 1989

Born in Sardinia in 1899, John Vattuone arrived in New York in 1922 and became an active anarchist and antifascist. He later moved to California and bought a chicken farm in Sebastopol, which he operated with his wife Elvira for twenty years, before retiring and moving to Santa Rosa. It was there that I interviewed him in 1989. Though saddened by Elvira's recent death, Vattuone, at ninety, was fit and alert when he picked me up at the bus station in his car. We saw each other again in 1991, when he came to New York to see his comrades, among them Valerio Isca (q.v.), a dwindling band of elderly rebels. Vattuone died of heart failure on February 13, 1994.

I WAS BORN in Cagliari, Sardinia, on November 11, 1899. My father's name was Luigi, and he worked as a baker. My mother was Giuseppina Pellini. I had six sisters but no brothers. I attended school in Cagliari from first grade through the second year of high school, and my sisters all went to high school. Most residents of Cagliari were literate, and the schools there were very good. Only one of my sisters is still alive; she was born in 1905 and lives in Cuneo in Piedmont. Mother died of pneumonia in 1908, and all the women in town with infants took turns in feeding my baby sister, a gesture of solidarity and compassion. Cagliari is a beautiful city with a Roman amphitheater.

My father was born near Chiavari in the mountains between La Spezia and Genoa. He was apprenticed to a baker, who visited Cagliari and saw a chance to open another bakery there. So he sent my father. My mother was born in Livorno but moved to Cagliari with her parents, who started a little restaurant there. When Father got to Cagliari, he heard of the restaurant run by Livornesi—Mother's parents—and went there to eat. He met my mother and got married and brought her back to Chiavari. After two kids arrived, they returned to Cagliari.

One day a man came from Carloforte, a small island (also called Isola San Pietro) off Sardinia inhabited entirely by Genovesi, descendants of sailors who had landed there. (They continued to speak the Genovese dialect.) He offered Father a job there. Father left all the children—seven by then; my oldest sister was sixteen—in Cagliari, but we managed to get along and joined him in 1910 or 1911.

I was then fourteen or fifteen. In 1915 I took to the sea. For years I sent all my earnings to my father to help the family. The ship's captain, impressed by my ability, suggested that I go to school and learn the wireless, but I preferred to remain a stoker. I remained a sailor for seven years, until 1922. In March 1918 my ship was torpedoed near Algiers and sank. I jumped overboard and hit my head but managed to reach a lifeboat and was saved. I went to Bizerte for a few days and then to Palermo (Easter 1918). Then I returned to the sea, working on a troop ship, until the war ended.

In 1922 I jumped ship in New York. I had been a socialist in Carloforte from the age of fifteen, and this was known to the fascists, who were growing in strength, beating and killing, especially in Sardinia. I wanted to go back to Italy—in New York there was a new language, different ways—and did not buy a suit of clothes for three years. But Mussolini remained in power. My first job was as a baker in Mount Kisco, New York, where I stayed for three years, from 1922 to 1925. I then moved to Brooklyn and got a job in another bakery. By now I was an anarchist. Already in 1919 and 1920 I thought the revolution was taking place in Italy. There were big meetings in Genoa and other cities, Malatesta came back, and so on.

I got interested and started to find out about Malatesta and his ideas. I began to read and my interest grew. In Mount Kisco I read *Cronaca Sovversiva*; my boss, an anarchist, had a complete set. In Brooklyn I joined the Italian group in Williamsburg, consisting of Giuseppe Carta, Valerio Isca [q.v.], Serio, and others, called the Anarchist Group of South Brooklyn. Another member of the group, Ovidio Sanvenero, spent eight years in jail for counterfeiting money. He died about seven years ago. Carta went to see Sacco and Vanzetti in prison. Carlo Tresca later said that Sacco was guilty—I can't explain why. Tresca was a dubious person; he never gave account of the money he received. Emilio Coda hated him, but I never liked Coda either. He acted like a superior being, but he was very close to Galleani.

In 1928 the group sent money to Bruno [Raffaele Schiavina] to come to the United States. Later—in the 1940s and 1950s—Salvatore Pernicone gave plays there, in the Galileo Temple on Montrose Avenue. Bruno was a dedicated anarchist, but he himself couldn't make a bomb, couldn't even kill a fly. He was very intelligent and very nice. He came in 1928, with the understanding that he should never appear in public. When Dick Perry [Ernesto Bonomini] came here, he and Bruno were very close friends. Bruno did nothing without Dick. He was also very close to Ciofalo, who was manager of *L'Adunata*. When Ciofalo died, Mike Magliocca took over.

Clemente Duval lived in Bruno's house for a while. When Duval's *Memorie autobiografiche* came out, the comrades in New London held a symposium about it and brought Duval there. Bruno was also there—I think it was 1929. They had a big group. There was lots of wine, a lot of talk, and of course a collection. Duval lived with a shoemaker, Olivieri, for a long time. He made orthopedic shoes. Dr. Guilhempe was active in those days and treated many of the comrades, including Duval.

In 1927 the postman accidentally left my copy of *L'Adunata* at the home of Antonio Ciminieri, a few blocks away, who also subscribed to it. I then had a bakery on Sixtieth Street and Third Avenue (Brooklyn), and Ciminieri came to give it to me. I was out delivering bread, and when I came back I learned that a man had brought the paper. I went to thank him. I met his daughter Elvira, then seventeen. We got together the next year, 1928. She died two weeks ago; she had always had a bad heart. We were together for sixty-one years.

In 1928 I gave up the bakery and went to drive a truck for a laundry concern on Cornelia Street in Greenwich Village. I worked there until 1949, twenty-one years. I quit and came to San Francisco, invited by Tony Martocchia and Osvaldo Maraviglia.[295] In 1950 I bought a chicken farm in Sebastopol for twelve thousand dollars. We ran it about twenty years. At first I sold chickens to a dealer, but I soon saw that the dealer got all the money and I got nothing. So I began to bring the chickens to Chinatown in San Francisco and sell them directly to the customers, both restaurants and individuals. In that way I eliminated the middleman and could make a decent living. But in the late 1960s it became illegal to slaughter chickens in San Francisco, so the business dried up. I sold the farm in 1970 for twenty-five thousand dollars. By then I had bought this house in Santa Rosa for twelve thousand dollars as an investment. We retired from farming and moved in.

Over the years I went to Italy a few times. Once I visited Vincenzina Vanzetti in Cuneo, where my sister lives. She had a picture of her brother on the table with a cross next to it. I couldn't stomach that, so I cut the visit short and left. I also went to Villafalletto [Vanzetti's birthplace]—a big courtyard with apartments around it.

Of all the Italian anarchists Malatesta was the best, and his ideas remain fresh today. Anarchism is still going on and eventually will find a way to eliminate all the bureaucrats, the union officials, the bosses—until the individuals themselves form the pedestal of society. Maybe in the next century—who knows? But it is bound to happen. Just look at all the changes going on in Eastern Europe right now!

• WILLIAM GALLO •

Highland, New York, May 9, 1987

William Gallo grew up in an Italian anarchist family in Paterson, New Jersey, a stronghold of immigrant anarchism during the late nineteenth and early twentieth centuries. His father, Firmino Gallo, was a silk weaver and one of the most prominent Italian anarchists of that city. Bill himself joined an anarchist youth group, the Francisco Ferrer Club, and opposed American participation in World War I. In 1917, like Sacco and Vanzetti, he fled to Mexico to avoid the draft, for which he spent six months in jail. After the war he dropped out of the movement, while retaining his anarchist sympathies to the end.

MY FATHER Firmino (Frank) Gallo was born in Mongrando in Piedmont in the 1860s. He was a silk worker, a "jacquard artist," as they were called, a weaver of jacquard cloth. His father was also a silk worker in Mongrando, both being highly skilled. Father and Mother—Ninfa was her name—were both anarchists in Italy and weren't legally married. The same was true of all of my aunts and uncles, and none of them ever separated or divorced, none of them. At that time Italy had a king, Umberto, the Catholic church was powerful, and this discouraged my parents, who were freethinkers. Some of their friends had already gone to America and wrote to them about it. They heard a good deal about America, about the freedom there.

They emigrated to the United States—they came in steerage—in 1889 or 1890. They went straight to Paterson because of the silk industry. Father got a job right away because of his jacquard skills. He worked for different mills, always jacquard work. He earned very little, though he left at seven in the morning and came home at six or seven at night, eleven or twelve hours a day. He operated two jacquard looms; on plain silk some ran four looms, but jacquard you had to watch. Many times, during my lunch break at school, I would bring his lunch pail to the factory and watch his looms as he ate. I was a small child then.

I was born in Paterson on August 25, 1897. I had an older brother, Henry, who died fairly young, as well as three younger brothers and a sister (Lena, who married Spartaco Guabello). Mother did not work in the mills but took care of the house and the children. We lived in a small apartment in Paterson (later my parents had a house in Haledon). The children attended public school. I recall that Mother, who did a lot of reading and a lot of deep thinking, said that the church was dogmatic and authoritarian, cardinals living like princes, crusaders stealing and looting and raping—all in the name of the Vatican. Father felt the same way. He was also a great reader and in fact ran a little *libreria*, a bookstore. People wrote in from all over the country to order books (in Italian) by mail. To my parents anarchism meant honesty and respect for others. Money was the last thing to be considered. Honest work and freedom—that's all they wanted. They didn't aspire to riches, to have bank accounts or wealth. They criticized exploitation of every kind. I remember that Mother respected the Bill of Rights. "This is wonderful reading," she said.

There were about three or four hundred anarchists in Paterson when I was a child, practically all of them Italians. All were weavers, with only a few exceptions: an insurance agent, a few machinists who worked for Van Vlaandren Machine Company. They made machines for the dye houses. I worked for them for a while, handling sales contracts. I started reading when I was five or six years old, always reading, reading, reading, a real bookworm. I read all the Russian writers—Dostoevsky, Artsybashev, Turgenev; and the Germans— Nietzsche, Schopenhauer. I never went to high school. I had to go to work—me and my older brother Henry. Our younger brother Jimmy (Severino), a brilliant boy, won a scholarship to Harvard, and we went to work to back him up. After Harvard he went to medical school and became a famous cancer surgeon. He died three years ago, a millionaire [said with distaste].

The Italian anarchists in Paterson started a *cooperativa*, a cooperative grocery store with a club upstairs, a little building. They met every Saturday and practically every evening. They played cards, had a drink of wine or beer, but not too much liquor. Every Saturday there was a dance, with music played by a little orchestra. I played the guitar, Henry the violin. My brother-in-law Spartaco ("Spot") Guabello played the mandolin. It was called the Piedmont Club and was located on Park Avenue. Father and Mother, especially Mother, did quite a lot of acting at the club, which had a small stage. Father was about five feet eight inches tall, thin, with a little mustache. He was a very quiet type. He never sought publicity. Alberto Guabello was more active and outgoing than Father. He also acted in plays, often with my mother. All the plays were about the life of the poor, and how they were oppressed.

When I was a tot, around ten or eleven, I worked for *La Questione Sociale*, the anarchist newspaper in Paterson. Guabello ran it as the manager. The editor was Franz Widmer, a printer, a tall man with a small wife. We used to fold the paper, address it, and bring it to the post office. Instead of going out and playing after school, I worked for the paper. I was working all the time.

Alberto Guabello was a good salesman, a persuasive talker. He didn't come too much to the club, didn't drink or play cards. He was always on the go, traveling here and there. Father would sit down, have a drink, talk. Not Alberto. He didn't work in the mills either, but was always well-dressed. I think he got a salary from the IWW. His brother Paul—Paolo—was quiet, like my dad. I liked him a lot.

Spartaco Guabello, Alberto's son—"Spot," we called him, though he took the first name Henry—was an anarchist, as I was. He had the same logical thinking as I did. We were raised in an anarchist milieu. We rejected religion and government, even democracy. And we rejected war. There were a number of strikes in the mills before the big strike in 1913. Emma Goldman would pass through town from time to time, a short woman and good speaker, a person to be reckoned with. I recall one strike—I don't know the year—when I went to have a look at the picketing. Paolo Guabello was on the picket line and was ordered to move by the police. He didn't move fast enough and was clubbed to the ground. Mother had come to get me and saw Paolo fall. She got down to help and the police clubbed her too. They threw them in a police wagon pulled by a horse. I ran after it crying, "Mama, Mama!" Paolo was bleeding all the way to the jail.

The big strike was in 1913. Bill Haywood,[296] Elizabeth Gurley Flynn, and Carlo Tresca came. They wanted to hold a meeting in Paterson but the authorities blocked it. So they went to Haledon. Tresca spoke from the balcony of the Botto house.[297] Elizabeth Gurley Flynn stayed at our house and insisted on sleeping on the floor. Haywood went to Paolo Guabello's. We didn't have money, you know, but they gave Haywood a set of used clothes. He and Tresca were both fine speakers, and Gurley Flynn too, in a different way. They stayed a few weeks and I remember them well.

The youngsters had a club with a library on Straight Street. It was called the Francisco Ferrer Club, I think. Spot and I were both members. I learned Esperanto and even started to learn Russian, but didn't get very far. I also learned to play chess. We talked about religion, science, astronomy. But federal agents came in, stole all our books (we never got them back), and closed the club down. It was snowing that night and they came in a horse and sleigh. I was about sixteen or seventeen at the time, so it must have been in 1919.

In 1917, after the draft was started, Spartaco and I went to Mexico, as we opposed all war. We were the only ones from Paterson to go, as far as I know. I refused to kill anyone or to shoulder a gun. The army had promised to make me a medic, but once I got to Kelly Field in Texas they put me in the infantry, and Spot too. They double-crossed us. So we ran away to Mexico. We were not in a group and did not meet Sacco and Vanzetti. We met one fellow, Al Ferrante, from Pasadena, California, and crossed over with him. He was a fellow Piedmontese and a good mechanic. On the way back from Mexico we swam the river and were picked up by Texas rangers and arrested. I got out on bail and went to San Antonio to talk to the prosecutor. We played chess. I told him I didn't want to kill, and he believed me. We plea-bargained and went to jail for six months. I got the jailer to get me a brush and some paint and I painted the whole inside of the jail—in Del Rio, Texas, it was.

The anarchists in Paterson were docile, quiet people. There was no bombing, no shooting. They still remembered Bresci, it is true. He left Paterson unannounced. Nobody knew. He told no one his plans. His ambition was to kill the king. But there was no conspiracy. That's what my parents said. None of the anarchists had a gun or a weapon of any kind. As far as dynamite bombs, that's a lot of malarkey. Dad, Guabello, Grandi, Baldiserotto,[298] and the others were gentle souls. Yet Guabello and Dad were picked up and taken to Ellis Island. They had an Italian lawyer from Paterson, a wonderful man, who got them off. The immigration authorities said to Father, "You marry your wife and we'll let you go back to Paterson." The lawyer accepted, and my parents got married. Before all this happened, a man called Leo Lemley had come to Paterson. He played the mandolin, ate at our house, but didn't sleep there. He wrote music for our little orchestra and was a brilliant and likeable fellow. But it seems he was a spy. The raids came. He never showed up again.

When I returned to Paterson in 1918, some scorned me as a deserter. But I got a good job at Van Vlaandren, handling contracts. That was after I had worked in the mills and with the Erie Railroad. I went to the Spencer Business School at night and took up shorthand and typing. I also took a correspondence course with Lasalle University in bookkeeping and accounting. I moved to Newburgh, New York, in the 1930s, and to Poughkeepsie in the 1940s, managing a textile dyeing and finishing plant. After that I did tax accounting until I retired five years ago.

I learned to fly and bought a plane and flew often to Paterson to see my family. Father died in the 1930s at the age of seventy-six, Mother at ninety-one. Both were cremated. After Father died, I went up in my plane with Mother and spread his ashes over Haledon, where they had lived. When she died I did the same with her ashes. During the 1920s, by the way, I had served as police commissioner of Haledon and as a councilman for eight years. When Paolo Guabello and other anarchists clashed with the fascists I was able to get them out of jail.

By the 1920s the Paterson mills were in decline and the anarchist movement was in decline. When you talk about the Constitution and Bill of Rights I'm skeptical and disappointed. We stole the land from the Indians, killed them off, put them on reservations. Is this democracy? Is this Christianity? Is this civilization? My early years, though, were times of happiness. We didn't have money or wealth, but we were contented. But anarchism has its limitations. You can't get people to work together collectively. They won't come out and protest. They'll complain about corruption, but won't do anything about it. And they'll still go to war when their country calls them. My own son signed up in the Second World War. I questioned it, but he wanted to fight. He landed with the first wave on D-Day [tears well up in Gallo's eyes] and was killed in battle ten days after.

• GUY LIBERTI •

Miami, Florida, December 21, 1972

Guy Liberti and his brother Ateo (both are pseudonyms) were Italian-born coal miners in Ohio, West Virginia, and Pennsylvania during the early decades of the century. Both were militant anarchists, and Ateo was once arrested at a mining camp in Pennsylvania during a clash between strikers and the police.[299] Both opposed the First World War and called for a social revolution to overthrow capitalism and the state, views expressed in the journal *L'Appello*, published by the group in Cleveland to which they belonged. Guy Liberti, who spent his winters in Miami after he retired, died in an Ohio nursing home on November 4, 1975.[300]

I WAS BORN in a village in Catanzaro province in Calabria in 1895 and came to the United States in 1912. I started to work in the coal mines when I was ten (I'll be seventy-eight next month). I mined in Pennsylvania, West Virginia, and Ohio. I knew Carlo Tresca when he was still a socialist and publishing *La Plebe* in Pittsburgh. It was at that time that someone cut his throat, so he grew a goatee.

Tresca was no anarchist. To my way of thinking he was an opportunist, a jumping jack. There was nothing in common between the followers of Tresca and the followers of Galleani. Galleani was the soul of the movement. He stood for anarchism without labels or adjectives. He understood the dangers of organization. The moment an organization is in its infancy there are rebellions; the moment the organization reaches adulthood it becomes conservative; and when it reaches full maturity it is reactionary. That has been the history of all organizations.

The trouble with the Italian movement is that they ignore the name of Galleani. Gods I don't care for; I am an iconoclast; I destroyed my idols long ago.

But Galleani is the one who created a real anarchist movement in America, and yet there is a conspiracy of silence against him. Galleani's son is living in the Miami area, but he's not worth seeing. The children were drawn away from anarchism because the influence of the school and the street is more powerful than any other. Galleani was the most forceful orator that I personally ever heard, and the most effective debater, especially against religion. My companion is from Lynn and knew him there.

I was active in Cleveland during the teens, twenties, and thirties. During the First World War our group published a paper called *L'Appello*. We also had an English-speaking Libertarian Group and a Fraye Arbeter Shtime Group; and there was a follower of Benjamin Tucker, an individualist named Horace Carr, a humble, intelligent printer. There was a Road to Freedom conference there in 1930. My former companion died there in 1933.

Alfonso Coniglio died in Tampa on November 7. He would have been eighty-nine on January 3. His father brought him to Tampa in 1888. He was a cigar maker and follower of Galleani and was persecuted by the government during World War I. Pedro Esteve was also in Tampa for a while. In Paterson he was the linotypist, not the editor, of *La Questione Sociale*. *Il Contro-pelo* was a scandal sheet. It criticized Galleani without mercy. It was against anybody and anything constructive—to advance the cause of the workers, to help them see their place in the universe, to further the struggle to better the lot of humanity, to help fight against the exploitation which humanity went through yesterday and is still going through today. *Germinal* in Chicago was neither a Galleani nor a Tresca type of paper but in line rather with Malatesta. Rudolf Rocker was a good man but was wrong about World War II.[301] Anarchism has always been antithetical to militarism. We must rely on people to rise up against dictators, not armies. Galleani was right when he said that Kropotkin lost much of his reputation because of his stand on World War I. Marcus Graham never vacillated from one side to another. He chose his road and stuck to it.

I haven't changed my anarchist views much over the years, but only modified some economic concepts. I'm not blind to the industrial and technological advances we have made. But that doesn't change the basic idea of anarchism. From a political standpoint I haven't wavered either to the left or to the right. Anarchism is an ideal, and humanity is heading toward it, and there is no force on earth that can stop it. So the philosophy of anarchism remains unchanged. We are gradually making more progress toward anarchism. But the goal is infinite. Revolution is still necessary in order to overthrow the capitalist system. We don't want to harm human beings, but if those human beings deprive us of our daily bread we must use revolutionary means to oust them.

The Miami Group now has only a half-dozen regulars, plus a dozen or more, mostly from Massachusetts and New York, who come down during the winter. We have weekly meetings and occasional picnics to raise money for *Freedom*, *The Match!*, *Umanità Nova*, *L'Internazionale*, and a few other publications. To take part in the joys and sorrows of the movement—that has been our reward.

• HUGO ROLLAND •

Elmhurst, New York, October 11, 1971; June 3, 1973

Hugo Rolland (real name Erasmo Abate) was born near Naples on February 15, 1895, and emigrated to the United States in 1912. During the First World War he was an active anarchist in Philadelphia, and he afterwards campaigned for the release of Sacco and Vanzetti. Deported in 1922, Hugo illegally reentered the United States, where he lived and worked until his death on August 15, 1977. In a letter to his family and friends, dated August 1, 1967, he defined what being an anarchist meant to him: "1. To be a useful and responsible member of the society in which I was born; 2. to be honest and decent with all persons with whom I come into contact; 3. to help whoever was in need, the best I could; 4. to respect everyone's ideas and beliefs, provided it is on the basis of reciprocity; 5. to strive to correct and eliminate ills and social injustices; 6. to oppose and fight—with arms if need be—all attempts to suppress freedom; 7. to never hide the truth, never be hypocritical or resort to falsehood."[302]

I WAS BORN on February 15, 1895, in Formia, near Naples, and came to the United States in 1912. I settled in Philadelphia and became a house painter. I drifted into anarchism instinctively. I was never a follower of anybody. I was opposed to terrorism and believed in the necessity of organization, in contrast to the Galleani groups, of which there were two in Philadelphia. Galleani wrote pamphlets advocating violence, and his followers engaged in illegal methods—even after the war they burned houses to collect the insurance—and opposed all organization.

Not long after arriving in Philadelphia, I started going to the Francisco Ferrer Group, which met in a rented store. It was basically an anarcho-syndicalist group, which supported the IWW and had some socialist as well as anarchist members. Its organ was *La Comune*, and I edited it (under my real name, Erasmo Abate) for the last few issues, during the First World War. Each of us set the type for our own articles. On the wall of the meeting room were pictures of Bakunin, Kropotkin, Marx, Most, and Bresci. We had talks and discussions, participated in strikes in Philadelphia and Camden, supported the Ettor and Giovannitti defense during the Lawrence strike of 1912,[303] organized demonstrations for Abarno and Carbone, who were arrested in New York in 1915 for plotting to blow up St. Patrick's Cathedral,[304] protested against the frame-up of Mooney and Billings, and organized demonstrations against the war.

There were many quarrels among the Italian anarchists in the United States: propaganda versus terror, organization versus no organization, and so on. Carlo Tresca once accused Ludovico Caminita—an excellent writer—of being a spy, but this was not true. During the Red Scare the government began to round up the anarchists, myself among them. In early 1922 I was deported to Italy. I traveled on the same boat as Riccardo Orciani, who told me that Sacco was guilty of the robbery but Vanzetti was not, though he knew about it and was part of the same group. Even Felicani intimated as much to me many years later. The fact that they shot at everybody was simply the mark of amateurs. Tresca, by the way, was killed not by fascists but by rival anarchists of the Galleanist L'Adunata Group.

After the assassination of Matteotti by the fascists in 1924,[305] I was part of a scheme—the Garibaldini affair, it was called—to land surreptitiously in Italy and assassinate Mussolini. But the others backed out and it fell through. Soon afterwards I returned secretly to the U.S. I lived in Stelton for two years, and then in Detroit. In 1926 I was an editor of *Germinal* in Chicago. Then I became a farmer in Michigan for twenty-five years. I knew Agnes Inglis and gave much material to the Labadie Collection, though after she died some of it was destroyed by the head of the library, a conservative.

I'm now terribly disappointed with what has become of anarchism. There is absolutely nothing left of the movement. Yet we must continue to combat tyranny and injustice. In this sense we remain true to our anarchist ideals.

• ESTHER TRAVAGLIO •

San Francisco, June 16, 1974

Esther Travaglio was the third wife of Eugene Travaglio (1876–1968), a handsome, versatile, and much-admired figure. His comrade C. V. Cook described him as "a dashing, graceful, vigorous son of Italy, with fine dark eyes and black hair."[306] A printer by trade, he worked as a compositor on *Free Society* in Chicago, and then edited a series of journals on the West Coast, including *La Protesta Umana* and *The Petrel* in San Francisco, *Why?* in Tacoma, and *The Dawn* in Seattle. Six years after his death, my wife and I visited Esther in their fine old house in San Francisco, where the interview that follows took place. In December 1981 my wife and I were again in San Francisco, and we took Esther to dinner in an Italian restaurant opposite Washington Square, which she enjoyed immensely despite poor health and failing eyesight. In December 1983, when I was yet again in San Francisco, to attend the annual meeting of the American Historical Association, I visited her in a nursing home on Broadway. She died there about two years later.

I WAS BORN Esther Hartz in Davenport, Iowa, in December 1893, of German Catholic parents. I was graduated from the University of California at Berkeley in 1922 and became the wife of Eugene Travaglio a few years later. We had one son, Dalny, an engineer.

My husband was born in northern Italy—in Milan, I think—on September

2, 1876. His mother was from a well-established family in Milan, and his father was an engineer from Piedmont who was knighted by Queen Victoria after participating in the Crimean War. His father was away a lot, and his mother ran off with Cesare Crespi, first to Scotland and then to New York, leaving Gene behind. They sent for him, though, and at the age of nine he arrived on Staten Island to join his mother, Crespi, and a baby half-sister Nina, who is now eighty-six and living in Santa Cruz.

They all moved to San Francisco around 1890. Gene went to the George Washington grade school (for boys) in the Italian district. He was raised without any religion. At fourteen he went out the Golden Gate on a sailing vessel as an apprentice seaman. The captain shot the sailmaker, and Gene refused to sign the log, which falsified and covered up the incident, and so he jumped ship in Siberia. He wanted to cross the country and visit Tolstoy, but he never got there. Instead, he spent three years with the International Geodetic Survey on the Yangtze River in China. He later made other trips—to Alaska, around the Horn, and so on.

Around 1900 Gene settled in Chicago and learned the printer's trade, becoming a first-class compositor. There he met his first wife, Frances ("Frankie"), who had been married before and had three children. They had three more daughters, two of whom are still alive. The oldest, Leah (born in 1903), was married to Radium LaVene [q.v.] of Home Colony, and afterwards to Dr. Arthur E. Briggs (now deceased), who mingled with the anarchists in Los Angeles. While on his first sailing trip, by the way, Gene's mother died. Crespi, who published an Italian newspaper in San Francisco, had several other children by another woman.

While in Chicago, Gene helped with the typesetting of *Free Society* and lived with the Isaaks. I think he was arrested with them after Czolgosz shot McKinley. He returned to San Francisco in 1902 or 1903 and worked as a printer. He also worked on an Italian anarchist paper with Giuseppe Ciancabilla [*La Protesta Umana*].[307] The earthquake of 1906 wrecked Gene's printing shop, so he moved to Stockton, where he published a paper called *Terra*, half in Italian and half in English, from 1906 till about 1909, intended for the farmworkers in the area. The coeditor was A. L. Cole, but I know nothing about him. I tried to locate copies of the paper, but without success.

Gene met his second wife—he was a ladies' man and could charm the skirts off any woman—Juliette Verrell in Stockton. They moved to Portland, Oregon, in 1909 or 1910, and Gene became foreman in the printing shop of *The Pacific Monthly*, edited by C.E.S. Wood. Soon afterwards, he moved to Tacoma and started his journal *Why?* He often visited the Home Colony and was fluent in Esperanto, which I think he may have learned at Home. His first wife, Frankie, moved up to Home to be near him, and Leah married Ray LaVene at Home. He loved Home and visited the place often.

In Tacoma Gene worked at night and then walked home about four miles. He became foreman at the Wobbly print shop. He knew Sam Hammersmark and the other anarchists and Wobblies well. Gene moved up to Seattle and started a small print shop called the Olympic Press. That's where I met him in 1924. He was a good friend of Harvey O'Connor's,[308] who published the Seattle *Record*, a labor paper. Gene published *The Dawn* in Seattle. I have a complete bound set and an unbound set (eight numbers). He did most of the writing himself and set it all by hand.

After we got together (we never legally married) we lived in Sausalito and San Francisco. When we lived at Sausalito, around 1925–1926, Gene would meet Eric Morton on the San Francisco ferry, but as far as I remember they never talked about anything important. He was about the same height as Gene, five feet eleven, but that's all I can recall.

Gene was fiercely anti-Bolshevik after the Russian Revolution and broke with some of his friends who became Communists. We used to visit Schmidty [Matthew Schmidt] in San Quentin and saw him several times after he came out. He had met Beth Livermore, from one of San Francisco's first families, when she visited the prison as a social worker, and they married immediately after his release in the 1940s. They used to take drives, with her at the wheel, and she was killed in a crash near Big Sur. He survived her by a few years, until the 1950s. He was a gentle and sympathetic person.

Gene had a great sense of humor and an ironic attitude towards the world. He was a craftsman as a printer and a painter and made model boats and cable cars from odd bits of wood. Coming to the United States as a boy, he was fluent in both English and Italian. He was a little too Italian for the Americans and a little too American for the Italians, and so he went his own way, somewhat aloof, while remaining on friendly terms with both. He didn't get along with Marcus Graham at all, but he and John the Cook [Vincenzo Ferrero, q.v.] were good friends. Gene died on July 6, 1968, at the age of ninety-one. He was cremated and his ashes were scattered at sea.

Angelo Luca, who died two years ago, was one of the most active comrades in the area. I really don't know how Luca lost his leg, but it was definitely by a bomb.[309] His wife Jessie was so close-mouthed about it. She is still alive at ninety-six, born in San Francisco of one of its leading families. She was one of the first graduates of Mills College in Oakland, and her grandfather endowed a chair there. Their son Mark [q.v.] teaches art at Berkeley.

Jonesie [Red Jones, q.v.] was a good comrade of the Lucas and of Gene. There were Chinese as well as Italian farm laborers in the San Fernando Valley and the Sacramento area. There was one German comrade in San Francisco, John Kassel. I have a plaque of Tolstoy for you by one of the French comrades here, Jules Scarceriaux.

• VINCENZO FERRERO •

Los Gatos, California, June 18, 1974

In April 1934 Vincenzo Ferrero and Domenico (Dominick) Sallitto (q.v.), who operated a restaurant in Oakland, California, were arrested as anarchists by federal officials and held for deportation proceedings. A nationwide protest campaign, in which the case was denounced as "a new Inquisition," a "renewal of the infamous Palmer policies,"[310] resulted in the liberation of Sallitto. Ferrero, however, was ordered deported to Italy, where, under Mussolini's dictatorship, he would likely have faced execution. Jumping bail, Ferrero went underground and worked as a cook in the San Francisco area, undetected by the authorities. When I met him forty years later, at the home of Sallitto in Los Gatos, he was introduced to me as "John the Cook," a small man of eighty-nine with grizzled hair and beard. Almost at once I realized his true identity, and when this became apparent to him he dropped the disguise. "At my age," he said with a twinkle in his eye, "I am beyond good and evil."

A Piedmontese by birth, Ferrero arrived in San Francisco in 1905, a year before the great earthquake, and immediately plunged into anarchist activities. Like a religious sectarian, a *fraticello* from the Middle Ages, he gave away his money to whoever needed it; years later, old friends would stop him on the street and hand him five or ten dollars in repayment. Ferrero, moreover, was a gifted writer and editor. From 1927 to 1932 he edited *L'Emancipazione*, a first-rate anarchist journal, and published single issues (*numeri unici*) of two other titles, *La Scolta* (July 1926) and *Golgota* (August 28, 1927), the latter marking the execution of Sacco and Vanzetti. Ferrero lived to be a hundred. He died on February 8, 1985, after a long life devoted to his ideal.[311]

I WAS BORN in the Piedmont region of Italy in 1885. I am now eighty-nine and came to San Francisco in 1905, a year before the earthquake. We had an active International Group—Italian, Spanish, French, Russian, Jewish—that lasted until the 1930s. There were only a few Germans, but one tall, thin comrade with a red necktie—I forget his name [John Kassel]—was always there. Each national group had its own members but attended picnics and lectures together and worked together in common causes. The Chinese came too, but none were as close to us as Jonesie [Red Jones, q.v.]. Some of the Chinese were artists who made drawings and woodcuts for *Man!* and other journals. *Man!* was a successor to *L'Emancipazione* but in a new language, as the group felt that a publication in English would be more valuable and have a greater effect.

The Volontà Group preceded the Emancipazione Group among the Italians. Though a small group, it had a meeting hall and it frightened the authorities. It had around thirty or forty regular members. From 1906 to 1909 there were three Italian anarchist papers in San Francisco: *Cogito, ergo Sum* and *Nihil*—both one-man papers put out by individualists—and *Aurora*.

Our comrade Dr. Rose Fritz had a nursing home with another doctor in the hills near Los Gatos before the First World War. It was destroyed by fire. It had 160 acres of land, with vineyards, and Dr. Fritz offered it to me, but I was young and had other ambitions. She had come to San Francisco in the 1880s, and before that had practiced medicine in Kiev. She was not licensed here and was arrested a few times as a result. She developed new medical techniques and as a woman was not fully accepted by the medical profession. She was active among the San Francisco anarchists and helped organize a group to aid Home Colony. She was quite old when she died in the 1940s.

Eric B. Morton was a nice fellow who liked to drink, a big, strong man and a good storyteller. Alexander Berkman was a fine, congenial man who was easy-going with people. While he was publishing *The Blast* here with Robert Minor, he issued a handbill *Down with the Anarchists!* We distributed twenty thousand copies in the San Francisco area. Freemont Older, editor of the *San Francisco Bulletin*, gave Berkman his paper for one day to print whatever he liked; he did the same for the socialists and the IWW. Berkman was a versatile man who knew what he was doing, keen-minded and a good speaker, though not a great orator.

Eugene Travaglio wrote a history of anarchism in the United States, but the manuscript has been lost. His mother was a countess and his father a general in the Italian army. As a boy he went to London and studied navigation. He went on a scientific expedition in China. On the same voyage was a French geographer, a friend of Elisée Reclus, from whom Travaglio learned about anarchism. He was a raconteur and bon-vivant. He became a rabid anti-Communist and blamed all ills on the Communists. On his voyage to China he was captured by Chinese pirates but was spared when he taught them navigation.

Travaglio edited *La Protesta Umana* in San Francisco together with Giuseppe Ciancabilla. Ciancabilla was so fluent a writer that he set his articles directly into print without a first draft. He fell in love with Travaglio's sister. He and Travaglio had a falling out—I don't know why, but Travaglio said that Ciancabilla called him a spy in *Protesta Umana*. Once when I printed a Ciancabilla issue of *L'Emancipazione* I asked Travaglio for his recollections. He said ask me anything but that. Ciancabilla was strongly anti-organizationist, in the same spirit as Luigi Galleani. I once had a trunk full of *La Protesta Umana* and *L'Emancipazione*, but I went away for a few months and when I returned the place was sold and the trunk gone.

The Italian anarchists in the United States came from all over Italy, from the south as well as the north, though certain towns (like Carrara) had more. They also came from Sicily and Sardinia (John Vattuone [q.v.], Angelo Luca). Some were anarchists already in Italy, but most were too young yet and became anarchists over here. It was the American experience of struggle that made them anarchists. Most came as young men with a sense of awareness of injustice. They began to read and listen and so became anarchists. Some came as socialists and became anarchists here. They represented a whole range of occupations, both skilled and unskilled.

The first man who influenced me towards anarchism was a worker in Denver, a cement mixer and a socialist who contributed to a socialist paper in Denver. He said, "I am a socialist, but the best thing is anarchism." He was a learned man. He knew plenty. So I began to lean in that direction. Among the famous men, though, the greatest influence on me came from Galleani. Galleani was not an individualist but was opposed to formal organization. He was for spontaneous cooperation and spontaneous action. Carlo Tresca was confused about his ideas; he had no particular philosophy, was not a real anarchist. The real Italian anarchists in America were Pietro Gori (who came to San Francisco), Errico Malatesta, and Galleani. They represented three different types of anarchism, each genuine in its own way.

I'll tell you what sort of man Galleani was. Galleani's lawyer describes an incident at the time of the last number the *Cronaca Sovversiva* was being prepared for distribution. Galleani was already under an order of deportation, and Palmer was questioning him. Palmer asked, "Mr. Galleani, what is your occupation?" Galleani: "I am the director of *Cronaca Sovversiva*." Palmer: "Mr. Galleani, what other activities are you engaged in?" Galleani: "I am the director of *Cronaca Sovversiva*." Palmer asks another question, and Galleani gives the same answer. Palmer (angry): "I have suppressed your paper!" Galleani (taking out the last issue of *Cronaca Sovversiva* and holding it up): "And yet it is here! *Viva l'anarchia!*" Palmer turns and flees the room.

Another type of anarchist was Sam Cohen, who never wrote a line. He was a nice man, but was incompatible with almost everybody—except me! During the time of Sacco and Vanzetti, around 1926, the Communists in San Francisco organized a big protest meeting to exploit the situation. They met in the San Francisco Auditorium. The place was full. It held eighteen thousand people, and there were more outside. I came and Sam Cohen too. I knew he would try something. As the chairman opened the meeting Sam called out from the back, "A word only. I have to admit that this evening is something out of the ordinary. All merit to those who organized it." Then came the bombshell. "Can we form a commission to collect the money and send it to where it belongs?" He was always making street-corner speeches criticizing Soviet Russia, and the Communists beat the hell out of him, shouting "Don't come back!" But the next night he reappeared all bandaged up to continue his speech: "As I was saying last night. . . ." He was very provocative and outspoken and insulted the Communists in the crowd, speaking of their "mental diarrhea" and so on. He was a tailor by trade, and a good one.

Jules Scarceriaux was a good comrade. Apart from French, he knew Italian and a few other languages. Jonesie was born here—or at least when they tried to deport him they couldn't do it because he produced documents to that effect! [He was actually born in China.]

Yes, I have changed plenty. In the beginning I thought that anarchism was knocking at the door. I still believe that humanity must attain anarchism if it is to survive. But the idea must be corrected. Today nearly all men live by profit, by domination, by the enslavement of others. Nearly everybody lives this way, most anarchists included. So there has been no basic change. Also, earlier anarchism was spreading more among working men, while now it is the other way around—among students and intellectuals. Yet every individual must be free to fulfill his needs, social, physical, mental. What is important is moderation: not too little but not too much. Man must be both a materialist and an idealist. If man cannot adopt a balance and live in moderation and without coercion, I see no salvation. A man can be free even in prison if he is free within himself, free in spirit. In a really free society there is room for all ideas, so long as they are kept in the mind and not forced upon others. For me it is easier to live this way than to explain about it. Any regrets? No! I would start again!!!

• DOMINICK SALLITTO •

Los Gatos, California, June 18, 1974

Dominick (Domenico) Sallitto, a gardener by profession, was born in Calatafimi, Sicily, the same town as Valerio Isca (q.v.), his boyhood friend. Emigrating to New York, Menico (as he was called) became an anarchist and contributed to such journals as *L'Adunata dei Refrattari* (of which he was briefly the editor) and *Man!* During the 1930s he was arrested and held for deportation with Vincenzo Ferrero (q.v.) but eventually released. I interviewed him in his attractive California home, where his wife, Aurora Alleva, from an anarchist family in Philadelphia, prepared an excellent Italian lunch, complete with freshly picked fruit and vegetables from their garden. Sharing in the food and conversation were Ferrero and Lino Molin (q.v.), whose words are recorded elsewhere in this section. Sallitto died on December 26, 1991, two weeks before his ninetieth birthday. Aurora died five weeks later.

I WAS BORN in Sicily on January 11, 1902, emigrated to New York as a young man, and came to California in 1930. Ninety percent of the Italian anarchists in America were poor immigrants, almost illiterate, so they couldn't communicate well with their children. There was a language barrier and a cultural barrier. Children of anarchists shied away from the movement because the parents themselves often failed to practice what they preached. The women seldom participated, and the Italian anarchist father was often an authoritarian at home. For the most part the anarchists were young immigrants who acquired their anarchism through contact with others. It was mostly by word of mouth and personal experience of the injustice of the system. Then they began to read the anarchist press and to attend meetings. Their hopes for a better life, a better society in America, were disappointed. It was just as ruthless and cruel a society as the one they had left.

When I came to San Francisco in 1930, Dr. Fritz was still alive. I visited her in her house, a mansion but with little furniture. She was still practicing medicine, a small, elderly, frail, grey-haired woman. Eugene Travaglio was an exceptional person. What impressed me was his command of English as well as Italian. Jonesie [Red Jones, q.v.] too was a fine comrade. One of the best pictures of Jonesie was at a lecture by Armando Borghi. Jonesie came before everyone else, set up the chairs, listened attentively to Borghi's lecture—never understanding a word—then put away all the chairs and was the last to leave. He always came on foot. He smiled but seldom said very much. We never knew what his inner feelings were. But that's dedication!

We used to see Bresci's daughter years ago but lost contact with her. There are now about twenty comrades in the Los Gatos area, and we have picnics from time to time to raise money for the Italian and English anarchist press. Ludovico Caminita was considered a turncoat in later years. I don't recall exactly why, but he was not taken seriously. Sam Cohen was the traveling salesman of anarchism, a hobo with a purpose. Wherever he went he would stop at street corners and lecture about anarchism. He didn't get along with anybody, either philosophically or personally, but that was his life. He lived by occasional tailoring jobs and by selling literature for a few pennies. He disappeared in Los Angeles about fifteen years ago and hasn't been heard from since.

No single anarchist influenced me most, unless it was Malatesta, and in his case as a human being more than as a thinker. I am suspicious of organizations, and I do not accept any qualifying label like anarchist-communist, anarcho-syndicalist, or anarchist-individualist. Anarchism is a beautiful philosophy, though I don't know whether it will be accomplished in my lifetime or even in my granddaughter's. But sooner or later it will come.

• LINO MOLIN •

Los Gatos, California, June 18, 1974

I interviewed Lino Molin on the same occasion as my interview with Vincenzo Ferrero, over lunch in the California home of Dominick and Aurora Sallitto. After years as an automobile worker in Detroit, he had migrated west and acquired a small farm in Los Gatos, where he raised apricots and prunes. A lean and handsome man, with white hair and mustache, he adhered to an unadulterated brand of anarchism that brooked no compromise or equivocation. In 1980 he was killed by a speeding automobile while crossing the street in Los Gatos.

I CAME to the United States from the Friuli region of northern Italy and worked here at various laboring jobs. I lived for a time in Detroit and worked on an automobile assembly line. During strikes I saw company police on horseback smashing right and left at the workers.

Carlo Tresca was a joker, an opportunist. He even shook hands with the President.[312] He enjoyed life and physical comforts, unlike Galleani. Emma Goldman was like Tresca in this respect. One should wait for the revolution to enjoy such luxuries.

Many of the Italians were anarchists by conviction but not by behavior or culture. They failed to apply it to their own lives, and so failed to hand it down to their children. But anarchism represents justice more than any other doctrine. I have no regrets, but fifty years ago there was more opportunity to realize anarchism than there is today.

• MARK LUCA •

Berkeley, California, June 11, 1974

Marc Luca is a painter and sculptor in Berkeley, California, where he lectured at the University of California. His father, Angelo Luca, born in Sardinia in 1895, was a veteran anarchist of the Luigi Galleani school, to which Sacco and Vanzetti adhered. He immigrated to San Francisco before the First World War and died there in 1972. Mark's mother Jessie, still alive at ninety-six when I interviewed him, came from an old and prominent San Francisco family and was one of the early graduates of Mills College in Oakland.

MY FATHER came to America from Sardinia as a young man. Immigration for him was a shattering experience and life was hard. Anarchism was his passion, his religion. He forbade me to paint on religious themes or to include churches or crosses in my work. He hated all that. Father was of the Galleani school, and they quarreled continuously with the Trescaites. Father went blind from glaucoma some years ago. Here's a record that he made with a story he told me on it. [The record contains a fifteen-minute talk on religion and government, on mental and physical enslavement, and on the free society of the future. Angelo Luca is a militant anarchist and atheist. He speaks in a beautiful, cultivated voice, without a foreign accent. He ends the record with a description of the future anarchist society: "complete freedom for every human being is the most precious thing in life."]

Father wrote poems, which Eugene Travaglio printed, and he sent them as New Year's greetings each year. Travaglio was more of an intellectual and reader of books than Father, for whom anarchism was on a more emotional and less rational basis. I knew Jonesie [Red Jones, q.v.], who still speaks English poorly after so many years in America, and Jules Scarceriaux, who tried to teach me French when I was a boy and who did some interesting sculpture work. Jonesie lived by himself on Joyce Street but used to get his mail at my parents' house at 650 Capp Street, San Francisco, until Father died. Now he has a small room in a Chinese rooming house on Broadway.

I did some drawings and woodcuts for *Man!* when I was young—in the Walt Whitman issue I think—but I never could accept anarchism, with its guerrilla tactics. I'm a pacifist (I was a conscientious objector in World War II) and something of a socialist. The anarchists were looking for a Utopia. I too wish I could find it—I lived in London and Amsterdam—but I doubt that it really exists.

• FRANK BRAND •

New York City, November 7, 1972

Frank Brand was the pseudonym of the Italian anarchist Enrico Arrigoni, who lived illegally in the United States from 1924 until his death in 1986. A bricklayer by occupation, he also went under the names of "Frank Branch," "Henry Arrigoni," and "Harry Goni" (from his surname Arrigoni). When I interviewed him in 1972, in his tiny apartment in the ILGWU Cooperative Houses in Manhattan, he asked me not to publish anything about him for the time being, "because I am not supposed to be alive." In 1977, when a reporter for the *New York Times*, Israel Shenker, asked him his real name, he replied, "Which one? What year?"[313] During the 1920s and 1930s Brand wrote for a number of anarchist journals, in Spanish and English as well as Italian, and in 1928 he founded a remarkable journal of his own called *Eresia.* In 1937 he went to Spain to take part in the struggle against Franco, and it was Emma Goldman who got him out of prison when he was arrested in Barcelona.

A confirmed individualist, Brand denounced not only Nazism and fascism but also what he called the "galley-slave world" of the Communists, whom he considered a greater menace to human liberty than any other political group. During the 1970s and 1980s he published a series of books—*The Totalitarian Nightmare* (1975), *The Lunacy of the Superman* (1977), *Adventures in the Country of the Monoliths* (1981), *Freedom: My Dream* (1986)—condemning centralized authority in all its forms. Asked by Israel Shenker when anarchism would come, he replied: "Not in my lifetime. Might be a few centuries from now. To be an anarchist, it's not important to realize anarchism immediately. Some day individuals will be free to regulate their lives by themselves, without intervention by the state—the greatest enemy of the individual."[314] In February 1984 the Libertarian Book Club, of which Brand was a longtime member, celebrated his ninetieth birthday with a party. Less than three years later, on December 7, 1986, Brand died in his apartment. His body was found on the floor near the bed by his old comrades Valerio Isca (q.v.) and Pasquale Buono. He was ninety-two years old. He left two daughters, a former companion, and a brother, his last, in Italy. Among Brand's passions had been travel and opera. He left his books and collection of opera records to the Libertarian Book Club. His body was cremated on December 11, 1986.

MY REAL NAME is Enrico Arrigoni. "Brand" is a pseudonym taken from Ibsen's character Brand, a strong individualist, and was given me by a girlfriend in the Black Forest in 1918. I was born on February 20, 1894, in the village of Pozzuolo Martesano, near Milan. My father was a tailor of peasant origin. I became an anarchist in 1908 at the age of fourteen. I was the only anarchist in a town of three thousand people. Some believe that anarchism is inborn, so perhaps that is true. In 1900 the signs already began to appear. When Bresci assassinated King Umberto and children denounced him as a murderer, I defended his deed as a natural act of rebellion and said that some day I too would be an anarchist. The very word "anarchist" fascinated me. I was only six years old.

At nine I finished third grade and went to Milan to work. I found a job as a baker's helper, going around at 6 A.M. distributing bread with a big rope on my shoulder, seven days a week, about a hundred hours of work for twenty lire (about four dollars at that time) plus room and board. There were no child labor laws to prohibit this yet. When I visited my native village a priest gave me books to read, and reading has always been one of my great passions.

At fourteen I began to work at a lathe in a locomotive factory. That year I read a pamphlet by Tolstoy called *I Cannot Keep Silent!*, an attack on tsarist tyranny. That pamphlet impressed me very deeply. I had been devouring books from the age of nine, reading two or three a week, carrying books on my bakery route, reading books in the street as I walked, a habit I still retain. By the age of fourteen I had read hundreds of books—histories, novels, adventure stories, and so on. I began attending a socialist course for young people, but at the conclusion I was the only one of a group of twenty to refuse to enter the Socialist Youth organization. When my socialist teacher asked me why I wouldn't join, I said that I considered socialism to be the last stage of capitalism, and that I wanted to be an anarchist.

So I already considered myself an anarchist at the age of fourteen. But I still had had no contact with anarchist groups or anarchist literature. I began to seek it out and started to read anarchist papers and books. I first came into contact with anarchists at a great protest meeting following Francisco Ferrer's execution in Spain. For a day or two the streets were filled with protestors. It was tantamount to a revolt. I met some anarchists then. My first anarchist act was to take part in a strike in our factory to reduce Saturday labor from ten to eight hours. In those pre-war years there was a period of great labor agitation in Italy. The workers did not want to come out, however, so I and two or three other young anarchists stood in front of the door and stopped them from going in. The strike was won but of course we were fired. We expected that, but we were not afraid. It was an honor to be fired—and so young! It was our badge of being a revolutionist. We anarchist youth took an active part in many strikes and street demonstrations, digging up cobblestones and throwing them at the police. We were the most militant group, and the Socialist Youth followed our lead. We were individualist anarchists, for Milan was a center of anarchist-individualism; the printer of the main anarchist journal was an individualist, and the first Italian translation of Stirner's *The Ego and His Own* was published in Milan.[315]

I was twenty when the war broke out. When my number was called I tried to escape from Italy with a friend. We went to Genoa and boarded a ship—we didn't even know where it was going—but were caught and arrested. My first arrest had been in 1909 or 1910 when I was selling anarchist papers at a band concert in a Milan park; I was kept in jail eight days and then released. I had quit working in the factory—I couldn't stand the routine and claustrophobia of factory life—and was selling fruit in the street. (I had refused to be a tailor, my father's occupation, because I hated sedentary work.)

When Italy entered the war in 1915, many socialists and radicals threw themselves behind the war effort. But the anarchists in Milan opposed the war to the very last. We did not follow Kropotkin and the others, but kept up our antimilitarist agitation to the end. The last big antiwar demonstration in Milan was organized by the anarchists. We printed five thousand leaflets saying, "All Come to the Piazza del Duomo to Protest Against the War." A handful of us went from factory to factory distributing the leaflets, and two of us were arrested. We got a large turnout. The square was jammed with young workers shouting, "Down With the War!" Fights broke out and I lost two teeth. It lasted for five hours, till one in the morning. I was drafted, but as a skilled mechanic was allowed to work in a factory (in uniform) and attended drill every Saturday.

That's when I began preparing to flee the country. My comrades Ugo Fedeli and Francesco Ghezzi worked in the same factory, but so far I was the only one in uniform. After two months as a soldier I and others decided to call a strike, and I was chosen head of the strike committee. The factory was under military control (it made reflectors for military use), so I had to escape. I and Ghezzi were the first of the Milan anarchists to escape. It took us two days to cross the Alps into Switzerland. I made my way to Geneva but was arrested with three comrades and spent three months in prison. Once, while I was lowering a tin of sardines to a friend below, a watchdog smelled the fish and set up a howl, so I was put in the hole where Luccheni[316] had spent six years, or so the guard told me. The four of us went on a hunger strike, and Luigi Bertoni[317] launched a campaign for our release, which eventually succeeded. There were a few hundred Italian deserters in Switzerland at that time, about half of whom were anarchists.

I wanted to learn German, so I went to Lucerne and worked as a lathe operator under close police supervision. Policemen used to escort me to and from work every day. After three months I moved to Zurich and worked in a factory for about a year. At the end of 1917, after the Bolsheviks took power in Russia, we Italian anarchists in Zurich got the idea to make a revolution there by organizing an antiwar demonstration that would spread through Switzerland into the warring countries. The idea seems fantastic now, but we were young, and at that time there was widespread discontent with the war and a widespread feeling of rebellion against the whole European social order. But after three or four days of demonstrations and violent encounters with the police, we had to give up. When a law was passed to intern all deserters until the end of the war, we decided to escape through Germany to Holland.

While riding the rails through Germany in February 1918, I was arrested near Karlsruhe and spent several weeks in jail, and then was released and allowed to work in a small factory in the Black Forest area as a lathe operator. As an antiwar gesture I sabotaged the machinery and was jailed again in Karlsruhe. I was charged with wartime sabotage and was in danger of being shot, so I began to plan my escape. I stopped eating to weaken myself, in the hope of being taken to the hospital. I intentionally scraped my head on the floor and then, bleeding, pretended to have fainted. The doctor was called. He examined me and said, "He's a bit undernourished, but otherwise quite healthy." I then wrote to the military commander in Karlsruhe demanding a trial or my release. For lack of evidence they decided to release me. I went back to work, first in Karlsruhe and then in Frankfurt, where I remained until the end of the war, working as a lathe hand.

With the war over, we Italians were burning to go to Berlin, expecting the revolution to break out there. I taught myself the violin and, pretending to be a musician, traveled to Berlin by train "to give a concert." Berlin was in the midst of revolutionary agitation. I sold the *Rote Fahne* of Karl Liebknecht and Rosa Luxemburg to make a living. When the Spartacus revolt broke out, in January 1919, I and other Italian anarchists and socialists joined in and occupied the *Vorwaerts* offices, while other Spartacists took over the railroad station and other key points around the city. We occupied it for eight days, and I was the only one to escape arrest by Noske's troops,[318] having been sent for fresh clothes and then pretending to be a native (by then I spoke fluent German) when I saw troops surrounding the *Vorwaerts* building. I hid out in various places—mostly in homes of Spartacists—for eight days. They conceived the idea of sending me and a comrade, Mario Mantovani, to Russia as repatriated prisoners of war.

We went to Russia for three months in early 1919. As we had no documents we were taken to the Cheka in Moscow, who thought we were spies. But I knew of Angelica Balabanoff,[319] who had lived in Italy, and I asked to see her. As soon as I mentioned her name it was like magic, and they released us immediately. The Third International was founded (March 1919) while we were there. Balabanoff, its secretary, embraced us warmly—she loved Italy and Italians—and helped us leave the country. She was disappointed already with the Bolshevik regime and very discouraged by the fate of the revolution. She sent us, in the guise of Hungarian prisoners of war being repatriated to Hungary, as couriers to Italy with documents of the International.

We arrived in Budapest in time for Béla Kun's[320] revolution. For us it was a complete surprise. We had a meeting with Kun himself and showed him the documents of the International. We then went on to Vienna and to the Italian consulate, claiming to be Italian prisoners in Hungary. We were thus allowed to return to Italy as heroes rather than deserters.

Once in Milan, I had to go into hiding for four months, as I was known there as a deserter. I returned to Berlin for about six months and taught Italian in a Berlitz school in order to make a living. I visited Rudolf Rocker, who helped me to get to Paris, where I spent a little more than a year before moving on to Spain. I worked briefly in a factory in Barcelona but got into trouble with the police and had to be smuggled on board a ship for Argentina.

That was in 1920. I lived in Buenos Aires for a year and a half, employed as a factory worker and carpenter. I lived in a room with Diego Abad de Santillán,[321] a fellow worker three years younger than I, for about five months. He became a member of the staff of *La Protesta*. I still visit him when I travel to Argentina. One day a German comrade named Wilckens,[322] who had been deported from the U.S., moved in with us. *La Protesta* sent Santillán to Berlin as a correspondent. He learned German, met Rocker, and married the daughter of Fritz Kater,[323] who still lives with him in Buenos Aires. I told Wilckens, who worked at the port as a dispatcher, that I wanted to go to the U.S., and he arranged to hide me on a British tanker, which dropped me off in Tampico (this was in 1921).

I crossed the Rio Grande on foot and entered the United States. But I was caught and jailed for seven months, brought to New York by the immigration authorities, and deported to Italy, in October 1922, as an illegal immigrant. In Italy—this was just before Mussolini came to power—I was still subject to a seventeen-year sentence. So I jumped ship in Palermo, then made my way to Rome, where Malatesta was editing *Umanità Nova*. He helped me get across the border into France. I remained in Paris till 1924, and then went to Cuba for several months. I wrote for an anarchist journal in Havana under the pseudonym "Brand," which I had adopted in Germany. I took a German freighter to New Orleans, my second illegal entry into the U.S. I went to New York, where I remained from 1924 to the end of 1928, and then returned to Paris. I came back to the States in 1930 and have been here—apart from frequent trips abroad—ever since.

In New York in 1924 I had gotten a job as a lathe operator in a small factory in Harlem, then became a housepainter, and then finally a bricklayer. I immediately became active in the anarchist movement, in the Spanish and Road to Freedom Groups on Twenty-Third Street and in an Italian group in Brooklyn, the Circolo Volontà. I wrote occasionally for *L'Adunata* and also for *Cultura Obrera*, edited after Esteve's death by Roberto Muller from Argentina, who later contributed to my journal *Eresia*. Perhaps, in addition, I wrote some short pieces in English for *The Road to Freedom*.

As I said, I mixed mostly with the Road to Freedom Group (I wanted to learn English as quickly as possible) and with the Spanish Group (I knew Spanish from Spain, Argentina, and Cuba, and my then companion, who died soon after, was Spanish). I was never actually a member of the Italian group; the Italian anarchists here were mostly southerners, and northerners like me didn't mix very well with them, while I felt quite at home with the Spaniards.

I founded *Eresia* in 1928, an eclectic journal with a strong individualist bias, though the contributors included anarchist-communists like Ugo Fedeli, my old comrade in Milan. Joe Conti, our treasurer from Brooklyn, taught me the bricklaying trade. I was the editor and wrote both as "Brand" and "Harry Goni." The drawings were done by another bricklayer, from New Jersey. We printed two thousand copies of the journal. Ghezzi, another old comrade from Italy and a fellow individualist, sent articles from Russia, from which we tried desperately but unsuccessfully to get him out."[324]

I later wrote regularly for *Controcorrente*, edited in Boston by Aldino Felicani, and helped found *Intesa Libertaria* during the late 1930s, which lasted only a year or two. It tried to bring together all anarchist tendencies but it failed. *L'Adunata* refused to cooperate, though a few *L'Adunata* people helped us as individuals. Carlo Tresca cooperated at first, but soon backed out. Finally the Tresca group in Philadelphia captured the journal, but it folded soon after.

I should also mention that I went to Spain during the Spanish Civil War. I was there for five months and wrote two articles a week for *Cultura Proletaria*. I was imprisoned in Barcelona, and it was Emma Goldman who got me out. But this is another story, which I'll save for another occasion. Finally, I wrote several short plays, published in Italy after the Second World War, under my real name, Enrico Arrigoni. I have been active in the Libertarian Book Club for the last twenty years, the only individualist in the group.

I remain an individualist anarchist. We believe in temporary organizations for specific functions that, once accomplished, the organization disappears. We don't accept permanent organizations because they tend to become authoritarian in spite of the good will of their members. But we are not against all kinds of organization; even Stirner believed in a Union of Egoists. But it is not only the question of organization that separates us from the anarchist-communists. We also have a different conception of freedom. For us freedom is the greatest good, and with freedom we make no compromises. Thus we reject all institutions with even a tint of authority. Yet each anarchist should follow the trend of anarchism which suits his own psychology. So I don't oppose anarchist-communism. Let the anarchist-communists remain anarchist-communists—I don't want to convert them! Individualist anarchism is not superior to communist anarchism. It all depends on one's temperament and psychology. Individualist anarchism suits me, but it may not suit others.

My view of anarchism has not changed much over the years. But Santillán, for one, has come to a point where he rejects revolution, just as we individualists do. We emphasize education. Some of us took part in revolution under the illusion that something better might come out of it. But through violent revolution we cannot inaugurate anarchism. Revolutions are inherently authoritarian. Moreover, in advanced countries like the United States we have many means of peaceful propaganda, so that we don't need revolution. I would always choose capitalism over Communism if the choice had to be made, for under capitalism we can write, speak, have forums, form cooperatives, and so on. When I see anarchists associating with Communists, I feel sorry for them, for they don't know what they are doing. In *Controcorrente* I conducted a campaign to have absolutely no contact and no relations with Communists.

I am an individualist by nature. Of anarchist literature, Stirner has been the main influence on me. The others—Armand,[325] for instance—didn't evolve new ideas, but were Stirnerites themselves. Indeed, you cannot go beyond Stirner because Stirner rejected every form of authority. He was the only anarchist who was able to unmask all forms of authority, whether of institutions or of conception—state, religion, duty, honor, fatherland—all that tradition holds sacred. For Stirner they are all "spooks." He was the only one who did not compromise in any form, the one who wanted a complete individual, an individual who would realize his complete personality and attain full freedom. I can mix perfectly well with other kinds of anarchists, but I am probably the only individualist left among the Italian anarchists today.

• ATTILIO BORTOLOTTI •

Toronto, Ontario, November 29, 1972;
North Miami Beach, Florida, December 10, 1988; January 19, 1990

I first met Attilio Bortolotti (also known as Arthur Bartell) in 1970 at a hundredth anniversary luncheon for Emma Goldman and Alexander Berkman, sponsored by the Libertarian Book Club of New York. I did not really get to know him, however, until 1972, when he attended a lecture on Russian anarchism which I delivered at the University of Toronto. At the conclusion of the lecture, Bortolotti, who lived in suburban Weston, invited me to his home for dinner. It was there that I conducted the first of three interviews with him; the other two took place many years later at his winter home in Florida. The son of humble parents in Italy, Bortolotti emigrated to Canada in 1920 and became active in the anarchist and antifascist movements in Windsor and Detroit during the agitation for Sacco and Vanzetti. Arrested in Detroit in 1929 for distributing a leaflet announcing a Sacco-Vanzetti meeting, he was held for deportation to Italy but jumped bail and fled to Toronto. There he worked as a tool-and-dye maker and resumed his anarchist activities, editing *Il Libertario* from 1933 to 1935 and *The Libertarian* in 1968 and 1969.

In 1934 Bortolotti met Emma Goldman, who was living at the time in Toronto, and the two became close friends. In 1939, when Bortolotti was threatened with deportation—and certain death at the hands of Mussolini—Emma immediately took up the fight, securing an able attorney and raising funds for her comrade's defense. Bortolotti, she said, was "one of the biggest men we have in our movement, intellectually and morally, besides being a tremendous worker. He is like so many of the Spanish comrades. He lives for nothing else but for his ideal."[326] Emma's campaign was successful, and Bortolotti was set free. A month later, however, Emma suffered a massive stroke, from which she died on May 14, 1940. The Bortolotti case had been her last battle against the state.

I WAS BORN on September 19, 1903, in Codroipo, a town of about four thousand (now thirteen or fourteen thousand) inhabitants in the center of Friuli, between Trieste and Venice. The name the Romans gave it 2,500 years ago was Quadrivium, because there are four roads that converge there, from the Alps to the sea and east and west. Codroipo is in the province of Udine, region of Friuli-Venezia Giulia. We were Friulani and our language was Romansch, similar to the Romansch in Switzerland and in a few towns in Austria close to the Carmic Alps. There is one valley there that is an anarchist valley, two kilometers from Austria—Pratocarnia, Val Peresina—where I go from time to time and we speak the same language. They are still anarchists, about five or six thousand of them, but they don't go to work in Austria as much as before. They own a building together with the socialists and use it as a meeting place. Most of the anarchists are construction workers, but there is one family, the Villaris, who have been making famous clocks that are used throughout the world. Libera and I were there in 1986 but stayed only five or six hours. We saw Petris and Del Fabbio, two of the oldtime anarchists. It's very beautiful in those mountains, a two-hour drive from Codroipo.

My father Luigi was a mason who became a builder and was in love with art. He took off two weeks every year to go to Venice, Florence, and Rome, and came back always with sketches of cornices and other objects. He was a good draftsman, with a skill which he learned by himself. Codroipo had a market every Tuesday; and the last Tuesday of the month was an animal market, ranging from pigs and goats to bulls and horses. Our town was in an alluvial valley with reddish soil fertilized with manure, both human and animal, as in China. My father made huge cement tanks to hold the manure. The grass all around would be blue, so rich it was from the manure. And there were grape vines all about. Every family had a cow and sheep for milk. Father made a relatively good living.

I was the fifteenth of eighteen children, and the only rebel among them. As a child I refused to go to church. At ten I and a friend heard a poor widow from our district say she had no manure to fertilize her land; and knowing that a neighbor had had a mound of unused fertilizer for years, we went and got some for her, and were reported to the police, who warned us with a smile. In 1917, during the First World War, we saw an Italian soldier hanging by the thumbs from a tree as punishment, so we cut him down. I became an antimilitarist and have remained so since. At the same time I remain strongly antireligious: how can "God" allow such tragedies to occur? I was fourteen, a born rebel.

Of my seventeen siblings only two are still alive: a sister in Ontario and another in Italy. I visit her from time to time. Out of eighteen children, seven died in infancy, and of the remaining eleven I was the only one who escaped being a victim of religion. My father was very religious; Mother, yes and no, as I'll explain in a minute. I was left-handed. My father was totally against it and would hit me as if I were a piece of stone. In return I hated him. When I was eight years old and in second grade, they passed a law requiring one hour of religious instruction (Catholic doctrine) every day in the church, from eight to nine A.M. So we went, four or five of us friends. One day I said: "Why go there? It's the same every time. Let's play doctor and nurse." We passed the word to four girls, and they liked the idea. We all went to a granary where corn was kept and studied each other's anatomy. It was beautiful, and we had a hell of a good time.

One morning it started to rain, and I saw my father come into the courtyard of the granary. I jumped downstairs and ran away for three days, sleeping in a box car at the railroad station. Finally two of my brothers found me and Father gave me the beating of my life. After that we had no relations. We never spoke. He made me do chores—clean the tools, take nails out of planks—but we never spoke. In 1913, when I wasn't quite ten years old, he got sick with bronchitis, which developed into pneumonia, and in a week or two he died. He was fifty-three years old. I felt no sorrow. It was a sort of relief for me. While I was waiting for the band to come for the funeral, a friend offered me a lira for my white rabbit, and I agreed and went to get it. When I got back the band was starting, the priest was there, and everybody was crying. But my eyes were completely dry. I didn't feel any remorse or sadness. Father was a very good builder, a good designer of houses, but he was so degenerated by religion that he didn't behave like a human being.

Mother, Maria Pittana, was a very generous woman. When I was fourteen years old, during the war, the Germans came into our village. That was in October 1917. We had a big two-story house with a big kitchen on the ground floor, bedrooms on the second floor, and a granary in the attic. In spring we raised silkworms, the biggest industry of the region. We all helped to cut the branches and take the leaves off the mulberry trees. Father had a two-wheel cart to carry the tools to and from his work. We used that to get the branches and leaves. During the Italian retreat from the eastern front, soldiers came in and asked for polenta. But we had only wine, and my mother gave it to them. Then the Germans came in, an officer and two men, and saw the Italian soldiers, who greeted them. But there was nothing left to give them, so the Italians threw grenades and killed them. Mother and I fled to my uncle in a neighboring village. When we returned the next morning we found the street littered with corpses. All the windows were shot out, the mattresses red with blood. The *arditi*, drunk with wine and spoiling to fight, had attacked and killed the Germans, along with Italian soldiers who didn't want to fight any longer but wanted only to go home.

Mother asked me to go out and look for food. I put on a helmet and overcoat, went to stores and brought home all kinds of stuff in our cart, trip after trip, carrying canned fish, cloth, spools of thread, cutlery. No one tried to stop me. Mother was amazed. "Tilio," she said, "we are rich!" She sent me out to see if I could find a cow for my two-year-old sick nephew, who lived with us. I found a cow and enticed her with grass, then put a rope around her neck and led her home. Two days later Mother sent me to find a four-wheel cart that I could attach to the cow and go to nearby towns and exchange knives and forks for wheat and corn. Mother and I went on back roads to her hometown. We passed corpses in a ditch. "Oh, my God!" she exclaimed. I said, "If there is a God, why does he allow wars and killing like this if he is so powerful?" She looked at me and said, "Oh, God must be a refugee." When I heard that, I felt like there were ten orgasms passing through my body, so happy I was to hear my mother say those words. Before the day was over, we had brought home grain and beans and hid it.

In addition to the cow I also found a mule. We exchanged it with a miller for a few sacks of wheat. A few days later a German officer, a captain, stayed at our house. It was a very cold day. We were warming ourselves around the fireplace when we heard the bells of the bell-tower. An air raid was coming. We huddled in the courtyard. Bombs fell close. Debris fell around us. My nephew got up and began to scream. He went haywire. The German captain jumped up, threw down the child and protected him with his own body. When I saw that, a revolution began in my head. "How come?" I thought. The propaganda said that the Germans were killing women and children, cutting breasts off women in Belgium and France. As soon as I saw that, I realized that it was mostly lies. When the all-clear sounded, we returned to the fireplace. I was looking at the captain with a queer look, a question mark on my face. He asked me why I was looking at him like that. I told him what I had read in the newspaper about the atrocities in Belgium and France. He said: "Young man, I want you to listen to what I have to say to you. I am a professor; I was teaching at the University of Berlin when I was called to serve in the army. I don't feel that I have the right to kill you because you were born here; nor should you feel you can kill me because I was born in Berlin. I want you to remember three words: *Freiheit über alles!*"

These words helped me, at the end of the war in 1918, to conceive the idea not to be a soldier for anybody. I was fifteen years old then. I wrote to my older brother William (Guglielmo), a contractor in Windsor, Ontario, to please send me papers to come to Canada, because I didn't want to be a soldier for any government. In a few weeks I got the papers. I went with another older brother, Umberto, to the British consulate in Venice. They gave us documents to enter Canada. But there was no room on any of the steamships. We had to wait till June 1920 to get passage.

I left home on June 19, 1920. I was sixteen years and nine months old. It took three days to reach Genoa because of a railroad strike. There were four of us: me, my brother Umberto, and two friends. I should mention that my father and brothers had wanted me to become a builder, like them. But I wanted to be a mechanic. I fell in love with the lathe. A friend of my father's had a shop in our town, and every time I passed it and saw the lathe I couldn't take my eyes off it. I fell in love as with a beautiful girl. In May 1915—I wasn't quite twelve years old—I became an apprentice to a blacksmith, who could do marvelous work with his hammer and file, without even a drill press. When he left for Bologna in 1917, I became the only blacksmith in town. Everybody came to me for keys, door locks, to sharpen tools, and the like. Farmers came to me for small anvils on which to sharpen their scythes. I accumulated a great quantity of tools which the Italian soldiers had left behind.

In any event, we arrived at Ellis Island, where we were kept for four or five days while the officials made sure I had a brother in Windsor. Finally we were allowed to proceed. We arrived in Detroit and slept in the railway station. The next morning I walked to the Detroit River and located the ferry to Windsor. I returned to the station for my three companions and we went over to Windsor, I with my wooden box with clothing and fourteen dollars in my pocket. We walked up an incline to Sandwich Street. I saw a streetcar with the sign "Walkerville," where my brother had a post office box. The conductor showed me where to get off. We sat there on the street. I bought oranges and sardines. At four o'clock I saw a man with a bicycle. It was my brother Guglielmo. I hadn't seen him in six years. He was now twenty-four.

Guglielmo knew an Italian contractor in Windsor who was excavating sewers and paving streets and who had a blacksmith shop. I worked there for three years as helper to a Ukrainian blacksmith, a wonderful man. I started to go to night school to learn English and machine-shop. I became a very good lathe-hand, and when they laid off the Canadian lathe-hand they gave me his job. In a sense that was my Waterloo. One day I was fixing a generator in the shop. My boss came in and told me to hurry up. For three years he had never called me by any name—just "dago" or "wop." I said I was doing my best. He wasn't satisfied. I told him to get the hell out of there and let me work. He began to shout. I threw my hammer, hit him in the leg, and he fell down. The next day I quit.

After that I couldn't get a job in Windsor. So I went to work at Chrysler in Detroit. That was in 1922. It was then that I became an anarchist. In the Windsor public library I had begun to study the history of religion. Also, my brother had a book called *Storia universale*, describing the solar system, the planets, the satellites—something entirely new to me. I didn't know that such a thing existed. I got interested, and by the time I got to Darwin and Spencer I had already traveled half the planet. One Saturday night, in 1921, when we used to congregate at a grocer's apartment, there was a guy who (I later found out) called himself an anarchist. He began to discuss religion. I took courage and put my two cents in. I said that "from tonight on I will be known as an atheist, not a Catholic." My brother broke in: "What did you say?" I replied, "I said what I feel."

A few months later, in early 1922, I came across a leaflet explaining why Sacco and Vanzetti were innocent and how they had been condemned without enough proof. I went to the library and tried to find out who Sacco and Vanzetti were and what "anarchism" meant. Slowly I succeeded in getting some papers, along with *Fra contadini* by Errico Malatesta and a pamphlet by Sébastien Faure.[327] It took me six months to digest this material, but it struck a profound chord. At the grocer's apartment, the same spot where a year earlier I had declared myself an atheist, I now said "I am an anarchist. I am against all government and authority." This time my brother said nothing. But two other men came over and shook my hand.

Soon afterwards, I got in touch with the comrades in Detroit. A bricklayer from Friuli had arrived in Windsor and my brother had given him a job. One

Sunday morning he asked me if I could get across to the States. I said yes, and he gave me a letter for a friend in Detroit. I was lucky enough to fool the immigration authorities and get in. The trick was not to hang back in the rear when the ferry docked but to stay at the front with the crowd and say with confidence, "Returning to Windsor same day!" I also wore a hat and looked more or less respectable. I had no trouble getting in. I went to the address on the letter (on Rivard Street). It turned out to be a candy store. I asked for the owner. "I am Cernuto," the man said. He was a Sicilian anarchist and the place was an anarchist hangout. I gave him the letter. He showed me a shelf of books and said, "Maybe you'll find something that you like." I took a few pamphlets.

And in those beginnings I became an anarchist. That was the period of Mussolini's march on Rome and the reaction in Italy. I became an antifascist besides calling myself an anarchist. Every Sunday morning I went to Detroit to Il Gruppo "I Refrattari." One active member, Bertoli, was a very good speaker, who got a lot of mail from Italy. Another was Ugo Baldi, an actor by profession, who organized a *filodrammatica* [theater group]. In Windsor, almost every Saturday, there was a dance and *una recita* [a performance] to send a few dollars overseas. There's where I learned to put my hand in my pocket, every Saturday and Sunday, and pull out as much as I could, usually four or five dollars, a tidy sum in those days. I didn't smoke, didn't go out on dates. I preferred married women. I read a book, *L'Amore libero* by Albert Berthelot, and created a revolution among half the Italians in Windsor—and the rest weren't too happy about me. Someone in Detroit gave me a copy of Emma Goldman's *Mother Earth*, and that made my idea of free love more complete.

In 1923, on July 29th—I forget a lot of dates but that one I'll always remember, the date on which Gaetano Bresci killed "*Re Buono*"—I attended a picnic in Detroit to commemorate the event. There was a big crowd, over two thousand persons, Italians, Spaniards, and a few Americans. I was with my girlfriend, the wife of somebody else. A tenor voice rang out, inviting us to gather round and hear who Gaetano Bresci was and who King Umberto had been. It was the voice of the chairman, Umberto Martignago [Libera Bortolotti's father], of the Libero Pensiero Group of Sault Ste. Marie. He was followed by two speakers, both from New York: the editor of *L'Adunata*, a Toscano named Arturo Galvani, and Pedro Esteve, who spoke in Spanish. There were five or six of us from Windsor, including Ghetti, an individualist anarchist, who said a few words.

It was at this picnic that I first met Ella Antolini, then in her early twenties. She was a beautiful young woman, a free spirit. She acted in plays in Chicago and Detroit. She went to live in Detroit with Pitton, an anarchist. She had been in prison at Jefferson City, Missouri, with Emma Goldman. After Emma and Ella left, Mollie Steimer came to the prison, and she and Ella began a correspondence. In later years, when Mollie was living in Mexico, Ella sent her two or three dollars with every letter. Ella lived in Florida for many years before her death in 1984. She was an interesting person. She was an avid reader. She did not indulge in small talk, but she had a lot to say. She never pulled her punches. She called a spade a spade. She still had a lot of her anarchism until the end. She brought her son Febo to the picnics in Crandon Park. She wanted to get him interested, but he never did. She had a stroke, which left her partly paralyzed, and died soon after of cancer.

As I said, I used to go to Detroit almost every Sunday, and never had any trouble getting in. One time, though, a U.S. immigration officer stopped me and called me aside. He asked me my nationality. I was tired of hearing this question. When I became an anarchist I also fell in love with astronomy and with Darwin's theory of evolution. I considered myself a human being, a creature of the universe. Besides, I am not an Italian. I'm a Friulian. I speak a different language. So to the question I replied, "I was born in a town that is located at forty-six degrees latitude and thirteen degrees longitude, east of Greenwich." The officer was astonished. He stood there for a moment with his mouth agape, then said, "Step into the office!" He asked me to repeat what I had told him to the other immigration officers. So I repeated it. "But what country is that?" one of them asked. I said, "Get the atlas and you'll find out where it is." They laughed. One inspector—Jewish, with a small beard—thought it over. He said, "It must be eastern Italy or western Yugoslavia." But they sent me back to Windsor. From then on, whenever I was stopped at the border, I always repeated that phrase.

In Windsor, due to my antifascist activities, the fascists sought to blacklist me. I tried to get a job at Ford, at the same place where Federico [Arcos] [q.v.] later worked. They refused. For a while I went back to blacksmithing, and then went to Detroit to work with my brother William on construction jobs. (He moved to Detroit in 1925.) There were three men ahead of me waiting for skilled jobs, so I started as a laborer. After six months my brother gave me a hammer and a trowel that he had bought and put me to work as a mason.

In 1926 the struggle with the fascists in Windsor was increasing and comrades asked me to join in. I attended a meeting addressed by the Italian consul, at which my former boss, Luigi Merlo, was chairman. I raised my hand, but the consul did not recognize me. I called him what he was—a coward. On the platform one of the fascist leaders in Windsor said, "If you have the guts, come here and speak." I got up as fast as I could and in five seconds I was there. I told the consul what they were—a bunch of killers, liars, and the rest. At my shoulder was a picture of the king. I tore it off the wall, crumpled it in my hands, and threw it in the face of the consul. That started a melee. In less than a minute the whole audience was fighting each other. The fascists retreated into one corner. My brother came over with a couple of comrades and said, "Tilio, let's go." We could hear the police sirens coming. "Let's go to Detroit and go to the opera and see *Rigoletto* tonight."

That was in 1926. Two days later my brother told me to go to Redford, a suburb of Detroit, to work on a house. Around ten in the morning I saw a big car stop across from where we were working. I said to myself, "God damn it, those guys are immigration officers." They came over and one of them asked for William Bortolotti. I asked him whether I could help him. He turned back his lapel and showed me his badge. I identified myself as Caligaris, a friend on Ellis Island. They let me go. They asked me to call over one worker at a time for identification. I called a citizen first, and to the others I shouted a warning in Friulian. All, including my brother Umberto, got away. Clearly the officials had been tipped off by the Italian consul or fascists.

A few days later my brother William called me (I was then living in Detroit) and warned that immigration officers were coming. He came over and we left for Windsor. Five minutes later an official came, but the people I boarded with told him that he had the wrong address. In Windsor I couldn't find work. I was completely blacklisted. I spent most of my time working for Sacco and Vanzetti. I collected money and put out a leaflet. Most of the winter of 1926–1927 I spent drawing a picture of Bakunin in black and white. I made a frame, very elaborate; it took me three months to carve it: thorns and needles carved into the frame, like Bakunin's own life. On the bottom of the frame I carved a skull, with ribbons emerging from the eyes, bearing the message, *Dio non esiste* (God does not exist). On the left side of the frame I carved Rodin's *The Thinker*, labeled *Anarchia è il pensiero e verso l'anarchia va la storia*. On the top was a young girl pulling up a black veil and the sun shining through (*il sol dell'avvenire*). The right side showed three naked women, with *Libertà e Uguaglianza* on the ribbon. It came out beautifully. My brother took it to Detroit, where it was used in a raffle. I could never find out who won it. I would give ten thousand dollars today to get it back.

One day, as I was finishing the frame, two policemen came to the door. "Bortolotti," one of them said, "the old man [chief of police] wants to talk to you." I went with them. When they opened the door, the chief said to me, "Come in, I've got something to tell you." On his desk I saw all the leaflets we had published in Italian, along with copies in English. I said, "You must like what we printed—you took the trouble to translate them." "Bortolotti," he replied, "I want you to clear out of Windsor and out of Canada. If I didn't know your brother Bill I would try you under the law passed during the general strike in Manitoba in 1919, with a twenty-year penalty. You can go now."

While I was walking home I said to myself, "What am I going to do?" I had no money. I owed my landlady $800. During the evening rush hour I spent five cents for the ferry and went back to Detroit. I got a room. The next day I saw an ad in the papers that Ford wanted a tool and dye maker. I applied and took a simple exam—fortunately, because I didn't know a thing about trigonometry in those days, a must for tool and dye making. They told me to come in the next day. I brought my tool box and a few tools and became Albert Berthelot— after the author of *Amore libero*—until arrested two years later.

During those two years, 1927–1929, I went back to Windsor occasionally to fight against the fascists. I did the same in Detroit, culminating in an incident on Columbus Day 1928. We found out that the fascists would come out in black shirts and full regalia and march through the city to Cadillac Square. We decided to see what we could do. The Communists and liberals said that they would join us. When the day came—a shame for Detroit—we found ourselves with only twelve persons, a Communist, two socialists, and nine anarchists. Seven of us were on the north side of the square and five on the south side. When the band began to play *Giovenezza*, the fascist hymn, we exploded in catcalls: "*Abasso il fascismo! Assassini!*" etc. The man who held the fascist flag put it down, took out his gun, and shot two comrades, both anarchists: Antonio Barra and Angelo Lentricchia. Barra was mortally wounded; Lentricchia survived.[328] As the fascists closed in on us I grabbed one of them by his long black hair and began punching him. I dragged him by the hair as far as I could. The police moved in on motorcycle and on foot with clubs raised. Someone called my name, a comrade in a fruit store. He shoved me behind four or five barrels of apples just before the police came in, and they didn't get me. It was a stupid thing to do—there were about sixty or seventy fascists—but we felt we had to do it. I still had a handful of black hair in the fruit store.

At Ford, meanwhile, there was a campaign for the union, to organize the shop. I never liked that idea in a way, but I helped pass around leaflets and talked to the workers, saying that a union might create a new ambience and things might be better. But I never became a member myself, because I was arrested.

During 1926 and 1927 I also worked to save Sacco and Vanzetti. On the night of the execution there was a mass demonstration—anarchists, Communists, and others—in Cadillac Square, with speakers on eight flatbed cars. Midnight came. "Sacco's dead," came the announcement, "and Vanzetti is on his way." Someone shouted, "Let's attack city hall!" The crowd started to move, but four hundred policemen came in on horses and motorcycles, and a struggle began. I struck a policeman with a two-by-two from a poster denouncing the execution, and he hit me with his club and opened my scalp. Somehow I managed to escape. I went to the office of the *Detroit News* and was told that Sacco and Vanzetti had indeed been executed. I don't know how I got home that night.[329]

After that, on every anniversary of the executions, we put out leaflets, eight by fourteen inches in size. The first anniversary we printed ten thousand leaflets and distributed them without any trouble. In 1929 I began to distribute leaflets on Fourth Street to workers coming out of the Fisher Body Plant. A police car stopped and arrested me. I spent the night in the Fourth Street station. The next day the head of detectives for Ford Motor Company came to pick up my worker's badge. The chief of police said, "How much an hour did Ford pay you?" "A dollar ten," I replied. "Would Mussolini pay you that much?" he asked. "Well," I said, "I have nothing to do with Mussolini." "You goddam anarchist bastard!" he yelled. "*You* may be a bastard, not me!" I said. At that point someone hit me on the head, knocking me unconscious, and I found myself locked in a cell. I was transferred to the county jail. After three weeks I was tried before twelve judges for breaking a city ordinance. One of them had a Polish name and face. He asked, "How come you were born in Italy and have a French name [Berthelot]?" I replied, "And how come you were born in America and have a Polish name?" "Do you believe in God?" he asked. "No,"

I said, "I am an atheist." "Do you believe in government?" "No." "Are you an anarchist?" "Yes, I am an anarchist!" They ordered me to be deported to Italy.

That was in the fall of 1929. My lawyer, Jacob Margolis,[330] tried to get me out on bail. Bail was set at $3,000. The comrades on Rivard Street got the money together, and I was let out. Two days later, Bruno [Raffaele Schiavina] arrived in Detroit. He said to me, "Tilio, your life is worth more than $3,000. Go back to Canada and get lost." My brother came with his truck and brought me back. One day I saw a comrade who had a wooden leg (he lost it in a coal mine explosion in British Columbia). He told me that the fascist consul was coming again to Windsor. Are we going to do anything? I wrote a leaflet and had it printed. We distributed the leaflet. The following Sunday the consul spoke. It was in the basement of a Catholic school. He wore a black suit. A few of the comrades attended. We shouted, "*Abasso il fascismo! Morte a Mussolini!*" The police called in reinforcements. We formed a double line on the sidewalk. When the consul came out we all spat at him. By the time he got to the police car his jacket was white with spit. Somehow they blamed this on me too. But nobody knew where I was.

I went to Toronto and checked my valise at the train station. I walked a few blocks and saw a library. It was the reference library of the University of Toronto. I went in. It was full of students. On the bulletin board were notices of rooms for rent. One was with a Finnish family at four dollars a week. I had fifteen dollars on me. I went back to the station, got my valise, and moved in, using the name Arturo Pittana (Pittana was my mother's maiden name). The landlord gave me the newspaper, which had an ad for a tool and dye maker, at sixty-five cents an hour. I got the job and worked there for eight years, making tools for automobile mechanics. That was still in 1929, two weeks before the Crash.

For my first year and a half in Toronto, I knew hardly any Italians. In August 1931, however, I printed five hundred leaflets on the anniversary of Sacco and Vanzetti's execution and distributed them in the Italian district. There I met Italian socialists and Communists, who told me about another Italian anarchist, Ruggero Benvenuti, with whom I soon became friends. They also told me that there was a Matteotti Club, composed mostly of socialists (when Matteotti was assassinated, in 1924, I burned my Italian passport). I went to one of their meetings and during the discussion put my two cents in. The head of the socialists said, "Hey, Pittana, I challenge you to a debate." A week later the debate took place. At the end, a group came up to me and shook my hand. "Glad to meet you," they said. Some were fellow Friulani, from near my home town, and together with Benvenuti we started an anarchist group.

The group, Il Gruppo Libertario, published a paper, *Il Libertario*, and organized a *filodrammatica*, of which I was the coordinator, and we put on works by Pietro Gori, Gigi Damiani,[331] and others. We left the socialists and Communists way behind when it came to plays and recitals—followed, naturally, by dancing—for twenty-five cents a person. Our group had about a dozen members, including Ernesto Gava and Cocchio (the only one still alive, apart from Benvenuti and myself). Most were anarchist-communists, though I considered myself an "anarchist without adjectives," adhering to no particular current or individual, Tresca, Galleani, or otherwise. I did not want anyone put on a pedestal.

There was also a Russian group, including a few Ukrainians and Bulgarians (of the latter Vasiliev was the most active), who had bought an old church and converted it into a meeting place. (The last member, Petrov, died about 1970.) We put on our plays there, and later at the Labor Lyceum, the Jewish trade-union hall. It was through the Russians and Ukrainians that I met the Jewish anarchists of Toronto—Seltzer [q.v.], Judkin, Desser, Langbord, Goodman, Steinberg, and others. The Jewish group was connected with the Workmen's Circle and the *Fraye Arbeter Shtime*, and later with an English-speaking group, called the Libertarian Group, which Emma Goldman organized when she came to lecture in Toronto in 1934. We met at the Dessers', a center for the movement, and occasionally at Vasiliev's place. Dorothy Rogers, a former socialist converted by Emma, was another active member, along with myself and Ahrne Thorne [q.v.].

In 1932 or 1933 Benvenuti and I decided to publish a leaflet to commemorate Sacco and Vanzetti. We took it to Simkin, a Jewish comrade who had a little printing shop, and had five hundred copies made and distributed. The following year, 1934, I first met Emma Goldman. I met her through Simkin—I was always in contact with the Jewish anarchists. She was staying at the Langbords' and was giving a series of lectures. I went to hear her and was flabbergasted by the way she spoke, with her energy, with the beauty of her sentences. She was nothing to look at—short, fat, unattractive—but when she spoke, with that fire in her, you forgot everything. In front of you was something that transcended looks. After she spoke, I went to the Langbords', where I was introduced to her.

The next time I saw her was in 1939. She was again in Toronto to give some lectures, early in the year. She stayed a month or two, and we became good friends. I was especially interested in hearing about her experiences in Russia and Spain. I drove her places in my car and arranged a few of her lectures, including two or three in Windsor, where the anarchists from Detroit could come across the border and hear her. One day, while we were there, I took her for a drive around the Detroit River, pointing out the sights. When we were parallel to Belle Isle, in the middle of the river, we stopped and I explained what we were seeing. I told her that Belle Isle was famous during the previous century when the black slaves were brought to Canada on the underground railroad. She was very interested in this. She was enthralled just to be near the United States. She looked at Belle Isle and Detroit as though through the eyes of a lover. It was then that I understood how much America meant to her.

Yes, she talked a lot about Berkman, and especially his attempt on Frick. One day she said, "If you had met Berkman you wouldn't have thought him capable of shooting at a fellow human being, but he was captivated by the ideal of anarchism and believed that Frick's behavior was antisocial and antihuman, so that he had to be eliminated."

Throughout the 1930s I was active in the antifascist movement. In September 1938 I was invited by the labor organization of Windsor to deliver a lecture on fascism and the activities of the fascists in Windsor, where they had organized a school to teach Italian with books printed by Mussolini. I succeeded in getting copies of these books, and there was more fascism than language in them, which I told the audience. The next day the *Windsor Star* had an article about my lecture, and the fascists were ready to destroy me. And when they found out that I had jumped bail in Detroit a few years earlier, they reported me to the American immigration authorities.

As soon as the war broke out, in September 1939, the fascists in Windsor and Toronto denounced me for spreading anarchist ideas: I was getting ten copies of *L'Adunata* at the time and passing them out, along with papers from France and Belgium. I was threatened with being "taken for a ride," and for the only time in my life—I detest firearms and killing—I carried a pistol for a few months. We organized demonstrations and street meetings at which I, Ahrne, and Dorothy Rogers spoke, and were attacked by mounted police. The authorities kept me under continuous surveillance, and they now tried in earnest to deport me.

At 5 A.M. on October 4th our house was surrounded by mounted police, and four of us were arrested, Gava, Benvenuti, Vittorio Valopi, and myself. Emma did more than anyone else to prevent the deportation. She organized meetings, raised funds, and immediately got the best progressive attorney, a Jewish lawyer named Cohen. He got Benvenuti, Valopi, and Gava out in two or three weeks. They kept me for three and a half months. The others had family—I was still single—and the fascists hated me the most; also, I took the burden on myself, insisting that I alone was responsible.

On the day of my arrest, the Toronto "red squad" came in and seized all my books and periodicals, a big collection of 1,500 volumes, along with all my correspondence. A big truck arrived and hauled it all away, and two years later they burned it. The day before the burning, two mounties came to my house and told me that they would be burning everything the next day. I said, "You think that by burning my library you will burn my ideals?" A few days later another mountie came, a young man born in Vancouver of Friulian parents. He brought me half a dozen pamphlets. That was all that remained of my collection. All the rest had been destroyed. If I live to be a thousand years old I'll never forget that. The mountie asked me what was anarchism. When I replied he said, "Why, that's democracy!"

That happened in 1941. I was now together with Libera; we had become companions that year. "Do you want to become a Canadian citizen?" the mountie asked me. "Then it's best to keep quiet. Forget about all this. And don't speak in public." I said that I want to be a citizen of the world. I had been helping two deserters from Detroit, and one of them was right there when the mountie came. Libera warned him in Italian to get away. We saved them from arrest and possible death. One was the son of Nick and Margaretta Catalano, comrades in Detroit. He now lives in California, and we still see him quite often.

After three and a half months, as I said, I was released on bail. Toolmakers were now in great demand because of the war, and they allowed me to work. At first I couldn't get a job because I was born in Italy, a country with which Canada was now at war. I promised Emma that as soon as I got a job I would rent a big apartment for her and Dorothy Rogers, her secretary. Emma was then living in cramped quarters with the Meelises, Dutch comrades, and didn't have enough money even for postage stamps. So that was foremost in my mind. I went to four or five factories, but they didn't want Italians. I went to one more place, the United Steel Corporation. On the way there, I met a friend, Bartello, and I took the name Arthur Bartell to sound more Anglo-Saxon. The man who interviewed me was Dutch, and he took me for a fellow Dutchman; I was blond, blue-eyed, and Bartell was a Dutch name. The next day I got a phone call from the superintendent, Joe Schainfeld, who was Jewish, and he asked me to come in. He interviewed me and told me to start tomorrow. So I took my tool chest and started to work. That was in early 1940.

By the time I had accumulated enough money to rent Emma an apartment, she had had a severe stroke. It happened on February 17, in the evening, the anniversary of Giordano Bruno's[332] being burned at the stake. Bruno had entered into my life quite early, and I had gathered quite a bit of information about him. I was going to speak about him to a group of friends at the Meelises' house at 295 Bond Road, where Emma was living. I went to pick up Jack and Sylvia Fitzgerald in my car—after that I was supposed to pick up Ahrne Thorne—when their phone began to ring. It was Dorothy: "Come right away! Emma has had a stroke!" I jumped in my car and raced over there. I found her lying on the bed. She tried to pull her skirt down because her knee was showing. Moments later the ambulance arrived and took her to the hospital. She couldn't talk. But her eyes talked a lot and her handshake was firm. Without Emma's help I would have been deported. Emma had a lot of charisma; even her political enemies respected her. She never regained her power of speech. She died three months later.

Yes, I still feel the same way about anarchism. At first I had been a real revolutionary. I was young and like quicksilver, enamored of Galleani and of terrorists like Emile Henry. But during the Sacco-Vanzetti tragedy, which had great repercussions in Canada and made a lasting impression on me personally, the small response that we got from the general population made me more reflective, more philosophical. Money and property never made an incision in my psyche; money is not for our own aggrandizement but to help those in need. Yet I still believed in the necessity of violence up to the time of the Spanish Revolution. After May 1937 in Barcelona I began to think. Tens or hundreds of thousands of lives were being sacrificed. For what? The anarchists had compromised their principles by joining the government. I began to see that anarchism cannot be imposed, that it can only be attained through education and propaganda. This remains our most important task. I am often sorry that I didn't take Ahrne's advice and take extension courses in literature and history at the University of Toronto.

For some reason fewer people come to anarchism these days than in the past. But I'm not disillusioned, even though the movement is not what it should be. Emma Goldman has been an inspiration to me. And Rocker too. I loved his way of speaking. I heard him often in Toronto. He used to come every year and deliver a minimum of six lectures. For a German he was very friendly.

· PART FOUR ·

Schools and Colonies

AMOUR LIBER • RÉVOLTE BERCOVICI • DAVID LAWSON

• MANUEL KOMROFF • BENJAMIN G. BENNO •

MAURICE HOLLOD • ROSE GOLDBLATT • GUSSIE DENENBERG

• CHARLES PLUNKETT • MORITZ JAGENDORF •

MORRIS BERESIN • HARRY MELMAN • EMMA GILBERT

• RICHARD GILBERT • MAGDA SCHOENWETTER •

RAY SHEDLOVSKY • EVA BEIN • MARY RAPPAPORT

• ANNA SCHWARTZ • HUGO GELLERT •

LILLIAN RIFKIN BLUMENFELD • SUZANNE HOTKINE AVINS

• ANATOLE FREEMAN ISHILL • BEN FRUMKIN •

SIEGFRIED ROLLAND • ESTHER WALTERS • RINA GARST

• MOLLIE ALBERT • MOLLY BOGIN • LALLAH BLANPIED •

DOROTHY RICK • JACQUES DUBOIS • HENRY FRUCHTER

• NORA HORN • JACOB LANDA • JO ANN BURBANK •

BEN LIEBERMAN • JACQUES RUDOME • LYDIA MILLER

• EVA BRANDES • NELLIE DICK • MACIE POPE •

DAVID DADISMAN • PEARL POTTU • RADIUM LAVENE

• PHILIP TRUPIN • LOUIS A. GITTELMAN • ELLIS GROSNER •

AARON ROCKOFF • ELEANOR LITWAK • SHAINDEL OSTROFF

• EMANUEL V. CONASON • BEATRICE MARKOWITZ •

DORA KEYSER

THE MODERN SCHOOL

774109

THE MODERN SCHOOL

WILLIAM J. DURANT, Principal, and child   Modern School.

4. Will Durant and pupils of the New York Modern School, 1912
(Paul Avrich Collection)

INTRODUCTION

ON October 13, 1909, Francisco Ferrer y Guardia, a Spanish educator and freethinker, was shot in the trenches of Barcelona's Montjuich fortress. Following a mock trial, at which no solid evidence against him was brought forward, a military court had found him guilty of fomenting a popular insurrection, which had raged for a week before being crushed by government forces. The execution of Ferrer, the founder of libertarian schools, provoked an international outcry. A little-known figure outside radical circles, he was catapulted into sudden prominence. On both sides of the Atlantic, there were meetings and demonstrations of protest. In a number of European cities streets were named after him and statues erected in his memory. Most important, however, a movement for libertarian education, spurred by his example, quickly spread throughout the world. In Brazil and Argentina, in Poland and Czechoslovakia, in China and Japan, not to mention England, France, and other Western European countries, schools were started on the Ferrer model. These schools, bearing Ferrer's name and promoting his philosophy of education, emphasized the rights and dignity of the child, a give and take between pupil and teacher, and the cultivation of both manual and intellectual skills in a libertarian environment.

The most extensive Ferrer movement, however, arose in the United States, where it endured for more than fifty years. Between 1910 and 1960, an assortment of radicals from New York to Los Angeles carried on a venture in learning that was unique in American history. Inspired by Ferrer's martyrdom, more than twenty schools were started in different parts of the country, where children might study in an atmosphere of freedom, in contrast to the formality and discipline of the traditional classroom. These Ferrer schools—or Modern Schools, as they were called—differed from other educational experiments of the same period in being schools for children of workers and directed by the workers themselves. Their founders, moreover, were mostly anarchists, who sought to abolish all forms of authority, political and economic as well as educational, and to usher in a new society based on the voluntary cooperation of free individuals. Their object, during an era of war, social ferment, and government oppression, was to create not only a new type of school but also a new culture, a new life, a new world.

In the wake of Ferrer's execution, anarchist and free-thought groups marshaled their resources in a campaign to spread Ferrer's teachings. By the spring of 1910, their efforts had crystallized into a national organization, the Francisco Ferrer Association (later the Modern School Association of North America), with Leonard Abbott as president and Harry Kelly and Emma Goldman among the charter members. Over the next few years the Ferrer Association prospered. Branches were started in all parts of the country, and membership grew with a rapidity that surpassed the most optimistic forecasts. By the outbreak of the First World War, moreover, Modern Schools had been opened in New York, Philadelphia, Detroit, Chicago, Salt Lake City, Seattle, and Portland, while additional schools were soon started in Boston, Paterson, San Francisco, Los Angeles, and other locations. In addition to English, classes were conducted in German, Yiddish, Czech, Italian, and Spanish. Near the larger cities, including New York and Philadelphia, summer camps were established as retreats from the squalor of ghetto life.

Most of the Modern Schools in America were ephemeral ventures, lasting only two or three years, although the school at Stelton, New Jersey, continued for four decades, and its counterpart at Mohegan, New York, for nearly two. Improvisation and experiment were the rule, and there was considerable variation from place to place, depending on resources and staff. Yet, for all the diversity, the schools shared a set of common practices and assumptions. Instruction was based on libertarian principles, with emphasis on learning by doing and on crafts as well as books. Rigid programs, curricula, and timetables were banished from the classroom.

Participants in the schools believed that traditional education restrained the spontaneous development of the child, stunted his growth, and brutalized his character. Shunning memorization and rote, the staples of conventional learning, they argued that freedom must be the cornerstone of education, that education was a process of self-development, a drawing out rather than a driving in, a means by which the child's unique spirit was nurtured rather than shaped or suppressed. As far as possible, they held, the pupils themselves must decide what to learn and how to learn it, that the function of the teacher was to allow them free scope, to encourage their self-reliance and independence. A favorite metaphor was that of a tree or a flower, growing, unfolding, blossoming, with nature alone to sustain it. In keeping with this philosophy, the students were treated with patience and understanding. Rewards and punishments were done away with, arbitrary rules abolished, and there were no marks or examinations which might engender hypocrisy or dissimulation or arouse feelings of envy among the pupils. Children, it was held, must be free to learn without fear and without the pressures of rivalry and competition.

In all the Modern Schools, education was conceived of as a never-ending process, extending from cradle to grave. Adults, accordingly, were encouraged not only to take part in the operation of the schools but also to attend evening and Sunday lectures by well-known speakers and writers, supplemented by courses on art, literature, and a range of historical and scientific subjects. In several schools, moreover, Esperanto was taught as an international language, promoting solidarity among the different nationalities, and nearly all the schools doubled as radical centers, involved not only with education but with a variety of social causes, from industrial unionism and freedom of speech to sexual liberation and antimilitarist propaganda. The prevailing ideology was a mixture of anarchism, socialism, and syndicalism, with Kropotkin as the most influential theorist. Apart from the Ferrer Association newsletter, a number of publications—notably *Mother Earth* and *The Modern School* magazine—carried news of the different schools, keeping them abreast of each other's activities. Contacts between them were frequent, including exchanges of teachers and equipment, and they shared a sense of common mission in their quest for educational freedom.

No school better exemplified the dual pursuit of children's and adult education than the Modern School of New York, familiarly known as the Ferrer Center. Established in 1911, it was a place where adults came to hear lectures by Clarence Darrow, Elizabeth Gurley Flynn, and other public figures, to see new plays staged by the Free Theatre, to listen to concerts of the Modern School Trio, and to debate the burning questions of the day. It was an outlet for men and women of talent, where Man Ray could experiment with camera and brush, Mike Gold read from Shelley and Blake, and Sadakichi Hartmann put on finger dances and perfume concerts.

Apart from a day school for children, supervised by Will Durant, the Ferrer Center offered evening classes for adults in literature, art, physiology, and psychology, as well as in Spanish, Esperanto, and French. The most successful of these was the art class, conducted by Robert Henri and George Bellows. Another popular course was the weekly forum on "Radical Literature and the Great Libertarians," organized by Leonard Abbott, who lectured on Maeterlinck, Shaw, and other writers of advanced views. Jacques Rudome, the teacher of the French class, remembers the Ferrer Center as "bustling with life and activity," and to Moritz Jagendorf, director of the Free Theatre, it was "a seething ocean of thought and activity, everybody working and creating." "I liked it at once," recalls the writer Manuel Komroff.[333] "One felt unfettered, one felt free. Views were freely exchanged between the speaker and the audience, and the air seemed charged with excitement."

The Ferrer Center was viewed by its enthusiasts as a model of what was desirable in human relations. In its structure and operations, in the behavior of its participants to one another, it provided a foretaste of the libertarian future, of what life could be like once the restraints imposed by authority had been removed. For some it was also a vehicle of rebellion, a means of altering social foundations by removing the fetters of ignorance, dogmatism, and convention. Its central aim, however, was to free the child. From this the rest would follow.

The progress of the school was interrupted, however, during its fourth year of existence. In April 1914, during a coal miners' strike in Colorado, a detachment of militia attacked a tent colony at the town of Ludlow, killing five miners and a boy. The soldiers then poured oil on the tents and set them ablaze; eleven children and two women were smothered to death. Following this, three persons, including a leader of the strike, were savagely beaten, then murdered. The Ludlow massacre, as the episode became known, touched off protests throughout the nation, directed at John D. Rockefeller, Jr., principal owner of the Ludlow mines. In the ensuing weeks, moreover, a plot took shape to blow up Rockefeller's mansion near Tarrytown, New York. Masterminded by Alexander Berkman, the conspiracy was hatched at the Ferrer Center. On July 4, 1914, an explosion occurred in a tenement on Lexington Avenue, a few blocks from the Center, killing three anarchists, Arthur Caron, Carl Hanson, and Charles Berg. A bomb intended for Rockefeller had gone off prematurely.

The Lexington Avenue incident had immediate repercussions within the school. In the wake of the explosion, police agents infiltrated the adult classes in an effort to sniff out the conspirators. Overnight the school acquired the reputation as a bomb factory, a hotbed of incendiarism and subversion. The number of visitors dwindled, and financial contributions dried up. The straits in which the school now found itself, combined with the presence of spies and the general atmosphere of anxiety and suspense, led to a decision to move the school outside of New York. A quiet, rural location was found in the village of Stelton, New Jersey, where an anarchist colony sprang into being. In May 1915 the Modern School moved from New York to Stelton, where it maintained a continuous existence for nearly forty years, the longest such venture on record.

Education at Stelton continued along the lines laid down in New York. There was no segregation of the sexes. Attendance was voluntary; the children came and went as they pleased, pursuing what interested them, ignoring the rest. There was no discipline, no punishment, no formal curriculum. Pupils as well as parents took part in the administration of the school, which formed the centerpiece of the colony, the focus of its life and main reason for its existence. In conformity with the principles of libertarian education, due emphasis was laid on handicrafts as well as books. Instruction was given in carpentry, weaving, and basket-making; a Belgian anarchist, Jules Scarceriaux, came from Trenton to teach pottery and brick-making; and Joseph Ishill started a class in printing. Under the guidance of Hugo Gellert, moreover, the children produced strikingly original art work. As in New York, much effort was devoted to experiment and improvisation. Furthermore, given the school's rural location, an outdoor education was more the rule than ever, featuring hiking, swimming, gardening, and a variety of games and sports.

Of the many teachers at Stelton during the school's prolonged existence, the most notable, perhaps, were Alexis and Elizabeth Ferm, the objects of much attention in the interviews. "The school was run by saints," Roger Baldwin remarks. "Alexis and Elizabeth Ferm were so dedicated, so self-sacrificing, that no setback or discouragement—and there were many—could stop them from carrying out their mission." The Ferms—Uncle and Aunty, as they were called—were among the earliest pioneers of libertarian education in the United States. In 1901 they started a free school in New Rochelle, New York, moving to Brooklyn and then to the Lower East Side, before ending up at Stelton in 1920. Both—and especially Aunty—were strong personalities who left a deep impression on the Ferrer movement, in which they were active for nearly thirty years. The Ferms left Stelton in 1925, only to return eight years later. Aunty died there in 1944, after which Uncle retired to a single-tax colony in Fairhope, Alabama, where he died in 1971.

Meanwhile, in 1923, a new colony had sprung up on Lake Mohegan, New York, with a Modern School of its own that lasted for two decades. The Mohegan school opened in 1924 under the direction of James and Nellie Dick, who were also in charge of the children's boarding house. Both had been ardent proponents of libertarian education in England, where they had founded Modern Schools in Liverpool and London. Emigrating to the United States in 1917, they supervised the boarding house at Stelton until their move to Mohegan. In 1928 they returned to Stelton as coprincipals, before starting their own Modern School at Lakewood, New Jersey, which continued for twenty-five years, closing in 1958. For half a century, then, the Dicks had played a major role in the Ferrer movement on both sides of the Atlantic.

The closing of the Lakewood school marked the end of the Modern School movement in America. To preserve its legacy, however, a group of former teachers and pupils met in 1973 and established the Friends of the Modern School. In September of that year the new organization held its first annual reunion at Rutgers University, a stone's throw from the defunct Stelton Colony. Since that time Rutgers has become the repository of the Ferrer movement archives, and hundreds of pupils and teachers, colonists and friends have attended the reunions, among them Nellie Dick, her son James Junior, and the children and grandchildren of Leonard Abbott, Harry Kelly, and Joseph Cohen, three of the principal founders of the movement. From all over the country the alumni of the New York, Stelton, Mohegan, and other Modern Schools have gathered each year to take part in lectures and symposiums and to deposit material in the Rutgers collection.

In addition to Stelton and Mohegan, residents of two other anarchist colonies, Home, near Tacoma, Washington, and Sunrise, in the Saginaw valley of Michigan, have been interviewed for the present collection. As in Stelton and Mohegan, the colonists at Home and Sunrise sought to recapture a more natural and harmonious life, unspoiled by industrial and urban blight, and to create a freer world in which they could direct their own affairs in accordance with libertarian values. A central assumption, as in Stelton and Mohegan, was that the anarchist ideal of a society without coercive authority or economic oppression would be realized, at least in part, through the education of children uncorrupted by the commercialism and selfishness of the capitalist system and undisturbed by political repression or by the indoctrination in religion or government practiced in the traditional school.

Both Home and Sunrise, accordingly, boasted schools of a libertarian type. Although not called Modern Schools or affiliated with the Ferrer Association, they were run on principles similar to those evolved by Ferrer and his disciples. At Home, founded in 1896, the execution of Ferrer was the occasion for mourning. One colonist named his son after Ferrer and kept a bust of the Spanish educator on his mantelpiece. *The Agitator*, a journal published at the colony, called itself "A Semi-Monthly Advocate of the Modern School, Industrial Unionism, and Individual Liberty," and carried articles on "The Martyrdom of Ferrer" and the "Necessity for the Modern School," as well as contributions by Bruce Rogers, director of the Modern School in Seattle. George H. Allen, one of the community's original settlers, contrasted public education with the "liberty of thought and action allowed in our school," of which he himself was the first teacher. As in the Modern Schools, crafts, play, field trips, and sex education had an important place in the Home curriculum. Nor was adult education neglected, with lectures, courses, and study groups offered on such subjects as eugenics, Esperanto, and oriental philosophy. Guest lecturers included Emma Goldman, who visited the colony several times, and plans were begun for the creation of a "Liberty University of the Northwest," a project that, however, remained unrealized.

Home Colony, situated on a small bay framed by sloping woods in a remote corner of the nation, endured for a quarter-century before its formal dissolution, making it one of the longest-lived American communitarian experiments. By contrast, the Sunrise Co-operative Farm Community, founded in 1933, barely outlasted the decade. Although farming was the main endeavor, the colonists were conspicuously unqualified for agricultural labor, being mostly city workers of East European Jewish background, bred in urban surroundings and skilled in industrial trades. A few, including the founder, Joseph Cohen, had previously lived at Stelton or Mohegan, while one, Yetta Bienenfeld, had been a teacher at the Detroit Modern School before the First World War. At Sunrise, however, the school was not the focus of community life; and cultural events, while not ignored (guest speakers included Rudolf Rocker, the foremost living German anarchist, and Agnes Inglis, curator of the Labadie Collection in Ann Arbor), took a back place to economic survival in the midst of the great Depression. From its inception, unfortunately, the colony was plagued by personal rivalries, factional quarrels, and economic hardship, causing many members to leave. In 1937 a remnant moved to Samos, Virginia, disbanding there in 1940.

• AMOUR LIBER •

Bronx, New York, April 17, 1973

Amour Liber was the first pupil to enroll in the New York Ferrer School when it opened in October 1911 on East Twelfth Street. He was accompanied by his father, Dr. Benzion Liber (1875–1958), a Rumanian-born physician, hygienist, founder of the Free Acres single-tax colony, treasurer of the Anarchist Red Cross, and author of a dozen books and scores of articles on diet, health, and the like.[334] Among Amour's fellow pupils were Magda Boris Schoenwetter (q.v.) and his cousins Hyperion, Gorky, and Révolte Bercovici (q.v.), the children of Konrad and Naomi Bercovici, Benzion Liber's younger sister. Amour, like his father, went on to study medicine. He taught at the Albert Einstein School of Medicine and served as chief pathologist at the Bronx Veterans' Hospital, where I interviewed him in his laboratory. He died in 1974.

MY FATHER was born in Rumania. His name was originally Librescu, which he changed to Liber in the United States; his brother changed Librescu to Liberty. From Rumania my parents went to Paris, where I was born in 1905 (French is my native tongue). We came to the U.S. soon afterwards.

In 1911, when I was six, Father brought me to the Modern School on East Twelfth Street. I was the first pupil, along with a pretty girl in a blue sweater named Ruth. We called her "Ruth the Beaut." Our first teachers were the Coryells,[335] and I was very fond of them. After school I visited their home. When they left after a few months, they were replaced by Will Durant. He was a fine teacher, but to be the Coryells' successor was an unenviable fate. The children all loved the Coryells, so at first he had a hard time. We played pranks on him, and he didn't know why. But with great patience and kindness he overcame our hostility and became very popular.

I was at the school only a few months and didn't go on to 107th Street. I don't know why Father withdrew me, but after that he taught me himself, at home, until I was ready for high school (Townsend Harris). I went on to Cornell, then studied medicine in France. While teaching me, Father started a small school at home for two or three pupils, which lasted intermittently for several years. He was a general practitioner till about 1925, when he began to specialize in psychiatry. He wrote a dozen books and was also a good amateur artist. He was a founder of the Free Acres Colony and we went there for the summers. We knew Bolton Hall well, a wealthy corporation counsel. Father mingled with all the radicals without ever adopting a permanent label. Unfortunately he did not save his papers.

Joseph Ishill's first wife was a relative of ours from Rumania named Sophie Sommer, who died around 1920. Then he got together with Rose Freeman.

• RÉVOLTE BERCOVICI •

New York City, September 29, 1977

Révolte ("Rada") Bercovici is the daughter of the Rumanian-born writer Konrad Bercovici (1882–1961), author of *The Story of the Gypsies* (1928), *Around the World in New York* (1938), *It's the Gypsy in Me* (1941), and other works of biography, travel, and fiction. Together with her brothers Gorky and Hyperion, Rada attended the Children's Playhouse School on the Lower East Side, conducted by Alexis and Elizabeth Ferm, and the Modern School of New York on East Twelfth Street, along with Amour Liber (q.v.) and Magda Schoenwetter (q.v.). Her sister

Mirel, present at the interview, had been married to William Morris Abbott, son of Leonard D. Abbott, a leading figure in the Modern School movement. Rada died in 1993, at the age of eighty-six.

I AND MY BROTHERS, Hyperion and Gorky, were at the Ferrer School from the beginning, along with our cousin Amour Liber [q.v.]. There were also Stuart Sanger, Magda Boris [Schoenwetter, q.v.], and Anne and Arundel, two girls from the South. Our teachers, the Coryells, were very nice. We were wild, very badly behaved. The janitor, Frank the Crank, chopped a cat's head off to teach us "about life." A lot of society people came to visit. It was like going to the zoo!

Will Durant replaced the Coryells. We didn't like him at all. He was not a good teacher. He was interested in lecturing to the adults, and all sorts of things, but not in teaching children. "There comes the faker," we said when we saw him approaching. We wanted to kill him. So we danced around him in a circle, like Indians on the warpath, drawing closer and closer. And that frightened him a little. We didn't like the school because we didn't like Durant.

The person I liked the best was Robert Henri.[336] He would talk to us about Paris, about art. The man knew color, the man knew life. So I used to get up and dance for him. He was a natural teacher. Emma Goldman came too. She was a lovely person, but wasn't interested in kids. She much preferred lecturing. But I liked to listen to her. She was full of fire. Emma, by the way, together with Alexander Berkman, came to see my parents in Paris during the 1920s. She was broken-hearted about Russia. She wept, and Sasha went over and patted her shoulder.

Before the Ferrer School, I can remember Aunty and Uncle Ferm's school on Madison Street. They were very sweet people, very nice people. Aunty played the piano—badly. Mr. and Mrs. [J. Stanwood] Menken used to come to the school. He was a wealthy man, and they came in a big car. She was a sweet woman, a little old lady who was interested in "doing good." Johanna Cook, a real American libertarian, came often to the school. We all loved her. My mother had her own school, in Hewlett, Long Island, for a few months around 1910.

• DAVID LAWSON •

Brooklyn, New York, November 17, 1977

David Lawson, a Scottish-born engineer, was the companion of Lola Ridge, "our gifted rebel poet," in the words of Emma Goldman, who thought her "a sweet and lovely spirit."[337] Ridge was the first organizer (i.e., manager) of the Francisco Ferrer Association in New York, where she and Lawson met in 1911. "There was a nice young man," said Gussie Denenberg (q.v.) of Lawson, "who always accompanied her. Without him she couldn't do much. He was on her right-hand side all the time." In 1912 Ridge became the first editor of *The Modern School* magazine, for which Lawson designed the cover. She herself contributed poems to the paper, as well as to Goldman's *Mother Earth*, and recited a poem to Goldman and Alexander Berkman at a farewell dinner on the eve of their deportation in 1919. In 1927 she marched on a picket line in Boston to protest against the death sentence for Sacco and Vanzetti and wrote some of the finest poems inspired by that tragic case.

I WAS BORN in Glasgow, lived in Boston, and came to New York around 1910 [he is about ninety-two]. I was interested in socialism at that time and heard about the Ferrer Association on St. Mark's Place. Bayard Boyesen gave up his job at Columbia University to teach there. He was a nice-looking man who liked his cocktails. Emma Goldman's niece Stella Comyn [Ballantine] liked him and tried her damnedest to get him—and probably did sometimes. James F. Morton[338] taught Esperanto. He was a man of medium height, on the blond side, with whiskers but no beard.

One night we had an affair there to raise money. There was a lot of food left over. "Why don't you bring in some people who need this stuff?" someone asked. So I went out to the Bowery and found hungry men, one after another, a whole procession of them, who followed me to the Ferrer Center and ate up everything. I met Lola Ridge at the Ferrer Association. We used to go there almost every night. It was Konrad Bercovici who conducted her around the Lower East Side, where she saw the Jews for the first time.

The school moved from St. Mark's Place to East Twelfth Street. I designed the cover and lettering for the first issue of *The Modern School* magazine, which Lola edited. And I was the first one to contact Will Durant. I went over to his home in New Jersey and invited him to come to the school. Lola and I met Jack London[339] at East Twelfth Street. Margaret Sanger[340] came too, and Ben Reitman and Bill Haywood. All the people who came were people with ideas and wide interests. Robert Henri taught art at night—gratis—to children and adults. Alexander Berkman—Sasha—was a beautiful person. You could see it all over him. You could see it in his face, his features, his character, his movements. I can see his face in front of me right now.

Lola and I left New York in 1912 and traveled around the country for five years. Before we left, there was a big benefit for the Ferrer Association at Webster Hall. We traveled all over the country. In New Orleans we sent for her son, who was living out West. We came back in 1917.

We rejoiced over the Russian Revolution. At that time it looked as if the whole world would open up. We had an ideal vision of the Revolution, of the possibilities that lay ahead. We were all for the working man, you know.

• MANUEL KOMROFF •

Woodstock, New York, September 29, 1972

As a young man of versatile gifts, Manuel Komroff was one of the most vital figures at the Ferrer Center in New York, where he attended the art class of Robert Henri and George Bellows, drew a cover for Emma Goldman's *Mother Earth*, and wrote avant-garde plays for Moritz Jagendorf's (q.v.) Free Theatre. During this time he also became an art critic for the *New York Call* and editorial writer for the *Daily Garment News*. When the Russian Revolution broke out in 1917, Komroff went to Petrograd and edited *The Russian Daily News*, published in English. After the Bolshevik seizure of power, he left the country by way of Siberia and went to Shanghai, where he worked on *The China Press* for several months before returning to America.

Back in New York, Komroff worked as an editor of The Modern Library, then owned by the firm of Boni & Liveright, while embarking on a career as a novelist and story writer that earned him a measure of fame. He published more than fifty books, the best known being *The Grace of Lambs* (1925), *Juggler's Kiss* (1927), and *Coronet* (1930). At the same time, he was an accomplished painter, carpenter, photographer, and cook. When I interviewed him at his home in Woodstock, New York, he prepared a delicious omelette with home-grown mushrooms and eggs from a nearby farm. An affable man of medium height, with a neatly trimmed white mustache, he was then engaged in writing his memoirs. Entitled "A Story Teller's World," it had not been completed at the time of Komroff's death from cancer on December 10, 1974.[341]

I WAS BORN in New York City on September 7, 1890. In 1911, when the Ferrer Center opened, I had been going to lectures at the Rand School[342] downtown on Fifteenth Street. I had attended Yale for two years and was interested in art, music, and wood crafts. But the Rand School disappointed me. I didn't like Marx: he was so cumbersome! I didn't like his materialist interpretation of history. I felt that it didn't explain Napoleon or St. Francis of Assisi or a lot of other important things in history. Nor did I care for his theory that the revolution would come first in advanced industrial countries. And he was autocratic and dogmatic. On the Rand School bulletin board I saw a notice of a lecture at the Ferrer Center. I liked the place at once. I then read *An Appeal to the Young* by Kropotkin. It just hit me, a young unadjusted man. I followed it with *Mutual Aid* and *Fields, Factories and Workshops*. I loved Kropotkin. I became a philosophical anarchist, but also a pacifist and opposed to terrorism.

At the Ferrer Center we all felt that what we were doing was important. I heard people speak on different subjects that I never dreamed existed: Joseph McCabe[343] on his thirteen years in an English monastery; Theodore Schroeder[344] on phallic symbols and free speech; Clarence Darrow, whom I introduced several times when Leonard Abbott was not there; Will Durant on "Havelock Ellis, Sex, and Society," a course of six lectures. After one of the latter Mrs. Konrad Bercovici got up and said in a thick Jewish accent: "Mr. Durant, I don't want to ask a question, and I don't want to make a discussion, but I myself have personally been in the sexual movement for fifteen years and I can see no progress."

The Ferrer Center became my whole education. It taught me everything I know and opened up new worlds. I attended the Henri-Bellows art class. The class had nude models, both male and female, unusual for those days. Henri spoke with hypnotic effect, sort of Chinese-looking with his high cheek-bones. He was a great teacher, though I always felt there was some shadow over him. Bellows was more direct, like the Yankee baseball player he was, without Henri's magnetism, nor as cultured. They gave me a sense of values that was not political, that was not tied up with money. You don't know what you missed! We had wonderful times—not a nickel, but wonderful times!

Leonard Abbott was tall, lean, and born in Liverpool. He spoke fine English and was a lovable man. He knew Kropotkin, Morris, the Fabian Socialists, and so drifted into socialism and anarchism when he came to the United States. Morris and Whitman were among his favorite writers. I spoke at his funeral in 1953. Harry Kelly was small and thin with a straw-colored mustache. He spoke with horse sense. After one of his lectures someone in the audience asked, "If everyone is free to do as he wants, how can an orchestra play one piece? What if I marched down the aisle playing 'Yankee Doodle Dandy' on the piccolo?" Kelly said, "Then we'd take you by the collar and throw you out."

Alexander Berkman was only a shadow of what he could have been, while Emma Goldman did fulfill herself. She did wonderful things. But she was a very jealous woman. She thought she owned anarchism and that we—the Ferrer Center—were poaching on her preserve. By the Ferrer Center I mean Abbott, Kelly, Joseph Cohen, Stewart Kerr,[345] and myself, as against the *Mother Earth* office nearby.[346] There was a certain rivalry between the two. Emma had a strong, powerful voice, but ugly with a guttural Russian accent. No one at her lectures ever said, "Louder, please." Ben Reitman went down the aisles selling anarchist literature. She was thoroughly unattractive and not an inspiring person, for all her good work. She didn't touch people the way Kelly or Abbott did.

Joseph Cohen was a former cigar maker from Philadelphia, and in New York he still rolled cigars for his friends. He was a wonderful fellow, quiet, never mixed up with violence. He spoke on occasion, but not too well. Hippolyte Havel was often maudlin and occasionally suicidal. In 1913–1914, when he edited the *Revolutionary Almanac* (the "angel" who paid for it was a Greek tobacco importer named John Rompompas, who came to the Ferrer Center lectures), he lived in the Hermitage on Fifteenth Street, where John Reed[347] also had a room. I visited him one day and smelled gas. The door was locked. Then Jack Reed came up the stairs. I called him—he was a big fellow—and he broke in the door. We opened the windows and Havel came to. He later was a dishwasher and cook—not a waiter—at Polly's Restaurant in the Village.

Sadakichi Hartmann was a tall, skinny fellow. His father was a German officer and his mother a Japanese girl, and he inherited the worst traits of both races. When I went to Hollywood to write film scripts I was warned not to let him know I was there, or "he'll touch you." But he had a fine, sonorous voice, which today would be thought too dramatic. He recited Whitman and Poe. When opened, his mouth was toothless except for two tusks. He played the main thief in Douglas Fairbanks Senior's *The Thief of Baghdad*, but disappeared near the end of the filming, then demanded more money to finish. On the other hand, Alfred Stieglitz[348] said his book on Japanese prints was fine and that he was one of the best photographers in the United States.

Other people at the Ferrer Center included Joseph Kucera, a Bohemian machinist and Voltairine de Cleyre's last lover. He had the manuscript of her translation of Louise Michel's memoirs, which was never published. Adolf Wolff[349] was a Belgian sculptor, a faker and poseur who left a trail of debts. He was in Henri's art class with me, and his former wife became the mistress of Man Ray,[350] who had also been in our class. Wolff wrote poetry too—lousy poetry. Both of the Durants were anarchists—she definitely so, he leaned that way. They were married before a judge at City Hall, and Ariel's mother was there too because her daughter was only fifteen. The judge shook his finger at Will and said, "Remember, now, don't sleep with her until she's sixteen!" It was not to City Hall that Ariel came on roller skates but to a lecture at the Labor Temple, after Durant told her to stay home and wash the dishes. She skated down all the way from the Bronx, then into the hall and down the aisle to the podium.

One of the Bercovici boys, Gorky or Rion, tried Durant's libertarian principles by standing on the classroom windowsill and threatening to jump. Konrad Bercovici once used the schoolroom on East Twelfth Street for a gypsy party and broke up the place. The walls were spattered with wine. Benno's father jumped bail in England, put up by Kropotkin, and fled to the United States. Eugene O'Neill often came to the Ferrer Center lectures. Bill Shatoff was one of the few Russians in the anarchist movement to come to the Center. He was a linotype operator for *Golos Truda*. He had a powerful voice and spoke without notes, yet they hung on every word. The Lexington Avenue bomb was intended for Rockefeller's offices in the Standard Oil building on lower Broadway.[351] The use of violence was much discussed at the Ferrer Center, and the expropriation of property was also a subject of heated debate: Was it or was it not right?

Before the First World War I was in dental college with Johann Most's son [John J. Most, Jr. q.v.], who graduated and became a dentist. I, fortunately, dropped out. I was John Reed's assistant at the Paterson Strike Pageant in Madison Square Garden in 1913. That same year I began my career as a journalist, as an art critic for the *New York Call*. In 1917 I went to Russia by way of Vancouver, Japan, and the Trans-Siberian Railroad, along with Shatoff and other Russians of the Golos Truda Group. Shatoff became the Danton of the Russian Revolution, a very powerful speaker. I occupied a room in his apartment, so I had a front seat for the Bolshevik Revolution. I was a journalist for a British paper. I left at the end of 1917, then spent a year in China. When I returned to the U.S. I reviewed silent pictures for *Film Daily*. Then I worked for Boni and Liveright, in charge of production and of the Modern Library series, which was later sold to Bennett Cerf. It took me two years to get over my disillusionment after the Bolshevik Revolution. I studied Gestalt psychology in Wolfgang Koehler's laboratory in 1927. I have two dishes of Kropotkin's from Russia, given me by his daughter Sasha [Alexandra Kropotkin, q.v.].

I am still an anarchist today. Our government is now more corrupt than Tammany Hall early in the century. I feel closer to Jefferson and Thoreau than ever. True, technology today hinders decentralization, yet anarchism is still a happy way of living in a small community—for artists, if not for businessmen. Businessmen are crocodiles who swim in a money stream.

• BENJAMIN G. BENNO •

New York City, September 24, 1972

Benjamin Benno (born Greenstein) immigrated to the United States from London in 1912 and attended the Ferrer School in New York, where he studied art with Robert Henri and George Bellows. Inspired by their example, he embarked on a career as an artist, acquiring a reputation as an original painter and sculptor. When I interviewed Benno in his small Greenwich Village apartment, cluttered with old filing cabinets, shoe boxes, and mattresses, he was long past his prime as an artist. Tall and lean, with a white beard on a young face, he wore a faded green beret and carried an ornately carved walking stick, giving the appearance of a typical Village "character." Although an interesting conversationalist, with vivid recollections of his youth, he was agitated by a dispute with his landlord, who was attempting to have him evicted. Benno died in March 1980, at the age of seventy-nine. Eight years later an extensive selection of his art work was exhibited at the Jane Voorhees Zimmerli Museum of Rutgers University.[352]

I WAS BORN Benjamin Greenstein on June 2, 1901, in London. My father, Abraham Greenstein, was a diamond setter and goldsmith and an anarchist. He knew Kropotkin well. In the United States he became head of the Jewelry Workers' Union during the 1920s. In London my parents split up, and I lived with Kropotkin from the age of two to five. I was kidnapped by my mother's new husband and taken through Europe to Odessa, where we lived for several years. I came to the United States in 1912. I was a seaman for twenty-four years, a watchmaker, a taxi driver, and an artist, and I taught art during the early 1960s at Montana State University.

When I arrived in New York I was enrolled in a public school but found it hard to adjust and was unhappy. An anarchist friend of my father's recommended the Ferrer School. I liked it at once. There I was at home! I could draw, scribble, model with clay. I studied in the art class of Robert Henri and George Bellows. Bellows gave me the best art criticism I ever got in my life. The other pupils included several future artists of distinction: Man Ray, Jean Liberté, Niles Spencer, Martha Gruening (sister of Ernest), William Gropper, Sol Wilson, and many more. Adolf Wolff sculpted; Man Ray stole his wife. Wolff turned away from radicalism and became a reactionary. Sadakichi Hartmann often lectured on literature and art and read poetry. He was opportunistic, a con-man who sought patrons and felt the world owed him something. But he was an important historian of art, especially his two-volume history of American art.

Leonard Abbott? I loved him. That was a man, a beautiful person, like Kropotkin. Robert Minor and Manuel Komroff were then artists who later turned to writing. Mary Hansen and her daughter Heloise often came to the Ferrer Center. Heloise was pretty and wanted to be a dancer. Mary radiated the same beauty and saintly quality as Leonard Abbott and Kropotkin, clear and pure. I also knew the Durants, who still write to me. Puck Durant, Becky Edelsohn, and Eureka Marchand were among the voluntary nude models in the art class. Many wonderful people came out of that "lunatic fringe."

• MAURICE HOLLOD •

North Miami, Florida, December 20, 1972

As a youth, Maurice Hollod attended the Ferrer School in New York, where he met such figures as Emma Goldman, Alexander Berkman, Hippolyte Havel, and Sadakichi Hartmann. He later mingled with the anarchists in Washington, D.C., where he worked as a chiropractor. It was Eva Brandes (q.v.) who advised me to interview him in Florida, where he had retired. He died there of a heart attack in June 1973.

MY FATHER was a Russian revolutionary of the old school. He hid from the tsarist police and finally smuggled his family out of Russia. I was three when we came to New York. Father died of tuberculosis a few years later, when I was eight or nine, after we had moved to Pueblo, Colorado, for his health. He was correspondent for the *Forverts* for that area. When he died, in 1909, Mother was left penniless with three kids, and we moved back to New York, where we had a large family.

We lived on 107th Street near Fifth Avenue. I was attending P.S. 188 on 106th near Madison. One day in 1913, when I was around twelve, I met a kid in Central Park (his name was Charles Marin; I think he later went with his family to Spain) who went to the Ferrer School on 107th Street between Lexington and Park. He told me about the school and took me over there. He led me upstairs to a classroom. There was a long table with a group of kids around it. In the center was a tall man [Leonard Abbott] peering through a microscope at a drop of blood on a slide, explaining to the kids what they were seeing under the scope. I became so entranced that I made up my mind on the spot that I'm going to this school. That was it! It opened my eyes to what a school could be.

I went home and said, "Momma, I'm not going to public school any more. I'm going to a private school a few blocks from here." I told her it was called the Ferrer School, and she had heard about it. "No, you're not going to that school," she said. And we had quite a tussle there, but I went. She was certain that my education would be aborted at that point, that it would go no further.

On my third day in the school I acted a little smart-alecky. Cora Bennett Stephenson[353] was the head of the school. She was the most lovable person I ever met. She said to me, "I don't think you're ready for class yet. I think you want to play. So why don't you go out in the yard today?" She said this calmly and without any hostility. I thought, what kind of school is this where they punish you by letting you play? I played in the yard all day. And the next day too. The next day I told Mrs. Stephenson that I didn't want to go into the yard again. She said, "Do you feel ready to sit down and work with the rest of the class?" I said yes. "All right, come in." Can you imagine the difference between this type of discipline and that in the public schools of that day, a military type of discipline, a barracks discipline? That was exactly the way it happened.

As much as that school meant to me, the Ferrer Center meant much more. That's where things were happening! I got to know people from all parts of the world and all parts of the radical spectrum. All of them found their way to the Ferrer Center. Living three blocks away, I was able to attend many of the evening affairs. I practically lived there. I was home so rarely that Mother went to Bill Shatoff and begged him to talk to me, which he did. But there was no keeping me away. It was more exciting than the school. The lectures by Will Durant always drew large crowds. Charles Sprading lectured there. Famous actors and artists came. There was a mumbo-jumbo of radical elements. The anarchist tendency predominated, but there were socialists and unaffiliated radicals too. Hippolyte Havel's *Revolt* was published there. I remember Sadakichi Hartmann giving a series of recitals from his five unpublished plays— *Christ, Buddha, Mohammed*, and so on. He was a tremendous booze hound. He fell in love with the Ferrer gang, for they were the very warp and woof of what he stood for.

It was during the winter of 1913–1914 that Sadakichi gave his series. They ran an ad in *The Call*. The first night limousines pulled up with women in fur coats and lorgnettes, things never seen on 107th Street before! During the intermission he drank a pint of liquor to get primed for the second act. During one particularly obscene segment, the rich ladies all got up and walked out. Sadakichi and Hippolyte Havel used to walk from the Ferrer Center to Greenwich Village, with dollar bills they had bummed in their jacket pockets, and never missed a gin mill on the way down.

I used to divide my time between the Ferrer School and Ferrer Center, and also between the Ferrer Center and the Mother Earth Publishing Association. Emma Goldman and Alexander Berkman were not often at the Center. In fact,

Emma hardly came at all, neither to the school nor to evening lectures, while Berkman lectured to the students on a few occasions about education. They evidently wanted to keep the school free from association with their activities. Not that there was any rivalry between the two places. On the contrary, they were complementary, and both Emma and Sasha were strong supporters of the school.

Berkman was a very lovable character. Everyone who met him immediately fell in love with the man. He loved children. He was an impeccable dresser in a light grey suit with a Panama hat and cane, mustache and glasses. Once I saw him in the street and I ran instinctively to him. He stopped me and quietly told me to go home. I was crushed. But he later explained to me that he was being followed and didn't want me hurt.

I was at Union Square the day after the big unemployed rally when the police beat up Joe O'Carroll.[354] Sasha, Emma, and others spoke. Then suddenly about twenty or thirty feet from where I was standing there was a terrific commotion. They were beating up Wild Joe O'Carroll! Emma protested and called for a march of the hungry and homeless up Fifth Avenue to the Ferrer Center. A black flag was flying, and Becky Edelsohn was marching arm in arm with Charles Plunkett [q.v.]. She was a tremendously fiery person, always two steps ahead of Berkman or Goldman. She called for the immediate destruction of the capitalist system—a real propaganda-by-the-deedist! She was famous for her red stockings, which she was wearing that day. We marched up Fifth Avenue from Union Square to 107th Street. At Fifty-Ninth Street a black limousine was crossing and stopped momentarily for the crowd. Becky opened the door and spat in the face of the plutocrats. When we got to the Ferrer Center everyone lined up for a free meal, and those who wanted to were allowed to sleep on the floor.

Emma Goldman was also—in theory at least—a propaganda-by-the-deedist, if not as radical as Becky or Plunkett. One night she was to speak at an antiwar rally in Carnegie Hall, a united front of anarchists, socialists, and other radicals. I was in the *Mother Earth* office that afternoon, and she said to me, "The socialists will have literature there. I'm going to give you a bundle of literature to distribute for us." It was a cold night. I had the bundle under my coat. When I got to the balcony, two detectives from the Red Squad grabbed me and frisked me. Emma rushed over and hit one square in the face. "You dirty dog," she said, "leave the child alone. If we have any killing to do we'll do it ourselves and not ask children to do it." These things are fresh in my mind—I'm reliving them.

I saw Caron, Hanson, and Berg the night before the explosion on Lexington Avenue. The Ferrer Center had a basement with a tea room, a first floor for lectures, a large yard in back, a second floor for the school, and a third floor with rooms for rent. Teenage boys from the school stood guard that night and made sure no one from the outside got in. Berkman was at the meeting upstairs with Caron, Hanson, and Berg. In fact, he was not only there but was the central figure. There had been a number of earlier meetings, and Berkman attended them all. He hadn't gotten rid of his propaganda by the deed bent. At 1 A.M. the men came downstairs. I was wearing a button that said "GENERAL STRIKE." Berg saw the button and asked me if he could wear it at a mass meeting the following day. That was the last I saw of him because the explosion occurred in the morning.

Caron was a vibrant fellow. He had boundless energy. In the basement tea room he was always the center of attention. Adolf Wolff designed the urn for their ashes. Earlier that year he had published a poem on Frank Tannenbaum's occupation of St. Alphonsus's Church,[355] for which he got thirty days in jail for "inciting to riot." [Hollod recites the poem from memory with great feeling.] He was a painter, sculptor, and poet of sorts. When World War I broke out he became a Belgian nationalist and even called for the deportation of Berkman, Goldman, and the rest. Later he and Joe Brandes[356] were in my class in chiropractor school.

After the funeral celebration for Caron, Hanson, and Berg, the ashes remained in the urn in the basement of the Center. I and another boy named Fagin took the ashes and scattered them in Central Park. I don't know what became of the urn. [It was taken to the Stelton Colony the following year.] Wolff also wrote a poem for the special issue on the bomb explosion in *Mother Earth*. I was in the *Mother Earth* office when he wrote it. They had to go to press, and Emma said to him, "Adolf, be quick, we haven't much time." So he hurried and finished it.[357]

Leonard Abbott, by contrast, was a mild person. The Ferrer gang referred to him as "Sister Abbott" because of his softness, a man who couldn't harm a fly. He had a house way up in the Bronx, and we kids used to go up there and pick cherries from his cherry tree. Alden Freeman[358] supported Will Durant, sent him to Europe and to graduate school. One of my patients in Washington turned out to be Freeman's former secretary, and she told me that in Freeman's last years he was indigent and only Durant sent him money.

There was also an Irishman at the Center named Sullivan, tall and burly, and the kids loved him. Some said he was a spy, but I never could believe that.[359] But there *was* a spy at the Center named Spivak. A letter he sent to the Burns Detective Agency was returned to the Center for insufficient postage. Abbott noticed the address, opened it, and saw it was a report on the Center by Spivak.

Dr. Charles Andrews, son of the nineteenth-century anarchist [Stephen Pearl Andrews], used to come to discussions and lectures. David Ross (Rosenthal) married a Yuster and became a famous radio announcer. Heloise Brown as a kid was the most beautiful, delightful girl you ever saw.

After two years in the school I went to Cora Bennett Stephenson and said I'm ready to go to high school. I got a diploma signed by her and Abbott and Kelly. I went to Townsend Harris High School and gave the diploma to the principal. As he read it his face got redder and redder, then he threw the thing in my face and yelled, "Get out of here or else I'll throw you out!" So Momma was right after all, I thought. While walking down Amsterdam Avenue, with tears streaming down my face, I ran into Sullivan and told him what had happened. He tried to comfort me, and bought me a soda. When I came home Mother said, "What did I tell you, what did I tell you?" I enrolled in Paterson (New Jersey) High School for a year, then transferred to DeWitt Clinton in the Bronx, where one of my teachers was Bertram D. Wolfe.[360]

During my year in Paterson, Emma Goldman and Ben Reitman hired a hall near one where Billy Sunday was meeting, a sort of counterpropaganda. I saw her in the alcove that afternoon, pacing up and down and going over her notes for the speech that evening. But the hall burned down (it was probably arson) and the meeting was never held.

After the school moved to Stelton, the Ferrer Center remained active until we entered the war. Then the police were there every night, arresting and harassing the boys. So much was happening, so much was packed into just a few years: that's what's so amazing to me.

Jack Isaacson lived on 102d Street, east of Lexington Avenue. Every morning he would go to the corner for the *New York Times*. On July 4 he heard an explosion and a piece of a body—a man's arm—fell at his feet. It happened in Louise Berger's[361] apartment. (She once gave me a copy of Berkman's *Prison Memoirs of an Anarchist*.) She knew of the plot, but one of the men, her brother if I'm not mistaken, had her spend the night with someone else. A Wobbly named Mike Murphy happened to be spending the night there, and when the place blew up his bed fell into the apartment below. He was dazed and shaken up and lost some clothing, but got away with minor bruises.

Jack Isaacson was an editor of the New York *Freedom* in 1919 and took responsibility for an article which the government called seditious. He was ordered deported but went underground and took the surname of his wife, Gussie Denenberg [q.v.]. He was active for many years in the Washington, D.C. group, which centered in the home of Lillian Kisliuk Dinowitzer and included myself, Wally Krimont, and others. Lilly Dinowitzer had a large, rambling house that was the radical center in Washington. It was also a nursery school from the late 1920s to the late 1940s—not a Ferrer School but a progressive school mainly on Montessori lines. Her father [Max Kisliuk] was a pioneer anarchist in Atlantic City, and she was the only one in the family to follow in his footsteps. During the Palmer era she and a few others tried to hire a hall to discuss the situation in Russia, and after much difficulty finally got one and held a series of meetings in defense of the Russian Revolution. She held regular soirées in her house for many years, and when Emma Goldman came to the U.S. in 1934 she stayed there. I saw Emma there and heard her speak, in a hall rented by Lilly. She was just as she had been when I knew her as a kid—the fire was still there.

Jack Denenberg inherited Max Kisliuk's library and had a large collection of his own. He had a little grocery store in Washington with a pot-bellied stove in the center and his books all around, and he would read when not waiting on customers. All those years, by the way, he was madly in love with Eva Brandes [q.v.]. Did she tell you that? After the Second World War his wife applied for her citizenship papers, and the authorities, while checking, discovered him and reopened his deportation case. They hounded him, you know. He was a very gentle, sensitive human being. I knew of no man who gave of himself as much as Jack. They don't make them that way any more. Finally he said, "If you want to deport me, then deport me." "Oh, no, Mr. Denenberg, we don't want to deport you." Yet they kept on hounding him, questioning him every other week, until he broke down.

One evening, in April 1946, I saw him at someone's house and he looked unusually cheerful, as if some heavy weight had been lifted from his shoulders. He was smiling, talking animatedly, but would often rub his neck with his fingers. That bothered me, so when I was ready to leave I went up to him and said, "It's good to see you in such good spirits, Jack, but why did you keep rubbing your throat?" At that his eyes opened wide, he reared back, and fled from the house. He hanged himself in his grocery the following morning.

• ROSE GOLDBLATT •

New York City, October 20, 1975

Rose Goldblatt was the sister of Helen and Lillian Goldblatt, young anarchists at the Ferrer Center in New York who were close to Emma Goldman and Alexander Berkman. In 1913 and 1914 Helen and Lil were involved in unemployed demonstrations and in protests against the Ludlow massacre, in which Colorado miners and their families were slaughtered by vigilantes and militiamen during one of the bitterest labor disputes in American history. In July 1914 Helen's boyfriend, Arthur Caron, was blown up with two comrades while preparing a bomb intended for John D. Rockefeller, Jr., the principal owner of the Ludlow mines. Helen later got together with Jacques Rudome (q.v.) and lived for many years at the Mohegan Colony.

MY OLDER SISTERS, Helen and Lillian Goldblatt, were active anarchists in the United States. They took part in the Tarrytown free-speech fight of 1914[362] and spent a short time in the Blackwell's Island workhouse, where Alexander Berkman corresponded with them. They knew Berkman, Emma Goldman, and Margaret Sanger, and were active in the Ferrer Center in Harlem. Helen was born in Warsaw on October 21, 1897, and died of leukemia at Mohegan on January 30, 1963. Lillian was born in 1895 and died on March 1, 1967. I was born in 1902, the youngest of the three.

Both of my sisters—especially Helen—were bright and did well at school in Warsaw. Father emigrated with his brother and went first to London, then on to the United States. He had studied for the rabbinate but threw it all over as nonsense and became a Zionist in America. Helen was five, Lil seven, and I six months old when he left. He sent for us in 1910. Prior to that, Mother had to take care of three small children. The wife of our doctor became interested in Helen, who was almost a genius, and asked Helen and Lil to tutor her children. In return, she paid their tuition at a Ferrer School in Warsaw, and it was there that they first came into contact with revolutionaries—the teachers were all revolutionaries—and revolutionary ideas. After the Ferrer School they went to the *gymnasium* and then came here.

We immigrated to New York in 1910 and lived on Orchard Street on the Lower East Side. Helen and Lil continued their education at night schools and worked as hat operators during the day. They met Jack Butler, Trauner, Morris Goldfarb (Bertha Butler's brother), and others who frequented the Ferrer Center. Margaret Sanger taught Helen and Lil to stop wearing the long skirts with tight corsets of the period and began to teach them to become comfortable.

So they went often to the Ferrer Center. And they walked all the way up to Tarrytown—it was a protest march—with Butler, Goldfarb, Maurice Rudome, Caron, Berkman, and several others. Caron came to visit us frequently at our apartment on Orchard Street. He was a very attractive young man, tall, dark, slender, part Indian, and an extremely fine person, charming and a gentleman in every sense of the word. He was crazy about Helen and became her boyfriend, though she was not yet his "sweetheart." She was small and he was about six feet tall, but she was quite a fighter and an extraordinary girl, and he adored her.

Helen and Lil were arrested with the group at Tarrytown. My parents were sick over the whole thing. But Mother, though religious, was very understanding and never interfered in our lives. They were at Blackwell's Island for a short period, and Berkman, then on a lecture tour, corresponded with them. They were horrified when the explosion occurred. They did not approve of such methods. What they wanted was protesting—a lot of protesting—but not bombing. They were deeply upset by exploitation and oppression by government and capital, but they were literally sick over the explosion and the loss of life. The horror of the whole thing for them cannot be exaggerated. In 1917 Louise Berger and many other Ferrer Center anarchists went back to Russia to take part in the revolution, and they were all slaughtered by the Bolsheviks.

After the Tarrytown episode, Helen and Lil moved up to 105th Street to live with Eva and Usher Bittelman, their dearest friends. But all of a sudden the Bittelmans gave up anarchism and became avid Communists. Lil for a time had hopes for Russia, too, and thought it was becoming a utopia along anarchist lines, with no exploitation or millionaires. Of course it was all a pipe dream. Yet in 1918 Lil went to Russia by way of Japan, though my parents tried to persuade her not to. She got to Japan and found that Russia had closed all entrances to the country, so she had to return to the U.S. after waiting vainly in Japan for about six months for Russia to open up. Helen wasn't interested in going to Russia. She never felt the same enthusiasm for the Bolshevik Revolution as Lil did, and at Mohegan was an active anti-Communist.

Lil's daughter by her first husband went to the Stelton school and hated Aunty Ferm, who was too authoritarian and a real disciplinarian. Uncle Ferm was just the reverse, always very sweet and gentle. Lil later remarried; her new husband was Howard Buck (not Jewish), who taught at Commonwealth College[363] and was an ardent single-taxer, a follower of Henry George, and talked about it morning, noon, and night—he really drove us crazy.

Helen got together with Jack Rudome [q.v.]—Morris's brother—sometime after Tarrytown. She went away with Eddie Cahill for a while, and that made Jack very angry. She and Jack went up to Mohegan in the later 1920s. They bought George Seldes's original plot and lived there for the rest of her life. They built the house there in 1937. Helen designed the plans and Bennett [Tony Di Benedetto, an Italian anarchist] built it.

Around that time the Communists were beginning to invade the place and take over. Helen was on the board, along with Anita Miroy and Eva Brandes [q.v.], and they fought them tooth and nail. It was a horrible period. Helen was so sick over it. She had a marvelous personality. She was very understanding, never judged or condemned anybody, never interfered with her friends' lives, but always defended them.

• GUSSIE DENENBERG •

Washington, D.C., March 20, 1973; New York City, August 25, 1973; Washington, D.C., December 29, 1976

From about 1910 Gussie Denenberg was involved in the anarchist movement in New York, Chicago, and Washington, D.C., and was acquainted with Emma Goldman, Alexander Berkman, and Voltairine de Cleyre, among others. Her husband, Jack Isaacson, threatened with deportation during the Red Scare of 1919–1920, adopted her surname and went underground. The two lived quietly for many years until his identity came to light. Hounded by the FBI, he committed suicide in 1946 (see interview with Maurice Hollod). Gussie died around 1980 at the age of about ninety.

I WAS BORN in Pinsk, Russia, eighty-two years ago and came to New York in 1906. Until 1911 I lived on St. Mark's Place near Second Avenue, next door to the first Ferrer School, which opened in 1910. I attended lectures there in the evening. Bayard Boyesen, a handsome young man, spoke on literature, with Dr. Paul Luttinger as chairman. Dr. Hillel Solotaroff lectured too. He was a well-known physician and an outstanding journalist, who died of cancer around 1917.[364] He and Dr. Michael Cohn were close friends, and Cohn treated his illness. Solotaroff wrote a weekly column for *Der Tog* for many years. Dr. Cohn had money but was very tight. Pryns Hopkins, from California, gave money to the school. These were all remarkable people, and it was during that time that I became an anarchist.

I moved to Chicago in 1911 and lived there for a year before returning to New York. Among the active anarchists there were Jake and Annie Livshis, William Nathanson, and Dr. Joseph Greer. I lived on Crystal Street, around the corner from the Livshises on Potomac Avenue, where Voltairine de Cleyre was living. Voltairine and Nathanson started a Modern Sunday School in Nathanson's mother's house on Twelfth Street, but it didn't last very long. Voltairine also gave private lessons in her room. My friend Fanny took English lessons from her in the evening. I went to her for a few math lessons. As she taught it, it seemed so easy compared with public school. She was rather tall, slim, pale, with a face you couldn't forget. Though she was not beautiful, she had wonderful eyes. She had a bullet in her since she was shot by a former pupil in Philadelphia in 1902. She was an intense speaker, overflowing with sympathy. When I went to her for lessons, I couldn't take my eyes off her, off the agony of her face. But you know, the Haymarket executions made her suffer more than the bullets in her body. I once attended a lecture in the Little Theatre of Chicago by Arthur Morrow Lewis, a socialist, who criticized Emma Goldman's *Anarchism and Other Essays,* and I heard Voltairine's voice call out behind me, challenging him to a debate.[365] After she died, there was a Voltairine de Cleyre Group in Chicago, including myself, Ida and Harry Miller, and a few others.

From Chicago I returned to New York and resumed going to the Ferrer Center, which moved to 107th Street in 1912. The place was a beehive of activity. Visitors included Jack London and Sidney and Beatrice Webb.[366] Lola Ridge, the poet, came every Sunday evening. She was fragile looking and intense and reminded me of Voltairine de Cleyre. She had the same spirit. There was a nice young man [David Lawson, q.v.] who always accompanied her. Without him she couldn't do much. He was right by her side all the time.

Joseph Cohen came to the Ferrer Center as the "organizer," which really meant the janitor or caretaker. He was called "the *shames*" [caretaker, in Yiddish], just as my husband Jack Isaacson was called "the rabbi," Alexander Berkman "the pope," and Emma Goldman "the red queen." The boys at the Center called Leonard Abbott "Sister Abbott," he was so gentle.

Cohen had been a cigar worker but was forced to quit because of his asthma and become the Center's custodian. He lived on the third floor of the building, while Jack and I lived on the first floor, taking Bill Shatoff's room after he left for Russia in 1917. Cohen fought with everybody and used to chase people away. During the war the Center became a haven for expatriates, and many young men came from France, England, and Italy, in order to escape the draft. But Cohen would chase them out. Pat Bannister, an Englishman, once got so mad at Cohen that he almost punched him. Cohen was a withdrawn person. He didn't get along with anybody. He had no special talent. His history of Jewish anarchism in America is lifted from Yanovsky. In the twenty-fifth anniversary book on Stelton he talks of a man who built the water tower single-handed but withholds his name—Moyshe Papagailo—because he didn't like giving people credit, unless it was himself.[367]

My husband Jack and Hippolyte Havel used to put out *Revolt* in the basement of the Center. (Jack later edited *The Hotel Worker*, a union publication.)
Jack and Hippolyte suspected Donald Vose[368] of being a spy. Jack saw a bulge
in his pocket where he kept a gun and said, "He is a hunter and he's going
hunting." At the *Mother Earth* office Vose heard Emma Goldman say,
"Schmidty, please fix the light," and he turned him in. Spivak [not Joseph
Spivak, q.v.] was another spy. He forgot to put a stamp on a letter with a report
to the police and it came back to the Ferrer Center. Leonard Abbott, seeing
the address, opened it, and Spivak was exposed. There was yet another spy,
Potocki, at both the Center and Stelton; he had been a spy in Philadelphia
before that. Minna Lowensohn lived[369] with him until he was exposed, and
they were supposed to go to Russia together.

Gussie Miller, who taught at the Ferrer School, was also a public school
teacher in Manhattan. Andrea Salsedo used to come to the Center. Adolf
Wolff, the sculptor, turned reactionary during the war and said that Emma
Goldman should be hanged from the nearest lamppost. Morris Becker[370] spent
two years in federal prison and then was deported to Russia. Anna Olay,[371] of
Chicago, committed suicide by taking an overdose of sleeping pills. Gray
Wu[372] was a cook at Stelton and at affairs in New York, a very brilliant guy, a
philosophical type. The Goodman sisters were twins who were raised in a Spi-
noza colony in Pennsylvania. Pryns Hopkins sent two teachers to Stelton from
his school in California, and they were caught shoplifting at Wanamakers' in
New York. The Stelton principal, William Thurston Brown, was so shocked, so
sick over the matter, that he and his wife left the colony. Louise Berger went to
Russia during the revolution and died of typhus.

In 1914 Louise had an apartment on Lexington Avenue and 102d Street,
where they were building a subway. My husband Jack then lived on 103d Street
a block away. One morning, on July 4, he was going for newspapers when an
explosion occurred. He saw an arm flying in the air and then fall to the street.
The bomb had been made outside the city and brought to New York the previous night. It was to be used on Rockefeller's house in Tarrytown that day, the
fourth. Louise (Carl Hanson's half-sister) was on her way to tell Berkman that
the bomb was ready when the explosion took place. Caron, Hanson, and Berg
were killed. They were fine comrades, but were so mishandled and mistreated
by the police at the Union Square unemployment demonstrations and Tarrytown free speech meetings that they were desperate and no longer cared. Berkman was the mastermind of the plot. He was outraged by Ludlow, Tarrytown, unemployment, police brutality. I liked Berkman better than Emma. She
was too self-centered, but she had great spirit. Before the Union Square demonstration, Plunkett [q.v.] told the comrades, "When you're arrested and asked
your occupation, tell them 'Killing cops.'"

Anarchism is a way of life, no matter what your view is of human nature. No
authority over you, no slaves under you—that's the anarchist life. So when I
think of Voltairine de Cleyre, when I think of Sasha and Emma—that's what
I think of. That was their way of life, a revolt against injustice and inhumanity.

• CHARLES PLUNKETT •

Long Valley, New Jersey, June 4, 1975

Charles Plunkett, a young activist at the Ferrer Center in New York, was involved in the Lexington Avenue conspiracy against John D. Rockefeller, Jr., in reprisal for the Ludlow massacre of 1914. He afterwards took a Ph.D. at Columbia University and became a professor of biology at New York University, where he wrote a standard textbook on the subject and served as chairman of the department. When I interviewed him at his New Jersey farm in 1975, Plunkett was eighty-two years old and nearly blind, with white hair and beard. Yet he retained a good deal of his youthful militance, calling Henry Kissinger the most dangerous man in the world and devoutly wishing for his assassination. Plunkett died in his ninetieth year in June 1981.

I WAS BORN in New York City, on West Ninety-Eighth Street, in 1892 (I'll be eighty-three this fall). My parents were also born in New York, and their parents in Cork County, Ireland. Father had been a plumber but became a building contractor, so we were a middle-class family, with a horse and carriage and an occasional servant. When I was a child we lived on 115th Street in Harlem, and then in the Bronx and in Queens. I attended public school and Morris High School in the Bronx, then Flushing High School, from which I was graduated in 1909 at sixteen. I won a state scholarship and a university scholarship at Cornell, class of '13. I was what they call a "brilliant student," always good at taking exams.

I always explored things and thought things out for myself. I never did anything by halves. As a child, brought up as a Catholic, I was intensely religious; if I pursued it I would have become a priest. That's the way I am. But at the age of eleven or twelve I read the Bible from cover to cover, and that finished me with religion. That was the end—bang!—of religion.

I'm not a skimmer or a picker, but like to read a thing through. From the age of fourteen to sixteen I began to think about social questions, about the rich and the poor. Why? I asked. And I came to the conclusion that property was the fundamental cause—I've never changed my mind about that—that the institution of property was a fundamental evil. That became, and still remains, the basic axiom of my political thinking.

During my years at Cornell I met people who called themselves socialists and anarchists. I joined the Inter-Collegiate Socialist Society, I read the *International Socialist Review* in the library, and I read *The Communist Manifesto*. From then on I adopted the communist label, which expressed my fundamental animus against private ownership. I also read the whole of *Capital*—all three volumes—just as I was later to read the whole of *Principia Mathematica*,[373] something very few people have done.

I also began to read up on anarchism. There was a sharp division between communist anarchism and individualist anarchism; and, though I have never liked the label, I began to consider myself a communist anarchist, with the accent on *communist*. From the age of fourteen or fifteen, as I said, I had no use for the doctrine of individualism, which was economically unjust, ethically vicious, and historically reactionary. The interests and desires of all individuals, I have since felt, must be subordinated to the general welfare.

Kropotkin was different, a communist as well as an anarchist, and I agreed with him to a large extent. I was very keen about his works, though I never accepted all of his ideas (I never agreed with anyone entirely). I especially liked *Mutual Aid*, which was strongly admired by a number of biologists, including my teacher at Columbia, T. H. Morgan,[374] who had a good deal of sympathy with anarchism. I equally admired *Fields, Factories and Workshops*, which became my social bible.

But, as I say, I never agree entirely with anybody. Why should one? One thinks things out for oneself even when one is influenced by others. To me there has always been one underlying theme: equality, to put it in one word. Liberty's a will-o'-the-wisp without equality. Economic justice has always seemed more important to me than freedom of speech, for example. More essential than being able to open one's mouth is being able to put some food in it. It is this criterion—equality, the economic criterion—that governs my definition of progressive and reactionary. If something tends to work against equality it is bad and in the opposite direction good. That hasn't changed with me over the years, not since I was fourteen or fifteen. In other respects, of course, I've changed—I'm not a dogmatist—but not that underlying concept.

In the summer of 1912, after my junior year at Cornell, I got a job in West Orange, New Jersey, with Thomas Edison. I was making moving pictures of the life history of insects. At the same time I became a member of the Socialist Party in West Orange, active in the election campaign of 1912, the high point of the Socialist Party in the United States. I regarded Edison as a reactionary, though he treated me nicely and invited me over for dinner, but I began to organize the workers in his shop, so that by the end of the year he had fired me.

By then I had become disillusioned with the Socialist Party, which was too conservative and reformist. So I went to New York and became an organizer for the IWW. The first place that I worked was in Paterson, during the 1913 strike, and then in Allentown and Williamsport, Pennsylvania. It was my own thinking that led me into all this, just as I had rejected religion at twelve and private property at fifteen. After the Bible I read Darwin and got interested in astronomy after hearing a lecture on the subject.

I always threw myself into things heart and soul. I never stopped halfway. I was no amateur. And so it was with the labor movement. In New York I began to organize among the textile workers, and especially for the Marine Transport Workers on West Street. Bob Warwick was secretary of the union, which had broken away from the conservative union and joined the IWW. Bob, who was also an anarchist and Wobbly, and I put out a few issues of a magazine called

The Social War in 1913. We wrote nearly all of it, though we probably used a few pseudonyms. We were anarchists in the general sense. There were no such sharp lines of demarcation in those days. We argued and scrapped, of course, we anarchists, Wobblies, and militant socialists, but we were able to remain friends. Jaime Vidal, an active anarchist, was the Spanish organizer for the Transport Workers, a man in his thirties or forties. Nearly all the Spaniards in that union were anarchists.

Unemployment was not as extensive or chronic in those days as it is now. But there was no unemployment insurance then, no welfare, but only soup kitchens. It was Frank Tannenbaum who started the whole unemployed movement going. He was a couple of years younger than me and worked as a busboy in a restaurant. In 1913 the IWW organized a strike of the hotel and restaurant workers. Frank joined the IWW and began his activity then. He used to listen to us talk—myself, Frank Strawn Hamilton, and others. (Hamilton had come from the West Coast, a friend of Jack London's.) Tannenbaum was just a boy and hung on our words. He didn't know anything and was anxious to learn. And he learned fast. In fact, he started the whole unemployment thing. It was quite spontaneous. No one put him up to it. It was his idea to occupy churches. But it grew very quickly and got too big for him. He couldn't handle it and came to us for help.

I was busy with my work for the Transport Workers and shouldn't have joined but did it anyway. At first things went smoothly. We went to a few Protestant churches without incident. But then we made the mistake of going to a Catholic church, St. Alphonsus. That brought the police—most of them Irish—crashing down on us. I got one month (on Blackwell's and Ward's Islands) and Frank got one year (on Blackwell's Island). I was a witness for the defense at his trial before an Italian judge named Freschi.

It was at this point that Arthur Caron and other unemployed workers joined the movement. He was about twenty-three or twenty-four with a slightly dark complexion and an aquiline nose, of medium height and strong build. We began to meet at Mary Heaton O'Brien's (later Vorse) house, and I stayed there for a few days. As it happened, on the night of our arrest at St. Alphonsus, there was a meeting at Mary O'Brien's where an organization was founded [the Labor Defense Committee] that was a forerunner of the ACLU. Frank Hamilton, who had slipped away from St. Alphonsus when he saw the police coming, went to Mary's house and told them what had happened. So ours became the first case. They hired Justus Sheffield as our lawyer. He had no sympathy for the anarchists or the IWW but was an old-style liberal who believed in free speech.

I'm the only one still alive who knows about Lexington Avenue, but I'm not going to tell you or anyone else. Why should I? After all, it was murder. But I can tell you some things. At the May First rally in Union Square, following the Ludlow Massacre, the police rode us down with horses and beat people so badly that it backfired on them when the victims showed up in court all bruised and battered. The cops were all Irish, all brutal, and hated everyone who was not Irish, especially Italians and Jews. I was injured, but not seriously. Joe O'Carroll was beaten very badly. Our response was ad hoc, a spur of the moment thing, nothing organized.

I had begun to attend the Ferrer Center in early 1914. I never belonged to the Ferrer Association and wasn't much interested in libertarian education—as I said, the economic question was uppermost for me—but it was a hangout, a place where people met and talked. Sadakichi Hartmann put on "perfume concerts," and Hippolyte Havel was often there; he was one of the more thoughtful of the anarchists and not to be laughed at.

We also went often to the *Mother Earth* office on 119th Street near Lenox Avenue, where Alexander Berkman was editor. I knew Berkman very well. He was not a great theoretician, like Kropotkin, but very intelligent, of medium height, and in his later forties. I liked him well enough, but he was too self-centered and dogmatic for my taste. He was no great man in any sense. A *really* great man was Bill Haywood, the driving force of the IWW. He was the heart and soul of the IWW from beginning to end. Did you know that the IWW never paid any of its officials more than eighteen dollars a week, Haywood included? He spent his last night in the U.S. in my house, before going to Russia.

Bill Shatoff was a Wobbly in spirit, but as an editor of *Golos Truda* he could not be a member of the IWW, since nobody who edited a non-IWW paper could be a member. He was often at the Ferrer Center, heavy-set, calm, capable. Carlo Tresca was never a member of the IWW, for the same reason, though Elizabeth Gurley Flynn was. I knew them both since the Paterson strike of 1913, and John Reed too. Flynn's remains are in the Waldheim Cemetery; I wonder why she didn't prefer to be buried in Moscow, where she died.

It was Berkman who started the free-speech fight at Tarrytown. That is, it was his idea to go up there, where Rockefeller lived, and protest and demonstrate against him. Berkman himself didn't go up there, though, as he was on probation for a previous arrest.[375] I went, and Caron, Hanson, Berg, Maurice Rudome, Jack Butler, two Italians named Frank and Jimmy—I can't recall their last names now[376]—and one girl, Becky Edelsohn. We all got arrested, and the next day we started a hunger strike in the Tarrytown jail.

It was a lark for us. We were young, cheerful, light-hearted, enjoying the excitement. But we were serious enough about Ludlow. The police were very attentive when we started our hunger strike. We were bailed out in May, and our trial was set for the end of July. We were in jail—Blackwell's Island—in August, about the time the war broke out. I was in jail for two months that time and was given a welcome at the Ferrer Center when released.

As I said, I'm the only one left who knows about Lexington Avenue. At the time only a few people were involved. They included Caron, Hanson, and Berg, of course. Hanson and Berg were Latvians and active in the Latvian movement. Louise Berger, Hanson's half-sister, knew about it; it was her apartment and she left it just minutes before the explosion. I knew about it, too, and in fact had spent the previous night, the night of July 2, in the apartment. Becky Edelsohn knew about it. And Alexander Berkman.

It was Berkman who organized it, though the others were to carry it out, as he was on probation. He was the only older man in the group, the only one with experience. Emma Goldman was not involved—in fact she was away on a lecture tour. Berkman still believed in the necessity of violence. Caron, Hanson, and Berg had been collecting dynamite for Russia and storing it in the apartment. It was the bomb that set it all off. I'll never know why they brought the damn thing back! They had brought it up to Tarrytown on the night of July 3. It was not intended for Rockefeller's house but for some other location in Tarrytown, the newspaper office perhaps. There was no intention of harming anyone but only to set off an explosion as a gesture of protest. Mike Murphy told me he knew nothing about it. It was my job to get him to Leonard Abbott's house in Westfield. From there we sent him to Chicago to lie low. He was asleep when the blast occurred and fell through to the floor below, but he still had his clothes on when I saw him.

I was at Abbott's place that day. So was Becky, and Helen Goldblatt, who was Caron's girl friend at the time—Helen of Troy, we called her. Caron, Hanson, and Berg were cremated out in Queens and their ashes put in an urn shaped in a pyramid with a clenched fist on top, designed by the sculptor Adolf Wolff. I was later married to Becky Edelsohn for nine years, and we had a son. Becky died in California about three years ago. She had lived in Emma Goldman's apartment since she was thirteen years old. She was the only girl at Tarrytown, kept in a separate jail. She was five feet four inches tall, moderately plump, with black hair; she was very pretty—beautiful, I should say—and very generous.

By the next year I had swung from dynamite to pacifism. I read Tolstoy. I became a conscientious objector when America entered the war and served another term in jail for refusing to register for the draft. For two years—in 1915 and 1916—I lived at Grantwood, New Jersey, part of Ridgefield actually. Manuel Komroff [q.v.] lived there too. It was a bunch of small houses, not a colony exactly, rented by artists, writers, and radicals.[377] There was also one big house, owned by Bob Brown.

I never went to Stelton. I wasn't interested in education but in the labor movement. It was in 1915 that I entered graduate school at Columbia, though I had never finished at Cornell. I got my Master's and Ph.D. (1926) in biology, working in genetics with T. H. Morgan. Then I taught at NYU for a dozen years and wrote an undergraduate textbook in biology. I retired and took up chicken farming in New Jersey, not far from here.

Leonard Abbott was one of the "New England liberals," a quiet man, rather bald, and had an income. He was not married to Rose Yuster, but his family threatened to withhold the legacy from his children unless he married. He asked our advice and we all said yes, except Berkman, who refused to compromise his principles. That's what I mean by his dogmatism. It was Berkman, by the way, who put all that stuff on Lexington Avenue in the July issue of *Mother Earth*. Emma was away and disapproved when she saw it. Did I mention Lingg in my Lexington Avenue speech?[378] Well, I'm not surprised. For many of us he was the ideal of the anarchist hero. The other Haymarket figures were not that special, but Lingg stood apart as an inspiration. He did not associate much with the rest.

Abbott did not engage in militant activity but was entirely sympathetic with it, not a pacifist, as I became, in the war. I didn't reject my pacifism till the Spanish Civil War, when the fascists launched their invasion. If 99 percent of the people are pacifists and only 1 percent are armed, the 1 percent will rule the rest.

Not that I had rejected revolution. I was very enthusiastic about the Russian Revolution and have admired the Soviet Union, Stalin included, ever since. I am a great admirer of Stalin to this day—not everything that he did, of course; Lysenko[379] was downright medieval. Stalin was necessary no matter how many were killed or imprisoned. He made the Soviet Union, and the Soviet Union was the only bastion to stop Hitler and fascism and to stop the United States from dominating the world, with its degenerate capitalism and morality.

But Kropotkin is also necessary. I hate big cities, and my ideal is a decentralized society with farms and small factories, as depicted in *Fields, Factories and Workshops* or William Morris's *News from Nowhere*. The concentration of private property must give way to economic equality, and for that to happen, revolution—and Stalin—are necessary, with Kropotkin's vision as the ultimate ideal. Barring a nuclear war, we may get there in about ten thousand years. Property, not government, is the primary evil. Government is secondary, existing only for the protection of property, a device of the privileged class to keep the rest of the people in subjection.

• MORITZ JAGENDORF •

New York City, April 14, 1972; May 28, 1973; February 23, 1978

Dr. Moritz Jagendorf, dentist, folklorist, and connoisseur of wine, was founder and director of the Free Theatre at the Ferrer Center in New York.[380] He wrote for Hippolyte Havel's *Revolt*, published in the basement of the Center, and afterwards for *The Road to Freedom* and its successor *Freedom,* of which he was coeditor with Harry Kelly and Louis Raymond (q.v.). He was also treasurer of the Mohegan Colony Association. When I first interviewed him, in the spacious living room of his apartment on Riverside Drive, he led me to a wine closet, "the best room in the house," he called it, and removed an 1889 Madeira. Over my protests not to waste it on a neophyte like me ("no time like the present," he insisted), he opened the bottle and poured its contents (it was excellent), consuming most of it himself. Jagendorf lived to the ripe age of ninety-two, dying in January 1981. In accordance with his wishes, his wake took the form of a wine-tasting party at the Cornell Club of New York.

I WAS BORN in 1888 in Chernowitz, Austria (now in the Soviet Union). I was always interested in the theater. At the age of eleven I organized a theater group among my friends and wrote plays for it. At thirteen I read Max Stirner's *Der Einzige und sein Eigentum*. The words "You can do as you wish" leaped out from the page, and I became the bane of my poor mother's life. We came to the United States in 1903. New York opened a new world to me. While an undergraduate at Columbia, I came across a copy of *Mother Earth*. Impressed, I wrote to Emma Goldman, who replied by advising me to come to the Ferrer Center. That was in 1911 or 1912.

The Ferrer Center was a seething ocean of thought and activity, everybody working and creating. Leonard Abbott, Harry Kelly, Joseph Cohen, and Hippolyte Havel were the mainstays of the place. Abbott was the first real Christian since St. Francis of Assisi. Havel was a friend of Eugene O'Neill's. O'Neill himself came only rarely to the Center, but we saw him often in Greenwich Village. One night he brought a bucket of beer to a party there. Christine Ell[381] boasted to all her friends that the taxi driver tried to rape her on her way over.

Many anarchists in those days habituated the Village. They went to the Liberal Club and Polly's Restaurant, both on MacDougal Street. Polly was Havel's lover, and he worked as a waiter in the restaurant. He was a heavy drinker and was once brought before a judge and fined five dollars for urinating in the street. He protested that the United States was the only civilized country without comfort stations. Havel used to hang around the Brevoort Hotel to cadge free drinks at the bar. One time, after Havel had been ejected by the bartender and had climbed back in through the window, an editor named Tom Smith bought him a few drinks and gave him his calling card. Havel got drunk, went outside, and sat down dazed on a stoop. A cop saw the card and brought him to Smith's house, where he fell asleep on a rug.

Sadakichi Hartmann also frequented the Ferrer Center and was a drinking pal of Havel's. He was very tall and very thin. He later acted bit and character parts in Hollywood. At the beginning of the 1920s I had a house on East Fortieth Street where Sadakichi read poems and gave lectures and often stayed the night.

Manuel Komroff [q.v.], another mainstay of the Center, was a talented writer but, though himself a Jew, had an anti-Semitic streak. He wrote one of the plays for the Free Theatre that I started at the Center. We also put on Pierre Louis and other radical playwrights, as well as the first production of Lord Dunsany in the U.S. In addition, we put on plays in the auditorium of Wanamaker's and did two performances on Broadway after being invited by a Broadway producer who had seen us at the Ferrer Center. I was asked to be the director of the Washington Square Players, which preceded the Provincetown Players, but I declined.

Apart from Havel, Hartmann, and Komroff, the regulars at the Ferrer Center included Bill Shatoff, with his booming voice; André Tridon,[382] who helped me with my plays, a tall, handsome newspaperman and poet; and Robert Minor, then an ardent anarchist, a big, slow-moving man. I also ran into him frequently at Romany Marie's restaurant in the Village. Another habitué was Adolf Wolff, the sculptor, a Belgian Jew, bearded and with a fat stomach. Wolff's former wife, Adon LaCroix, moved in with Man Ray at the artists' colony in Ridgefield, New Jersey, to the great inconvenience of his roommate. He was susceptible and fell in love with her, but she bullied and dominated and used him terribly. We visited Ridgefield a number of times, and she would brutally abuse him before everybody, while he would sit and say nothing. Man Ray was nothing until he got rid of her.

After the Ferrer Center closed, Wolff went to chiropractic school, but he never started a practice. He dropped out of the radical movement, never earned a penny, and lived by the sweat of the vagina of his girlfriend Vera, who was a successful designer and had a house on 113th Street. She always suspected him of betraying her, so she once rented a studio for him in what is now Lincoln Center, where the El passed by, and she could look in the window and see if he had another woman with him.

Havel, in the basement of the Ferrer Center, published a little paper called *Revolt*. I wrote for it, as did Adolf Wolff and Benjamin De Casseres,[383] among others. I knew De Casseres well. Once when in Paris he had a bad toothache. He said, "I'll never have a toothache again." He went to a dentist and told him to pull out all his teeth. The dentist objected, but De Casseres said that if he didn't do it he would go elsewhere. So all his teeth were pulled. He learned to eat with his gums. He later wanted dentures, but his mouth had contracted and they wouldn't fit.

July 4, 1914, was a nice, sunny day, and we had all arranged to go out to Leonard Abbott's place in New Jersey for a picnic. I lived with my parents on 109th Street, with a nice little garden in the back. Suddenly, that morning, there was a great crash. I rushed out and ran down Lexington Avenue about six or seven blocks and saw rubble and smoke. A crowd had gathered and the police were hustling everyone away. I started home but saw detectives questioning my father. They wanted to talk to me. So I didn't go back but went straight to Abbott's place.

Abbott served us corned beef and tongue sandwiches and beer. Everyone was hushed. There was an undercurrent of excitement. No one knew what to say. Besides, we knew that there were spies among us. One had come to my office for dental work, and when he brushed against me I felt a gun in his hip pocket. Another was Dave Sullivan, a New York City police detective. Becky Edelsohn lived with him before taking up with Plunkett. What scoundrels they were, talking with us, laughing with us, sharing our ideas, our hopes, our excitement—or at least pretending to!

Leonard asked me about the explosion. I told him that the "Dicks" had come to my house to question me, and he offered to put me up, but I preferred to go home. Abbott was crushed by the tragedy. I'm positive he didn't know about their plans. I myself knew something was afoot, and I'll tell you why. A few days before the explosion, I met Caron at the Center. "Let's have a cup of coffee," I said. "No, Moritz," he replied. "I'm too busy with something very important." He had a set face, very tense. They were working at it—they must have been working at it from the way he looked and spoke. The Ferrer Center was the heart of anarchist activity in New York and had anarchists of all kinds, including the dynamiters. Was Alexander Berkman involved? Well, he was very straightforward, practical, a man of action and organizing strength. I honestly feel that Berkman was involved, that he helped, at least with the planning.

I'm still an anarchist, but a philosophical one. Look at life. Particularly since I began to study myths and lore since ancient and prehistoric times, I find the same follies, the same wrongs, committed throughout human history. The only progress is in the individual, in you yourself; and through that progress you better the whole world. And that is as far as you can go. I said that in 1914 to Leonard Abbott, and again in the 1920s and 1930s, and I still say it today.

• MORRIS BERESIN •

Philadelphia, November 28, 1971

As a teenage anarchist in tsarist Russia, Morris Beresin took an active part in the Revolution of 1905, mostly in Kishinev and Odessa. Exiled to Siberia, he managed to escape by way of China and to sail for the United States, an episode described in his book *Fun keyten tsu frayhayt* (From Chains to Freedom) (New York: Anarchist Red Cross, 1916). Settling in Philadelphia, Beresin became a member of the Radical Library Group, along with such well-known Russian-Jewish anarchists as Chaim Weinberg, Boris Yelensky (q.v.), and Joseph Cohen, with whom he organized a branch of the Anarchist Red Cross to aid political prisoners in Russia. He was later active in the Baltimore branch of the Union of Russian Workers, an anarcho-syndicalist confederation, and contributed to the Russian anarchist press. As "B. E. Resin," moreover, he wrote for Marcus Graham's journal *Man!*, published during the 1930s. He died in Philadelphia in 1973.[384]

I WAS BORN in Kishinev in 1888 and joined the anarchist group there during the 1905 Revolution. I knew Altman, Mets, and Taratuta very well and considered them the finest type of revolutionist.[385] Altman was the man who threw the bomb into the Café Libman in Odessa in 1905. No one was killed, but Altman himself was wounded by fragments. The doctors refused to treat him. Finally he was given poison by his merciful sweetheart. Other members of the group were arrested, myself among them, and exiled to Siberia. My cellmate was Egor Sazonov, the famous Socialist Revolutionary. I managed to escape and made my way to America by the Pacific route. I arrived in 1912 and settled in Philadelphia.

I became a dental technician and joined the Radical Library, which had been organized near the beginning of the century. It had about two hundred members, mostly Jewish with a few Italians and Russians. They were largely garment workers and tailors, some of them from the London East End, as well as cigarmakers and a few construction workers (painters, electricians). There were also teachers, librarians, and students. It was a cultural as much as a political organization. It sponsored lectures (every Sunday, in English) and forums, had a Sunday School for the children, distributed literature, and published books and pamphlets, including Joseph Cohen's history of the Jewish anarchists in America. The majority were moderates, engaged in propaganda work, but we had a small minority of militant revolutionists, including Marcus Graham.

The leading figure was Joseph Cohen, a cigarmaker by trade, who served as the group's librarian. He and Harry Kelly and Leonard Abbott, who often came down from New York, formed a sort of *troika* and were dedicated to the Modern School movement. Will Durant of the New York school also came to speak. His *Story of Philosophy* is an outgrowth of lectures delivered over a two-year period in New York and Philadelphia. Other speakers included Rudolf Rocker, Charles Dana, Harry Overstreet, and Chaim Weinberg (called "*der folksredner*" [the people's tribune]), who held the audience's attention with his humor and treasure of anecdotes. George Brown, from England, was another able speaker. We had close ties, incidentally, with the Italian group in Philadelphia, and held joint meetings, picnics, and other affairs. In addition, Cohen and I organized an Anarchist Red Cross branch to assist political prisoners in Russia.

In 1917 I moved to Baltimore, where I lived for the next three years and was active in the local branch of the Union of Russian Workers. It was a bad time because of the war and antiradical repressions. Our branch fell victim to the Palmer raids, and all our materials were seized. I was jailed for three months and threatened with deportation. But things quieted down and I returned to Philadelphia, where I've been for the past fifty years.

• HARRY MELMAN •

Philadelphia, November 28, 1971

Harry Melman and his wife Celia were members of the Radical Library Group in Philadelphia, which in the early decades of the century boasted a Modern Sunday School and a summer camp (Camp Germinal), both attended by their daughter Ethel. When I asked for any relevant documents, Celia produced the membership ledger of the group, now housed in the Avrich Collection of the Library of Congress. An hour or so later, as I got up to leave, Harry had an idea. Reaching into the hall closet, he extracted a group of old photographs, among them a striking one of the pupils and teachers of the Sunday School, dating from 1910 or 1911. *"M'ret un m'ret un m'shushketsakh,"* said Celia (We talk and talk and remain silent). Harry died on July 10, 1974, at the age of eighty-five.

I EMIGRATED to Philadelphia in 1910, before Voltairine de Cleyre left for Chicago, but I knew no English then and have no recollection of her talks. I don't remember Samuel Gordon, Nathan Navro, or Joseph Kucera. I do recall Natasha Notkin,[386] who was friendly with Chaim Weinberg, but that's all I remember. Voltairine de Cleyre was a member of our Workmen's Circle branch, the Radical Library. In 1911, at a meeting of the branch at 424 Pine Street, Joseph Cohen read us a letter from her from Chicago, asking us to make a collection for the Mexican revolutionaries, and we sent her a hundred dollars.

The Radical Library was composed mostly of garment workers, cigarmakers, teachers, and construction workers. It became a branch of the Workmen's Circle in 1909. Around 1910, it organized a Modern Home and School Association, whose aim was to build a Ferrer School for our children and also so women could be free to work. The plan was never realized, but we did have a Sunday School and later a summer colony, Camp Germinal, in Jamison, Pennsylvania, about thirty miles north of the city. It lasted until 1934. Our daughter Ethel was there. Anarchism was not specifically taught at the camp, but a libertarian atmosphere prevailed. The camp had a children's theater, organized by Richard Gilbert [q.v.], and lectures for adults by Will Durant, Rudolf Rocker, and others.

• EMMA GILBERT •

White Plains, New York, September 23, 1974

Emma Gilbert (named after Emma Goldman) was the daughter of Joseph J. Cohen (1878–1953), an editor of the *Fraye Arbeter Shtime,* founder of the Sunrise Colony in Michigan, and participant in the Modern Schools in Philadelphia, New York, and Stelton (Emma attended all three). Entering New Brunswick High School in 1917, Emma made a brilliant showing, leading her class in all subjects. She was graduated as valedictorian and went on to study at Radcliffe, eventually becoming a child psychologist. She died on December 29, 1986.[387]

I WAS BORN in Philadelphia on August 9, 1904, and was named after Emma Goldman. My brother's [E. V. Conason, q.v.] middle name is Voltaire, after Voltairine de Cleyre. My parents, Joseph and Sophie Cohen, immigrated from Russia in 1903. Both learned English from Voltairine de Cleyre, and though I was only a small child when they were taking their lessons from her, my memories are quite vivid. My own first language was Yiddish, and I can remember standing up in my crib and reciting a Yiddish poem, but my parents were determined to learn English, so my Yiddish dropped away very quickly. When they went to Voltairine's apartment for their lessons they would take me along, and I sat in her lap as she taught them.

My whole understanding of "elegance" goes back to Voltairine. It was the first time I saw a room with curtains, with little pieces of décor, though nothing expensive of course. She herself had an ascetic kind of beauty. And she smelled very good, like lavender. She wore a dark, long-sleeved dress, and every gesture of hers had a kind of beauty, especially in contrast to Emma Goldman, whom I always found repulsive. When Voltairine was sick we kept all her things in our attic in the Radical Library on Pine Street, and I can remember what they looked like to this day: mother-of-pearl and beautifully shaped shell things and clothes that smelled like her, like lavender, which made it so nice to go up there. Father never cared about possessions, about things. Only books—and even that was not to possess them but to use them, to learn from them.

Mary Hansen was another wonderful person. She and Voltairine were physically somewhat alike, tall, thin, and bony. She was rather severe-looking but with a wonderful smile. She told us how she came to America from Sweden [actually Denmark] and worked as a servant girl in a rich house. When George Brown died, she and Heloise came to live with us at the Ferrer Center. She told marvelous stories to the children.

The Radical Library consisted almost entirely of Jewish immigrants. My first recollection of a black person was of Lucy Parsons, who came through Philadelphia several times to lecture and would stay with us at the Radical Library where we lived, at 424 Pine Street. The Radical Library had a Sunday school, which made more of an effort at indoctrination than Stelton did. We sang the *Internationale* and other revolutionary songs and recited revolutionary poems. But it had few distinguished figures. It was not the yeasting place of New York Bohemianism that the Ferrer Center was and did not produce the writers and artists that emerged in New York. One of my earliest memories of the Radical Library was of Father and a group of men sitting on boxes in the cellar, warming themselves by the furnace and talking earnestly about "the crisis."[388] That is one of the first English words that I can remember. It must have been in 1907 or 1908. I remember going to a meeting where Voltairine de Cleyre spoke and being handed out the window when the police came along and broke it up.

Alexander Berkman was a warm, loving person that children as well as adults took to. He was extremely forceful and persuasive. I detested Emma Goldman: she was so repulsive and extremely domineering, extremely self-centered. There are people you meet whose eye engages you and you feel they are interested in you. Sasha was like that, but not Emma. She was completely egotistical. Of course she had great capacity, but not on a personal basis.

Dad became manager of the Ferrer Center in New York, and Cora Bennett Stephenson was the teacher when I first came there. She always carried a book under her arm. She was much less an influence at the time than people thought. She had a greater effect on us, perhaps, after we left the school.

During the Lexington Avenue affair I was questioned by women detectives who were introduced to me by Dave Sullivan. He had gone to Tarrytown and even to Blackwell's Island for thirty days, but later turned out to be a police spy. The detectives offered me ice cream and tried to wheedle information out of me. In *Transition* Will Durant portrays himself as the young man who got out of the apartment alive.[389] That was actually Michael Murphy, who used to hang out at the Center. Mom used to feed him, and he took the children out for walks. The sound of the explosion could be heard from over on 107th Street. Soon afterwards Murphy turned up naked but with a police overcoat. Mike told me that Louise Berger had gone out for bread and that these guys [Caron, Hanson, and Berg] had gotten up early in the morning and were having a pillow fight, just like children, they were so happy. He wasn't in on the plans and didn't know what was happening. The dynamite went off and he emerged naked. The police arrived, and one of them put his coat over Murphy, who then slipped away and came to the Center.

Murphy talked to Dad and Sasha. I am convinced that neither my father nor Berkman had known what these boys were up to. But to protect Murphy, Dad brought him out to Leonard Abbott's picnic in Westfield, New Jersey. Before leaving New York he called Harry Melman [q.v.] and other comrades in the Radical Library in Philadelphia to meet him at Westfield. He delivered Murphy to them at the railroad station. Murphy was a very suggestible and simple boy, and they feared he might be used by the police. He was kept in Philadelphia for a while, then taken to England by way of Canada. He wrote to Father from England shortly before the Second World War asking, "Is it safe for me to come back?" Dad gave a double-take when he read that, and figured that if he had to ask such a question after all that time he had better stay there, so he answered no. The people at the picnic weren't told about Murphy, but they had probably heard about the explosion. It was all kept very quiet.

I'll tell you why I don't think Berkman was involved. Shortly before Lexington Avenue there was a group of Italian anarchists at the Center who wanted to go with guns to Tarrytown and make an attack on Rockefeller's estate. I was swinging in the yard while Sasha was trying to calm them down. He told them that such an *attentat* would have no meaning for ordinary people—no doubt he was thinking of his own experience with Frick—and that it would not draw the masses to the anarchist cause but rather achieve the exact opposite. He was very persuasive and they didn't go. So I doubt that he was involved in the Lexington Avenue affair, but I may be wrong.

Robert Henri taught art at the Ferrer School, but he was more than an art teacher. He was a hero to us kids because he got us tickets to Isadora Duncan. George Bellows used me to pose for his class. I believe that Edna St. Vincent Millay lectured at the Center. Gussie Miller wore the most fabulous opal, but

I don't recall anything else about her. We had a microscope and a set of the *Book of Knowledge* but little else in the way of equipment. You know that later, as a psychologist in Washington, D.C., I took part in a group therapy conference, and some of the people there had been at the Ferrer Center and trying the same technique even then. The Center had all sorts of influences in later years—on education, psychology, and the arts.

The main thing about the Ferrer School in New York and at Stelton was that the children were told that they were absolutely free to do anything they wanted, so long as it did not hurt anyone else. Bobby and Deedie Hutchinson[390] were my teachers at the school in New York after Cora Bennett Stephenson, and they came out with us to Stelton. Bobby was a rather passive teacher. I wanted to study astronomy, so Bobby got books for me, but he really wasn't interested at all. He just stood there nodding and saying "Great." Deedie, with her dietary theories, practically starved their first baby, and all the adults were up in arms over it. Bobby remained entirely in the background, giving as little direction as possible.

Leonard Abbott and Harry Kelly were never at the center of things like Father. They would pay an occasional visit, but Father was left with the hard day-to-day work. Abbott was one of the most charming people in the world, but he never gave a strong or definite opinion. No matter what anyone said to him, he would answer, "Quite so, quite so." That was his favorite phrase. And Harry Kelly's stand on the war—he wanted Britain to be beaten at all costs—left him completely out of phase with the colonists.

William Thurston Brown was badly treated in Laurence Veysey's book.[391] The kids *did* like him. He told wonderful stories about early American history. He was a great admirer of Mark Twain, and we devoured Mark Twain, read everything he wrote. Brown told us what America was like in the early days, and it was all perfectly real and wonderful. His wife, you know, was caught shoplifting and there was an awful scandal.

I learned to print from Joseph Ishill. I learned illuminated letters from him and how to set type. He was an artistic genius. Pryns Hopkins taught me to tango, and dancing the waltz with Jim Dick was the greatest experience of my life! Henry Schnittkind[392] was only there a couple of months, until Thanksgiving, but in that short time he made an everlasting impression on the school, and the school left an everlasting impression on him. He taught us the most unbelievable word games, he taught us Dickens, he taught us algebra. He was a classics scholar and an extraordinary teacher. Years later, when I went to high school, I could still recall his algebra, and that made it very easy for me. I think he was the most gifted teacher I ever met. He enjoyed every bit of it, and we adored every bit of it.

I was one of the first group to go to New Brunswick High School from Stelton, though Elsie Kelly was a senior there by then. I was valedictorian of my class, and after graduation I spent a year under Aunty Ferm as her assistant. After that, Richard [Gilbert, q.v.] brought me up to Radcliffe. I married him before entering and thus was Radcliffe's first married undergraduate. It was in the fall of 1922 that we left Stelton. Richard became an economist at Harvard. Before the Second World War he was an advisor to Harry Hopkins,[393] and then served in the OPA [Office of Price Administration]. I was raising a family and worked as a child psychologist at Children's Hospital in Washington. I had a Master's degree and did most of the work for the doctorate, but never finished.

There's no denying that Aunty Ferm was a great woman. She had a strong spiritual quality that came out of her. But she was a mystic and didn't always make sense. She had no flexibility. That was true of Uncle too, to a lesser degree. And they both had a kind of anti-intellectualism and distrust of theories, except for those of people they accepted, like Froebel. Both were extraordinarily gifted. She expounded all sorts of Froebelian principles that were way out—though absolutely real to her—and had nothing to do with anything. Stelton was essentially a Jewish community with a traditional Jewish feeling about education, but with a libertarian slant and without Aunty and Uncle's anti-intellectualism. The school was designed to instill the idea of freedom. The colonists had a beautiful belief in the perfection of man through libertarian education.

• RICHARD GILBERT •

White Plains, New York, September 23, 1974

Richard Gilbert, husband of Emma Cohen Gilbert (q.v.), was an economist at Harvard, an advisor to Harry Hopkins during the New Deal, and an official at the Office of Price Administration (OPA). As a child he attended the Radical Library Sunday School in Philadelphia, of which Emma's father, Joseph Cohen, was a founder. He and Emma were head counselors at Camp Germinal, operated by the Radical Library.

As a CHILD in Philadelphia during the First World War I attended the Radical Library Sunday School. Abe Grosner was then in charge, and afterwards he went to teach at Stelton. There were a number of Wobblies at the Radical Library, and also a few terrorists, but no one famous or to become famous in literature or the arts, as in the Ferrer Center. We youngsters had very serious discussions there, particularly about the war, the main issue of the time and which we were all against. Later, during the 1920s, Emma and I were the principal counselors at Camp Germinal, north of Philadelphia, which had been started by the Radical Library.

The fundamental point about Stelton was that it was not an anarchist colony but a community populated by anarchists. The one thing that tied them together was the school. In other matters they largely went their own way, most of them working in New York rather than collectively in the colony. Sunrise was entirely different. People worked cooperatively and lived cooperatively. The school was incidental. The situation was totally reversed. The driving motive to band together was the Depression, and as soon as things opened up again, these people, with their urban occupations and skills, ran from the hard life on the farm.

Joseph Cohen took an active part in both of these communal ventures. He was a good speaker, an articulate but not a loquacious man. He was also a good man. But God help the poor creature who tries to establish a leadership role in the anarchist movement!

• MAGDA SCHOENWETTER •

Brooklyn, New York, January 5, 1973

Magda Schoenwetter, together with Amour Liber (q.v.) and Révolte Bercovici (q.v.), was one of the original pupils at the Modern School of New York, which opened in October 1911. She moved with the school to Stelton in May 1915 and afterwards attended New Brunswick High School and lived with the family of Joseph Cohen.

I WAS BORN in New York City in February 1907. My name was Magda Boris, though my real father was Pavel Orleneff, the Russian actor whose troupe was managed by Emma Goldman when it came to New York. I entered the Ferrer School when it opened on East Twelfth Street in October 1911, moved with it to Stelton, New Jersey, in 1915, and went on to New Brunswick High School.

My mother's radical background goes back to the 1880s. She came from a well-to-do Jewish family in the Ukraine. Her tutor, named Starodvorsky, was a Populist, who spent twenty years in Schlüsselburg fortress. Her family came to New York in the 1880s, and she mingled with the anarchists of the Lower East Side. She was a good friend of the Bercovicis, so she knew of the Ferrer School on Twelfth Street and sent me there. It later moved to a brownstone on 107th Street. There was a kitchen in the basement, a lovely big room. It was the children's dining room during the day and a tea-room for adults in the evening. The parlor floor had a platform, or stage, in the back. Sadakichi Hartmann recited there in the evenings. Upstairs there were two rooms—the two classrooms. The back one had all sorts of Montessori equipment for the kindergarten. Above that was a third floor with rented rooms.

I think Esther Wolff was Adolf's daughter and that Homo and Human Davidson were cousins of Luna Dunn. I adored Will Durant. He was my first love, my favorite teacher. He used to take us to Central Park, and after I got home

I would nag Mother to take me to the park—maybe Will would be there! We had picnics and nature study there, he told us stories and sang "Way Down Upon the Swanee River."

In the backyard of the school we walked on stilts and on the fence. We read books about cave dwellers and tree dwellers. Robert Henri was a friend of Isadora Duncan's, and he got us free tickets to see her dance. Once we saw her dance in *Oedipus*. We were often taken to dances and plays, and I remember seeing Maeterlinck's *Bluebird*. Every time Luna Dunn's mother made lunch it was Wheatena or cornmeal mush, and I still love them. We had a cooking class and made desserts and other things.

What everybody is yowling about now—freedom in education—we had then, though I still can't spell or do multiplication. Robert and Delia Hutchinson used Montessori methods and equipment. On the way home from school, I, my sister Sophie, and Esther Wolff used to stop at the *Mother Earth* office. Sasha was nice to us, but Emma was a pain in the ass. I couldn't stand her red face and dumpy figure. She was busy and would chase us out. Jacques Dubois [q.v.] had a summer school for the Ferrer Center kids in Maplewood, New Jersey, around 1912 or 1913, and I went.

We moved down to Stelton on May 16, 1915, a cold, rainy, nasty day. It was mud all over. I blame Harry Kelly for choosing that awful, dumpy place. Yet I loved it there. William Thurston Brown was the principal after the Hutchinsons left. I'll tell you something about Uncle Will, the silly thing! His wife told him to give the girls some kisses—and they were chocolate kisses! I remember giggling stupidly at a sex lecture he gave, and I was so ashamed of myself. I liked Jim and Nellie Dick [q.v.], but the one I loved best was Fred Dunn,[394] a Cockney. He taught us about Aztecs and Mayans, and I've been interested in them ever since. In fact, we're going down to Mexico next month to see the ruins.

I hated Joseph Cohen, though I adored his daughter Emma [Gilbert, q.v.]. He almost ruined my life. I was going to New Brunswick High School and living with the Cohens. During the Christmas vacation I stayed late in order to see Gorky's *Lower Depths*—I loved the theater—and Cohen wouldn't give me a note of excuse. So I never went back to the high school, which I liked and where I was doing well. And he also did something else: he broke up a romance between Ray Miller [Shedlovsky, q.v.] and Richard Gilbert to get him for his daughter Emma. He was devious and a self-seeker.

At the Living House each older child was in charge of a group—they rotated every few days—that helped in the kitchen and set the table and washed the dishes, and so on. I had had a crush on Stuart Sanger in the New York school. His brother Grant was my age, and Grant and his sister Peggy were at Stelton, where Peggy died of pneumonia. I myself had malaria there in 1918.

Henry Schnittkind taught us about cloudbursts—that it could rain in one spot and not another. Sherwood Trask used to call me "Mazda Electric Lamp." Joseph Ishill taught me printing, and I still remember how to set up type. And there was also a very handsome guy—I can't recall his name [Bernard Sexton]—with a beautiful wife, and he was steeped in Indian lore and taught us Indian chants. We loved that! Pryns Hopkins sent us a teacher from Santa Barbara, Marie Travis, who taught us table manners. Hopkins came to visit. He took the whole school to the Hippodrome in New York, and we ate at the Russian Tea Room. Dudley Field Malone, the ACLU lawyer, and Maude Malone lived at Stelton for a while.

Gray Wu was one of those I loved best. When he got mad he'd reach up and grab the door jamb and swing back and forth until he got rid of all his frustrations. He had a crush on Lucy Vinnick. He gave me Tolstoy's *What Is to Be Done?* He took us to New York to Chinatown and bought us Chinese slippers. He was an exchange student at Columbia and worked in a Chinese restaurant but was fired when he organized a waiters' strike. A bunch of Chinese, his friends, came out to visit the colony. He was on a par in my affections with Fred Dunn.

We lived in an open dormitory at first. Then it was enclosed. But we loved it open. Mary Hansen told us wonderful stories, dear Mary Hansen. Hers was the only house with a peach orchard. One night we went and stole all her peaches and carried them home in our bloomers. Henrietta Rodman,[395] a close friend of Mary's, once wrote a poem about her daughter Heloise:

> Heloise Hansen hyphen Brown,
> Never stands up when she can sit down,
> Never sits down when she can be dancin',
> Heloise Brown hyphen Hansen.

Emma Goldman told me, when things are bad, scrub floors.

• RAY SHEDLOVSKY •

New York City, October 14, 1972

Ray Shedlovsky, born in 1903, is the widow of Dr. Leo Shedlovsky, a chemist, and the daughter of a Jewish anarchist couple in Philadelphia, where she attended the Modern Sunday School of the Radical Library Group. In 1915 Ray moved with her parents to Stelton and enrolled in the Modern School there. She afterwards graduated from New Brunswick High School and became a professional singer, specializing in German *lieder*. Her mother, Bella Miller, was a member of the Libertarian Book Club in New York, where I met her in 1969, a year before her death at the age of ninety.[396]

My PARENTS were members of the Radical Library in Philadelphia, and I attended its Sunday School from 1912 to 1915. We had singing, stories, art class. We all became great friends. That's where I met Emma Cohen [Gilbert, q.v.], whose father was in charge of the library. Abe Grosner was in charge of the

Sunday School, which was held during the afternoon. Sunday evenings were reserved for adult activities, such as lectures by Will Durant and Scott Nearing.[397] Voltairine de Cleyre had just died. She was thought of with great reverence, as a kind of god. George Brown was a very peppery fellow, and Mary Hansen, his companion, quiet and unassuming, a marvelous person, so generous and friendly, so understanding. All the kids there and at Stelton were crazy about her.

I visited the Ferrer Center once. It was during a visit to Emma Cohen, whose family had moved up there. Emma was very excited about the school and the teachers. The war had just broken out, but everyone was more excited about an explosion that had taken place a few weeks before. On entering the Ferrer Center I remember vividly a black metal pyramid with a fist on top. It made a terrific impression on me. Alexander Berkman was there that morning. It was the only time I ever met him. Emma Cohen took me into the yard of the school and he was there. She introduced us, and he said, "What dreamy eyes you have." I was eleven years old.

We moved from Philadelphia to Stelton and lived there from 1915 to 1918. I attended the school from 1915 to 1917, then New Brunswick High School in 1917 and 1918, before we moved to New York. The Hutchinsons were in charge when I came. Deedie was pregnant that summer. On walks we sat down in the middle of the road and she explained conception and childbirth, all this to little five- and six-year-olds. They left for Stony Ford soon after. Deedie was very charming, and Bobby was tall and slender. All the people there were so loving! They all seemed to have a passion for children, and the children were mad about them!

Uncle Will [William Thurston Brown] came next, with a woman named Elsie [Pratt], who was not his wife. They stayed several years, then left for California. We used to go to his house on winter nights, made fudge, popped corn; he read us Dickens and Mark Twain and laughed so hard he had to stop reading, and we all just sat there and watched him laugh. I still remember how he enjoyed that book!

There were so many unusual people there. Hippolyte Havel was very charming when sober. We never knew what he was doing there, but we all liked him. No one ever said anything derogatory about him, despite the fact that he had "no visible means of support" and was not always sober. On the contrary, everyone treated him very gently. He often wore one of those flowing black anarchist ties.

Henry Schnittkind was my favorite teacher. He taught writing and math and had a natural talent for teaching. One day Pryns Hopkins came to Stelton. He heard me singing—I was always singing—and sent me to New York for singing lessons, which he paid for. He was tall, thin, wealthy, and later had a school in California. I became a professional singer; I gave many concerts and specialized in *lieder* with some opera.

I was deliriously happy in the Stelton school. My mother had sent me there for only one summer, but I refused to come home. The first year I lived in the

Living House, and woke up on winter mornings with my hair frozen to the pillow. That first winter there was a fire in the Living House but no one was hurt. I loved the other children, and Emma Cohen, Heloise Brown, and I were particularly close friends. Mary Hansen was modest, never talked about herself, very solid. Heloise sent me a poem Mary wrote before she died, in the 1950s I think. Her son George seemed mentally retarded.

In the early years the school was completely disorganized. In the New York Ferrer Center and at Stelton one heard little about Francisco Ferrer's educational theories, though a good deal about his anticlericalism and martyrdom. They talked a good deal more about the Montessori method. We did everything as a community. Instead of reading A *Midsummer Night's Dream* we put on the play, and put it on outdoors. The grownups got involved too. I never avoided taking part in anything, whereas in high school everything seemed a chore, even though I always got good marks. The only thing I liked was French. I went through four years of high school but didn't make a single real friend. In Stelton everyone was a friend. And I went to grammar school for six years before coming to Stelton, yet I can't remember anything we did or any of the teachers, except that they read Bible to us every morning and that three Civil War veterans visited school one day. I read at home avidly, but school is a blank. On the other hand I remember a great deal about Stelton. Stelton was not only a school but a community; it wasn't just education—it was living.

Joseph Cohen was a very bright and capable man, though he was one of the few in the colony who were not hail-fellow-well-met but rather remote. You never felt terribly close to him—and I lived in the Cohen house for more than two years, after a year at the Living House, and became fast friends with Emma. But he had a good sense of humor and was an able organizer, conducting meetings with Harry Kelly and Leonard Abbott. (They didn't live in the colony— Kelly came off and on and Abbott hardly ever.) In that period Cohen also worked every day in a New Brunswick cigar factory.

Harry Kelly was a charming fellow who could talk for years on end without stopping for breath—and it was always interesting. Leonard Abbott had some of the qualities of a minister. You always had the feeling that you were talking to a holy man, terribly friendly though, always seeming so interested in what you had to say. After his wife got sick he devoted all his time to her when not working. His active life just stopped. He asked me to come up to his house in the Bronx and sing for her, which I did on several occasions.

I met his sister-in-law Romany Marie in Stelton, which she visited often. Her husband, A. D. Marchand, who was something of a kook, collected pottery. She was a very flamboyant person, always dressed in an extravagant gypsy style, and had a booming voice. When she came into her Greenwich Village restaurant her personality would take over the whole place. She fed down-and-outers, sometimes for months on end.

Margaret Sanger's daughter got sick at Stelton and died. The Dicks, who came in 1917, went back to England, and returned again to Stelton, were very warm, friendly, and easy-going. Jimmy Dick was a marvelous dancer. He would always put on his dancing pumps for Saturday night dances, and we were very impressed. I got the impression, from later visits, that Aunty Ferm was very rigid. She lived by a great many rules and regulations and expected people to conform to her ideas. Most people were fonder of Uncle than Aunty, though they felt she was an important person.

Joseph Ishill taught us printing. We printed our own magazine. We did everything ourselves—we were gardeners, we were typesetters, we were cooks. We did everything with our own two hands. I remember how I enjoyed setting type. Ishill was an artist—he showed us many beautiful things he had printed.

We had some characters there too, Havel, for instance, and Anyuta Krimont, who once took over the Living House kitchen and decided that the children would eat only nuts and raisins for a while. Vegetarianism was strong among the colonists. Most were vegetarians, and I was one all the time I lived at Stelton. We used to bake our own bread, had our own vegetable gardens, lived close to nature and to the soil. Boys and girls swam together nude, to be natural and avoid hang-ups. I felt the anarchists were the only people with the right attitude towards life. Personal relationships were the most important thing. People were allowed to develop their own potentialities. You didn't live according to rigid rules but could do what you wanted as long as you didn't interfere with the rights of other people.

• EVA BEIN •

New York City, January 13, 1973

Eva Bein attended the Ferrer School in New York in 1914–1915 and in Stelton, New Jersey, in 1915–1916, and then the Stony Ford School in 1916–1918. After that she attended New York City public schools, James Madison High School in Brooklyn, and Hunter College. She became a champion swimmer, the holder of national titles, and a social studies teacher in New York high schools. The woman swimmer in Paul Gallico's *Poseidon Adventure* is modeled on her (she met Gallico with a group of swimmers in Europe during the 1930s).

I WAS BORN in New York City in 1910. My parents were radical and hadn't married. Father was a cigar worker, an IWW, and then a socialist with anarchist leanings. He had left Poland because of his activities in the Jewish Bund. He named my younger brother Eugene Victor (after Debs)[398] and always had pictures of Emma Goldman, Rosa Luxemburg, and Karl Marx.

When I was two, my parents sent me to summer camp in Maplewood, New Jersey [run by the French anarchist Jacques Dubois (q.v.), later at Stelton and Mohegan], and when the Ferrer School opened my mother shifted me there.

It was a brownstone house, and many of the activities took place in the yard. I remember being taken to Central Park often and being outdoors a great deal, but I was barely four and all this is very vague. I remember pandemonium, noise. It wasn't restrictive but spontaneous, easygoing, permissive. It's all very dim, but that's what I remember about the place, and that there were people there who were interested in the kids. Puckie Durant was warm and friendly and used to hold my hand and wipe away the tears if I fell down and got hurt. Anna Schwartz [q.v.] was a mother figure for me, though it wasn't until later, at Stony Ford, that I really became close to her. The Albasis, with two children in the school, had a grocery store on 106th Street between First Avenue and York, I think. My parents used to take me to lectures and to meet people. I heard Emma Goldman speak, and Father introduced me to her. She didn't seem very interested in me. She looked mannish and seemed terribly excited.

I went with the original group to Stelton when the school moved there [May 16, 1915]. The place was quite primitive. We lived in a partly open dormitory, and I slept next to the two children of Margaret Sanger, a boy and a girl. We had only one stove in the middle of the dormitory. The Sanger girl came down with pneumonia, and Mother feared that I would catch it too. In the morning, when we went to wash, there was ice. The toilet was outside. Everything was unpainted wood. The adults as well as the children went bathing nude, and Mother was taken aback and left the same feeling with me, and to this day I'm more modest about it than perhaps I should be. I remember many grownups there, always talking among themselves a great deal. In the school there was one room; we sat on benches and there were wooden tables. I liked Stelton more than the city school, but probably because I wasn't living with my parents. Also, there was a lot of activity, a lot of zest, vitality, experiment. It was like pioneering, and I think I felt a part of it.

I went to Stony Ford at the age of six, and I remember that well. I remember that the Hutchinsons were very interested in health and diet, in the body as well as the mind. We had two meals a day, at a quarter to eleven and at five. To this day I have never enjoyed breakfast. The ideas of that school were so strong and I held on so hard that when I came home I couldn't touch a morsel of breakfast. My parents were so insistent that they took me to the insane asylum at Welfare Island and threatened to leave me there with those people behind the bars. When they turned away and began to leave, I ran after them terrified. Another thing is that we didn't eat any meat, and I remained a vegetarian till eighteen. We ate Protose and Notose in cans—mostly nuts, beans, and the like—and all sorts of Kellogg's cereals, which they would buy at Macy's and have shipped to Stony Ford, and bread without yeast. And they always emphasized that we shouldn't overeat.

We slept in a dormitory with the back and sides sheltered but the front open. They would put us in sleeping bags tied at the neck, then put us in bed. We swam naked and could go swimming in winter too if we liked. I had learned to swim at Stelton and swam often at Stony Ford and got to love it. I later became a champion swimmer and won several national awards, and I moved into London Terrace [on West Twenty-Third Street, where the interview took place] because it has a pool in the basement.

We were all assigned household tasks each day. They never used the word "school." It was all play. We worked for weeks making Dutch shoes, skates, windmills—everything to do with Holland. We had to touch and feel and smell and become acquainted with everything about it; and then we read the story. We went through *The Dutch Twins*, *The Spanish Twins*, and so on. Yet there was a kind of leisurely feeling about the place. We never felt pressured, rushed, harassed. I don't remember anybody raising his voice at Stony Ford. There was no hostility in their voices. Those were my happiest years.

Deedie's [Delia Hutchinson] brother Dana[399] came up from Columbia, where he taught. He took us for an overnight outing—we slept outdoors on a hill—and he taught us all about the stars; he had a story about each star. Dana was a pacifist and lost his position at Columbia, and I think was even put in jail as a conscientious objector. They used to discuss these things with us, things you would think pertinent only to adults. We discussed everything together and were always told just what was taking place. They really respected us as people. The teaching was quite informal and centered around play and projects. One boy wanted to look for rabbits and just got up and walked away. We often went on hikes and picnics. We had a dog named Bucky, a cow, and a horse. They liked us to get close to the animals in a friendly way. When my parents came up to visit I used to say, hours ahead of time, "You're going to be late for your train." A man named Hugo, such a kindly person, gave us piano lessons for a quarter.

The men at the school wore knickers, which at that time was considered radical, and the women wore dresses only down to their knees and had their hair short. When we would go into Middletown, in an old Ford with a crank, and we got to the outskirts of the town, I would lower my head so as to become invisible to the townspeople because I felt we were always creating a commotion by our entrance, all conspicuous with knickers and short dresses and hair. I remember clearly when Bobby Hutchinson told us that the place was to be disbanded. I cried and the other children cried. There was no corporal punishment. Instead, we were put in a room and not given any food, just fruit juice, for a few hours, and that was the worst punishment we ever got.

When I went back to Stelton I was eleven, and I was boarded with Anna Schwartz's sister, a very attractive woman. I remained with her for about a year. I was quite surprised by what a community it had become and how many houses had sprung up. I liked Stelton, but Stony Ford was the best experience I had as a child. I loved it, and many of the ideas I hold to this day were conceived and nurtured there. I'm very conscious of my health, of exercise, of the love of learning. As a teacher I always had great rapport with my students. I think it helped a great deal in my life. They were more conscious of food than other people. Now it's quite common to eat whole-wheat bread and the like, but then it was new. I never ate a frankfurter or drank tea or ate penny candy. In fact I was a vegetarian until eighteen, and that all started at Stony Ford.

After the Ferrer School, Stelton, and Stony Ford, public school was a traumatic experience. Susan Dubois, my good friend, was sent to Ethical Culture, and that would have been much better. Public school was conventional and rigid. The teacher once told me that if I came late again I shouldn't bother coming to school. I once made a blotch with the pen-point on the paper and the teacher slapped me in the face. I was a good reader but I knew very little math. I didn't seem to fit. They called me the "wild Indian." I had a Dutch haircut with short bangs and looked different from the other girls, and I wore the oldest rags for clothes. I was very fidgety because I wasn't accustomed to sitting still in the classroom all the time. And maybe I spoke out, as we all did at Stony Ford and Stelton. I got the most horrible headaches at that school, and would cry all day, and sometimes even fainted, which I had never done at the other schools. It was extremely hard to adjust, though after the first year I had no further difficulties. In New York and Stelton they had a picture of Francisco Ferrer on the wall. They told us that he was a martyr, that he was executed for wanting free education, to separate the schools from both church and state. I always remember that.

• MARY RAPPAPORT •

Brooklyn, New York, January 5, 1973

Mary Rappaport (known as "Marucci") was the daughter of Anna Schwartz (q.v.), the last principal of the Modern School at Stelton. Marucci and her brother Zack were pupils at the school as well as at the Ferrer School in New York and the Stony Ford School, run by Robert and Delia Hutchinson. Marucci died of cancer in Palo Alto, California, on April 24, 1982.

MY MOTHER, Anna Schwartz [q.v.], was an anarchist, and she enrolled me in the Ferrer School in 1914, when I was ten. Cora Bennett Stephenson was the principal. She taught us how to use a fan and said, "Whenever you go to the theater, that's the sound you hear, of the fans swishing." Her successors the following year were Bobby and Deedie Hutchinson. Bobby was tall, thin, and good-looking, from a prominent Philadelphia family. His wife Delia was the granddaughter of Henry Wadsworth Longfellow and of Richard Henry Dana. Her brother Richard was an architect, who designed the American wing of the Metropolitan Museum of Art. Deedie was a nurse and demonstrated how to bathe a baby, using a big doll. Bobby taught us how to dance—"Down and up and one, two, three." At Harvard he had always played the female leads in the Hasty Pudding Society.

I went to Stelton when the school moved in 1915, and then on with the Hutchinsons, who established their own school at Stony Ford, New York, the following year. As in Stelton, we followed a vegetarian diet and slept in a dormitory that had a roof but no walls and was open all year, even in winter. But we had plenty of quilts and blankets, and we loved it. The pupils, besides myself and my younger brother Zack, were Bruno and Marie Albasi, Benny Hegel, Eva Bein [q.v.], Jessie, Rosie, and Barney Mendelson, Nora Huebsch, and a few others, about fifteen kids in all, many of them from Stelton.

Bobby and Deedie were vegetarians and believed in eating only two meals a day. The school had 137 acres, bordered on one side by the Wallkill River, near Goshen. There was an old Dutch farmhouse with a great big fireplace. Across from the house was a big barn in which we had workshops. I made a desk for my room there. Upstairs in the barn was a most wonderful place: all Bobby and Deedie's things were up there, and they let us rummage through them. He had at least thirty pairs of white gloves that he had used as an usher at weddings. Deedie's brother designed a new wing to the house that was larger than the original house. In it we had our dining room and the Hutchinsons had their living quarters and a nursery—beautifully designed with a sandpile and slide—for their own child and brother's child. The house was brilliantly lit all the time, and the neighbors called it the Light House. Off the new wing was our dormitory, overlooking the river. We used to use carbide cans as rafts and float in the river. My mother taught there, and Deedie was the nurse. Helen Lund taught there too. Stelton was too messy, too unmannerly for the Hutchinsons.

This was dairy country. Up the hill was a big dairy farm owned by the Bull family. They had a stone house with a spinet, and a treadmill with dogs. We had such wonderful times there. Each week a group of three kids would be responsible for getting supplies. Bobby drove us into town (Goshen) to get the stuff, and if the group didn't function correctly we had no food. We also did the cooking. We had a wonderful deep brook that made gurgling noises. The Hutchinsons put a dam in and that made a swimming pool for us. But the dam had to be broken up because it flooded the farmers' pasture land.

I don't recall much about the teaching, but I remember one thing: we drew a big map of Greece on the floor—we were all on our hands and knees doing it. We were doing a Greek play at the same time, which had to do with Greek history and which we ourselves made up. So we were learning theater, geography, history, reading, and writing at one stroke. There was beautiful china and fine chairs and an oval table in the dining room—there was nothing impoverished about this place! The school lasted about three years, and then the Hutchinsons moved to Mamaroneck. I was then about fifteen, and I lived with them there for a year or so. They were starting to break up. He afterwards married Hesper Le Gallienne, the actress Eva's half-sister.

A few miscellaneous points. The pyramid urn by Adolf Wolff was taken from the Ferrer Center to Stelton when the school moved there in 1915. One time, in 1917 or 1918, the mounted police came to Stelton to look for draft dodgers, who were in fact hiding at the colony, though the police didn't find them. The disputes that went on there between anarchists and Communists were dreadful. Many of us (including myself and Magda Boris [Schoenwetter, q.v.]) became Communists because the anarchists were bourgeois and the Communists were the only ones who seemed effective, the only ones who were doing anything to change the world.

• ANNA SCHWARTZ •

Palo Alto, California, June 17, 1974

Anna Schwartz, an immigrant from Russia, headed the Modern School of Stelton during its final years, from 1948 to 1953. One of Stelton's original settlers, she also attended adult classes at the Ferrer Center in New York and taught at the Stony Ford School, run by Robert and Delia Hutchinson. Her children Mary (Rappaport, q.v.) and Zack attended the schools at New York, Stony Ford, and Stelton, and Zack taught at Stelton and Mohegan. Afterwards Zack and his wife, a former pupil at Stelton, were teachers at the Peninsula School of Creative Education in Menlo Park, California. Anna died in Palo Alto on October 7, 1978.

I WAS BORN Anna Druz' on May 22, 1887, in the village of Shvirnevo near Konstantinovka, Kherson province. The nearest big town was Voznesensk. Father had a dry goods store. He had gone to Hebrew school and was very conservative in his views. I was raised very strictly and severely by a strict and severe father. My libertarian philosophy is in part a reaction against this upbringing. Father hired a local druggist to teach his three girls (I was the second, and there were other children later) the Russian language and arithmetic. Every Friday Father would examine us, and he hit me—I daydreamed a lot during the lessons— if I failed to give the correct answers. My older sister went to live with relatives in Odessa—how lucky she was!—but died suddenly on the eve of her wedding. So Father married me off against my wishes. I was seventeen and I never forgave him.

During the Russo-Japanese War my husband, an army reservist, was going to be called into service, so he went to America. He settled in St. Paul, Minnesota, and became a barber. I was pregnant when he left. Marucci [Mary Rappaport, q.v.] was born in 1906, and that year we came to New York, where my husband joined us. Our second child, Zachary, arrived, and my husband took up his barber's trade in the city.

My younger sister married an intelligent young man named Sigmund Brodsky. They brought young people to our house from the needle trades, and I began to see things in a new light. In 1909, when Francisco Ferrer was executed, I was already reading the *Fraye Arbeter Shtime*, and through these young people I began to attend anarchist meetings. When a movement arose to protest against Ferrer's execution, I joined it. I separated from my husband, and when the Ferrer School opened on 107th Street I moved to Fifth Avenue and 106th Street to be near it so my children could attend. Before that, Marucci had gone to public school. Once when denied permission to go to the bathroom she made in her pants, and I went and complained to the principal, a big, red-haired Irishwoman, who called me a "greenhorn" and all sorts of names. So I transferred her to the Ferrer School and enrolled Zack also.

The school had a little yard in back, and my son would climb the fence to celebrate his freedom. I often attended the lectures in the evening. Leonard Abbott was a delightful man, a dreamer, and his wife was a simple woman. Harry Kelly was a joy to listen to, and he loved to talk. Minna Lowensohn, a big, hefty woman, became my close friend. I heard Emma Goldman speak. Alexander Berkman was a very fine person. They were people from heaven for me. They were so different from the people with whom I had grown up. It was a completely new world.

I once met Voltairine de Cleyre while visiting the Cohens in Philadelphia, but I can't tell you anything about her. Cohen came to manage the Ferrer School later. He was a domineering personality, but he knew what he wanted and was an anarchist in spirit and action. Mary Hansen also came from Philadelphia. She taught at the school in Stelton, a delightful storyteller both for children and adults, a wonderful woman.

I moved to Stelton at the very beginning, in 1915. Robert and Delia Hutchinson were in charge, a beautiful, idealistic socialist couple. They did not fully accept the anarchist standpoint, and they wanted to establish their own school in accordance with their own ideas. Without telling anyone, they began to search for a site and found one at Stony Ford, New York. They were loved by the children and quietly wooed them away to their new school. I didn't like that. All of a sudden my own children announced that they were going with Deedie and Bobby. So I let them. Pretty soon the Hutchinsons invited me to come up and work with them.

Stony Ford lasted three years. It had good ideas. Deedie had theories on diet and believed in only two meals a day. For a week one group would cook, for the next wash dishes, and so on. They went to neighboring farms with cans for milk. They did the shopping in town with Bobby. They slept in a dormitory that was open on both sides. Deedie taught nursing and baby care. The school was a success, but Bobby fell in love with another girl, and the breakup of the marriage led to the breakup of the school. Deedie was deeply hurt. They had three children of their own. Bobby later left the new girl and married a sister of the actress Eva Le Gallienne.

We came back to Stelton. The Ferms came a year or so later, remarkable teachers and people. They put themselves out to make me understand the principles of freedom in education. There were differences in their character, which I think had mainly to do with her early life and Catholic background. She was always proud of that—of her Irish-Catholic name, Elizabeth Byrne Battle Ferm!

We didn't have a schoolhouse yet, but we had set aside land for one. Meanwhile the school was in the farmhouse, and Aunty Ferm made the barn, or carriage house, into a kindergarten. If a ten-year-old came around he was free to work there. She brought Froebel "gifts"[400] and the ideas from Froebel's books. Both were followers of Froebel. See that woodcut above my [kitchen] door? Uncle Ferm made it. Look at the inscription: "Be *thy* aim to give bread to men; let *my* striving be to give men to themselves. Froebel." It used to hang in the Stelton school.

But to have a group of parents—a whole colony—telling you what to do didn't agree with individualists like the Ferms. The community of tailors and dressmakers wanted a free school, but they wanted academics. With the Ferms there were workshops and printing but not enough academic work for immigrant Jewish workers, who themselves had always yearned for an education and who wanted their children to become educated professionals.

So the Ferms left. And without them the school began to fall apart. The Dicks [q.v. Nellie Dick] tried to put it back on its feet. But they too, like the Hutchinsons, wanted their own school. Meantime the Mohegan Modern School had opened, and it attracted some families who wanted more academic training for their children. Cohen left too—he went to Sunrise.

Camp Kilmer was the final ruin of the school. Several young children were raped by soldiers. So the remaining families began to move away. I took over in 1948, when Uncle left for Alabama, and remained until it closed in 1953. It was just a nursery with a few children at the end. Those curtains were woven by the children when I left. But I am still an anarchist, nothing else but that. I have never changed, and doubt that I ever will. People with true convictions do not change.

• HUGO GELLERT •

Freehold, New Jersey, December 28, 1972

During the First World War and its aftermath, Hugo Gellert, the Hungarian-born artist, did striking covers and sketches for Max Eastman's *The Masses* and *The Liberator*. From 1920 to 1922 he taught art and helped direct the children's theater at the Stelton Modern School in New Jersey. A supporter of the Bolshevik dictatorship, he joined the John Reed Club in New York, painted murals on social themes, engaged in antifascist activity, and drew regularly for the *Daily Worker*, *New Masses*, and other Communist publications. In later years he lived with his Australian-born wife Livia, an artist and pianist, in an eighteenth-century house near Freehold, New Jersey. When I interviewed him there in 1972, he was still reciting the orthodox Communist line—that the Soviet Union was a workers' state, that workers' councils controlled the factories and ran the economy, that

Stalin was a great leader who saved the world from Hitler, and so on. Clinging to these beliefs to the end, Gellert died at his home on December 6, 1985.

I WAS BORN in Hungary in 1892 and came to the United States as a young man before the First World War. It was Mike Gold who told me about Stelton. I had just come back from California after slacking during the war in Mexico. Mike said, "I think you'd be good with kids, and they need an art teacher at Stelton." I was interested in kids, and they took to art like ducks to water. I always felt that if a good scientist had gone out there they would all have been interested in science.

We had a great big table with different colors in one-quart jars. Little three-year-olds would say, "Please pass the magenta." They would pose for each other. I would draw too, and they made drawings of me while I was drawing or painting. Bill Pogrebysky was my star pupil, the most talented of them all, a real genius. He took over after I left—I was there about two years, between 1920 and 1922—and later worked as an artist in the Soviet Union. We had a Stelton art exhibition at the City Club in New York, in 1922 I think; see Floyd Dell's article about it in *The Liberator*. Alfred Stieglitz came and said to me, "What did you do to them? Every one of them is a genius!" There was also a two-page spread in color of the kids' work in the Sunday magazine section of the *New York World* around that time.

I knew about the theories of Ferrer, Montessori, and others, but they had very little to do with our teaching. It was a libertarian school, and one tried to give the child as much freedom as possible. Vaguely I had a theory that everybody has some natural artistic ability and merely needs the opportunity to bring it out. Old Art Young [the political cartoonist] used to say, "Every kid is a genius, but on the way they blast it out of him and destroy his creative spirit." I went on my own experiences as a child. I just encouraged them, praised their work, and they began to produce beautiful things. At the same time, I learned from the children. I was an academic product, and with them I loosened up completely. My dragon design for *The Liberator* cover was originally part of a curtain designed for the Stelton players.

In Greenwich Village Sadakichi Hartmann gave "scent concerts" that I attended. I was at a meeting of the editorial board of *The Masses* in 1917 where we voted on whether to publish a certain poem. Hippolyte Havel objected: "Phooey! Voting on poetry! Bunk!" "What about *Mother Earth*?" we asked. "We make decisions," he said, "but we don't abide by them." That's what I knew about anarchism. We had no political quarrels when I was at Stelton. It was still almost entirely an anarchist colony; the Communists came in little by little over the years. We all favored the Russian Revolution. We didn't argue much. We were concerned about the kids. I had only a hazy idea of the differences between anarchists and Communists. Later on there were disputes, but in the early years we were all excited about the revolution and too busy building up the colony to waste time quarreling.

I liked Alexis Ferm very much. As for Mrs. Ferm—well she was firm! I think she was well-meaning, but she had a dictatorial streak. Some of the children didn't take to her, while they all liked Uncle. Yet she would have done anything for the kids. She was honest and thought she was doing the right thing. Incidentally, she really believed in fairies and said she could see them under the table, and so on, and that was a nice side of her character. Alexis was gentle, easy-going, considerate. Paul Scott, who later taught at the Walden School in New York, was a very good influence. He got them interested in writing poetry by teaching them how to print it.

• LILLIAN RIFKIN BLUMENFELD •

New York City, October 15, 1975

Lillian Blumenfeld, an active figure in progressive and libertarian education, taught at the Organic School in Fairhope, Alabama, the Modern School in Stelton, New Jersey, and the Walden School in New York City, among other places. A graduate of Bloomsburg State Normal College in Pennsylvania, she studied at Columbia University's Teachers College with John Dewey and William Heard Kilpatrick and afterwards published books on children and education. In an interview on WBAI (New York), aired on October 11, 1975, she likened the child to a flower or plant, which must be allowed to grow naturally to reach its fullest development.

I WAS BORN in Wilkes-Barre, Pennsylvania, on April 9, 1897. My parents came from Moscow, where father had been a banker. They arrived in 1892 and father became a successful businessman in Wilkes-Barre. Mother's brother, Abe Heller, was a Communist and founded the International Publishers. I attended public school. We lived in a fifteen-room house, and the whole attic was my playroom. When friends came I enjoyed having them and became a kind of teacher to them. I was always, even as a child myself, interested in children and in what children can be.

I was graduated from Bloomsburg State Normal College (Pennsylvania) in 1917, then taught at a public school in Chester, near Philadelphia. My astronomy teacher at Bloomsburg always emphasized respect for the children, and that made a great impression. I was given forty children in first grade. All were Polish and many couldn't talk English. Their parents worked in ammunition plants—that was Chester's main industry at the time, during the war. I put a table in front of my desk and had a saw, a hammer, and nails, and gave each child drawing paper and crayons. Of course, it was noisy—and who had noise in first grade then? So the administration opposed these methods, and I had to resign after one year.

In 1919 I attended an international education convention in Heidelberg. There were educators from all over the world, some Montessori people, and Carl Jung[401] was the featured speaker. He said you have to look at the internal rather than the external, and I agreed with that immediately. At Heidelberg I met Martha Gruening,[402] sister of Ernest Gruening and a reporter for the Paris *Herald*, who had had a private school near Albany during the war. In Paris, after the convention, we became very good friends. I established an outdoor group for American children in Paris, and she wrote it up in her paper, and that attracted all the embassy children and others, so that it worked out very well. I lived in a little hotel near the Eiffel Tower and got to know Paris. With Martha, by the way, I visited Odenwald Schule, a progressive school near Heidelberg, which is still in existence. She enrolled her adopted black son there— she had founded the upstate New York school because of him—while she lived in Paris.

I stayed in Paris about six months, until news came that Father died, and I came back to Wilkes-Barre. We had a barn in back of our house, and I turned it into a school for poor children and brought down all my toys from the attic. Then I rented rooms for it and ran it three years (1919–1922). After that, I came to New York and went to Teachers College and took courses under John Dewey and William Heard Kilpatrick. I read in Dewey's *Schools of Tomorrow*[403] about his visit to Marietta Johnson, so I went up that summer to her school in Greenwich, Connecticut, Rosemary Hall. She said everything that I always felt about the child. She was like an evangelist, but very simple and modest—a marvelous person. That fall she gave me a job at Fairhope.[404]

I taught for one year at Fairhope (1922–1923) and loved it. Many northern single-taxers put their children in the school there. I had the eight and nine year olds. I got great big wooden cases and the children sawed out windows and doors, and we papered and painted and carpeted, and made a whole street, with a post office and store. Reading, writing, and especially arithmetic were all gotten in that way. Fairhope is on Mobile Bay, and we were Indians there for a whole week. We slept on the beach, cooked over an open fire, made beads out of chinaberry trees and clay dishes from the gulley banks, in all colors. We made small boats out of palm tree bark and sailed out into the bay. Marietta Johnson didn't want to force the children to read till they were eight. Their eyes weren't ready for it, she believed. Everything she did was in accordance with this "organic" principle, with different equipment for different age groups. The result was that the children were more creative. She also didn't like exams and didn't give any. They were too much of a strain on a child, too much worry, so you don't sleep at night. We had dictionaries and geographical magazines.

Fairhope was down south on a bay, and I couldn't take the climate, so I returned north after a year. I don't remember how I found out about Stelton— probably read about it in some education magazine. It was a boarding school, and that attracted me. The Ferms were anarchists and the environment was free. I fell in love with some of their methods. They believed in not pushing the children and not teasing or talking down to them. There was only one street, you know, with the school at one end and the boarding house at the other. The colonists worked mostly in the garment center in New York. I was there for one year, in the early 1920s, probably 1923–1924. In the Living House Aunty had the children do the cooking, the dishes, and so on. My main objection was that they were largely vegetarian and were fed peanuts from morning to night, and once a week a frankfurter or something like that. I got ringworm all over my hands as a result.

The Ferms, though, were very nice people, although she was a bit hard and authoritarian. They were idealists, and with her teaching was such an easy thing for us. There was only one room, and you could just sit down with the children and read and write. It was a very free atmosphere. Aunty never talked down to the children, and that's what I loved about her. Nellie [q.v.] and Jim Dick were there, and Sherwood Trask, who was with me at Fairhope and later at Walden. He's now in a nursing home in Naples, Florida, his mind completely gone. He was very enthusiastic and stimulated the children no end. At Walden he was the one that started trips with the children, on foot or bicycle.

I was invited to go to Mohegan, and also to Walden, and I chose the latter, which was then called the Children's School and headed by Margaret Naumann. I was there almost fifteen years. I went to Russia in 1929 with the head of Walden, Margaret Politzer, to see the schools there, and I loved it. They were using the Dalton plan and other progressive methods. They were warm-hearted people and loved the children. Most of the experimentation was scrapped during the thirties under Stalin.

I left Walden when I married a widower from Austria with two daughters. But I continue my activity in education and published a book, *Our Planet the Earth* (New York, Shepard, 1938) and a series called *When I Grow Up I'll Be* (1938–1940).[405]

• SUZANNE HOTKINE AVINS •

Bronx, New York, March 5, 1973

Suzanne Avins taught French and music at the Modern School of Stelton, New Jersey, in 1924 and 1925, when Alexis and Elizabeth Ferm were coprincipals. She also played the piano at morning assembly, a daily ritual at the school, and assisted the children and parents in other ways. After leaving Stelton, she attended the Juilliard School of Music in New York and gave piano lessons in the Bronx, where she lived with her husband Will, a sheet-metal worker, who died of a heart attack in 1975. Suzanne died of cancer four years later.

I WAS BORN in 1906 in Russia of Jewish parents and came to Paris as a small child. We came to America in 1924, when I was eighteen years old. I began to study music at Juilliard. I liked the freedom of American schools, but a roomer in our apartment told me about a *really* free school, at Stelton, New Jersey.

Coming from France, with its rigid school system, the idea drew me at once, and I went there for a visit. It was an experience of a lifetime. I went on a beautiful June day. I was impressed by the warm, friendly atmosphere, the peacefulness and play. In front of the Living House (formerly the farmhouse) I saw a lady dressed in white, with a white ruffled hat and sparkling blue eyes, sitting out front shelling peas. "I'm Aunty Ferm," she said with a radiant smile. (But she could be a son-of-a-bitch too, I soon found out.) I saw a little naked boy on the road with blond curls and asked him for the school. He said, "You walk and see a beautiful house. That's the school."

Aunty asked me to stay for the summer and play the piano at morning assembly. I went home and told my parents. My father—a shoemaker, free-thinker, and poet—agreed. But when I got back to Stelton, there was a tremendous wall of coldness from Aunty. She was aloof, unapproachable. I wanted to go home. The next morning she didn't even come to assembly. Yet it wasn't long before she came to love me. I stayed all summer, and at the end, the children, in tears, begged me to remain. So I stayed for two years, traveling to Juilliard in New York three days a week. In addition to playing at assembly, I taught music and French. I stayed till the end of 1925, when the Ferms left. After that I came back occasionally to teach on weekends and in summertime after the Ferms returned. But by then the magic was gone from Stelton. It had come to an end in the mid-twenties.

I was sublimely happy in that place during those two years. At morning assembly we sang greetings to the sun, then nature songs, followed by improvised dancing. Ethel Butler danced beautifully (she later joined Martha Graham's troupe). I organized a small band in 1924. I produced by hand fifty copies of "Stories from Music Land" for the children.

In the schoolhouse Aunty insisted on rainbow colors—primary colors—as in Froebel "gifts." It brought out the positive side of people, of life, she said. No other colors were allowed. There was something mystical about this, as with Froebel himself, but it was very beautiful. Her mysticism was powerful. She was still full of religion, full of the convent from which she had come. She had a horror of sex. She was puritanical, with a repressed sexual drive and a strange attitude towards men. She was far stronger than Uncle, a bigger person, more complex, more profound than he was, but harder too. If a child came to school without a shirt on a hot day she would send him home. And she objected to nudity in the colony—even at swimming—and tried to stop it. She was a fiery Irish woman who would brook no interference from anyone and looked down on the immigrant colonists as somehow inferior. She even had a deep-seated anti-Semitic streak, stemming from her Irish Catholic upbringing. Despite her break with the church, she was still a Catholic, and Catholicism meant a great deal to her. Yet at the same time she had a broad outlook, a wide scope.

Of the two, Aunty and Uncle, she was the visionary; it was she who inspired him. She had ten pairs of eyes. She didn't mix much with the colonists, but knew what was going on in every household. She was very Irish. She recited Gaelic poetry, sang Gaelic songs, marched in St. Patrick's Day parades. She was a twisted genius. She spoke French fairly well and played the piano with verve, especially Beethoven. Her playing, though lacking technically, had spiritual greatness about it. We played duets for hours—Haydn, Beethoven, Mozart. Uncle too loved music. I played "The Moonlight Sonata" for him on his 101st birthday and the tears came streaming down his face. He was softer, sweeter than she, but she was the heart of the educational experiment.

The Living House was immaculately kept by the Ferms. There were no electric lights then, but nice kerosene lamps, with murals on the walls, as in the school. Uncle made much of the furniture, and it was beautifully finished. I still think of it with excitement. Next to the school were four shops: weaving, carpentry, printing, art. Bill Pogrebysky was in charge of the last, and it was the most popular. The children brought art exhibits and plays to New York City. John Dewey came to visit Stelton. During the five years under the Ferms no doctor ever had to be called. But Uncle carried his distrust for doctors too far. Once he refused to call a doctor when Minnie Bluestein got a rusty nail embedded in her knee and insisted in pulling it out himself, which was very painful and left a permanent scar. The teachers included Paul Scott, Anna Koch, and Erica Feist, now in Pennsylvania, the sister-in-law of Charles Garland.[406] I have a good caricature of Aunty Ferm by Erica. Hans and Anna Koch[407] were separated and did not live together. She was an excellent gardener as well as weaver. Hans was also very competent, very German, dignified with a long mustache.

The Ferms had run a school at Dyker Heights [in Brooklyn] from 1902 to 1906, then on Madison Street on the Lower East Side from 1906 to 1913. They had land in Newfoundland, New Jersey, where I visited them often. They had a farm in Connecticut—after Madison Street and before coming to Stelton— and ran it very successfully. She got tired of it and responded to the children's need for a director. The same with Stelton: she got bored when it reached its height. As soon as it was a success she left, like a rolling stone. She was a great woman, a difficult woman. She left the school in the lurch. They packed themselves up and went off.

Uncle also was director of the Pioneer Youth Camp in the early thirties and taught at the Manumit School. He and Aunty hated the term "progressive" education, and they disliked the Montessori method, with its authoritarianism and emphasis on early reading. Progressive to them implied goody-goody sugar coating, whereas their education implied a situation where the individual has to face himself. Progressivism implies that there is no growth, no pain, no struggle. Progressivism was to cover up pain, overprotect the children. They preferred public schools to progressive.

Uncle was an old single-taxer, though he was never able to explain it to me. He spent his last years at Fairhope, the single-tax colony in Alabama (his address was 515 Equality Avenue). He greatly admired Ernest Crosby[408] and often spoke about him in later years. And Aunty quoted Emma Goldman to me all the time. I came to Stelton for a day, I stayed two years, and it has remained a part of me forever.

• ANATOLE FREEMAN ISHILL •

Staten Island, New York, September 23, 1975

Anatole Freeman Ishill is the son of the anarchist printer Joseph Ishill (1888–1966), known for his magnificent hand-produced volumes on Peter Kropotkin, Elisée and Elie Reclus, and others, and of Rose Florence Freeman, a lyrical poet. Anatole was a pupil at the Modern School of Stelton, where his father taught printing to the children and printed *The Modern School* magazine.

I WAS BORN in the Bronx in 1918. Father had built a one-room house at Stelton at the beginning of the colony, in 1915 or 1916. He got together with Mother in 1917. They moved to the Bronx in 1918, and then to Berkeley Heights, New Jersey, the following year. We lived in Stelton for a few years in the mid-1920s, while keeping the house in Berkeley Heights, and I attended school there under the Ferms. I found Uncle a warm person. Aunty was more firm, but I liked her too. I was very happy in the school because there was a sense of freedom as to what you could do, yet it was very orderly and harmonious. I was interested in weaving, and Anna Koch was my teacher. I can't remember any public school teacher so vividly. Every child had a little project, and I had mine. That appealed to me. I liked the way things were taught—the activity, the story-telling. Bill Pogrebysky was another fine teacher that I can remember. And my father taught printing. I stayed at the Living House at times, sleeping on bunks with straw mattresses.

We left Stelton around 1927. There was some kind of crisis or conflict at the school,[409] and I was never a student there again, though Father went back and forth for many years and I sometimes went with him, making the journey from Berkeley Heights on foot. We also visited the Ferms at Newfoundland in the late 1930s, and I was very happy to see them.

Father was stubborn, strong-willed, unbending, even towards his own children. We always took a back place. Mother, too, was distant and remote. She was a true genius and did much of the writing and revising that appears under Father's name. Few people came to visit our house, though Father carried on an extensive correspondence with anarchists all over the world. Father was a strict vegetarian and a Thoreauvian. He belonged to the Thoreau Society and we all visited Walden Pond in 1962, which was for him a kind of mystical experience. He also saw himself as a successor to William Morris, whose work he greatly admired. Ernst Bloch, the composer, came to visit us, and we went to Pennsylvania to visit Bertha Johnson[410] and her husband at their dairy farm. We stayed there two or three days at a time and saw Oriole Tucker [Riché, q.v.] there. What lovely people they were. Mother converted to Catholicism in 1968, two years after Father's death.

• BEN FRUMKIN •

Rockaway Park, New York, April 20, 1981

Ben Frumkin, the son of a veteran anarchist, Leibush Frumkin, who took part in the Russian Revolution of 1905, attended the Stelton Modern School and was a member of the Rising Youth Group in New York. During the 1930s, however, he abandoned anarchism as vague and ineffective and, to the consternation of his father, became a supporter of the Soviet Union.

I WAS BORN in London in 1911, in Whitechapel. Both of my parents were garment workers and anarchists from Russian Poland. My older sister Rose attended Nellie Dick's [q.v.] nursery school run on Ferrer lines. My parents knew all the anarchists involved in the Houndsditch affair,[411] and Luba Milstein's son, Alfred Driscoll, is one of my oldest friends. We came to the United States in 1912, when I was one year old. My father, Leibush Frumkin, was an active member of the executive board of Local 22 of the ILGWU and of the *Fraye Arbeter Shtime*. Mother was on the executive board of Local 38. So you can see that I grew up in an anarchist and labor milieu.

In 1919 my sister and I were sent to Stelton, where we stayed in the Living House until 1923. When we arrived, Fred Dunn was in charge of the Living House, and Gray Wu was the cook, a quiet, studious young man. I liked the school and liked both Uncle and Aunty Ferm, though she once expelled a young boy and girl who were fooling around in the high grass. When I came back to New York in 1923 to live with my mother, I was put in grade 6B. During the summers I went to the Ferms' place at Newfoundland, New Jersey, a beautiful place, where we lived in a tent, hiked, climbed mountains, picked cherries (my sister baked pies from them), and hunted for copperheads. I was graduated from elementary school in 1926 and from the High School of Commerce in 1930.

The Goodman twins, Sara and Elizabeth, started *The Rising Youth* in 1928. I knew them from childhood, and our parents knew each other from London. Catherine Karpoff knew them too. They smoked a lot. They always supported each other. Both of them were interested in Spinoza and seemed to know all about him. We started the paper together and used to go to Union Square and distribute it in front of the Workers' Cafeteria. The workers came out and argued with us and wanted to beat us up. The older anarchists had a club on East Twenty-Third Street, the International Center. That was sort of our headquarters. The twins later went to Chicago. Both married and died there.

After about 1930 I was no longer involved in the anarchist movement. When I attended meetings with Harry Kelly or Joseph Cohen or some other well-known anarchist, I found that they all had different ideas about what anarchism meant. And they never seemed to get anything done. Anarchism didn't seem to be effectual. I had read Alexander Berkman's *ABC of Communist Anarchism*.[412] It sounded good—but what do you do from here? That was my reaction.

My sister Rose had married Bill Pogrebysky, whose mother was a charter member of the Communist Party. I went to one of their meetings, and the place was packed. There were thousands, not forty or fifty like the anarchists. I thought: They can attract people; that's power! You need solidarity, where people march together and follow a single line that keeps them in step, as in the Soviet Union. Whatever its faults, it works. It gets things done. My father, old-time anarchist that he was, was very disappointed in me. After the Nazi-Soviet Pact he didn't speak to me for six months. But the pact didn't trouble me. I supported the Soviet Union. They kept on going—and didn't have capitalism. That's the important thing.

• SIEGFRIED ROLLAND •

Elmhurst, New York, June 3, 1973

Siegfried Rolland, the son of Hugo Rolland (q.v.) and Bertha Blackman, attended the Modern School of Stelton during the 1920s and went on to become a professor of history at the University of Idaho. He died of heart failure on January 19, 1989.

I WAS BORN in New York on February 12, 1918, and attended the Modern School at Stelton during the 1920s, when the Ferms were in charge. Aunty Ferm was an extremely harsh disciplinarian. Once I was with a group of older boys who broke into one of the shacks and took some things—I took a water pistol—and she scolded me, worked me over. If a child wet his bed, she made him sleep in the wet sheets. Also, I didn't learn to read until the eighth grade, after I had left Stelton. But she had a way, you know. We occasionally hiked up to Green Pond, near Newfoundland, New Jersey, some thirty miles north of Stelton, and stayed at the Ferms' house.

At Stelton the boys and girls slept in the same dormitory, showered together, swam naked together. Isadora Duncan's brother Raymond Duncan often visited the colony in his flowing robes. The Young Pioneers were organized by the Communists at Stelton in the mid-1920s. They sang Communist songs, read Communist books, and so on. It was all very dogmatic and authoritarian. I couldn't join that! Bill Pogrebysky went back to Russia and died in the Second World War. His father drowned in Birobidzhan.

The whole experience at Stelton made it possible for me, more than anything else, to live with the current generation of college students, to sympathize with them, to adjust to their informality and permissiveness. It also gave me an opportunity to become interested in a tremendous variety of things that you couldn't get in a regular school.

• ESTHER WALTERS •

New York City, October 19, 1972 (telephone)

Esther Walters, formerly of Stelton, was a member of the April Farm community in Quakerstown, Pennsylvania, founded by Charles Garland in the 1920s. She left the community in 1929, a year or so before its dissolution. She died in New York in 1975.

CHARLES GARLAND came into a large inheritance which he wanted to repudiate, but Roger Baldwin [q.v.] persuaded him to put it to use in worthy causes. He set up Vanguard Press and established a small colony in Massachusetts in 1924, which soon moved to Pennsylvania. He called it April Farm, and it lasted until about 1930.

It was a small colony, with about thirty or thirty-five regular members, including many anarchists, two or three of whom (including myself) came from Stelton. We had beautiful peach and apple orchards, a vegetable garden, and a communal dining room. The first spring there was the happiest of my life, so I was all the more hurt and disappointed when the colony fell apart.

The regular members worked very hard, at least at first. But there were many, many visitors, who came for a weekend or a summer. For them it was a vacation. They ate, slept, sat under a tree philosophizing, and didn't work. Under such circumstances a colony cannot survive. Marital problems arose, and bitter personal quarrels, and the community fell apart. I left in 1929, and it failed a year or so later. To this day I remain bitter and disillusioned. Most people are parasites.

• RINA GARST •

New York City, October 24, 1972

Rina Garst is the daughter of Abe Winokour and Anna Sosnovsky, both of them ardent anarchists, who named her after Voltairine de Cleyre and her sister Tisa after Sacco and Vanzetti, and who chose to be buried in Chicago's Waldheim Cemetery, near the graves of Emma Goldman and the Haymarket martyrs. Rina

attended the Modern School at Stelton, where she was born, and afterwards lived
in the Mohegan Colony, where she knew such well-known anarchists as Rudolf
Rocker and Harry Kelly.

I WAS BORN in Stelton in 1931 as Voltairine de Cleyre Winokour, the second
daughter of Abe Winokour and Anna Sosnovsky, both dedicated anarchists
who are now buried in Waldheim Cemetery, Chicago. My sister's name is Tisa,
"ti" from Vanzetti, "sa" from Sacco. She now lives in California. At Stelton I
recall in 1937 driving through the colony with Father collecting clothing for
Spanish anarchist refugees. We also went to the Johnson & Johnson factory in
New Brunswick to buy bandages and medical supplies to send to Spain. Spain
was the overriding issue at that time, and I was weaned on anti-Communism,
the Communists being the betrayers of the Russian Revolution and now of the
Spanish Revolution. There was a big fight in the colony during the thirties
between the anarchists and the Communists, even when I was a baby. Ma was
so upset that her milk became poisoned and she almost died. Dr. Stretch saved
Ma by putting me on goat's milk, and we then kept a goat in our back yard. It
was Dr. Stretch, though, who may have been responsible for Ma's death, but
we'll come back to that later.

I started school at Stelton as soon as I was able to walk. My parents worked,
so my sister Tisa (she was three and a half years older, born ten days after the
execution of Sacco and Vanzetti and hence named after them) took me. I was
very happy in the school, and especially in the print shop. There were, of
course, big holes in my knowledge, but in terms of attitude, of our way of
looking at life, these gaps were counterbalanced. I can't separate the school
from the colony—I can't tell what in my thinking is attributable to the school
and what to the colony and the way we lived. Our house was a political center
with constant visitors, meetings, etc. Whenever a conference was held in the
colony our house was filled with people and talk. We were vegetarians, though
by that time very few members were vegetarians, in contrast to the early years.

In 1936 or 1937 Mom had a nervous breakdown and we went to Florida for
two or three months so she could recuperate. We settled in West Palm Beach.
The neighbors thought us strange: we were vegetarians, we didn't go to school,
we had unorthodox views, and so on.

When we returned to Stelton the Ferms were still in charge. I liked Uncle a
lot but didn't care for Aunty. She was too strict. In fact she was one of the few
people who ever punished me in my life. One day I skated to school without
bringing my shoes, and to teach me to remember things she made me walk
around all morning on skates. I had great admiration for Aunty, but I didn't
think she was a warm person; I couldn't love her the way I loved the other
teachers. Though I learned things from her—she was a good teacher—I saw her
mainly as a cranky old lady. Uncle could be fun, but she didn't laugh much. He
used to take us camping, hiking, and riding around in the rumble seat of his old
car. I didn't care much for Anna Schwartz [q.v.] either. I couldn't warm up to
her and, unlike Aunty, she was not a good teacher. We were the last generation

of the real Stelton children. The school was already deteriorating, with only fifteen or twenty kids: me and Tisa, Lenny Rico, Jo Ann's [Burbank, q.v.] children, etc. Camp Kilmer was built in 1941. The place was no longer a closely knit community.

My parents had been in California years before and always planned to go back. But with the danger of a "Japanese invasion" and other reasons we moved to Mohegan in May 1942. The school had already gone under, so we were enrolled in public school for the first time. The experience was absolutely shattering: the discipline and routine and rigid structure. In Stelton we would spend half a day on a project if we wanted; there were no time periods, which are artificial and confusing. I also had a reading and writing shock, not knowing formal grammar—I didn't even know what an adjective was. That and other differences from the regular kids made us a bit self-conscious and uncomfortable.

We lived in Mohegan from 1941 to 1948. I attended Peekskill High School for the seventh and eighth grades and did very well. But we didn't have any feeling of colony at Mohegan. Yet what a beautiful place it was! Helen Rudome was Mom's best friend. Rudolf Rocker was the most respected resident there, and I loved him. He was a warm person and exuded humanity. Whenever Pop said, "I'm going to see Rudolf," I would try to tag along. I liked Harry Kelly but I adored Rudolf. He never talked down to me but spoke on an equal level. Harry Kelly was a real talker. In 1947 there was a huge blizzard and at the railroad station people were snowed in, so he talked for twelve hours and got everyone together. Apart from Rocker, the French were the most interesting people in the colony.

We moved to California in 1948, to Los Angeles. Mother got sick en route and died of breast cancer in 1949. She had already been ill in Mohegan and went to Dr. Stretch for consultation. He said it was nothing serious and prescribed a diet remedy. Rocker came to California in January or February 1949 and talked to her with kindness and gentleness. She died in May. She had been born in 1900 in the same *shtetl* as Rose Pesotta, the third of five daughters; three were active anarchists: Mom, Fanny Breslaw, and Lisa Luchkovsky.

The family name was Luchkovsky, but one branch took the name Sosnovksy to avoid conscription into the tsarist army, and Mom adopted it, as she told a judge in the U.S., because it was easier to spell! She was a little woman, five feet tall, and nice-looking. She came to America in 1912. She lived on the Lower East Side and went to work in the garment industry, where she got her anarchism: the *Fraye Arbeter Shtime*, the Ferrer Center, etc. She rose in the ILGWU to the position of organizer (in New Jersey) and manager of her local. She took part in the colony movement and was secretary of many conferences and meetings. She attended Brookwood Labor College for two years with Rose Pesotta when A. J. Muste was its head.[413] She came to Stelton and got together with Dad around 1925. They married officially in 1944 so she could get her citizenship papers. She and Dad were very active in the Sacco and Vanzetti campaign. She was a thoroughly dedicated anarchist. When she was a young girl Sasha Berkman teased her that the revolution would begin at 3 A.M. on such and such date in Union Square, and she, Rose Pesotta, and Helen Rudome (then Goldblatt) actually went there!

Dad was born of a middle-class family in the Ukraine in 1894. He came to the U.S. around the same time as Mom, 1911 or 1912, and settled in Philadelphia. He became a paperhanger and member of the Radical Library. He spent the First World War in Mexico as a conscientious objector. He went to Stelton in 1922 and built a house there. He got together with Mom, went to California in 1927 (after the Sacco-Vanzetti execution), and returned in 1930 to Stelton, where I was born. He was an active rank-and-filer in the painters' union and was later president of his local in Peekskill.

• MOLLIE ALBERT •

Bronx, New York, October 7, 1972

Mollie Albert and her husband Jack, both Jewish immigrants from Eastern Europe, were active anarchists in New York during the early decades of the twentieth century. They frequented the Ferrer Center in Harlem and were among the first to go to the Stelton Colony in New Jersey when it was established in 1915. During the mid-1920s they moved to the Mohegan Colony, near Peekskill, New York, and from 1933 to 1935 were members of the Sunrise Co-operative Farm Community in Michigan, founded by the Jewish anarchist Joseph Cohen.

I WAS BORN in Przemysl, in Austria-Hungary, on October 15, 1892, into a religious family with rabbis on both sides. My father's father was a furrier. Father went to school, started a bank, and prospered. But he had compassion for the poor. Felix Frankfurter was his cousin. Father emigrated to the United States but was greatly disappointed, as he was unable to found a bank. We came to New York in 1907. Father returned to his father's trade, becoming a furrier. At sixteen I met Jack Albert, who was twenty-one, an accountant who wrote for the *Fraye Arbeter Shtime*. He introduced me to anarchism. He left the *Fraye Arbeter Shtime* to work for Dr. Liber's *Unzer Gezunt*, published for three years in Yiddish, then two years in English, as *Our Health*.

Dr. Liber was an anarchist and a psychiatrist at the Polyclinic Hospital in New York. He was the author of books and editor of journals on health, physical and mental, the warmest person in the world; he loved children and made friends easily with disturbed children. He was active in the Ferrer Center, lecturing on hygiene, diet, and the like, and also taught art. We became vegetarians because of Dr. Liber. We were devoted to him throughout his whole life and gave a party for him on his eightieth birthday in 1955. He died a few years later. He had a brother named Liberty Liber and a son named Amour Liber [q.v.] (Free Love), a Cornell graduate, now a doctor at the Veterans Hospital in the Bronx, where he is a pathologist and a professor at the Einstein Institute. Dr. Liber suggested the name of Freethought for our son; he insisted on it.

We knew Bolton Hall very well and lived at his Free Acres Colony (in New Jersey) for a while. He gave away most of his land in the course of his lifetime. We also knew Leonard Abbott, who was the most outgoing and generous person in the world, very soft. When his wife Rose got ill no one helped him. He devoted himself to her, read to her.[414] Harry Kelly was a wonderful speaker and human being. His daughter Elsie was a marvelous little girl and also a good speaker.

I was in the first group to go to Stelton and had frequented the Ferrer Center in New York before that. My husband built our house there, and we lived there during the summer for seven years. During that period we had a vegetarian restaurant in Harlem and later one at Bushkill. Dr. Stretch was influential at Stelton. Anna Sosnovsky died because of him: she had a breast tumor and he treated it with massage. He was an extremist—raw vegetables, fresh air. Lydia Gordon was his most devoted follower.

We went to Mohegan colony in the mid-twenties. We conducted a separate kindergarten there, not part of the school. We lived in George Seldes Senior's house until our own house was finished. He was a fine man. His wife died young of tuberculosis and he lived alone at Mohegan. We lived there two years and then several summers. It was wonderful. We had the most wonderful times at the beginning. For a while I was in charge of the Living House with forty children. We had entertainments, dances, parties; we gave dinners to raise money for the school. But wealthier nonanarchists like Bern Dibner[415] wanted county water and county roads. So taxes went up and the poorer members were forced to move out.

We were at the Sunrise colony in Michigan from the beginning and stayed two years. Jack was in charge of the grain elevator. We knew Joseph Cohen in Stelton and liked him, though he was a heavier, duller speaker and writer than Saul Yanovsky. Yanovsky was a vibrant, inspiring speaker, and his columns and editorials in the *Fraye Arbeter Shtime* had pep. Cohen's daughter Emma [Gilbert, q.v.] spent a lot of time in our house. Cohen was refused membership in Mohegan, but he had a summer camp near the colony, Camp Sharon, which lasted a few summers. His son-in-law Richard Gilbert [q.v.] helped him, and some blamed Gilbert when the camp failed and left debts. Cohen was no longer editor of the *Fraye Arbeter Shtime*. He was at loose ends. So he got the idea to form a colony. He wrote to Eli Greenblatt in Philadelphia. Greenblatt bought ten thousand acres for $135,000 from the Pittsburgh Glass Company, which sold it cheap after Greenblatt and Cohen explained their purpose. The Depression was on, and people flocked to us from all over. But Cohen was very obstinate. One time he didn't let anybody go into the office. We left because of the friction. Jack couldn't stand it. He tried to talk to Cohen privately and persuade him to be more lenient, more flexible, but to no avail. So we decided to leave. When the farm was sold to the government, each sharecropper—

there were about fifteen or twenty of them—got a forty-acre plot. For city folk it was backbreaking work. When the garment industry revived and jobs opened up in New York, they all rushed back to the city.

• MOLLY BOGIN •

Peekskill, New York, November 8, 1983

Molly Bogin, an immigrant from Russia, was acquainted with Emma Goldman, Alexander Berkman, and other prominent anarchists in New York through her husband, Sidor Bogin, a devotee of Bakunin and Kropotkin, who had been imprisoned as an anarchist during the Revolution of 1905. For many years Molly and Sidor were residents of the Mohegan Colony near Peekskill, New York. In 1973 I was introduced to Molly by her friend Eva Brandes (q.v.) at a *Fraye Arbeter Shtime* luncheon in New York. A decade later, accompanied by Eva, I interviewed her at a nursing home near Mohegan. Molly died in April 1992, a month before her 105th birthday.

I WAS BORN Marisia Skliar eighty-six years ago [she is actually much older] in the village of Kazar in Chernigov *guberniia*, near the city of Nezhin. Father worked for a tobacco company in Nezhin. Mother was a housewife. She died when I was fourteen. I had three brothers and two sisters. When I was sixteen I went to work in a dress shop as a finisher. My stepmother, whom I didn't care for, made me learn how to sew. I wanted to get away, so, still sixteen, I left home and went to Nezhin and got a job in a store, selling dry goods. I made enough to save money to go to America. In 1906, when I was seventeen, I went to Odessa and boarded a ship for America.

I was alone when I landed in New York. But a friend in Nezhin had given me the address of her sister, so I had a place to go. I soon got a job in a dress shop. I knew how to sew and was able to make a living, though it wasn't easy. I began to go to meetings of the Yiddish anarchists. I don't remember why—maybe a friend in the shop brought me. I also read the *Fraye Arbeter Shtime* and other anarchist papers. I liked what they had to say. Once, at a lecture, I met Emma Goldman. She was in the audience; a man was the speaker. She liked me, and when I saw her at later meetings she always came over to talk. She was short, spoke very fast, and I didn't always understand what she said. I also met Alexander Berkman. He was my husband Sidor Bogin's friend. Berkman was a very nice person. I liked him better than Emma. She talked too much about herself. Berkman was more modest and more intelligent. He was ready to listen.

I met my husband Sidor at a lecture. He was also from Nezhin, and we had a lot to talk about. In Russia he had been a printer. He had been arrested during the 1905 Revolution and had been in prison. When he came to America he took up the trade of housepainting. He also taught himself carpentry. And he loved farming. He never liked the city.

We visited Stelton a number of times, but didn't live there. After the Mohegan colony was started, we bought a plot of land and built our own house. That was in 1925. Sidor did all the work himself. I worked in a dress shop in Peekskill, while Sidor was a painter. We also raised chickens—Sidor built the chicken coops. He loved to read—he read Bakunin and Kropotkin in Russian—and was a real anarchist, much more than I. Harry Kelly was our good friend. He knew a lot and loved to talk. But he had no airs and he always tried to help when needed. We also knew George Seldes, Joseph Cohen, and other active anarchists. We had picnics at the colony, brought in famous speakers, held meetings, had arguments. Rudolf Rocker came to the colony during the 1930s. He was a very intelligent and interesting man. Like Harry Kelly, he had no airs about him. He would talk to us as equals, even if we knew nothing. He never tried to make himself big. His wife Milly was also very nice and took part in everything we did. The anarchists were in general honest and intelligent people—more so than most. They were idealists. You could learn a lot from them.

• LALLAH BLANPIED •

New Rochelle, New York, April 7, 1972

Lallah Blanpied, an intelligent and articulate woman, served as director of the Mohegan Modern School in 1935–1936 and was a close friend of the American anarchist Harry Kelly, a founder of the Mohegan Colony, located near Peekskill, New York. I interviewed her at her home in company with Eva Brandes (q.v.), a longtime resident of the colony.

HARRY KELLY, whom I knew well at Mohegan and here in New Rochelle, was born in St. Charles, Missouri. His father died when Harry was eight, and he got a job in a grocery to help support a large family. He was self-educated and very well-read. He rode the rails through the U.S. His first glimpse of Pittsburgh from a boxcar reminded him of Dante's inferno. He was of a very generous nature. He took in the son of his first wife, Mary Krimont, who had left him briefly for another man, and raised him as his own child, Wally Krimont.

Harry visited the Whiteway colony in England in the 1890s, a foretaste of his own later ventures with colonies. He supported the United States war effort in both world wars. He loved children and adored his grandchildren. He had a marvelous sense of humor. He could swear like a trouper. He loved to talk. He liked parties. He knew baseball from A to Z and wouldn't miss a game on TV in his later years, until his eyesight failed. He refused to compromise his anarchist principles or even to consider other points of view on the subject. He was an arbitrator of family quarrels at Mohegan. He didn't want the law involved. He always spoke of "discipline from within," personal discipline. He opposed having the police in the colony.

Harry never lost faith in anarchism or changed his fundamental principles. He was an individualist. He believed that everyone in the colony should have his own house and plot of land. He didn't care about his food or clothes. He knew the French Revolution from beginning to end and read everything about it. When he was old he was interviewed by Harry Hopkins in Washington for a job in the Roosevelt administration, in the TVA,[416] I think. On his application form he filled in his politics as "anarchist." Hopkins said that that would offend the president. Harry refused to write anything else. "I've been an anarchist all my life," he said.

I met Harry about 1930. He brought me to Mohegan in 1935 as director of the school. The job lasted only one year, 1935–1936. I had a terrible time up there. I was disillusioned. I had previously swallowed anarchist philosophy hook, bait, and sinker. I had read Kropotkin and Dewey and was familiar with Froebel, Ferrer, and Pestalozzi.[417] The parents interfered with the teaching and with my administration. Political differences among them had an adverse effect on the school. I commuted from New Rochelle, attended all the meetings, got worn out, got sick, and quit. There was a continual fight between colonists who wanted the state to take over the school so as to get more money for teachers and to improve the school (Bern Dibner was one of these) and those (mostly anarchists) who firmly opposed state control. On the positive side there was freedom to teach and for the child to talk and learn. There were small classes, twelve to fifteen maximum. Jacques Dubois [q.v.], the shop teacher, did wonderful things with the children. Those children were the most worldly wise I had ever taught. They knew as much about the Spanish Revolution as most adults and could discuss it intelligently. Some of the alumni did well. Iris Miroy got a doctorate in biology at Harvard. Billy Stevens became an outstanding engineer.

John Scott had been my sociology teacher at Kansas State College. He called himself a "Thoreauvian anarchist" and had first editions of all of Thoreau's books. He was born in the coal mines of Virginia. The police shot his father, a miner, dead before his eyes during a strike. He was a brilliant boy. He finished high school in two years. He was Phi Beta Kappa in college and later got a Ph.D. He named his son Jon Thoreau and his daughter Shelley. He edited *Mother Earth* with Jo Ann Wheeler [Burbank, q.v.], and later edited *Money* in New York, which he called in the paper "Jew York." Among the finest colonists was Sophie Bannister, a genuine anarchist, extremely considerate and generous to other people. André Miroy, a translator, was one of the truest anarchists in the colony, clear-headed and responsible.

I always felt that Harry Kelly should have married Minna Lowensohn rather than her sister Leah. Minna was devoted to him, a real anarchist who shared his philosophy. Leah, by contrast, disliked colonies and wanted legal marriage (they were married in Italy). Sam and Hilda Adel [q.v.] of Mount Airy colony in Croton are the uncle and aunt of Leon Edel, the biographer of Henry James. They were staunch anarchists. Sam was a fine cabinetmaker.

• DOROTHY RICK •

Lake Mohegan, New York, September 19, 1972

Dorothy Rick, a woman of Quaker background, taught at the Mohegan Modern School from 1933 to 1939. She died at Mohegan in 1976.

THE COMMUNITY and the school were one—one big family. The children didn't feel they were being held in. They loved the school. They didn't look upon it as most children look on school. Yet there was enough structure so that the children did not feel at loose ends. If you wanted to punish a child, you would threaten to keep him home from school. Most of the kids did exceedingly well in high school. At first they would keep interrupting, asking questions, having ideas of their own. But the teachers—some at least—began to appreciate this as valuable to the class.

We knew little of Ferrer's theories; not many people had even heard of Ferrer. I had studied Dewey, but not much theory was involved here. It was a progressive school, not a libertarian or Modern school. Reading was taught when the children were ready for it. It wasn't pushed on them. "Projects" were a big thing, something they're trying to do now in most schools. We studied Egypt as a unit, not its geography, history, etc., separately. We had a similar project on American Indians. We made trips to New York to study city life and did a large mural about our impressions. We had hiking, camping, and other outdoor activities. The grown-ups put on plays. Once they did Gilbert and Sullivan's *Mikado*, in which "Three Little Maids from School" was sung with a Jewish accent and one of the little maids was five feet nine inches tall. One man in the audience laughed so hard he fell off the windowsill.

• JACQUES DUBOIS •

Lake Mohegan, New York, September 19, 1972

Jacques Dubois, a sturdy man with white hair and mustache, was one of a half-dozen or so French anarchists who resided in the Mohegan Colony near New York between the 1920s and 1970s. Before settling in Mohegan, where he taught carpentry to the pupils of the Modern School, he had frequented the Ferrer Center in Harlem and lived at the Stelton Colony in New Jersey, where he helped take care of the children.

I WAS BORN in 1888 and left Paris at seventeen or eighteen. I had already been an anarchist, in the L'Endehors Group,[418] and had gotten into trouble with the law. I spent three years in London, where I knew Tom Keell,[419] Errico Malatesta, and Rudolf Rocker, whom I knew again later at Mohegan. I came to New York in 1910 and worked as a jewelry designer. There were no French groups in New York at that time; the French anarchists here were mostly individualists, who were not for the "working class" or "revolution." I went to see Emma Goldman at the *Mother Earth* office, attended the Ferrer Center, and took part in a protest for Kotoku at the Japanese consulate.[420] At the Ferrer Center we were happy; you could meet whomever you wanted.

From the Ferrer Center I went to Stelton and took care of the children for a time. In the mid-twenties I went with some comrades to Costa Rica to establish a colony there; I remained for a year and a half, while others stayed much longer. When I returned to the U.S., the Mohegan colony had already been established and I went there. During that period a Modern School had been planned also for the Bronx and a house rented for the purpose, but it fell through.

The Mohegan school was better than the one at Stelton. I wanted a libertarian school for my kids, and I served as custodian and a member of the board. All of our children enjoyed the school, loved it. I lived anarchism. That's what I wanted—not when I'm dead. I'm satisfied. I never had as good a time as I had here in the colony. But as property increased in value and people made money, the spirit dissipated, the movement declined. Anarchism was a movement of poor immigrants. As soon as the children made money, they lost anarchism.

• HENRY FRUCHTER •

New York City, May 1, 1972

Henry Fruchter, a half-brother of Emma Goldman's secretary Pauline Turkel (q.v.), frequented the Ferrer Center in New York, lived at Stelton, and moved to Mohegan, where he was a trustee of the Mohegan Colony Association. In 1922 he became head of the Naturalization Aid League, in which he remained active until his death in 1974 at the age of eighty-three. Although he early abandoned anarchism for socialism, he worked with the anarchists throughout his life and was a member of the Libertarian Book Club, serving briefly as its executive secretary.

I WAS BORN in Galicia in 1891 and came to New York in 1901, the year of President McKinley's assassination. I got a job in the New York Public Library and taught myself typing and stenography. I then got a job in the New York District Attorney's office, where I worked until 1917. I lived on East 112th Street, near the Ferrer Center, which I attended frequently. It was open every day and in the evenings. There was always something interesting going on— lectures, concerts, plays—and interesting people to meet. My half-sister Pauline Turkel [q.v.] became Emma Goldman's secretary at *Mother Earth*.

At the Ferrer Center I met Harry Kelly. What impressed me most about him was his sweetness. He was gentle, and it was a joy to listen to him. He wasn't as sharp as Emma Goldman or as aggressive in his pronouncements. He was more like Leonard Abbott, though half his size. Kelly, Abbott, and Will Durant lectured often at the center. Bill Shatoff came a lot, loquacious and able. I followed Kelly to Stelton in 1915. The ideas of Ferrer appealed to me. I built a house and spent the summers there. After the First World War I became active in the Socialist Party. I ran for many local offices, but never won. In 1923, following Harry Kelly, I left Stelton for Mohegan.

I was president of Mohegan Colony for many years. I bore the brunt of the debates and battles, as the man in the middle. The cooperative store failed, but the school was quite successful for some years. George Seldes was a philosopher and the father of Gilbert and George Junior. He had a fine character and opinions galore on every subject. Neither Stelton nor Mohegan was a colony in the nineteenth-century sense, as members mostly did not work on the premises. Stelton was purer, more naive, more isolated, and poorer than Mohegan. At both, people were warm, friendly, comradely. Rudolf Rocker was a scholar; he did not take an active part in the social or administrative life of Mohegan Colony.

Anarchism is unthinkable in the United States. It is close to some primitive Christian faith. When I see Catholic nuns being arrested in St. Patrick's Cathedral I think of the anarchists.

• NORA HORN •

Lake Mohegan, New York, September 19, 1972

As a child Nora Horn attended the Ferrer School in New York and went to the Stelton Colony for the summers. Afterwards she lived for many years in the Mohegan Colony, where her husband taught at the Modern School.

I WAS BORN in New York in 1905. Both my parents were anarchists, and they named me after Ibsen's "Nora." My mother, Sarah Kramer, was a seamstress and was custodian of the Ferrer Center on East 107th Street. I was a student at the school under Will Durant, along with Puck Kaufman (Durant's future wife), Joe Ostrom, the Bercovici children, and others. The thing that school taught me most was curiosity. They didn't shut you up. And I never lost it. I entered the school in 1912 and stayed a year and a half. Alexander Berkman carried me on his shoulders at the *Mother Earth* office when I was four years old. The school had a backyard with all sorts of toys, and we could go and do what we wanted. We had a microscope there. I still remember that microscope! It impressed me deeply as a child. We lived nearby on 105th Street. Louise Berger lived with us at that time. She was a marvelous woman. She later moved to an apartment on Lexington Avenue but was not in the apartment when the explosion occurred. In 1917 she went back to Russia, willingly, eagerly, to take part in the revolution.

I went to Stelton for the summers starting in 1916. Mary Hansen was a marvelous person. The colonists had something to live for and look forward to, but they failed their children and ultimately themselves. All dedicated people in some way do their families wrong. The same was true at Mohegan. The Depression affected the parents and also the school. Some of the children felt neglected. They were left to their own devices and lacked the guidance and attention that children need. Our principal, Miss Davis, said that the parents lacked a cultural background. And the school did not give the kids basics. There was no money to pay teachers, let alone to purchase equipment. On the other hand, the kids got outdoors and were not bound to a seat in the classroom or to iron discipline.

The staff was constantly changing. Some of them were marvelous, some positively awful. My husband Herman taught metal and wood crafts during the thirties. The children made furniture, did copper work, had a printing shop, and did leather work. But they got an erratic education. Lallah Blanpied [q.v.] was an ineffectual director, and Robert Bek-Gran was awful. Yet some of the students became well-known professionals: Pauline Mont is a professor of engineering at the University of Michigan, Iris Miroy got a Ph.D. in biology at Harvard, and many of the boys became doctors, scientists, and engineers. Daniel Bell, a nephew of the Monts, is a well-known sociologist.

• JACOB LANDA •

New York City, September 24, 1972

Jacob Landa (known as "Styopa") was a socialist who lived among the anarchists. During the 1920s his daughter Lydia attended the Ferrer School at Stelton, where he himself spent the summers. He later moved to Mohegan, becoming the caretaker of the Modern School there, in addition to teaching carpentry. He died in a nursing home in Baltimore on November 13, 1976.

I WAS BORN in Kiev province eighty-four years ago and came to the United States in 1907 to avoid recruitment into the Russian Army. As a young man I was a Bundist, and I never became an anarchist, though I was close to them. I attended Emma Goldman's lectures—she had a tongue like Bella Abzug's.[421] The anarchists held antireligious balls on Yom Kippur. In 1914 I took part in the unemployment protests at St. Alphonsus's Church on Tenth Street, together with Isidore Wisotsky,[422] Frank Tannenbaum, and the others.

At Stelton my daughter Lydia boarded with Sally Axelrod[423] during the 1920s, and I spent the summers there. The local industry didn't work; the colony's economy was tied to New York, and the garment shop lasted only a few years. Almost all the members commuted to work, though some did a little farming on the side. The school children were happy, as children are happy everywhere, but especially with the lack of discipline. Aunty Ferm, unlike Uncle, was something of a disciplinarian, contrary to the basic aim of the school. Most of the teachers were amateurs. Occasionally they would get an educator of experience and training, but they seldom stayed very long. Ninety percent of the Steltonites were anarchists, basically ignorant and uncultured, but attracted by the ideals of freedom, no government, and sympathy with the poor. They were searching for a cure-all: "anarchism will solve everything." But colonies in the twentieth century could not succeed. There was no longer any place to escape. Land was unavailable and too expensive, and the national economy too integrated.

I went to Mohegan in the late 1920s. I met my wife Frieda there, a milliner and devout Communist. Dr. [B.W.] Barkas, the principal of the school, hired me as the caretaker, and I also had a class in carpentry. I took the children for hikes and told them stories in the Living House at night. Frances Goldenthal (then the wife of Abe Winokour) taught music. It was a "play school," and the children could not help but like it.

Harry Kelly was the soul of both colonies, their spiritual leader. Joseph Cohen was also a founder of colonies; he also had a dream. He was a clever man, assertive, and wanted to be a writer. George Seldes was a devout anarchist, an older, scholarly type. He knew Russian, Yiddish, and Hebrew well. Nellie Dick [q.v.] was the more active and vital of the Dicks. The non-Jews couldn't find mates among their own people, and so often married Jews. Jim Dick was one example, André Miroy another. He was the intellectual among the Frenchmen at Mohegan. He even studied Russian and Hebrew. The Finns were mostly carpenters and builders. César Vega, a Spanish anarchist at Mohegan, returned to Spain in 1936 or 1937 but was immediately shot.

I went back to Russia in 1929 for two years and lived in Gorky with Frieda. I returned to the U.S. in 1932. I went to Mohegan for the summers and lived with Herman and Nora Horn [q.v.]. The school was already going downhill. There was a financial crisis caused by the Depression, arguments between anarchists and Communists over Russia and Spain, over the school, and other matters. Everything communal was shattered. They could no longer support the school, pay the teachers, or support the Living House. In the early years Mohegan had a good spirit, a spirit of unity, a sense of community. Then came rifts and the Depression.

• JO ANN BURBANK •

New York City, January 12, 1973

Between 1929 and 1946, Jo Ann Wheeler Burbank was a teacher at the Stelton and Mohegan Modern Schools. She was also a devoted supporter of Alexis and Elizabeth Ferm, pioneers of libertarian education in the United States. With her companion, John Scott, she edited a journal called *Mother Earth* (1933–1934), "A Libertarian Farm Paper Devoted to the Life of Thoreauvian Anarchy," as it described itself. She was later active in the Friends of the Modern School, established in 1973 to promote the idea of freedom in education.[424]

I WAS BORN Jo Ann Wheeler in Philadelphia on November 22, 1905. My father was an Englishman, a master mechanic—a mechanical engineer, they would now say—in knitting mills, who invented a precision gauge to measure stitches and also machinery to make lace stockings. Mother was from an old Rhode Island family that went back to the days right after the founding of the colony by Roger Williams. We left Philadelphia when I was four years old, and Dad came to work for Gotham Gold Stripe in New York. We bought a farm out on Long Island, where we lived for a few years, then another one in Craryville, New York, in 1916, which has remained in the family ever since. John Cowper Powys[425] lived there, in Craryville, at the time. I went to public school in New York City and in East Taconic, was graduated from high school at twelve and passed all the regents exams. Too young to go to college, I stayed and studied at home. Both my parents were well-read. Father was especially learned in languages and science, and as a boy had taught himself math and how to use a slide rule.

When I was seventeen I took a job as a teacher in the same one-room schoolhouse in East Taconic where I myself had gone. I loved art, both painting and sculpture, and I often went by myself to New York and spent hours in the Metropolitan Museum. I had twenty-four pupils, from three-year-old nursery tots to two high school students who had failed algebra. That was the hardest year I ever put in. I taught there for four years and a fifth year in a neighboring district, but I became disgusted with the public school system. We got a syllabus from Albany and day by day, week by week, everything was laid out for us.

When I was nineteen I took a summer course at Teachers College from a woman who had been infected with the ideas of progressive education. I went back and tried to introduce some of those ideas, but soon got into hot water.

You were supposed to keep the children quiet and well-behaved. I had the older ones help the younger, introduced art work, and the children wrote and illustrated their own newspaper and made up their own plays. My greatest pride is that I got some of them to like to read on their own. I was later impressed by how similar all this was to the Modern School.

One winter we were in Reading, Pennsylvania, a mill town where Father was working and where we lived on and off for about three years. John and Kate Edelman[426] came as union organizers, and it was from them that I learned about Stelton and Mohegan. I immediately became interested and wrote to Dr. Barkas, the principal at Mohegan, who interviewed and hired me. That was in 1929, an important year for me: I met John Scott and I met the Ferms. John was working partly at Manumit and partly at Mohegan, as the nature teacher. I worked in the Living House, a hard job that taxed my strength, but I liked it. I also taught the children piano.

Barkas was a well-meaning man, tall and lean with a loping walk, who lent himself to caricature. But "well-meaning" is about all I can say for him. The Ferms were far more interesting. They came up from their place in Newfoundland, New Jersey, and had a discussion group on education. I was very much taken with them, though a little daunted by Aunty's spirit. She was so full of spirit, so full of fire. Uncle was much easier going. That's why they made such a good team, I guess. That was my first experience with radicals. I had always lived in an atmosphere where people found me a strange and unconventional person. But in this group I was slightly conservative, and that was interesting too! My parents' house had always been open to people of different political stripes, and in Reading we had many friends who were black.

At that time, the division in the colony between anarchists and Communists was beginning to be seen, but was not yet very strong. I loved George Seldes, Sr. Once we moved books into the garage and lightning struck and they were all burnt up. He came in and picked up the remains and put the pages together. "You should all cherish books," he told us. Once John Scott led the children in a debate over whether life was worth living. The "no's" won. Then we all went out and had a wiener roast!

Scotty, as you may know, believed in free love and multiple loves. I had known many conventional men in Craryville, and I was considered queer and fast because I didn't want to stay with the same boy after one or two dates, as the town expected. I was a young girl, and the older women in the colony must have been hurt. He was visiting me, and also Anna Schwartz [q.v.], Lillian Buck, and Celia Bushwick. They were very angry about that, and I was quite disillusioned about radicalism as a result. We never legally married. John had grown up in Missouri, in the Ozarks. He had three years in a one-room schoolhouse, then went to college where he was Phi Beta Kappa. He was a strong individualist, and also quite a mystic with a vague pantheism and a theory of dreams: that after death you went on living in your former dream world.

Scott, as I say, was raised in the Ozarks. His father sold charcoal and had fought in the Civil War. After Missouri, John went out to California, where he

knew William Thurston Brown and taught in his Modern School in Los Angeles. He was a fine naturalist. He knew a great deal about nature, and that he
passed on to our son Jon Thoreau, who is now an ecologist at the State University of New York in Albany. Our daughter Shelley (after the poet) is now living
in Norway.

In the fall of 1929 Scott and I went to Stelton. That was the noisiest place!
We stayed until October 1930, just before Shelley was born. The Dicks were
there then. But the money ran out and they couldn't pay Scotty, so we decided
to move up to Craryville, where both of our children were born. Scotty built a
cabin on my family's land. It was very primitive, really, one room with a small
coal stove, yet we stayed until 1934. We saved up money and bought a mimeograph machine. I typed *Mother Earth* on an old typewriter which belonged to
my father. I did it late in the evening, after the children were asleep. We tried
to get the cabin warm enough to get the ink to run.

That was during the Depression. We grew most of out own food. We had
been brought up in my family on Emerson and Thoreau and Bronson Alcott—
the Fullers were cousins of some sort. I was much impressed by Thoreau's essay
on *Civil Disobedience*, but *Walden* was our bible and, given the Depression, we
tried living on the land. It wasn't easy, but we did it. We tried to follow the
authority from within, rather than any external authority. We hadn't much
money but we had a great deal of spirit and high thinking. We were precursors
of what young people are trying to do today. It stemmed from the same feeling,
except that ours was an individualist venture rather than communal.

Among our contributors to *Mother Earth*, Scotty had known Tom Bell in
California and liked him very much. We visited Laurance Labadie [q.v.] in
Suffern, and he also came to see us. He was trying to do in Suffern the same
thing we were, though all by himself. We knew Warren Brokaw[427] only by
correspondence, and the same for Ewing Baskette.[428] We also met Ammon
Hennacy[429] at that time. Scotty, by the way, although an individualist, had
known Eugene Debs in the early days in the Middle West, but he broke with
the Socialist Party during World War I. He was a pacifist all his life. His first
son, with another woman, was named Marx Scott. A son named Marx, then,
seventeen years later, another son named Thoreau—that's an interesting evolution! Marcus Graham also came to visit us. He was a vegetarian—in fact, a
fruitarian. He would fill his plate with nuts and raisins and start to eat, passing
up Mother's delicious roast beef!

I went back to Stelton in 1934. Scotty and I had parted in a friendly way—he
went to Camp Germinal in Pennsylvania—but he came to stay with me at
Stelton from time to time. He was twenty-six years older than I was, and a
family with two obstreperous children was much more than he could take. He
became interested in the Social Credit movement,[430] worked for *Social Credit*,
then founded his own journal, *Money*, a journal of monetary reform. He was
neither a fascist nor an anti-Semite, yet he was willing to publish the Protocols
of Zion[431] in his paper, and there was much hostility in the colony against him.
That was his blind spot. He was politically naive, and could be taken in by

anyone who was willing to work with him. He was never in the Silver Shirts, but he wanted to start a party called the Green Shirts because that was the color of Mother Earth. He ran for President on the Greenback Party ticket in 1948 and became a Quaker towards the end, a member of the Taconic Meeting. He died in November 1953 at the age of seventy-four.

Stelton was the most wonderful place I've ever been in. It wasn't drab. The mud and mosquitoes just didn't matter because the spirit was there, the walks, the singing, the moonlight. I was deeply influenced by the Ferms and completely devoted to them. Their idea of creative development from within, rather than the child as a receptacle for information poured into it by others, was a confirmation of what I was aiming at. The philosophy of the individual and of growth from within was something I could wholeheartedly accept.

Uncle was a very easy person to love. He lived by reason. I never knew him to lose his temper or raise his voice in anger at anyone. He was a steadying influence on Aunty. She was more emotional: If you're not with me you're against me. He could compromise. Nevertheless, I owe more to her than to him. She was a fighter. He was more Emersonian than Thoreauvian. Emerson fit his ideal more than anyone else. Those eleven years from 1935 to 1946 had a tremendous influence on me. I left in 1946 because of the deepening disruption in the colony, the hostility against Scotty, and so on. I felt that if people believe in freedom they should be able to accept what they disagree with, even what they abhor and detest.

I loved to hear Mary Hansen talk. She had a quiet sense of humor, nothing cutting or sharp. I knew that her life wasn't easy, yet she never uttered a complaining word. She was like Uncle—easy to love. She once told me that her husband in Philadelphia [George Brown] repaired the shoes of Coxey's army[432] free on their way to Washington [in 1894]. Hippolyte Havel? A lot thought he was just a drunk, but he was warm and loving. He took my hand and kissed it and said, "Good morning, princess." Once I gave him a curtsy and he was so pleased. He was a good man. Yat Tone and Eddie Wong visited us in Craryville in the early thirties. I heard that Yat Tone was killed in a Japanese bombing raid in Shanghai, and I cried when I heard it. He was no inscrutable oriental. He would effervesce. He took our children for walks, one on each hand. After that he went back to China. Hans Koch once gave a talk on Frank Lloyd Wright at Stelton; he was working for him then. Edgar Tafel[433] used to make beautiful buildings out of the Froebel "gifts," and the Ferms predicted he would become a great architect.

I learned a bit about Francisco Ferrer after I came to the colonies: about his anti-dogmatism, his idea of rational education, and his martyrdom. I thought it was a horrible thing that he should have been executed for these principles. But I wasn't influenced much by educational theory. I found theories—including those of Froebel—incredibly dull and without life, though that was probably the fault of those who wrote about them, not the theorists themselves.

I still consider myself an anarchist as far as philosophy is concerned. I was never part of the anarchist movement, though, but always on the fringe of it.

My brother William Wheeler fought in Spain as a Communist, a lieutenant in the Lincoln Brigade. For pragmatic reasons I will vote and discuss politics. I'm still an individualist. Anything that binds the human spirit cannot stand. But I'm not opposed to collectivist economic experiments, for collective experiments succeed only in so far as you have strong individuals who are willing to work in cooperative effort without trampling on the rights of others. You can make communism or socialism or cooperatives work, as long as they are not too authoritarian. But capitalism is basically dishonest, and in a large society tends to become fascistic; and socialism in a large society tends towards totalitarianism. I'm strongly antipatriotic and non-nationalist. Patriotism is one of the great chains binding the people. The same holds for organized religion, yet in my own personal way I'm deeply religious. Individualism and socialism are not that far apart. But the people are asleep. That's the trouble.

• BEN LIEBERMAN •

New York City, April 28, 1972

Ben Lieberman taught at the Modern School of Stelton under Alexis and Elizabeth Ferm, and both he and his wife Esther taught at the Modern School in Mohegan. Esther died in January 1977 and Ben not long after.

BOTH I (now sixty-eight) and my wife Esther were teachers at the Mohegan school in the early 1930s, and I also taught at Stelton. At Mohegan I was a general teacher and also taught music. At both colonies the day began with everybody—teachers, children, some parents—meeting in a great circle. We sang songs to nature, greeting the sun, and the like, and played games about birds and flowers. All this had a complete loveliness about it. It was Froebelian in approach, owing to the Ferms. One day I was bored and stood there slightly apart. Aunty came over and poked me in the chest with her finger. "You're a dead tree," she said.

The children were free to come and go as they pleased. There was no curriculum, no methodology, and above all no follow-up. Things were left hanging, or were dropped, even when interest was aroused. It was very amateurish. Some ten or eleven-year-olds couldn't read or write. Everybody, students and teachers, was a primadonna.

At music sessions the children and adults made up their own songs and dances. Forty-year-old women with big hips and dressed in shorts went out and made like fairies. It was funny yet beautiful. There was a close relationship between pupils and teachers. To this day a special feeling remains, and we are still friends. We still gush with feeling about the school and colony. The kids had a good time, and what's wrong with that? At both schools the kids had their own magazine, which they printed themselves. Stelton was a dreary place, though, and the poverty of the environment had a depressing effect. Mohegan's setting, by contrast, elated us; its hills, brooks, lake, and scenery were invigorating.

The school was at the center of things. The idea was to mold a new man. Man was intrinsically good; he was corrupted by the environment: in their theory of human nature the anarchists were utter and complete environmentalists. It is the capitalist and statist environment that makes the child bad. Get the child away from it and his goodness will emerge. Hence colonies and free schools. They were not educational experiments, but articles of faith. The colonists tended to be utopians, not experimenters. Their activities were grounded in a theory of man and society, and education flowed from that. The progressive movement was essentially middle-class, while libertarian education was essentially a working-class movement. Mohegan emphasized the former, Stelton the latter. What is interesting is how it persists, this idea of colonies.

One striking thing was that there was very little victimization of one child by the others. The kids were kinder, more generous. The one mongoloid at Mohegan was never persecuted. Kids who would have been the butt of jokes and persecution in public school—big, clumsy, odd—were liked and treated well. For some kids, of course, it was not a happy time, but most liked the school. But by and large the results differed little from other schools, except that the children emerged a bit more humane, a bit less prejudiced, easier to talk to, nicer, kinder, gentler to this day.

There was no racial problem whatsoever at the colonies. Mohegan had Finns and Frenchmen, as well as Italians and Jews. There were no ethnic frictions. It was almost like an extended family, a European village, a kind of community that the young generation of today misses. Different age groups, too, mixed more readily, without the hostility and stratification of today. Harry Kelly was an idealistic, old-fashioned anarchist. John Scott was a handsome *sheygets* [gentile], a Don Juan with six women on the string at the same time.

Why then did it break up? Chiefly because the world was too much with us. Try as we might, we could not divorce ourselves from it, could not build utopia and the new man. Nobody knows how, and too few among us appreciate the extent of man's quarrelsomeness. Before the First World War, radicals of different stripes could still argue about their differences, could still have their different groups and theories and yet agree about a common enemy (capitalism) and be friends—could even start colonies together. But after the war and the Russian Revolution this became more difficult. Earlier, if an anarchist got into trouble, the socialists would come to his defense; all rallied to Haymarket and Johann Most, for example. But with the Russian Revolution came an event which forced you to put up or shut up. Also the war: between patriots and internationalists no peace or compromise was possible. Bitter quarrels divided them for life. Among the anarchists themselves there were divisions. The trouble with the anarchists was that each one went his own way. Every meeting had a dozen viewpoints, and it was immensely difficult to agree on things. I am convinced that the First World War was the great watershed of the modern period. The result of the split in the radical ranks was an irreconcilable legacy of bitterness and enmity. A line of blood was drawn between them, with charges of "traitor" and "renegade."

All this poisoned the colonies. The Ferrer Center would hide anarchists, pacifists, socialists, and conscientious objectors. Even after the war some cooperation was still possible. Things still hadn't gotten that hot. The real split occurred during the late 1920s and the 1930s with the emergence of Stalin and Hitler. With Stalin something happened of a special nature that divided radicals irrevocably. Thus the main reason for the breakup was political, not educational. All this politics tore the colonies apart. What the Communists brought in was expediency, expediency to the nth degree: "I may love you, but if I have to kill you I'll kill you." Some anti-Communist anarchists (like Joe and Eva Brandes [q.v.]) were just as adamant and even worked with local Peekskill citizens against the Communists during the Robeson riots.[434]

Not even the Popular Front[435] could heal the breach. Most anarchists, syndicalists, and Trotskyists refused to accept it. Besides, the damage was already done; totalitarianism was already entrenched. All these issues deeply affected the colonists, who took their politics very seriously. Block voting occurred on every question, however trivial, even school questions. The teachers and students were caught in the middle. Quarrels made community life difficult and ultimately impossible. People weren't talking to each other. Occasionally fistfights broke out. The outside world kept impinging on the colony. There was no way to avoid the goddam world!

• JACQUES RUDOME •

New York City, February 10 and April 5, 1972

Jacques (Jack) Rudome, who emigrated from Paris to New York in 1907, frequented the Ferrer Center and the offices of *Mother Earth*. Afterwards he and his wife Helen (see interview with Rose Goldblatt), who participated in the Ludlow protests of 1914, lived for many years in the Mohegan Colony. Rudome died in 1985 in a nursing home in Great Neck, New York.

I AM SEVENTY-EIGHT years old, a former house painter by trade, and came from Paris to the U.S. in 1907. An older brother, in Paris, was a socialist and in 1905 took me to Louise Michel's funeral. In New York I lived in Harlem and frequented the Ferrer Center and the offices of *Mother Earth*. I knew both Emma Goldman and Alexander Berkman. Sasha was very gentle and soft-spoken, especially in contrast with Emma. When Sasha came out of prison he was confronted by a new world. The world had changed, his friends had changed. Young people took to him, more than to Emma. Helen and Lillian loved him.

The Ferrer Center was bustling with life and activity. People gathered there every day for lectures, art classes, and good conversation. Sadakichi Hartmann and Hippolyte Havel were often there. They were close friends and kindred spirits, both drinkers, spongers, Bohemians, and wasted talents. Sadakichi was a tall man for a Japanese, with an arresting face, but he looked like a gargoyle in the end. His combination of German and Japanese blood made him a remarkable character, half-authoritarian, half-libertarian. He was a half-baked genius with great promise that blew up in smoke. Charlie Chaplin helped finance him for a while. He died around 1950, in his eighties, on an Indian reservation in Banning, California, near Palm Springs.

Max Baginski, unlike Hartmann and Havel, was not a drinker. He was close to Emma and Sasha, the sage of *Mother Earth*, always called upon for information on European labor, radicalism, and the like. He was handsome, middle-aged, with a shock of white hair and a mustache.

During the summer of 1914, I worked my way across to Paris as a deckhand on a ship. I arrived in June and helped with the mailing of *Le Libertaire*, whose editor, Pierre Martin,[436] was a bearded hunchback with a beautiful head and a wonderful character. One day Kropotkin came in to visit his old comrade, and the two beards got entangled as the two Pierres embraced.

It was while I was in France that the Lexington Avenue explosion occurred, one of the causes of the Ferrer Center's demise. I knew the three men—Caron (an American Indian), Hanson, and Berg—who got killed. While walking with one of them a few months earlier, he said to me, while passing a subway construction site, that it would be a good place to get dynamite. I was in Paris when the bomb went off, and I read about it in the papers. I immediately knew what had happened. Their plan was to bomb Rockefeller's mansion in Tarrytown in reprisal for the Ludlow massacre in Colorado.

Another blow came with the Palmer raids in 1919 and 1920. You have no idea what mayhem they committed, intellectual mayhem too. They frightened a lot of people. The Sacco-Vanzetti affair was the aftermath of the Palmer period.

During the early 1920s I visited the Home Colony near Tacoma, Washington. I was impressed with Jay Fox,[437] an exceptionally fine person. Home had a different quality from Stelton and Mohegan. Most of its members were westerners, each a distinctive character of his own. Caplan was arrested there, and Schmidty in New York, where he had worked as a carpenter fixing up the offices of *Mother Earth*. They *were* involved in the *Los Angeles Times* explosion; they brought the "stuff" by rowboat from Seattle across the bay and hid it in Home Colony. A few of the colonists knew about it. Joe O'Carroll, an Irish Wobbly, jumped Donald Vose in court during the Schmidt and Caplan trial.

I moved with Helen to Mohegan and lived there for many years. What ruined the colony was letting in outsiders—relatives and friends—who had nothing in common with anarchism and didn't belong. Eventually they became the majority—liberals, socialists, Communists—and took over and ran things in their own way. But more than any other group it was the Communists who wrecked Mohegan. The best period of the colony was the early years.

Yet there were still quite a few anarchists in the years between the world wars. The Spaniards had quite a large group in New York, living mostly in lower Manhattan, on Cherry Street, near the waterfront. Many were sailors, stevedores, and cigarmakers. The seamen's organization of Spaniards was largely anarchist. Pedro Esteve was the main figure, quiet, soft-spoken, dignified, thoughtful, never violent. Another important figure was José Rubio, heavy-set and lively, a cigarmaker. The Italian anarchists were even more numerous than the Spaniards. They lived mostly in East Harlem, Brooklyn, and other Italian neighborhoods. The women worked in the needle trades, the men in construction. The French anarchists were much fewer in number. There was no real group in New York, and most were individualists. After the First World War I met in San Francisco a group of former Paris Communards, who had been exiled to New Caledonia and then come to the United States.

Yes, my ideas have changed over the years. I am still an anarchist, but I am an individualist anarchist rather than a communist anarchist, and I no longer believe in revolution. As Flaubert wrote in *L'Education Sentimental*, "In every revolutionist beats the heart of a policeman." We develop ourselves if it's within us to do so, if the quality is there, not through force or compulsion. In the early years Proudhon influenced me more than anyone else; later it was E. Armand. Revolution breeds terrorism; violence breeds violence. This is proved by the French Revolution, the Paris Commune, the Russian Revolution.

I still accept the libertarian education of Faure and Ferrer. (The Pelletiers of Mohegan, incidentally, went to Faure's La Ruche school in France.) And prisons should be abolished. But private property is sacred. What a man has earned is his—rewards according to work, not need. Individualism is the only true anarchism. Anarchism and communism are antithetical. Even Rudolf Rocker, towards the end of his life, was becoming an individualist, as he told me in frequent conversations at Mohegan.

I believe in the nuclear family, but I also believe in free love, a fine, wonderful idea that has been vulgarized and misunderstood. Above all else it is based on tolerance. As for the labor movement, I have never believed in it. I was a union member only from necessity, in order to get work. As the labor movement grows, it becomes a big monopoly. It has reached that point in America, with big salaries and nice fat jobs.

• LYDIA MILLER •

New York City, February 12, 1972

Lydia Miller, a half-sister of Eva Brandes (q.v.), attended the Modern School of Stelton and afterwards lived at Mohegan. She later moved to Manhattan (where I interviewed her) and worked in the photographs division of the New York Public Library.

I WAS BORN in 1914, the daughter of Harry and Lydia Gordon and the half-sister of Eva Brandes [q.v.] and Sophie Bannister. My father, Harry Gordon, was born in Vilna in 1866 of a prosperous Jewish family. He was a man of few words and strong principles. He was a machinist by trade but refused to make machinery related to the military during the First World War. He instilled in me a great deal of his idealism. When he talked I was always impressed. He was almost a saint.

We moved to Stelton in 1919 and had a small house there. I didn't like it. The Living House kids were the center of attention; the rest felt like day-school kids and not as important. The school was boring, with not enough to do. How many years can you weave baskets? They wouldn't let me read; the library was closed to children under ten. So I learned to read by myself.

I didn't like Aunty Ferm. I felt intimidated by her, afraid of her. Uncle was very nice, a kind person, soft, gentle; he never raised his voice. Aunty had her own ways and strong ideas about education and discipline. She once caught a boy masturbating and sewed up his fly. She was not a libertarian, as we were not free to do as we pleased, not free to read. She imposed her own ideas and methods on us, just as in other schools, only different ones.

Most of the kids liked the school and its comparative freedom, especially those who had come from public school. For some it was good, for others not. I needed more guidance and order. No one system fits all children, not the Ferms', not the public school's. At Stelton the emphasis was on spontaneous learning and self-education. One day at assembly Aunty complained when I danced that "someone has been giving you lessons," as if that were bad. One must learn by oneself, not be taught. I was much happier afterwards in public school.

The people at Stelton, for all their modern ideas, were still very Victorian, with roots in the nineteenth century. One of my favorites was Mary Hansen. She was a very warm person and I liked her very much. She had stained glass windows in her house. Her daughter Heloise and son George Brown, Jr., lived with her, but not her husband. [George Brown, Sr., had died before she came to Stelton.]

We left Stelton after three and a half years for New York City. I was then eight and a half. I went to public school, but over my mother's dead body. I liked it, despite the crowding and discipline. I wouldn't recite the pledge of allegiance to the flag because it was against our principles.

When I was eleven and a half Gordon got pneumonia, so we moved to Mohegan. Mother begged me to go to the colony school. I went one day and didn't want to continue, so I was enrolled in a one-room public school, which I liked. At the Mohegan school Jim Dick was a good teacher. But if the children got bored, with algebra, say, they got up and left, and nobody tried to stop them. Nobody at either Stelton or Mohegan knew anything about how children really learn.

Apart from the school, Mohegan was a wonderful place. It was more bourgeois than Stelton, more prosperous, and didn't have a strong anarchist identity. Many socialists, Communists, and even liberals moved there. Everyone was friendly in the early years. The children got along well, and friendships remain close to this day. We had a reunion there in August 1971, and all of us had fond memories of the colony; and it wasn't mere nostalgia. It had a free, healthy, rural atmosphere. We all felt like one big family. There were clubs, theater, dancing; Moritz Jagendorf [q.v.] put on plays. I always thought highly of Harry Kelly, and Elsie Kelly (the daughter of Harry and Mary Krimont) was a soft, lovely person.

Over the years, of course, Mohegan changed, though boys from the neighborhood still drove through the colony looking for "free love" girls. Under the impact of World War II many anarchists returned to their Jewish heritage; even Gordon thought it was a just war. Mohegan now is just another middle-class suburban community, with IBM junior executives and New York City commuters of every political persuasion. The houses are all decorated at Christmas. When I saw one man reading the *Daily News* I knew the colony was finished.

• EVA BRANDES •

Bronx, New York, January 7, January 12, February 1, April 4, June 13, 1972;
Lake Mohegan, New York, September 19, 1972;
Brooklyn, New York, September 9, 1974;
Bronx, New York, September 20, 1979

The child of anarchist parents, Eva Brandes attended Elizabeth and Alexis Ferm's Playhouse School in the Dyker Heights section of Brooklyn and afterwards lived at the Ferrer Center in Harlem, the Stelton Colony in New Jersey, and the Mohegan Colony in Crompond (near Peekskill), New York. She knew Emma Goldman, Alexander Berkman, Harry Kelly, Hippolyte Havel, Sadakichi Hartmann, and many other prominent anarchists, as well as Robert Henri, George Bellows, and Will and Ariel Durant. While residing at Mohegan with her husband

Joe (a cousin of the Communist writer Mike Gold), she commuted to New York City, where she worked for many years in the offices of the International Ladies' Garment Workers' Union. Small, articulate, with an astonishingly accurate memory for people and events, she was a woman of unassailable integrity, absolutely trustworthy in everything she said and did. She died at her daughter's home near Mohegan in 1988.

I WAS BORN in Chicago on July 18, 1898, and in 1901 moved to New York. Both of my parents were anarchists. My father, Boris Sachatoff (born in Tula, Russia, 1873, died in Winnipeg, Canada, 1952) was of Jewish birth but became a "Tolstoyan Christian anarchist," as he called himself. In 1910 he went to western Canada with me and my older sister Sophie—Mother remained in Chicago— to live among the Dukhobors.[438] We were there when Tolstoy died. Father was expecting him to visit the Canadian Dukhobors. Father was a jeweler and watchmaker up there, and Sophie and I went to school for six months. Then we returned to the States to live with Mother. We came back to Canada for two years in 1917–1918, and I went to the business school in Yorkton, Saskatchewan. I still correspond with my Dukhobor friends, especially the Petroff sisters, whose mother was Jewish.

My mother, Lydia Landau, was of Russian-Jewish birth. In 1901 Harry Gordon, another Russian-Jewish anarchist, came to Chicago and met her, and they stayed together forever. Gordon was a machinist from Pittsburgh and had been the first person to visit Alexander Berkman in prison after his attempt on Frick.[439] After President McKinley was assassinated in September 1901, he was almost lynched as an anarchist by a mob in Pittsburgh, but was saved when someone shouted, "He's a union man. Let him go!" After that he went to Chicago and met Mother. He saw other women as well as Mother, and when she questioned him he said, "But I love you too." She didn't like that "too," a commentary on the free love doctrine to which she herself adhered.

I thought the world of Ma and Gordon and the others in the Chicago anarchist group. For me they could do no wrong. I had implicit faith in them, which I still haven't lost. At the center of the English-speaking group was the Isaak family and their journal *Free Society*. Abe Isaak, Sr., was tall, broad-shouldered, and bespectacled, and he loved children. His wife Mary was small and dainty. They had three children, Pete, Abe, and Mary. They later lived in the Bronx, and Yanovsky, the editor of the *Fraye Arbeter Shtime*, bought their house there when they left for California.

I can still remember visiting the Isaaks as a little girl in Chicago. Both Abe Senior and Abe Junior wore green eyeshades and cuffs as they worked preparing their newspaper. Mary Junior had two daughters, Dorothy and Grace [Umrath, q.v.], and Abe Junior had two sons, one of whom became a Communist. During the 1930s Abe Junior came up to Mohegan colony and told me how disappointed this made him. My father also drifted in that direction. Although he had been a Tolstoyan and single-taxer, he turned towards Soviet Communism and remained a sympathizer even under Stalin!

I can also remember the Czolgosz-McKinley affair, though I was only three years old at the time. Czolgosz was not a true anarchist but was disturbed, deranged. I heard that he went to see Emma Goldman in Chicago, but she was wary of him and pretended to be someone else. He talked of bombs and violence, and she denied any interest in it and would have nothing further to do with him. After McKinley's assassination the Chicago anarchists were rounded up and imprisoned. I visited them in the jail, all herded together in one large cell like cattle. Mother handed me a ladle and I gave them water from a bucket.

The year before, when I was two and Sophie three, Emma Goldman made us two little blue dresses. We loved them, of course, but Emma was hard to warm up to personally. Later, in New York, I heard her speak at Cooper Union, among other places. There were a lot of mounted policemen outside the hall, and inside there was a ring of police, so many that it left me with a fear of police that I've never lost. I also heard Emma speak at Columbia University in 1934. John Dewey was sitting near me. After she finished he got up and said, "I admire your courage!"

Emma, by the way, was jealous of my mother, who was exceptionally good-looking and much sought after by men. Yet they were very close, and Mother always went to her for advice. I often heard Alexander Berkman's name as a child in Chicago, when he was in prison. The anarchists there were always talking about him. He had been in prison so long, suffered so much. They felt so bad about it. When I was still a child, in New York after his release, he came over and took me around. I felt at home with him. He was a very nice man. Ben Reitman was in New York at that time and was Emma Goldman's lover. The women were crazy about him. They were all over him, in his lap and everywhere.

We moved to New York in late 1901, after McKinley's assassination. Though still very young, Sophie and I were often taken to lectures by Emma Goldman and others. Sometimes we fell asleep but nevertheless absorbed something. Once we passed a Salvation Army meeting and I said to mother, "Let's go in there." It seemed just like our lecture meetings. To this day, words are more important to me than music, pictures, or anything else. We went to concerts and balls sponsored by *Mother Earth* and the *Fraye Arbeter Shtime*. The kids put on skits of capitalists and priests in a carriage pulled by the workers. It was obvious propaganda, but we did it very willingly, and it was not as blatant as what the socialists were doing. At the socialist club the children were systematically indoctrinated. At the end of their weekly meetings they were always asked, "And who was that great man?" They replied in unison, "Karl Marx!" and then ran out. Sophie and I attended a few times, but dogma and indoctrination were not for us.

In 1905, when Sophie was eight and I was seven, Harry Kelly recommended a school for us to Ma and Gordon. It was the Playhouse School in Dyker Heights, a neighborhood in Brooklyn, run by Elizabeth and Alexis Ferm. It was a boarding school, and Sophie and I were enrolled. Miss Otis, a Philadelphia philanthropist, had bought a house for the Ferms as a school to try out their ideas. Aunty Ferm was strong-willed, cranky, and very prudish, but not Uncle, who was always decent, soft-spoken, and easy to approach. He taught us how to plant things in the garden, and we enjoyed it so much. Aunty was lovely to look at, worked very hard, but was too sharp. She once washed a boy's mouth with soap for using foul language, and she hit another boy—Walter was his name—for peeking at nude girls on an overnight outing in Newfoundland, New Jersey, where the Ferms had some land. We slept in sleeping bags and ate raw oatmeal. Aunty was deeply upset by sex; and when she caught Walter peeking at the girls in the outhouse she made a horrible scene. She hit him so. We were all terribly frightened. Then she began to cry, and that made things even worse.

Aunty once asked us when we were born. I said July, and she said, "Anyone born in July is lazy." I was very hurt, and still am to this day. Once when we played a game hiding in a closet, she rushed in and warned us against masturbation; it was bad and we would lose our minds. The Ferms discouraged reading and did not teach it. The emphasis was on games and physical activity. We were always on the swings, rings, and trapeze. But this was just as authoritarian as forcing someone to read. Aunty discouraged even a spontaneous urge to read: "You don't really want to read that—your mother wants you to."

Sophie and I spent two years at Dyker Heights. Miss Otis, our benefactress, was a kind, soft person. Her four adopted children, Edith, Alla, Laura, and Miriam, were pupils in the school. Edith, the oldest, was a cellist and a lesbian. Miss Otis left the children much to themselves. She took us to the theater to see Maude Adams in *Peter Pan*. After that we ourselves put on the play over and over again, and we had a big picture on the wall of Maude Adams as Peter Pan. The Ferms invited Miss Adams to visit the school, but she couldn't make it and sent a dancing instructor instead. Besides *Peter Pan*, we also saw *The Wizard of Oz*.

With Miss Otis we always had a relaxed feeling, a feeling of ease, no fears or pressures. She prepared a special dinner for us each week; the dessert was always a slab of ice cream, and we could eat as much as we wanted. She also gave us a box of chocolates and candy canes to last the week. Mr. and Mrs. Potter, whose son Lloyd was a pupil, ran the Living House, located next door to the school. They were extremely nice people, but Aunty argued with them and they had to leave. Aunty also quarreled with Miss Otis, who was such a nice person. I got much more kindness from her than from Aunty. The Ferms were interesting and good people, but neither was particularly affectionate, an important drawback when dealing with children. She talked of fairies and leprechauns, which aroused our interest.

The Ferrer Center began as an adult school and meeting place on St. Mark's Place. It moved to East Twelfth Street in 1911 and to East 107th Street the following year. There was a day school and a Sunday school, which Sophie and I attended. Our first teacher was Dr. Solomon Bauch, a physician from Brownsville in Brooklyn and a very fine person. Anita Spiegel, later Anita Miroy at Mohegan, was a pupil in our group. The children, both of the day school and the Sunday school, had outings in Central Park and picnics in Van Cortlandt Park in the Bronx. Maurice Hollod [q.v.], now a retired chiropractor in Florida, loved the school, and you ought to go talk to him.

Will Durant was the teacher in the day school, and Ariel, his future wife, was a pupil. She was fifteen years old, and her real name was Ida Kaufman, though Will called her Puck, from A *Midsummer Night's Dream*. She was very lively and affectionate; instead of shaking hands, she would give you a hug. Will was twenty-seven, charming, calm, understanding. He fell for her. "I don't know whether to marry her or adopt her," he said. After their marriage they left the school, but he continued to lecture to the adults. Some of his lectures were published by Haldeman-Julius[440] as "blue books" and formed the basis of the larger works that made him famous. The Durants never really considered themselves anarchists; they were humanist and nonpolitical.

The Ferrer School was an exciting place for adults as well as children. It was a hangout for radical intellectuals like Manuel Komroff and Sadakichi Hartmann, the Eurasian poet, a very heavy drinker. He often recited poetry at the center, as did Harry Kemp[441] and Mike Gold, who read from William Blake. Robert Henri and George Bellows gave art lessons, and Hippolyte Havel published his journal *Revolt* in the basement, where he lived. David Rosenthal published poems in *Revolt* and, as "David Ross," went on to become one of the best-known early radio announcers. Becky Edelsohn, Berkman's former girlfriend, also came to the center. She had dark hair and brown eyes and was a lively, free spirit. Joseph Kucera, a Bohemian, also came, Voltairine de Cleyre's last lover. He lived in Greenwich Village and was tall, fair, nice-looking, and soft spoken. He later got married and had a son. Stewart Kerr was a salesman for New York Telephone Company and close to Emma Goldman, Berkman, and Leonard Abbott. Arthur Samuels was Rose Yuster's first husband, before she got together with Abbott. Anton (really Hyman) Rovinsky played the piano, and I had a crush on him. Apart from these regulars, there were lots of hangers-on, including some who came to see all the "free love" business.

Donald Vose frequented both the Ferrer Center and *Mother Earth*. He looked like a real westerner, with his western-style hat. He came to New York around 1914. My mother almost at once suspected him of being a spy because he had "too much money." He went to see Emma Goldman, who happened to mention that "Schmidty" (Matthew Schmidt) was coming to visit her. Vose informed the authorities and Schmidty was arrested.

Before he went to Stelton in 1915, Joseph Cohen acted as custodian of the Ferrer Center. When he left he asked Mother to take over: rent out rooms and keep the place in order. She accepted eagerly. So we moved in and lived there, and later in an apartment on 106th Street, from 1915 to 1917, when Sophie and I went to Canada. A number of interesting people lived at the Center, including Bill and Anna Shatoff, who had a room next door to our apartment, and Bernard Sernaker, a machinist, who worked for a while with Gordon and who went back to Russia to take part in the revolution. Another room, next to our bedroom, was occupied by Terry Carlin,[442] who knew Eugene O'Neill. He was an alcoholic and was very noisy when drunk. He had little money (his sister in Chicago sent him some from time to time) and stopped paying the rent. He had been living with a woman named Marie. She went to California and married a Jewish businessman, but she committed suicide not long after. Meanwhile Terry had moved out of the Ferrer Center and lived in a rented room. He came to Mohegan colony some years later for a visit, but went back to New York the next day. Soon afterwards he got pneumonia and died.

The war and the Red Scare caused the downfall of the Ferrer Center. A lot of anarchists who habituated the Center evaded registration for the draft. This was true not only of American anarchists but of anarchists who came here from Europe, such as Fred Dunn and Jim Dick from England and André Longchamp and André Miroy from France. Spies soon began coming around, including a young woman, and Longchamp had an affair with her. Jack Isaacson, an American, also avoided the draft and was ordered to be deported, but he went underground and lived under his wife Gussie's surname, Denenberg. Many years later he was discovered when Gussie [q.v.] applied for citizenship papers. The FBI kept him under watch and questioned him from time to time, until he finally committed suicide.

Mother, Sophie, and I lived at Stelton for a while, and before that at Fellowship Farm, a socialist colony across the road. My half-sister Lydia, Mother and Gordon's child, went to school at Stelton and didn't like it much. Like my daughter Hilda, who went to the Mohegan school, Lydia preferred public school. Hilda felt the same way. Ironically she found public school liberating after attending the Modern School at Mohegan. Uncle and Aunty Ferm were teaching at Stelton when we lived there. Uncle was relaxed, quiet, warm, and loveable. You couldn't call him anything except "Uncle." Aunty too was remarkable and hard-working, but was critical and overbearing, not a true libertarian teacher.

Of the others at Stelton, Joseph Cohen was intelligent and capable and got things done, but the colony had too much poverty to keep good teachers and principals. Margaret Sanger had a little girl, Peggy, who stayed at the Living House but died of pneumonia. Bill Pogrebysky left for Soviet Russia and went to the Jewish colony of Birobidzhan; he died at the front during World War II. Mike Gold visited Stelton and Mohegan and, even after joining the Communists, retained his ties and affection for the anarchists. Chaim Weinberg of Philadelphia was full of jokes and had a great sense of humor. His wife Yetta was an excellent speaker and a first-rate organizer; she organized the cloakmakers' and cigarmakers' unions. Gray Wu was the only oriental in the colony. He went back to China and was never heard of again. Abe Winokour was so devout an anarchist that he sent the ashes of his wife, Anna Sosnovsky, equally devout, to be buried in Waldheim cemetery, near the graves of the Haymarket anarchists. Their daughter, Rina [Garst, q.v.], is named after Voltairine de Cleyre. Abe had previously been with Frances Goldenthal, who now lives in Mohegan. Anna Sosnovsky was an out-of-town organizer for the ILGWU and a member of the board of directors.

The Mohegan colony was established in 1923, largely on the initiative of Harry Kelly. Kelly had a passion for organizing colonies, and towards the end of his life began even to plan for one in Florida for elderly anarchists. He was able to start colonies because people trusted him, but once a colony got going he moved on to his next project. His companion was Mary Krimont, and they had a daughter Elsie. After Mary died Harry married Leah Lowensohn. Kelly was also the driving force behind the Mohegan school, which was built in 1925 and now carries a plaque in his honor. He loved to talk, loved baseball, and inspired unquestioning trust. He, Leonard Abbott, and the others were a special breed of wonderful people. There are few like them anymore.

The first members of the colony, including us, lived cooperatively in one big house until we could build our own homes. At its height at the end of the twenties, the colony had 450 acres of land with about three hundred families. The big house became the Living House, as in Stelton, for boarding children. Jim and Nellie Dick [q.v.] came up from Stelton to take charge of it, but after a few years they left because the colony board refused to make them principals of the school, considering them unqualified.

The colonists consisted of people from different nationalities. The Frenchmen included Miroy, Longchamp, a translator, and Henri Dupré, a chef. Longchamp is still alive, prospering somewhere near Paris; the Durants visited him there in 1972. Jacques Rudome [q.v.] is a Polish Jew by birth, who came to Paris as a child. There were six or seven Finns, including Gus Alonen, a builder by trade, who built one of the first houses there and helped in the building of the school. He believed in health foods, sauna baths, and chiropractic. He was killed in an automobile accident on Crompond Road during the 1950s. There was also a larger group of Russians, both Jewish and non-Jewish. Rose Dodokin (Jewish) and I ran the big house for summer guests; one summer Angelica Balabanoff, David Isakovitz,[443] and Alexander Schapiro and his wife stayed with us. Rose's husband William (non-Jewish) made orgone boxes for Wilhelm Reich. He and Rose moved to Florida, where he died in 1972. Isidore (Sidor in Russian) Bogin died a few years ago at eighty-seven. His wife Molly [q.v.] is still living at the colony. Sidor escaped from Siberia in 1905, lived in Paris for five years, then came to the United States. He and Molly were among the first Mohegan settlers. Arnold Krimont, Mary's brother, died in California in 1973, at the age of ninety-two. George Seldes, Sr., was a longtime anarchist, but his sons, George Junior and Gilbert, were not. George Senior had been a druggist in Pittsburgh and was very active during the early years of the colony.

A few other items may be of interest. Many of the colonists—Harry Kelly, George Seldes, Minna Lowensohn, Marc Epstein, Jack and Helen Rudome, Moritz Jagendorf [q.v.]—had been associated with the Ferrer Center in New York. Some colonists commuted to work in New York; some lived at the colony only during the summer and sent their children to our summer camp. A number of the women at the colony followed the teachings of Dr. Stretch, a New Jersey chiropractor and health faddist. The colonists held a farewell party for César Vega, who went back to Spain to fight in the Civil War, and gave him guns as a present. He and several other Spanish anarchists from America were seized when their boat landed and shot. Lucy Parsons once visited Mohegan during the 1920s to see my mother, whom she had known very well in Chicago. Daniel Bell, the sociologist, is the nephew of Jacob Mont, a Mohegan colonist, and lived with him for a while as a child.

For quite a few years we had the most wonderful times, in warm friendship with one another. Lectures, concerts, costume balls were held every Saturday night for the benefit of the school. The school was at the center of the colony, and we did everything possible for it. But, starting in the late 1920s, a rift developed between the Communists and fellow travelers on the one hand and the anarchists and some socialists on the other. During the earlier years, when the colony was poorer and more idealistic, the members were more closely knit and communal-minded than later. Our admissions committee tried to keep out the Communists, on the one hand, and the well-to-do, on the other. But gradually they trickled in, and the colony began to change. Far more than at Stelton, the Communists were responsible for the breakup of the colony and school. And the liberals must take a share of the blame. They were not committed to genuine libertarian ideals or to libertarian education. What they wanted was merely a middle-class progressive school with a professional staff. The anarchists, for their part, were too apathetic to resist these incursions. We had to drag them to election meetings to vote. Harry Kelly at one point suggested using the label "libertarian" rather than "anarchist" so as not to frighten off potential supporters.

The climax came after the Second World War with the Paul Robeson affair. Robeson had come occasionally to sing at Communist affairs, and the neighboring townsmen were up in arms. In the early days of the colony the local KKK had already burned a cross opposite the barn where we held our meetings. Now gangs came through in cars looking for Communists. A reign of terror began. The Communists on their side imported "goons" from New York City who were armed with clubs and baseball bats and patrolled the colony, stopping even residents, especially anarchists, from walking freely. The Peekskill riot [1949] was a traumatic experience and the last great blow to the colony. After this, the anarchists founded a Civic Association and dissociated themselves from the Communists. We still had enjoyable times, but never the same as in the past.

Those years in Mohegan, though, were by no means wasted. We tried things, we experimented, we attracted many interesting people. Anarchism is still our religion. You have to have the inner feeling, a strong sense of integrity and responsibility, of doing what we must, freely and without any sense of guilt.

• NELLIE DICK •

Miami, Florida, December 17, 1972;
Oyster Bay, New York, December 26, 1972,
September 16, 1974, November 18, 1990

Nellie Dick's involvement in the movement for libertarian education goes back to 1912, when, still in her teens, she started a Modern School in the Whitechapel district of London. Her soon-to-be husband, James Dick, had himself opened a Modern School in Liverpool in 1908, having met the Spanish educator Francisco Ferrer the previous year. After coming to the United States in 1917, Nellie and Jim played a major role in several educational experiments in this country, including the Modern Schools of Stelton, Mohegan, and Lakewood, which they started in 1933.

Nellie was seventy-nine when I first interviewed her in 1972, seven years after her husband's death. A woman of astonishing vitality, with white hair, rosy complexion, and alert blue eyes, she had vivid memories of the anarchists—among them Peter Kropotkin, Errico Malatesta, and Rudolf Rocker—reaching back to the turn of the century. On the wall of the den in her Miami house hung a large composite photograph of the various schools and colonies with which she and "Big Jim" had been associated. Not long before, she told me, a visitor from Brazil, noticing Ferrer among the faces in the photograph, said that when his father lay dying in Spain he insisted on having a picture of Ferrer buried with him in his coffin. In 1973 Nellie sold her house, moved into an apartment, and threw herself into senior citizens' affairs. Every year, meanwhile, she came north to visit her son, James Dick, Jr., a Long Island pediatrician, who had attended the Stelton School as a child. She also took part in the annual reunions of the friends and alumni of the Modern Schools, at which she invariably spoke. In 1990, in her ninety-eighth year, Nellie left Miami and moved in with "Little Jim" and his family, where she celebrated her hundredth birthday in 1993.

I was born Naomi Ploschansky in Kiev, Russia, on May 15, 1893, and came to London at the age of nine months, along with my brother, while two older girls were left in Russia. More children were born—there were eight in all—and we were very poor. My father, Solomon Ploschansky, had no trade; he worked as a baker's helper. The bakers went on strike—I can still see the huge *khaleh* they were carrying and father leading the parade in his blue sash with gold letters. When I saw that, I thought to myself that when in trouble I would tell my friends that my father was a general. Afterwards he became a cap maker and was active in the trade-union movement. They would sing the *Internationale* as they dipped the caps in water and put them on the mold. Mother was Hanna Kiselevsky from the town of Lipovets near Kiev. She came from a rabbinical family which owned a small flour mill. Neither of my parents was an anarchist.

Mother, in fact, was an Orthodox Jew. Yet she had a strong rebellious spirit and would fight for her rights, though normally a quiet person.

We lived in poverty in the East End. My parents went to lectures in the radical clubs, and eventually my mother took off her orthodox wig and left the synagogue. The *Arbeter Fraynd* was published in our house upstairs, so we got to know the Rockers very well and also the other anarchists who went in and out. I was sent by them to mail letters. I could barely reach the opening, yet I knew I must not let anyone help me or give a letter to anyone.

Living in this milieu, my parents soon became anarchists. I used to go to Rocker's lectures, and though I didn't understand much I loved to listen to his voice and thought what a wonderful actor he would make. The audience was always spellbound. I wanted to learn German, and Rudolf offered to teach me. When I went up to his room for a lesson I saw a group of people sitting there and looking up at him, worshipful and open-mouthed as he spoke. So I quietly left and never went back for lessons. I don't believe in gods. I felt the same way about the Ferms at Stelton. Don't set them up on a pedestal. I've always felt that part of the deference to Rocker, the Ferms, Leonard Abbott was because they weren't Jewish, not just "one of us."

When I was eight or nine we lived in Leeds for a while, in a house where William MacQueen[444] and his sidekick Henry had published a journal called the *Free Commune*. I remember the detectives coming one day and asking us about MacQueen and where he was, but we didn't tell them anything. We knew Rudolf Grossmann,[445] too, another friend of MacQueen's. He used to come to the *Arbeter Fraynd* office in our house in London. One day I found that my beautiful Bible was missing, and I always felt that he had taken it.

In London I used to recite poems in Yiddish at the Jubilee Street Club, which opened in 1906. Once I recited a humorous poem about Kropotkin, and he was in the audience! How he laughed! Kropotkin used to play games with us kids, dancing around in a circle. I was scared to death he'd have a heart attack.[446] Malatesta also came to the club sometimes, a small, slight man with dark hair and beard and eyes so sharp you'd think he could look right through you. Pryns Hopkins once came from America and wanted to see Malatesta. I was sixteen then and was asked to take him. He called a cab; that was the first taxi ride I ever had, and I felt that the whole town was looking at me!

I heard Voltairine de Cleyre lecture in London when I was about twelve [it was in 1903 and Nellie was ten]. She was a rather tall figure, wearing outlandish clothes that interested me. Mary Hansen of Stelton was a very close friend of hers and used to talk about her a lot. David Isakovitz lived in London and worked on the *Arbeter Fraynd* before going to America.

Once we went to the Rockers' apartment and the place was dark because they had no shilling to put in the meter. So one of us put in a shilling, and then we went and got cold cuts and bread and had a party. We had light and we had food, but we had no money for books or toys. That's why later in Stelton every holiday that came along we celebrated—Christmas with a tree, and so on—and that got me into trouble with some of the parents.

At the lectures in the club I noticed that mostly older people attended, and I asked Father what will happen when they die. What of the younger generation? Father suggested that I talk to the grown-ups about it. I visited their homes and sang Yiddish songs to put them in the right mood. Then one night at the club I suggested that we start a Sunday School. It was just after Ferrer's death. Alexander Schapiro was on the platform and he opposed the idea. "We have enough public schools," he said. "Ferrer wanted to establish schools because they had none. But we have secular schools here and don't need our own. Besides, we don't have the money." "I'll do it with pennies," I said.

So I went ahead. We used Father's house at 146 Stepney Green, and believe me we had some wonderful gatherings there! We had a room downstairs with sliding doors. We opened these doors and the kids came. I taught them radical songs from a book called *Chants of Labour*.[447] The rabbis told the parents not to send their children to "that anarchist school." But we would have dances and entertainments at the club, and they kept on coming. We started with a handful, but before long we had to hire New King's Hall, and the *Arbeter Fraynd* group began to help with a little money.

In Liverpool at this time, James Dick was writing a children's column for the anarchist paper *The Voice of Labour*, which he signed "Uncle Jim," which gave me the impression that he was an older man. Actually he had been born on October 7, 1882, in Liverpool, of Scottish parents (his father was a policeman and his mother a gentle-type Quaker). Jim spoke in a soft Lancashire accent. He later worked in London for John Turner's Shop Assistants' Union, and in New York for the Seamen's Union in 1917–1918. When Bernard Sernaker of the Ferrer Center wanted to go back to Russia, Jim got seaman's papers for him.

Jim attended Liverpool University, where his Spanish teacher was Lorenzo Portet, a disciple of Ferrer and the executor of Ferrer's estate after his execution. Jim met Ferrer, who visited Liverpool in 1907, and became interested in the Escuela Moderna. In 1909 he went to Spain with Portet to help settle Ferrer's estate. He also organized a short-lived Modern School in Liverpool. Jim played in a temperance band, was a teetotaler, a tea taster, and a manager of a grocery store.

After Liverpool University, Jim went to Ruskin College at Oxford, then to the Central Labour College in London, where he got to know George Davidson. Davidson was the director of the British Eastman Kodak Company and a real anarchist. He had a mansion on the Thames and another in Wales, as well as a villa at Cap D'Antibes on the French Riviera. He took men out of the coal mines and sent them to college with the idea that they would go back to the mines and educate the workers—which, of course, they never did! He told me that Jim, whom I wanted to invite to the Sunday School to talk to the children, was at the Labour College.

On May Day 1910 [actually 1913], when I was seventeen, I took the kids to demonstrate in the May Day caravan (we carried a banner, "Anarchist-Socialist School"). I was distributing antimilitarist leaflets on the Thames embankment when I saw the "Central Labour College" banner, so I went up to ask for Uncle Jim. I saw a young man with grey hair who looked gentler than the rest, and I asked him if James Dick was there. He bowed: "I'm Jim Dick." He was then twenty-eight [actually thirty]. We walked along the embankment and streets and talked until we got to Hyde Park, where Father and a group of comrades were speaking. That evening I recited a poem by Voltairine de Cleyre at the Jubilee Street Club, and Jim came. It was his first contact with the Jewish group. A few days later a Jewish artist, Sam Goldenberg, asked Mother, "How would you like Nellie to marry a *sheygets* [gentile]?" I overheard him and asked him what he meant. He said, "I saw you talking to him at Hyde Park gate and I knew he was the one."

Jim got to know Rudolf Rocker and the other London anarchists, and he began to read anarchist literature—he was a great reader. I invited him and his friends from the Labour College to talk to the Sunday School about the coal mines, labor, and so on. Before long Jim joined me in running the school, which was still in New King's Hall. We had loads of kids—they just streamed in. Bonar Law[448] once came and recited "The Ballad of Reading Gaol." After the outbreak of the First World War Jim and I began to live with each other, without getting officially married. We got a small house at 24 Green Street, Whitechapel, and used the downstairs for the school, which went on until we left for America. Rudolf Rocker wanted his older son, Rudolf Jr., a tall, blond, and handsome young man, to take part in the school. He did, and took charge for a while when Jim and I were in Newcastle for a visit. Later in Canada, where he opened his own school, he wrote us that it was terrible for him to have to live in the shadow of his father, being asked by the comrades to speak and write.

Before and during the war, I worked in the office of the Invalid Children's Aid Association, located in the Toynbee Hall settlement house. I got very little pay, so in the evenings I would teach English to foreigners at the Jubilee Street Club. (I also learned Esperanto during this time.) One man I was supposed to teach was a Russian, but for some reason my parents talked me out of it. Soon after, the Houndsditch affair took place, and he was one of the men involved.

Our school kids went to antiwar meetings and often came back beaten up. A lot of our anarchist boys refused to register for the draft and had to go into hiding. Once we had a garden party which was raided by the police—there was a spy in our group—who arrested everybody without a registration card. Rudolf Rocker was arrested and sent to an aliens' camp. Jim and I got married so he could avoid conscription. But then they started taking married men, so in January 1917 we decided to go to America.

When we reached New York we immediately got in touch with the comrades. We went to a lecture on Dickens at the Ferrer Center. We went to a Prisoners' Ball at the Armory. We had heard Emma Goldman speak in London, so we went to the office of *Mother Earth*. She invited us to lunch in a room at the Hotel Brevoort on lower Fifth Avenue, and we were served fried chicken by a colored maid. I was shocked and disappointed! As anarchists in England we never knew any luxury, never wore jewelry, earrings, or anything. My sister had a jacket with fringes, and we cut them off. Nothing fancy. But Emma had a girl to wait on us, with a little white cap. I couldn't get over it—an anarchist with a hired maid.[449] I didn't care for Emma. She was too cold, too hard, and didn't like children. She wasn't interested in them. Berkman was softer and nicer than Emma, a warmer person. Rocker, too, was a finer person than Emma. He was gentle; he was interested in people; he was very fair in his judgments and in his criticisms of people.

It was Harry Kelly who suggested that we come to Stelton. It was in March 1917 that we went, and Fred Dunn and Gray Wu were on hand to greet us. Before leaving for the States, Fred had lived with us in Marsh House[450] in London, along with Lilian Wolfe,[451] Gaston Marin (a Belgian), and other comrades. He was one of a group of Englishmen at Stelton, most of them conscientious objectors, who had come to the U.S. to avoid military service. He and Jim were very good friends, and Jim was devastated by the news of Fred's death in 1925.

Gray Wu had heard of the colony through *Mother Earth* and came as a cook. He was slim and pleasant, very shy and very charming. When Jim and I came from England, we had been invited to a party at the *Mother Earth* office, and I remember eating Chinese food that he had prepared. He was a good cook and a true anarchist, intelligent, fine, clean, a student of philosophy at Columbia. He played a Chinese musical instrument and spoke fluent English, though with a Chinese accent. He once had to make a speech at Stelton, but felt shy and wasn't sure of his English. So Fred Dunn read it, and every time the audience applauded Gray would stand up and bow. It was very funny. He was quiet and modest, but got on well with the children. He once took a group of us to New York to see a show. I feared he might get into trouble, being Chinese and with young American girls, but all went well. His uncle had a Chinese restaurant on Broadway, upstairs. Jim and I went there to eat with him, along with Tessie Sapir, a woman from Fellowship Farm. It was a beautiful restaurant, a big place with a dance floor.

Jim and I took charge of the Living House and were paid $6.50 a week each, which I often spent taking the children for ice cream and movies in New Brunswick. Once when they played the *Star-Spangled Banner* in the theater, the kids refused to stand and we got into a big argument with the manager. I, Jim, Fred Dunn, and Gray Wu slept in one room in the Living House. Sometimes Gray's Chinese friends would come to visit. They worked in the Jade Mountain restaurant in New York. Jim and I once went there to eat, and they brought out all kinds of fancy dishes for us but wouldn't allow us to pay. Gray once picketed his uncle's restaurant during a strike and got into trouble with the authorities. He left the colony during the early twenties, I think, and went back to China, where he later became the dean of the University of Peking. He sent me a pair of Chinese slippers and kept up his correspondence with Uncle Ferm.

What a mess the colony was then! When we first came, the Living House was just filth! You never saw such filth in your life! The kids said it was a "free school," which meant to them that they could make a mess of the place. They had no idea how to behave. They were just dropped there by their parents, who stayed in New York. They would go around unwashed. One of them threw a plate of soup at a teacher when scolded. They had a saying: "There is no shame at Stelton." This meant more than just naked swimming. Jacques Dubois [q.v.], so we were told, used to come down to eat naked. Oh, the dirt that we had to clean up in that place—it was something terrible! There was no toilet but only a pail for the kids to make in at night. That was what we had to contend with. But freedom without responsibility doesn't go. Many of the early teachers left because they became exhausted and would not sacrifice their own lives and interests as the children demanded of them. They were battered— emotionally and intellectually—by underdisciplined children.

I played "Lords and Ladies"—an English children's game—with the Living House kids to teach them manners. I read them modern poetry before bedtime, which they didn't understand but loved the sounds and rhythms of the words. I kept house and did a little teaching. Big Jim taught basketry and metal work. William Thurston Brown was in charge of the school when we came. He seemed a rather ordinary man. The Ferms were much more dynamic—at least *she* was. I disagreed with her often. Her *theories* were great; once I heard her lecture in New York and I was enthralled. When she spoke I was transfixed. She was charming and beautiful, and there was fire when she spoke. But she didn't act as she spoke.

She and Uncle were never anarchists, but they professed freedom in education, which is an anarchist ideal. She was the one who objected to the name Francisco Ferrer School and changed it to the Stelton Modern School. She never shook off her Catholic upbringing. She was raised in a convent and never lost that—she always remained a mother confessor. With her everything had a religious undertone, and she couldn't shake it off. And she communicated it to the children in candlelight processions and so on. She was imbued with her religious upbringing. And she would scold a child in front of the others. Once the kids in the Living House took candy from a jar. Do you think she didn't make a big thing about that? She kept bringing it up to the kids long afterward. Another thing: some kids wet the bed, but you don't bawl them out for that. Aunty made them sleep under the floor of the house so their urine could drain into the earth. That's no way to punish a child. All kids are great if you handle them right. She was too strict. Uncle was different, a much gentler, softer person.

Joseph Cohen lived in the colony and worked in a cigar factory in New Brunswick. He was very clever, very able, very competent, yet in later years when he had a summer camp on the other side of Lake Mohegan he left owing money to everybody. He was a good organizer, but he liked to have his own way—a bit too authoritarian for me. Hans Koch was a handsome fellow with a shock of white hair. He had been sick with tuberculosis and was supposed to die from it but seemed healthy on the whole. His wife Anna did the weaving and afterwards went to Antioch College and still wove the most wonderful designs even when blind. They had a son, Inko, and a daughter, Gerda, at the school. Rose Freeman walked around in sloppy clothing, her hair a mess, writing beautiful flowery poetry, Japanese things, I think. Hippolyte Havel made his best speeches while drunk. He was very irascible, very short with people. He ended his days raving mad in Marlboro State Hospital in New Jersey.

John Edelman, the son of John H. Edelmann, an anarchist architect, was born in New Jersey, but his father died and his mother, Rachelle Krimont, took him to Whiteway Colony in England, where he was brought up. Big Jim met him there when he was visiting the colony and John was then a boy of fourteen. John produced the first children's play at Stelton, *Practice Pot* by Padraic Colum, followed by *The Idol's Eye* by Lord Dunsany. He married Kate Van Eaton, who taught at the school and is now bedridden with a stroke. He himself died last year [1972].

Of course we had many hardships in those early years, but we were young and enthusiastic, and we had the pleasure of overcoming the hardships. Visitors to the colony included Max Eastman, Art Young, Mike Gold, Joe Freeman,[452] and John Dewey. Jo Davidson, the sculptor, had his children there, and a child of Charles Garland lived under our charge in the Living House, and Jim and I once visited Garland's April Farm community in Pennsylvania.

There was a good deal of suspicion among the neighbors of the colony. I once got a lift from Stelton to New Brunswick, and the man said: "Oh, yes, you come from that free-love colony where a bell rings at midnight and everyone changes partners." In 1917 and 1918 government agents came around to look for conscientious objectors who were hiding in the colony or in the surrounding woods. One time they climbed up and took down our red flag.

After the war, in 1919, Jim and I visited England, where Jimmy Jr., our only child, was born. Then we returned to Stelton until 1924, when we went up to Mohegan. We returned to Stelton in 1928, then opened our own school in Lakewood, New Jersey, which we operated for twenty-five years, from 1933 to 1958. And the idea of a free school came with us wherever we went.

Our treatment by the Mohegan board hurt us very badly. We were there from 1924 to 1928 and built up the Living House until we had fifty kids. We became well-known in progressive education. Visitors came to see our school. Jim spoke at a Progressive Education Association convention in Baltimore. Yet the board decided to replace Jim as principal. They complained that Jim didn't know how to raise money for the new school building. They wanted somebody who could go out and make speeches, and we weren't interested in that sort of thing. The Mohegan colony was richer and more beautiful than Stelton and did not have the distinctive stamp of the Ferms, but the theory in running it—freedom in education—was much the same.

We returned to Stelton after the Ferms left in 1928 and were coprincipals for five years. In 1931 Jim went to a progressive education convention in England. We had read *The Dominie's Log*, A. S. Neill's first book,[453] during our first years at Stelton and had liked it very much, and now Jim visited Summerhill. Neill had invited him, and they continued to correspond in later years.

Jim and I had long wanted to set up our own school, and we finally did so in 1933. We called it the Lakewood Modern School, and it lasted for twenty-five years. We didn't follow theories much but experimented on our own, except that we remembered that Ferrer was a rebel, that he was shot, and that he believed in giving the child a wider scope. We weren't aware of other Modern Schools in the U.S., apart from Stelton and Mohegan, and had no contacts with Modern Schools in Europe. We had children from nursery age—three or four—through the primary grades. After that they went on to Lakewood High School (like our son Jim) or went home.

It differed from Stelton in that it was in a town rather than in the country, and we had a bit more academic structure. We were a household of ourselves, a huge family affair. The children who came to board were from broken homes or couldn't stand the air in New York—asthma, allergies, and so on. Most were from New York but some came to day school from Lakewood. A few had been at Stelton. We believed in freedom of education, as in Stelton. The children were never forced to attend class. If the kids got rowdy, Jim would simply walk out. As in Stelton, the worst punishment was to tell a child he couldn't go to school. I handled the nursery and kindergarten and housekeeping, and Jim had the grades. Many of the kids went on to become doctors, lawyers, scientists—I still keep in touch with many of them. The children were happy. It was not just a school but a home, a big family, and when we sold the place the kids cried. Once a psychiatrist praised me for the wonderful job I had done with Bruce Gilson, and when I told this to one of the girls at the school she said, "Yes, we did do a good job." She said "we," and she was right.

Jim taught the kids Shakespeare—he was a Shakespeare man—and nine-and ten-year-olds could recite his plays and sonnets. We took them to Shakespeare plays in New York and they knew the lines. But freedom in education didn't mean license. One of our little girls said, when I wouldn't let her do what she wanted, "Take that sign off your door! This isn't a Modern School!"

During the summers we had a Modern School camp, first at Montrose, New York, for one year, then at Carmel, New York, until about 1943, and finally at Stroudsburg, Pennsylvania, for a year or two. From then on we stayed at Lakewood and had camp there. The camp was run on the same principles as the school.

About the Rosenberg children,[454] two little boys. A friend of the Rosenbergs living in Lakewood—there were lots of Communists in the Lakewood area—asked me if I could take them and shelter them from publicity in the wake of their parents' execution. If I had said no, I never could have lived it down. They stayed for the summer. My son was the only one who agreed. Even Big Jim said, "Why do you want to stick your neck out?" That was in 1953. In the last years, like Stelton and Mohegan, Lakewood became only a nursery and kindergarten, as Jim had grown older and didn't have as much patience and energy to carry on with the grades. The school closed in 1958, and we moved to Miami soon afterwards. Jim died there in 1965 at the age of eighty-two.

Some other points may be worth mentioning. Our son Jimmy was an intelligent little boy, but he didn't learn to read until ten. A great majority of the former pupils at Stelton, Mohegan, and Lakewood have pleasant and enthusiastic memories of the time that they spent at the school. John Scott joined the Silver Shirts, a fascist outfit, and ran for president of the United States on a right-wing fringe-party ticket in 1936 or 1940. He was a great nature man, a wonderful farmer, but we had lots of trouble with him. So much of the destiny of the colonies was determined by private lives and interests and needs rather than by theories or ideals. William Bridge, an Englishman, came to Stelton while the Ferms were in charge. He had been chased out of Hunter College because he had an affair with a student. One of his daughters, Joan Bridge, was the singer Joan Baez's mother.[455] Bridge's school at Chatham, New Jersey, was not really a Modern School. For Bridge as for many other people Stelton was a temporary sanctuary. People came for a variety of reasons: politics, diet, broken marriages.

My father, by the way, left London and went back to Russia in 1917 to join the revolution. He became an ardent Communist, died in 1937, and was buried with military honors. Afterwards, though, one of my sisters spent fifteen years in Stalin's prison camps. I made three trips to Russia to see my family, in 1930–1931, in 1933 (with both Jims), and in 1960. During the first trip I went to see Bill Shatoff, who was on the board at the Ferrer Center and at Stelton when Jim and I first came there and who returned to Russia in 1917. He was husky, strong, a hail-fellow-well-met, always with a slap on the back. He was wearing all his medals and decorations, which stretched from one side of his chest to the other. He seemed happy to see me and told me that he was still an anarchist, even though he worked with the Communists, which he said was a necessary step on the road to freedom. The second time I came to Russia, in 1933, I went to his apartment but wasn't allowed in. He was arrested a few years later during the purge.

My views on education have remained essentially the same over the years: just being human to the children. When children are treated with respect and are given responsibility they will be happy. We were interested in the children. We were concerned with their lives, their whole beings, and with their being happy. But you can't attribute the child's successes or failures to the school alone. You must know his whole background and how he grew up. A few years ago the former Stelton children had a reunion at young Jim's house on Long Island and the question was asked, What was it about Stelton and the other schools that stays with us so much, that makes us feel as we do about them? Love? Freedom? I thought of it later, and it struck me that the answer was security, the security of the family, of being part of one big close-knit family, which they had lacked before they came to the school. That's what they had, the feeling of security, of a family, of home.

• MACIE POPE •

Huntington Beach, California, June 23, 1974

Macie Pope, born in 1884, was the daughter of Oliver A. Verity, a founder of Home Colony near Tacoma, Washington. She and her brother Kenneth set type for the colony paper, *The New Era* (1897), and her husband, Charles L. Govan, edited and printed its successor, *Discontent* (1898–1902).

I WAS BORN in 1884 and will be ninety come December. I came to Home at the start, when I was eleven years old. The men cut cordwood for a living. They built a flume and flumed it down to the bay, put it on a raft, and sold it to the steamer. Captain [Edward] Lorenz, who ran the steamer, was a good man. He took the kids free to town. It was hard sledding at first. B. F. Odell was the blacksmith. He had one daughter. They moved away. We three families divided our milk right to the cupful. We shared and shared alike. Later on, greed came in as new members came in and bought up land for speculation.

My brother and I helped set type for *The New Era*, the first colony paper. We had a little hand press. Then we had paper-foldings when we'd all get together and fold the paper for mailing. I also helped set type for *Discontent*, the next paper published at Home. We got our own groceries by a steamboat called the *Otto*. We used to meet it in rowboats. We finally got our own store and butcher shop.

I went to school to Morton.[456] He taught high school at Home. He was a learned man and a good teacher, quite strict. He didn't have much patience. Once when a boy gave the wrong answer Morton said, "Billy, are you an idiot?" The boy snapped back, "No, are you?" There was an art teacher, Miss Mint, and adults took lessons as well as the children. We had lectures. Mr. Morton taught an Esperanto class that I attended.

We had a band at the colony, with Allen at the head. It was a good place. All our children turned out well. We used to swim, go to dances, and had a baseball team. Huckleberry picking was one of the main livelihoods. We picked the berries in the fall and shipped them to Alaska and different places.

Charles Govan came out and printed *Discontent*. I was much younger than he was. He didn't know much about homesteading. All he knew was printing— a city guy. He went to Tacoma twice a week to take dancing lessons so we could go dancing together. We separated, and I came down with Kenneth to Los Angeles. Govan died up there around 1949.

Father was a good man, noted for his good deeds. He would run a mile to help someone. I'm very angry that Mr. LeWarne called him an anarchist in his article.[457] Father was a good carpenter. My brother was a good carpenter, and I'm a good carpenter too. I helped split the shakes for our first house at Home. I taught domestic science—cooking and the like—to the school children at my house. Liberty Hall was up on the hill. The first floor had the print shop and the school. The second floor was the dance hall. A new schoolhouse was built, and Liberty Hall burned down years later.

I remember that Emma Goldman came out in a launch to visit. She seemed more masculine than feminine. We were no anarchists. We criticized that Czolgosz when he killed the President. Yet the townspeople wanted to wreck the colony and would have if Captain Lorenz hadn't stopped them. When Tom Geeves and his family lived in a rundown shack, they all got together and built a new house for them.

They were dreamers who wanted to reform the world. But when you get people coming in from all over, there has to be friction. People got money-hungry. They bought up land for speculation. If it could have stayed the way it was at the beginning, things would have been all right.

They were idealists. They always seemed to want something beyond or better than the way it was. That's why they named the paper *Discontent*. They weren't satisfied with the world as it was, and without discontent, they said, there would be no progress. "Discontent—The Mother of Progress." That was their motto. Yet I raised my daughter there, and she turned out to be wonderful.

• DAVID DADISMAN •

Home, Washington, June 7, 1974

When I visited David Dadisman in 1974, he was the last of the oldtime residents of Home Colony, the principal anarchist community on the Pacific coast, established in 1896. Dadisman was planting vegetables in his garden when I arrived, a sturdy little man of eighty-four. He had built his house all by himself, he proudly informed me, and installed the wiring and plumbing. He cherished the old values of honesty, independence, and hard work, deploring laziness and corruption. Dadisman died at Home on March 3, 1985, at the age of ninety-five.

I CAME to Home from Virginia in 1899, when I was nine years old. I came with my father, Martin Dadisman, who had had a farm in Virginia. The twelfth of this month will be the seventy-fifth anniversary of our arrival. Dad was a very good mechanic and invented a new seed drill. I still have a copy of the patent. But McCormick stole the idea and never paid Dad a cent. Dad was way ahead of his time. His ideas are in general use today, but in those times they were almost unheard of. On our farm in Virginia Dad had a black man working for him and he sat at our table and ate with us. The neighbors found out and threatened to tar and feather Dad and ride him out on the rails. He was so aggravated by their attitude that he decided he was going to get out of there.

Dad first landed at Equality, a socialist colony on Puget Sound, but he didn't stay there very long. A few people did all the work, while the rest of them idled and profited at the expense of the laboring. My dad was a very hard worker, and that didn't set very well with him. I share that philosophy. So Dad decided to move to Home. There were about a dozen residents when he arrived, including Verity, Allen, and Odell. They were ordinary people, pretty intelligent and hard workers. They did whatever they could find to do: some worked in the woods, Allen taught school for a while.

My dad came about a year before I did. I went to school in Liberty Hall, which burned down many years ago. Gracie Allen was my teacher. Liberty Hall was up on the hill. The dance hall occupied the entire second story. The first story had two school rooms and the print shop of Charlie Govan. The school was nothing different from ordinary schools. I'm the only one of the oldtimers left here. One of the Allen girls, Georgie Evans, is still alive. She was living at Horsehead Bay, but now she may be living in Tacoma.

My father was not an anarchist, or never called himself one. No, I never heard of Francisco Ferrer. I never heard of Stelton. James F. Morton was another teacher, a red-headed fellow, a kind of crackpot. I remember an incident at school one day. A kid my age named Adius Smith—he was full of the devil—was cutting up one day. "Adius, are you an idiot?" asked Morton. "No, are you?" he answered. Morton was an intelligent fellow. I don't know what became of him after he left the colony.

I was well-acquainted with Jay Fox. He edited the paper for a time. He was a good guy, a printer. His wife Cora was a very smart woman and a hard worker. She was also an artist and worked in ceramics. I'll show you some of her work [he shows me a beautiful teapot inscribed by Cora]. She was a very good-hearted person. I ran the cooperative store here for twenty years, and she worked for me candling eggs. She died about three or four years ago. The store burned down a couple of years ago. I've worked hard all my life. I built this house from top to bottom. I have three children, and they each have three children. I have five great-grandchildren. If I may say so, I have a very nice family.

When McKinley was shot [September 6, 1906] the townsfolk of Tacoma threatened to come out here and destroy the place. The only thing that prevented them from doing it was that the captain of the steamer [Ed Lorenz] knew what kind of people were living here and he dissuaded them from coming over and raising the devil. Allen died here and Verity moved away. His son Kenneth is still living in California. He visited me a couple of years ago. He's about ninety years old now. I can give you his address.

Donald Vose? He was a shyster, that guy. He did his darnedest to get these people into trouble. He was the cause of several of them being arrested. He was no damn good. Nobody had any use for him. Jim Tillman was the same kind of guy. Gertie Vose wasn't first class either. She was a kleptomaniac. Every time she came into the store she would steal a bar of soap or anything else she could get her hands on. Her husband, if she had one, never was here. Her father,

O. B. Vose, lived here and she kept the Vose name, so I have an idea she was never married. That Donald Vose—his real name was Donald Meserve. But Meserve never lived here.

Charlie Penhallow was a good, simple, hardworking fellow and jolly. His wife Mattie was postmistress here when they took the post office away at Lakebay. And it was never restored. Shortly after they took the post office away they installed R.F.D., and we were served by R.F.D. till ten or fifteen years ago. Now we have a post office at Home. My youngest son carries the mail up here.

There was strife among the people here, and they finally decided to disband. There were no racial or religious antagonisms—that wasn't it. There was one old fellow came here who dressed like a woman. They had a pretty hot meeting up there in that old Liberty Hall. One fellow shouted, "You can go to hell!" Another added, "I second the motion!" There weren't any antagonisms either between the anarchists and Communists. As far as I know there were no Communists here.

I'm well-satisfied with my life here. You know, I haven't had time in my life to do anything except work. There've been all sorts of people here—people of every nature. There've been a lot of very fine people here and a lot of shysters too. But the good people were in the majority.

• PEARL POTTU •

Home, Washington, June 7, 1974

Pearl Pottu grew up near Home Colony on Puget Sound. She is a member of the Key Peninsula Historical Society and has photographs and clippings relating to the colony.

I WAS RAISED next to Home Colony in a family of nonmembers. We came from a different background. Father was a minister, and we didn't see eye to eye with the colonists, who were strongly antireligious, for the most part, and made no bones about it. But they were hard-working and decent folk, who minded their own business, and we got along well with them.

The school at first was in Liberty Hall, but they needed more space and built a separate schoolhouse around 1910. It's still standing but is a private home now. Liberty Hall burned down years later. Another social center, called Harmony Hall, was built, but it collapsed a few years ago.

Joe Koppelle and Franz Erkelens built a tree house in 1908. Erkelens moved out in 1910 and Koppelle in 1917.

• RADIUM LAVENE •

Los Angeles, June 22, 1974

Radium LaVene, the son of anarchist parents, was raised in Home Colony, near Tacoma, and attended the school there. He died in Los Angeles in 1991 at the age of eighty-eight.

I WAS BORN in Tacoma in 1903. My parents had come to Home Colony the year before. My father, Nathan Levin, was an anarchist and had read about Home in the anarchist press. The three founders, you know, had come in 1896 with a boat, a five-dollar piece, and a dream—the sum total of their resources. My parents named me Radium, which had been discovered about that time.[458] My younger brother, born in 1911, was first named Revolt and then Ferrer. He's now a policeman in New Jersey. We had a little bust of Ferrer—with a goatee, I remember it yet—in our house. There was an Albert Parsons Grosse in the colony, who now lives in Seattle.

I went to the school at Home. George and Sylvia Allen and their daughter Grace were my teachers. When I started, the school was in Liberty Hall, and then we moved into a new schoolhouse about half a block away (Mrs. Van Tyle lives there now). The education was fairly traditional. It was not called a "Modern School." I went there till the seventh grade. Then we moved to Tacoma.

Donald Vose was maybe ten or twelve years older than me. He was a weak person who saw a chance to make some money by becoming a stool pigeon. After it was all over, he used to sneak out to the colony to see his mother and a few friends—beer-drinking buddies—who stood by him. We had a baseball team that played all the teams around Tacoma and gave a good accounting of itself. On one of Vose's visits he was crouching on the sidelines watching us play when one of the older French colonists, Gaston Lance, went up and spat in his face. Donald didn't make a move in return. He just took it.

Burns[459] came up posing as a book salesman, looking for Dave Caplan. Actually he was hiding on Bainbridge Island on the Sound, and Frankie (Frances) Moore was keeping house for him there. I met Caplan many years later at a picnic down here in Los Angeles. I can't recall the year—maybe it was 1945—but he was growing old.

After Joe Koppelle left the tree house in 1917, he built a house way back in the woods. He and his wife were very small, so they built the whole house very small—to scale.

Alexander Berkman visited Home, and Emma Goldman too. She stayed at our place and Ben Reitman was with her. Emma was very jealous of any attention that other women paid him. When Mother was talking to him out in the yard, Emma couldn't stand it and kept calling him to come into the house. Reitman told ghost stories around a bonfire to us kids.

It was an exciting place. We lived near the water and Mother was one of the "nude bathers." We colony kids all bathed nude. One fellow at the colony—not an anarchist—took pictures and sold them to the Tacoma papers. That created a scandal and "free love" accusations. He hid by the road and tried to photograph Mother on her way to her swim, but she always outsmarted him, and Dad caught him and almost threw him into the bay.

The kids sang Wobbly songs around the campfire. Miss Mint had art classes every summer. There were building parties when all the men got together and put up a house for a newlywed couple. Ernest Falkoff at thirteen was the youngest student ever to enter the University of Washington. He had a sister named Emma, after Emma Goldman.

Dad had a cleaning store in Tacoma, and Andrew Klemencic[460] worked for him as a tailor. He was bald, middle-aged, and lived in Tacoma. Many of the most active anarchists at Home—Klemencic, Jay Fox, Sam Hammersmark,[461] Dr. Reznick (Esther Fox's first husband, a dentist; she later lived with Fox, then with William Z. Foster)[462]—came there from Chicago. Hammersmark went back to Chicago in the 1930s.

It was a beautiful spot. Groceries and supplies were cheap. So all kinds of people came to live there. Factions formed, disharmony developed. The grocer, Oscar Ingval, drank and the store got into trouble. I remember Father borrowing money from a friend in Seattle and turning it over to the store, but it failed anyway. Law suits followed. David Dadisman [q.v.] started it up again later. Finally the Mutual Home Association was dissolved. Families left, the older folk died out, and the colony days were over.

• PHILIP TRUPIN •

Nutley, New Jersey, May 31, 1972

Philip Trupin, a graduate of the National Farm School in Pennsylvania and of New York University, was the principal of the Sunrise Colony school in Michigan during the 1930s. He also served on the executive board of the colony and succeeded Joseph Cohen as general secretary when the colony moved to Virginia in 1937. During these years Trupin's eyesight was failing, and he was totally blind when I interviewed him in 1972. He died on September 5, 1983.

I AM NOW seventy-two and am a graduate of the National Farm School in Bucks County, Pennsylvania, which I attended from 1918 to 1921. I am also a graduate of New York University, with an M.A. in workers' education. I do not consider myself an outright anarchist, though I have a tinge of anarchism in me. Before the Sunrise colony was founded, during the late 1920s and early 1930s, I attended anarchist meetings in New York. The English-speaking anarchists, the Road to Freedom Group (Walter Starrett, Hippolyte Havel, and the rest), met on lower Broadway, and the Jewish anarchists met on Second Avenue below Fourteenth Street.

I came to Sunrise in January 1934, when I was thirty-four, with my wife Eva and two-year-old daughter. Our son, Joel Sunrise Trupin, now a professor of biology at a Negro college in Tennessee, was born at the colony in 1934. Another son was born in 1940. I was the teacher in the Sunrise school and also worked in the dairy, tended cows, and did other chores. I am "the Professor" in Joseph Cohen's book, *In Quest of Heaven*.[463] I served on the executive board of the colony, and after the move to Virginia I succeeded Cohen as general secretary and thus inherited the colony archives [which he later deposited in the Bentley Library of the University of Michigan at Ann Arbor].

I supported J. J. [i.e., Joseph J. Cohen] throughout. Not that he was always right, but he had a constructive outlook, not destructive. The oppositionists, by contrast, were bent on destroying the colony. Cohen was a self-proclaimed assimilationist. He watched the experiment at Llano and other colonies carefully. He was a very able administrator but not tolerant enough of other people's views and mistakes. But now I have some regrets for supporting Cohen so strongly. He was too aloof, abrupt, cold. "If you put a glass of tea by him, it would freeze," said his *Fraye Arbeter Shtime* associates. He had a streak of vanity, arrogance, intolerance. Yet he was a man of unimpeachable honesty and integrity, if too individualistic and not really fit for communal life.

One reason that Sunrise failed was that it did not act according to its stated principles. We never really learned the meaning of the word "we," of togetherness. We did not know how to live together. The oppositionists were even worse. Eli Greenblatt ("Yoine" in Cohen's book) sat there like King Tut. Chaim Weinberg, the dean of the anarchists at the colony, thought Cohen too severe. Even the anarchists forgot what anarchism was, forgot responsibility and mutual aid, and emphasized individual self-interest.

An opposition existed from the start. The first question put to me when I arrived was, "Are you a septic-tankist or a sewerist?" Talk about opposition! I had no idea what they were talking about. When the first opposition left the colony in April 1934, Cohen thought his troubles were over. But a new opposition arose immediately, headed by Stein.[464] And even after *he* left, there was an opposition of some sort. Take the case of Rose Dubin. Here Cohen's account is biased. She and her husband, a butcher, came from California with their two children in November 1933. They arrived in the middle of the night after driving an old jalopy cross-country, and Cohen refused to come down to greet them. After she wrote her letter to the press, Cohen and his supporters were out to punish her, forgetting their anarchist principles—just like the outside world. She could have been reasoned with, had Cohen tried. Nor should Peter Wolff ("the manufacturer") have been victimized—called up before the general meeting, insulted and humiliated. Cohen was a vindictive man by nature. Those "victories" of his spelled our downfall. Another victory like that, I told Cohen, and we are through.

The colonists were mostly garment workers from New York, Detroit, Philadelphia, Chicago, and other cities. At most 10 percent were real anarchists. Several came from Stelton and Mohegan and one from Home. Among the Steltonites were the Cohens, the Farbers, the Keysers, the Bluesteins, and Minnie Markowitz. Freethought ("Freddie") Albert had been at Mohegan. The other anarchists included Chaim Weinberg from Philadelphia, Yankl and Sarah Katzenelenboygen from Florida (they worked in the dairy), Sima Rosen, Cohen's bookkeeper from the *Fraye Arbeter Shtime*, and Mendel and Shaindel Bluestein [q.v., Shaindel Ostroff], who ran the Children's House. Angelo Di Vitto and Silvio Boccabello were dedicated Italian anarchists from Detroit. Paul Boattin, another Italian anarchist, left the colony and became a Communist. When he returned for a visit, during the Spanish Civil War, Angelo ran after him with a shotgun, so bitter was the hatred of the anarchists against the Communists at that time.

There were quarrels between the anarchists and the Communists in the colony, but this was not as conspicuous as in Stelton or Mohegan. We were all very concerned about what was happening in Spain. The murder of Berneri[465] especially infuriated the anarchists against the Communists. Communists were supposedly not permitted in Sunrise to begin with, yet some did get in, in spite of every effort by the admissions committee to keep them out. There were quite a few socialists (the anarchists had no objection to them) and Labor Zionists (Poale Zion), however. We undertook to feed strikers—thousands of them—in the great General Motors strike of 1937. We sent truckloads of vegetables, beef, bread, and cheese to Flint, thirty-five miles to the south. We were part of the labor movement in a very real way.

There was just one school, with an elementary and a high school group. I was the principal. It was not "modern" but progressive, stressing activities and method. Children under four and over twelve lived with their parents, with the others in the Children's House. Look at this photograph of the elementary and high school children. I was looking sad because the colony was coming to an end. Cohen came over to console me. "Sunrise will never die," he said, "because anything I start doesn't die."

The school was part of the state system and had to conform to state requirements, thereby saving an annual tax of two thousand dollars. The high school teachers included Esther and Joe Swire, Eddie Kolchin, and Sam Perlis. The elementary teachers were Minnie Bluestein, Joe Swire, and one or two others. Rachel Stone taught music and Sam Gittelman art to both groups. Gussie Davidson was the librarian. Some of the teachers also did farm work: I worked in the barn, Joe Swire in the fields, and so on. The school was a member of the Progressive Education Association. The total number of students was about sixty. They went on to become doctors, lawyers, academics, workers, musicians.

For adults, too, there were occasional classes, lectures, and discussions, and we put on plays and musicales. On several occasions Harry Kelly visited the colony to speak, and Rudolf Rocker came once. Rocker also came to Ann Arbor to speak at Yankl Katzenelenboygen's funeral. Italian anarchists from Detroit held conferences at Sunrise, and there were picnics and other gatherings. Israel

Davidson, a nephew of Jo Davidson and also a sculptor, was a member of the colony and a real nut. He made a bust of Joseph Cohen, gave it to him, then later smashed it to bits, a symbol of his disillusionment in Cohen.

The Sunrise experiment, whatever its difficulties, enriched our whole lives. It was the most meaningful experience in our lives. We all felt that way, even those with whom we didn't agree. You live intimately with other people, plan with them, think with them. Communal life is different: one for all and all for one. There is no stronger bond to me. It meant real intimacy, closeness. To this day we remain close. Some of the best times we have are to relive those experiences, those years. We visited the site in 1969. Nothing of the colony remains. It's now just a large family farm.

• LOUIS A. GITTELMAN •

Bronx, New York, October 25, 1972

Louis Gittelman, the son of a Russian-Jewish anarchist, went with his family to the Sunrise Colony in Michigan at its inception in 1933 and remained until its demise in Virginia in 1940. He afterwards became a podiatrist and lived in the Amalgamated Cooperative Houses in the Bronx, where I interviewed him in the apartment of his neighbor Ahrne Thorne (q.v.).

MY FATHER, Boris Gittelman, was from Kiev province, Russia. He was a cap maker, a lifelong anarchist, and a self-educated philosopher who came to the United States in 1909. When I was born he named me Elisée Reclus Gittelman, after the great French anarchist and geographer. The county clerk asked, "What kind of name is that?" My father said it was French. "Oh, a Frenchman," the clerk replied and recorded it as "Louis." But as a kid I was always called "El," for Elisée, which sounded like "Al" with a Yiddish accent. So I became known as Al, though officially my name is Louis.

Dad was a nature lover and had a farm in Bethel, New York, for about a year. He always wanted to be close to the soil, and I inherited some of that quality. We went to the Sunrise colony in Alicia, Michigan, when it was founded in 1933. We stayed there five or six years and then spent another year in Virginia where it moved, remaining almost to the end. I was sixteen when we arrived in Michigan, attended the high school, and worked in the stable tending to the horses. We had a breeding barn with purebred Belgian horses of good stock. The colony sent me to Michigan State University at East Lansing to take a four-month course in agriculture, with emphasis on horse-breeding, plus two months at the college's breeding plant working with breeders.

Dr. [Jacob] De Geus, a Dutchman, was advising the colony on breeding, and it was he who arranged for my schooling. When I returned to Alicia, I took over the horse-breeding plant from the hired hand. I got no extra pay—nobody did.

A few other boys were trained in different specialties, dairy in particular, and we also took correspondence courses in animal husbandry from Penn State. In addition, the county agricultural agent helped us with modern methods and we got booklets from the state capital in Lansing. By 1937, from a small group of untrained individuals we had two thousand head of pure beef cattle and two thousand purebred Shropshire sheep, as well as two thousand Leghorn cattle, a dairy barn of fifty Holsteins and Jerseys, and over a hundred horses and many goats. We also had a beekeeper, a Russian named Dan, who doubled as a wagon maker. Each year we showed our animals at the East Lansing fair.

Joseph Cohen was a great man, a man of strong character and few words, but a brilliant man. Yet he was a hard man in the sense that he set high goals, unattainable goals, which were bound to lead to frustration and disappointment. He tried to mold a hodgepodge of men and women in a preconceived cast. But not all of them were idealists like him. Far from it. For many, Sunrise was merely a chance to escape the Depression-ridden city and to find a new and better way of life. When we got to Sunrise, in 1933, there were no streets, no electricity, no plumbing. The idealists could take it, but the others wanted to flee at the first opportunity.

I loved the outdoors, the sound of the wind, the sunrise and sunset, the change of leaves, the dirt, the animals—and I was very happy. I worked in the peppermint distillery, as a teamster, a blacksmith, a bricklayer, a cabinetmaker. I also attended the high school, as I said, and liked it very much. When some of us were sent to Saginaw High School for a time, it was very hard to adjust to the discipline and routine, and we returned to our own school.

The teenagers lived in a building called "The Hotel," while smaller children lived in "The Children's House." A lot of the parents—the nonidealists—wanted the children to live with them and always asked, "Why can't they stay with us?" In this and other respects it resembled an Israeli kibbutz, a pioneering venture in community agriculture. Not every city dweller could take to the farm, let alone take orders from a hired hand. They milked a cow with one hand and read the *Forverts* with the other. This meant considerable inefficiency and waste of time.

But on the whole it was a beautiful experiment, and up to a point a successful one. We had a workshop where we made our own clothes and a shoemaker who repaired our shoes. Our school differed from public schools. We didn't have a rigid syllabus. We often studied outdoors. We were less inhibited than in public school. My older brother Sam was the art teacher. He's now a mechanical engineer. My brother Sol ran the power plant for irrigation and pumping out water as needed. He became a precision machinist. And I became a podiatrist.

But as soon as things began to pick up in the city the colony began to collapse. It was a product of the Depression and disappeared with the disappearance of the Depression. When it began to break up I went to study veterinary medicine in East Lansing for a year. I returned to the colony until it moved to Virginia and stayed there for a year. When I left for good I missed it very much.

Like every farm we had fires, floods, drought, insects which destroyed crops. But our worst enemy was the human being. There were Zionists who you couldn't get out to the fields and Yiddishists interested only in *kultur*, without manual labor. The oppositionists held constant meetings, often till late at night, so it was left to dedicated workers like Yankl Katzenelenboygen and Angelo Di Vitto—who worked from sunup to sunset—to carry the load.

Yet there were no police, no crime, no locks on doors. We had our own entertainment—singing and dancing, concerts and plays. We went to town in trucks for movies and ice-cream parlors, singing to and fro. The spirit can't be denied: it was very much like what was later to take place in Israel. I think it was the adults who missed out. The young people adjusted better to the hard work and had a better spirit. It was the adults, not the youth, who couldn't get along. If it had been organized by young people, who were less set in their ways and less easily lured back to the city and the garment trade, it might well have succeeded. We had help from cooperative exchanges, such as the Wolverine Exchange in Lansing. During the summer and harvest periods people came from the cities to help out, and they prolonged the life of the colony. When we went back to society, nearly all of us went to college and most became professionals: one girl a child psychologist, another a professor of sociology, and so on. Most of us did very well at college, despite the fact that we had attended a nonaccredited high school and had to take special exams to get in. But only one or two stayed on the land.

• ELLIS GROSNER •

Atlantic City, New Jersey, July 3, 1972

Ellis Grosner and his brother Abe were active members of the Radical Library Group in Philadelphia during the first two decades of the century. In 1933 Ellis went to the Sunrise Colony in Michigan, where he worked in the fields and in the dairy. When a group of colonists moved to Virginia in 1937, Ellis was among them, remaining until the end in 1940.

I WAS BORN eighty-one years ago in Poltava *guberniia* in the Ukraine and came to Philadelphia in 1906 when I was fifteen. My brother Abe was two years older than I. He was active in the Radical Library from the years before the First World War, organizing lectures and concerts. Later he was a fund-raiser for the *Fraye Arbeter Shtime* in New York and was active in Stelton. He died twenty-one years ago.

The Radical Library had a Sunday School and Abe was the head. I taught science, a subject in which I always had a strong interest, offering a course in astronomy with the aid of a slide lantern. Afterwards Abe went to Stelton as temporary director of the Ferrer School. He was very disappointed when he was replaced [by William Thurston Brown], and he and I and a younger brother bought a small farm near Pottstown, about thirty miles from Philadelphia, and set up a little school with a handful of students that lasted a year and a half. It followed Ferrer principles but had no name.

I was at the Sunrise colony from the beginning to the end, including Virginia. Joseph Cohen had come to Philadelphia, where I worked as a watchmaker for many years, to propagandize about the colony. It appealed to me at once. I love the country, I love nature, I love to work with the soil. So I joined.

The colony had a helter-skelter population, like the world as a whole. It had anarchists, socialists, progressives, and Zionists. The issues dividing the colonists were not basic. Human nature was the crucial factor. They always found something to fight about. There were even fistfights at the general meetings. The majority came to the colony because they had no livelihood due to the Depression. They had to feed themselves and their families. They were starving. They did not have the necessary ideals or principles. As soon as they began to hear that things were looking up, they began to leave, one by one, rather than work with cow manure or dirt in the garden. It was doomed to fail from the beginning. They were not the right kind of people. Try to find them! You'd have to look for them like Diogenes with a lamp! All that 97 percent of people care about is Food, Fame, Fortune, and Fucking. The 3 percent with ideals are hard to find. I am one of them.

Cohen too had his failings. He made passes at other men's wives. He rarely paid attention to anybody else's ideas. Yet I was with Cohen whatever his faults. He was the only one who could handle complex business, like negotiations for loans with the government. Once when he threatened to resign the members almost fainted.

In 1934, when Rudolf Rocker was lecturing in Detroit, we brought him by car to Sunrise to speak. He stayed three days. When we went to fetch him, Emma Goldman was also in Detroit. It was the last time I heard her speak.

At the colony I milked cows and started a vegetable garden with forty-five different vegetables. I also worked in the dairy and for three years sold butter and dairy products from a truck on a route in Detroit. I consider my years in the colony very worthwhile. I learned a great deal about human nature. I have a full set of *Sunrise News* and *Out at Sunrise* and often reread them. My whole heart and soul was in it. I tried to organize a new colony in Pennsylvania after the colony dissolved but couldn't find the right people.

I am a firm believer in cooperatives and peaceful change. I am a thoroughgoing pacifist. I reject revolution and war; both mean violence and killing. I refused to register for the draft in 1917 and had to hide to avoid prosecution. I am also an individualist and am opposed to trade unions. Strikes hurt innocent people.

• AARON ROCKOFF •

Roosevelt, New Jersey, January 5, 1974

Aaron Rockoff, a Labor Zionist, spent three years at the Sunrise Colony during the 1930s, where he worked primarily in the dairy. He was a strong critic of Joseph Cohen, the principal founder of the community.

I WAS BORN in Russia eighty-two years ago, and when I came to America I settled in New Brunswick, New Jersey, and started a dairy farm and milk route. I was always a dreamer, and when I heard about the Sunrise Colony I got in touch with Joseph Cohen at the *Fraye Arbeter Shtime*. Some of the other people at the *Fraye Arbeter Shtime* had no faith in colonies, but Cohen did. He thought it was a bargain, but actually the company that owned the farm wanted to get rid of it.

The farm had some ten thousand acres surrounded by dikes. You entered it across a small bridge. There were three sections: Alicia, with the offices and living quarters; Pitcairnia, with the peppermint distillery and barns; and Clausedale, where we raised our sheep. Sometimes there were severe floods. We had a pumping station run by diesel motors. During one big flood Angelo [Di Vitto] and two other colonists stayed there for two weeks to pump out the water.

I went to Sunrise in the fall of 1933 and left in January 1937. I was in charge of the dairy and for the last two years was also labor manager. Our biggest crop was peppermint. We also planted sugar beets and raised sheep and cattle, but none of this paid, even though the government gave us two hundred dairy cattle as a grant.

Only a few of the colonists were anarchists or otherwise dedicated to the experiment (I was a Labor Zionist myself). The rest were ordinary people. Some were out of work because of the Depression. Now at least they had a roof over their heads and a decent school for their children. But they didn't kill themselves. They thought that God Almighty would send them everything from heaven. But it didn't turn out that way. You have to work. But many of them didn't want to. "Let George do it," they said. And they saw it as a temporary haven. At the first opportunity they left. Also the climate was bad (fifteen degrees in December), the soil was bad, the people lacked experience and were not fitted for hard work.

Stein, Rubin, and myself were the opposition leaders. We printed the *Sonrayz Shtime*. But they were fanatics—about Yiddish and about their hatred for Cohen—while I was more moderate. I could talk to Cohen. Many times he would say, "What do they want from me?" He was a capable man, but he was dogmatic and didn't like to be criticized. If he thought something was good, it was good! The opposition resented him and his high-handedness. He couldn't make friends. Even Peter Wolff, who at first looked on Cohen as God, would tear him to pieces; and in Virginia, Angelo, one of his staunchest admirers, once threatened his life, so disgusted did he become! Cohen left and went to Stelton, where he started a small poultry enterprise. I visited him there and he was glad to see me.

At Sunrise I came down with pneumonia and was in Saginaw hospital for four months. The colony paid for everything, three thousand dollars, which at that time was a great deal of money. By the end of the third year I knew the colony would fail. So I decided to leave.

I went to Jersey Homesteads in 1937. It all belonged to the government, but the land was sold to the members. I managed the dairy with five people under me. I got forty-five dollars a week, plus a house. When we incorporated as a borough we renamed it Roosevelt. But I was a dreamer, as I said, and I look back on Sunrise as worthwhile, a good dream, not a nightmare. I still have good memories of the place, no regrets.

• ELEANOR LITWAK •

New York City, November 2, 1972

Eleanor Litwak is the youngest daughter of Joseph and Lena Smith, members of the Fraye Arbeter Shtime Group of Detroit and friends of Emma Goldman and Rudolf Rocker. As a child during the 1930s, Eleanor, now married to a sociologist at Northwestern University, spent nearly two years with her family at the Sunrise Colony in Michigan.

MY FATHER is from Zabludovo, near Bialystok, the same *shtetl* as Israel Ostroff [q.v.]. He came to the United States in 1913 on the same boat as Rose Pesotta. He met my mother in New York, and both became anarchists around 1920. He was a painter and she a garment worker. His father, though, had had orchards, which Father loved, and this love of the soil later contributed to his desire to go to Sunrise.

My parents moved to Detroit in 1925, a year before I was born. They joined Branch 111 of the Workmen's Circle, an anarchist branch called the Fraye Arbeter Shtime Group. It had about ten active members and thirty or forty others, and maintained friendly relations with the Italian, Spanish, and Russian groups, though actual contact was infrequent. The Russians had a beautiful balalaika orchestra, and we often went to hear them. Among the Spanish anarchists the Vivas family, Emilio, Aurora, and their children, were close friends of ours, and we occasionally went to picnics and social events. The Spaniards, as you can imagine, danced magnificently in ethnic costumes. In those days we were still concerned with the Mooney-Billings case and of course with the Sacco-Vanzetti case and its aftermath.

We went to Sunrise in August 1934 and stayed till May 1936. Zina and I went to Esther Swire's school (Philip Trupin [q.v.] was more involved with the older children). All grades met together in a small house behind the large Children's House. There were around thirty or forty kids. I did third and fourth grades there. We did learn spelling, reading, and arithmetic, but there was an emphasis on verbal expression—not that many of us needed it! I was happy at school, but I did not want to leave my mother and live in the Children's House. I even went to the cucumber fields with her.

I remember Joseph Cohen warmly, and Father admired him too, and supported him. He had an accent, but his English was excellent. I sensed an articulateness, a beauty in his speech that was not common in our working-class and petit-bourgeois milieu. We remained friends with him afterwards. Some people hated Cohen—*s'gehalten groys* [he held himself aloof], they said. The Farbers also stand out in my memory. She [q.v.] was active, bustling. Angelo Di Vitto was a hard worker but a man of violent temper, who once took a knife to someone.

My father came to the colony with strong ideals and beliefs, and with a willingness to do agricultural work. He was Labor Manager for one of the two years we lived there, but he came to feel that, for an experiment like this to be a success and to live up to anarchist ideals, a more careful selection process was needed. Many of the people who came were simply goldbricks for whom it was a means of obtaining food and shelter. They didn't like working in the fields. Yet if they had the $500 fee, they were accepted.

Beyond this, the weekly meetings disintegrated into verbal abuse and occasional fisticuffs. Father felt there was a breakdown of communication, that there was an insufficient number of people wedded to the ideological core. Animosities were ugly and poisoned the atmosphere. So we decided to leave. Father had worked hard, and his disillusionment was very deep.

We returned to Detroit. We occasionally visited Emma Goldman over in Canada. She was a strong woman with an overwhelming power, even in those later years. Rudolf Rocker visited us from time to time. My parents adored him, and so did I. He took me in his lap and hugged and kissed me; and he talked to me like a person, without condescension, treated me as a human being. He was a gentle, human person.

During the Spanish Civil War there was close contact between the Spanish and Jewish anarchists in Detroit. But at the end of the conflict and with the outbreak of the Second World War divisions began to appear, especially when Jewish anarchists tried to help other Jewish anarchists get out of Europe. The Spaniards and Italians saw this as ethnic bias on our part and refused to help. Father never forgave them, particularly as Jewish anarchists had helped so much in the Spanish Civil War. Because of the war and the extermination of the Jews, some Jewish anarchists, especially those with earlier Zionist inclinations, were given a push towards Jewishness, Israel, and the like. Ethnic differences were thus accentuated by the war. In any event, the movement was rapidly dying out. Eventually the anarchist branch of the Workmen's Circle merged with a socialist branch, and today there are only three or four old comrades left.

• SHAINDEL OSTROFF •

Bronx, New York, September 28 and October 3, 1972

Shaindel Ostroff, Israel Ostroff's [q.v.] wife, was a member of the Radical Library Group in Philadelphia and afterwards lived in the Stelton Colony, where her daughter attended the Modern School. During the 1930s Shaindel and her then companion Mendel Bluestein spent two years at the Sunrise Colony in Michigan, founded by her old Philadelphia comrade Joseph Cohen. At the age of sixty-two Shaindel took up sculpture under the tutelage of René Shapshak (q.v.). Her work, including busts of Rudolf Rocker and George Bernard Shaw, was exhibited at the Amalgamated Houses in the Bronx. She died, aged ninety, on August 2, 1985.[466]

I WAS BORN Shaindel Kaplan and came to the United States from Russia in 1909, at the age of fourteen, settling in Philadelphia. My family was inclined towards anarchism, and we were immediately drawn to the Radical Library, founded by Joseph Cohen and others. Cohen was one of the first people I met in the group. I also met my first husband, Mendel Bluestein, there, and Harry Melman [q.v.], who came from the same *shtetl* as Bluestein.

The Radical Library was a beautiful thing—it had lectures, concerts, and other activities. Wonderful personalities, like Scott Nearing, came to talk, and the cellist Kindler of the Philadelphia Orchestra gave recitals. We had *boyern-beler* [peasant balls], tea parties, and the like. In 1909, the year I arrived, Emma Goldman tried to speak, but the police interfered.[467] This was a major incident in our group. Emma was fearless, defiant. But she was hard—not like Voltairine de Cleyre, who lived in Philadelphia and belonged to our group. The human qualities were just shining out of Voltairine's eyes, while Emma was a political being. Voltairine's personality was fascinating. You could not help but admire her. But you could not get too close to her.

The Radical Library was very poor. It rented an unfurnished room without books for the library and only slowly built itself up, with used furniture and donations of books. It started a Sunday School for the children. Mary Hansen was one of the key figures at the school. She was shy, quiet, withdrawn, but a soulful, very good and kind person. Her daughter Heloise was a talented dancer. They lived in great poverty in Philadelphia and later in Stelton.

Abe Grosner, another active member, was scholarly and musical, with a good voice; he sang operatic arias. But he had a tragic life, and his talents were left unfulfilled. The group also started a summer camp, Camp Germinal. It was a regular children's camp with summer houses nearby, a beautiful place in contrast to Stelton. We named it Germinal after Rudolf Rocker's journal in London.

I lived at Stelton from 1920 to 1933. Financially it was poor, and it was not much to look at, but in spirit everything was rich and beautiful. We lived in a shack, but had wonderful times. The school was the whole thing. We came there because we wanted our children to have a modern education, not the American public school education. Freedom in education, living with playfulness, creativeness—with freedom. My daughter Diana was born there and went to school there. None of the children were delinquents. Artists and intellectuals came out for weekends and summers. Isadora Duncan came to dance. We had beautiful times there!

Joseph Cohen also lived at Stelton. I knew him intimately; after our daughter was born we left our shack and lived in his house for two years. He was also involved in Camp Germinal and often went down there. He was intelligent and able but a cold person; if he didn't like what you were saying he would lower his head and pull his cap down over his eyes to shut himself out. Hippolyte Havel was one of the intellectuals who came to Stelton. He came and stayed. He was very nice, but an alcoholic. He lived there for many years. Elizabeth Ferm—Aunty Ferm—was set in her ways. You couldn't get close to her, as you could to her husband. Yet they were both admired, especially Uncle. Marcus Graham lived next door to us. There are some people who must needle others, pick out the bad points. That was him. But he was very close to some of the more militant anarchists, like Havel, Abe Winokour, and Anna Sosnovsky.

When the Sunrise Colony was started in Michigan in 1933, a group of Steltonites, including us and the Cohens, went there as pioneers. The Stelton comrades gave us a big send-off. We stayed only two years, till 1935. At Stelton it was mainly the school that kept the colony together. At Sunrise it was not the school but the communal life and economy. Stelton was a product of the twenties, Sunrise of the thirties, the Depression. It was not an anarchist colony, moved by the anarchist ideal, but a group of people very badly off with no means of livelihood. Anarchists formed a minority, though the leadership was mostly anarchist. So, without ideals, we tended to look out for ourselves.

There weren't enough dwellings at first; and though we had sheep, cattle, and horses, most members knew nothing about them. But they learned quickly, at least those who were willing; the others never learned, and never wanted to learn. They just talked, argued, and complained. The good members cut wood in the forest and sang as they worked. It was a marvelous thing to see. We had a communal kitchen and dining room for more than three hundred people. I and Minnie Markowitz worked in the kitchen as cooks.

The farm had three separate sections: Alicia, which had the office and communal house and most of the members; Clausedale, where the cattle and sheep were kept; and Pitcairnia, with the big Living House with some forty children—Mendel and I were in charge. Mothers used to come and butt in. Mendel and I also worked in the fields. I got sick from sunstroke, and we were forced to leave the colony.

It lasted only a few more years. Many members resented Joseph Cohen's aloofness, and resented the anarchist core. Stein, although an anarchist himself and a writer for the *Fraye Arbeter Shtime*, made a lot of trouble. It was not just an ideological dispute. Stein didn't trust anybody—especially Cohen. The oppositionists went into the fields, leaned on their hoes, and talked against the leadership. One issue was the use of Yiddish in conversation and the newspaper, another was resentment of Cohen's high-handedness, and there were personal feuds as well.

After returning to New York, we spent a lot of time at the Mohegan colony. Rudolf Rocker was my favorite. He had great knowledge, was a great speaker, yet so plain in his manner towards ordinary people—he was one of the comrades. He was also the life of the party. And yet he was very sentimental. When he was speaking, after his wife died, he would sometimes break into tears. He was an example of a human anarchist. You felt that you knew him for years, and he was admired by nonanarchists as well.

Mendel died in 1957. After his death, I got a letter from Uncle Ferm. He wrote that many of the older comrades were dying: "So we come, make a fuss, and then pass on."

• EMANUEL V. CONASON •

White Plains, New York, September 23, 1974

Emanuel Conason (called "Red," owing to his red hair and florid complexion) was the son of Joseph J. Cohen, a leading Jewish anarchist and editor of the *Fraye Arbeter Shtime*. During the 1930s Conason took part in the Sunrise Colony in Michigan, of which his father was the founder and his wife was a teacher in the school. An interview with Conason's half-sister, Emma Cohen Gilbert, also appears in this collection.

I WAS BORN in 1910, the son of Joseph Cohen in Philadelphia, and was at the Sunrise colony in the 1930s, as well as at Stelton and Camp Germinal before that. My middle name is Voltaire, after Voltairine de Cleyre, whom my father knew very well. My wife taught at the Sunrise school. Now we run a gift shop in White Plains.

There were no issues at Sunrise that made any sense. Some of the colonists who were the most bitter and vocal opponents of my father—like Aaron Rockoff [q.v.]—later told me that they wondered what they were fighting about. There were no deep issues. It all started when Eli Greenblatt was elected president and Dad secretary. Greenblatt couldn't run things properly, so the duties of running the place devolved on my father. The first dissatisfactions and accusations started there.

Dad wasn't a good enough politician. In fact he hated politics and politicians. He loved humanity in the abstract, but not individual people. Some felt he didn't say hello warmly enough. You needed that to keep people happy. Meetings ran till two in the morning, night after night, with arguments over small matters, when we had to run a farm. They divided not over issues so much as among those who were with Dad and his administration (such as Mendel Bluestein) and those who were opposed. It always ended with quarrels over who could do things better.

But don't exaggerate the members' unwillingness to work. Most performed their tasks fairly cheerfully. When I was work manager there was very little malingering.

• BEATRICE MARKOWITZ •

New York City, September 12, 1972

Beatrice Markowitz, born around 1924, lived at the Stelton and Sunrise Colonies and attended the schools at both. She afterwards worked at the Lakewood Modern School under James and Nellie Dick (q.v.). Her mother, Minnie Markowitz, an anarchist in New York and at Sunrise, died on March 18, 1990, at the age of ninety-eight.

I SPENT the summers at Stelton from 1927 to 1930, lived for two years (1931–1933) in the Living House, and attended the Ferrer School. Jim Dick was principal of the school, and he and Nellie [q.v.] ran the Living House. I can still do printing, pottery, and silver crafts. We all swam in the nude and sometimes even went to school nude. The colony had quite a few vegetarians and diet faddists (one woman, hooked on grapes, even ate them mashed). I loved the school. We did no reading, but Jim Dick read Shakespeare to seven-year-olds; he loved Shakespeare. We learned weaving, basketry, and the like. The older kids built a canoe in shop and tried to harpoon fish. The colony and school was continually changing as people with different ideas came and left. We learned some reading and writing by setting up type of our own stories with the aid of the older children. There was no feeling of being "in class." Hippolyte Havel always sat on the porch, with his beard and protruding stomach, looking very dignified.

In August 1933 we left Stelton for Sunrise and lived there for three and a half years. The school there was not a Ferrer School, though it had some libertarian features: little discipline, no compulsory attendance, no imbuing the children with patriotism, and so on. The colony did not center on the school, as in Stelton. I can recall great floods in 1935 and a plague of Japanese beetles in 1933, which ate the crops and stampeded the cattle.

There was an "in group"—the Cohens, the Farbers, the Lifschitzes, the Bluesteins, etc.—and an "out group" in the colony. Some people Cohen could not accept; he tolerated them, at best, and sometimes shunned them. I loved the colony, being close to nature, with the feeling of one big family. The children helped with farm work if they liked. In a sense, the periods of hardship were the best time, as everybody pulled together and opposition dissolved. We left in 1937, when the colony moved to Virginia.

The Dicks had a summer camp at Carmel, New York, where I was a counselor for four seasons, from the age of fifteen through eighteen. They founded the Lakewood Modern School in 1933; it lasted until the late 1950s. About twenty children lived there; some were former Steltonites and nearly all working-class. The parents came out on weekends from New York and Philadelphia. The school and living quarters were in the same building. Nellie and Jim were the teachers, along with one or two others. I taught nursery school and arts and crafts at the age of seventeen. It was a happy place, run as a family. Unlike Stelton, there were classes and some degree of structure. I taught there for two or three years. Nellie still keeps in touch with the former pupils.

• DORA KEYSER •

Los Angeles, California, June 24, 1974

Dora Keyser, seventy-five when I interviewed her, was one of the few oldtime anarchists still active in social causes. Earlier in the century she had been at the Stelton and Sunrise Colonies and taken part in a number of anarchist groups. During the 1970s and 1980s she was a tireless worker for César Chavez's United Farm Workers, for which she made and sold ceramic eagle medallions, the union's emblem. In addition, she helped organize food cooperatives and was active in the City of Hope and in the Kropotkin Branch of the Workmen's Circle in Los Angeles. She also taught weaving at a local Quaker school on a loom that she had brought with her from Stelton. Dora died of a stroke on July 20, 1983.

I WAS BORN Dora Stoller on July 4, 1899, in a family of eighteen children in the town of Sokolka, Grodno province, Russia. My father eked out a living as a bookkeeper in a leather factory and as a baker. We all helped with the baking and selling. Father never laid a hand on any of the children. He died when I was twelve years old. My mother used to bring our groceries all the way from Bialystok in a little wagon. I was a very religious little girl, but in 1905 all the young people were involved in the revolution and I joined them. My older brother Max took an active part in the revolution, and as a little girl I carried the forbidden literature that he and his friends kept buried in a yard around the corner from our house.

My father died in 1912, and we emigrated to America, settling in Brownsville, Brooklyn. My older sister Lisa, already a revolutionist in Russia, joined the Union of Russian Workers, and my brother Max was the secretary of the Anarchist Red Cross in New York. He organized *boyernbeler* [peasant balls] and other events to raise money for political prisoners in Russia. He was later very active in the American labor movement.

I started to come to anarchist *vecherinkas* [parties] in Brownsville when I was fourteen or fifteen. I knew the Brownsville anarchists well, like the Raiva brothers, Misha and Grisha. As a gesture of opposition to the capitalist system Misha refused to work and refused to eat. When he went back to Russia after the 1917 Revolution, he died of starvation.

Around 1916 I moved to the Bronx and joined Zalman Deanin's [q.v.] anarchist group. I think it was called Germinal. We had lectures every Sunday. Trotsky and Bill Shatoff lectured for us. I heard Alexander Berkman speak in New York, and also Margaret Sanger, and I never missed a lecture by Emma Goldman. I went to the Ferrer Center and learned English in Will Durant's class. Around this time I met my husband Lyova (Louis), and we lived in a commune on Eleventh Street; Abe Winokour was a member. I worked as a finisher in the clothing industry.

Around 1920 Lyova and I moved to Philadelphia and joined the Radical Library. Many of its members went to Stelton, and we came there in 1922. I remembered how when I went briefly to public school in New York I had a mean, red-haired old-maid teacher, and I never wanted my children to go to public school. I had a very rigorous education with Aunty and Uncle Ferm. She had a class with the parents—I still have the notes—and I think I got more out of the school than the children.

Aunty and Uncle had a common goal and were great individuals in their own right. But he was very gentle, while she was very strong. She was a great woman, a strong personality, and she knew what she was after. She seemed to know the parents without even visiting their homes. Many of them felt that the children should be learning reading and writing, that crafts were not enough. But the Ferms created a whole atmosphere for the children in which they could move freely without being molested. She had no use for petty gossip. It was the kind of atmosphere in which I could learn together with my children.

But people do not stay the same, and a school does not stay the same. When the Ferms left, the school changed. And in 1934 we went to Sunrise. The life of that colony was a study in the cooperative communal principles in which we believed. That's what we learned there—at least those who practiced it. But the Cohens were not right for such an experiment. Sophie was an ordinary woman who always pulled for her own family. Cohen himself was sitting there *mit'm hitl* [with his cap] down, doing nothing to smooth over the differences among the colonists. When Rudolf Rocker visited, he was just the opposite. He greeted everyone, went to visit the sick members, while Cohen never even said good morning! Cohen, by the way, had no use for Rocker. Nor did Marcus Graham, who criticized Rocker for not speaking in public on anarchism after coming to the U.S. Graham called Rocker a "traitor" to the cause. But Rocker told me that Graham himself was the traitor, since if he had lectured on anarchism he would have been deported.

Lyova was not a political man but a dynamic and hard-working man, an electrician by trade. Abba Gordin[468] came to Stelton a few times, and we organized lectures for him in Perth Amboy and other towns. But Gordin made everyone work while boasting that he never did a lick of work in his life. He used people and had little respect for them—a very difficult man, a house guest who gave orders to everybody. Maximilian Olay[469] was a very gentle and beautiful person. Around 1920 we had a vegetarian restaurant on 103d Street in New York, and he and his wife Anna used to eat there often, even though they were not vegetarians. She was Jewish and he Spanish. When Olay died she took it very hard. And their only son died as a young man. She committed suicide in Los Angeles, in February 1957 I think it was.

We came to Los Angeles from Sunrise in 1938. We were active in the Kropotkin Branch of the Workmen's Circle and in the Rocker Publications Committee. Dr. [Arthur E.] Briggs of the Ethical Culture Society and Dr. [Frederick W.] Roman of the University of California used to speak, and some anarchists attended their forums. But there was much pettiness and bickering among the comrades. They quarreled for years—and haven't stopped quarreling yet.

Jules Scarceriaux was an artist and a fine anarchist. He had a discussion group for the youth and tried to infuse them with anarchist ideas. He was a devoted anarchist in his whole attitude. Hans Koch, who had been at Stelton and worked with Frank Lloyd Wright in Taliesin, lived with us during his last years. When we aided refugees after World War II, he made contact with surviving German anarchists and published a book of poetry and two other books in Germany near the end of his life. When Koch came here he took care of Alfred Sanftleben, a sweet old man with thousands of books. He wrote poetry in fourteen languages.

When Koch died, Sanftleben came to the funeral with a tiny bouquet of flowers. It was so pathetic. We took care of him after that. When he died, I was left to take care of his library. I wrote to Rudolf Rocker and sent him a list. He chose some, and some Sanftleben had sent to Agnes Inglis at the Labadie Collection. The rest were given to the City of Hope.

The anarchist philosophy is a natural philosophy, and my views on that cannot change, except that whatever you can't put into practice does not mean much to me. I keep in contact with young people. I try to live an anarchist life to the best of my ability. That to me means anarchism. I want a cooperative way of life. That's what I am striving for.

PART FIVE

Ethnic Anarchists

SAM DREEN • RENÉ SHAPSHAK • LENA SHLAKMAN

• JULIUS SELTZER • JOSEPH SPIVAK • REBECCA AUGUST •

IDA LEHRER AND SONYA TUCKER • ZALMAN DEANIN

• SONYA DEANIN • PAUL ROSE • IDA RADOSH •

CLARA LARSEN • BESSIE ZOGLIN • SONYA FARBER

• ISIDORE FARBIASH • ISRAEL OSTROFF •

ABRAHAM BLECHER • CLARA HALPERN

• MORRIS SCHULMEISTER • DAVID BABICH •

VICTOR LYNN • WANDA SWIEDA • MORRIS GANBERG

• MORRIS GREENSHNER • MARK MRATCHNY •

JOHANNA BOETZ • LEON SHAPIRO • BORIS YELENSKY

• MARCELINO GARCÍA • SIRIO ESTEVE •

JOSÉ HERNÁNDEZ • LOUIS G. RAYMOND • JUAN ANIDO

• MARCELO SALINAS • GUSTAVO LÓPEZ •

JOACHÍN EDO • FEDERICO ARCOS • H. L. WEI

• RED JONES • BELLA WONG •

5. The Frayhayt Group, New York, 1918 (Paul Avrich Collection)

INTRODUCTION

ANARCHISM, for all its international pretensions, for all its faith in the unity of mankind, has always been divided into national and ethnic groups. There have been French anarchists and Spanish anarchists, Russian anarchists and Polish anarchists, Japanese anarchists and Chinese anarchists, united by language and tradition in addition to their political beliefs. Nor should this be surprising. For anarchists, cherishing diversity against standardization and uniformity, have always prized the differences among peoples—cultural, linguistic, historical— quite as much as their common bonds. "Anarchism," as Israel Ostroff puts it (see interview), "does not wipe out nationality."

This principle applies equally in the United States, with its varied multinational population. During the late nineteenth and early twentieth centuries, when foreign-born artisans and laborers constituted the mass base of the anarchist movement, groups were organized largely on ethnic lines and their activities conducted in native languages. On occasion, it is true, different national groups took part in joint social and cultural events, and they invariably banded together in times of crisis (Haymarket, Sacco-Vanzetti, the Spanish Civil War). Generally, however, they tended to go their own way. "We had little contact with other anarchist groups," recalls the Spaniard Marcelino García, "the biggest mistake we ever made in this country."

Be that as it may, immigrants from Europe and elsewhere played a major role in the emergence of the American anarchist movement. Germans and Czechs, Italians and Spaniards, Russians and Jews, nearly all of them of humble background, they provided fresh recruits from decade to decade, beginning in the 1870s. The influx of foreigners also brought writers and speakers, who came either as permanent settlers or on extended lecture tours. From Russia, for example, Bakunin escaped to the United States in 1861, Kropotkin came to lecture in 1897 and 1901, and Emma Goldman and Alexander Berkman, arriving in the 1880s, remained until their deportation in 1919.

The names of émigrés from other countries are hardly less familiar. From Germany came Johann Most and Rudolf Rocker, Robert Reitzel and Max Baginski, to say nothing of the Haymarket martyrs. From France came Joseph Déjacque and Anselme Bellegarrigue, Elisée and Elie Reclus, Clément Duval and Michel Dumas. From Italy came Luigi Galleani and Errico Malatesta, Pietro Gori and Saverio Merlino, Carlo Tresca and Armando Borghi, Nicola Sacco and Bartolomeo Vanzetti. From Austria came Rudolf Grossmann, from Rumania Joseph Ishill, from Spain Pedro Esteve, from Mexico Ricardo Flores Magón, from Japan Denjiro Kotoku, from India Har Dayal. From Britain came Samuel Fielden and William Holmes, W. C. Owen and Thomas Bell, William Bailie and James L. Walker, Miriam Daniell and Helena Born.

And so it went from country to country around the entire globe. In the half-century from 1870 to 1920 more than twenty million aliens entered the United States, of whom tens of thousands joined the anarchist ranks. Up to the 1880s the great majority originated in countries of northern and western Europe, but shifting patterns of immigration saw a decline in French, Germans, and Britons, who had formed the backbone of the anarchist movement, and a rise of southern and eastern Europeans, primarily Italians, Russians, and Jews, who furnished a new generation of recruits. They flocked predominantly to industrial cities and became unskilled or semiskilled laborers. Some had been anarchists in their countries of origin and brought with them their radical creed. Most, however, were converted after their arrival. "It was the American experience of struggle that made them anarchists," says Vincenzo Ferrero of his Italian compatriots, the exploitation and oppression of the workers, the poverty and squalor amidst abundant wealth.

The Italians (see Part Three), of whom Ferrero himself is an example, comprised one of the largest and most militant of the ethnic groups which made up the immigrant anarchist movement. They came from every corner of Italy (including Sardinia and Sicily) and settled in all parts of the United States, from Boston and New York to San Francisco and Los Angeles, where they engaged mostly in manual trades. They did not, however, play a notable part in the organized labor movement, differing in this respect from their Russian and Jewish comrades, who were prominent in the construction and textile unions. Not that the Italians were completely estranged from the unions, but their role was inconsiderable, mainly because of their suspicion of formal organizations that might harden into bureaucratic shape, with their own bosses and officials.

To a large extent the Italian movement remains a shadowy subject, draped in impenetrable mystery, a "great dark forest," in A. William Salomone's phrase,[470] echoing Dante's Inferno. Originating in the 1880s with the first wave of Italian immigration, it reached its zenith between 1900 and 1920 under the tutelage of Luigi Galleani, a man of magnetic personality and ultramilitant views, whose disciples included Sacco and Vanzetti. Galleani, it has been noted, edited the foremost Italian anarchist periodical in the United States, the Cronaca Sovversiva (Subversive Chronicle), which ran for fifteen years before its suppression by the authorities, followed by Galleani's deportation.

From 1920 to 1927 the plight of Sacco and Vanzetti was the chief preoccupation of the Italian anarchists, who labored in vain to save their comrades from execution. Afterwards the menace of fascism became their overriding concern. In Little Italys throughout the country the anarchists emerged in the forefront of the antifascist struggle, heckling pro-Mussolini speakers, disrupting rallies, and engaging in fistfights and gunplay. On occasion they also employed dynamite, attacking fascist clubs and Italian consulates.

Their main weapon, however, was words, as printed in Carlo Tresca's Il Martello, Aldino Felicani's Controcorrente, and Raffaele Schiavina's L'Adunata dei Refrattari. L'Adunata, conceived as a successor to Galleani's Cronaca Sovver-

siva, was founded in 1922, the year in which Mussolini came to power. Apart from rallying the Galleanists, scattered and demoralized by government repression, its dual aim was to campaign for Sacco and Vanzetti and to combat the forces of fascism, in Italy as well as in America. For the next two decades the paper was feared by Mussolini and his agents because of its uncompromising militancy and belief in direct action. Capably edited by Schiavina, it continued to appear until 1971, when declining circulation caused it to cease publication.

The Italians, for all their activity, were by no means the only major component within the immigrant movement. Equally important were the Germans and Jews, with the Russians and Spaniards close behind. Bringing up the rear were such smaller groups as the Chinese, Finns, Portuguese, Serbs, and Koreans. Nearly all nations and languages were represented, cropping up throughout this volume. The present section, however, confines itself to four: Jews, Russians, Spanish, and Chinese.

The Jewish branch of the movement, dating like the Italian from the 1880s, came into being as a direct consequence of the Haymarket tragedy. Indeed, it was the sentencing of the Chicago defendants, on October 9, 1886, that precipitated the formation of the first Yiddish-speaking group, the Pioneers of Liberty (Pionire der Frayhayt). Situated on the Lower East Side, the predominantly Jewish quarter of New York City, the Pioneers boasted an array of talented writers and speakers—David Edelstadt, Hillel Solotaroff, Alexander Berkman, Saul Yanovsky, J. A. Maryson—which made it one of the most effective propaganda circles in anarchist history.

In February 1889 the Pioneers launched the weekly *Varhayt* (Truth), the first anarchist periodical in Yiddish. This was followed by a flood of antireligious tracts, based on a parody of Jewish liturgy and ritual. To the Pioneers, attacks on religion were inseparable from attacks on government and capital. Just as every state, they argued, was an instrument by which a privileged few wielded power over the immense majority, so every church was an ally of the state in the subjugation of humanity. In their speeches and writings the Pioneers upheld reason and science against ignorance and superstition, which lay at the root of every religion. Their most dramatic weapon, however, was the Yom Kippur ball, which, featuring dancing, merrymaking, and atheistic harangues, openly travestied the Day of Atonement, the most sacred of Jewish holidays. This aroused the fury of the orthodox community, for whom nothing could be a more direct attack upon their faith.

The *Varhayt*, meanwhile, proved a short-lived venture, enduring only five months. Its successor, however, the *Fraye Arbeter Shtime*, founded in July 1890, was destined to survive for nearly nine decades. The *Fraye Arbeter Shtime* played a vital role in the Jewish labor movement in America, and throughout its long life it maintained a high literary standard, publishing some of the finest writers in the history of Yiddish radical journalism. Its editors, an impressive group, included Edelstadt, the most popular of the Yiddish "labor poets"; Saul Yanovsky, whose administrative as well as editorial talents put the paper on a solid footing; Joseph Cohen, a founder of the Stelton and Sunrise Colonies (see Part Four); and Ahrne Thorne, converted to anarchism during the agitation for Sacco and Vanzetti (see Part Two).

In contrast to their Italian comrades, the Jewish anarchists, from their earliest days, took part in the formation of labor unions. They were especially active in the International Ladies' Garment Workers' Union and in the Amalgamated Clothing Workers of America, participating in strikes, rooting out corruption, and fighting against bureaucracy and indifference. During the 1920s, moreover, they joined forces with socialists and liberals to prevent a Communist takeover of the unions, denouncing the arrogance of Communist officials and their fraudulent election practices.

Like the Jews, with whom they were closely linked, the Russian anarchists in America set their hopes on labor unions and cooperatives to achieve their libertarian goals. During the years before World War I, the Union of Russian Workers in the United States and Canada emerged as the largest organization of its kind, with a membership of almost ten thousand and branches in virtually every industrial center in North America, most notably in New York, Detroit, Chicago, Philadelphia, and Baltimore. The members, predominantly poor peasants from the overcrowded western provinces of the Russian empire, intended in most cases to return to their homeland and become independent farmers. "They were young, unmarried," says Victor Lynn, himself a typical example, "and came to America, as I did, to earn enough money to go back and buy land and some cows."

More than a few, however, were political refugees from the 1905 Revolution, who, like Vladimir (Bill) Shatoff and V. M. Eikhenbaum (Volin), had languished in tsarist prisons. Shatoff and Volin, for whom the U.S. was a temporary haven until conditions in Russia were ripe for a new upheaval, became the union's most popular speakers, as well as writing for its paper *Golos Truda* (The Voice of Labor). Beyond this they were active in the Anarchist Red Cross, founded in 1907, which sent aid to their exiled and imprisoned comrades. With the collapse of the autocracy in 1917, the Anarchist Red Cross disbanded, and many of its members, including Shatoff and Volin, returned to Russia to take part in the revolution. In the United States, meanwhile, the Union of Russian Workers fell under the heel of government repression. During the Palmer raids of 1919 and 1920, the organization was broken up and its principal activists deported, only to be imprisoned or shot in the cellars of the Bolshevik secret police. Victims of the Red Scare in America, they ended as victims of the Red Terror in Russia.

For all the persecution to which they were subjected, the ethnic anarchists in the United States led a rich and active existence that continued for nearly a century. Anarchism, as they conceived it, was not something to dream of for the future. It was a guide to everyday life, a doctrine to be applied within the interstices of American capitalism. It would not do to sit back and await the millennium. What mattered, as Malatesta put it, was "not whether we accomplish anarchism today, tomorrow, or within ten centuries, but that we walk towards anarchism today, tomorrow, and always."[471] Such was the position of the anarchist immigrants. Within their circles and groups, within their cooperatives and colonies, they created an alternative society which differed sharply from the regime that they opposed. They formed, in effect, a network of anarchistic enclaves, which they hoped would quickly spread throughout the land.

To disseminate their libertarian message, the immigrants, between 1870 and 1980, issued some four hundred periodicals in more than a dozen languages, several of which—Most's *Freiheit*, Yanovsky's *Fraye Arbeter Shtime*, Schiavina's *L'Adunata dei Refrattari*—ran for decades and achieved a measure of literary distinction. The number of Italian papers alone, including the *numeri unici* published on special occasions, approached sixty or seventy, an astonishing figure when one considers that they were produced by ordinary workers in their spare time, mainly in the evening and on Sunday. Furthermore, there were some twenty journals in Yiddish and comparable numbers in German and Spanish, of which Pedro Esteve's *Cultura Obrera* is the leading example; and in addition to periodicals, a flood of books and pamphlets were printed and distributed, including anticlerical (e.g., Most's *The God Pestilence*) as well as anarchist works.

Beyond their publishing ventures, the ethnic groups engaged in a range of cultural activities that enhanced their feeling of solidarity while enriching their daily existence. Life was hard for these working-class immigrants, but there were moments of happiness and laughter. They had their orchestras and theater groups, their debating clubs and literary societies, involving hundreds if not thousands of participants. They arranged concerts, picnics, dances, plays, and recitations, in which children as well as adults took part, imparting a new revolutionary content to customary social activities. "The picnics," recalls Joachín Edo, "were a mixture of Spanish and anarchist traditions, with Spanish dances from different regions, Spanish guitar music, singing, plays, contests (such as putting a pig on top of a greasy pole as a prize for the man who could climb it)." The plays, adds Edo, followed a familiar format: "the oppressive *señorito*, the handsome and brave peasant who opposed him, the beautiful girl whom the peasant loved and the *señorito* tried to make his concubine, and so on."

Attending lectures—in those days the longer the better—was another favorite pastime. Large audiences came to hear Emma Goldman, Johann Most, Luigi Galleani, Pedro Esteve, and Carlo Tresca hold forth on the evils of government and the virtues of the anarchist commonwealth that would replace it. Anarchist schools, as we have seen, formed another part of this alternative culture (see Part Four). In addition to English, such schools, in which the pupils learned how to think and live according to their own lights, were conducted by immigrant groups in Italian, Spanish, German, Yiddish, and Czech.

By the 1930s, however, these schools had largely ceased to exist. Time had been taking its toll, and the immigrant movement was now a mere shadow of what it had been only a decade or two earlier. Its adherents, mostly in their forties and fifties, had seen better days, while their children, born and raised in the United States, were entering the mainstream of American life. The civil war in Spain provided the last great cause for the older generation. Apart from furnishing financial and moral support to their Spanish comrades, the anarchists in America, especially those of Spanish and Italian birth, raised a scattering of volunteers who went to fight against Franco. Some died, among them César Vega of the Mohegan Colony and Michele Centrone, a veteran militant of fifty-seven, who had distributed *Cronaca Sovversiva* in San Francisco twenty years before. For the survivors the victory of Franco was a devastating setback. The coming of the Second World War seemed to many the ultimate madness, yet they managed to cling to their ideals.

Following the war, however, the decline of the movement accelerated. Many of the older comrades had already passed from the scene, and no one had emerged to take their place. "Those were wonderful days and years," says Joachín Edo of the prewar period, "with a sense of purpose and comradeship and togetherness that has since been lost. The Spanish anarchist movement and culture are now gone, forgotten by the younger generation, who cannot even speak Spanish and who have no interest in the events of the past or the ideals in which their parents and grandparents so deeply believed."

One by one, the immigrant journals were forced to shut their doors. *Cultura Proletaria* (Spanish) closed in 1953, *Delo Truda-Probuzhdenie* (Russian) in 1963, *Controcorrente* (Italian) in 1967. In May 1977 the *Fraye Arbeter Shtime* held its last annual banquet, an event recorded in the *New York Times*.[472] In December of that year it ceased publication. After eighty-seven years, it was the oldest Yiddish newspaper in the world and, apart from the London *Freedom*, founded by Kropotkin in 1886, the oldest anarchist periodical in existence. It was also the last of the foreign anarchist papers in the United States, its Italian counterpart, *L'Adunata dei Refrattari*, having folded in 1971.

• SAM DREEN •

Tom's River, New Jersey, August 17, 1974

In 1900, at the age of fifteen, Sam Dreen emigrated from Vitebsk, in White Russia, to London, where he worked as a pants maker in Whitechapel. Soon after his arrival, young Dreen became a member of the circle around *Der Arbeter Fraynd*, the Yiddish anarchist paper edited by Rudolf Rocker, a non-Jewish German who had mastered the Yiddish language and taken a Jewish woman as his companion. Dreen at once was drawn to Rocker, became his friend and disciple, and revered him for the rest of his life. "He united us," Dreen said, "filled us with revolutionary ardor, inspired us with his clear thinking and wide knowledge, his love and understanding of art and literature and the values of culture."[473] In 1956, two years before Rocker's death, Dreen helped arrange for the publication of Rocker's *The London Years*, for which he contributed an epilogue; and in 1973 he helped organize a Rudolf Rocker Centenary Celebration at Toynbee Hall in London. Dreen emigrated to the United States in 1961, and I interviewed him in 1974. He was a small, well-knit man of eighty-nine, with white hair, blue eyes, and a florid complexion, spry, alert, and clear-headed. He died in Milwaukee on February 3, 1979.

I WAS BORN in the city of Vitebsk, Russia, on December 12, 1884, the youngest of five children (I had a brother and three sisters). Father, a religious man, died at forty-nine, when I was five years old, so I never had a chance to know him. So of course we had a very hard time. Mother worked as a seamstress. I was nine when she gave me as an apprentice to a tailor for six years. Every penny I earned went to the family. I did extra work as a delivery boy in the market to earn a few copecks. My brother was a couple of years older than me. When he was in his teens my mother began to worry about his being called for military service. She would have done anything to prevent that. So she sent him to her brother in London. He soon began to work and earn money, and sent us tickets for the whole family to emigrate to England.

Meanwhile I had joined the Jewish Bund.[474] I was twelve years old at the time, and an apprentice tailor. I used to distribute their leaflets at meetings in the woods and was very useful to them. I used to read the literature myself, and liked what I read, so when I came to London I knew something about socialism and the labor movement. I didn't have time for school. Labor was my class, my university.

When I came to London, in 1900, I was fifteen years old. There were many *landslayt* [townsmen] there from Vitebsk, and they greeted me very warmly. The *Arbeter Fraynd* had just started to appear under Rudolf Rocker, who had been there already a few years. One of our Vitebsk friends, Zalman, took me to a meeting where Rocker spoke. He was a tall, heavy-set, imposing man. Milly was also tall, but thin. Rocker had a mustache and curly hair. He was not a speaker but an orator. Whatever he spoke about—literature, for example—you could feel that you were living through the people he described. Though he spoke a Germanic Yiddish—he later mastered the language and even used Hebrew words—and wasn't easy to follow, I was deeply inspired. He made an impression on me that has lasted all my life.

It didn't take long before I joined the Arbeter Fraynd Group. Right up to 1914, when Rocker was interned, I was an active member, collecting money, selling the paper, organizing meetings, and the like. The other active members included Wolf Wess, Lazar Sabelinsky, Shatz, David Isakovitz, Alexander Schapiro, Milly Rocker, and later Abraham Frumkin. Rocker also published *Zherminal*—the name comes from Zola's novel—with Isakovitz taking an active part. (He later came to America.) The Arbeter Fraynd Group used to meet every Thursday, and we all chipped in to pay the printer.

The Workmen's Circle—Rocker was one of its founders in London—had a Modern Sunday School. There was also a Russian Library in the East End, kept mainly by Socialist Revolutionaries. They had a daily reading room, and if you wanted to find anybody Russian you went there. Teplov, an SR, was the librarian. Cherkezov came there, and Chaikovsky, and also Schapiro and Kropotkin. I met Kropotkin there twice. He also spoke a few times at our club on Jubilee Street. Malatesta came to our meetings at the club, a very excitable man both in his movements and his speech. I saw Voltairine de Cleyre at a meeting when she came to London [in 1903], a tall, slim woman, very nice looking—not like Emma—and a good speaker. She was highly regarded by the comrades. John Turner was one of the few Englishmen who came to our club, a fine English gentleman, always well-dressed. He loved Rocker. Wess belonged to both circles: the Arbeter Fraynd and Freedom Groups. I once chaired a meeting at which Louise Michel spoke. She was short, plain, and bent over. She spoke in French and someone translated into Yiddish for us.

I got to know the Rockers well. I was closer to them, in fact, than to my own family. I ate there, sometimes slept there, even played cards there—but the "money" was matches! One day Rudolf and Milly were walking in Whitechapel and passed my house. They stopped in and he told my mother, "Don't worry, your son is in good hands." Rocker got visits from Spanish anarchists and from comrades from all over. He spoke at picnics and demonstrations. You know, some people still have vivid memories of him, especially of his speeches, like Kossoff the baker, who supplied refreshments for the Rocker centenary last year. For my ninetieth birthday this coming December I'm going to London to spend it in the East End. How I loved that man! When he embraced you it was with real warmth and you could feel it. In the general strike of 1906 he was an active member of the strike committee. He picketed with us, slept with us, explained the meaning of "general strike" to workers who didn't understand it. For him it was the millennium. He also took a leading part in the 1912 strike.[475] I was active in the garment union and was shop steward in that strike.

Meanwhile I helped to get out the *Arbeter Fraynd*. But the *Fraye Arbeter Shtime* was a better paper, you know. Yanovsky was a fine journalist. I wrote to him in 1902 saying I wanted to distribute the *Fraye Arbeter Shtime* in London. He sent me two hundred copies a week, and I sent him the money every month. I used to sell it on the streets of the East End. At that time it was *read*. There were lots of readers.

I wanted to get to know the American comrades, and in 1904 I crossed the ocean. There was a price war between the shipping companies, and my round-trip fare cost only five pounds! The *Fraye Arbeter Shtime* office I think was on Rutgers Street. I was greeted by Mintz, a blind comrade whom I knew from London. He introduced me to Yanovsky. Yanovsky was writing. He looked up and said, "Ah, Sam Dreen. Have you got money for me?" "Oh, yes," I said, and paid him for the last month. "You're a Rocker follower, aren't you?" he asked. He disliked Rocker intensely. I answered, "I came here not as a Rocker follower but as an anarchist." I stayed in New York about nine months, then returned to London, to my job as a sewing-machine operator, to my union activities, to the *Arbeter Fraynd*.

During that time I worked closely with Alexander Schapiro. He was very intelligent and capable, but I didn't care for him. He was too stubborn and overbearing, an intellectual who didn't always appreciate the problems of the workers. The Arbeter Fraynd Group divided on the question of participating in trade unions, which I, as a worker and shop steward, strongly favored. Rocker remained impartial, but Schapiro was uncompromising in opposing the submerging of anarchist principles in trade unionism. We used to argue, but it didn't interfere with our friendship.

In 1929, when I went to a Zionist conference in Zurich, I stopped in Berlin to visit Rudolf and Milly. He embraced me with such warmth, so tightly that he wouldn't let go. They gave me Schapiro's address in Paris, where he was living illegally. I went to his apartment and knocked on the door. A young woman opened it, a very nice girl but not his wife Tanya, whom I had known well in London. You know that in London Kropotkin loved Schapiro, was very close to him, and there used to be talk about his marrying Kropotkin's daughter [Alexandra Kropotkin, q.v.], but that never happened. Schapiro came out and I had a brief visit with him, but he was a changed man.

When Rocker was interned in 1914 *Zherminal* closed down. The *Arbeter Fraynd* went on for a few years, edited by an anarchist rabbi! During the war I moved towards Zionism. The Balfour Declaration[476] and the Russian Revolution, which occurred at about the same time, made a great impression on all of us. I joined the Poale Zion[477] in 1916 or 1917. All Jewish organizations in London received a letter from Weizmann and Sokolow[478] to support a Jewish home in Palestine. The Bundists in our union were strongly opposed to Zionism, and when I suggested to our union committee that we send a delegation to Weitzmann they bitterly opposed it. A heated debate took place, and the committee rejected my proposal. So I requested a general meeting of the union. A meeting was called and I asked that the letter from Weitzmann and Sokolov be read. It was read aloud, over the objections of the Bundists, and the membership overwhelmingly supported my proposal to sent a delegation. Not that I had abandoned my anarchism; my fellow Zionists in fact called me "the anarchist." Up till today I'm still a dues-paying member of the Farband [Labor Zionists] in Milwaukee, but in my heart I remain an anarchist. There's no conflict between the two. In fact my Zionism is my anarchism.

I visited Palestine three or four times between the wars and even considered settling there. I also visited the States and saw the Rockers at Mohegan. It was not until 1961 that I finally emigrated. My wife had a big family in Milwaukee, and in 1948 my older daughter and her husband went to live there. My son followed. (My younger daughter still lives in London.) So we went too. My wife died four years ago and I am very lonely. [He proposed to Nellie Dick—q.v.— whom he had known in his London years, but she declined.] But I go twice a year to London to see my daughter and my friends.

No, I haven't changed my ideas about anarchism. In fact I have improved them. Rocker, when he began his activities among the Jewish people, was an extreme revolutionary. He supported terrorism both in writing and speeches. Ravachol[479] was for him a hero. Yanovsky's opposition to Rocker was partly because of that. When I began my activities I also admired terrorism. But after a while that changed. I don't believe that violent revolution brings any good results. I strongly believe that the coming world will be a different world and that some day we may have a free society instead of what we have now. What is necessary in order to realize such a world is that people must change their hearts, their thoughts, their attitudes. They must get hatred and prejudice out of their system. Only such men can live in a free society.

How can that be accomplished? Only by education. It cannot be otherwise. Future generations will have more and more opportunity for a better education, and that will bring about a better world. Even now people are disappointed in politics and distrust politicians. Right now is a good time for anarchist propaganda. Too bad Rocker is not alive! A change will come. No doubt about it. It may not come in your generation, but maybe in the next. I am much encouraged that students, especially students of history, are so interested in our movement. Change is on the way.

• RENÉ SHAPSHAK •

New York City, May 10, 1975

René Shapshak is a sculptor who lives in the Chelsea Hotel on West Twenty-Third Street and has a studio a few blocks away. Around 1958 Shaindel Bluestein (later Ostroff, q.v.) called and asked if he would give her lessons. She had done some sculpture on her own, she explained, and wanted to improve her technique. Shapshak agreed. They made an appointment, and he asked her to bring a sample of her work. Choosing a plaque she had made of Rudolf Rocker, she brought it to Shapshak's studio. "Why, that's Rocker!" he exclaimed. It turned out that Shapshak, an artist of some repute (he had done busts of Harry Truman, Charles de Gaulle, and Queen Elizabeth), had been an anarchist sympathizer since his childhood in Whitechapel. In 1975 Shaindel introduced me to him at the annual luncheon of the *Fraye Arbeter Shtime.* He vividly recalled the well-known anarchists he had known, about whom he spoke with unbounded enthusiasm.

I WAS BORN in Paris, but as a child moved with my family to London and settled in the East End. One day, in 1913 or 1914, someone on the street asked me for directions. I conducted the man to his destination and inside saw Rocker, Kropotkin, Schapiro, and other anarchists. They looked so interesting—the most interesting people I had ever seen—that I went in and stayed and listened eagerly to their talk, impressed by their warmth and friendliness. I saw Kropotkin on another occasion—small, broad-shouldered, with a beard—and visited Rocker after his internment by the British authorities in 1914. I went often to anarchist circles and meeting halls; on the wall of one of them was a picture of workers breaking through the floor of a fancy-dress ball of the rich.

After the First World War I returned to Paris to study and practice art. There I got to know Alexander Berkman, Emma Goldman, Makhno,[480] Volin,[481] and other well-known anarchists. Makhno was a short, simple peasant with a kind and generous nature. He spoke French haltingly and had a Jewish girlfriend. Volin was a real intellectual and poet and Berkman a wonderfully fine man. I visited Makhno several times in his rooms. I also met a group of Chinese students but cannot recall their names. I knew Sholem Schwartzbard[482] and was with him in a café just a few hours before he killed Petliura. He was very calm and self-possessed and gave no sign of what he was about to do. He was a fine watchmaker; all the comrades went to him to have their watches fixed. I later knew him well in South Africa, where he died in the 1940s. I came to the U.S. in the early 1950s.

I still remain enthusiastic about anarchism, though I never took part in the movement. As a young man I read Marx (including *Capital*) and other socialists and anarchists. I found the anarchists the most sympathetic, the most attractive, the most to my taste, the nicest also as people, with their beautiful ideal. There ought to be an anarchist museum in New York for anarchist literature and art, something like the Kropotkin Museum in Moscow, for there is a close relationship, I feel, between anarchism and the arts.

• LENA SHLAKMAN •

New York City, January 23 and 24, 1974[483]

In 1973, when Rudolf Rocker's son Fermin (q.v.) returned to London, the city where he was born, he asked me to visit an old comrade of his father's, Lena Shlakman, who lived in the Jewish Home and Hospital for the Aged, not far from my apartment in Manhattan. One afternoon, having received a letter from Fermin, I walked over to the nursing home to convey his regards to her. I found her an alert woman who appeared to be in her eighties. In fact, she had celebrated her 101st birthday the previous month. I had meant to stay only a few minutes, but her personality was so charming and her conversation so vivid that I took out my pen and wrote down what she said. I stayed well over an hour and had to return the next day to hear the rest of her story. Lena died on June 14, 1975, at the age of 102.[484]

I WAS BORN Lena Hendler in Vilna in December 1872. My father died before I was born, when my mother was in her fifth month. Mother remarried and I went to live with my grandparents. As a teenage girl I got a job in an envelope factory, pasting on the glue. That was in the late 1880s, under Tsar Alexander III, when the socialist movement in Vilna was just beginning. Students from the *gimnaziia* [academic high school] and from the university of St. Petersburg came to the factory to talk to us about socialism. They formed little discussion circles (*kruzhki*) of four or five working girls with a student as the "teacher." Sometimes the teacher was a literate worker who had been initiated by the students.

My own teacher was a shoemaker named Berkovsky, whom I ran into later when I came to New York. And that was the way it started. He taught me—and he himself had teachers. We read the little books (*knizhki*), which were passed from group to group until they were read to bits. There were books on socialism, on cooperatives, on the labor movement, on the sun, the stars, and the planets. It was all very elementary, but how we devoured those little books! You can imagine how little we knew and what wonderful new worlds were opened before us.

I was then about sixteen. Life was hard: we worked twelve hours a day for a ruble and a half a week. At night we read until the sun went down, and then by candlelight. We read books by Engels, by Kropotkin, by all the great ones. Engels's book on cooperatives was the first book I read about England. Berkovsky lived outside of Vilna, and I and two or three other girls had to walk at night to his house to take our lessons. He taught us how the earth moved, using a pitcher filled with water that he turned around with ropes. We thought the water would fly out of the pitcher, but it remained. It was a miracle to us! So we learned how gravity works, how the earth rotates on its axis, and how it revolves about the sun. Another teacher, a girl, read to us from socialist writers, from the major thinkers, the wonder-people (*vundermenshn*).

We celebrated the First of May, which was a very important event. It was forbidden by the authorities, so we met in one of the girls' rooms upstairs to celebrate it and ate herring and bread while we talked, or we walked for an hour out of town and had our meeting in the woods, where our teachers, the students from the university, made speeches. At these meetings in the rooms or the forests one of us always stood guard to watch out for the police. Sometimes they lasted all night, and we walked back to town as the sun came up.

So life was not easy. But we were happy. We were friends, like sisters, and worked together in the factory, and studied together in our circles, and took part together in our first strike. Our heroes were the *narodniki*[485] and the European socialists. My future husband was a Social Democrat, and we named our first daughter Eleanora, after Eleanor Marx.[486] Our son was called Victor, after Victor Hugo, and our second daughter was Vera, after Vera Zasulich.[487] You know, you're the first person I'm telling all this to. In the old days who would want to hear? That was the way we all lived then, and now no one is interested—until you came.

I came to New York in 1897, the year the *Forverts* started. I was a socialist then, and was completely on my own, though I met friends from Vilna who had come here before me. I rented a tiny room with an anarchist family, the

Rudashes.[488] He was from Vilna and she from Moscow. All the anarchists came there to talk—Dr. Solotaroff, Dr. Maryson,[489] and other intellectuals—and I found myself gradually drawn to their ideas. That same year I went to hear Kropotkin, who had come to speak in New York. It was a big meeting, and the hall was packed. He spoke in English with a Russian accent, which somehow made it easier for me to understand. I also heard Johann Most speak a few times. He was not liked by many of the comrades, but I can't recall why [because he had criticized Alexander Berkman's attempt on Frick]. Two years later, in 1899, Yanovsky came from London and started the *Fraye Arbeter Shtime*, which we all read every week.

Soon after coming to New York, I got a job in a glove factory owned by my friend's brother on the Lower East Side. For the first six months I worked without pay to learn the trade. I worked by a window, stitching the gloves on a machine, and the people outside would watch as they passed by. Then I got a job in another glove shop. I worked on gloves for quite a while, but I didn't make much from the gloves. After that I went to work in a shirtwaist factory, where I learned to make silk waists with corduroy, then with tucks. Here I began to earn more money, ten dollars a week with three times a week overtime and half-days on Saturday. I was able to pay back my cousin in Vilna for my passage to America; and I invested a couple of hundred dollars that I had saved in a little bookstore that Rudash opened, but it soon failed.

I met Louis Shlakman the first day that I came to New York. He was from Pinsk, and he came here by way of London. He was a ladies' tailor and a lifelong Social Democrat, yet always friendly with the anarchists. We got married a few years later, and our first daughter, Eleanora, was born in 1900. Then came Victor, an engineer at General Electric who died not long ago of multiple sclerosis, and Vera, who taught economics at Queens College and now teaches at the School of Social Work at Columbia.

In 1901 we moved to Montreal, where my husband was offered a job as foreman in a shirtwaist factory. We stayed there thirty-six years. There was a small anarchist group, mostly Jewish garment workers, and whenever Emma Goldman and Rudolf Rocker came to Montreal to lecture they stayed with us. Emma had a strong character, too strong for some, but she was honest and fine, and I liked her. Alexander Berkman also came once to lecture. Rocker was a lovely man and a great speaker. He stayed with us several times, the first when my children were still babies.

All three of my children were educated at McGill, but they all went to New York to find jobs. Meanwhile, my husband and the head of the Montreal anarchist group, Kars, had opened up a cooperative contracting shop. But Kars died, and the shop burned down. So we followed the children to New York. We went to anarchist lectures and to picnics at Mohegan Colony. When my husband died I went to live in Brooklyn with Vera, and two and a half years ago I came here.

Last month I had my 101st birthday and everybody made such a fuss! I have been a socialist and anarchist all my life. But now I am discouraged. I don't believe that "it"—the free society—will ever come. People are not getting better; they're getting worse. We tried many experiments—schools, colonies—but only the ideas remain. Ideas—the ideas of the anarchists and socialists—can remain forever. But it will not come in my time, and not in yours. If it does come, we won't be there.

• JULIUS SELTZER •

West Orange, New Jersey, May 9, 1972

Julius Seltzer, who rose from poverty in Eastern Europe to become a clothing manufacturer in Canada (Emma Goldman called him "the only 'millionaire' in our ranks"),[490] was active in the Jewish anarchist movement in Toronto. A few months after interviewing him at his son's house in New Jersey, I met him while speaking at the University of Toronto. He was seated in the front row with Attilio Bortolotti (q.v.) and the three of us had dinner together. Afterwards we drove to the senior citizens' residence where Seltzer lived and bid him good night. Bortolotti gently embraced the old man, as if for the last time. He died in his sleep on February 21, 1973, at the age of ninety-two.

I WAS BORN in 1881 in Shereshev, near Bialystok. I knew the anarchist Zeydl there. He lived in London in 1898 and 1899, and Rudolf Rocker converted him to anarchism. He returned to Bialystok and was active in the movement. He was an excellent speaker and a great reader, though he never went to school. He was a laborer, carrying bundles. I worked as a wood-carver at his sister's place. So I was already exposed to anarchist ideas before leaving Russia for New York in 1900.

In New York I started attending anarchist lectures. I heard Rudolf Grossmann, who spoke in a Germanized Yiddish. He was fair, handsome, and an inspiring speaker. In 1902, during a textile strike in Paterson, a scab was killed and Grossmann and William MacQueen, a tall English anarchist, were arrested for inciting the violence. Both escaped, MacQueen to England and Grossmann to London, then Vienna. MacQueen, after settling his family in England, returned to the United States to face trial. He was tall, energetic, and a good speaker. Theodore Roosevelt, who read of his case, summoned him and freed him. But the damage had been done. He had contracted tuberculosis in jail and died within six months of his release.

But it was John Most who really confirmed my anarchist convictions. Most, more than anyone else, made an anarchist out of me. He was fire! After McKinley's assassination he was imprisoned on Blackwell's Island. On the day of his release we went out in a small rented boat to meet him. His mouth was twisted, but you forgot all about it when he started to talk. He spoke with enormous power and had great influence on his audience. He could say to a crowd, "Let's burn New York," and they would follow him.

In New York I sold newspapers for a while, and then turned corn-cob pipes. I left in 1902 for the Alaskan gold rush, but on the way stopped to visit my brother in Spokane. I remained and established a lending library there. While in Spokane, I made a one-day visit to Home Colony. I was disappointed: it was mostly *goyim* [gentiles] and I was a *yid* [Jew]. Also, it wasn't really an anarchist colony. The anarchism was already fading out. But I was still young then, a greenhorn, and maybe didn't appreciate it. Ben Capes lived there much later. He had been a Chicago roughneck who once heard Emma Goldman speak and immediately became an anarchist, following Emma wherever she went to hear her speak.

In 1907 I left Spokane and moved to Schenectady, New York, where I had a restaurant until 1911. I organized a lecture for Emma Goldman; it was an enormous success, with an overflow crowd. Emma was always very sexually inclined, affectionate, always hugging and squeezing me. In 1908 I organized a lecture for Alexander Berkman.

In 1911 I moved to Ann Arbor for a year and had a restaurant. In 1912 I went to Toronto, where my wife's brother had opened a knitting mill. I became his partner. The factory was very successful, and I have lived there ever since. Marcus Graham was there when I arrived, but left a year later.

Toronto had a mixed Jewish and English-speaking anarchist group, including Italians, a few Bulgarians, and others. Of the forty-two in the Jewish group I am the only survivor. Joe Desser was the secretary and the top man in the Toronto movement. The members were mostly garment workers. It was Branch 339 of the Workmen's Circle, and I still attend Workmen's Circle conferences. The activities included fund-raising for the *Fraye Arbeter Shtime*, lectures (including Emma Goldman and Rudolf Rocker), and the like. I. N. Steinberg[491] lived there for many years; he was really an anarchist, as was his daughter Rada.

Other Canadian cities also had anarchist groups: Montreal, Winnipeg, etc. Winnipeg's was the most active group, headed by the two Prosoff brothers, very able and active until the 1950s. They had a department store. Other members included a jeweler, the owner of a newspaper, and garment workers—a more intellectually inclined bunch than in other cities. In Toronto we had only one intellectual—Graham—and he left early.

Dr. Michael Cohn visited Toronto in 1936 to deliver a eulogy to Alexander Berkman. Cohn was a heart specialist, and he refused to take money from comrades who couldn't afford to pay. The same was true of Dr. Solotaroff and of J. A. Maryson's wife, also a doctor.

Emma Goldman lived in Toronto before her death, and she had also visited us frequently and lectured. She was always nervous before speaking. She would not eat but took a stiff drink to brace herself. She was a homely woman, but once she mounted the rostrum she became a different woman, beaming with fire, beautiful in her Spanish shawl.

The people in the anarchist movement were the most wonderful in the world. That alone made the movement great. It was one big family. Some of the best were not well-known but were dedicated, simple people, such as Lillian Kisliuk of Washington, D.C., a schoolteacher and daughter of a veteran anarchist. The anarchist ideal is *zaftig* [juicy]. I am in with it all the time, all my life, always getting great pleasure from it, from the ideas, the people, the comradeship. You meet an anarchist and a socialist and they are completely different. The anarchist is soft, mild, warm—the other dried out.

There really was never any violence in the movement per se. There were only individual, personal acts committed by men who were driven by outrage or despair, who could stand injustice no longer. But this had nothing to do with the anarchist ideal, with anarchism itself. And there has been less emphasis on violence since Kropotkin took over from Bakunin, and that saved the movement. The ideal is still floating all over the world. I have never been disillusioned. I am always optimistic.

• JOSEPH SPIVAK •

Bronx, New York, October 5, 1971

Born in Uman', Russia, in 1882, Joseph Spivak emigrated to the United States in 1902, settling in New York. During the 1905 Revolution, however, he went back to his native town, taking part in anti-tsarist agitation and in the defense against anti-Jewish pogroms that swept the area. When revolution gave way to reaction, Spivak returned to New York and worked in a cigar factory while studying chemistry at night at Cooper Union, from which he received a B.S. degree in 1915. (He afterwards became a pharmacist.) During the First World War he was active in American anarchist circles, taking part in the anti-conscription movement launched by Alexander Berkman and Emma Goldman and in the agitation for Tom Mooney and Warren Billings, falsely charged with exploding a bomb during the San Francisco preparedness parade of July 22, 1916. Hounded by the authorities, Spivak was threatened with deportation, his apartment was raided, and his papers and personal belongings were seized. But he refused to be silenced. Moving to Los Angeles, he joined the Kropotkin Branch of the Workmen's Circle as well as a local group of the Industrial Workers of the World. With Tom Bell, the Scottish-born anarchist, he organized a weekly libertarian forum and a Free Workers' College, and he also contributed to *The Road to Freedom*, the *Fraye Arbeter Shtime*, and other anarchist periodicals.

Meanwhile, with the rise of the Bolshevik dictatorship, Spivak lost his faith in mass revolution and became, in his own words, "a complete Stirnerite," adopting for his credo Max Stirner's dictum that "nobody is higher than myself" (*mir geht nichts über mich*), which he considered "the basic anarchist truth." At the same time, however, he continued to take part in anarchist-communist and anarcho-syndicalist activities. Returning to New York in 1927, he joined the Francisco Ferrer Branch of the Workmen's Circle, the Jewish Anarchist Federation, and the New Trends Group, organized at the end of the Second World War by Alexander Schapiro. But his most important work, perhaps, was in the Libertarian Book Club, of which he was the driving force and instrumental in the publication of its four books: Volin's *The Unknown Revolution* (1954–1955), James J. Martin's *Men Against the State* (1957), Paul Eltzbacher's *Anarchism* (1960), and Max Stirner's *The Ego and His Own* (1963), in which, as an avowed Stirnerite, he took particular pride. Small, lively, energetic, Spivak remained active to the end. Only a few weeks before his death he lectured to the Libertarian Book Club on the cooperative movement, a subject in which he had a lifelong interest. He died in the Bronx on November 7, 1971.[492]

I WAS BORN on March 2, 1882, in Uman' in southern Russia. When I was eleven years old I was impressed by my father's demand that I should behave and obey him so long as he fed me. I resolved at that point to be independent. Later, Max Stirner's "No one is higher than myself" struck a responsive chord. I emigrated to the United States in 1902 but returned to Russia in 1905 and witnessed the revolution. This firsthand exposure stimulated the development of my revolutionary ideas. When I returned to New York, in 1906, I formed a discussion and propaganda group. I enrolled in Cooper Union and studied chemistry (I later got a degree in pharmacy) and worked as a chemist in New York, Cleveland, and Niagara Falls. In 1917 I took part in the anti-conscription movement and in the Mooney-Billings campaign. At a Mooney-Billings rally in Chicago I proposed a general strike as a means of saving them. My apartment was raided, but I was not arrested.

I moved to Los Angeles in 1921 and lived there for several years. I helped organize the Libertarian Forum, which held well-attended weekly lectures and discussions on diverse subjects. We also organized a labor college—the Free Workers' College—around 1925. I wrote articles for *The Road to Freedom* and was close friends with Thomas Bell, a tall, asthmatic Scot.

I became disillusioned with revolution after the establishment of the Bolshevik dictatorship and became a complete Stirnerite. The basic anarchist truth is, as Stirner said, "There is nobody higher than me." You cannot change people or society overnight and not by compulsion. Evolution is the only way. Revolution cannot succeed. After I moved to New York in 1927, Tom Bell wrote me a letter: "If the comrades in New York are not yet using that store of dynamic energy called Joseph Spivak they are overlooking a good thing indeed."[493]

• REBECCA AUGUST •

Los Angeles, California, June 20, 1974

Rebecca August, a Jewish immigrant from Russia, arrived in Chicago in 1904, attended lectures there by Emma Goldman, Alexander Berkman, and Voltairine de Cleyre, and assisted Jane Addams at the Hull House settlement. Moving to the West Coast, she lived for a time in Seattle and worked in a tailor shop. An anarchist since her days in Chicago, she now joined the Industrial Workers of the World and participated in strikes and demonstrations. After Seattle, she lived at Home Colony, an anarchist community near Tacoma, then settled finally in Los Angeles, where she took part in the local anarchist movement.[494]

I WAS BORN in 1883—Beck was my maiden name—in Kovno province, Russia. I came from a poor, ignorant family. Father was a traveling tailor who carried his machine on his shoulders and went from place to place making suits for people. We emigrated to London, and I attended the Berner Street School for three years and learned English. I came to Chicago in 1904. I went to Hull House to see Jane Addams, and since I spoke English and Yiddish she sent me to talk to immigrant workers about trade unions. Most of the young people from Russia were rebels, and from them I became an anarchist. Emma Goldman came to lecture in Chicago. She seemed a bit despotic, coming to your house and wanting to be fed well, no matter what it cost. But she was a real rebel.

I also saw Voltairine de Cleyre in Chicago. She was a wonderful person. She was slim, slender, and delicate-looking, about 5'5" tall. When I went to Seattle in 1911, I asked her to come there to lecture, but she said she didn't want to take money for her fare from us poor people. She was a more philosophical speaker than Emma Goldman. Emma was more the agitator. I admired Voltairine greatly. I learned a lot from her.

Alexander Berkman also came to Chicago to lecture, a very nice fellow. But I didn't care for Ben Reitman much. He once took me home from a lecture and immediately asked me to sleep with him. I said no, and he said, "Don't you believe in free love?" "Yes," I answered, "I believe in choosing my lovers."

In Seattle I worked with Louise Olivereau[495] in the Labor Temple. She was of French origin, tall, nice looking, with short hair. "Why do you wear such short hair?" I once asked her. "To distract attention from my big feet," she replied. Her father was a minister.

At that time I was working in a tailor shop. I had been working in tailor shops since I was twelve. They had a forty-hour week for women, but when we left each day the men had to stay and work two more hours. I couldn't stand that! So we girls decided to strike. The regular unions wouldn't help, so I went to the IWW. Yes, Rebecca, we'll help you, they said. And they did. So I joined them. They were fine people. I helped organize the trolley workers. I went on a car and talked to the driver—Come on in and get organized! Once I was arrested for striking and picketing. A girl scab struck me on the head and cut it open. The judge asked me why I wanted to interfere with capital, and I said without labor there would be no capital. The case was dismissed.

After Seattle I lived at Home Colony for about two years, before the First World War, and visited it often afterwards. I was Jay Fox's proofreader on *The Agitator* and lived in his house. Gertie Vose was a nice person, kind and hospitable. Her son [Donald] was a spy. I told people in the colony to be careful—he's asking too many questions. There was another spy there, a Jewish fellow named Frank Greenfield. Margaret Sanger came to lecture on birth control. Anna Falkoff's son passed the entrance exams for the University of Washington at thirteen, but he had to sue to be admitted. Jay Fox's little house on the hill is now an evangelical church. David Edelstadt's aunt and uncle lived for a long time at the colony. Their daughter, Sonya Keene, is still alive.

I left Home Colony in 1931 or 1932. I went back to Seattle, then came to Los Angeles in 1934. I worked as a hand-sewer and buttonhole-maker in men's clothing factories. I was arrested here too for striking. I knew the anarchists, such as C. V. Cook (I had known him in Chicago before 1911), Charles T. Sprading, and Walter Holloway. But the movement was disappearing.

I have no regrets. I did what I felt like doing. I call myself now a humanitarian. I want to see the world at peace. I still belong to the International League for Peace and Freedom, founded by my old friend Jane Addams. I believe in mankind. My motto is, "Down with hatred! Love to all mankind!"

• IDA LEHRER AND SONYA TUCKER •

Los Angeles, California, June 20, 1974

Ida Lehrer and Sonya Tucker were both born in tsarist Russia, both emigrated to the United States in the wake of the 1905 Revolution, both heard Emma Goldman lecture, and both joined the Jewish anarchist movement, Ida in Detroit and Sonya in Philadelphia. Both, finally, moved to Los Angeles, where they continued their anarchist activities as members of the Kropotkin Branch of the Workmen's Circle, founded in 1923. I interviewed them at the Jewish Home for the Aged at 325 South Boyle Avenue, not far from the defunct Walt Whitman School, an affiliate of the Francisco Ferrer Association. Two days after the interview, I attended, at Ida and Sonya's invitation, a luncheon of the Kropotkin Branch, accompanied by Marion Bell (q.v.).

IDA: I was born eighty-two years ago in Vilna province. During the 1905 Revolution, when I was fourteen years old, I carried illegal literature to different towns, and was briefly arrested at the age of fifteen. I came to America and settled in Detroit, where I joined the Fraye Arbeter Shtime Group (Branch 181 of the Workmen's Circle). Emma Goldman lectured to us. I came to Los Angeles in 1923 and joined the Kropotkin Group, also a Workmen's Circle branch. In Detroit I married my husband, Boris Dobser, and we lived together for thirty years.

SONYA: I was born eighty-three years ago in Cherkassy in Kiev province. I came to the United States in 1906 and lived in Philadelphia, where I was a member of the Radical Library on Pine Street. I attended Emma Goldman's lectures on literature. She was a great orator and a very capable woman. I moved to Detroit in 1916 and was a member of the Union of Russian Workers. I knew Bill Shatoff, who spoke to our club. My younger brother went back to Russia with Shatoff in 1917, and both were later purged by Stalin. Shatoff was a dynamic personality, a strong and convincing speaker. William Thurston Brown and his wife Elsie Pratt had the Walt Whitman School for four years right here on Boyle Avenue, a block or two away. We raised money for the building. It was a day school, and all our children went there. Hyman Yaffe, later active in the Rocker Publication Committee, was well-to-do and contributed a great deal of money to the school. We also ran bazaars to raise money.

• ZALMAN DEANIN •

Farmingdale, New York, September 18, 1974

Zalman Deanin, a patriarchal figure with his white beard and scholarly appearance, had suffered a stroke a few years before I interviewed him. But, though his speech was halting, his memory remained intact, and he had interesting recollections of the period from 1910 to 1920, when he was active in the Jewish anarchist movement in New York. He died on February 9, 1978.[496]

I WAS BORN in Mogilev, Russia, eighty-two years ago and came to America in 1909. I worked in a clothing factory and began reading the *Fraye Arbeter Shtime* and the London *Arbeter Fraynd*. I was at once drawn to the idea of complete freedom and became active in Jewish anarchist circles. I founded the Germinal Group in Brownsville, where I lived, and we published a paper by the same name for a few years, from about 1912 to 1915. Another group in Brownsville at that time was Broyt un Frayhayt [Bread and Freedom]. I also took part in the Friends of Art and Education Group.

In 1918 I helped publish the *Frayhayt* with Jacob Schwartz, Mollie Steimer, Jack Abrams, and others. Around the same time, Abrams, who thought we were not revolutionary enough, founded his own paper, *Der Shturm*. Both papers opposed the war and the intervention in Russia. But Abrams was an extreme militant. He and Schwartz were tough and fanatical. Whoever disagreed with them was an enemy to be beaten up. It didn't matter whether they were capitalist enemies or anarchist enemies. Yet on a personal level we got along well with them. Other members of our group were Sam and Hilda Adel [q.v.], Sam Lipman, Sam Hartman, Katz, and Shatz. Mollie Steimer was also very militant but not as wild as Abrams.

I heard Voltairine de Cleyre lecture a few times in New York, a wonderful, charming woman. We all liked Emma Goldman, a good speaker and writer, though of a different type from Voltairine. Alexander Berkman was strong and impressive, and he fascinated all of us because of his history. I didn't like Yanovsky, a very strict and angry man, but also a very good journalist.

No, I have no regrets about my anarchism, none at all. It was my whole life, and if I had to live it over again I would not behave any differently. We are still interested in anarchism. Men still want freedom. They will always want it.

• SONYA DEANIN •

Farmingdale, New York, September 18, 1974, October 31, 1975 (telephone)

Sonya Deanin, together with her husband Zalman, was a member of the Frayhayt Group in New York. In a major civil liberties case, four other members of the group, Jacob Abrams, Mollie Steimer, Hyman Lachowsky, and Samuel Lipman, were deported to Soviet Russia in 1921 (see interviews with Hilda Adel and Clara Larsen). Sonya died at Mid-Island Hospital in Bethpage, New York, on February 12, 1977. She was eighty years old.[497]

I WAS BORN in Vitebsk, Russia, on June 13, 1897, and came here in 1911. My older brothers had come to Newark by way of London, where they had joined the anarchist movement, and I went to live with them. I too became interested in anarchism. There wasn't much activity in Newark, so I began attending lectures in New York. Around 1913, when I was only fifteen years old, I went to the Ferrer Center. It was interesting, and I liked the idea behind it, but it was also chaotic and lacked organization and planning. It all seemed very haphazard. I read anarchist literature in Yiddish and Russian, especially Kropotkin and Tolstoy. I went to Dr. Maryson's office on East Broadway—his wife was also a doctor—and asked him for anarchist books. He took me under his wing and sent me out with Sam Margolis[498] to sell anarchist literature around the country. But we only got as far as Philadelphia. Sam didn't behave nice. What a big fool! He had three dollars a week for expenses—I got nothing—and was expected to save something to send his wife and baby.

Berkman was a true revolutionary and, I felt right from the beginning, too revolutionary, although I considered myself a rebel. I felt there were other methods, since methods of terrorism never won many friends for anarchism. Zalman organized a band of Jewish anarchists in Brownsville to go throw stones at Rockefeller's mansion in Tarrytown, but he says that Berkman had no part in the Lexington Avenue affair, as far as he knows.

I met Zalman in 1915 on an excursion to Bear Mountain. We both missed the boat. That's what started it all! I was a straw hat operator because I wanted seasonal work that would leave me part of the year free. I took a few lessons in making straw hats, then went from factory to factory looking for a job. At each place they put me at a machine and told me to make a hat, which I couldn't yet do properly. I was thrown out of ten factories in one day. But I was learning at each place, and at the end of three months I was an expert.

In 1918 I was in the Frayhayt Group with Zalman and the others. Shloyme Bunin was a member of the group, and Zalman and I lived with him and his wife for a short while. He was mentally disturbed, suffered from hallucinations, a little, argumentative fellow who suffered from persecution mania, quarreled constantly with his wife, and picked quarrels with members of the group. Schwartz and Abrams beat him up more than once as a result, until he finally quit the group. He died young a few years later. We also had trouble with the treasurer of the group, whose name I can longer remember. He refused to hand over three hundred dollars needed to release the paper and took a shotgun from the wall and pointed it at the committee when we went to his apartment in Harlem. He said he had spent the money and threatened to shoot us if we didn't clear out.

Our group printed the *Frayhayt* illegally. We folded it up very tightly and stuffed it at night into mailboxes. One night in Brownsville the police chased us but we got away, so we were not arrested with the others. It was holy work, you know, to distribute our literature, to spread the word. The detectives were after us, there were spies in our groups, and finally, as you know, Abrams, Mollie, and the others were arrested.

Joseph Cohen was a sincere man, devoted to the cause, a great idealist. He was an independent person. He had a mind of his own and fought for his beliefs. I liked him, though many didn't. Harry Kelly was a much softer person, but you never knew when he would take a stand. Leonard Abbott was an intellectual, well-read and well-informed, who knew what he was talking about.

We were among the first of the colonists at Mohegan. I had had three acres in Stelton when still single but didn't go there much. Now we bought six acres in Mohegan, leaving our chicken farm at Mount Ivy, New York (near Pomona), which we had operated since 1919 under the guidance of the Jewish Agricultural Society. We felt isolated from the movement, so we went to Mohegan with our baby son Rudolf (after Rocker), leaving the farm to a brother of mine and his family. We wanted to start a chicken farm at Mohegan, but no one wanted to help, so it never got off the ground. Instead, we bought a farm near the colony with another couple, but suddenly we got word that our farmhouse at Mount Ivy burned down, so we went back to rebuild it and take care of the chickens. We temporarily left our two-year-old son at the Mohegan boarding house, where we had lived for a while as a commune. Hippolyte Havel lived there too and waited on tables. We all went in for health fads—Dr. Tilden, Dr.

Stretch, Dr. Firth—and Zalman was a vegetarian. Hippolyte asked him, "What will you drink?" "Water with a little milk," said Zalman. "What's that?" said Hippolyte in horror.

We never returned to Mohegan. We did go to Sunrise to look the place over—Zalman already had big plans for raising chickens there—but there was so much bickering and so much loafing that we decided not to stay. They argued till three o'clock in the morning over trifles. Some read books instead of working in the fields. Once a horse made on the dining hall steps and everyone walked around it rather than cleaning it up. There was no screening process: anyone who had five hundred dollars could join. It lasted as long as it did because the farm was big, the soil was rich, and they had good cattle and horses—everything they needed to make a success.

Our farm at Mount Ivy prospered, and in 1945 we sold it for fifty thousand dollars. Then we came out here to Long Island—a wilderness in those days—to build homes. We made a good deal of money and have become devoted to Israel, but without abandoning our ideal. As a philosophy anarchism is still beautiful. I'm not at all sorry for the years I gave to it, and I think it enriched my life. If I didn't believe in the dream, that eventually the world would come to it, my life wouldn't be worth living. But it is not a practical matter at present. There are immediate issues—the struggle for food, the struggle against disease—that cannot be remedied by anarchism. I'm glad, though, that there are still anarchist papers and books to keep the ideal alive.

• PAUL ROSE •

New York City, January 25, 1974

Paul Rose, already an anarchist as a teenager during the Russian Revolution of 1905, continued his radical activities after coming to the United States in 1906. He was a member of both the Industrial Workers of the World and of a Jewish anarchist group in New York (Jacob Abrams and Mollie Steimer were fellow members) which opposed the First World War and criticized American intervention in Soviet Russia. He died in New York on May 27, 1977.

I WAS BORN in Tula, Russia, on February 23, 1890. My father was a worker in a Belgian-owned light bulb factory. As a boy I was apprenticed to a cook. During the 1905 Revolution I helped distribute leaflets and arms. My father was an anarchist and my older brother too. I left for America in 1906, working my way around the world as a seaman.

When I arrived in Boston, I and some shipmates went for some beer. We saw an IWW sign and walked in. The place was full of seamen, and Henry D. Cohen was the manager. There weren't many Jews in the IWW, but in Boston the Wobblies organized the bakers, raincoat makers, and barbers, so there were quite a few. I remained in Boston, shipping out of there, for the next two years, and I attended the 1907 IWW convention in Providence.

I was later in Everett, Washington, during the massacre,[499] and I cooked in an IWW club in Seattle. I knew Bill Haywood quite well and saw him fall off the speakers' platform when drunk. Once when I was with him in San Francisco a drunk asked him for a handout. When Bill gave the fellow fifty cents, he said, "God bless you, sir." Bill then asked for the money back and said, "Go fuck yourself." I also knew Charlie Ashleigh[500] and met him later in Moscow in 1932. He was deported to London for homosexual activities.

On a trip to London in 1914 or 1915 I visited Peter Kropotkin. He served us tea, which he made himself, and though I called him a chauvinist because he wanted to kill Germans, he was very hospitable and friendly. In Paris we visited Plekhanov,[501] but he saw our rough seamen's clothes and said, "I'm very busy."

I used to attend meetings of the Union of Russian Workers in the *Narodnyi Dom* [People's House] at 133 East Fifteenth Street. Adolf Schnabel[502] was a fine man. Volodya Shatoff was a heavy drinker, like Haywood, and a printer for *Golos Truda*. He was an outstanding writer and speaker. He came originally from Odessa. I also knew Oradovsky, Perkus, Brailovsky—whom I later met in Rostov where he was a Communist official—and many others in the Union of Russian Workers. Some of us used to go occasionally to the Ferrer Center uptown. Perkus and Shatoff never became Communists, though they cooperated with the Bolshevik government. Shatoff was purged during the 1930s. Perkus wasn't, but he took to drink.

A group of us in New York during the war had a paper called *Der Shturm*, which lasted almost two years—1917–1918—though illegally. It was anti-conscription and then anti-intervention. We also distributed leaflets. The group consisted of Abrams, Steimer, Lachowsky, Schwartz, Lipman, Prober, and a few others.

Abrams was a wonderful boy. He claimed to be an anarchist but wanted to be the chief. He left Moscow in 1926 and went to Mexico. Did you know that when he got throat cancer he was brought twice to New York in secret to see specialists, but it was too late. Mollie was a little, lively, and brave young girl. When Emma Goldman was freed from Jefferson City jail, Mollie occupied her cell. In Paris during the 1920s Mollie was Makhno's girlfriend for a while.

I used to go to Stelton quite often and pitched a tent there during the summers. I knew Joseph Cohen there and previously also in the Ferrer Center in New York. He always was looking for business. In Stelton he made right away a chicken farm and did quite well for himself.

In 1919, before Abrams and the others were shipped off to prison, someone in Stelton suggested that I help them. So I took Abrams and Lipman to New Orleans with the intention of smuggling them over to Mexico. Abrams was "Mr. Stone" and Lipman "Mr. Green." I got a job on a boat. We were supposed to sail at nine o'clock in the morning, but the time was changed to 3:00 P.M. Abrams or Lipman went to mail some letters and was spotted by federal officials. They let us sail, then stopped the boat. Abrams and Lipman were arrested and taken off, but they let me go. Lipman, by the way, was a Communist, not an anarchist. He became a professor at the Far Eastern University in Moscow and was purged by Stalin during the 1930s. I lived in Russia from 1928 to 1938—working as a cook—and saw him there. Lachowsky wasn't purged and may still be alive.

Berkman was one of the nicest men you could meet, and Fitzi was a very fine woman. I offered to take him along that time with Abrams and Lipman. But he said, "Let them go. I don't want to spoil things. I've been too long in the movement to run away. Whatever will happen to me will happen."

• IDA RADOSH •

New York City, October 21, 1975

Ida Radosh is a cousin of Jacob Abrams, a defendant in the Abrams case of 1918, which resulted in his imprisonment and deportation. In 1924 Ida and her husband visited Abrams in Moscow. By then he had become disillusioned in the Bolshevik regime, of which he had been an enthusiastic supporter. Soon afterwards he left the country and settled in Mexico, where he became a friend of Leon Trotsky. He died of throat cancer in 1953.

JACOB ABRAMS was my mother's brother's son. Jack's wife Mary was working at the Triangle factory the day of the fire.[503] She had already gone down with a friend, who went back for her pocketbook and never came out alive. Jack was close to Alexander Berkman and Emma Goldman and was active in the bookbinders' union. He was an anarcho-syndicalist. He and his friends distributed leaflets in 1918 protesting the American intervention in Russia. After the trial he jumped bail and tried to flee to Mexico but was caught and taken to prison in Atlanta, where he shared a cell with Eugene Debs for a while. He was deported to Russia in November 1921.

At first Jack wrote us that he and his comrades were wonderfully received. He organized the first steam laundry and operated it in the basement of the foreign ministry. He was an excellent organizer, learned languages readily, and spoke beautiful Russian, English, and Spanish. He was a fine man, knowledgeable and kind. When he formed an opinion you couldn't budge him, but when something had to be done, he did it!

In 1924 we visited Russia and arrived in Moscow on August 11. Jack and Mary had just been evicted from their apartment, so we all moved in with the Perkuses. We were in Russia five weeks. In Leningrad we met Oradovsky and other anarchists from America. By now Jack and Mary were disillusioned with Bolshevism. We were defending the regime and they were crying against it.

Abrams had great foresight and knew already that Trotsky was on his way out. "You won't hear him speak," he said. He told us also that anarchist clubs and bookshops were being closed. He knew what was coming. He took us up to the Lux Hotel to see Bill Haywood.

Jack and Mary left Russia not long after and stayed in Berlin for a while before going to Mexico. We visited them in Mexico City in 1945. Abrams had often visited Trotsky at his villa, and once the subject of Kronstadt came up. Abrams criticized the suppression of the sailors, but Trotsky said, "If I were faced with the same situation today I would do the same thing." Trotsky liked Abrams very much and always looked forward to seeing him.

Jack was a chain smoker and got throat cancer while in Mexico. He wanted to come to the United States for treatment, but they wouldn't let him in. Anarchists and socialists in the garment unions worked hard to secure permission for him to go to the Temple Hospital in Philadelphia, and through the efforts of David Dubinsky and Sasha Zimmerman[504] permission was finally granted.

When Abrams's plane landed in Dallas, he was met by an FBI agent, who was ordered never to leave his side. Abrams at first protested—"I'm not a prisoner," he said—but finally yielded. They allowed him to see a specialist in New York and to spend the night at our apartment on Ninety-Seventh Street and Broadway. We invited all their old friends to come and see Jack and Mary, and the FBI man, a decent sort, did not interfere. Jack was so elated to be in New York and to see them! The doctors in New York, and afterwards in Philadelphia, told him that it was too late to do anything. He remained at Temple Hospital a couple of weeks, the FBI man with him, and his friends came down to visit. Abrams returned to Philadelphia the following year for an operation, which was unsuccessful. He died a few days after returning to Mexico.

In 1972 we visited Moscow again, and Ethel Bernstein[505] came to see us in the Hotel Rossiia. Her husband and son are dead, and she lives in an old room.

• CLARA LARSEN •

New York City, May 21, 1974

Clara Larsen, a native of Russia, was an anarchist in New York City during and after the First World War. A close friend of Mollie Steimer, deported to Russia in 1921, she later raised money for her support and visited her regularly in Mexico, until Mollie's death in 1980. For many decades Clara was active in the International Ladies' Garment Workers' Union, serving on the executive board of Dressmakers' Local 22. In 1980 she appeared in *The Free Voice of Labor: The Jewish Anarchists* (Pacific Street Films). Clara died in New York in 1993 at the age of ninety-six.

My MAIDEN NAME is Clara Rotberg, and I was born in 1897 into a Jewish family in the town of Volochisk in southwestern Russia. We moved to Aleksandrovsk after the pogroms of 1905. Father had been a rabbinical student, a very intelligent man, and we were twelve children in all. Nearly all of us became radicals of one sort or another. My brother, Solomon Davidovich Rotberg, lives in Moscow and remains an ardent Communist to this day. When I visited him there in 1970 he showed me his party card and said, *"Eto ia!"* [That's me!]. In the 1920s and early 1930s he was Krupskaya's[506] secretary, and there is a photograph of them in the Museum of the October Revolution on Red Square.

I came to America all by myself in 1914. But one of my brothers was already here, a worker in the garment industry. I too got a job as a garment worker, in an old factory on Broome Street. The work week was sixty-five hours and beginners got no wages, only carfare, fifty cents a week. I later worked in a children's clothing factory, then in a dress factory. I became active in the union almost from the beginning and have remained active ever since.

During the First World War, I started attending lectures at the Rand School and met Morris Hillquit[507] and other socialists there. I also met anarchists there and in the industry, and I took to them at once. Around 1917 a group of us—Isaac Radinowsky, Rose and Ethel Bernstein, and others—started a club and published a Yiddish anarchist paper. We opposed the war, distributed leaflets, held *vecherinkas*, and had a hell of a good time. We were also members of the Union of Russian Workers, and I was at its house when it was raided by government agents in 1919.

I attended Emma Goldman's lectures at Cooper Union and at the Labor Temple on Fourteenth Street. But she didn't appeal to me much. She was so preoccupied with sex—and we were too serious for that! I also heard Alexander Berkman speak occasionally. I had great respect for him. He was a hero in my eyes, because of Frick. He was a very strong individual. What he said he meant.

I met my husband, Christ Larsen, in 1926. He was a Dane, a sailor, an IWW, and a wonderful man. Tomorrow will be the tenth anniversary of his death. We used to go to Stelton and often saw Hippolyte Havel. He was a drunken bum. He used to get drunk in the Village and come over to our place on Eleventh Street at two in the morning and tell Christ to take him home.

I spent two years at Commonwealth College, in 1925–1926, just before I met Christ. The union sent me there on a scholarship. Kate O'Hare[508] was there then, and Covington Hall,[509] William Zeuch, and many others. When I returned to New York, there was a struggle in the union between the Communists and their opponents. The struggle was a very ugly one. For several years the union was practically ruined. Among the anarchists, Mendel Bluestein, Simon Farber, Nicholas Kritzman, and Rose Mirsky were active in opposing the Communists.

At the same time, we were very active for the defense of Sacco and Vanzetti. Years before, Vanzetti used to come to the apartment that Rose Mirsky and I shared on Eleventh Street. Rose knew him well because she had lived in Boston and had mingled with the anarchists there. He was a very simple man, a fine person. We went often to Boston to petition, picket, and work for their release. We attended the funeral, were among the few to witness the cremation, and marched up front with flowers in the procession. There was no truth whatever to the charges against them.

Christ and I had a house at Mohegan for over twenty years. Of all the anarchists I loved Rocker the best. He was a wonderful person, very simple—so simple that I would sometimes get angry at him. He knew only one world, writing, lecturing, and the rest; the other world, he never knew. He had guts, though. But when Milly died he was all alone. I used to go over and cook for him and take care of his needs.

When Jack Abrams got cancer of the throat while in Mexico, he was allowed to come to Philadelphia for an operation. He was a dying man who could barely move, and don't you know that he was guarded by a detective twenty-four hours a day!

When I went to see my brother in Moscow in 1970, I also saw Ethel Bernstein, who had been deported from America on the *Buford* with Emma Goldman and Alexander Berkman. When she came into my room in the Rossiia Hotel she put her finger to her lips, then pointed to a recording device on the floor near the wall. We went outside to talk. She told me how Stalin had killed her husband [Samuel Lipman] in the purge, how her son had been killed in the war, how she had spent ten years at hard labor in a Siberian prison camp. Her whole life had been a tragedy, and she was now a broken woman. She told me that Lachowsky had died of natural causes, but that Shatoff, Lipman (her husband), Perkus, Novick, and Bondarenko had all been killed by Stalin. None of them had survived.[510]

• BESSIE ZOGLIN •

New York City, February 3, 1977[511]

Bessie and Isaac Zoglin were anarchists in Kansas City, Missouri, where they supported the *Fraye Arbeter Shtime* and arranged lectures by Emma Goldman, Rudolf Rocker, and other speakers. In 1917 Bessie founded a committee to aid antiwar prisoners in Leavenworth penitentiary, among them Louis Raymond (q.v.) and Ricardo Flores Magón.[512] During the late 1920s Bessie became a Labor Zionist and a friend of Golda Meir, whom she visited in Israel on several occasions. Bessie died in 1985 at the age of ninety-two.

I WAS BORN in Gomel, Russia, in 1892, of a family with thirteen children. My father was a shoemaker and a Zionist. After the pogroms of 1905 and 1906, he wanted to take the family to Palestine. There were two pogroms in Gomel, and I remember them vividly. During one of them, five revolutionists, three men and two women, were put up against a wall and shot. A mass meeting was held in an open field, and the Cossacks rode in and whipped them almost to death. So Father went to Palestine, but came back after two years, then went to America. Two years after that he sent for us.

We came to the United States in 1909. We landed in Galveston, Texas, and went right on to Kansas City, Missouri. Father had a job in a shoe factory there. He took me in and got me work, but I hated it, especially after a needle went through my thumb, so I quit after a week. I then learned tailoring, which I liked better, and became a buttonhole maker, working on men's coats by hand. I was good and very fast, and stayed with it a few years.

I belonged to a cultural group in Kansas City. In 1911 Isaac Zoglin came there. I showed him around, and very soon we became close and got married. He had been an anarchist since the age of sixteen in Russia, and was arrested and jailed in Chernigov province, where he was born. There were only about a half-dozen active anarchists in Kansas City, all of them Jewish and supporters of the *Fraye Arbeter Shtime* as well as the Workmen's Circle. We arranged lectures by Emma Goldman, Yanovsky, Rocker, and others. Isaac was always ready to help with money, but I did the organizing. The speakers usually stayed at our house. Emma came during the First World War. She was short and stocky and not at all good-looking, but what a speaker!

Yanovsky came a few times. He was very clever and very sharp in his answers. He could give you a dig that you could see stars! He would play pinochle with me and my nephew, and was an excellent player. Once, when I had a bad cold, he lost the game on purpose. "I want you to get well," he said. Rocker came three times and always stayed at our place. I have a beautiful picture of him made by his son Fermin [q.v.]. That was a man you couldn't forget, a great personality, but down-to-earth too, with all his languages and knowledge, and a wonderful speaker. I met Alexander Berkman once; he came with Emma Goldman, but not to speak. He seemed quiet and yet impressive. At all these meetings we raised money for the *Fraye Arbeter Shtime* and other anarchist causes.

During the First World War, Earl Browder[513] and Jim Cannon[514] started a paper in Kansas City, *The Workers' World*. They were socialists then, and we became close friends. I used to go out and get subscriptions for their paper. One of the Kansas City policemen used to inform on us and have our meetings broken up. Once, at a dance—I was a very good dancer!—the policeman showed up, and I told Browder that I was going to talk things over with him. Browder said, "If you do, I'll never speak to you again." I told Jim Cannon, and he said it was okay. So I went over and asked the policeman to dance. I promised not to tell his chief and get him into trouble. So we began to dance. "May I ask you a question?" I said to him. "I understand that you're the one who's been turning our fellows in at their meetings. Why are you doing that?" "Because they're mean to me," he said. "Every time I go by they ignore me or are ready to spit at me." "Maybe you deserve it," I said. "They're really your friends and will defend you if anyone does you wrong."

At that point the chief came in. I immediately went over and told him that I forced his man to dance with me. "Don't hold it against him." The chief said okay, and I went back to dance with him. He promised he would not turn our boys in again. And do you know that he kept his word. From then on our meetings were undisturbed. But Browder wouldn't speak to me any more, though Cannon remained a good friend.

After America joined the war, Browder and Cannon, who opposed the war, were arrested. When Isaac put up bail, he too was arrested but soon released. Three groups of antiwar militants were tried—from Sacramento, Chicago, and Wichita. Many were sent to Leavenworth, including Ricardo Flores Magón and his brother Enrique. The other antiwar prisoners got two to five years, some-times ten, but Ricardo they gave twenty. In 1917 I organized a group called the Ladies' Tea Club, which was really to help the Leavenworth prisoners. We visited them and provided food and clothing, and also helped their families. The prisoners' wives did very little. Only our Jewish women—there were eigh-teen in the club—helped. The prisoners included anarchists, socialists, and Wobblies. Among them were Charles Ashleigh, Ralph Chaplin, Mortimer Downing (he was our "manager" inside: he told us what the men needed and wanted), Big Thompson, and the two Magóns.

I visited Ricardo Flores Magón many times. He was short, dark, and good-looking. But he was getting sick. He complained of stomach trouble and weak-ening eyesight. And he felt neglected by the comrades. "What's the matter with our anarchists?" he asked me. "They don't come to see us. They're not interested in us political prisoners." He felt bad about the movement. So I wrote an article about it in the *Fraye Arbeter Shtime*.

I went to the prison as often as possible. I even dragged the children with me. One day the guard stopped me and said, "You can't go in. You have to see the warden." "What's the matter?" I asked. "I can't tell you. Speak to the warden." I went to his office and demanded, "What's going on here?" "You're not allowed to come here any more," he replied. "For what reason?" "You wrote an article filled with lies about this prison." "You'll have to show me where I lied, but I'm coming to visit these prisoners."

For nearly a year I didn't go to Leavenworth. But then I went back. What could they do—only throw me out. I went to the warden, who loved publicity, loved to see his name in the papers. "Mr. Biddle, I'd like to ask you a question. You have 284 political prisoners." He broke in: "We have no political prison-ers." "Don't you know the difference between men who refuse to kill and men who want to kill? These men are intellectuals, idealists." But he could not—or would not—get the point.

Two of our fellows were working in the prison hospital as orderlies, Elbert Preshner from England and a Spaniard whose name I can't recall, both of them anarchists. They found out that Ricardo Flores Magón was being fed poison instead of medicine, in small doses, bit by bit, in order to get rid of him. So they poured out the poison and replaced it with water. The authorities found out because it was taking Ricardo too long to die. The two boys were replaced, and the prison officials resumed the poison. After he died, an autopsy was performed in Mexico and traces of poison were found.[515]

To improve his image, Warden Biddle once showed me around the prison. You see what a nice person I am, he was trying to tell me. He loved publicity— you can catch flies with honey! "Yes, I shall put in the paper what kind of man you are," I said. As we walked through, I heard the marching in unison of the prisoners going to the dining room, like a military march, a sound you cannot forget. "There are many," I said, "who take an interest in these political prisoners. You should do the same. Promise that from now on you'll be good to them. I got a letter informing me that they'll soon get amnesty. So you may as well be nice to them. They may come back. Once I find out that you're treating these boys as human beings, we'll remember—and they'll remember."

Over the next year or two the boys were let out. A few years before, Isaac and I had bought a forty-eight acre farm in Independence, the home of Harry Truman, where we spent the summer. We had it for thirty-five years. When turned loose, the prisoners would come to the farm and stay to rest and eat. They told us that the warden had improved. He treated them better, with more consideration. Mortimer Downing stayed on the farm about six weeks. He had an anti-Semitic streak—always "goddam Jew." "Pack up and get out," I finally said. And he went. A few years later we visited San Francisco and were invited to a lecture of his, but we refused to attend. I lost my appetite for these so-called "internationalists" who hated Jews. I was disappointed with revolutionaries of that type. I was growing ripe for a change.

I continued working for the *Fraye Arbeter Shtime*, arranging lectures, raising funds, and selling pamphlets for the Sacco-Vanzetti defense. I later organized a meeting for Sholem Schwartzbard, who stayed three days in our house. When a dinner was held for him in Chicago—they had a big group there—I went and met Yelensky [q.v.] and other comrades. I wasn't yet a Zionist in 1927 when Dr. Rabelsky came from Chicago, a very inspiring speaker. I was very impressed. The women of the Workmen's Circle asked me to become local chairman of the annual Histadrut campaign. After much hesitation I finally accepted and served for three years, from 1927 to 1930.

At the end of 1927 Golda Meir[516] came to Kansas City and I introduced her to the audience. She was a fine speaker. She stayed at our place [Bessie shows me a photograph of Golda and others in Kansas City]. "Bessie," she said, "I can see an organizer in you. Would you promise to organize a branch of the Pioneer Women here?" I had lost my god in the anarchist movement, the international revolutionary movement, and was looking for another. Here it was. I organized the Kansas City Pioneer Women in 1928. Since then I've been to Israel six times and visit my anarchist and Zionist friends, including Golda. I just saw her on my last trip this year.

Isaac died last year, and I miss him. As for my years in the anarchist movement, I have no regrets. I'm glad I had the experience. It was the chance of a lifetime. I've been a pretty good student of human nature. Anarchism is a philosophy, an ideal. We want to see life organized on the principle of social justice, as in the kibbutz, for example. True anarchism will never materialize as long as ignorance exists in this world. So I think it is a long, long way to Tipperary. But who knows what the future will bring?

• SONYA FARBER •

New York City, April 11, 1972

Sonya Farber was an active participant in the anarchist movement from her arrival in the United States from Russia in 1906 until her death in New York in 1983, at the age of ninety-one. Small, pert, and lively, she was a member of the executive board of the *Fraye Arbeter Shtime*, a member of the Libertarian Book Club, and a resident of the Stelton, Mohegan, and Sunrise Colonies, not to mention her role as a striker and picketer for the International Ladies' Garment Workers' Union, of which she was a devoted member. Sonya's husband, Simon Farber, was also active on the *Fraye Arbeter Shtime* and served as editor of the ILGWU newspaper *Gerekhtikayt* (Justice).[517]

I WAS BORN in Kiev on March 26, 1892. My brother was a social democrat and printed the local social democratic paper. Through him I took part, as a young girl, in the 1905 Revolution, acting as a courier and going on marches and demonstrations. I came to New York in 1906. Soon after I arrived I got a job in the garment industry, working as a finisher and baster, and attended socialist meetings. My cousin, a Poale Zionist, gave me the *Fraye Arbeter Shtime* to read. I liked it at once. The dogmatism of socialism never appealed to me. I argued with my cousin. One day he said, "What are you, an anarchist?" That did it. I attended lectures by Emma Goldman. I realized that even as a child I had leaned that way. I had always resented people giving orders.

I began to attend *Fraye Arbeter Shtime* meetings and stayed with them ever since. Later I was active in other anarchist groups, including the Libertarian Book Club. Anarchists were very numerous in the garment industry—in the dressmakers' union, cloakmakers' union, and so on, people like Freedman, Shane, Rothman, Farber, Kritzman, Rose Pesotta, Anna Sosnovsky, Fanny Breslaw. They were a dynamic force in the ILGWU and the Amalgamated.

In 1919 I met my husband, Simon Farber, who strengthened me in my anarchist beliefs. He said, "You are a natural anarchist." Simon was born near Bialystok in 1887. He went to the yeshiva to prepare for the rabbinate, but ran away, became a Socialist Revolutionary, and organized the workers in Bialystok. In 1902 he went to London, met Rudolf Rocker and Solo Linder, and became an anarchist. He was on the board of the *Fraye Arbeter Shtime* during the 1920s, labor editor of the *Forverts*, and editor of the ILGWU *Gerekhtikayt*. He died in Miami in 1960.

In 1920 Simon and I moved to Stelton and built our own house. Our son and daughter went to school there. Simon and I commuted to our jobs in New York. We were very happy. Simon was on the Stelton board of directors with Joseph Cohen, Harry Kelly, and Leonard Abbott. Cohen was always thinking, always full of ideas. Kelly was good-natured, generous, genuine—a real anarchist. He never dominated anyone or told you what to do. Abbott was pleasant, well-spoken, soft, like Uncle Ferm. Uncle I especially liked. In Aunty there was a domineering streak that he lacked. She was not as approachable as he. I never got to know her as I did him. She wasn't involved with the parents as much as he was. He was warmer, she more aloof. Our children liked the freedom of the school.

We lived at Stelton for four years, then followed Harry Kelly to Mohegan. That was in 1924. We stayed till 1928. We lived in a tent at first, while building our own home. George Seldes was one of the founders, together with Kelly. He had been a druggist in Pittsburgh. He knew eight or nine languages, was a translator and writer, very intelligent and capable, but took to drink. In 1928 we moved to Belle Terre, Harry Kelly's colony in Croton. We all lived in one big house with fourteen rooms—us, Seldes, Kelly, the Epsteins, and the Mirskys. Rocker stayed with us for a while during one of his visits from Europe. We had symposiums every Saturday.

From Croton we went back to Mohegan. Then, in the early thirties, we went to Sunrise. We were there for three years, from the beginning in 1933 to 1936. We believed in the cooperative life. That's why we joined all the colonies. They were all happy years, despite inevitable hardships. Many came to Sunrise to escape the Depression. They were not interested in colonies per se, and had no ideals. Some refused to work—they said their money was working for them. There were other tensions and divisions. Yiddishists insisted on speaking Yiddish at meetings and in ordinary conversation. Even the cow was given a Yiddish name! My son, who was studying Yiddish, got so fed up with them that he abandoned his studies. Another problem was the Depression itself: we couldn't get credit and were always financially pressed. In the end the colony failed for lack of money. Less than half of the members were anarchists, and of those only a few were dedicated to the anarchist ideal. There were 350 families in all, a hundred of which were anarchist. The great majority were Jews, but we had a few Italians and other nationalities. They came from all over the country— New York, Philadelphia, Detroit, Chicago.

Many years have gone by since that time. I'm neither disappointed nor disillusioned in anarchism. Some day, I feel, it will prevail. The same for the cooperative life. I consider myself an anarcho-syndicalist. I'm a firm believer in trade unions. At present I'm on the board of the *Fraye Arbeter Shtime*, just like my husband before.

• ISIDORE FARBIASH •

Miami Beach, Florida, December 20, 1972

Isidore Farbiash, eighty years old, was working at his sewing machine in his small rented room in Miami Beach when I came to interview him in 1972. Born in Poland in 1892, he had been exiled to Siberia in the wake of the 1905 Revolution and emigrated to the United States after his release, becoming a garment worker and member of the International Ladies' Garment Workers' Union. In New York he attended lectures by Emma Goldman and Alexander Berkman and joined the Anarchist Red Cross, which assisted political prisoners in tsarist Russia. He later took part in the Mohegan and Sunrise experiments, moving to Florida after the Second World War.

I WAS BORN in Poland in 1892 and as a youth worked in a shoe factory in Warsaw. In 1907 the Bund called a strike of the shoe workers, which failed. The PPS (Polish Socialist Party) took it over, but they too failed. So the anarchists started planting bombs in the factories that resisted a settlement. Moyshe Londoner, a well-known anarchist, lived in our house and was active in the strike. The police came and questioned me about him and beat me so hard I started to holler, so my older sister ran out and fought with them. We were both arrested and sat for eleven months in prison, and were then sent to Siberia for three years. When I returned to Warsaw I had to report to the police every month.

I left for America in 1911 and became a garment worker, active in the ILGWU. I took part in organizing the Frayhayt Group in New York in 1913 and also belonged to the Anarchist Red Cross. I heard Emma Goldman and Alexander Berkman speak. In 1917 I intended to go back to Russia, but when the Bolshevik Revolution broke out I instinctively distrusted them and remained in the U.S.

At a conference at Unity House in 1923, Simon Farber told me about Mohegan colony (he was already a member) and I joined. At the end of 1924 quarrels broke out in the ILGWU between the anarchists and the Communists, and I was the only anarchist who joined the Communists in the struggle, because I thought they were more effective and also I liked their slogan of a maximum of two years for all union officers. I was in the Action Committee of the Communist Group in the ILGWU, and you can imagine how angry my anarchist friends were at me! In 1925 I overheard one Communist leader tell another, "We must see that the failure of the strike [a cloakmakers' strike then going on] falls on Sigman."[518] That was enough for me and I quit.

Meanwhile we had a nice little house in Mohegan from which I commuted to New York City. Harry Kelly was a plain, honest man who never raised his voice. The idea was a good one, but it wasn't fulfilled because the Communists came in and there were fights which poisoned the atmosphere of freedom and destroyed the possibilities for a true libertarian school.

But I didn't give up on communities. I joined the Sunrise colony at the beginning, in 1933. Joseph Cohen made one big mistake. He didn't pick the people carefully, but let anyone who had the money come in. He admitted people who simply didn't fit, who had no ideals, and who weren't able to do the necessary physical labor. The possibilities were marvelous. We could have had there a heaven if not for the oppositions and fights. Cohen was honest, he meant well, but he wanted to do it himself. People came there because of the Depression. They did not have the Idea and could not do the work. Some of us gradually got accustomed to it, but most members looked for easy labor or for management jobs. That's where the fights started. It could have been one of the richest establishments that radicals had ever been involved with. It had big livestock, rich land. Yet it failed.

The place was very large and we needed at least fifty more families. Less than half were anarchists. There was a quarrel between Yiddishists and non-Yiddishists. Eli Greenblatt had a personal grudge against Cohen because he himself wanted to be head. But most people didn't like Greenblatt—he would have been a real dictator. The anarchists made one big mistake: they started to organize gatherings for themselves and didn't invite the others, who felt left out, and this helped to wreck the community spirit. I nearly cried when we left; I knew it could have been good. We had five thousand sheep, two hundred horses, as well as pigs and other animals. The main crops—peppermint and sugar beets—could have been a great success. Everything could grow there except fruit (it was too cold).

We went back to Mohegan at the end of 1934. But there too there were bitter quarrels. The fights with the Communists were worse than before. People started to leave. Slowly the community broke up. The Paul Robeson riot [in 1949] marked the end. Afterwards there was a large exodus to New York City and Miami. Stein, the shoemaker and chief oppositionist at Sunrise, lived in Miami for a number of years and died two years ago in the Workmen's Circle Home in the Bronx.

• ISRAEL OSTROFF •

Bronx, New York, September 28, 1972

I first encountered Israel Ostroff on May 3, 1969, at the annual luncheon of the Libertarian Book Club. Following a lecture on Bakunin by a lawyer named Burton Hall, a young man got up and shouted that what anarchism really meant was "Up Against the Wall Mother-Fucker!" This he repeated several times, in an effort to *épater les anarchistes*. Thereupon a white-haired man on the other side of the room—it was Israel Ostroff—rose and said in a heavy Jewish accent, "I've been an anarchist for sixty-four years, and for the first time I think maybe I made a mistake." At the conclusion of the luncheon I went over to Ostroff and introduced myself, and we soon became friends. He died in Miami Beach on April 21, 1974.[519]

I WAS BORN in the *shtetl* of Zabludovo, near Bialystok, on January 4, 1892. In 1907, at the age of fifteen, I became an anarchist. I was then a tannery worker. I had been a Zionist but heard an anarchist lecture and was immediately converted. He quoted Isaiah on beating swords into plowshares and Samuel on not needing a king,[520] and he emphasized the dignity of the individual. In 1914 I emigrated to the United States and settled at first in Chicago. I was in a Workmen's Circle branch with many anarchist members. Anarchism gave the immigrants a sense of belonging, of family, community, common ideals and aspirations, which we desperately needed.

I came to New York in 1918. I became a cutter of women's dresses and active in the ILGWU, especially in the fight against the Communists between 1924 and 1928. I was also active in the office of the *Fraye Arbeter Shtime* and helped organize the Amshol Group, a merger of the Amalgamated and Sholem Aleichem branches of the Workmen's Circle in the Bronx. It had about sixty members, some of them anarchists, such as Benjamin Axler and Morris Ganberg [q.v.], the secretary.

The anarchist faction in the ILGWU included Nicholas Kritzman, Mendel Bluestein, Simon Farber, and Rose Pesotta, as well as myself. We published a Yiddish paper, the *Yunyon Arbeter*. There were anarchists in the Amalgamated too. The *Fraye Arbeter Shtime* was also involved in the labor movement, always preached unionism rather than being isolated from the workers. There was a Kropotkin Literatur-Gezelshaft in New York, which published anarchist and socialist works. Its members included Dr. Globus, Dr. Michael Cohn, and Morris Shutz and Benjamin Axler of the *Fraye Arbeter Shtime*.

Saul Yanovsky was the first major editor of the *Fraye Arbeter Shtime*. In Russia, like Joseph Cohen, he was a talmudic student; in the U.S. he fought against terrorism. For him anarchism was a philosophy of human dignity and human rights, a philosophy of love and brotherhood, not bombs. His attitude caused a split in the Jewish movement over the issue of violence. He was an excellent speaker and debater, with a sarcastic, biting wit. He immediately found the weakness of his opponent. During the 1920s he edited *Gerekhtikayt*, the Yiddish paper of the ILGWU (he was succeeded by Simon Farber). Once, at a concert, he asked the pianist why he didn't play the violin. "I don't know the violin," was the reply. "And the piano you know?" said Yanovsky. Yanovsky had a feel for good literature. He was a good man, but when he hit you he hit too hard. He was a little Jew, with a little beard, who looked like an insurance agent to me.

J. A. Maryson was even more moderate and opposed to revolution and violence. He was one of the first to say that anarchists must take part in American life and that anarchism is an ideal for the future. Dr. Herman Frank[521] was not active in the anarchist movement but had a libertarian philosophy. Solo Linder's specialty in London was theater criticism. He was expelled from England with Rudolf Rocker in 1918 and was close to Rocker in Berlin. During the Depression, after returning to the U.S., he was manager of the Manhattan Beach Hotel in Brooklyn, owned by Dr. Cohn. Dr. B. Liber played a significant role in the anarchist movement during the early part of the century. He wrote and lectured on diet, hygiene, and child rearing, a sort of Jewish Dr. Spock. Bernard Fliesler was secretary of the Ferrer-Rocker Branch of the Workmen's Circle in the Bronx. In Yanovsky's time everyone who could read and write was considered a philosopher. The rank and file were barely literate and revered writers like Yanovsky and Rocker. Education and schools were of vital importance for them, as was the cooperative movement, especially cooperative colonies and cooperative housing (above all the Amalgamated Houses in the Bronx and the ILGWU Houses in Manhattan).

Anarchism does not wipe out nationality. Despite anarchism's international ideal, there are Jewish anarchists, Italian anarchists, Spanish anarchists, and so forth. Anarchism is different from socialism: it has no laid-out plan of how we should live. It stands for a continuous evolutionary struggle for more freedom. When we reach the top of the mountain, we must begin to climb a higher one. It is a way of life, a way of thinking, rather than a specific goal or achievement. It is the climbing and not the peak that counts. Rocker came to believe this in the last years of his life.

• ABRAHAM BLECHER •

Miami Beach, Florida, December 16, 1972

Abraham Blecher, a native of Kiev province, emigrated to the United States in 1910. He became a garment worker in New York, where he joined the Golos Truda Group as well as the Industrial Workers of the World. During the 1920s he lived in the Stelton Colony in New Jersey and was a frequent contributor to *The Road to Freedom* and the *Fraye Arbeter Shtime*. He later veered towards Trotskyism, without completely abandoning his anarchism, for which he thereafter retained a nostalgic affection.

I WAS BORN in Belaia Tserkov' in Kiev province eighty-four years ago and came to the United States in December 1910. I roomed in a house that Simon Farber often visited, and he introduced me to anarchism—and also to his sister Yetta, who became my wife. I soon joined the Golos Truda Group in New York. Avgust Rode-Chervinsky was its outstanding member, a devoted anarcho-syndicalist. He was of German descent and had participated in the big railroad strike before the 1905 Revolution and was wounded in the ear. He was the oldest and most experienced member of our group. By contrast I had no re-spect for Bill Shatoff. He was an adventurer who loved wine, women, and song. He was talented, intelligent, and a good speaker and debater. He typeset *Golos Truda* in the Russkoe Slovo plant, where he worked.

At the same time, I was secretary of a local IWW group, of which Isidore Wisotsky, Frank Tannenbaum, Sam Klatchko, and others were members. Misha Raiva of the Golos Truda Group died on ship while returning to Russia in 1917. His younger brother Grisha returned to the United States and became a Communist. They had published *Pravda* in Brooklyn during the war as well as a Yiddish anarchist paper. The Jewish Anarchist Federation published *Fray-hayt* around 1915 [1913–1914]. I was secretary of the federation for a time.

Of all the well-known anarchists, Kropotkin appealed to me most because of his attitude towards the people. He really idealized man, and at that time that appealed to me, though I've since altered my views on human nature. Leonard Abbott, by the way, was a strong admirer of the Bolsheviks and wouldn't stand for any criticism of the Soviet regime for several years after the revolution.

During the 1920s I was active in *The Road to Freedom* as treasurer and a writer of articles on labor. Most of the group were anarchist-communists, though Hippolyte Havel, the editor, was basically an individualist. We moved to Stelton in 1921 and lived there for sixteen years, and our daughter went to school there from the age of four to ten. I commuted to New York as a garment worker. Uncle Ferm loved the children. Aunty believed in children but I don't know how much she loved them. She was stern and strict, but most of the kids liked her, though they liked Uncle more—he was softer. The anarchists and Communists got along all right in those early years. They had a common inter-est in the school, the cooperative store, the jitney service. They may have ar-gued a bit but never came to blows. Hans Koch, a German, taught woodwork-ing, a very intelligent man and an ardent anarchist. Anna Koch taught weaving and sewing, and there were also a few other Germans in the colony. Marcus Graham was an individualist and naturist and raised his own vegetables.

During the twenties I was also on the board of the *Fraye Arbeter Shtime*. Joseph Cohen was then the editor. He had a good mind, was capable and respected, but I don't think he was loved. He held grudges and was intolerant of different opinions. One time I wrote two articles and he published the first but not the second because he disagreed with me. Yanovsky would never have done that! He was staunchly opposed to centralization. Federalism was a sa-cred principle for him. When Cohen had something against a person he never let go. He was very vindictive.

I resigned from *The Road to Freedom* in 1927. I didn't see any constructive work from the anarchists—only abstract propaganda. I was looking for activity. So I became active in the Amalgamated Clothing Workers. I still believed in the philosophy of anarchism, but I did not believe in anarchist organization, because it does not lead to any established order. I thus became a freelance anarchist, though basically an anarcho-syndicalist, the only constructive type of anarchist. During the 1930s I wrote for *Vanguard* and *Challenge* (under the pseudonym of Albert Orland), and also for the Trotskyist *Militant* and for *Unzer Kamf*, a Yiddish Trotskyist paper. I was no longer a member of any anarchist group, and in fact was a Trotskyist. But I found the Trotskyists too dictatorial and was soon arguing with [Max] Shachtman[522] and [James] Cannon. I wanted free soviets. So I quit. Nor did I agree with Trotsky's belief that the ends justify the means, for in reality this does not differ from Stalinism.

I still believe in taking part in all phases of radical activity, but I am no longer an idealizer of the working class. I know the worker too closely to idealize him. When the workers get power they do the same as any other class. I still adhere to anarchism as a philosophy rather than as a practical solution. Anarchism can only work in small groups but not on a large scale, because it will then lack stability, and there will always be clashes and quarrels. Thus there cannot be an overall anarchist society. There can at best be small anarchistic groups within society. But even they never last very long. You cannot trust a man just because he pretends to be an anarchist. Yet, despite all this, the years at Stelton, working on *The Road to Freedom* and the *Fraye Arbeter Shtime*, were the best years of our lives.

• CLARA HALPERN •

New York, January 13, 1973[523]

In January 1973 Sam Dolgoff's (q.v.) son Anatole telephoned me and said that he had just met a woman who called herself a "Maximalist." Would I be interested in talking to her? I got over there as fast as I could. The Maximalists, I was aware, had been an extreme left-wing group in revolutionary Russia, akin in some respects to the anarchists. As far as I knew they were extinct. The person I now met, Clara Halpern, was a lovely blue-eyed woman in her eighties, the last survivor of that militant sect. What she told me was of absorbing interest. Clara died, aged ninety, on January 20, 1978.

I WAS BORN on February 28, 1888 of a middle-class Jewish family in the town of Novozybkov in Chernigov province, Russia. My father was a prosperous timber merchant. I was the youngest of four daughters and a son, and we all went to a *gimnaziia*. The town was relatively progressive: it had no ghetto and was an active educational as well as commercial center, with several good schools. And it was there that I got my first lessons in revolution.

The main force that drove me to the revolutionary movement was my compassion for the oppressed peasantry. It was a feeling derived not so much from personal observation as from my reading of Turgenev, Tolstoy, Uspensky, Nekrasov, and other writers, who so vividly described the unbearable conditions under which the peasants were living. There developed within me a strong sympathy for these downtrodden and abused people. I came to idealize the Russian peasant, whom I knew primarily through my reading. Everything about him seemed lofty and enchanting, and his suffering became my own.

My last year in the *gimnaziia* coincided with the 1905 Revolution. The whole city came out to fight against the tsar and the authorities. It was a wonderful sight! Social Democrats and Socialist Revolutionaries spoke to us students and tried to draw us into their movements. I became a member of a self-education circle, in which we studied social, economic, and political questions. But before long an ideological divergence emerged among us. Some of us leaned towards the Social Democrats, others towards the Socialist Revolutionaries. I belonged to the latter group. I devoured the literature distributed by the SR agitators. My older sister, Dora Lazurkina, had studied in St. Petersburg and was already a dedicated Marxist. She tried without success to convince me that only the working class was capable of liberating Russia from capitalist exploitation, and that the peasant, with his disposition towards private ownership and his petty-bourgeois psychology, would only be an impediment to the revolution. My sister, by the way, remained a lifelong Bolshevik, one of seven young women whom Lenin prepared in Switzerland for important roles in the party. She is still alive in the Soviet Union, and a few years ago she appeared at a party congress and told of having seen a vision of Lenin, who said to her, "I don't want Stalin next to me in my tomb," after which he was removed.[524]

To me, however, Marxist theory seemed too rigid and entirely unjust to the peasantry. I couldn't bear the thought that the peasants were unable to become true socialists without first being converted into factory hands and undergoing proletarianization. I argued that we would have to educate the peasant to understand his own plight, and that this understanding would confirm his own instinctive feeling of communal ownership—of socialism. We also differed on other important questions, such as the role of the individual in history and of terrorism in the revolutionary struggle. My sister rejected terrorism. That made me extremely disappointed in her, and I even began to dislike her, as I did all other Marxists.

By the time I finished the *gimnaziia* in 1905, I had joined a small student cell of Socialist Revolutionaries. I wanted more than anything else to play an active role in the revolutionary movement. I did not want to go on to the university. My university was the revolution! Instead, I went to the town of Borisov in Minsk province to teach in an elementary school and to seek contacts with other SR groups. Meanwhile, a friend of mine from Novozybkov wrote the SRs in Minsk, where there was a flourishing movement, and told them about me. They soon sent an emissary, a young girl named Roza Shabat, to invite me to join them. I returned with Roza to Minsk, and she brought me to the home of one of the SR leaders, Katya Izmailovich, whose father was a lieutenant general in the Far East, taking part in the war against Japan. Her sister Alexandra was then in a St. Petersburg prison, beginning a life sentence for an unsuccessful attempt to assassinate the Minsk governor, Kurlov.

Katya was a marvelous person—so dignified, so sophisticated, while I was so young and inexperienced. In her mid-twenties and not pretty, she was tall and slender, with smoothly combed brown hair, and always wore the same simple calico dress. She seemed to have some hidden source of energy within her, as well as a very strong will. All of the comrades, even the veteran revolutionists, showed her great respect. I idolized her. I lived with her for two weeks and she taught me many things.

At last the day came when Katya asked me to speak before a group of workers, my first test as a revolutionary agitator. Roza Shabat brought me to a small smoke-filled room with ten or twelve bakers, and I spoke to them about the revolution. There was a book, a kind of revolutionary ABC, that I had read over and over so I would know what to say. But I was only seventeen, and extremely nervous. I began to talk about revolutionary ideas and programs when suddenly I couldn't remember the book, which I had learned practically by heart. I became confused, upset, and finally began to cry. I will never in my entire life forget my mortification. It meant everything to me to succeed as a propagandist, and if I failed, I thought, my whole life was a failure. But the bakers started to cheer me up. "That's nothing, *baryshnia* [miss]. You'll remember. Don't worry." They understood my situation and sympathized with me, and through their encouragement I regained my composure and was able to finish.

On the way back to Katya's house I was afraid to look at Roza, afraid to ask her what she thought, afraid she would say that it wasn't any good. Yet two days later, to my immense delight, Katya told me that they were assigning the bakers to me as my group. It was a great moment for me—the beginning of my revolutionary career!

I remained in Minsk for several months, carrying out agitational work. During that time I learned from Katya that a split had occurred in the ranks of the SRs, that an opposition group had emerged in Bialystok, a group of young revolutionaries led by Lipa Katz and Meyshka Zakgeim called the *Molodye*, the "Young Ones," who were later to take the name of Maximalists. The Young Ones rejected the parliamentary struggle and partial reforms, and they waged a campaign of terrorism against the police and government officials. They called for a social rather than a political revolution, a mass uprising that would usher in a dictatorship of the proletariat. They distrusted intellectuals in the revolutionary movement and said that the workers and peasants must make the revolution themselves by seizing the factories and the land.

The Young Ones resembled the anarchists in their revolutionary spirit and their belief in terrorism, but disagreed with them on the question of organization. The anarchists didn't believe in organization. They didn't believe, as the Young Ones did, in a dictatorship of the proletariat. They refused to accept *any* dictatorship, and called instead for a federation of autonomous communes. The Young Ones, on the other hand, felt that some degree of organization, of centralization, was necessary. They were not much concerned with ideology, but they were influenced less by Bakunin than by Lavrov,[525] and especially

Mikhailovsky,[526] who, in spite of his moderate views, was their main theorist. Like Mikhailovsky, they emphasized the role of the individual, of the human personality, in shaping history. They were also strongly influenced by the revolutionary syndicalists in France, above all by their notion of direct action and the general strike.

The program of the Young Ones struck a responsive chord in me. I talked to Katya about them, and she got word to the Bialystok group that one of her comrades was eager to work with them. Soon afterwards, an emissary came from Bialystok—"Michel," we called him—and told me all about the "opposition" and its activities. Many of its members, he said, had already been arrested, and they needed new speakers and organizers. I decided to go and immediately packed my things.

Katya too was planning to leave Minsk for another destination, and she arranged a little farewell party. Handing me a glass of wine, she said, "This will be our swan song." That was the last time I saw her. The next day she left for Sevastopol to assassinate Admiral Chukhnin of the Black Sea Fleet. Dressed as a widow of a sailor, she went to Chukhnin to ask for relief. She drew her pistol and fired, but succeeded only in wounding him in the leg. In a fury he ordered his orderly to kill her, and he cut her to pieces with his sword. Her sister, as I told you, was already in prison for an attempt on General Kurlov, and when their father heard the news about Katya he committed suicide.

I was in Bialystok when I heard of Katya's death. It was heartbreaking news, but I continued my agitational work, lecturing to groups of workers and students. And it was not long before I won their confidence and affection, and we became great friends.

In an effort to expand the oppositionist movement, Lipa Katz, one of the leaders of the Bialystok group and my future husband, went to Ekaterinoslav to organize a group among the factory workers there. Lipa soon sent for me to help him, and we often spoke to the workers at the factory gates, arranged mass meetings on the outskirts of town, and succeeded in forming a small but active cell with about twenty members, nearly all of them of Russian nationality. In Bialystok, which had the first and largest Maximalist group, the membership was mostly Jewish, with a sprinkling of Russian and Polish workingmen and a small following among the peasants of the surrounding countryside. In addition, there were groups in St. Petersburg, Moscow, Kiev, and other large cities, as well as one in Yuzovka organized by "Mortimer" Ryss.

In order to maintain and expand our revolutionary activities, "expropriation" became an important part of our tactics. One of the first of these "ex's" was carried out in Kiev under Mortimer's leadership. He was an intelligent but nervous man who moved about as if mounted on springs. He was short and unprepossessing but with bright, burning eyes and an enormous personal magnetism which attracted young radicals to his side. At the same time he was extremely polite and gentle, almost effeminate. In Kiev he organized the holdup of a government courier, but trying to assist a wounded comrade, he was himself captured and taken to prison. Azef[527] had long wanted to plant an agent in our organization, and he now hit upon Ryss as his instrument. Mortimer pretended to go along, and the police allowed him to escape from prison. But instead of going to St. Petersburg, as agreed, he went south and organized a small group in Yuzovka. It was soon rounded up, however, and Mortimer was hanged.

The principal leader of the Maximalist movement was known as *Medved'*, the Bear, a nickname he had acquired during the Moscow uprising of December 1905, in which he played a very prominent part. In contrast to Ryss, he was a handsome young man, tall, blond, and blue-eyed, with a face that radiated vitality. His real name was Sokolov,[528] and he was the illegitimate son of a nobleman and a servant girl. When the split occurred in the SR ranks, he immediately joined the opposition and became its most dynamic leader, organizing a Fighting Brigade (*boevoi otriad*) modeled after that of the parent party. In March 1906, jointly with the SRs and the Bolsheviks, he engineered our first big "ex" in Moscow, which netted nearly a million rubles.

The Bear was constantly preoccupied with devising new adventures. He was the epitome of the revolutionary militant—dynamic, forceful, energetic, an idealist and activist combined. The most famous act of his Fighting Brigade was the attempt on Stolypin[529] in August 1906. Our comrades were dressed in uniforms obtained by Natasha Klimova, the beautiful daughter of a member of the State Council, who had joined the Maximalists while a student at Moscow University. For her the struggle was important in itself, quite apart from the ends which it was to achieve. In revolutionary action she saw the highest beauty, a source of vibrant experience, almost a form of art. The young men threw bombs into Stolypin's *dacha* in St. Petersburg, and several of them were killed, along with more than twenty people in the house, although Stolypin himself escaped unharmed.

The last of the "ex's" took place in Petersburg in October of 1906. It was carried out on the Fonarnyi Pereulok in broad daylight by a group of Maximalists from Petersburg, Bialystok, and Ekaterinoslav, some of the finest comrades in our movement. They attacked a messenger with government funds guarded by mounted police. One of them threw a bomb while the rest opened fire on the police. The raid netted 460,000 rubles, but at the cost of eight comrades killed or captured.

Part of the money was used to finance the first and only Maximalist conference, which took place in a farmhouse in Finland.[530] More than sixty delegates attended, workers and intellectuals from various cities. I was a delegate from the Ekaterinoslav group. At the conference we officially proclaimed our independence from the SR party and shed the name of Young Ones for SR Maximalists. We also drew up a program that emphasized the importance of terrorist activity. A pall hung over the meeting because of the loss of our comrades in the Fonarnyi "ex." Of the proceeds of the raid the Bear said: "There is blood in every kopeck, comrades. Let's make it all count."

After the conference, the members of the Fighting Brigade met with the Bear in Helsingfors to plan its next move. It was decided, at the Bear's suggestion, to blow up the main police headquarters in St. Petersburg. I was thrilled when the Bear asked me to take part. Natasha Klimova (who was by then the Bear's companion) was to obtain the dynamite in Finland, while Comrade Lukich and I were to smuggle it into the capital. We did this by pretending to be a newlywed merchant couple returning from our honeymoon in Finland. I sewed some of the dynamite into my petticoat, and Lukich fastened the rest to his belt. On the train, however, we were watched by a police spy, and when we got to St. Petersburg we found that our hideouts had been raided the previous day and all of our comrades arrested. Lukich tried to return to Finland but was seized at the railroad station. I was chased in the street and caught just before I could jump into a carriage. Natasha too was arrested the same day, and in prison I found that the cell next to mine was occupied by Nadya Terentieva, who had gone to Odessa with Meyshka Zakgeim and three other members of the Fighting Brigade to kill the governor there, but were caught before they could execute the deed.

So I never did kill anybody—though not from lack of trying. And now our entire organization had been smashed. Everyone had been either killed or arrested. The Bear was executed in the police station without trial. The rest languished in prison until June 1908, when a mass trial, the Trial of the Forty-Four Maximalists, took place in the capital. Natasha Klimova was tried separately and sentenced to life imprisonment at hard labor. The news caused her father—a member of the State Council—to die of a heart attack. The rest of us got sentences ranging up to fifteen years at hard labor. I received the lightest sentence, two years with time already served deducted, because of my age and a lack of evidence against me.

While I was serving the remainder of my sentence, Lipa Katz escaped from prison and made his way to Paris. After my release in 1909 I joined him there, and we mingled with a whole colony of exiled revolutionaries—Chernov, Savinkov, Breshkovskaya, Figner, Grossman-Roshchin, Martov, Lenin.

Lipa and I came to Boston in 1914, on the eve of the First World War, and we have remained there ever since. In 1926 I visited Soviet Russia and saw Nadya and Meyshka, who had married in Siberia, where they were imprisoned until 1917, when the Revolution gave them amnesty. They were both members of the Organization of Political Prisoners and worked in its bookstore in Moscow. Natasha Klimova, who had escaped from prison and joined us in Paris, was all packed to return to Russia in 1917 when she died suddenly of influenza. My husband died in 1971 at the age of eighty-eight.

So I am the last of the Maximalists, as far as I know. Those who remained in Russia were exiled, purged, executed; those who went abroad have all passed away. They were the greatest idealists, revolutionists of the highest moral caliber. They sacrificed all the comforts of life to serve the cause of freedom, and many chose the path of martyrdom. Yet so much was packed into those few years in Russia—so much of life's excitement, of high ideals and hopes. They were wonderful years, you know. Without them, without those few years, my life would have no real meaning.

• MORRIS SCHULMEISTER •

Bronx, New York, April 8, 1975[531]

When I interviewed Morris Schulmeister at the Jewish Home for the Aged in the Bronx, he was one of a handful of anarchist survivors of both the 1905 and 1917 Revolutions. An opponent of all governments, he had the distinction of taking part in armed "expropriations" against tsarists and Communists alike. I interviewed Meyshka (as he was called) together with Ahrne Thorne (q.v.), editor of the *Fraye Arbeter Shtime*. For three hours he reminisced about the past, speaking in Russian and Yiddish. Two years after our visit, Meyshka fell ill with cancer, for which he received radiation therapy. But there was a time to live, he said, and a time to die. The time to die had come, and he refused all further treatment. At the same time, he stopped eating. While strapped in his bed to be fed intravenously, he was visited by a comrade, Hannah Spivak. "Give me a knife," he pleaded, "so I can cut these bonds." Hannah replied that she had no knife. "Then give me a match and I'll burn them away," he said. The end came not long after. Meyshka died on June 9, 1978, in his ninetieth year.

I WAS BORN in a village near the town of Kleshchel', Grodno province, on April 10, 1889. When I was about four years old, I went to live with my grandmother in Brest-Litovsk and remained there till the age of nine or ten. At that time my father went to work for a wholesale sugar distributor in Bialystok, and he took me to live with him. I began to study in the seventh grade of a talmud-torah and completed the eleventh grade at the age of thirteen, when I was bar-mitzvahed. I then attended a yeshiva for one year, during which I started losing my religious faith. So I quit the yeshiva—I was fourteen then—and my cousin, my father's brother's son, gave me a job as a weaver in his small factory. I was there for about three years, until the age of seventeen, and began attending radical meetings, held mostly in the woods outside of town.

That was during the great period of social ferment that culminated in the 1905 Revolution, and Bialystok was a center of radical activity of every sort. In 1906 I witnessed a pogrom in the city. By then I had read Kropotkin's *Appeal to the Young* and *Conquest of Bread* and other anarchist works and was a member of the Anarkhistishe Veberishe Federatsie [Anarchist Weavers' Federation]. Yuda Grossman (Roshchin) came from Western Europe and debated with the Bundists and Socialist Revolutionaries. Nobody could beat him in debate, and he confirmed me in my anarchist faith. He walked the streets of Bialystok with his pockets full of leaflets and papers, absent-mindedly reading some revolutionary brochure. I met him later in Moscow, in 1918, well-dressed in a suit and with a well-groomed beard, a totally different man. He was ten or twelve years older than me, one of three brothers who were anarchists; one of them—Avram—was killed by the police. Yuda himself never took part in "ex's" or other militant activities. His specialty was speaking and debating, in which he was an undefeated champion. He made a great impression. Zeydl and also Yasha "Shlumper"—who knew his revolutionary Talmud—were other anarchists who debated effectively against Bundists and SRs, as well as Maximalists like Lipa Katz, winning many new adherents to the movement.

The anarchists in Bialystok were known as the Chernoe Znamia (Black Flag) Group, composed of members of the Weavers' Federation (like myself), the Bakers' Federation, the Tanners' Federation, the Cabinetmakers' Federation, the Tailors' Federation, and other trade federations, each of which had an anarchist group or contingent, that of the weavers being the largest. There were about sixty or seventy active anarchists in all. Most of us—especially those like myself with common first names—had nicknames. I was Meyshka "Polzhidok," another was Meyshka "Konke," still another Meyshka "Damf." This last was a reflection of the introduction in 1905–1906 of new weaving machines, powered by electricity (though called "damf"—steam), in place of our old hand machines. Many of the bosses—even Jewish bosses—preferred to hire Polish weavers because the Jews wouldn't work on Saturday. Jewish and Polish workers armed themselves and sometimes fought over the right to work. That is how we won the right to a job.

We were armed also for our revolutionary activities. Among the anarchists we all had Brownings (I once had an accident with mine) and engaged in gun battles with the police. Aron Elin ("Gelinker") was particularly active, and also Yudl, who was a good speaker. Grossman used to call them *Vort un Tat* (Word and Deed)—Yudl and Elin. Yudl later emigrated to America and became the manager of Camp Tamiment. Striga and Meier "Babe" and another comrade were blown up by their own bomb in a *drozhki* in Bialystok. Yankl "Presser," a tanner, and his comrade Meishl, were surrounded by police who raided their house. Yankl threw a bomb down from the roof, and when the police cornered them Meishl shot Presser and then himself. He killed himself but Presser survived. We once made an "ex" against a liquor store collector—a government employee, as liquor was a state monopoly—and took money at gunpoint from private manufacturers, and sometimes killed them if they didn't pay. The money was used mostly for propaganda—to hold conferences, buy paper and print for our literature, and so on. Now I look at all this with different eyes. It wasn't necessary.

The following year, 1907, I went to Minsk, as the police in Bialystok were looking for me and things were getting hot there. The anarchist group in Minsk had a printing press and a bomb laboratory and carried out propaganda both of word and deed. The printing press [called *Anarkhie*] was run by Boris Engelson, together with a girl who afterwards went to London and is mentioned by Rudolf Rocker in his autobiography. Mikhail Kukuts-Kovetsky ("Feliks"), a Latvian, made the bombs. In 1904, in a convoy of political prisoners en route to Siberia, he was liberated by anarchists in the town of Slonim who gave him a loaf of bread with a Browning inside. Other members of our group, besides myself, were a girl named Liza and a young man named Savitsky.

On April 1, 1907, Feliks and one of his comrades went to a little park to try out the bombs. Feliks spotted a detective and winked to his comrade to warn him, but they were surrounded and caught, after a shootout in which Feliks had wounded a few detectives. The rest of the group (including myself) were arrested soon after and locked up in Minsk prison. Under pressure from the police, Kukuts-Kovetsky had turned informer and was responsible for the arrests. Knives were smuggled to three other anarchists in the prison—Fomin, Stakh, and Solov'ev—who got out of their cell, went to the special tower where Kukuts-Kovetsky was being held, killed the guard, then killed Kukuts-Kovetsky. The alarm was sounded and they were caught. After a trial they were sentenced to be hanged. Boris tried to organize their escape but was himself captured, taken to Vilna, and shot by a firing squad. His three comrades in Minsk had meanwhile been hanged.

I had almost evaded arrest but was seized by two gendarmes in the railroad station at Vilna. They found on me revolutionary proclamations to peasants produced by our printing press in Minsk, as well as a false passport in the name of "Zakhar Nefidov." Thereafter my police dossier would read, "Zakhar Nefidov, alias Schulmeister." I asked if I could buy an apple, as I had not eaten in some time. They said all right, and I made a break for it, only to run smack into the arms of military police. Returned to Minsk prison, I was sentenced to four years at hard labor. I spent the first eight months in chains, day and night, never taken off. Our trustee was an anarchist named Kirill Pavlovich Grodetsky, who had been a fellow university student of the district procurator, who recognized him when he visited his comrades in prison. Leivick,[532] the poet, a Bundist, shared my cell with me. During our three years together he wrote numerous poems and plays, while the others talked or played chess.

In 1910 I, Savitsky, and a few other comrades were transferred to Moscow, where I spent the next two years in prison at hard labor. From there, in 1912, I was taken on my next *étape* to Minsk, Slonim, and Bialystok, where I had been falsely accused of shooting a policeman. I was made to stand in a lineup, but my accuser picked out a different man. Nevertheless, I was sentenced to eternal banishment in Siberia. But first I was returned to Moscow, to my same old cell, to await transportation. Finally, in 1913, I was deported to the village of Mukhtin, Kerensk district, Irkutsk province, near the city of Yakutsk, with the Lena River on one side and the *taiga*—where I once got lost overnight but met a hunter who led me out—on the other. There were eight of us politicals in that village, and we lived communally, three anarchists and five Maximalists, all very nice fellows. I remained there one year, until the outbreak of the First World War. During that period we built a local school as part of our labor sentence.

Three weeks after the war broke out I received one hundred dollars from the Anarchist Red Cross. I was overjoyed. In my high spirits I thought I would take a chance. I left the village on foot and walked for sixty-three hours to a small city, from which I made my way to Irkutsk. There men were being mustered for the army, so I bought a military outfit and joined them. The station was packed, so I paid a conductor ten gold pieces for his cap and lantern and boarded a train bound for Brest-Litovsk, where I had lived as a child. My grandparents had since died, but their family still lived there, and I went to the house of an aunt. At first she didn't recognize me—she took me for another of the many soldiers who were on their way to the front—but I called her name and she embraced me and gave me fresh civilian clothes.

From Brest-Litovsk I took a train to Bialystok and went to the sugar store where Father worked. He brought me home and Mother kissed me and cried, kissed me and cried. I managed to get another false passport—not "Zakhar Nefidov" this time, but "Moyshe Kaplan"—and took a train to Odessa, where my younger brother worked in a factory that made epaulettes. At the last station before the city—Razdel'nie, it was called, and famous for its thieves—I returned to my car to find that my money and passport had been stolen. I was left with only eighty copecks and the ticket in my vest pocket. But I soon got a job in a pen-point factory and remained in Odessa more than two years, until the outbreak of the revolution.

One day, in 1916, I was stopped by a policeman who asked me, "Why aren't you at the front, fighting? Come with me to the station." I gave him three rubles and he let me go. The next Friday he came to my factory and demanded more money or he would take me "to the station-house." I gave him my watch as collateral till pay-day, when I gave him three rubles and got the watch back. The pen-point factory failed, but I found a new job in a factory that made canvas sacks. I didn't like it—it made sacks for the war, which I opposed—and I soon quit. I then taught Russian and Yiddish to the children of a Bialystok baker who had come to Odessa, until the revolution erupted.

The sailors of the Black Sea Fleet had numerous revolutionaries—SRs, anarchists, Bolsheviks—and when one of them asked me why I wasn't in uniform I told him my story. He and his friends telegraphed to Sasha Taratuta—Olga's husband and a *sovetskii anarkhist* [pro-Bolshevik anarchist]—in Petrograd, and he vouched for me. I was told about the amnesty for revolutionaries and that I was excused from military service. But I went anyway, and served in a watchtower by a bridge in Bessarabia. One day a comrade came to fetch me. He told me that anarchists were returning from London, from America, and to come home to join the revolution. So I returned with him to Odessa.

From Odessa I went to Yalta, then north to Moscow and Petrograd, meeting with comrades in each city, including Sasha Taratuta, Bill Shatoff, and Sanya Schapiro. I settled down with the Moscow anarchists and plunged into active work. A group of us went to the front to spread propaganda among Krasnov's troops, who were seeking to crush the revolution. Trotsky arrived, and one of the first things he said was, "There are too many anarchists here." We were sent back, and I worked in the transport department of the Union of Cities and was active in the Moscow anarchist group, which carried out expropriations, just as we had previously done against the tsarist government.

The largest "ex" took place in 1918 against a state bank and insurance company, and forty anarchists (myself among them) took part. One comrade, Stokozov, gained entrance through a guarded iron door by wearing the uniform of a Red Army officer. The guard opened the door a crack and we pushed our way in. There were twenty-five Bolshevik soldiers there, but one of our men displayed a bomb and ordered them not to move. "Who are you?" one asked. But we did not answer. And they did as they were told. As clients entered they were rounded up and put under guard. We opened the safe with a blow-torch and removed several million rubles. I stood at the switchboard and made sure that the operator did not sound the alarm. It took four hours to open that safe! It was our last successful "ex." We tried one more—at the Textile Union—but that failed. I gave Abba Gordin some of the money to be used for his newspaper, *Anarkhiia*, and he took it, though he knew where it came from. Part of the rest was used to buy food and goods which were brought to Dmitrov and given to Kropotkin, who would not have accepted them had he known their origin.

After that the Bolsheviks began to raid anarchist clubs and many comrades were arrested. I went to Kozlov to lie low at the house of an anarchist. Three *chekisty* [secret policemen] came around and asked for me. My host told them I had been there but already left, and they apparently believed him. But they might return, so I had to move on. I went to Kharkov for a while, and saw Mratchny [q.v.], Moshke [q.v.] and Becky Greenshner, and other comrades of the Nabat Confederation. From Kharkov I returned to Bialystok. The Poles were there at the time—it was in 1919. Mother had died. Father was in Kleshchel'. All of his relatives were later to be killed by Hitler, except one, who is now in Israel.

In 1920 the Red Army came through town on their way into Poland—then came back when the Poles drove them out. While there they made me head of the *revkom* [revolutionary committee] for a while. In 1922 I smuggled myself across the border and made my way to France, where I boarded a ship for Argentina. I lived in Buenos Aires a year, met Moshke and Becky again, and worked at my old trade as a weaver. I came to New York in 1923, but could not take part in the movement any more. Many of my old comrades had become Bolsheviks, ready to do anything "for the Revolution"—worse than the Bolsheviks themselves! I had lost my faith in anarchism, in the working people, in mankind as a whole, and could be close only to individuals whom I knew and who appealed to me without regard to their ideology. What possibility was there for the realization of a free society if men could behave so badly? Men should be more humanitarian. But they aren't. They haven't progressed—they've regressed!

• DAVID BABICH •

Bronx, New York, January 28, 1977

David Babich, who emigrated to the United States from Russia on the eve of the First World War, was a member of the Union of Russian Workers and of the Kropotkin Literary Society in New York. A clothing worker and member of the International Ladies' Garment Workers' Union, he knew both Emma Goldman and Alexander Berkman, as well as other important anarchists, including V. M. Eikhenbaum (Volin) and William Shatoff. I interviewed him at his home in the Amalgamated Cooperative Houses in the Bronx, where I was introduced to him by a fellow resident, Ahrne Thorne (q.v.).

I WAS BORN in 1891 in Boguslav, Kanev district, Kiev province, Russia. My father sold piece goods. I had six brothers and sisters. My parents were religious, and I attended *kheder* [Yiddish elementary school]. There were no rebels in our family—except me!

One fine day, I took a piece of bread and walked to the railroad station. I was nine years old. I was fed up with *kheder*, with the synagogue, with the whole way of life. The conductor let me off at Fastov, and I boarded another train to Odessa, where my third cousin was a rabbi. He had intelligent children. Another cousin was Ahad Ha-am,[533] the famous Zionist. He and other Zionists took me with them to Palestine. I was nine and a half and remained there four years.

After returning to Russia, I spent a few years in Odessa, then returned to Boguslav, only to be drafted into the army. I deserted and lived in Moscow for two years, always wearing my uniform (in Moscow everybody wore a uniform). Then I smuggled myself across the border into Germany and made my way to Hamburg. It was in 1914, at the time the Archduke was assassinated.[534] I boarded a ship for America, arriving in Philadelphia on July 14, 1914, two weeks before the war broke out.

From Philadelphia I went immediately to New York and settled in Brooklyn, near the Williamsburg Bridge, with a *landsman* from Boguslav. At first I worked as a laborer for the *Morgen Zhurnal*. Then I became a cutter of coats and joined the ILGWU, local 10. I met anarchists and socialists and immediately joined the Union of Russian Workers and also the Kropotkin Literary Society. The executive committee of the Kropotkin Literary Society consisted of Benjamin Axler, David Isakovitz, myself, Volinsky, Hillel Solotaroff, J. A. Maryson, Max Maisel, Sam Margolis, and two or three others.

In the Union of Russian Workers we published works by Bakunin and Kropotkin. When the Lusk Committee[535] began its investigations, we stored this literature at the *Fraye Arbeter Shtime* office. Once, during the war, I attended a Union of Russian Workers conference in Pittsburgh. Some Russian peasants and workers there asked, "Why bother publishing books? Let's go make the revolution!" Bill Shatoff was one of our best speakers and very active in the movement, an outstanding agitator. But a spiritual leader he wasn't. Volin was far superior in this respect. Peter Bianki was simply a class-conscious worker—nothing more. He became a Communist in Russia. The Russian anarchists did not consider Yanovsky and the *Fraye Arbeter Shtime* group to be real anarchists or revolutionists and had a low opinion of them.

I heard Emma Goldman and Alexander Berkman speak many times. Both were good rebels, but one couldn't learn much from them. I later saw Berkman and Alexander Schapiro in Paris, on my way back from a trip to Russia in 1929. There we saw [Hyman] Perkus and his wife, who had become Communists. I also visited the Kropotkin Museum that year.

• VICTOR LYNN •

New York City, June 15, 1972; Astoria, New York,
September 25, 1972; New York City, December 10, 1976

I first met Victor Lynn in May 1972 at the annual luncheon of the Libertarian Book Club. A fit-looking man of eighty, with alert eyes and white mustache, he was sitting in the lobby outside the dining room, a copy of my book *The Russian Anarchists* in his hands. Introducing himself as an old Russian anarchist from Minsk province, he at once offered to give me all his money. It was a considerable sum, he explained, he had no surviving relatives, and he did not want it to go to the state. There would be no strings attached, but he hoped that I would use it to compile a biographical dictionary of anarchism. I thanked him but declined: I was a total stranger, I did not need the money, he would need it himself as he grew older, and so on. Over the next few years, however, I kept in touch with Victor and interviewed him on several occasions. We lost contact around 1980. Given his advanced age, I imagine he died not long after.

MY ORIGINAL NAME was Viktor Demianovich Linko, and I was born into a family of poor peasants on February 6, 1892, in the village of Samizhovo in Minsk province, about thirty miles from Slutsk. We all worked in the fields and lived in a small cottage. My grandfather's wife died (his name was Zakhar), and he remarried. His new wife made life a hell for me and my mother. My father and grandfather once came to blows over this. Grandfather's wife finally threw Mother out. It was winter and we lived in a shed until the wife of a Jewish shoemaker (he had left for America) took us in. Mother, Anna Prisakova, died around 1907, when I was fifteen. The rest of the family, including my two sisters, Agafa and Elena, were killed during World War I. My Uncle Pavel (Father's brother) and his two horses were killed when lightning struck his plowshares while he was working in the fields.

My family were poor and illiterate. They attended church every Sunday. They were good people. I also went to confession as a child. The priest would ask, "Do you behave?" "Do you listen to your father and mother?" and so on. But he also asked: "What do your parents talk about?" "What do they say about the government?" "Do they have visitors?"

As a boy I worked in the fields and also tended the cows of our family and of our neighbors. The cows were thin and hungry and raided the vegetable garden, and I felt so sorry for them that I didn't stop them. In 1912, when I was twenty, I decided to go to America. My idea was to stay there about two years, earn a thousand dollars, and return to my village and buy enough land, along with a few cows and horses, for my family to live in comfort. At that time the landlords felt that something was coming and they were selling land. I did send five hundred dollars to the State Savings Bank but lost it all when the revolution came.

Anyway, I came to America in 1912. I worked laying railroad track in Michigan, as a grinding-machine and punching-machine operator in Toledo, Ohio, and as a porter in New York hotels. I worked for many years at the Plaza on Fifth Avenue and Fifty-Ninth Street. Ella Tyler (born in rural New Jersey in 1886) worked there as a chambermaid. When I broke a rib and was in the hospital, she came to visit and invited me to rent a room in her and her husband's apartment in Astoria. Mr. Tyler was an Englishman and he returned to England soon after the Second World War. He died ten months later.

Ella and I became companions. We lived quietly (with our canaries) for thirty years until her death in 1971. We had willed our money to each other; we both had pensions and savings, especially Ella, who had inherited fifteen and twenty thousand dollars from a woman and then a man for whom she had worked as a helper and unlicensed nurse. She is buried in Pinewood Cemetery on Long Island.

Ella didn't know that I had been an anarchist since my first years in America. We never talked about it. Shortly after my arrival I joined the Union of Russian Workers in the United States and Canada. The New York branch had rooms at the Russian People's House at 133 East Fifteenth Street. There was a classroom, a library, and a school for automobile mechanics in the basement. The journal *Khleb i Volia* was published there. There were lectures, buffets, concerts, and dances. I went there often.

Avgust Rode-Chervinsky, editor of *Golos Truda*, was one of its most active members, but in 1917 he returned to Russia with a group from the paper. He was arrested several times by the Bolsheviks. He became sick and returned to his hometown in Belorussia, where he died in the early 1920s. In 1918 I too wanted to go back to Russia and join Makhno's army in the Ukraine, but I could not raise the fare.

Another important figure was Adolf Schnabel. He was of German origin and came from the Ukraine, and he worked in New York City as a mechanic. He was the editor of *Kolokol*, of which only two numbers appeared. He didn't write much; he was more the manager of the paper than the editor. *Kolokol* was suppressed by the government, as was *Nabat*, which he also edited.

Schnabel was tall, well-built, wore a mustache, and was a good speaker. He went to Detroit and debated a Bolshevik named Shturman. Schnabel was the clear winner, so much so that Shturman was expelled from his group. Whenever Schnabel spoke the hall was full. He was always ready to talk on three subjects: anarchism, Marxism, and religion. He was one of the nicest comrades in the U.S. and a true anarchist. It was his idea that the staffs of Russian anarchist newspapers should all get equal pay, so that the seven men working on *Rabochii i Krest'ianin* and the six on *Amerikanskie Izvestiia* each got twenty-five dollars a week.

Schnabel returned to New York from Detroit in 1918 and remained active in the Union of Russian Workers. He was arrested two weeks before the Palmer raids began and deported on the *Buford* in December 1919, along with Emma Goldman and Alexander Berkman. Also deported with them was the entire editorial board of *Khleb i Volia*: Peter Bianki, the editor, Nikifor [Hyman] Perkus from Cleveland, the two Shatz brothers, and Arthur Katz. Bianki, a Russian of Italian parentage [Bianchi], was a window-washer by trade and was secretary of the Union of Russian Workers in New York. He and Schnabel were the guiding spirits of the organization, but Bianki was tougher and more authoritarian. Once, while at Schnabel's house he swept his cat from the windowsill. Schnabel was furious.

Others who worked on *Khleb i Volia* were Peter Kravchuk, an ordinary workman, who had been secretary of the Union of Russian Workers in Detroit but moved to New York and became secretary of the housewreckers' union. He died in 1919. Markus Oradovsky came to the U.S. from South America and served as a distributor of the paper. Perkus, who was Jewish, was a carpenter and a friend of Emma Goldman and Alexander Berkman. Kushnarev, also Jewish, had organized a branch of the Union of Russian Workers in New Haven, along with K. F. Gordienko. Rose Pesotta was also active there. All three came to New York, where Kushnarev was on the editorial board of *Khleb i Volia* and became secretary of the Union of Russian Workers.

In 1919 a nonparty convention of the Russian colony took place in New York. At this convention *Rabochii i Krest'ianin* was established, with Adolf Schnabel as manager. It served as the organ of the Soviet of Workers' Deputies of the United States and Canada, with headquarters in the Russian People's House. The first editor, Alexander Brailovsky, was dismissed when he tried to make it a Bolshevik paper. Zubovich, a member of the editorial board, was also a Bolshevik. Ivan Okuntsov, an SR with anarchist sympathies, became the new editor. On the board was M. Korneev, an anarchist seaman, and Gordienko, the anarchist from New Haven mentioned earlier, who later edited *Amerikanskie Izvestiia*, *Delo Truda*, and *Probuzhdenie*. He afterwards died in Florida.

Amerikanskie Izvestiia was first edited by Dumashkin, a Bolshevik, but when Gordienko took over it became a good anarchist paper. There were other anarchist papers as well. *Rabochaia Mysl'*, edited by Schnabel, was in close touch with A. A. Karelin in Paris, who contributed most of the articles. *Burevestnik* was a Bakuninist and Kropotkinist journal edited by Victor Bondarenko, a mechanic who now lives in Los Angeles. Only two numbers appeared. Later, in 1922, Bondarenko organized the Souiz Edinykh Anarkhistov [Union of United Anarchists], inspired by the ideas of Volin as expounded in *Anarkhicheskii Vestnik* in Berlin. Maliuta Gromm and I were members. It lasted only a few years, and we sent money to Volin for his paper.

Svobodnoe Obshchestvo was edited by Vasili I. Dodokin in Canada. Dodokin came to Detroit, and then to New York, where he edited *Volna*, organ of the Federation of Anarchist-Communist Groups. Another editor of *Volna* was L. Lipotkin (Lazarev), who had been the last editor of *Khleb i Volia*. He was a Jew in Rochester, New York, nice, friendly, and before 1917 he had been with Volin in Detroit, where Volin was on a lecture tour and debating with social democrats.

Other papers included *Vostochnaia Zaria* and *Pravda*, the latter edited by the brothers Misha and Grisha Raiva, both Jewish and former members of the Union of Russian Workers. There was also *Golos Truzhenika*, an IWW paper edited by Yakov Sanzhur, who later lived in Mohegan, where he died of heart failure. He was a builder by trade, from Siberia, with a good command of English.

Relations between Russians and Jews were friendly till after the 1917 Revolution, when among some of the Russians a note of mysticism, nationalism, and anti-Semitism crept in, with the "Jewish Bolsheviks" seen as betrayers of the revolution. The Rassvet Group of Detroit was an example of this. *Rassvet* was the worst Russian anarchist paper; in fact it was not really anarchist. Its editor, Moravsky, was a mystic and anti-Semite. The first editor had been F. Kraemer, a Russian-German anarchist with Bolshevik leanings. Moravsky also edited *Probuzhdenie*, and in Chicago Grigori Maximoff edited *Delo Truda*. *Delo Truda* and *Probuzhdenie* had different outlooks; *Delo Truda* was anarcho-syndicalist, while *Probuzhdenie* was Moravsky and mysticism. But when Moravsky died they merged as *Delo Truda-Probuzhdenie*. His death made the merger possible.

Detroit had the largest Russian anarchist colony, even larger than the one in New York. Many were automobile workers; in New York they were garment workers, hotel workers, housewreckers, and the like. Detroit at its height had five branches of the Union of Russian Workers. Stotsky, a poet, helped organize ROOVA[536] in Detroit in the mid-1920s. It was then an anarchist group but turned towards Moravsky and his ideas. After the Palmer raids, the Union of Russian Workers was renamed the Union of Russian Toilers, but it soon lost its revolutionary fervor. Many of its members turned to nationalism and the church, and many of its branches became branches of ROOVA, which was also increasingly nationalist and religious.

Most of the Russian anarchists in the United States were peasants from the western and southwestern provinces. They were young, unmarried, and came to America, as I did, to earn money and then go back and buy land and some cows. When the revolution broke out, everybody wanted to go back to share in the new freedom and in the distribution of the land. And many did go, either of their own accord or as deportees, only to be persecuted by the Bolsheviks. Rode-Chervinsky died of illness, after being imprisoned by the Cheka. Bianki joined the Communist Party and was killed as a member of a food-requisitioning squad, trying to get hay and fodder in a village. Schnabel, rumored to have gone to Siberia to manage a factory, disappeared without a trace.

• WANDA SWIEDA •

Woodside, New York, January 11, 1972

Wanda Swieda, a retired librarian and social worker, was active in the anarchist movement in Los Angeles and in New York. Her husband Vasya, a carpenter and draftsman, was an anarchist in Newark and Philadelphia before coming to Stelton and New York, where he and Wanda joined the Libertarian Book Club, of which Vasya was president until his death in 1971. Wanda died at her home in Woodside on October 24, 1987.

MY HUSBAND, Walter ("Vasya") Swieda was born in 1895 in a village in Minsk province, about forty kilometers from Minsk. His real name was Vasili Filippovich Svirida, a Belorussian. At eight he was put to work in the fields. He had a tremendous thirst for knowledge. He went to the local village school and then to agricultural school, which he had to give up for lack of money. He read avidly and wrote and read letters for his mostly illiterate fellow villagers. He loved to sing, dance, and play the balalaika. His Uncle Nikolai, the village blacksmith, was a revolutionist, and his shop served as a radical center. Populists lectured there to the peasants. The revolutionists had a hectograph in his shop, which issued leaflets that Vasya and the other boys left at the doors of the peasant huts. He also read them aloud in the village streets. He had his ears wide open and learned new ideas as well as revolutionary songs, which he loved to sing. With his meager savings he bought books by Tolstoy, Nekrasov, and others.

Vasya emigrated to the United States in the summer of 1914. From New York he went to Newark, where he was one of the founders of the local Soiuz Russkikh Rabochikh [Union of Russian Workers]. He also belonged to the Golos Truda Group, which published *Golos Truda* in New York. He had imbibed anarchism with his mother's milk in his village, where mutual aid and hostility to government were bywords. Among the theorists, he drew his greatest inspiration from Kropotkin and Tolstoy. He was a lifelong anarchist-communist.

During his early years in the United States, Vasya's revolutionary name was "Stalyov." He was arrested during the Palmer raids but not deported. He moved to Philadelphia and then to Willow Grove, living near Chaim Weinberg, his closest friend during the 1920s. He was a member of the Radical Library in Philadelphia and participated in Camp Germinal, along with Weinberg, who was a labor organizer for cigar and cap workers.

Vasya was an expert carpenter, and during the late 1920s he helped the colonists at Stelton (John Scott, for example) build houses. Scott later turned fascist and anti-Semitic. Vasya, by contrast, had absolutely no ethnic prejudice whatsoever. This was unusual among lower-class Russians, and even many anarchists among them had anti-Jewish feelings. Others, however, intermarried with Jews, especially the self-made intellectuals who couldn't find the sort of intellectual and ideological lifemate among the Russian girls that were common among the Jews.

Vasya always believed in education, and especially admired Tolstoy's school at Yasnaia Poliana. He had been involved in the Ferrer School since 1915, the year that it moved to Stelton. Some of the colonists went to Philadelphia to ask about the red clay (shale) in the soil there, and if it could be used to make bricks, but Vasya told them no. He was associated with the school from then until its demise in 1953.

I myself was born in 1898 in the Ukraine of prosperous Austrian parents (my surname was Tiger). German was spoken at home. Father was an engineer, the director of a sugar factory. I rebelled against the oppression of peasants and workers at an early age. In 1923 I married Morris Greenberg, a Jewish anarchist, an ardent follower of Emma Goldman and Alexander Berkman in New York, who had returned to Russia to take part in the revolution.

In 1924 he left Russia and returned to the U.S., settling in Los Angeles, where he became active in the Kropotkin Literary Society. He sent for me the following year. I became acquainted with the anarchists in Los Angeles, and was especially encouraged by Tom Bell, who considered me his pet and hoped that I would do big things in the movement. I was secretary for a time of the Libertarian Society, but I couldn't throw myself into it completely—only with one foot. Bell was old, sick, and unhappy; he lived alone, separated from his wife and children. C. V. Cook, another active member, was large, florid, and bombastic, and wrote resolutions for meetings and conventions. The Jews there were mostly garment workers.

My husband and I drifted apart, though we remained on friendly terms; he died in 1934. In 1929 I came to New York to study for the M.A. at Columbia University, having received the B.A. that year at U.C.L.A. For a while I was the guest of Abe and Anna Winokour at Stelton, where I met Vasya. He too had been married to a Russian-Jewish anarchist (both of us were of gentile background). We got together and remained companions until his death last year.

In New York Vasya worked as a carpenter, as a draftsman for a precision tool company, and as a model maker for the Metropolitan Museum of Art. He made the scale models from which the Cloisters was built, and he also restored antiques for the museum. In the 1940s he worked in the maintenance department of Sears Roebuck. I worked as a librarian and research assistant in the Child Guidance Institute of Teachers College for six years, during the 1930s, then for the New York City Department of Welfare, in day care and child placement, for twenty-five years, until my retirement.

Vasya became president of the Libertarian Book Club in the 1960s and served until his death in 1971. We had a summer home in Stelton for many years. Aunty Ferm was opinionated, self-assured, and thought that whatever she preached was gospel. She was intolerant of differing views. Uncle was much easier to get along with. One day, incidentally, while Vasya was doing carpentry work at the colony, a delivery man asked him if "free love" was practiced there, and Vasya said, "Isn't all true love free?"

During the 1930s I wrote a weekly column, "Semi'ia i Vospitanie" (Family and Education) for the Chicago anarchist journal *Rassvet*. I also wrote for the *Novoe Russkoe Slovo* in New York. The Russian anarchist group in New York, once very numerous and active, became two branches (16 and 25) of ROOVA, the Russian mutual aid society, and is now completely defunct, though ROOVA still has its cooperative farm in New Jersey.

• MORRIS GANBERG •

Bronx, New York, February 2, 1974

Morris (Moyshe) Ganberg became an anarchist during the 1905 Revolution in Russia, as a teenage boy in Bessarabia. Emigrating to the United States in 1910, he resumed his activities in the movement, becoming a friend of Alexander Berkman and joining the Anarchist Red Cross in New York.[537] In 1917 Ganberg returned to Russia to take part in the revolution. With the rise of the Bolshevik dictatorship, however, he returned to the United States and served for many years on the executive board of the *Fraye Arbeter Shtime*. He died in the Bronx of heart failure on May 11, 1979.

I WAS BORN in 1888 in Khotin, Bessarabia, near the Austrian border, and I attended high school there. My father was a wine salesman, an intelligent, freethinking man, who read German as well as Yiddish and got newspapers in these languages. Some of my school friends—Samsonov, Gordenko, the daughter of Malsky the letter carrier—belonged to an anarchist group and invited me to join. My older sister, who lived in Warsaw, was already a member of the Bund. After 1905 she was arrested and banished to Siberia. She afterwards came to America and became an anarchist and then a Bolshevik.

The Khotin anarchist group carried out a few expropriations and was hunted by the police. Most members were arrested and sent to Siberia. Bibi Samsonov, the son of a peasant, escaped and fled to Liverpool, England, where the Anarchist Red Cross sent him money. He later became a Bolshevik and an aide to Stalin. My wife looked him up in 1926 or 1927 when she went to Russia to see her parents. When she told him who she was, he at once helped her to give clothing and other things she had brought to her family.

Twenty miles from Khotin was a peasant village where a family lived named Rybak. Rybak and a group of fellow anarchists smuggled revolutionaries and revolutionary literature back and forth across the Austrian border. It was by that route that many anarchists and Socialist Revolutionaries—Burtsev, "Babushka" Breshkovskaya, Arshinov—passed, with Rybak as their guide. Once he and his comrades were chased by peasants, who thought they were ordinary smugglers or thieves. Rybak was wounded, and he disfigured himself with a knife so that he wouldn't be recognized; then he shot himself. His picture and an article about him are in the anarchist *Al'manakh* edited by Nikolai Rogdaev.[538]

One time in Khotin the police raided my apartment. We kept our revolutionary literature in the cellar, but they didn't find it. Things were getting too hot, with raids and arrests, so in 1909, during the height of the repressions, I left Russia for Argentina. I lived in Buenos Aires about a year, laying track on the railroad. My fellow workers included a group of Russians, among whom was Zhenia Federenko, an excellent mechanic. We became good friends. I told him all about my background, but it was months before he said anything about himself—that he had been a sailor and a revolutionary who had taken part in the *Potemkin* mutiny in 1905.[539] One day he said we ought to leave Buenos Aires and go to North America. He found jobs for us on a freighter, and in May 1910 we arrived in Boston, from where we took a train to New York.

In New York I got a job in a chandelier factory for three dollars a week. Federenko went up to Winnipeg, Canada, where cousins of his got him a job on the railroad. At that time the Russian government had spies all over. Federenko's cousin worked for the local Russian Orthodox priest and mentioned his new guest from New York, Zhenia Federenko. The priest, an agent for the tsarist government, had Federenko's name on his wanted list, and he alerted the authorities. One day a fellow—a detective, as it turned out—came to the railroad site and struck up a conversation with Federenko. Then they had a drink in a saloon. Federenko always carried a pistol, so the detective left his watch on the table, said it was getting late, and left. He returned later to Federenko's room, knocked on the door, and said he had left his watch behind. When Federenko opened the door, he and two other detectives jumped him and put him under arrest.

Federenko refused to say anything except that he was an anarchist. This was reported in the Winnipeg press, and the local Jewish anarchist group saw it and went to the jail to see him. Meanwhile the Russian government was trying to extradite him on the false charge of killing a police officer. The Jewish group asked Federenko whom he knew in New York, and he said only one man knows me there. He gave them the address of Weitzman's restaurant where I used to take him to eat. (I later took "Weitzman" as my pseudonym in the Anarchist Red Cross.)

The group wrote to Alexander Berkman, who came to the restaurant. When I went to eat supper the manager said, "There's a man waiting for you at the table in the back." I and my friend went over and sat down. Berkman, whom I didn't know, asked me if I knew a man named Federenko. My friend poked me under the table, and I said no. Berkman then said that Federenko was in prison in Canada and that the Russian government wanted to extradite him on a murder charge and he needed help. I insisted I knew nothing. Berkman suddenly stood up and said, "I can see that you're afraid to talk. Well, here's my card. Come to see me." And he left.

Bystanders came over and said, "He just came to America, a *griner*, and already he knows Berkman!" They told me who Berkman was, and about his fourteen years in prison, and I said to myself that I must see him. So I went to the address on his card, but there was no name "Berkman" on any box. In the street was a man—a detective—watching the house. He asked me who I was looking for and I said Alexander Berkman. He told me, "Ring this bell." It was the apartment of Becky Edelsohn. I went up and rang the bell. Becky opened the door and I told her who I was. She invited me in and asked me to wait, as Berkman was not at home. A half-hour later he came in, saw me, and gave me a broad smile: "I knew you would come. Good fellow!"

I told Berkman about Federenko and his history. Berkman went to Isaac Hourwich,[540] who got in touch with lawyers in Winnipeg. Berkman arranged a protest meeting in Cooper Union. Vladeck[541] and De Leon[542] were among the speakers. The lawyers in Winnipeg got Federenko out on bail. He immediately went to Vancouver and sailed to London. He wrote to me from there. When I went back to Russia in 1917 I tried to find him. For three years I asked, wherever I was—Moscow, Petrograd, Kiev, Odessa—but he had disappeared without a trace. I never saw him again.

Above everything else, Berkman was a good comrade, a dedicated man (*ibergegebene mensh*). He would do anything for a comrade. He was physically a very strong man. He loved to eat, and he ate and talked with everyone, without airs. Incidentally, I heard Voltairine de Cleyre speak one time in New York. She was rather tall, with brown hair, a beautiful person who left an impression.

The Anarchist Red Cross was founded in 1911, and I was active from the start. The center was in New York, with branches in Detroit, Chicago, Philadelphia, and other cities. We all had *boyernbeler* and *arestantenbeler* [peasant balls and prisoners' balls] and raised large sums of money, which we sent to anarchist prisoners in Russia. At one *arestantenbal*, in a big casino on Fourteenth Street, five or six thousand people came, and we took in a few thousand dollars, all of which we sent to the political prisoners. Sometimes we sent hollowed-out books with false passports and papers to allow the prisoners to escape from Siberia (for example Jacob Mont, who died a few years ago at Mohegan Colony).

The New York branch had about sixty or seventy members and met every week on East Broadway. We particularly needed people who knew Russian to serve on the correspondence committee, of which I was a member until I returned to Russia in 1917. Only the correspondence committee could write to the prisoners, and each member of the committee had ten or twelve prisoners to write to. We pretended to be brothers, sisters, fathers, or mothers, otherwise the Russian government would not deliver the letters and money. The secretary of the committee was Ginsbursky, and we met in his house. Only the members of the committee knew the names of the prisoners, and each only knew his own names. Both Ginsbursky and his wife had themselves escaped from Siberia, where they had been in *katorga* [penal labor]; Ginsbursky shared a cell with Bogrov,[543] the assassin of Stolypin.

The whole thing got started when we heard that socialists were being helped in Russian prisons but that the anarchists got nothing. So we founded our own organization. We also published a paper once a year, called *Di Shtime*, which lasted about four issues, until 1917, half Yiddish and half Russian, like the *Hilf-Ruf*, the organ of the Anarchist Red Cross in London. All the money was sent from the New York center. All the branches agreed to this and sent us whatever they raised—all, that is, except Yelensky [q.v.] in Chicago, who insisted on sending the money himself. We also sent false documents, as I said. Once in Irkutsk they were discovered, and ten or twelve anarchists were tried there. We arranged for lawyers to defend them, but in the midst of the trial the Revolution of 1917 broke out and the case was dissolved.

Quite a few Anarchist Red Cross members—myself, Perkus, Yarchuk, Yelensky—returned to Russia in 1917, and we met many former prisoners. How they embraced us when they found out we were from the Red Cross! They couldn't do enough for us. Yet in New York, with all our hard work, Yanovsky wrote in the *Fraye Arbeter Shtime* that the young boys and girls of the Anarchist Red Cross were gathering money and didn't know how to use it properly. How indignant we were! We challenged him and called him, along with Berkman and Rode-Chervinsky of *Golos Truda*, to the Bronx and showed them our books. Yanovsky wrote an apology in the next issue, then helped us advertise our *boyernbeler*. He was an outstanding journalist, and I once saw him dictate a whole "Oyf der Vakh" [On Watch] column directly to the typesetter, who set it up as he talked.

Whenever I came to the Ferrer Center and Shatoff saw me he would say, "The Red Cross is here!" To tell the truth, though, I didn't care for him. He was from Kiev, like Ginsbursky's wife, and she once told me that he had been an ordinary criminal there, not an anarchist expropriator but for his own personal gain. And he insisted on cooperating with the Bolsheviks even after the raid on *Golos Truda* in Moscow in April 1918, despite our protests.

In 1917 I went up to the *Mother Earth* office on 125th Street. Berkman was there. I remember he had a bad foot, and I told him I'm going to Russia. He said he had something to give me for the Russian comrades, a declaration for Tom Mooney and instructions to the comrades to organize demonstrations to save Mooney. Fitzi (with whom Berkman was then living) typed it up and I came back for it a few days later. Berkman also gave me his *Prison Memoirs of an Anarchist*, which he inscribed to me. But someone later borrowed it from me and I never saw it again.

I went to Russia in May 1917 by the Pacific route via San Francisco. Berkman gave me a letter to Robert Minor, and I stayed with him in San Francisco for three days while waiting for my ship to sail. I told Minor about the declaration, and the next day he took me to visit Mooney and Billings in prison. Minor told Mooney, "This man is going to Russia and will do something there to help free you." Mooney shook the bars and said very loudly, "I hope you Russian people will help me."

Once in Russia, I traveled from Khabarovsk to Moscow and then to Kiev, and gave Berkman's appeal to the Kiev anarchist group. They distributed it to Moscow, Petrograd, and Odessa, and demonstrations were organized, especially at the American embassy in Petrograd. Then I went to Bessarabia to see my parents. From there I went to Odessa, where I remained for nearly three years.

In Odessa there were several anarchist groups. The one I joined, called the Anarkhicheskii Otriad [Anarchist Detachment], was headed by Sholem Schwartzbard, who had been decorated for heroism in the French army during the war. He was a brave man and a first-class marksman, who never wasted a bullet. Our detachment fought against the *Petliurovtsy*, the *Denikintsy*,[544] and other White forces during the Civil War. Once I was almost captured by Denikin's troops and barely managed to escape. Though I spent most of my time in Odessa, I traveled to other places, and in early 1918 spent three months in Moscow working on *Golos Truda* under Alexander Schapiro's supervision. I lived with Raiva and helped get out the paper. I was there during the Bolshevik raid of April 1918, and many of our comrades were wounded or arrested. I also met Abba Gordin in Moscow, but him I didn't like.

When Denikin entered Odessa in January 1920, I hid out for three days, then escaped to the Crimea. In Sevastopol I posed as a wine merchant. Our comrades there got us false passports and smuggled us out on a small cutter after bribing the captain.

When I came back to America I met Robert Minor, who was then a cartoonist for the *World* and still an anarchist. He lived in Provincetown with Mary Heaton Vorse[545] and sent me a ticket to visit them. I stayed for two months in his house. Nearby lived Eugene O'Neill with his wife Agnes. Minor knew them well, and one night he took me there. A storm broke out, so we stayed for dinner and had to spend the night. O'Neill had a big library with many English translations of Russian writers, a whole wall with books. He asked me everything about Russia, Russian society, and Russian literature, which fascinated him, and we talked for hours.

In New York Minor and I went often to the Medved' restaurant on Second Avenue and Thirteenth Street. While we ate he made sketches on the menu. Once he called me and said we must meet; it was important. He said an office manager was needed for a new journal, at $100 a week. "Who's the owner?" I asked. "The Communist Party," he said. "Bob, I will not work for the Bolsheviks," I replied. He left and I didn't see him for a long time. Yet at a memorial meeting for Kropotkin in 1921 he spoke and defended Makhno!

Joseph Cohen was a difficult man. He sat in the *Fraye Arbeter Shtime* office on Canal Street with a cap over his eyes, smoking cigarettes, writing, looking at no one and talking to no one who came into the place to visit. In 1926 or 1927 Shatoff's wife Anna came in. She had been sent by the GPU to ask the paper to stop criticizing the Bolsheviks. I was there. Cohen said, "Nothing doing," and told her to leave.

In Paris my comrade Schwartzbard shot Petliura and was tried and acquitted. In 1937 the French government sent World War I veterans to a convention in New York, and Sholem, who had been decorated for bravery, was among them. He stayed with me for seven months. He published his memoirs here in two volumes in Yiddish, helped by Yelensky and me: *In krig—mit zikh aleyn* (1933) and *In'm loyf fun yorn* (1934). He told me that he had told only one man about his plan to kill Petliura. That was Makhno, who followed Petliura and recorded all his movements for Sholem to plan his attack. Sholem was a watchmaker by profession. He tried to go to Palestine, but the British wouldn't let him in. So he went to South Africa, where he was a salesman for a publishing company and died many years ago.

• MORRIS GREENSHNER •

Miami, Florida, December 19, 1972; January 13, 1985

I first interviewed Morris ("Moshke") Greenshner in 1972, at the suggestion of Sally Genn, secretary of the Libertarian Book Club. Over a delicious lunch, prepared by his wife Becky, he told me of his activities in the Anarchist Red Cross in New York during the First World War and of his return with Becky to his native Russia in 1917 to take part in the revolution. I did not see Moshke again until 1985, when I visited him in a Miami nursing home. By then Becky had died, and Moshke, almost ninety-two, was in frail health. As I entered the garden, unannounced and unexpected, Moshke, seated in a wheelchair, called my name. He had recognized me at once, before I could look around for him, after an interval of a dozen years. He died only a month later, on February 15, 1985.[546]

I WAS BORN on January 18, 1893, in the city of Kamenets-Podol'sk, Russia. My father, Mikhl, was a bookbinder, my mother, Sarah, a housewife. I had three older sisters. It was a beautiful town, with a river, the Smotrich, running through it. It had two theaters, a park, a *gimnaziia* for girls, another for boys, technical schools, and later a university. The population was around forty-five thousand. There were no factories, but handicraftsmen—tailors, shoemakers, and the like—were numerous. I attended elementary school and junior high school. Then I began to work in a transport office, doing paper work for ten rubles a month. I was fifteen years old. But already I belonged to a group. It was called the Podol'skaia-Bessarabskaia Gruppa. When I was fourteen I had attended a meeting of the Poale-Zion, but I didn't like it—I never did like what they had to say. A schoolmate recommended a different group, an anarchist group. It was a small group, maybe fifteen people in all, and I liked it right away. I read anarchist proclamations—no books yet. But it was in my nature. I fell in love with it. I still love it. I still dream. But thanks to the Bolsheviks we lost that dream.

I became quite active in the group, distributing leaflets near the theater, near the schools. That was in 1908. Three years earlier occurred the Revolution of 1905. We had a pogrom in our city. No one was killed, but many were beaten. They beat my father and ruined his lungs. The city was very excited about the revolution. Don Cossacks and soldiers were stationed in our town, the 74th Pekhotnyi Polk [Infantry Regiment]. One member of the anarchist group that I later joined threw a bomb into a store and was caught and sent to Siberia. He later came to America, but by then had left the movement. In Siberia he wore chains on his feet—*katorga* [penal labor].

I left Russia in 1909, when I was sixteen years old. My sister was arrested that year—she was a Socialist Revolutionary—and imprisoned for five or six months before being released for insufficient evidence against her. My father said we should go to America: "Your friend was sent to Siberia. Your sister was arrested." I made my way alone to Belgium, boarded a ship to Montreal. From there I went to Troy and then New York. I stayed with a cousin, Avrom, in Brownsville. His son was a presser and got me a job. So I began to learn the trade.

Avrom took me to a meeting of the Arbeter-Ring [Workmen's Circle]. There I met a friend from Russia, Sidney Blackman, who had belonged to the same anarchist group. Was he glad to see me! He told me to move to Manhattan and join his organization. He found a room for me on First Avenue for five dollars a month. He brought me to a meeting of the Anarchist Red Cross. I became a member. He brought me into the correspondence committee. One man objected—"We don't know who he is." But Sidney backed me up, and they accepted me. I had twenty prisoners with whom I corresponded, all over Russia. I brought Moyshe Ganberg [q.v.] into the group. We had more than a hundred members in the New York branch, including myself, Ganberg, Izzie and Fanny Wishnak, Bill Shatoff, and the Raiva brothers. Every year we had a ball, an *arestantenbal*, and raised a few thousand dollars. We published a small paper, in Russian and Yiddish, the *Shtime*. We sold tickets, collected money, and sent aid to tsarist prisoners. That was from 1910 to 1917. In 1917 we had our last ball, in the Harlem Casino. It was a great success; all the Jewish writers, the Russian intelligentsia, attended. Then came the revolution. The Anarchist Red Cross went out of existence. Many members went back to Russia to help the revolution.

Besides the Anarchist Red Cross, I was also active in the Union of Russian Workers, during approximately the same years. It was primarily an educational organization, with several thousand members. Rode-Chervinsky, a leading member, was of Polish origin, a quiet, pleasant, intelligent man. But he had consumption and died in Russia in the early 1920s. Our group had several hundred members. One of them, Mukhin, went back to Russia and became secretary of the metal workers' union in Petrograd. Shatoff was among the most active speakers.

I met my wife Becky in 1910 at a May First demonstration. We fell in love at first sight. Two years later we got married. Our only child, a son, was still-born, in 1912. Becky and I attended anarchist meetings and lectures: *Mother Earth*, the *Fraye Arbeter Shtime*, the Union of Russian Workers, the Anarchist Red Cross. We went to the annual *boyernbal*, sponsored by the *Fraye Arbeter Shtime*. David Shub[547] came once with a lantern as Diogenes looking for an honest man. We went to the Ferrer Center. Puck Durant's mother used to sell the *Fraye Arbeter Shtime* in the street. We also had a literary anarchist group in New York, which included myself, Ganberg, and a few other Russian and Jewish comrades, and which sold *Burevestnik, Khleb i Volia*, and other European periodicals and sent them money that was essential to their survival. There was also a Yiddish Group "Frayhayt" in Harlem, with Zalman Deanin [q.v.] its most active figure, and a "Broyt un Frayhayt" Group in Brownsville, Brooklyn.

As I said, we went to *Mother Earth* gatherings and to Emma Goldman's lectures. Emma didn't appeal to me. She was too much of an intellectual—she looked down on ordinary workers. But I later changed my mind. I met her in Toronto in the 1930s, after she had been in Russia and Spain (there was a big picture of Durruti on her wall). She had changed. Anyway, I used to attend her lectures; she was a very good speaker. I also heard Alexander Berkman speak a number of times. He was no match for Emma. But he was a first-rate person. He had no airs. It was in our apartment in the Bronx, by the way, that Berkman organized the New York Mooney-Billings Defense Committee. I later met him in Moscow. He was a fine man who made you feel that you were part of him, just like you.

Around April or May of 1917 Becky and I decided to go back to Russia. We went by train to the West Coast, and on the way members of the Anarchist Red Cross and the Union of Russian Workers, from Detroit, Chicago, and other cities, joined us. We had a special train, reserved for us alone. The Provisional Government in Russia paid for it. Shatoff was the main organizer, and he himself took a later train. We had the printing press of *Golos Truda* on board.

The train took us to San Francisco, where we stayed five days and visited Mooney and the McNamara brothers in prison. Then we sailed on a Japanese ship to Honolulu. We stayed there two days, then went on to Yokohama. There we stayed two weeks, took a train to Tsuruga, then sailed on a Russian ship across the Sea of Japan to Vladivostok. In Vladivostok a committee of all radical parties welcomed us. We took a train to Irkutsk, from Irkutsk to Krasnoyarsk, and then to Petrograd. It was the beginning of July when we arrived. There was a terrible shortage of food, and we stayed only ten days. During that time we met Yarchuk and the Kronstadt sailor Zhelezniakov.[548] He was a good boy—an anarchist. I met him later at an anarchist meeting in Odessa. He said he was sorry that he dispersed the Constituent Assembly. He didn't think the Bolsheviks would go as far as they did in smothering civil rights. He was killed at the front in 1919.

From Petrograd Becky and I went to Odessa, a beautiful city on the Black Sea, with wide streets and trees on both sides. There was a special hotel for political immigrants, and we got a room. The first day, near the hotel, I noticed a name on a door—Isaak Golovin. He had been one of my correspondents in *katorga*. Now he was a factory worker in Odessa. I waited for him to come home from work. He invited me in. "I don't remember you," he said. "But I remember you," I replied. I told him that I was "Grisha," my pen name in the Anarchist Red Cross. He embraced me. He couldn't do enough for me. He took me and Becky to his family. My letters had meant everything to him, he told us. They had kept him going.

Golovin got me a job in his factory. I worked on a lathe. The factory had a Red Guard unit, and I became a member. Rumor had it that there would be an officers' rising. We were on watch all night. But nothing happened. It had rained all night, and I was on guard outside. I fell ill. But I returned to work. After a few days I couldn't get out of bed. The doctors said it was a form of polio, an inflammation of the nerves [*vospalenie nervykh*], and that I couldn't go back to work. I was taken to the Jewish Hospital [Evreiskaia Bol'nitsa], a very fine hospital. I was there two months. But they couldn't help me. One of the doctors, a good nerve specialist, told me: "You need two things—time and patience. We can't give you anything here. But if you can go to the Crimea it may help." It was December, just before Christmas. The Crimea was then a battleground between the Whites and the Reds.

One of my prisoners as a correspondent for the Anarchist Red Cross was called Iosif Savitsky. He was now in Moscow and found out that a group of Anarchist Red Cross members were in Odessa. He wanted to find me and thank me for what I had done while he was in prison. He went to Odessa, found our hotel, and Becky took him to see me in the hospital. I was very glad to see him, and he to see me. I told him what the doctor said. "Oh, we'll get you to the Crimea," said Savitsky. "How will you take me?" "You'll see."

Savitsky told anarchist sailors that we needed a boat. They found one for us, and Savitsky, Golovin, Becky, and I sailed for the Crimea. We intended to go to Yalta, but when we reached Evpatoria we ran out of fuel. Sailors took us ashore, got an automobile, and drove us to Simferopol. There we stopped in a hotel. The next day Savitsky went to the soviet and told them my story. They said that Livadia was the best place; it was no longer a tsarist palace but a sanitarium for political prisoners. The next day we went to Livadia. I didn't stay in the palace, which was for consumptives, but in a guest house nearby. I stayed only two weeks. Savitsky was with us all the time. [Moshke shows me a photograph of Savitsky, a young, impressive looking man with a beard, wearing a Cossack-style shirt.] A doctor said it was not for me and sent me to a sanitarium in Yalta. I lay in bed for six months. A few days after I arrived, a man, a patient from Minsk, came into my room. He knew who I was. He had a room with a terrace and invited me to sit there with him. So I did—every day. They all helped me. I was a *rabochii* [worker]! After a while I began to walk. I had no medication, only the sun and good food.

In due course we returned to Odessa and were active in the Odessa anarchist group, supporting the Bolsheviks against the Whites. Savitsky chided us for this. He said (it was 1919), "You are dancing at a strange wedding." And he was right. During the early 1920s the Bolsheviks clamped down on the anarchists, even those who had helped them.

In 1923 Becky and I returned to the United States. But the anarchist movement here was only a shadow of what it had been before. There was the Ferrer Center branch of the Workmen's Circle in the Bronx (founded around 1920 or 1921; it became the Ferrer-Rocker branch after Rudolf Rocker died in 1958); the Amshol branch, also in the Bronx (founded around 1929); the Fraye Gezelshaft branch, once again in the Bronx, which included Wisotsky, Isakovitz, and others. We occasionally attended meetings of the Italian comrades. They were pure, strict, fanatical anarchists, who absolutely refused to associate with anyone who employed hired labor; and they later opposed the Second World War just as vigorously as they had opposed the First. The Amshol group, incidentally, published the speeches of the Haymarket martyrs in Yiddish translation.[549]

We moved from New York to Detroit in 1925 or 1926. I had been in Detroit in 1910, and there was a Yiddish group there then called Anarkhie. A new group had formed in the mid-1920s with about twenty members, called the Fraye Arbeter Shtime Group: Rebecca Warren, Joseph and Lena Smith, Fein, Zubrin, and others. There were also Russian and Italian groups. In New York at this time the anarchists were fighting with the Communists in the ILGWU; Nicholas Kritzman, Joe Schneider, Sima Rothman, Louis Levy, Leibush Frumkin, Mendel Bluestein, and Simon Farber were among the most active.

I never cared much for Stelton, which we visited a few times. In Stelton they all thought that young Abe Bluestein [q.v.] would become a second Bakunin. In Sunrise, Joseph Cohen took whoever had the money. Cohen was a dry person, lacking in warmth. At parties he would sit and read the paper. In later years he came to visit us in Miami when we had our guest house. In 1945–1946

Alexander Schapiro and Isaac Radinowsky were business partners in a firm that sent parcels to Russia.

Anarchism as an ideal is excellent. But the methods we dreamed of years ago—terrorism, revolution—are of no use now. They bring no positive results. Even in Chile, Allende's election[550] is not to my taste. Fifty years ago I would have shouted hurrah, but now I fear another Lenin, another Castro.

• MARK MRATCHNY •

New York City, February 15, 1974

Mark Mratchny was an important figure in the anarchist movement during the Russian Revolution and Civil War. Aside from being a member of the Nabat Confederation in the Ukraine and editor of its newspaper, he established a clandestine press in Siberia and joined Makhno's guerrilla army in Gulyai-Polye. In November 1920, when the Cheka rounded up the leaders of the Nabat Confederation, Mratchny was arrested and sent to prison in Moscow. In February 1921 he was released for one day to attend the funeral of Peter Kropotkin; and in July of that year, after an eleven-day hunger strike, he was allowed to leave Russia for Berlin. Before his departure, he met Alexander Berkman and Emma Goldman, who themselves were about to leave the country. For Goldman, Mratchny was among "my special favorites" of her Russian comrades, owing to his "sparkling vitality, ready wit, and understanding of human frailty."[551]

In Berlin, where he studied psychoanalysis, Mratchny assisted Gregory Maximoff in publishing the anarcho-syndicalist journal *Rabochii Put'* and collaborated with Berkman on the Joint Committee for the Defense of Revolutionists Imprisoned in Russia. In 1927 he emigrated to Canada, and from there to the United States, where he edited the *Fraye Arbeter Shtime* from 1934 to 1940. After that he dropped out of the movement and, as Mark E. Clevans (from his real name, Klavansky), practiced psychoanalysis in fashionable Gramercy Park. It was Alexandra Kropotkin (q.v.), in 1965, who suggested that I interview him, in connection with my research on Russian anarchism. Mratchny, cherishing his privacy, refused. Several years later, however, he had second thoughts, and we arranged to meet for lunch in Oscar's restaurant on Third Avenue. Owing to some mixup, we failed to find each other. After waiting for more than an hour, I telephoned Mratchny's apartment. Mratchny answered and accused me of standing him up. Subconsciously, he said, I was getting even for his refusal to see me in 1965. "Please don't psychoanalyze me," I said. "To prove that your theory's mistaken, I'm coming right over." I went immediately to Mratchny's apartment. He greeted me with a smile, and we spent a few hours in pleasant conversation. I visited him again in 1974 to conduct the interview that follows. Mratchny died of a stroke on March 29, 1975.[552]

I WAS BORN Mark Klavansky in Kovno in 1892. My father had studied for a time in Leipzig and was a shipper of wood from Russia to Germany. I attended *gimnaziia* in Vilna at a time when radical ideas were in the air. Some of my classmates were already socialists and some anarchists. My roommate, Bogin, was a tall, emaciated musician, who later died in New York. One morning, soon after I moved in, I woke up and found a copy of Kropotkin's *Zapiski revoliutsionera* [Memoirs of a Revolutionist] on the table. I started to read and was at once enthralled by it. Bogin, of course, had left it for me. He was connected with an anarchist group in Vilna and soon began taking me to its illegal meetings in the woods outside the city. I became deeply interested in anarchism and read further into anarchist literature. I was quite a reader! I started to read when I was four, and never stopped.

At that time I felt that Kropotkin, though a great man, was too moderate, though I drew closer to his viewpoint later on. I was young, you know, and for romantic youth emotions weigh more heavily than knowledge. We were youngsters and more interested in action than in ideas. One member of the group used to keep a revolver on the table of the restaurant in which we ate. When I asked him why, he said, "In case the police come—I'll shoot them." And, in fact, not long afterwards, he and a few other comrades were surrounded in a house by the police and tried unsuccessfully to shoot their way out, but were captured and sent to Siberia. It was all so romantic, so exciting, you know, to go to the woods, discuss revolutionary ideas, debate with the Bolsheviks.

In 1911 I left Russia illegally and went to Paris to study languages at the Sorbonne. In Paris I continued reading anarchist literature and attended some meetings but wasn't active, though later, in Kharkov, Volin said that he remembered me from Paris. When the war broke out I went back to Russia from Marseilles by boat to Odessa. From Odessa I went to Kharkov, where I gave private lessons in French and one of my star pupils was an aide to the governor. I was arrested, however, for not registering for the army and expelled from Kharkov. I went to Vilna, where my parents were living, and resumed teaching French.

The German army was advancing, so I returned, with my parents, to Kharkov. There, in 1917, I went to an anarchist meeting and met Volin and other comrades, who accepted me at once. One evening a comrade asked me, "Mark, why are you so gloomy?" [a pun on "Mark" and *mrak*—*Mark, pochemu vy tak mrachnyi?*] So I took Mratchny as my pseudonym and began to write under it in *Nabat*, the Kharkov anarchist journal. Volin was the editor, and when he left for Moscow I succeeded him. This was around 1918. And so it happened that I became an editor of an anarchist paper, *malgré moi*. I was teaching, making a living, content, with no strong urge for the limelight, just caught up in the drift of events. In fact, I am quite embarrassed to be talking about myself at such length.

In 1919 Nestor Makhno needed someone to edit his paper, *Put' k Svobode* (The Road to Freedom), and I was sent to Gulyai-Polye to undertake the job. But I spent no more than a week there, since Denikin's army was advancing and we had to leave in a hurry. Makhno was short, thin, and already consumptive. His attitude towards me was friendly and jocular. I stayed in Gulyai-Polye with a Jewish family named Zalkind. I asked Zalkind, "What is Makhno? An anti-Semite or what?" He answered, "Our only prayer is that the *bat'ko* should stay with us." They had only praise for him. He was in no way at all a *pogromshchik*. He was always indignant when he heard the charge, and he fought against it fiercely. After all, he was the man who killed Grigoriev, a notorious *pogrom-shchik*. I started to prepare an issue of the paper, but it wasn't printed, as we had to move on. I saw no communes or other social experiments while I was there. There was a war going on—what kind of communes! For me the *makhnovshchina* was not an anarchist revolution. It had no theoretical content. It was rather a rebellion, a *bunt* [spontaneous rising] pure and simple.

I returned to Kharkov and resumed editing *Nabat*. The Nabat Confederation had perhaps fifteen or twenty activists in Kharkov, as well as branches in Odessa and one or two other southern cities. Aaron Baron was in Odessa and helped get out the *Odesskii Nabat*. He came to Kharkov and joined our group. He was a short fellow, quite intelligent, and we had a friendly relationship. Ivan Kabas-Tarasiuk was also active in our group. But Volin was the key man, a fluent speaker and very knowledgeable. I liked him, but at the same time I felt a certain shallowness in him. He spoke and wrote easily, but always on the surface and without real substance. We Litvaks, you see, are skeptics.

I went for a few months to Ekaterinburg in the Urals with the intention of starting a *Nabat* there, but it never got off the ground. I was there about three months, and also in Omsk for a short while, earning a living as a teacher. Once I went to Moscow. There was a small group of militants there who planned to throw a bomb into the Communist headquarters on Leontievskii Pereulok.[553] They included Sobolev, and Lev Chorny was their theoretician. They invited me to join them, but I decided not to. They were disappointed in me and called me an "armchair anarchist" (*kabinet-anarkhist*), but we parted on friendly terms. After the bombing, it became very dangerous to stay in Moscow, so I left and returned to Kharkov.

In Moscow, Kharkov, and other places, I met Maximoff, Yarchuk, Yelensky [q.v.], and many others. In 1920 the Bolsheviks launched a series of raids against us. Volin and Maximoff were arrested in Moscow and I and a dozen others in Kharkov. I was considered a particularly dangerous anarchist—editor of *Nabat*, a *makhnovets*, and so on. I was sent first to Lubianka, the Cheka headquarters and the worst prison in Moscow, where I shared a cell for several months with David Kogan (*Khristosik*, "Little Jesus"). He, I, and a few others were released for a few hours to attend Kropotkin's funeral. It was a cold, clear day [February 13, 1921]. I was asked by some comrades to stay with them overnight, but I had promised to go back to prison and I did.

While in Lubianka I expected to be shot. You see, the movement had to be punished, and as editor of *Nabat* and an active member of the Nabat Confederation I was a likely target. But to my surprise I was transferred to Butyrki, then to Lefortovo (where I met Boris Nicolaevsky),[554] then back to Lubianka, and finally to Taganka. That was where we staged our hunger strike, ten days with no water, no food, nothing. That was during the Profintern Congress, so Trotsky decided to deport us. Ironically, he showed Stalin the way and was himself to become a victim.

Maximoff and Volin were in our group. Maximoff was educated, intelligent, and a gentleman in every way. He knew only Russian. He was a true believer. Anarchism was an essential part of his life. Volin was a different type: a former SR, a Jew, more cosmopolitan in roots and outlook, knew languages, and not as deep or serious as Maximoff about his anarchism.

In January 1922 we were deported. In Stettin we were arrested and detained for a few days, but then allowed to go on to Berlin. Once there, I adhered to the anarcho-syndicalist group, which included Maximoff and Schapiro and published *Rabochii Put'* and was active in the new International Working Men's Association (Berlin International). Volin and his group (including Fleshin) published *Anarkhicheskii Vestnik*, based on the notion of *edinyi anarkhizm* (united anarchism), which rejected anarcho-syndicalism as too narrow; they did not take part in the Berlin International but did not oppose it either.

I had met Alexander Berkman and Emma Goldman briefly in Moscow, and we now renewed our acquaintance. Berkman was a strong fellow. I worked with him on the Relief Fund for anarchist and revolutionary prisoners and wrote most of the Russian articles for its bulletin, which Berkman translated into English. In the International we worked closely with Rudolf Rocker, Augustin Souchy, Fritz Kater, and others.

I had already been interested in the psychoanalytic movement, and once in Berlin I plunged deeply into studying it and went through analysis for several years, working in a bookshop for a livelihood. I remained interested in anarchism, and what I spoke and wrote I meant, but it was not at the center of my being, as with Maximoff or Berkman. I was always a Litvak, always something of a skeptic. I saw Makhno once at Rocker's place, and he wanted to quarrel with me because I had criticized his movement in *Rabochii Put'*.

I came to Canada in 1927 and spent about a year in Windsor, teaching in a Workmen's Circle school. Then I smuggled myself into "God's country" for a summer and worked as a laborer in Brooklyn. When I returned to Canada I was sent to Detroit—that was in 1928—again to teach in a Workmen's Circle school. There I met Carl Nold[555] —already old and disillusioned—and Agnes Inglis, whom I sent material for the Labadie Collection. Beginning in 1928 I also became a steady writer for the *Fraye Arbeter Shtime*. At the beginning of the 1930s I went to Los Angeles and taught for a while in a Workmen's Circle school. Then, in 1934, I got an invitation to edit the *Fraye Arbeter Shtime*, which I did until after the defeat of the Spanish Revolution, which was a crushing disappointment to me. I had also become disappointed with my work. I felt like a rabbi in an empty synagogue. So I resigned from the *Fraye Arbeter Shtime* and from the anarchist movement.

Anarchism is a nice dream—but a dream nevertheless. There is no chance that it will be realized. It has no future, except as an ideal. Yet it was not so easy for me to give it up. The best thing about the *Fraye Arbeter Shtime* was that they paid me so little that it wasn't so hard to resign. Anarchism is good only in connection with other things. As in medicine, it is a necessary ingredient to make something work. It is good when mixed with something else—education, for example, or the labor movement, or even politics. Anarchism is essentially an ethical ideal, but in practice ethics usually goes out the window. If the anarchists had won in Spain, then Durruti or somebody like him would have become the leader. Power corrupts—even the anarchists.

• JOHANNA BOETZ •

New York City, December 4, 1972

Johanna Boetz, a native of Germany, was a social worker in New York City and the wife for many years of Mark Mratchny (q.v.), a well-known anarchist who took part in the Russian Revolution and Civil War. In Berlin during the 1920s, Mratchny was associated with Emma Goldman, Alexander Berkman, and Rudolf Rocker, and he later edited the *Fraye Arbeter Shtime* in New York. Johanna, as Mratchny's companion, was well-acquainted with these celebrated figures, as well as with many other anarchists in Germany and the United States, including Augustin Souchy, Agnes Inglis, and Carl Nold.

I AM SEVENTY years old, born in Hesse, Germany, in 1902. I met Mark Mratchny [q.v.] in 1922 after he had left Russia and come to Berlin. I gave him German lessons. I was then a young reformer (not Jewish) with a special interest in education, and I wanted to write an article about Francisco Ferrer, so Mark introduced me—it was in 1924—to Rudolf Rocker, who knew a great deal about him. Milly and I fell sort of in love. I enjoyed being with them, and often went to Augustin Souchy's place, where I met Alexander Berkman and Emma Goldman. I do not have a favorable memory of Emma: she always used people—to type her letters, to mend her clothes, etc.—and she didn't live badly either.

Mark and I came to the United States, first to New York, and then to Detroit, where we spent four years (from 1928 to 1932) and where Mark was a teacher in the Workmen's Circle school. He revived and mastered his Yiddish, and so was able to become editor of the *Fraye Arbeter Shtime* in the mid-thirties. Rocker lectured in Detroit in 1928, the year that we arrived, and all the *khasidim* gathered around the *rebbe*.

By then there were just a few German anarchists left in Detroit, and some of those, like Dr. [Urban] Hartung, were anti-Semitic. We met Carl Nold, a Swabian, a small man with a wonderful sense of humor. There was no real movement left, and Carl spent a good deal of time and energy collecting materials in German for the Labadie Collection. Nold was a tool and dye maker by trade and designed and built his own house. We also met Agnes Inglis at that time—a marvelous woman. The anarchist movement there was on its last legs. There was a Jewish group attached to the *Fraye Arbeter Shtime* (it was a branch of the Workmen's Circle), of which Abe Zubrin was an active member, and also some Italians and Russians. It was Carlschen, dear Carolus, who took us to Agnes, and we became warm friends. Later, when Mark was editor of the *Fraye Arbeter Shtime*, we sent her much material about Spain in the Civil War.

In 1932 we moved to Los Angeles, where Mark again taught at an Arbeter-Ring [Workmen's Circle] school, and stayed there till 1934, when we moved to New York. Alfred Sanftleben, a Slovak, already old, shrunken, underweight, worked as a carpenter, mending old furniture for Good Will Industries. He lived alone, very frugally, and loved cats, a gentle, kindly man. He died around 1956, and his papers came to Rudolf Rocker, who asked me to go through them. I gave some, including a card and photo from Martin Buber, to the manuscript division of the New York Public Library. They showed the essential loneliness of the man, and his essential shallowness. Stephanus ("Steve") Fabijanovic was a Yugoslav pastry baker in Los Angeles, previously in London, charming and friendly but a little cracked. We also met Tom Bell, at a picnic.

Joseph Cohen looked like an old bird of prey: hawk nose, hunched shoulders, glasses, tall, owlish look. You could almost feel the wings. He and Mark didn't get along, and he didn't get along with Rocker. Rudolf had what you would call *neshome*—soul. He was a genuine person, but he had a temper and constant meetings exhausted him. Without Milly he could not have held out. She was his support. They were very closely interwoven.

• LEON SHAPIRO •

New York City, January 25, 1983

Leon Shapiro, a Menshevik, studied law at the University of Kiev, from which he graduated in 1924. He was arrested by the Bolsheviks, but the wife of Maxim Gorky intervened and he was allowed to leave the country. In Paris he met such anarchists as Nestor Makhno, Alexander Schapiro, and Sholem Schwartzbard. Emigrating to the United States in 1941, Shapiro taught Russian and Jewish history at Rutgers University until his retirement in the 1970s. He died in New York in 1984 at the age of seventy-nine.

I WAS BORN in Kiev in 1905. My father worked in the sugar industry and we lived in a comfortable household. We spoke Russian at home, but Father knew Hebrew and Yiddish. I knew only Russian and Ukrainian then, but later learned Yiddish and Hebrew perfectly. I had an older brother and sister who remained in Russia after the revolution. I was the only one who left. I attended *gimnaziia* in Kiev. The revolution came when I was twelve years old. I was a capable young man, and I passed the examinations for Kiev University at the age of fifteen. I studied social science and law and graduated in 1924.

It was at the university that I became a Menshevik, although at first I was not aware of it. What I wanted was free soviets, democratic soviets. I knew I was a socialist. I found *diamat* [dialectical materialism] and the Komsomol [Communist Youth League] highly distasteful. Some of our best professors were executed by the Bolsheviks—as "saboteurs." We started to protest. A few of the teachers and older students were Mensheviks. It became clear to me that I was one of them. I was not against the revolution itself but what was happening to it. Because of the protests I was arrested (in 1924) and spent a year and a half in Siberia, charged with being an "English spy" and sabotaging railroads and telephone lines. Before being sent to Siberia I spent a few weeks in Butyrki and Taganka, where two anarchists—not Jewish but fine men—organized a hunger strike.

Peshkova, Gorky's wife, intervened, and they threw me and my comrades out of Russia. We ended up in Palestine. There I organized a group of young Mensheviks. The director of Histadrut's medical institute was Victor Mandelberg, a Social Democrat in the First Duma, and Abraham Benadir edited *Vozrozhdenie*, organ of SERP [Jewish Socialist Workers' Party]. I met them. They were older and had gone through many disappointments. I was still a revolutionary. We ran a candidate for the Tel Aviv city council and made speeches to the workers in Russian.

I was in Palestine over a year. From there I went to France and attended the University of Toulouse, graduating in law. It was a beautiful city with a beautiful university. I graduated in 1929 and went to Paris, where there was an active Menshevik group with a library on the Avenue de Gobelin. Tsereteli was there, and Peskin, Ivan Lodyzhensky and his family, Chkheidze, Zhordania, and so on. In the 1930s Dan, Abramovitch, Yugow, Nicolaevsky, and others came from Berlin and joined us—an extraordinary group of men!

We had a political Red Cross in Paris, sponsored by the whole liberal and socialist emigration, from Miliukov[556] to the SRs and Mensheviks. It was through this group that I met Makhno. That was in about 1930. I asked him about the responsibility of his army for pogroms. He said that there were such atrocities but that he did what he could to prevent them. I was convinced that he was telling the truth. *Makhnovtsy* took part in pogroms—of that there is no doubt. But he personally did not. After all, he was accepted by the Red Cross as a candidate for assistance. He did not drink or smoke, as he suffered from tuberculosis.

I also met Alexander Schapiro and Sholem Schwartzbard. Schapiro had a good job with the Hebrew Immigrant Aid Society. When the Germans came, I went to Toulouse, then through Spain to Portugal. There, in Lisbon, I renewed my acquaintance with Schapiro. He was there with his wife, who was a bacteriologist by profession, very beautiful, who later worked in Mount Sinai

Hospital in New York. Schapiro did not want to go to America, since he feared filling out the questionnaire asking if he was an anarchist. But eventually he did go. I had the impression when he was here that he never felt quite secure, and that his anarchism was a thing of the past. He operated a parcel service to Russia on Forty-Second Street, together with a Menshevik friend of mine.

• BORIS YELENSKY •

Brooklyn, New York, August 19, 1971; August 12, 1972
Miami Beach, Florida, December 21, 1972

I first met Boris Yelensky in 1963 at the offices of the *Fraye Arbeter Shtime* on Union Square. I was seeking information on the history of Russian anarchism, in which Yelensky himself had played a part. At first, to my dismay, he seemed unfriendly, resenting my nonpartisan approach to the study of a movement to which he had dedicated his life. Born with boxing gloves on, as Sam Dolgoff (q.v.) described him, Yelensky was unbending, at times belligerent, in defense of his ideal, of which he refused to countenance the slightest criticism. Before long, however, we became good friends, and I interviewed him on several occasions.

Born in southern Russia in 1889, Yelensky at sixteen joined a small group of SR Maximalists (see interview with Clara Halpern) and fought in the 1905 Revolution. In the reaction that followed he fled to the United States, becoming a member of the Radical Library in Philadelphia. At the same time, he joined the Union of Russian Workers and, together with Joseph Cohen and Morris Beresin (q.v.), organized a branch of the Anarchist Red Cross. In 1917 Yelensky went back to Russia to take part in the unfolding revolution, an episode he later described in an interesting memoir.[557] With the rise of the Bolshevik dictatorship, however, he returned to the United States and settled in Chicago, where he became secretary of both the Free Society Group and the Alexander Berkman Aid Fund.[558] Yelensky, in addition, contributed to a broad range of anarchist and labor publications, including *Golos Truzhenika, Delo Truda-Probuzhdenie,* the *Fraye Arbeter Shtime, Dos Fraye Vort,* the *Industrial Worker, Freedom,* and *The Match!* He died of cancer in Miami Beach on June 18, 1974.[559]

I WAS BORN on February 17, 1889, in Ekaterinodar, now Krasnodar, in southern Russia, the son of a cap maker. When I was five years old we moved to Novorossiisk. At the age of twelve I began to read revolutionary literature. During the Revolution of 1905 I became an SR Maximalist and took part in the Novorossiisk Soviet. During the reaction that followed, in 1907, I emigrated to the United States and settled in Philadelphia. There I was drawn to anarchism by its antiauthoritarianism and beautiful ideal. I became an anarchist in 1909 or 1910, joining the Radical Library, a branch of the Workmen's Circle with about 150 members, including Mendel Bluestein, Bernard Shane, Sam Rothman, and Simon Farber, all of whom were later active in the ILGWU. I heard Voltairine de Cleyre speak and was deeply impressed. Some kind of glow came from her. But the main influences on me were Joseph Cohen and Saul Yanovsky.

Cohen was a builder, like Ibsen's "Master Builder," the initiator of many important projects. He was an organizer of great ability, though privately he could pick and choose his friends, ignore you, and this aroused bitterness. Yanovsky, who used to stay with us when he came to lecture in Chicago, had a sharp eye and wit, which opened up many things for me. His *Fraye Arbeter Shtime* column, "Oyf der Vakh," was outstanding.

While a member of the Radical Library, I read John Henry Mackay and thought my own ego was more important than anything else. I was working as a paperhanger, and when a local of the paperhangers' union was organized, I refused at first to join because I considered it an organization that would impose itself on me. But Cohen came and talked to me about mutual aid, cooperation, solidarity, and persuaded me to join. Now I believe that the only way for humanity to come out of its dead end, to avoid being dominated and pushed around or to live according to somebody else's taste, is to create a free society, or anarchism.

In Philadelphia I helped organize the Anarchist Red Cross with Morris Beresin [q.v.]. In 1913 I left Philadelphia for Chicago, where another Anarchist Red Cross branch had been formed. I became its secretary in 1917. In July of that year I returned to Russia to take part in the revolution. I traveled by the Pacific route on the same boat as Volin, Bill Shatoff, and John Reed. Many of the Russian anarchists were returnees from the United States, including Louise Berger, who had been involved in the Lexington Avenue explosion of 1914, when a group of anarchists made bombs to be used against Rockefeller. Isidore Wisotsky was involved too but was blown out by the force of the explosion. Back in Russia Louise took part with *naletchiki* [armed robbers] in carrying out "expropriations" in Odessa. She had been Senya Fleshin's girlfriend for a while.

I went back to Novorossiisk and took part in establishing workers' control in the factories. I also served as a courier for Tsentropechat', the government publishing agency, though I remained a loyal anarchist. But in 1923, after the Bolsheviks consolidated their dictatorship, I came back to the United States and to Chicago. There I helped organize the Free Society Group, which lasted until 1957. There had been an earlier Free Society Group in Chicago, formed at the beginning of the century. Its members included the Isaak family, Jake and Annie Livshis, Joseph Goldman, and Isaac Blum. Our group, which had about eighty members at its height, took its name from this one, but the membership was not the same. One of the members, Jack Denenberg, was hiding from the police. His real name was Jack Isaacson, and after the Lexington Avenue explosion he had gone underground to Canada, and then returned to the U.S. using his wife Gussie Denenberg's [q.v.] surname and settled with her in

Chicago. They were both active in the Free Society Group, where he gave good lectures and took part in all other activities until the mid-1920s, when they moved to Washington, D.C.

I also helped organize a Committee to Aid Political Prisoners, which was renamed the Alexander Berkman Aid Fund after Berkman's death in 1936. We published *In the Struggle for Equality* and helped publish Maximoff's *The Guillotine at Work*, his *Constructive Anarchism*, and his anthology of Bakunin, as well as pamphlets by Emma Goldman, Voltairine de Cleyre, and others. In addition to this, we helped arrange the fiftieth anniversary memorial to the Chicago Martyrs in Waldheim Cemetery in 1937, and we raised money and other assistance for Spain. Our comrade Maximiliano Olay was the "ambassador" of the Spanish anarchists in the U.S.

I am a *edinyi anarkhist* [united anarchist], like Volin, with the aim of uniting the anarchist movement, for I believe that differences among various kinds of anarchists are not insuperable. Many of our younger anarchists left the movement because they became economically successful: Jack White became a union official, Louis Genin [q.v.] a plumber, David Koven [q.v.] an electrician, Sidney Solomon [q.v.] a book designer, Abe Bluestein [q.v.] a co-op manager, David Wieck a professor, and so on. For them anarchism was a temporary thing, a phase of their youth. As for me, I'll remain an anarchist to the end.

• MARCELINO GARCÍA •

Palmerton, Pennsylvania, December 18, 1971

An immigrant from Spain as a boy, Marcelino García worked at a variety of hard jobs before settling in New York and meeting Pedro Esteve (1866–1925), editor of *Cultura Obrera* and the foremost Spanish anarchist in America. After Esteve's death, García emerged as a leading figure within the Cultura Obrera Group. For more than two decades he edited *Cultura Proletaria*, which succeeded *Cultura Obrera* as the principal Spanish anarchist journal in America. He was also a popular speaker at anarchist picnics and meetings, with his lilting voice and jet black hair and flowing mustache. During the 1920s and 1930s, García was active in the campaign to save Sacco and Vanzetti, in the Solidaridad Internacional Antifascista, and in other libertarian causes. In 1937 he spent several weeks in Spain (where he met Emma Goldman) and provided an eyewitness description of the social revolution for the readers of *Cultura Proletaria*. With the victory of General Franco, however, and the outbreak of world war, the Spanish anarchist movement in America entered a period of decline from which it never recovered. In 1952 *Cultura Proletaria* suspended publication. A few years later García's companion Gloria developed a blood clot which left her paralyzed. Moving to a small house in Palmerton, Pennsylvania, García nursed her until her death after five years of suffering. Tragedy struck again in 1975 when his son, who lived with him in Palmerton, was killed in an accident. On April 1, 1977, Marcelino himself passed away in his eighty-fourth year, bringing to an end his long and active career as a libertarian socialist.[560]

I WAS BORN in 1893 in San Martín (Oviedo) in the Asturias region of northern Spain, where all the rebels come from. My father was a socialist. We came to the U.S. twice, the first time illegally when I was thirteen, then again soon after. At fifteen I was a zinc worker in West Virginia. Our family moved a lot; we were like gypsies. I worked on the docks, stoked coal furnaces, and was an elevator operator in New York. My favorite places are the town where I was born and New York. All I learned was in New York.

When did I become an anarchist? As far as I am concerned I was born an anarchist. It was in my nature, my emotions. I didn't have to read about it; it was within me. At seven or eight years old I already had great admiration for the anarchists. I saw in them men who were willing to fight for the poor. Angiolillo,[561] for example. He once came to my town. He was my angel! At the time I thought anarchism was a secret society. What kind of anarchist am I? A simple anarchist. The Italians say they are individualists, but they are as collectivist as you or I. A syndicalist? No. A more precise term for anarchist would be libertarian socialist. That should be the name.

The greatest influence in my life was Pedro Esteve. Look at his picture and you will see why. He was a great moral influence. I got to know him well only during the last few months of his life, though we had met several times previously and I had read his journal *Cultura Obrera*. He was the outstanding leader of the Spanish anarchists in America, an educated man who could speak in simple terms. He devoted his life to educate peasants like me.

Esteve had a serious, calm, dignified demeanor. Catalans are composed people. But he had a sense of humor. Only once did I see him blow his top, and then he was like a tiger. He spoke English and also Italian—his wife Maria was Italian. He was born in Barcelona in 1866. He planned to study medicine, but when he was fourteen his father died and he had to go to work. He became a printer, a typesetter. In 1891 he met Errico Malatesta at a convention in Milan, and also the woman he was later to marry. During 1892 he toured Spain with Malatesta until the Jerez uprising. Malatesta fled to Portugal and then England. Esteve went into hiding and the same year made his way to the United States.

Starting in late 1892 Esteve edited *El Despertar*, an anarchist journal in Paterson. Around 1895 he went to Tampa, where Spaniards from Cuba worked as cigar makers. There was a stipulation in their contract that they be read to while working. Esteve sat on a high stool and read them anarchist literature. He also published a small anarchist paper in Ybor City, next to Tampa. Esteve was warned by a socialist friend that vigilantes were out to hang him, so he hid in his friend's house for three days, shaved his beard and mustache, and returned to New York.

Esteve began publishing *Cultura Obrera* in 1911 or 1912. He wrote for the paper, set up the type, and did other tasks. He also became the secretary of the IWW in New York, in order to serve the many Spanish sailors and dock workers in the city, who needed an organization that was open to them. He was paid ten dollars a month. But he was soon disturbed by the authoritarianism of the IWW and, not wanting to make a public issue of it, quietly resigned.

Esteve, like Malatesta, was an internationalist, and he opposed America's entry into the war. As a result, *Cultura Obrera* was shut down and Esteve, together with Frank González, was arrested. The two men were questioned separately, but González could hear Esteve's answers; he spoke intelligently, knew his rights, and was unmoved by threats of deportation. "But you have eight children," they said. "They are all Americans," he replied. And he refused to stop propagandizing. "Then you won't publish any more," they said. There was no rule of law in those days.

But Esteve was not deported. After four hours in jail he was released, with a twenty-four-hour guard placed at his house. He was out of work, but a Russian anarchist on Fourteenth Street gave him a job and persuaded him to cut off his beard and mustache again. In 1921 *Cultura Obrera* resumed publication. Esteve remained the editor until his death in September 1925, at the age of fifty-nine, about six weeks after he delivered a speech at Stelton (here is a picture). His oldest son was an anarchist, but he died. The others are still alive but aren't interested.

Spaniards like Esteve began coming to the United States in large numbers during the 1890s. Many settled in port cities, like New York, Boston, and Baltimore, and worked as sailors and dock workers. Spanish seamen were masters of the Port of New York. Over the years many moved inland to the mines and factories of West Virginia, Pennsylvania, and Ohio, and took up their former occupations. They were an important element in steel, mining, and metallurgy, as well as in cigarmaking. Of course not all Spaniards were anarchists, but even those who were not tended to be sympathizers. Spanish workers are by nature anarchists; Spaniards joined no other radical groups in any numbers in the U.S.

At the height of the movement, during the 1920s and 1930s, there were about 2,500 active Spanish anarchists in the United States, as well as about 2,000 sympathizers. The top circulation of *Cultura Proletaria*, which I edited from the 1930s till it closed in 1952, was 4,000. But we were largely isolated. We had little contact with other anarchist groups, the biggest mistake we ever made in this country. We engaged mainly in propaganda—journals, lectures— and little participation in strikes. We were a small minority wherever we were.

In Spain itself the situation was different. Spain, in fact, was the only nation in the whole world where anarchism was truly a mass movement. I myself went to Spain during the Civil War and met Emma Goldman there. When I returned I wrote about Spain in *Cultura Proletaria* and made speeches to raise money for our comrades. I had done the same a decade earlier in behalf of Sacco and Vanzetti. The movement in Spain has been suppressed, but it will rise again in three or four years. The doors are opening.

In America the movement is dead. Many comrades have died, and after the Second World War many moved to California. They too are dying out. And the younger generation is not interested.

• SIRIO ESTEVE •

Asbury Park, New Jersey, March 28, 1973

Sirio Esteve, a tall, gaunt man with a neatly trimmed white beard, was one of eight children of Maria Roda and Pedro Esteve, the leading Spanish anarchist in the United States. A few days after the interview, Sirio wrote to me of his father's "idealism, his kindness, and his firmness."[562] Sirio, a retired music teacher, and his wife Eugenia, the daughter of an Italian anarchist in South America, lived in Asbury Park, New Jersey, where he died in 1974.

I WAS BORN in Paterson in 1902 and taught music in Weehawken for twenty-seven years. My father, Pedro Esteve, was born in Barcelona in 1866 and came to New York and Paterson (via Paris and Cuba) in the early 1890s. A few years later he went to Tampa, but came back to Paterson, and then went to Tampa again. Around 1911 he was forced to flee Tampa during labor disturbances there. Vigilantes broke up his printing shop, where he had been editing an anarchist paper, and beat a worker with a big belt from the linotype machine. In New York he spoke at IWW rallies during a seamen's strike and had a printing shop on West Street (where he published *Cultura Obrera*) while living in Weehawken. Mother was Italian, and Father spoke Italian fluently. Over the years he was active in two important Spanish anarchist labor groups: the Tampa cigarmakers and the New York seamen.

Father had regular Sunday gatherings at our house in Weehawken, at 611 Gregory Avenue. The comrades were mostly anarchist and IWW seamen. He was the embodiment of his beliefs, idealistic and gentle. He spoke of Kropotkin more than any other anarchist writer. Mother preferred Stirner and had a mystical streak, later turning to Rosicrucianism. I too consider myself an anarchist, with a mystical streak like Mother's. Random House will soon publish my first book, *The Jesus Experience*.[563]

• JOSÉ HERNÁNDEZ •

New York City, April 5, 1977

Although no longer active in the movement, José Hernández was one of the few Spanish-speaking anarchists remaining in New York in the 1970s, when I interviewed him on the Lower East Side, where he lived. I was introduced to him by Sam Dolgoff (q.v.), his comrade and fellow house painter, who had maintained close contact with the Spanish groups since the 1930s.

I WAS BORN in northern Mexico, near the border at Laredo, Texas, in 1896. In 1919 or 1920 a friend sent me a copy of *Regeneración*, the paper of Ricardo Flores Magón. I liked what it said and began to read it regularly. By the time I came to the United States, in 1921, I was an anarchist. First I worked as a miner for five years, in Scranton and then Wilkes-Barre, Pennsylvania. Then I moved to New York City and became a house painter, a trade that I kept until I retired.

I was an active member of the Cultura Proletaria Group from its formation in 1927. We had a hall on East Twenty-Third Street, El Centro Internacional. Marcelino García [q.v.], then a carpenter, edited our paper, *Cultura Proletaria*. He was also a good speaker. When we had to mail out the paper each week, we all got together in the Center. There was a long table, and we all wrapped and addressed the paper and mailed it the same day. To raise money for the hall and the paper we also had a monthly supper in the Center. The group had about twenty-five or thirty active members, but many more were anarchist sympathizers or readers of the paper. In 1937 Marcelino went to Spain for a few weeks and wrote about it in *Cultura Proletaria*.

Many of the comrades have died, and others have moved to Florida or California, and a few to Mexico and Europe. They were miners, tobacco workers, seamen, house painters, and steel and construction workers by occupation. The movement here is now dead and has little future. But it has a big future in Spain.

• LOUIS G. RAYMOND •

Stelton, New Jersey, December 5, 1971; December 14, 1989

Louis G. Raymond, whose real name was Manuel Rey y García, was born in Spain in 1888 and came to the United States in 1910 as a seaman on a freighter. Settling in New York, where he worked as a house painter, he became an anarchist and a member of the Industrial Workers of the World. In 1917 Raymond was arrested for opposing the war and was a defendant the following year in the notorious trial of the 101 Wobblies in Chicago. After five years in Leavenworth prison, he was deported to Spain. Returning clandestinely to the United States, he was deported a second time, only to reenter again. Adopting the name of Louis G. Raymond ("G" for García and "Raymond" for Rey), he found sanctuary in the Stelton Colony, where he lived for more than fifty years with his companion Lilly Sarnoff, who had visited him when he was at Leavenworth.

A writer as well as a manual laborer, Raymond published poems and articles in anarchist and IWW journals, including *Cultura Proletaria, One Big Union Monthly, The Road to Freedom, Man!*, and *Freedom* (New York, 1933–1934), of which he was coeditor with Harry Kelly and Moritz Jagendorf (q.v.). Raymond, the last anarchist in Stelton (Lilly and their daughter Louisa Vansa, named after Louise Michel and Sacco and Vanzetti, died in the early 1980s), remained there almost to the end. In February 1990, at the age of 101, he fell ill with pneumonia and was taken to the Workmen's Circle Home in the Bronx. When his condition worsened, he was transferred to Jacobi Hospital, where he died on March 28, 1990.[564]

I WAS BORN on October 26, 1888, in Castrofoya, a village in Galicia, Spain, on the river Miño. My father, José Rey, died in the Cuban Revolution; someone shot him down. My mother's name was Javiera García. Both were *campesinos*. It was a small village and life was hard, but there were holiday celebrations and fiestas. The schools in Spain were all religious. "Feed the hungry, give shelter to the poor"—I believed in that, but the church never practiced it. The priest had fancy glasses and drank expensive wine.

I left Spain as a youth as a seaman on a freighter. I lived in Buenos Aires, Montevideo, and Rio de Janeiro. I went back to Spain in the crew of a ship, then traveled through Europe—Holland, Scandinavia, Germany, France. I can speak several languages, including French and Italian and some German. I learned Esperanto in no time.

I came to the United States in 1910 as quartermaster on a freighter. I was an anarchist and a Wobbly. I have always been opposed to terrorism, yet I can understand how desperate and courageous men can be driven to such acts by the cruelty of men who hold power. Around 1912 I tried to dissuade a comrade from going back to Spain to assassinate Canalejas,[565] but in vain. And in Buenos Aires I had known Kurt Wilckens, an anarchist and Wobbly like myself, who later shot a brutal police officer who had forced his prisoners to dig their own graves. "I killed Colonel Varela," he said, "because he was not a man but a beast."

During the First World War I was arrested as a radical and spent six years in Leavenworth prison before being deported to Spain. Although I was a Wobbly, I was never a syndicalist. Syndicalism is not true anarchism but has a built-in hierarchy and authoritarianism. As the Spanish proverb says, "*Aunque el mono se vista de seda, mono segueda*" [Though the monkey may wear silk, it remains a monkey].

Anarchism is as old as man. There is an ancient saying of a primitive African tribe: "He whoever is hungry, come and partake in the meal I am about to take." Anarchism is the natural philosophy of life; and through the process of education we may be able to make of every human being a *man*, a man who can think freely and do the best he can for himself and his fellow human beings. But we must be patient, for this education is a slow and gradual process. Another century may go by before the public really understands the true meaning of anarchism. Don't get discouraged.

• JUAN ANIDO •

New York City, December 7, 1974

Juan Anido was one of a small group of Spanish anarchists in the Mohegan Colony near New York City. Although he joined the Industrial Workers of the World after his arrival in the United States in 1920, he was at heart an individualist anarchist, who distrusted formal organizations and championed the sovereignty and independence of the human personality.

I WAS BORN in 1898 in the mountains of Galicia in Spain. I did not know anything about anarchism, as I left home at thirteen, though I remember hearing about the killing of Canalejas. At the end of 1914 I left Spain and spent a few years in Cuba. I worked on the railroad, in the sugar mills, and in a restaurant at the port of Havana. There I met anarchist seamen and began to attend their meetings and even signed on as an ordinary seaman on one of their ships. I went to America in 1920, joined the IWW, and carried revolutionary literature to Mexico. I got thrown off a couple of ships for that! We were all sympathetic to the Russian Revolution at first. We even planned to save money, buy tools, and go to Russia to work for the revolution. But when Emma Goldman's pamphlet came, telling of the crushing of the revolution,[566] that was the end of it.

Life then was very hard. Anarchism looked like the dawn of a better life—Aurora! Germinal! It also appealed to my instinctive sense of justice. My first three or four years in the U.S. I continued to work in the merchant marine. I got interested in individualist anarchists—not [Pedro] Esteve, but Jorge Vidal, Pedro Clua, and others. After leaving the sea, I worked on construction jobs, in the mines and steel mills of Pennsylvania and Ohio—Lackawanna, Cambria, Youngstown. I read Stirner and Benjamin Tucker and admired them very much. I liked Bakunin and Malatesta, too—there was plenty of individualism in them—but I was drawn mostly to the individualists, to Emerson and especially Thoreau. The individualists published *Aurora*, and also *Algo*, a mimeographed sheet in Lorain, Ohio; six or seven numbers appeared. The editors were Jorge Vidal and Emilio Vivas. That was around 1925. Emilio and Aurora Vivas were jailed for speaking out for Sacco and Vanzetti. I never met Esteve, and did not agree with his philosophy—he was not radical enough for us—but he was a good man and we read his paper, *Cultura Obrera*. Yes, I read about Voltairine de Cleyre, and what I read interested me greatly. I think we even printed something by her in *Algo*.

I heard about the Mohegan colony from Boran and Vidal in a union hall in New York. I went up there with César Vega, who already lived there, and I decided to stay. There were a few Spaniards there, four or five. Vega went to Spain in 1936 to fight in the Civil War, and he and four comrades were killed when they arrived. My little girl went to the Modern School and she liked it very much. Ferrer was shot, but his ideas were not wasted. Progress has been made toward the sort of libertarian ideas that originated with him. I was especially close to the French anarchists up there, above all André Miroy, a great guy.

It was prosperity, I think, that led to Mohegan's decline. At first the colonists were mostly workers, but it became more and more middle class. I left in 1965 and sold my house, the smallest in the colony, I think. There were happy times and sad times, but all in all they were good years and I'm glad I was there. But when I think about anarchism now it makes me sad. People don't seem to want to accept the responsibility. They want something made to order. And that's what they are getting. And that's what will probably continue in the future. With anarchism the individual has to think for himself and try to realize that he must accept responsibility in order to be himself. It's too bad. The fruit was wonderful, the flowers were beautiful, but the tree did not grow.

• MARCELO SALINAS •

Miami, Florida, December 22, 1972

In December 1972, when I visited Gustavo López (q.v.) and other Cuban anarchists in Miami, they urged me to talk to "El Viejo," the old man. El Viejo turned out to be Marcelo Salinas, a fine-looking man in his eighties, warm-hearted and highly intelligent, who lived in a tiny room in Little Havana. Born in Cuba in 1889, Marcelo worked as a farm laborer and factory hand before emigrating to the United States. While working as a cigarmaker in Tampa, he shared a room with Manuel Pardinas, who, on November 12, 1912, assassinated the Spanish prime minister, José Canalejas. Salinas himself fell under suspicion and was deported to Havana in 1913. During the First World War he smuggled himself into New York where, under the name of George Gallart, he frequented the Ferrer Center in Harlem. During the Red Scare of 1919, he was accused of taking part in a plot on the life of President Woodrow Wilson and summarily deported to Spain. Expelled in turn from Spain, he returned to his native Cuba and resumed his radical activities in Havana. Apart from writing poetry and fiction, he edited *Los Tiempos Nuevos*, a weekly anarchist journal, in which he criticized the Bolshevik dictatorship. When Fidel Castro came to power in 1959, Marcelo left Havana for Miami, where he lived out the remainder of his life. He died on April 5, 1976, at the age of eighty-six.[567]

I WAS BORN on October 30, 1889, in the small Cuban town of Santiago las Vegas in Havana province. I am of Spanish ancestry, though one of my grandfathers is buried in a Jewish cemetery in Oriente province. From 1910 to 1913 I worked as a cigarmaker and *lector* [reader] in Tampa. I helped organize an IWW local there and was driven out by the authorities, like Pedro Esteve. When still under Spanish rule, during the 1880s and 1890s, many Cubans had come to Tampa, and many of them, as well as the Spaniards there, were anarchists of the Esteve and Kropotkin type. My roommate in Tampa was the man who went to Spain to kill the prime minister, Canalejas.

There were also a smaller number of Italian anarchist cigarmakers in Tampa at this time, mostly Sicilians, like Alfonso Coniglio. They were more excitable by temperament than the Spaniards and Cubans and were partisans of Luigi Galleani. Galleani was an outstanding writer and speaker and exerted a strong influence among the Italian anarchists all over the United States.

When Esteve was driven out of Tampa, he went back to Paterson, New Jersey, where, though not an admirer of Galleani or his crowd, he worked as a typesetter for *La Questione Sociale*. I myself went to New York, where I often came to the Ferrer Center. I was at the Tarrytown protests against Rockefeller with Maurice Rudome, Jack Isaacson, Charles Plunkett [q.v.], and the others. Louis Levine and Rose Rogin, both of whom attended the Ferrer Center, had a son named Valentine.[568] Louis left them and I moved in. How I loved that boy! I later lived with Gussie Miller, another of the Ferrer Center crowd.

I went under the name of Georgie (Jorge) Gallart in those days. In 1919 I was arrested and deported to Spain. Mollie Steimer and I were on Ellis Island together when I was awaiting deportation. Soon afterwards I was expelled from Spain and went to Cuba, where I was active in anarchist circles until Castro took power and began imprisoning the anarchists. At that point I returned to the United States and have been living in Miami ever since. After the Second World War, by the way, our group in Havana got several letters—in French, I think—from Li Pei-kan in China. What has become of him?[569]

• GUSTAVO LÓPEZ •

Miami, Florida, December 22, 1972

An immigrant from Cuba, Gustavo López worked as a waiter in New York during the 1950s and 1960s, when he attended meetings of the Spanish Group and of the Libertarian League, founded by Sam (q.v.) and Esther Dolgoff. Moving to Miami, he continued in his occupation as a waiter while assisting political exiles from Castro's dictatorship.

THE CUBAN REVOLUTION started out as a libertarian revolution, as in Russia. Castro's own father was an anarchist, and there were many anarchists in his movement, some of whom took part in the famous assault on the fortress. Castro himself was a rebel and in close touch with the anarchists. But when he took power he didn't know what to do with it. He didn't like the Communists, and it was the Communists, not Castro himself, who were responsible for driving the anarchists into prison and exile. Before anything else, Castro was anti-American and anti-imperialist. As a result, he became paranoid about this country, to the extent that he was ready to join with the devil.

The Cuban anarchists in exile raise money for prisoners' relief. They have contacts in Cuba through whom they send money and medicine to prisoners and their families.

[At this point, Gustavo called in a man named González, who was painting his house outside. González is a Cuban anarchist who was in contact with his comrades in prison until he left Cuba for Mexico, then came to the U.S. last year. Now seventy-one, with grey hair and florid complexion, González is a sturdy house painter who had come to Cuba from Salamanca as a child. He was well-informed about anarchism. He knew that Malatesta visited Cuba and knew of Max Nettlau, Ricardo Mella,[570] and others. All, he said, left a legacy in the Cuban movement. But now, he said, the movement was dead. Everybody left for Mexico or the United States. Whoever remains is either in jail or too old to be active anymore.]

• JOACHÍN EDO •

Windsor, Ontario, June 20, 1987

Between the 1880s and 1950s, Spaniard and Spanish-speaking Latin Americans comprised one of the largest segments of the immigrant anarchist movement in the United States, although very little has been written about them. Joachín Edo, a retired librarian and son of a Spanish anarchist family in Detroit, provides a brief glimpse of their active cultural life.

I WAS BORN in Detroit in 1924 of Spanish anarchist parents. My father, Casiano, and mother, Manuela, came from a village in Aragón and were anarchists before coming to the United States. Father came here in 1917, worked as a miner in Utah and in West Virginia, and returned to Spain in 1921 to fetch his wife and children. I was born here three years later. Father got a job as an auto worker in Detroit, which he kept until he retired. He earned good money and we had a large, comfortable house, where anarchists came and went and spent the night or several days. We children were allowed to sit and listen to their discussions—though we seldom joined in—which we did with great interest and a sense of participation. We also attended conferences, picnics, plays, musical events, and the like. All these events were in Spanish; in fact, my parents never learned to speak English, although they lived here for forty or fifty years, and this was true of many of the older generation.

Nearly all the Spanish anarchists in and around Detroit were workers, mostly in the automobile industry. Apart from Detroit, they were numerous in Youngstown, Gary, Akron, and other industrial cities, as well as in mining communities. Their conferences and picnics drew a thousand people or more. They read and supported *Cultura Obrera* and later *Cultura Proletaria*. Sometimes the Italian comrades would join these events, but few others, though we did visit the Sunrise Colony in the 1930s. The picnics were a mixture of Spanish and anarchist traditions, with Spanish dances from different regions, Spanish guitar music, singing, plays, contests (such as putting a pig on top of a greasy pole as a prize for the man who could climb it).

Activity reached a climax during the Spanish Revolution of the 1930s, when meetings were held to raise funds for the CNT-FAI. (Before that, the biggest event was the trial and execution of Sacco and Vanzetti, when money was raised for their defense.) We put on plays, written by Spanish writers in Spain, in which children as well as adults took part; there were costumes and scripts (I still have some of the scripts) which followed a familiar format: the oppressive *señorito*, the handsome and brave peasant who opposed him, the beautiful girl whom the peasant loved and the *señorito* tried to make his concubine, and so on.

Those were wonderful days and years, with a sense of purpose and of comradeship and togetherness that has since been lost. The Spanish anarchist movement and culture are gone, forgotten by the younger generation, who cannot even speak Spanish and who have no interest in events of the past or the ideals in which their parents and grandparents so deeply believed.

• FEDERICO ARCOS •

Bayside, New York, September 10, 1989

Born into an anarchist family in Barcelona, Federico Arcos joined the Confederación Nacional del Trabajo (CNT) at the age of fourteen, was coeditor of an anarchist youth paper (*El Quixote*) at seventeen, and fought in an anarchist youth battalion during the Spanish Civil War. With the victory of General Franco in 1939, Arcos took sanctuary in southern France, where he was interned in a refugee camp. He escaped in 1941 and worked in a tool and dye shop in Toulouse before returning to Spain and taking part in the anti-Franco resistance. Emigrating to Canada in 1952, Arcos was hired as a tool and dye maker by the Ford Motor Company, where he worked until his retirement in 1986. During the 1960s and 1970s, he was active in the Black & Red and Fifth Estate Groups in Detroit. He has contributed to a range of anarchist publications, in Europe as well as in America, and in 1976 he published a volume of poems, *Momentos: compendio poético* (Detroit: Black & Red). His home in Windsor, Ontario, boasts an extensive collection of anarchist literature, manuscripts, and photographs, including important material on Emma Goldman.[571]

I WAS BORN on July 18, 1920, in the city of Barcelona, in the Clot district, a working-class neighborhood. (On my official papers it says July 22, the day when my father went and registered it.) My father, Santos Arcos Sánchez, came from Castille, from the village of Uclés in Cuenca province. He was a peasant who worked for a landowner. He never went to school and could not read or write. At that time there were oral contracts (*apalabrados*) between worker and landlord: so much flour, oil, chickpeas, cash, in return for a year's labor. My mother, Manuela Martínez Moreno, came from the neighboring village of Tribaldes, the daughter of a peasant. She did not go to school either, but could read and write a little. After their marriage, when father made the contract, she had to work in the landlord's household, doing housework, sewing, and taking care of the children.

I had two brothers and two sisters, all born in Uclés. When I was ten or eleven I got sick and my mother took me to live there for a month. The village was situated on a hill, at the top of which was a convent and castle. At the center of the village was a fountain with five pipes of water. After four o'clock in the afternoon the old folk would sit around the fountain and talk. There were no toilets in the village and little electricity; we used candles and oil lamps for light. We stayed in my uncle's house. I slept in a high bed on a feather mattress, and really sank in! Onions, peppers, and other vegetables hung from beams on the ceiling. Outside there were lots of chickens, pigs, and other animals. In the house, near the entrance, was a fireplace and a big pot for cooking. The houses in the village were painted with whitewash by tall sticks with brushes. I went back to Uclés just last year for the first time since my childhood. The streets are now paved and the convent has become a seminary. During the Civil War Franco quartered soldiers there and used it as a prison. Next to it are buried the corpses of prisoners executed by Franco.

I was the youngest child in my family and the only one to be born in Barcelona. It happened this way. My father's brother went to Barcelona for his military service, got married, and had a child. Father followed him about 1910. He walked from his village all the way to Valencia, where he took a boat to Barcelona. There he got a job as a stevedore, working at the docks. Then he brought his wife and children to join him. Soon afterwards he became a tanner (*curtidor*) in a leather factory. So I was born in Barcelona. In addition to my brothers and sisters, the husband of one of my sisters also lived with us, a fine man named Juan Giné. He bought a blackboard and chalk and taught me the alphabet and numbers, so when I went to school at six I had the edge on my classmates.

I went to school across the street from where we lived, at the Academia Enciclopedica. I was the baby of the family, and I don't think anybody could have had more love than me, from my brothers, sisters, and sister's husband as well as my parents. I went to school till thirteen and was very good in mathematics. I learned to play chess and was good at that too. For sports the favorite game was soccer, which we played on empty fields. My parents were not religious, and I did not receive communion because of this and because my father had no money to buy a suit. Nobody in our house went to church.

At thirteen I left school and started working as a cabinetmaker. One of my brothers was a cabinetmaker, a very good one, and got me the job. I learned the trade on the job and at fourteen became an apprentice. The moment that happened, in 1934, I became a member of the CNT. My ambition was to be an engineer, but there was no money for me to study. I was happy, though, to be a mechanic. I worked from 8 A.M. to 6 P.M., with a two-hour break for lunch. At 7 P.M. I went to a trade school—Artes y Oficios—five evenings a week, learning mathematics and drafting, which you need in order to work as a skilled mechanic. The first year in the school I got a rating of "excellent" and I won a prize. My employer was interested in my studies, and we did mathematical work together. He was an engineer and wanted me to be one too, but my family did not have the means to allow that. I worked five days for eight hours and four hours on Saturday afternoons, plus school five evenings a week. That was an exhausting routine. More than once I went to bed Saturday evening and got up Monday morning. The second year I cut my wrist on the cutting machine. I learned how to work all the machines—lathe, drill press, cutter, shaper—as well as to forge my own tools. I worked there until the end of 1937. At the request of the CNT I then went to work as a machinist in a brewery, where they wanted to strengthen their ideas. I remained there until I went to the front in April 1938. After the defeat of Aragón, the republic called up my year and I volunteered for a CNT battalion.

As I said, I became a member of the CNT when I received my apprenticeship at the age of fourteen. My father was a CNT member, as were both my brothers and my brother-in-law. So it was natural that I should become a member too. Besides, we used to get anarchist papers in our house, including *La Revista Blanca*, so I grew up with it, you might say. During the 1930s there was a feeling of agitation in the air, of hope that the revolution would come. I read the papers aloud to my father and some of our neighbors who came to listen. I remember, for example, when Durruti was banished to Africa. I read about it aloud in *Tierra!* Though still a child at the time, I already knew about social questions as an adult did.

There were other influences. Like other districts of Barcelona, Clot had an Ateneo Libertario. My brother was a member and took me along. In another street there was an Ateneo Eclectico, and I began to go there and applied for membership in June 1936, on the eve of the revolution. I remember a pharmacist—Castels was his name—near the Ateneo Libertario, who gave discounts to CNT members. He later became a doctor. He was a generous, wonderful man, who made a lasting impression on me. Of course there was my brother-in-law Juan Giné. He taught me all he knew about mechanics. He was a brother for me and a father. He was a CNT member and in 1939 was sentenced to death by Franco. He was not executed but spent four and a half years in prison. He is still alive, and I visit him whenever I go to Spain. We remain very close. My brothers and sisters are all dead. I'm the only one still alive.

There were other things as well. I recall going to CNT meetings in a bull ring where the crowds were always large. I went with my father or brother or alone. When someone spoke there was silence—no applause to feed the speaker's vanity. The crowd preferred to listen, digest, think. Occasionally voices cried out, *"Viva el comunismo libertario!"* Also there was the Dam brewery, where Durruti used to work. The men went out on strike and boycotted the beer. *"Boycott a la Dam!"* read signs all over the city. The workers won the strike and got a role in hiring and firing as well as other benefits. Another recollection still agitates me. All this was before the revolution. I saw some policemen chasing a man in the street. One took a rubber truncheon and struck him in the back. I was running alongside them. I wanted to jump at the policemen, I was so angry. I should have done that—jump at the policemen!

The uprising began on July 19, 1936. The next morning, a Sunday, factory whistles blasted to summon the workers. The CNT issued calls on the radio. Cars with loudspeakers circulated throughout the city—"CNT, FAI! CNT, FAI!" Someone threw a bomb in a church and got away. People burned money. What use would it be after the revolution? I told my mother, "I'm going to keep fifty pesetas as a souvenir to show my children. Think of it, people used to kill one another for money!"

That fall I joined the Juventudes Libertarias of Catalonia, a section of the Cultura y Propaganda de la FAI, whose purpose was to educate the youth in accordance with the principles of the FAI. The Juventudes Libertarias had a social hall, theater, and library. I joined it together with my friend Liberto Sarrau. One day we attended a plenum of the CNT-FAI at the Casa CNT-FAI. They sent us to the Comité de Defensa, where we were given old rifles and six bullets each. We were indignant. "We want to fight for the revolution as much as you do!" we told the men there. They said, "There are people here much older than you who will need the newer rifles. When they die you will take their place. That is your responsibility and our trust in you." I was moved by this statement. I felt that if I failed or weakened I would not be worthy of our great ideals, the beautiful ideals of anarchism.

That was shortly before Durruti died.[572] I was sixteen years old. My best friends were Liberto Sarrau, Diego Camacho ("Abel Paz"), and Germinal Gracia ("Victor García"). At the Ateneo Libertario we set up a table with pamphlets and other literature. We wrote and printed an anarchist leaflet. In 1937 we published three issues of *El Quixote*, which promoted the ideas of anarchism for the youth. It was very critical of the government for its counterrevolutionary attitude, and of the CNT for participating in the government. We presented the paper to the censor, who cut out objectionable articles. But we kept the type and printed uncensored copies for circulation. One issue is in the International Institute of Social History. It belonged to R. Lone,[573] who gave the Institute his huge anarchist collection.

Liberto decided to join a collective in the village of Cervía, in Lérida. Germinal and Diego went there also. I wanted to go, but my mother convinced me to stay. (I was the only son left at home, etc.) I remained at my job in Barcelona, though I went to Cervía to help them once or twice. The collective survived for quite a while. Only when the front was broken was it dissolved, and they had to leave Cervía and return to Barcelona. We were very critical of the CNT at that time. We thought they had betrayed us by joining the government, as the only purpose of government was counterrevolution. We youth wanted to carry on the purity of anarchism, lest it degenerate and become corrupt. It was the duty of the youth to look to the future; the CNT was taking steps backward. We also objected to the militarization by the CNT, its desire to create a formal army. The FAI was almost as bad. The one we admired was Durruti. His column was elected; everybody had the same pay. I did not know him, but I met his companion and daughter.

In April 1938 my class was called for the army. Liberto and Germinal volunteered for the Twenty-Sixth Division, formerly the Durruti Column. I volunteered for a new anti-gas battalion. My brother-in-law Juan Giné was in the same battalion as a provisional sergeant. For a while we remained in Barcelona. Then we were sent to Vellver de Cerdaña, south of Andorra. From there we were sent to the Twenty-Fourth Division, the "Jover Division," in the Pyrénées, as instructors. When I got to the front I met the barber from Cervía. He had no footwear, so I gave him a pair of shoes. I had an old rifle and bayonet. They made me the Miliciano de Cultura, and I taught the men how to read and write. I served on night watch often and slept in my uniform. Mice chewed away at my pants. Our equipment and clothing left much to be desired.

In November 1938 I was sent to the lower Ebro, to the city of Tortosa, where I spent the winter. The city had once been beautiful, but now it lay in ruins. It was surrounded by orange groves and the ground was full of oranges. Otherwise food was scarce. I found a blackboard and a two-volume set of *Don Quixote*, illustrated by Gustave Doré, a beautiful edition. There was a flood on the lower Ebro and the trenches were filled with water. Our commissar was a Communist. We were moved to a new position north of Tortosa, where the worst fighting took place. Our front was broken and we had to move back, all the way to Tarragona. Tarragona fell. We were almost encircled. Messerschmidts flew over and repeatedly strafed and bombed us. We had to fight our way out. There were bodies all over the roads, dead horses and mules. I received a shrapnel wound in the back, but it was not serious. My comrades were dying all around me.

After the retreat I found my way back to Barcelona. My mother was over-joyed to see me alive. On January 24, 1939, I went to the Libertarian Youth Center where a truck was leaving for the French border. I got aboard. Two days later Barcelona fell. The truck got as far as Figueras. From there I walked with three girls to the border. Along the way I met three male comrades and walked with them over the mountains and across the border, along with a dog that attached himself to us. We passed a dead man hanging from a tree. That night we could see the lights of French villages.

We got as far as Le Boulou. From there we were taken to a refugee camp at Argelès-sur-Mer. Eleven of us slept together in one blanket. For a while I worked in an aircraft factory (from November 1939 to June 1940). Then we returned to the camp. French police came in and took away all members of the International Brigades, but they left us alone. We attended classes taught by prisoners—teachers, engineers in civilian life. I learned trigonometry, which proved useful in my trade as a machinist. There were poetry recitals. I learned French. Whatever I learned at that time I really remembered.

In 1941 I escaped and went to work in Toulouse as a fitter in a tool and dye shop in a turbine factory. There I remained till 1943, living in a rented room. Police came around looking for men to work in Germany, but I managed to evade them. Meanwhile Liberto Sarrau and Diego Camacho came to Toulouse from the camp. There was a notice in the papers that all Spaniards in France should return to Spain for military service. We decided to go. In Figueras I was put in jail for twenty-one days, fourteen prisoners in a tiny cell. There was no running water. Priests came every day and tried to get us to go to communion. Some went, but I refused. One day an officer came around and took a cigarette from each of our packs. I said to him, "I did not offer you one," and he actually put it back. But then he hit me in the face. I wanted to kill him.

From Figueras I was taken by train to Barcelona. There I was put in the army and sent to Morocco, to the same city and same barracks where my father and brother before me had been. I remained there till the end of the war a year and a half later. It was high in the mountains, very quiet and clear. I learned a bit of Arabic. I read a lot and enjoyed it. After the war I was released from the army and returned to Barcelona, where I at once made contact with the CNT. Mean-while Liberto, Diego, and Germinal had been arrested—Diego was sent to prison for eleven years. In 1947 or 1948 I attended a meeting of the Libertarian Youth in the mountains. Forty people were there. I was elected as a member of the secretariat. The secretary and I did most of the work, issuing circulars, arranging meetings. Little by little everyone was arrested, except me and the secretary.

Yet we still had many groups in Barcelona, one in every district of the city. Germinal was released from prison, and he and Raúl Carballeira came to see me. Raúl was a dedicated organizer and printed *Ruta*. We were like brothers.

He was a real activist. He once came to my place with a thousand-peseta bill. Pura, my *compañera*, changed it for hundreds. He came back again. When there were no more hundreds, he asked for his pistol. But soon afterwards he was surrounded by police in the Montjuich mountains and shot himself rather than be taken.

In 1948 I went to France and served in the Maquis for six weeks. In January 1949 I crossed the border into Spain with a group of fellow militants: Marcelino Massana, Ramón Vallacaldevila, José Sabaté (Francisco's brother), Francisco Martínez, José Perez Pedrero, José Pons, and three more—ten all together. Yes, one was José Massip. Massip, Sabaté, Martínez, and one other went to Barcelona. Martínez was shot while making contact with comrades. Sabaté was also shot. Massip survived (he's still alive). Pons and Pedrero were both captured and executed by firing squad.

Massana and I made our way back to France. He had a fever and could barely walk. We stopped to rest in the Pyrénées. It was nighttime. We could hear voices of soldiers nearby. Dogs barked in the night. But we weren't caught. I had the best two hours' sleep in my life. Then we crossed the border and approached our base, a farm in Oseja. We saw two gendarmes, so we waited till they left before entering. From there we went to Toulouse. There we rejoined the Libertarian Youth. I served on the national committee and was secretary of the organization in 1950. To earn a living, I worked in a factory—the same one as before. By now most of my best comrades were dead, though in addition to myself Liberto, Diego, and Germinal were still alive.

In 1952 I emigrated to Canada, where I hoped to start a new life. When the boat docked in Montreal, I was hired by the Ford Motor Company and sent to work as a tool and dye maker in Windsor. They needed skilled mechanics. I became ill with tuberculosis of the kidney, which had to be removed. I spent fifteen months in the Essex County Sanitarium until I regained my health. In 1958 I became a Canadian citizen. With my new passport I went to Europe and reunited with Pura. She and our daughter came to Canada and lived with me in Windsor.

In Detroit around this time I met Francisco Riveras (his wife is still alive at ninety-five). He was reading Rudolf Rocker. When I told him that I had read *La Juventud de un rebelde*[574] his face lit up. I told him I was a comrade of José Peirats, and he asked me to come back as soon as possible. I did and I met the Grupo Libertad, about a dozen comrades. José López Rios was the spirit of the group; he knew Pedro Esteve, Marcelino García [q.v.], Eusebio Carbó. Every month we met in a different house and made a collection for the movement. In 1960 I went to the conference of the Libertarian League in Youngstown and met Sam [q.v.] and Esther Dolgoff. There were many comrades there, mostly Spanish. One was a Russian named Perry Shumko. He had been in the 1917 Revolution. He was now an old man near the end of his life. He hugged me and kissed me with tears in his eyes. He saw me as the hope for his ideals.

In 1960 I also met Attilio Bortolotti [q.v.], in Toronto. A friend took me to see him and Dorothy Rogers, who gave me letters and other materials relating to Emma Goldman. I also got to know the Italians in Detroit, the Gruppo Refrattario (Boattini, Crisi, Catalano, Puccio), and also a few Russians, like John Cherney. Bortolotti and I became close. He's now the best friend that I have.

• H. L. WEI •

New York City, January 11, 1975; Flushing, New York, February 22, 1975

Dr. Wei, an anthropologist, came to the United States from Taiwan in 1973. An anarchist since his teens, he took part in the May Fourth movement in 1919 and in the May Thirtieth movement in 1925, together with the writer Pa Chin (Li Pei-kan). In 1927 he and Pa Chin went to study in Paris,[575] where he completed a thesis on Proudhon. After their return to China, Dr. Wei and Pa Chin remained close friends and saw each other often. In 1936 Wei led a general strike against the Nationalists in Wuhan and later fought the Japanese and the Communists. In 1949, following the Communist seizure of power, he and his family left China for Taiwan, leaving behind his entire library, including his thesis on Proudhon. Assisting the Weis in their flight, Pa Chin, who himself stayed behind, spent four days at the Nanking railroad station until he could acquire tickets. "I think every anarchist is first and foremost a good man," said Dr. Wei when recalling this incident. In Taiwan Dr. Wei published articles on such subjects as "Categories of Totemism in Ancient China" and "The Descent Principle and Kindred Category," as well as a four-hundred-page book on the Chinese family structure.

I WAS BORN Wei Hwei-lin in Shansi province, China, in 1900. My father was a schoolteacher. When I was eighteen I read *Hui-ming lu* (The Cock Crows in the Darkness), a collection of anarchist essays edited by Shi-fu.[576] I immediately accepted it. My convictions were further stimulated by the May Fourth movement in 1919. The following year, 1920, I went to Tokyo to study at Waseda University. My main subject was anthropology, but I was also interested in the utopian socialism of Owen and Fourier, which had a strong influence on the anarchist movement. In Tokyo I met a Chinese anarchist group and joined their discussions and activities. I also met leading Japanese anarchists, such as Osugi (murdered after the earthquake in 1923) and Yamaga, who became my close friend.

Back in China, I took part in the May Thirtieth movement in 1925. At this time, the mid-1920s, anarchism was still on the rise. Every big city had at least two or three groups. I had personal contact with two in Peking, both composed mostly of students. There was also a School of Esperanto in Peking, started by a blind Russian writer and musician named Eroshenko. All anarchists in China were Esperantists; in those days the two words were almost synonymous. Each group had thirty to fifty members. I organized a meeting in Peking in 1923. More than one hundred people attended, mostly male students, but there were some middle-aged and even old men there. Li Shi-tsien was there (he died last year). He organized a Comtist school and later became prominent in the Kuomintang. The same year I went also to Shanghai, where there were at least four anarchist groups.

In Shanghai I took part in the May Thirtieth movement with Pa Chin (we had gone to the same high school in Nanking, but I was four years older). In the repressions that followed, we went together by boat to France to take part in the work-study movement in Paris. We lived together in the same hotel. I studied anthropology at the University of Paris, but also spent much time studying anarcho-syndicalism. I met Pierre Besnard[577] and other French syndicalists. Pa Chin and I also met Jean Grave,[578] Sébastien Faure, and Paul Reclus.[579] We once met Nestor Makhno, a plain, direct workman, who spoke very little French. I did not meet Emma Goldman or Alexander Berkman, but Pa Chin, I believe, met Berkman. Pa Chin was a quiet young man. He had no girlfriends. He read much but spoke little. He also began to write his first novel before leaving Paris in 1929.

I remained there another year. When I returned to China in 1930, the anarchist movement was still flourishing. Its real decline did not begin until the Sino-Japanese War. I helped establish two Modern Schools in Fukien around 1934, both high schools. The first was called Li Ming (Aurora), the second P'ing Ming (The Common People). I taught social sciences at Li Ming. Both schools continued to exist until the 1949 Revolution, but after the outbreak of the Sino-Japanese War their character changed and they ceased being anarchist.

During the 1930s and 1940s, my wife and I lived mostly in Nanking. Here we knew Jacques Reclus, the son of Paul Reclus, who lived in China for many years and visited us often in Nanking. We left China in 1949 and spent more than twenty years on Taiwan, where I taught at the university and did field work in social anthropology. Pa Chin remained in China because he had obligations to family, friends, and his bookstore, Culture and Life. I came to America two years ago and live in Flushing, Queens, not far from your college.

Chinese anarchism derives from both native (especially Lao-tsu) and Western sources. The first generation of Chinese anarchists had been brought up on the native philosophers, fusing their ideas with those of Western writers whom they read as students. Rousseau probably knew of the ideas of Chinese philosophers. He influenced utopian socialists and liberals of the nineteenth century, whom Chinese students of the twentieth century read, so that it all started in the East, traveled to the West, and then came home again!

No, I did not know Yat Tone[580] or Gray Wu, or any Chinese anarchists who had returned from the United States. I did know a Chinese anarchist who, like Yat Tone, went to Spain. He was Chuang Chung, who went there in 1937 and married a Spanish anarchist woman, whom he brought back with him to China after the Sino-Japanese War. They were arrested several times by the Communist government but are probably still alive now.

I also knew Chu Cha-pei, a sort of Chinese Makhno from Yunan province in the south, near Burma and Indo-China, the son of a soldier. Following his father's occupation, he too became a soldier and attended Whampoa Military Academy. He read Pa Chin's translations of anarchist classics and became an ardent anarchist. He later met Pa Chin and visited me and my wife in Nanking in 1936. He told us that some day he would welcome us in an anarchist utopia in the south.

Chu Cha-pei actually knew about Makhno from Bao Puo,[581] who wrote about him in the paper *Kuo Feng* (National Folkways) after returning to China from Moscow in 1923. Chu was tall, strong, intelligent. Like Pa Chin, he was a man of few words. He fought in turn against the Japanese, the Nationalists, and the Communists, just as Makhno had fought against the Austro-German occupiers, the Whites and Nationalists, and the Communists. Again like Makhno, his base of activity was in the mountains of his native district in the south, from which he continued to launch attacks against the Communist authorities throughout the 1950s. He is probably still there, still alive, hiding in the mountains of Yunan, though his precise whereabouts are unknown.

• RED JONES •

San Francisco, California, June 12, 1974

The Chinese anarchist with the improbable name of Red Jones—"Jonesie," he was usually called—was born Lau Chung-si (hence "Jonesie") in the village of Lung-du, near Canton, in 1892. At the age of seventeen he emigrated to the United States and at once fell victim to what Emma Goldman called the "brutal and barbarous persecution" of Asian laborers on the Pacific Coast.[582] Before long Jonesie became an anarchist, for which he barely escaped deportation during the Red Scare of 1919–1920. In 1925 he was a founder of the Equality Group (P'ing-she) in San Francisco, of which he was the most active member. Between 1927 and 1929 the group published a journal called *P'ing-teng* (Equality), whose outstanding writer, Li Pei-kan, was soon to become famous as the Chinese novelist Pa Chin, a pen name formed from the first syllable of Bakunin and the last syllable of Kropotkin. Pa Chin, it is interesting to note, published an essay "To Comrade Chung-si" in the February 1928 issue of *P'ing-teng*.[583]

In the face of government harassment, the Equality Group also published books and pamphlets on anarchism, as well as seven numbers of a monthly journal *Wucheng-fu kung-ch'an yüeh-k'an* (Anarchist Communist Monthly), which appeared in 1934. From his meager earnings as a laborer, Jonesie contributed money to *The Road to Freedom, Man!, Spanish Revolution*, and other anarchist periodicals of the 1920s and 1930s, and attended the lectures and picnics arranged by Italian and English-speaking groups in the San Francisco area. The Equality Group was long since defunct when I visited Jonesie in 1974. He lived alone in a tiny room in a Chinese rooming house on Broadway. On the wall was a picture of Emma Goldman inscribed with a quotation from Bakunin: "I am not free until all men are free."[584] After translating it for me, Jonesie showed me a composite picture of Chinese anarchist periodicals displaying the faces of Bakunin, Kropotkin, and other celebrated anarchists, among them the Haymarket martyrs. Jonesie seemed sad and lonely in his little cell-like room. He said little (possibly because of his meager English) but made a strong impression, with his obvious sincerity and quiet manner. Three years after the interview he left the United States for Macao, not far from his native village, where he died in 1979.

I AM EIGHTY-TWO years old. I came to America from China in 1909 and did various jobs—as a laborer on the railroad, a farm hand near Sacramento, and so on. P'ing-she was a very small group, with about ten or twelve members. We put out the paper together and distributed it free of charge. We sent it to China and all over the United States. Pa Chin was our most important writer. Yes, I met Yat Tone, who visited San Francisco. He was one of the finest and most loved of the Chinese anarchists. I do not know what happened to him after he returned to China in the 1930s.

We had contacts with the Italian and English-speaking groups in San Francisco, at picnics, lectures, and other affairs.[585] I gave a set of P'ing-teng to the San Francisco public library, but no archives or photographs have been saved. I think I was born an anarchist. The idea was in me from the start. Anarchism is still the most beautiful ideal, and I think someday it will come.

• BELLA WONG •

Jackson Heights, New York, January 24, 1991

Mrs. Wong, born Bella Friedman in Poland, is the widow of Eddie Wong, one of a small complement of Chinese anarchists in the United States in the decades before the Second World War. Born near Canton in 1900, Eddie arrived in San Francisco in 1921 and was active (with Red Jones, q.v.) in the Equality Group (P'ing-she). He moved to New York in 1929 and took part in the Road to Freedom and Vanguard Groups while working as a waiter in a restaurant. He died in Queens, New York, in 1988.

MY HUSBAND was born Wong Chay-tin near Canton, in March 1900. He later took the name Edward from the English socialist Edward Carpenter and was called Eddie by his friends. His mother died in childbirth, so he never knew her. His father was a shopkeeper, who married him off when he was seventeen. He hated his father for that. He and his wife had a son, but they soon separated, and Eddie went to Hong Kong to live with a cousin, a radical. Eddie himself already had radical leanings. As a little boy, in 1912, he cut off his queue as a sign of liberation, and he was now influenced by his cousin's ideas.

Not long afterwards, Eddie came to the United States and spent the next few years in the San Francisco area. He lived in humble, unbelievable poverty. What little money he earned he paid his father back for the trip. He worked fourteen to sixteen hours a day in the fields, picking peas. When his knees began to bleed he stopped. Then he worked as a busboy in a restaurant for five or six years. During this time he attended night school and engaged in radical agitation, speaking in Chinese on street corners as a soapboxer.

Eddie came to New York at the beginning of the 1930s. His best friend at that time was Yat Tone, a very devoted anarchist. Yat held back the money from his own food and gave it to the movement. He was of medium height, wore glasses, and spoke little English. He was a waiter in a Chinese restaurant. He went back to China in the mid-1930s. We heard from him for a while but then no more.

Eddie also worked in a Chinese restaurant, and he and a few other waiters pooled their resources and opened their own restaurant, the Jade Mountain, on Second Avenue near Twelfth Street. It was a partnership rather than a cooperative, and they used some hired labor. During the Second World War Eddie worked in an ammunition factory in Brooklyn. After the war he worked for a Chinese jade company. He went to New York University and took business courses, graduating in business management. He took over the jade company, importing jade for jewelry. We lived then on Thirteenth Street, near Ida and Valerio Isca [q.v.], and moved to this apartment in 1954.

I was born Bella Friedman in Kalisz, Poland, eighty-five years ago and immigrated to New York. I had a girlfriend who was interested in anarchism, and she took me to a meeting on Second Avenue. I met Eddie there, sometime in the mid-1930s. I met him again in the same place soon afterwards. I found him personable, charming, and kind. He spoke fair but not really fluent English. I was interested in anarchism but leaned more towards Communism. Anarchism had a big failing: the anarchists didn't go through with anything they started.

Yet Eddie stuck to it till quite recently, maybe ten or twelve years ago, though he wasn't active. He saw that anarchism didn't accomplish anything; things never seemed to change. He was disappointed that the comrades were busy with their own lives, had nice apartments, and were concerned with material things. He himself was very frugal, had no use for luxuries, and wouldn't even buy a car. He never wanted any of that. Material wealth was not important. In spite of his disappointment, though, anarchism remained his beautiful ideal. We went to Stelton and Mohegan a few times and spent a whole summer at Mohegan in a tent.

There were only a few Chinese anarchists in New York, four or five at most. Each lived separately, and there was not much contact between them. Franklin Wong was not Eddie but a different person. We saw him occasionally. He liked the girls. Another was a very old man without teeth. I can't remember his name, but he visited us here a few times. He was a truck driver and came from the Canton region. He was very frugal—even more than Eddie. He carried all his money—several thousand dollars—on his person. Eddie begged him to put it in the bank or to will it to his relatives, but he didn't. When he died it all went to the state.

Eddie made a good living from his jewelry business. We owned our apartment and lived comfortably but not lavishly. Eddie financed an elementary school in his hometown in China, of which his son was the director. When we visited it in 1976 we got a very warm reception [she shows me photographs of Eddie and herself at the school with smiling teachers and children]. Eddie retired in 1971. He died on Labor Day weekend in 1988.

6. *The Relevance of Anarchism to Modern Society,* pamphlet by
Sam Dolgoff, 1989 edition, Charles H. Kerr Publishing Company
(Paul Avrich Collection)

INTRODUCTION

By the 1920s, as we have seen, the anarchists had fallen into disarray. The First World War and its aftermath had inflicted irreparable damage on the movement. *Mother Earth*, *Cronaca Sovversiva*, and other leading journals had been suppressed, and with the Palmer raids of 1919 and 1920 the most prominent figures, among them Emma Goldman, Alexander Berkman, and Luigi Galleani, had been silenced by prison and deportation, together with many from the rank and file. Nor were there fresh recruits to take their place. Declining immigration and new restrictions on southern and eastern Europeans reduced potential adherents to a trickle. The pull of Communism likewise took its toll, despite Berkman's warning that authoritarian methods, such as those used by Lenin and his associates, "cannot lead to liberty, that methods and aims are in essence and effects identical."[586] At the same time, the older generation was waning, while most of the children were becoming assimilated to American values and losing touch with their anarchist roots. The anarchists, as a result, never recovered their former place in the radical spectrum. By the end of the 1920s, the fear which they had previously generated had been transferred to the Communists, still basking in the glow of the revolution.

Yet the anarchists by no means vanished from the scene. Weakened and scattered though they were, they struggled to regroup their forces. And though not as conspicuous as in the past, they concerned themselves with the whole range of issues that confronted the world during the twenties and thirties: the growth of the Bolshevik dictatorship, the rise of Mussolini and Hitler ("the most vicious clown in the whole obscene brood of European politicians," as one anarchist paper described him),[587] the martyrdom of Sacco and Vanzetti, the impact of the great Depression, and the overriding questions of violence, revolution, and war.

Proof that the movement had not expired came with the launching, in 1924, of *The Road to Freedom*, "a periodical of anarchist thought, work, and literature," as it described itself. Edited by Hippolyte Havel, an erstwhile lover of Emma Goldman, it was the first major English paper to appear since the suppression of *Mother Earth*, a journal in which Havel had played a part. A central task of the new publication, which continued until 1932, was to attract a complement of younger readers to whom the torch of anarchy might be passed. Towards this end *The Road to Freedom* started a special "youth page," as did the *Fraye Arbeter Shtime*, printed in English to make it accessible. These efforts, however, were unavailing. For to younger readers who sought a libertarian viewpoint, both youth pages seemed obsolete. "The English-language youth page of the *Fraye Arbeter Shtime* didn't interest us much," Louis Slater recalls, "as it was not really a youth organ but old-fashioned and outdated, almost a translation of the Yiddish into English."

Spurning the efforts of their elders, the youngsters took matters into their own hands. As one of them, Sara Goodman, put it: "The youth is the rising sun of the tomorrow that will come to take the place of the setting sun of yesterday."[588] In 1927 Sara and her sister Elizabeth, twin daughters of anarchist parents, formed the Rising Youth Group in New York, a short-lived venture with a journal of the same title and meeting places in Brooklyn and the Bronx, as well as in Manhattan. During its brief existence, noted W. S. Van Valkenburgh, who had replaced Havel as editor of *The Road to Freedom*, the Rising Youth, and especially the Goodman sisters, had "bitter fights" with his paper and the *Fraye Arbeter Shtime*, their attitude being that "they will brook no advice or suggestions from the old fogies."[589]

After two years the Rising Youth disbanded. It was followed, however, by the Friends of Freedom, a tiny circle in the Bronx. The Friends, in turn, evolved into the Vanguard Group, which, augmented by its teenage affiliate, the Rebel Youth, became the leading youth group of the thirties, surviving until the outbreak of the war.

Vanguard, like Rising Youth before it, scorned what it considered the backwardness and narrow parochialism of its elders, who, clinging to outworn doctrines and "cooped up within the confines of little national colonies," were unable to "think in terms of American life." Their own group, Vanguard asserted, heralded the anarchism of tomorrow, "rebellious, critical, iconoclastic." Impatient with the "smug generalities of the older generation,"[590] Louis Slater, Abe Bluestein, and others vowed to formulate a concrete program of action, from which a totally regenerated society would emerge. In such a society, they declared, compulsion would give place to cooperation, and the bureaucratic state, whether Communist or capitalist, would be shorn of its arbitrary power.

Such a program was never forthcoming. On the contrary, the ideas evolved in *Vanguard*, the organ of the group, differed little from those in *The Road to Freedom* or its foreign-language contemporaries; the denunciations of totalitarianism, the support for the anarchists in Spain, even the picnics, dances, and lectures announced in *Vanguard*'s pages—all bore a familiar ring. Among the journal's most perceptive contributors, it might be noted, were such venerable figures as Rudolf Rocker and Emma Goldman; and Rocker's arrival from Germany in 1933, followed by Goldman's lecture tour the next year, provided a source of inspiration which sustained the group throughout its existence.

Vanguard dissolved itself between 1939 and 1941. What brought about the group's demise, more than anything else, was the coming of the Second World War. Once again, as in 1914, the war issue divided the anarchist movement. A quarter-century earlier, when Kropotkin declared his support for the Entente, fearing that German authoritarianism might prove fatal to social progress in Europe, his stand had been challenged by those who, like Luigi Galleani, rejected all wars except the "social war," which would overthrow capitalism and the state. In 1939, by the same token, while Jewish anarchists overwhelmingly supported the war effort, most of the Italians and Spaniards remained true to their antimilitarist convictions, denouncing the war as an imperialist struggle for power and profit, with the workers serving as cannon fodder, so that it was absurd to favor either side against the other.

Rudolf Rocker sharply dissented from this view. A refugee from Nazi Germany, he argued that Hitler had to be defeated if liberty was to survive. "The present war cannot be measured by the standards of military conflicts of the past," he wrote. Rather, "the struggle against totalitarian slavery and its bestial achievements is the first duty of our time, the first condition for a new social development in the spirit of freedom and social justice." So far as German militarism was concerned, Rocker admitted, Kropotkin had, twenty-five years before, "judged things better than I and others did."[591]

The Vanguard Group, with its predominantly Jewish membership, tended to side with Rocker's position. A few, indeed, went so far as to join the United States Army, considering Nazism the ultimate evil. Others, however, left in disgust and ultimately cast their lot with the Why? Group, established in 1942. Why? itself disbanded shortly after the war, a remnant forming the Resistance Group, which survived until 1954.

The divisions caused by the war left the anarchists in a shambles, and what had once been a flourishing movement shrank to the proportions of a sect. Throughout the 1940s and 1950s, anarchism in America was in the doldrums. Apart from a few active propaganda circles, such as the Libertarian Book Club in New York, the chief evidence of its continued presence lay in a succession of cultural and literary magazines—*Retort* and *Resistance* in the East, *The Ark* and *The Needle* in the West—that published writers of the caliber of Saul Bellow, Paul Goodman, and George Woodcock, as well as such poets as Kenneth Rexroth, Kenneth Patchen, and Allen Ginsberg, to mention only a few. A related publication was Dwight Macdonald's *Politics*, which "forsook the true Marxist faith," as Macdonald put it, "to whore after the strange gods of anarchism and pacifism."[592] Its remarkable list of contributors during its five-year run (1944–1949) included George Orwell, C. Wright Mills, Jean-Paul Sartre, Simone Weil, Victor Serge, and Albert Camus, in addition to Paul Goodman and George Woodcock.

Among the new anarchist groups of the period, the Libertarian Book Club was perhaps the most important. Founded in 1945, it devoted itself to disseminating anarchist literature among the postwar generation, a task accomplished by a combination of mail-order sales and the publication of such important books as Volin's *The Unknown Revolution* (1954–1955), James J. Martin's *Men Against the State* (1957), Paul Eltzbacher's *Anarchism* (1960), and Max Stirner's *The Ego and His Own* (1963). For a number of years, moreover, the club held annual luncheons, addressed by such individuals as Roger Baldwin, Paul Goodman, and Alexandra Kropotkin. Beyond this, it launched a series of monthly lectures and discussions, featuring speakers like Herbert Read, Dwight Macdonald, James T. Farrell, Murray Bookchin, and Daniel Guérin.

By engaging in such activities, the Libertarian Book Club kept the traditions of anarchism alive during an otherwise dormant interlude. At the same time, it provided a bridge, fragile though it was, between the older generation of the twenties and thirties and that of the sixties and seventies, soon to make its entry onto the stage. A similar function was performed by the Libertarian League, which, founded by Sam and Esther Dolgoff in 1955, sponsored forums, distributed literature, issued a journal (*Views and Comments*), and corresponded with anarchists around the globe. According to its statement of principles, "the only salvation for a world satiated with exploitation and war and threatened with atomic destruction lies in a new, free, classless social order yet to be created."[593]

For the time being, however, the efforts of these groups seemed unavailing. Until the coming of the Vietnam War, anarchism remained a half-forgotten movement, its membership scattered and declining. Some historians, indeed, had begun to write its epitaph, when the social ferment of the 1960s saw it gain a new lease on life. To the dissidents of the Vietnam era, the "warfare state" and "military-industrial complex" seemed to be fulfilling the anarchists' most despairing predictions, while the formulas of self-determination and direct action exercised a growing appeal. Of particular relevance, after the lessons of Russia, China, and Cuba, was the message that social emancipation must be attained by libertarian rather than authoritarian methods, that socialism without freedom, as Bakunin put it, is the worst form of tyranny and exploitation.

In campus demonstrations from Berkeley to Columbia the black flag was once again unfurled. Anarchist groups revived and multiplied, their adherents taking part in many forms of social protest, from the campaigns for racial equality and nuclear disarmament to resistance to the draft and the war. New anarchist journals made their appearance—*The Match!* is a notable example—as well as pamphlets, books, and manifestos, which provided, as in the past, a fundamental criticism of state power and questioned the premises of virtually all other schools of political thought.

As of this writing (1993) interest in anarchism, both its doctrines and personalities, shows little sign of abating. The moral stature of the anarchists, combined with their vision of a free society, continues to exercise an appeal, particularly among students and intellectuals, if not manual workers as in the past. The older generation of anarchists, although vanishing from the scene, have been encouraged by this revival, which they themselves did much to bring about. Reading their interviews, one is struck by their persistent warnings against the dangers of concentrated power, economic and political alike. To their credit, they were among the earliest and most consistent opponents of totalitarian rule, indeed of injustice and tyranny in all its forms. And, despite a life of hard experience, their integrity and optimism have remained intact. "Clara and I remain anarchists," says Sidney Solomon. "There are grass-roots sentiments everywhere that indicate that a libertarian movement can catch fire. People are getting tired of rigid bureaucracies and social formulas. In anarchism there is an underlying idea that relates to virtually every aspect of life. We have no regrets about those early years. We threw ourselves heart and soul into the cause. It was writing and working, it was personal involvement, it was hitchhiking and travel, it was organizing and demonstrating—it was all the energies of our youth."

• SAM DOLGOFF •

New York City, November 2, 1971; November 30, 1971;
December 10, 1971; December 18, 1971; August 12, 1972

Sam Dolgoff, a house painter by trade, was both an anarcho-syndicalist and a member of the Industrial Workers of the World. During the 1920s, as an itinerant propagandist, he rode the rails from town to town, subsisting on odd jobs. He spoke on street corners and in lecture halls, agitating for Mooney and Billings, for Sacco and Vanzetti, and against reformist socialism and authoritarian communism. In 1925, while in Chicago, Sam joined the Free Society Group, the largest contingent of anarchists in the city, and fell under the influence of Gregory Maximoff, a veteran of the Russian Revolution, whom he referred to as his "mentor." In Chicago he also encountered such figures as Lucy Parsons, widow of the Haymarket martyr Albert Parsons, and Ben Reitman, lover of Emma Goldman. In 1930, while passing through Cleveland on a speaking tour, Sam met a young anarchist named Esther Miller. The two became lifelong companions and settled in New York, where they raised their two sons, Abraham and Anatole.

Adopting the pen name of Weiner, Sam began to write for anarchist and labor publications, some of which (*Vanguard, Spanish Revolution, Views and Comments, News from Libertarian Spain*) he helped to found and edit. Over the next sixty years his writings appeared in a wide range of periodicals, in Europe as well as in America. He and Esther, in addition, founded the Libertarian League and were active in the Libertarian Book Club, both located in New York. After 1970 Sam published a series of books: *Bakunin on Anarchy* (1972), *The Anarchist Collectives: Workers' Self-Management in the Spanish Revolution, 1936–1939* (1974), *The Cuban Revolution: A Critical Perspective* (1976), and *Fragments: A Memoir* (1986). During the 1970s and 1980s, usually accompanied by Esther, he lectured at colleges and universities around the country and spoke at memorial meetings for Bakunin, Emma Goldman, and the Haymarket martyrs. With his gruff voice and unruly hair, his checkered shirts and wide suspenders, he cut a colorful figure on the platform. Sam died on October 24, 1990, at the age of eighty-eight, in the small apartment on the Lower East Side where he and Esther had resided for twenty-five years. During that time they received a steady flow of visitors from all over the world, who would always find a comradely welcome, a place to sleep, and a lively exchange of ideas. Esther herself had died there almost a year before Sam, and her death undoubtedly hastened his passing.[594]

I WAS BORN on October 10, 1902 in the *shtetl* of Ostrovsky in Vitebsk province on the Dvina River. My father's brother, Tsadik Dolgopolsky, was a well-known Yiddish teacher and writer. Father was a railroad worker, nonpolitical but humanitarian. In the U.S. he became a house painter. We followed him here in 1905 or 1906. I started working at eleven and was apprenticed to a house painter at fourteen. I attended public school in New York and some night school, but I was largely self-educated. I took language courses at the Rand School but acquired languages mainly by reading.

At the age of thirteen or fourteen I liked to listen to radical soapbox speakers. I joined the Young People's Socialist League in 1917, when Morris Hillquit campaigned for mayor of New York on the slogan of "Better milk for babies." I thought this timid and beside the point. What was needed was fundamental social reform. I began to criticize the socialists. A few years later I was expelled from YPSL. "You're not a socialist but an anarchist," I was told. This aroused my interest in anarchism. I began to read anarchist literature. I became an anarchist in 1920 or 1921 and a Wobbly in 1922.

I joined the Road to Freedom Group around this time, but found their ideas too vague and utopian. I was especially put off by their antiorganizational position. Hippolyte Havel was one of the best-known members of the group. He was an able writer and a man of broad culture. He fit the bourgeois image of an anarchist, almost a character, who adorned anarchist meetings and gatherings. He was of medium height, with long hair, a thick mustache, spade beard, pince-nez, spats, cane, black ribbon tie, and narrow, tight-fitting trousers. He was witty and used colorful language enriched by drink. He and Tom Bell didn't get along; he called him Tumbell. He spoke with a Czech accent. He was a drinker and bon vivant, supported by friends, mostly Jews and Italians. He never had a regular job, except as a dishwasher. He went on frequent drunks in Greenwich Village, returning from his drinking sprees looking like a drowned muskrat. He was a typical bohemian anarchist. He loved the theater. He sponged regularly off Eugene O'Neill, and it is said that he was the model for the anarchist editor in *The Iceman Cometh*. Ideologically he was an eclectic anarchist. He wrote mediocre pamphlets that contributed nothing to anarchist theory. Max Nettlau accused him of chopping up his biography of Malatesta. But he had a sane and humane streak in him. He deplored that the Italian anarchists engaged in bootlegging and racketeering. With all his idiosyncracies he was an ethical anarchist, close in spirit and friendship to Rudolf Rocker.

Havel was the editor of *The Road to Freedom*, the organ of the group. The writers included Samuel Polinow, a member of the Radical Library Group in Philadelphia and a bit of a screwball—an anarcho-moron. E. Bertran was another oddball, a Frenchman who had a scheme of marketing his own special brand of aspirin. He went to Brazil [Costa Rica] to found an anarchist colony, but nothing came of it. Grant Lowry's real name was Louis Genin [q.v.], a plumber by trade. His wife was Abe Bluestein's [q.v.] sister Minnie, who was going blind and jumped off the roof earlier this year [1971]. Abraham Blecher [q.v.] was treasurer of the group. He later flirted with the Trotskyites and now lives in Miami Beach. Grace Wellington, not an anarchist, was a poet from Pittsburgh; she wrote poems on Sacco and Vanzetti. Dr. Liber was a vegetarian and nature faddist. Donald Crocker was a notorious drunkard but a first-rate printer and radical journalist. Pat Quinlan was a Wobbly anarchist, mainly interested in the labor movement; he hung on the fringe of the group. Harry Block was a doctor living in Chelsea, Massachusetts, a poet and friend of

Havel's and Abe Winokour's. Dr. Globus was a dentist, an erudite and fine man. Apart from *The Road to Freedom*, he also wrote for the *Fraye Arbeter Shtime* and gave frequent lectures. He was a philosophical anarchist, a cultured man, a good writer and speaker. He was not a spellbinder, but was well-informed. When Hitler came to power, he took to wearing a skullcap to honor his fallen people. He was undogmatic, of moderate temper, friendly with all the groups.

Louis Raymond [q.v.] was a Spanish anarchist and IWW who was arrested during the Palmer raids, one of the so-called class-war prisoners. He was married to Lilly Sarnoff of the Road to Freedom Group, and they still live at Stelton. He wrote articles and poems for *Cultura Proletaria* as well as for *The Road to Freedom* and was a house painter by trade. Walter Starrett (Van Valkenburgh) came from Schenectady, where he organized Emma Goldman's lectures. He lost a leg in a railroad accident. He had a job in the Wall Street area, knew Havel well, and succeeded him as editor of *The Road to Freedom*. He was also friendly with Carlo Tresca, and so the *L'Adunata* group hated him; they threatened him and made life miserable for him. This is another example of how many anarchists recapitulate all the evils of the state which they themselves condemn. The *L'Adunata* crowd were fanatics who hounded moderates; they were petty and vindictive; they gossiped about other groups. Starrett had a Jewish wife named Sadie Ludlow. He was a good man. He died of a heart attack in the 1930s.

Archie Turner was from England. He and Van [Valkenburgh] hated each other; they got along like fire and water. Van once pulled a gun on him and I took it away. Turner had no trade and no special talents except being a ladies' man, an anarchist Don Juan. He and most of the other Road to Freedom members belonged to the lunatic fringe of the movement. One believed that human beings were unfinished organisms, yet to be perfected; another believed that there was no society, no people, only "me." There were quarrels over trivia or nothing at all. Marcus Graham was always spoiling for a fight. Rudolf Rocker called him a "wretch," an extreme term for Rocker. Graham was a terrible scandal-monger. He was supported mostly by Italian anarchists of the Galleani school, who admired his militancy, rather than by the more moderate Jews.

Among the saner anarchists was Harry Kelly. He was a friend of Max Nettlau, gentle, quiet, unassuming, friendly, intelligent. His main work was establishing colonies and Modern Schools. He was also active in the Sacco-Vanzetti case. Another good comrade was Jules Scarceriaux, a Frenchman who lived near Los Angeles and was affiliated with the Italians of the area. He was an amateur potter and sculptor. He made clay plaques of Bakunin, Kropotkin, Malatesta, and Reclus. He left all his money to anarchist newspapers.

As you can see, I was not entirely happy about the Road to Freedom Group. Around 1924 I started my own mimeographed paper, *Friends of Freedom*, a one-man Young Turk affair that lasted only a few months. No copies survive, as far as I know. Then I went to Chicago and joined the Free Society Group, a polyglot group, mainly Jewish, Italian, Spanish, and Russian, that held weekly lectures and forums. I soapboxed for them in Bughouse Square, opposite the Newberry Library. The secretary of the group was Boris Yelensky [q.v.], a crusty paperhanger, born with boxing gloves on. He was active in raising money for political prisoners in Russia and Italy. Through him I met Gregory Maximoff, my mentor. Maximoff took me in hand. He taught me about Bakunin and about anarcho-syndicalism. For me Free Society's brand of anarchism was too visionary and vague, like that of the Road to Freedom. I drew up my own anarcho-syndicalist manifesto, which Maximoff supported, and read it before the Midwest anarchist conference, held that year, 1926, I think, in Chicago. Few delegates attended. As one of them, Rose Krutchkoff of Cleveland, remarked of her own group: "Well, the Italians don't believe in conventions, and the two Jews aren't speaking to each other."

Besides Yelensky and Maximoff, the Free Society Group included Irving Abrams, a lawyer, and Maximiliano Olay, a Spanish anarchist born in Asturias who came to the United States before World War I and spread anarchist propaganda among the cigar workers. He was thin, nervous, emotional, a regular jumping-jack. In Chicago he operated a translation bureau, but when the Spanish Civil War broke out he became the CNT-FAI representative in New York. He traveled among the Spanish groups in the midwest as a sort of liaison, keeping them in touch. When Barcelona fell, according to Rudolf Rocker, who was with Olay at the time, he broke into tears. He had a Jewish wife, Anna, and a son Lionel, a hippie who wrote for the Los Angeles *Free Press*. Olay died of an ulcer during the Second World War. His wife later committed suicide.

I spoke several times at the Free Society forums during the mid-1920s. I met Lucy Parsons, who attended my talk on "Is Anarcho-Syndicalism Possible?"—I thought it was not only possible but inevitable. She found the talk excellent, one of the best she had ever heard. She later became a Communist sympathizer, lending her name to their affairs, petitions, and causes. I shared the platform with her in 1937 at a fiftieth anniversary commemoration in Chicago of the Haymarket Martyrs. Another person I met in Chicago was Ben Reitman, the "clap doctor from Chi." You couldn't possibly have too low an opinion of him. He was a cheap opportunist, who took advantage of Emma Goldman. The one good thing about him was that, during Prohibition, he wrote a good prescription for whiskey.

During the late 1920s I was often on the bum, riding the rails as a Wobbly soapboxer, speaking for Mooney and Billings and other causes. Passing through Cleveland in 1930, I met Esther Miller, who became my lifelong companion. She was born in Volynia province, Russia, in 1905. Her father's cousin had been an anarchist who "went to the people." She came to America at the age of six months, and her family settled in Cleveland. Esther helped form the Social Studies Club with the idea of reading and discussing radical literature. She received an A.B. at Western Reserve University in 1927 and joined the Anarchist Forum in Cleveland the following year. She was accepted to medical school but the Depression prevented her from going. Another member of the Anarchist Forum was Luba Fagin, the sister of Fanny Baron, who had been shot by the Cheka in 1921.

I returned to New York in 1930, and Esther followed me a few months later. Between 1932 and 1934 we lived at the Stelton Colony, where our older son Abe was born. Esther and I were dissatisfied with the Stelton school and started a mimeographed paper called *Looking Forward!*—only a few numbers appeared—together with Albert Weiss and other young people who were critical of the way the school and colony were run. Many of the young people felt that the school did not give them enough. Some were attracted by communism or socialism, and we sent our son to the Fellowship Farm school for a while. Alexis Ferm replied to our criticisms, and I replied to him in turn.

The trouble with Stelton was that it wasn't really an anarchist colony but a hybrid with a libertarian streak. People owned their own houses, worked for wages, and worked outside the colony. The school was the only thing that held them together, but even that was no more anarchist than many progressive schools of the time. All this was true of Mohegan as well, which had even less of an anarchist identity. In fact, there never was a true anarchist colony in the United States. All such experiments were disparate, mixtures, vaguely libertarian in their ideas and aspirations, and diluted by the presence of non-anarchists—socialists, liberals, sympathizers. Stelton, like other colonies, was infested by vegetarians, naturists, nudists, and other cultists, who sidetracked true anarchist goals. Marcus Graham always went barefoot, ate raw food, mostly nuts and raisins, and refused to use a tractor, being opposed to machinery; and he didn't want to abuse horses, so he dug the earth himself. Most Steltonians worked in New York and New Brunswick, though the colony did have a cooperative garment contracting factory.

Until the early 1930s Joseph Cohen was a key figure at Stelton. He was tall, slender, and very intelligent and able. He was as keen as mustard. But he envied Rudolf Rocker for his reputation as a writer, speaker, and ideologist, and for his standing in the anarchist movement. Cohen criticized Rocker in the *Fraye Arbeter Shtime*, of which Cohen was then editor. He once told a group of us at the *Fraye Arbeter Shtime* office: "You're making a god of him. No one's infallible. He's a man, after all." Rocker himself had never sought this kind of worship. He was humble, modest. Cohen, by contrast, was egotistical and conceited; he cared very much about his esteem and reputation. Cohen resisted extreme reaction against bolshevism and criticized many of his *Fraye Arbeter Shtime* colleagues for becoming "the right wing of the State Department," defenders of the capitalist system. Cohen was thus accused of being an apologist for communism. After the collapse of Sunrise, Cohen's wife died. He remarried and moved to Paris after the war and published *Fraye Gedank* there in the 1950s. He criticized the *Fraye Arbeter Shtime* for defending the U.S., for its cold war mentality, for its friendliness to the social democrats. He died in 1953.

Beginning in 1930 I wrote a few articles for *The Road to Freedom*. Then, in 1932, I helped organize the Vanguard Group, together with Mark Schmidt [q.v.], Louis Slater [q.v.], Abe Bluestein [q.v.], Sidney Solomon [q.v.], and Clara Freedman [Solomon, q.v.], whose father was the manager of the *Fraye Arbeter Shtime*. The group also included Glenn Carrington, a black homosexual who wrote under the name of George Creighton; "Jack White" (real name

Jack Schlesinger), who wrote on literary subjects; and "David Lawrence," a Portuguese Jew whose real name was Leonard Dal Negro. Alexander Schapiro was our European correspondent. There were also a few Chinese members, who worked in a cooperative restaurant on Second Avenue called Jade Mountain. Its main figures were Yat Tone and Eddie Wong, who had come to New York from the Equality Group in San Francisco. Both were dedicated and idealistic. They held Chinese dinners in their restaurant to raise money for the movement. Yat Tone traveled to Spain in 1933, and then returned to China to set up a Modern School but was arrested and executed.

Basically Vanguard was an anarchist-communist group, propagating the ideas of Bakunin and Kropotkin. It disagreed sharply with the Stirnerites, individualists, and bohemians. Under the influence of the Depression, it believed it necessary to prepare for the social revolution. It believed that what was needed was a realistic program of action, to win support from the workers and intellectuals, to organize an anarchist-communist federation throughout the United States as a prelude to the social revolution.

The Vanguard Group held weekly forums. It favored a united front with progressive groups—especially the IWW and the socialists for specific purposes. Its biggest deficiency was its hero-worship of Schmidt, a textile salesman by occupation, the oldest member and guiding intellect of the group. (He wrote as "Senex" for our journal, *Vanguard*.) He began to drift towards the Communists and advocated a united front with them. In 1939 he went so far as to support the Molotov-Ribbentrop pact. This caused a deep rift with some of the younger members, especially myself and Abe Bluestein, and we began to fight him. We had the support of Maximoff, while Schmidt was supported by Slater and by Roman Weinrebe, the son of an old Jewish anarchist [B. Rivkin] and a Georgian gentile mother. He was a millwright, a fine mechanic, and worked with the retarded and handicapped. The group split apart and eventually broke up completely. Abe Bluestein had already broken away and in 1938, after returning from Spain, started a new paper, *Challenge*.

Challenge was a group as well as a journal. Many of its members were later active in the Libertarian Book Club. Robert Bek-Gran was one of the writers, and that was his real name. He was a German, inclined towards council communism, and a friend of Paul Mattick.[595] The other names in the paper are pseudonyms. Another new periodical was called *Spanish Revolution*, published by the United Libertarian Organizations, a group that included members from the IWW as well as anarchist groups such as Vanguard, Cultura Proletaria, Fraye Arbeter Shtime, Il Martello, and Delo Truda, banded together to support the Spanish Revolution. The treasurer was Isaac Radinowsky, a construction foreman and good administrator, who represented the Fraye Arbeter Shtime Group. I raised the bulk of the money on speaking tours through the east and midwest, as far as St. Louis. We were divided over whether the anarchists in Spain should join the coalition government. Jews tended to favor it; Schapiro and Maximoff were opposed; and the Spaniards themselves were split.

There were other active groups and individuals during the 1930s. There were several Italian groups in New York and other cities, a few Spanish groups, and Portuguese groups in Newark, New Jersey, and New Bedford, Massachusetts. Abba Gordin was a one-man movement. He published his own paper [*The Clarion*] and had his own disciples. He was strongly individualist and stayed away from the main movement. Joe Zack, a glazier and good comrade, spoke among both Russian and Jewish groups. And Mateo Rico was active among the English, Spanish, and Italian groups. Rico, though a Sicilian, was active in the Spanish Cultura Proletaria Group. He lived at Stelton and managed the cooperative garment workshop. He was the companion of Rose Pesotta and later of Anna Schwartz [q.v.]. At Stelton he got into an argument over a woman, shot a man, and I think did a stretch in prison. He died about fifteen years ago.

The Why?/Resistance Group was founded during the war. They were mostly Greenwich Village bohemian types, ox-cart anarchists who opposed organization and wanted to return to a simpler life. Luigi Fabbri once called this type "bourgeois anarchists," as opposed to his own "classical anarchism." Most were pacifists during the war; and when Rudolf Rocker, who had opposed the First World War, came out against Hitler, they heckled him. I agreed with Rocker and broke with them, though we remained on friendly terms. I am sick and tired of these half-assed artists and poets who object to organization and want only to play with their belly buttons. They were also strongly influenced by Wilhelm Reich, the psychoanalyst. David Wieck went to jail as a conscientious objector. Most of the L'Adunata Group were also opposed to the war.

The journal *Why?* was founded around 1943 by myself, Franz Fleigler [q.v.] (pen name "Lead Line"), Dorothy Rogers, a Canadian proofreader from Toronto who had nursed Emma Goldman and accompanied her funeral cortege to the Waldheim Cemetery in 1940, Audrey Goodfriend [q.v.] and her husband David Koven [q.v.], David Wieck and his wife Diva Agostinelli, Jackson MacLow, a pacifist poet, Daniel DeWeis, a black Brooklyn College student, and Paul Goodman, who remained on the fringe of the group. Most were students and intellectuals. They held weekly lectures and forums in the hall of the Spanish group at 813 Broadway, later used by the Libertarian League. *Why?* was renamed *Resistance*; some in the group took to Buddhism and mysticism, and some, such as Dave Dellinger, had links with the Committee of Non-Violent Revolution.

In 1955 Esther and I founded the Libertarian League, and it lasted for ten years. Together with the Libertarian Book Club, of which we were also members, it became the main source for the distribution of anarchist literature in the United States, selling over ten thousand dollars' worth of literature during the decade of its existence. It also issued a journal, *Views and Comments* (the last issue, number 50, was titled *Towards Anarchism*) and reprinted Errico Malatesta's *Anarchism* and George Woodcock's *Anarchism or Chaos*, among other works.

The Libertarian League was based in New York, sharing a hall at 813 Broadway between Eleventh and Twelfth Streets with the Cultura Proletaria Group, formerly the Cultura Obrera Group, founded forty years earlier by Pedro Esteve, whom I met before his death in 1925. The name of his paper was changed from *Cultura Obrera* to *Cultura Proletaria* and edited by Marcelino García [q.v.] and Frank González, both very fine men. The Spanish comrades were generous and hospitable. They had a monthly dinner without admission charges and simply passed around the hat. If you couldn't contribute they knew you would do so when able.

The League had about ten regular members, including old-timers like us and Russell Blackwell and newtimers like William Rose, Richard Ellington, [q.v.] Walter Caughey, and Jonathan Leake. Our position was essentially anarcho-syndicalist, with a nostalgia for anarchist-communism. We sponsored weekly lectures (on Fridays) on various subjects, attended by twenty to fifty people, as well as the dinners prepared by the Spaniards, chiefly to raise money. The group consisted mostly of students and a few workers. Most of the articles in *Views and Comments* were unsigned but written by me, and I also translated materials from French and Spanish anarchist papers.

Apart from the forums, the journal, and the distribution of literature, our activities were diverse. We demonstrated against Franco by picketing the Spanish consulate and tourist office and organizing a committee to save workers in Spanish prisons; Norman Thomas[596] and other socialists were among the members. We saved at least five lives of anarchist workers condemned to death. Russell Blackwell and I wrote anti-Franco letters that William Green[597] signed and read at the AFL-CIO convention in Washington. We criticized the suppression of the anarchist movement in Bulgaria and maintained contact with Bulgarian anarchists in Parisian exile. We criticized the Castro regime in Cuba from the outset, as we had been in contact with the correspondence bureau of the Cuban anarchist movement in Miami, and in Havana before Castro took power, and knew what was going on. When Dave Dellinger supported Castro, a split took place and a debate ensued in *Liberation* magazine. Roy Finch, a professor of philosophy at Sarah Lawrence College and a pacifist like Dellinger, came over to the League's position and resigned as one of the editors. I and Russell Blackwell made a tape for WBAI on "Cuba: A Third View," but the station decided not to run it as being "too controversial and one-sided."

The League maintained close liaison with anarchist groups in Europe, including the Noir et Rouge Group in Paris and a group in Milan. We had a mailing list of over three hundred names, many of them in American colleges and universities. Though our group expired in 1965, it paved the way for the anarchist revival that began about that time.

The League had a number of affiliate groups in the U.S. with which it kept in contact: one in Youngstown, Ohio, mostly Spanish, Italian, and Russian steel workers; another in Detroit, mostly Spanish and Italian; one in Albany, New York, mostly students at the State University; one in Cleveland, old anarchists and Wobblies; and others in Vancouver, British Columbia, and Donora,

Pennsylvania. The Seattle Group, led by George and Louise Crowley, kept in touch with us and issued a bulletin. There was a convention in Youngstown in 1960 attended by Spanish and some Italian comrades. We got financial support from all over the country—from Italian anarchists in California and from students and professors at Rice University in Houston.

Among the younger members of the League in New York, William Rose (who wrote as "G.W.R.") was a graduate of Yale who studied in Spain, where the anarchist underground converted him. He married a Spanish girl, returned to the U.S., and was a reporter in Ohio before coming to the League, which he left for the *National Guardian*. He became a strong sympathizer with Castro. Richard Ellington was a science-fiction bug who ran a multilith. He was a good technician, moved to California and became secretary of the San Francisco Opera Company.[598] He and other League members who went west helped start the anarchist movement there in the sixties. They organized demonstrations at Berkeley and helped inspire the Free Speech Movement and student rebellion. Walter Coy (his real name was Caughey) was a militant pacifist from Louisiana, a graduate of Antioch College in Ohio, and arranged for me to speak there. He took part in rent strikes on the Lower East Side, where he was murdered by hippies. Jonathan Leake came from a wealthy family; his father was a UN official. He became a Trotskyite, then a Maoist, and named his son Lenin. He was a nut and was expelled from the group.

Why did the group dissolve? People like Leake aroused the hostility rather than the support of the neighborhood. Some of the best members, like Ellington, moved to the Coast. Russell Blackwell grew less and less active as his energies were diverted to neighborhood groups and civil rights. A new element of crazies, nuts, acid-heads, and junkies, some with authoritarian tendencies, came in. Their talk was dominated by sex, drugs, and violent action. They were disruptive and did little constructive work. The problem became how to remove or expel them. They forced a change in the title of *Views and Comments* to *Towards Anarchism* to show their militant stance. The group then collapsed amid bickering and quarrels.

The crackpots, faddists, and terrorists have always given anarchism a bad name. And they are still with us today. For people on the west coast like Ed Stover and among the Solidarity Group in Chicago and even here in New York, the fascination with terrorism remains to plague us. With friends like these we don't need enemies. They're worse than *agents provocateurs*. Ravachol, Bonnot,[599] and their ilk were nothing but anarcho-bandits. The *L'Adunata* crowd, especially Galleani, glorified criminals like Duval. And Kropotkin, Emma Goldman, and Malatesta refused to condemn them. But Maximoff did, and rightly so.

Since the Second World War, older groups, mostly echoes of the past, have been trying to keep the movement alive and to adapt it to a rapidly changing world. But the movement is dying out. It's a paradox. The interest in anarchism grows as the movement declines. Then the historians enter on the scene to write its obituary. Anarchism becomes, for intellectuals, fashionable, even respectable, but there is no working-class support. The irony is that at a time of unprecedented interest in anarchism the movement is virtually defunct.

Yet the anarchists have not lost hope. It's too early to write their obituary. New seeds are being planted by the new histories and the old reprints of anarchism. If there's so much interest in our ideas, we must be saying something of fundamental and lasting importance. A whole generation, as Rudolf Rocker pointed out, was lost in wars and the rise of totalitarianism. This hindered the transmission of the anarchist tradition to the next generation. Now the survivors are too old and too few to carry on. No new thinkers have appeared to take the place of Bakunin and Kropotkin and to bring anarchism up to date. But it must be remembered that other radical movements—socialism, Communism, Trotskyism—are also dying out. All are mere shadows of their former selves. And they are bankrupt, discredited, unlike anarchism. We at least are going down with our colors flying.

The anarchists have a distinctive voice, a definite ideology, different from that of other radicals. Yet there are many varieties of anarchism, some more pertinent than others. I myself believe in workers' control but not in community control. Control must be in the hands of those who are engaged in specific tasks, who know what they are doing. Community control amounts to control by the mob, like Rousseau's "general will." What, after all, is "the community?" The community is an abstraction—one of the most dangerous of all abstractions. Not that I'm an elitist. Far from it. I believe in a functional democracy— administration by the people who work at specific tasks and know what they're doing. I'm not going to have a pants presser prescribe medicine for me. Can the community fix my TV set? All this talk of community control emerged during the education crisis in New York in the 1960s, where incompetents wanted to control the schools. One must have the necessary knowledge and skills. I'm sick of all this criticism of experts, technicians, and even bureaucrats. Skilled administrators are essential for a comfortable and orderly society. A complex world cannot rely on voluntary help alone. Essential services must be delivered on time and with reasonable efficiency, and this requires stable and responsible organizations.

The trouble lies not with the bureaucrats but with the lawmakers. The bureaucrats are themselves only cogs in the machine and not to be blamed. The engineers and technicians are not our enemies. The anarchists must face up to the problems of a complex industrial society. They must deal with the intricate questions of health, food, coordination of production and distribution, and so on. Even if there is a social overturn, these problems will not vanish. We'll still have to grapple with them. But without force or compulsion—or goodbye anarchism! Too many anarchists have been preoccupied with side issues and have failed to confront the basics of life.

Yes, my views have changed somewhat over the years. In the early days I had been enthusiastic over Kropotkin's anarchist-communism. But I've come to believe that anarchism per se is not a well-defined social system that we'll soon reach, but rather a permanent unfolding, a permanent transitional period. Kropotkin's ideas cannot fit everywhere, given the differing conditions and stages of development among the people of the world. The masses of people aren't ready to accept Kropotkin's ideas—there's a kind of social and cultural lag. No system, in fact, will suit all people. There is no single answer. Anarchism, rather, should be seen as an amalgam of theories which must be adjusted to modern life. I am more concerned now with practical problems and with deeply rooted prejudices and habits that are uncongenial to our ideas. We have to recognize and face this fact. Nor is anarchism realizable immediately. We will have to have all sorts of economic systems existing side by side, and this means inevitable friction. I'm willing to settle for a little less than the millennium. But we must try to propel things more and more in a libertarian direction. We don't, above all, want to compel, to dictate. When I was young things seemed much simpler.

• SARAH TABACK •

Bronx, New York, November 11, 1976

William and Sarah Taback, longtime anarchists in New York, became president and secretary, respectively, of the Libertarian Book Club in 1971. In 1975, however, they were voted out of office because of what the members deemed their authoritarian behavior. All official titles were thereupon abolished and everyone was declared to be simply a "member," on equal terms with everyone else. Bill, a retired electrician who had worked out an elaborate theory regarding the cause of earthquakes, was so hurt by his dismissal that he took to signing his correspondence "Bill Taback, Plain Member." He died in 1976 in his seventy-fifth year.[600] Sarah died in a Bronx nursing home about seven years later.

I WAS BORN on April 15, 1900, in the *shtetl* of Felshtin, near Proskurov, in the province of Kamenets-Podol'sk. My father, Moshe Kuman (later Cohen), was the steward of the village and an agronomist and made a good living. I had two brothers and three sisters, but Shprintse and I were the only ones who became anarchists. Mother died in childbirth with my younger sister Rose. I was frail and suffered palpitations of the heart, so I didn't go to school but had private teachers who came to the house, university students, one of them from Odessa.

We left for America in 1914, before the outbreak of the war. We settled in New York on East Tenth Street near Avenue A. Father was fifty-four years old. Shprintse was here already. She and all the other children worked, one brother in a shirt factory on Twenty-Third Street, Shprintse in a dress factory as a sewing-machine operator (she was then seventeen years old). I also worked for a while in a dress factory, doing unskilled labor.

When Shprintse came to America and began to work in the garment industry, she met anarchists and began to attend lectures by Emma Goldman and other speakers. At once she found herself. She recognized that she had always been an anarchist. She became an organizer for the union and was often laid off from her jobs. It was through Shprintse that I too became an anarchist. In Russia I had read Tolstoy, Korolenko,[601] and other great writers who were sympathetic to the people. Shprintse now took me to anarchist lectures and introduced me to her friends, whom she loved. She was very enthusiastic about them. Once, in 1917, she introduced me to Alexander Berkman. He had just come out of prison and was having trouble with his leg. "You have a weak heart," he said, "but join the movement and do what you can, distribute leaflets, and forget your troubles. Here I am with an injured foot, but my mind is intact and I remain active. Anarchism will give you life."

I didn't like Emma Goldman as much as Berkman. She was too much "I, I, I." I once heard her lecture in the Forward Building. It was one of her last lectures in America. She was a good speaker, a powerful personality. She possessed you when she spoke. Reporters and detectives sat in the front row, writing down everything she said—or trying to, she spoke so fast! When the *Buford* sailed I went to see them off. When Emma returned to New York in 1934, I saw her again. She looked old, but was still vigorous.

One day, in 1918, Mollie Steimer came to my house—we lived then on Seventeenth Street and Second Avenue—and handed me a batch of leaflets to distribute to workers on the streets, leaflets against the intervention in Soviet Russia. When she left, my father said, "What did that little girl want?" When I told him, he said, "Let Shprintse do it. She's older and stronger and could stand prison better." I refused, and he threatened to kill himself. But I went out to distribute the leaflets myself. After an hour I returned with the whole bundle, and he was quite relieved.

After the war I attended meetings of the Union of Russian Workers and of the Zhenskoe Obshchestvo [Women's Society]. For a while I lived with a Russian named Mikhailov, who helped get out the *Amerikanskie Izvestiia*. I often went to Stelton, where Shprintse lived in those years. I met Harry Kelly and Leonard Abbott, who were nice. But Joseph Cohen I didn't like. Even his face scared me then—like a stern old man. The first English-speaking group I belonged to was the Freedom Group, in the early 1930s. I became its secretary. We had a paper called *Freedom*, edited by Harry Kelly with the help of Dr. Jagendorf [q.v.] and Louis Raymond [q.v.]. The young people of the Vanguard Group resented us as "oldtimers." *Freedom* was the successor to *The Road to Freedom*, edited by Walter Starrett. He drank very heavily. One day while walking to a meeting I saw him lying in the gutter on Fourteenth Street, drunk and dirty and mumbling to himself.

After *Freedom* I was involved in *Challenge* and *Spanish Revolution*. Then came *New Trends* during the forties. Alexander Schapiro, its editor, had been brought up by Kropotkin in London. He was a highly intelligent person, devoted to his paper, but he had a weak heart and died a couple of years after it started.

The Libertarian Book Club was started in 1945. Bill and I were among the founding members, along with Jack Frager [q.v.], Shprintse, Joseph Aronstam, Brand [q.v.], Valerio [Isca, q.v.], Maliuta Gromm, and a few others. It grew very quickly. Bill worked nights for the Domino Sugar Company (as an electrician), so he was home in the daytime. He had a car and worked very hard for the group. We both worked hard. I got together with Bill in 1929. I was working in the office of Unity House, the union resort. Bill was on vacation at Camp Tamiment and came over to visit. He was working at that time as a title searcher in the New York City Hall of Records. We met at breakfast. I had recently broken up with Mikhailov. We played chess, went for boat rides. We began to see each other in the city. We remained together forty-seven years, till his death this past June.

• JACK FRAGER •

New York City, November 28, 1971; January 4, 1972; October 28, 1972

Jack Frager, a slender man of medium height with clear blue eyes and a soft, high-pitched voice, left his native Russia in 1921, having witnessed the revolution and civil war. Settling in New York, he became a house painter and a member of the Road to Freedom Group, contributing articles to its journal of the same name. Well-read in a range of radical literature, Frager was most strongly influenced by Gustav Landauer, the German anarchist martyr (see interview with Brigitte Hausberger), on whom he lectured often and whose famous essay on revolution he published in a Yiddish translation. Landauer, however, was not the only anarchist whom Frager admired. In 1976, on the centennial of Bakunin's death, he published in pamphlet form Bakunin's letter to Sergei Nechaev,[602] criticizing the latter's immorality. And in 1977, to commemorate the fiftieth anniversary of the execution of Sacco and Vanzetti, Frager brought out a reprint of Vanzetti's autobiography, *The Story of a Proletarian Life*. A dedicated anarchist— he named his daughter after Louise Michel—Frager served on the executive board of the *Fraye Arbeter Shtime* from 1970 to 1976 and as president of the Libertarian Book Club from 1971 to 1973 (he had been a member since 1945). Moving to Florida around 1980, he lectured on anarchism to senior citizens' groups, before returning to New York in 1993.[603]

I WAS BORN in 1902 in Podol'skaia *guberniia*, Russia, and brought up in Mogilev. I was not converted to anarchism but was born an anarchist; it was in me. As a teenager during the Russian Revolution, I was already told by friends that

I "talk like an anarchist." I left Russia in 1921 and went via Rumania to Buenos Aires, which had a large anarchist colony. I met Russian anarcho-syndicalists there and began to read anarchist literature, especially Bakunin and Kropotkin. *Zapiski revoliutsionera* (Memoirs of a Revolutionist) was the first of Kropotkin's works that I read, and it made a deep impression. But I don't consider myself, like Kropotkin, an anarchist-communist, or an anarcho-syndicalist or anarchist-individualist for that matter, but rather an "anarchist without adjectives." I reject all dogma and rigid theory. Life is a great teacher. I believe in the sanctity of the human person above all.

I moved from Buenos Aires to New York in 1922. I became especially devoted to the ideas of Gustav Landauer and I. N. Steinberg. I came to know Steinberg personally, a Left Socialist Revolutionary with a strong anarchist bent. As for Landauer, what impressed me about him was his idea not merely to talk about or preach anarchism but to start living an anarchist life within a capitalist framework. My first lecture in English, at the Stelton Colony, was on Landauer, and I later published a Yiddish translation of his *Die Revolution*.[604]

In New York I became a house painter and a member of the Road to Freedom Group, the first anarchist organization I ever belonged to. I wrote articles for its journal and was active at its center on Twenty-Third Street and later on Broadway. It was also called the International Group, a mixture of Italians, Spaniards, Jews, and Americans. It held regular open forums and published Hippolyte Havel's pamphlet on anarchism[605] but little else aside from the journal. Havel was a short, stocky Czech with an intelligent face. He was a heavy drinker, constantly putting the touch on his friends. Max Eastman once gave him a decent suit of clothes so he could go to the library.

Rose Pesotta was secretary of the group and its most dynamic force, but its literary luminary and best speaker was Walter Starrett (his real name was W. S. Van Valkenburgh, known as "Van"). Starrett, like Havel, was a heavy drinker, and he had a wooden leg. He succeeded Havel as editor of the journal, *The Road to Freedom*. He was a good soapbox orator with a sharp tongue; he was an acid critic of his opponents and refused to show tact or pull punches.

The group contained about twenty members, with an active nucleus of eight or so, including Pesotta, Starrett, Starrett's companion Sadie Ludlow, and myself. The journal had about three thousand subscribers. Its main thrust was anarchist-communist, in the tradition of Bakunin and especially Kropotkin. Marcus Graham was a member but on the fringe, always alone. Abe Winokour once told me that in 1918 or 1919 Graham decided to launch the social revolution in New York. He met on a street corner on Madison Avenue with Anna Sosnovsky, Mollie Steimer, and a few others—Abe Winokour himself couldn't make it—to start the revolution. "But what do we do?" someone asked Graham. And that ended the whole affair. When he was arrested and persecuted by the federal government, which wanted to deport him, he claimed to have been born in a small American town which through hard research he had found had burned down with all its records.

Leonard Abbott spoke at our forums and wrote for the paper. He was tall, erect, dignified looking, and handsome, the sort of man that people turn to look at in the street or on a bus or train. He was extremely well-spoken; he never chose the wrong word, even in ordinary conversation. There was no distance between him and other people, regardless of their social class or occupation. He came from an old and distinguished family. His wealthy father disinherited him when he turned to the cause of social justice and equality, though his children inherited a fortune after his death. He was charming, sincere, generous, and decent. You never heard a bad word about him, not even from political opponents. He eked out a living by journalism, editing, and ghostwriting. He was burdened by a crippled wife, Rose Yuster. He named his son after William Morris. He loved flowers and often carried some. "There must be something right about our movement," said Alexander Berkman on first meeting Abbott, who was carrying a bouquet of flowers.

Harry Kelly, like Abbott, was of old American stock, and though small and slight, commanded respect because of his honesty and integrity. He was soft-spoken, sincere, genuine. Like Abbott, he barely made a living. For a time he had a small real estate office. "One can make a lot of money in real estate," he once told me, "but not in my corner." He was not as eloquent or impressive as Abbott but was an effective speaker in small groups because of his warmth, humor, and sincerity.

Bolton Hall often attended our forums, a tall, lanky libertarian of American stock. He always wore a top hat and long coat to meetings and lectures, even before a working-class audience, a habit that irritated some of his intellectual friends, though he insisted that it commanded attention and respect.

Of the writers for *The Road to Freedom* Michael Cohn often contributed money to the movement; Samuel Polinow drank; E. Bertran was a French individualist; "Grant Lowry" was the pseudonym of Abe Bluestein's [q.v.] brother-in-law Louis (Whitey) Genin [q.v.], a plumber from the Bronx; and Archie Turner was an English anarchist, handsome and cynical. Dr. Globus was a dentist who also wrote for the *Fraye Arbeter Shtime* and was a frequent lecturer. Though he was an anarchist, he admired Karl Marx. He was a nice, fine, sincere man, though not an original thinker like Abba Gordin. Harry Block was a Chelsea, Massachusetts, physician who wrote poems and neglected his profession for his activities in the movement. Jack White (his real name was Schlesinger) had pretensions of being a literary critic and writer on the cultural scene.

Starting in the late 1920s there was a succession of other anarchist groups in New York. The Rising Youth Group of 1927–1929 included the Goodman sisters, who were twins; Joe Floria, the leading Italian member; Galileo Tobia [q.v.], now in Albany; Alexander Schapiro's daughter Helen; and a few others. The Goodman girls tried to take a westerner for money for the group, and he came in with a pistol and threatened to shoot them. Soon afterwards they left the movement and joined the Spinoza Institute. The Militant Anarchist Youth (MAY) of 1929–1930 included Whitey Genin, myself, and four or five others.

We had a youth page in *The Road to Freedom* in 1929, with Genin ("Grant Lowry") as the main contributor. The International Group was formed in the early thirties and published *Freedom* in New York, a successor to *The Road to Freedom*. I and Lilly Raymond were active in forming it.

The Vanguard Group was the main youth movement of the thirties. The main figure was Mark Schmidt ("Senex") [q.v.], Jewish, well-read, of intellectual bent. Roman Weinrebe's father, B. Rivkin, had been a Russian anarchist and editor of *Burevestnik*.[606] Abe Bluestein was editor of the paper, a Stelton product and fine person. Sam Weiner [Dolgoff, q.v.] was a good soapboxer but not much of an organization man. We worked together as house painters. He is neither petty nor vain, like so many anarchists, but honest, dedicated, and intelligent. But Vanguard had deep divisions. Mark Schmidt set up a group of spies, including his own companion, to spy on the others, including Sam and Esther Weiner. There was an element of Nechaev in Schmidt's makeup, a sign of his growing Stalinism.

The anarchist youth of the twenties and thirties left much to be desired. They were young in years, but their spirit was old. Carlo Tresca was three times their age but younger in spirit. Also, their behavior in many ways was communist, though outside the Communist Party. During the late 1930s some split off from Vanguard and started the Challenge Group. I was one of the members, and Abe Bluestein was editor of the paper. Its headquarters was on Fourteenth Street and Avenue A. Like the Road to Freedom Group, it had Spanish, Italian, and English-speaking members, and held lectures, forums, dinners, and picnics.

At about the same time, *Spanish Revolution* was published by an anarchist propaganda group of all factions to aid the anarchists in Spain. During the 1940s there was a group around the paper *New Trends*, of which I was a member. Alexander Schapiro was its leading intellect, and Lisa Luchkovsky, Jack White, and Sidney Solomon [q.v.] were other members. Schapiro's aim was to direct the paper against Dwight Macdonald's [q.v.] *Politics*. Schapiro, as a leading intellectual with an international reputation as "Kropotkin's darling," tended to look down on the others and had an elitist streak.

Between the 1940s and 1960s two other groups were important: the Libertarian Book Club and the Libertarian League. The book club still exists and remains quite active but is not as effective as before, mainly because Bill and Sarah Taback [q.v.] are in charge. Back in the 1930s Yanovsky said, after they asked some questions at a lecture of his, "*Er iz a ferd un zi a ku*" [He is a horse and she a cow]. At another meeting Maximoff said to me about Bill, "*Mne kazhetsia, chto on durnoi paren'*" [He seems to me a bad lot]. The Libertarian League was started in the 1950s by Russell Blackwell, together with Sam and Esther Weiner. Blackwell, a former Trotskyite, was converted to anarchism in Spain during the civil war. He was the mastermind and driving force. He was of Yankee origin and a cartographer by profession, an intelligent and dedicated person. He worked at the United Nations but was fired because of his anarchist ties.

During the 1930s I visited the Sunrise Colony and gave a lecture. The members came from all over the country. Nearly all were Jewish, but there were a few Italians. About two-thirds were anarchists, the rest workers of different political hues. Few were skilled in farming; some were lazy. The main reason for the colony's collapse was that everyone was accepted who could make a down payment. Joseph Cohen was intelligent and hard-working but cold and domineering. The largest group, from New York, brought their factional quarrels with them, so there was a built-in opposition from the start. On the language question there were assimilationists—Cohen, Simon Farber, Chaim Weinberg, and most of the other anarchists—against the Yiddishists, who wanted to make it a Yiddish colony with Yiddish as the official language. The assimilationists tended to be the harder and more reliable workers. Cohen, I should mention, allied himself with those who accused Rudolf Rocker, who came to America in the 1930s, of nourishing a cult of personality, and Rocker in return was extremely insulting toward Cohen.

During the 1920s I was strongly for a social revolution—but not for terrorism—for a revolution not dominated by anarchists any more than by Communists or any other group. I still favor revolution and hope that the anarchists will exert a positive libertarian influence in it and prevent the emergence of any new dictatorship. Like Landauer and Elisée Reclus, I believe that anarchism is a civilization, a culture, not just a new economic and social order. I strongly favor the nuclear family as the only warm, natural cell of society. I am opposed to a laissez-faire economy, which gives some a chance to exploit and profit from the work of others. I am opposed to wage slavery, but I favor private property in the form of personal belongings, including houses and gardens.

The anarchists have the foibles and failings of all human beings, but as a group they are nicer and more decent than most. The reason is that ethics and humanitarianism always played a central role with them, in contrast, say, to the Marxists, who were chiefly concerned with power, success, and organization. We wanted not "success," not a political takeover, but a change, a transformation of human beings, a better society with better people.

• ABE BLUESTEIN •

New York City, December 9, 1972

Abe Bluestein is the son of Mendel (Max) Bluestein, a leader of the Anarchist Group in the International Ladies' Garment Workers' Union and a member of the Stelton and Sunrise Colonies. Abe was brought up in Stelton, and was an editor (as Abe Coleman) of *Vanguard* and *Challenge* during the 1930s. In 1937 he went to Spain and served as an English-language correspondent for the CNT-FAI in Barcelona, where he encountered Emma Goldman (whom he had first met in

New York in 1934) and the German anarchist Augustin Souchy. Abe never lost his interest in Spanish anarchism, lecturing and translating books on the subject (including Souchy's *With the Peasants of Aragón*). Following the death of Franco in 1975, he coedited *News from Libertarian Spain* (1977–1980) and its successor *Anarchist News* (1980–1982). Active in the cooperative housing movement in New York City, Abe was a manager of the ILGWU cooperative houses in Manhattan and of the Amalgamated and Co-op City houses in the Bronx. His wife, Selma Cohen Bluestein, he met in the Vanguard group, and she drew cartoons for *Challenge*.

I WAS BORN in Philadelphia on November 1, 1909. Both of my parents were anarchists and members of the Radical Library. They were very close friends of the Melmans [q.v.]. The Radical Library was a lively group with a very active social life among the immigrants. I can remember going to the Sunday School for a while, but I was a small child when we left. My sister Minnie and I were taken to Stelton in 1917. My parents separated, and we lived with Mother but saw Father often, as he too lived at Stelton. He was an official of the ILGWU and was later at Sunrise. I had a very close relationship with him all my life.

I was brought up in an anarchist milieu, and was an anarchist already as a child. I had many lengthy discussions with my father—even before I was in my teens—over whether society could exist without government or laws. He insisted that the strongest guides or codes that people could have were internal, within themselves, and that the best social order was one which was freely arrived at by the people themselves, rather than being imposed by some external authority. Thus in the home he promoted the same educational philosophy as the Modern School itself was practicing. Our house was filled with anarchist literature, and Kropotkin's works—especially *The Conquest of Bread, Mutual Aid*, and *Appeal to the Young*—made the strongest impression on me. Thus all three sources—my father, the Modern School, and Kropotkin's writings—combined to shape my anarchist upbringing, something which has never left me.

I went to the Stelton school from 1917 until 1924, then to junior high school and high school in New Brunswick for three years. An interesting fact is that for about fifteen years in a row a Stelton kid was valedictorian in the junior and senior high school, of only three or four kids who went from Stelton into the New Brunswick schools each year. I was valedictorian in junior high school and was headed in the same direction in high school, but we moved to New York in 1928 for my senior year. We lived in Coney Island and I graduated from James Madison High School. I spent two years at Brooklyn College, and then we moved to the Amalgamated co-op's in the Bronx, so I transferred to City College, from which I was graduated.

The Stelton school was conducted in an atmosphere of almost total freedom. We went there each day and did exactly what we wanted to. This could mean playing all day or periods of frenzied activity in the weaving shop or the carpentry shop or the printing shop. But there was very little interest in academic classes, and there was unending concern among some of the parents over this lack of academic training. In response to their pressure, Uncle and Aunty Ferm would intermittently conduct classes, but only half-heartedly, so that we never approached reading with the same enthusiasm as the manual arts. I would guess that at least 75 percent of the children put in nearly all their time in arts and crafts, despite our freedom to do whatever we wanted—or nothing at all. Only a small minority, and a constantly changing minority, took advantage of the freedom to do nothing.

I liked both of the Ferms, though Aunty was much firmer, almost dogmatic, in her educational philosophy, while Uncle was a more gentle soul who talked little but inspired the children by his personal example. He was warm, dignified, and highly skilled, and always had a crowd of children working with him. He never told you what to make, but when you came to him with an idea, he was always encouraging and helpful. I remember his helping me once to make a wheelbarrow. When we were finished he asked, "Do you realize how much you have learned of arithmetic and geometry?," and he explained how that was so. He was a warm and good man.

One of my pleasantest memories is of publishing the *Voice of the Children*. I worked the presses, and loved every minute of it, under Paul Scott's gentle guidance. He was another warm person with a great deal of love for children and for graphic arts, in which he was a proficient man. John Edelman produced several plays with the children. We brought *A Midsummer Night's Dream* to New York and put it on in the old Hippodrome Theatre (I acted in it) and the place was always filled to capacity. Sherwood Trask was another of the fine teachers and human beings of whom I have fond recollections.

One of the most unpleasant memories I bear with me was of the bitter fights between the anarchists and Communists in the colony. It expressed itself in all phases of colony life—in the school, in the cooperatives—where people came face to face with each other. They were always in conflict and I particularly deplored that as a teenager growing up. The same fight was going on simultaneously in the ILGWU, and ours was a sort of extension of it. Father was involved deeply in both places. Without the three leading anarchists—Bluestein, Nicholas Kritzman, and Louis Levy—the Communists would have succeeded in taking over the union, as Dubinsky himself admitted. On the other hand, I cannot forget how a group of simple garment workers with modest resources could organize and maintain not only the school but a whole range of cooperative enterprises, including a cooperative milk delivery, a cooperative bus service, a cooperative grocery and vegetable store, and a cooperative ice-cream parlor. And during the Depression, after I left, a cooperative dress factory was also set up.

Hippolyte Havel was already a superannuated figure, no longer active in the anarchist movement. Though he did edit *The Road to Freedom*, he had no active role in the colony, neither in the school nor in the cooperatives. He was a sort of passive bystander, though wonderful to talk to and to watch as he walked down the road. When drunk he often made anti-Semitic remarks, despite the fact that he was supported by Jewish comrades all those years. This was the last phase of his life, and he was a declining man. Many were moved by pity for him at this point.

Joseph Cohen was by contrast an active figure. I never heard him referred to in any sense as a dictator. (These charges probably arose from the bitterness of the Sunrise experience during the Depression.) On the contrary, he was frequently quoted and was regarded with respect.

We sometimes had picnics at Leonard Abbott's house in Westfield, but he was already fading out of the movement by the mid-twenties. Finally, I should say something about the physical conditions in the colony. When we moved there, the nearest telephone was a mile away; there was no electricity and no central heating; we had outhouses for many years and unreliable running water. Dirt roads became impassable during the spring. It was all very primitive.

We moved to New York, as I said, in 1929, at the beginning of the Depression. One of the first things I did was to start going to the forums at the Libertarian Center on Second Avenue and Thirteenth Street. The Vanguard Group was formed there in 1932. At that time I still had all the arrogance of youth and I criticized the more utopian aspects of anarchism and of libertarian education, which provoked Anna Sosnovsky to call me an "anarcho-bolshevik." My criticisms were harsh and were received with deep resentment. Moreover, *The Road to Freedom* was too vague, too loose, and gave no clear picture of anarchism and was not attractive to us youth. Not that there was a deep gulf between the old and the new generations, between the fathers and the sons, but there was one between the immigrants and the American-born. Once Harry Kelly spoke to our group and I asked him: "You have given your life to the anarchist movement. Don't you think, in view of the movement's decline, that your life has been a failure?" To which he replied: "Each man must live according to his own views and has to be true to himself. If one believes in liberty, one must live according to its principles." Kelly also emphasized the warmth of fellowship and fraternity, the common bonds and shared ideals, with anarchists all over the world.

Mark Schmidt [q.v.] was the mentor of our group. He had been in Russia during the revolution and emigrated to the United States during the twenties. He was a highly intelligent man with a sound and logical way of approaching social problems. He was well read and well informed and brought his knowledge to bear effectively on a wide range of subjects. He was au courant with events all over the world, on which he had very definite ideas. He also had great energy and drive and kept us together as a group more than we would have been if left to ourselves. I met him in the street about ten or twelve years ago, and he was still an apologist for Stalin for whom the Soviet Union represented the wave of the future and the U.S. the height of fascism and imperialism.

In addition to our magazine, we conducted forums and lectures and made soapbox speeches on street corners, getting into fights with the Communists all the time, protected by Wobblies with iron pipes wrapped with handkerchiefs. *Challenge*, unlike *Vanguard*, a theoretical monthly, was a weekly tabloid dealing with current events. Louis Slater [q.v.] and I were the key figures, with Simon Farber helping out. Robert Bek-Gran taught at Mohegan and at the Walden School but remained on the fringe of the movement. Eddie Wong, a waiter at the Jade Mountain restaurant, was married to a Polish Jewess [Bella Wong, q.v.]. We were also active at Carlo Tresca's center on Fifth Avenue and Fifteenth Street. Selma painted murals there.

I went to Spain with Selma in May 1937 and remained there until January 1938. On our way there we visited Emma Goldman in London. When we got to Spain we met Brand [q.v.], and it was amazing how he could move about and get into and out of places where no one else could go. I was in charge of the English-language desk of the CNT-FAI, giving radio broadcasts and sending weekly news bulletins to U.S. and British publications.

With the outbreak of the Second World War we faced a great dilemma. As antimilitarists we could not support the war, but we regarded Hitler and fascism as the greater danger. Our group dissolved during the war. I have never abandoned the anarchist cause, though I became inactive as the movement itself was dying out. But I still retain my anarchist ideals. I regard anarchist-communism and anarcho-syndicalism as complementary rather than contradictory. I don't think that a violent upheaval can ever break the chains of dictatorship and lead to real freedom. Spain showed that the libertarian tradition is deeply rooted and has vast constructive possibilities. But I've never accepted class struggle as the explanation of historical development, nor any theory of violent confrontations. Rather, I see history as a slow, tortuous climb by humanity striving toward liberty and brotherhood. But men have themselves been responsible for their own sufferings over the centuries because of their ignorance, prejudices, and fear of the unknown and unfamiliar. Thus the answer lies primarily in education—"freedom through education," as Elizabeth Ferm put it. All my life I have put my faith in trade unions, cooperatives, and education as constructive channels. Is this inconsistent with anarchism?

• LOUIS GENIN •

Bronx, New York, April 15, 1975

In 1929 Louis ("Whitey") Genin, not yet twenty years old, was writing for *The Road to Freedom* under the pen name "Grant Lowry." Joining the Vanguard Group in the 1930s, he wrote as "Gike Mold" (a takeoff on the Communist writer Mike Gold) for *Vanguard* and for *Challenge*, edited by Abe Bluestein (q.v.), whose sister Minnie was Genin's wife. The Genins spent more than two years at the Sunrise Colony in Michigan. Returning to New York, where Whitey became a licensed plumber, they lived in the Amalgamated Cooperative Houses in the Bronx.

I WAS BORN in New York City on February 19, 1910. My father was a political prisoner in tsarist Russia and was on his way to Siberia when he escaped and came to America a few years before my birth, becoming a custom ladies' tailor. He was liberal or radical in outlook, but had a very mild personality, a nonviolent socialist. Once when we were having a discussion of social questions he said, "You know something, you're an anarchist." He had got my point of view. I was then about fifteen.

When I become interested in something I go to the sources and study it. I wanted to go to the Rand School and joined the YPSL [Young People's Socialist League] to get in there. But then I heard Sam Dolgoff [q.v.] lecture, so I joined his group and began to study anarchism on my own. I read everything that I could get my hands on. The two greatest influences were Proudhon and Kropotkin. I leaned towards anarcho-syndicalism and read a good deal about the IWW. I could not see anarchism by itself, as a mere philosophy, but rather as something to be practiced, to be put into effect, and so had to be tied to the labor movement. What was to happen after the revolution? What was the social and economic structure going to be? These were the important questions. And my position is still that way: organizations have to be functional, not geographic, trade unions and consumer organizations rather than local communes. If they are geographic, they tend to outlive their usefulness. This is not so if they are organized according to function.

I was against authority, against the state, against organization being imposed on me whether I like it or not. I always shared Jefferson's "That government is best which governs least," and also the views of Thoreau and Emerson, the American liberal heritage. So I turned away from socialism and communism and towards anarchism. We had our own liberal tradition right here in America, and a fantastic one!

I was about seventeen at that time, a senior at Stuyvesant High School. I wasn't surprised by the Sacco-Vanzetti case—the outcome, I mean. What had a greater influence on me, though, was the autobiography of Lincoln Steffens,[607] just as true today as it was in his time. As for Sacco and Vanzetti, I followed the trial and figured that the authorities were out to get them and that they didn't have a chance. It all came out of the Palmer witch-hunts. I began to read about Malatesta and the Italian sit-down strikes. He had a great influence on me. He wasn't a great writer, but an activist, and that appealed to me.

I was taught justice by my father, the old Judeo-Christian concept of justice, of "Do unto others," that every man is holy and deserving of respect. I inherited this idea, and it had a deep effect on me. I was once down in Philadelphia in the mid-twenties during a free-speech fight. I jumped up and started reciting the Declaration of Independence. The police arrested me and took me from one station to another so I couldn't get help, and after two weeks kicked me out of the city with the threat not to come back. I got a job at Camp Germinal under an assumed name—it was too close to Philadelphia—"Grant Lowry," from my initials in reverse. That was during the summer of 1927. The rest of the year I was a college student, first at NYU and then at the University of Michigan, studying engineering and economics. I graduated in 1930. At the Labadie Collection I read anarchist periodicals and the old *Masses*. Agnes Inglis, the curator, was very pleasant, very helpful. One thing college taught me: how to do research.

Rising Youth was not much of a group. The Goodman sisters were children of devout anarchists and inherited a traditional religion with all the ritual that goes with it. But apart from their paper, they didn't do very much. But the old Road to Freedom Group was still important. In 1929 I started a youth page in its journal under my alias Grant Lowry. I had known Yiddish from Workmen's Circle schools, and I'd always liked to write, poems and prose, in Yiddish or English. So I went to Walter Starrett and proposed a youth page in *The Road to Freedom*. He liked the idea, and all went well till I did a piece on Christian anarchism, which *The Road to Freedom* had little use for. I thought, take Christ out of the church so as to mean peaceful, nonviolent anarchism, and that was close to the true spirit of anarchism. I had quite a run-in with the Road to Freedom Group over that!

I attended the Road to Freedom conferences at Stelton and spoke there a few times on anarchism. I found that out there a lot of people had joined the movement not for its general philosophy but for some specific aspect of it, especially free love, and weren't genuine anarchists. I also found quite a few individualist anarchists who opposed organizations of any kind. This seemed to me to confuse freedom with license. They didn't realize that if you have liberty you have *more* responsibility than otherwise. Again, it's the old Judaistic concept: once you're a man you must be responsible for your actions; you can do good or evil, but you are responsible. You have the right to swing your arm as far as you want, but only to the point where the other fellow's jaw begins. Freedom with restraint. In many ways Judaism is an anarchistic philosophy, an ethical concept, in fact the whole concept of ethics. Take the ritual away from Judaism and take only its ethical philosophy, and it is very anarchistic.

A number of us who were influenced by Sam Dolgoff, including his own brother Tommy, decided to form a group in the Bronx as an alternative to both YPSL and YCL [Young Communist League]. Sid Solomon [q.v.], Abe Bluestein [q.v.], Tommy Dolgoff, myself—we called the group the Friends of Freedom. We had street-corner meetings and meetings in the anarchist center on Second Avenue. Some of the older anarchists—Sam Dolgoff, Harry Kelly—came to lecture to us. Harry Kelly was a talker but also a doer: he organized Stelton and Mohegan. Joseph Cohen, on the other hand, was more a talker than a doer, like an old school rabbi with a retinue around him, looking up to him. At Sunrise he was not practical, as Harry Kelly had been at Stelton and Mohegan.

We decided to put out a paper in English, the *Vanguard*, so we became the Vanguard Group. There was a Jewish paper, an Italian paper, and so on. But they did not reach a younger audience and did not say enough about what was happening here in America. We struggled—we were all working at the time.

Thinking back on it, it seems fantastic how we did it! How could I—working, married (to Abe Bluestein's sister Minnie)—write a weekly column? Where did I get the time? When I read it now, it's a funny thing: it's as if somebody else wrote it. I used the name "Gike Mold" in *Vanguard* and *Challenge*, a takeoff on Mike Gold, who wrote for the Communist press. I always had a sense of humor. Again, I admire the Jews for that. They never lost their humor, but poked fun at themselves and also used it as a weapon. That was the idea behind my column: humor used as a weapon to ridicule corrupt institutions.

Mark Schmidt [q.v.], a Russian, was the theorist of our group. I didn't care for him personally. I always had the impression that when he spoke "God had spoken," that we were getting the Word. But he did know what he was talking about. He certainly knew about Communism and got me interested in Communist literature, in Lenin and Trotsky, especially Lenin on the state—he had a keener understanding of the state than many anarchists had, and he knew how to use it! Schmidt disturbed me, though. I couldn't completely trust him, and we sometimes even felt he was a Communist planted in our midst.

Eddie Wong used to come to our meetings once in a while. The Chinese were not very talkative. They had a cooperative restaurant; some of them were students at Columbia. We ate there all the time, on Second Avenue and Twelfth Street.

I went to Sunrise with Minnie in June 1933, almost at the very beginning. I thought the experiment would work. I had gone to school in Michigan, and I had had some farm experience while a student, following the harvests to earn some money. Minnie was a teacher, and we thought it would be a wonderful experience. It certainly was an enlightening one! My wife did an excellent job in the school. She created a dual classroom, for academic work and for play. Play activity was related to the academic work, but they were doing it in the form of play.

Joseph Cohen was very impractical and was surrounded by other impractical people like Simon Farber and Mendel Bluestein, well-meaning men but without the practical knowledge and experience for success. Much of the work was done by hired labor or by young people. We were there about two and a half years, leaving at the end of 1935. Most of the older people didn't do much work. They couldn't run the machinery. We did that and took care of the peppermint distillery, working late at night while the old folks talked. There was no selection of members. Most were out of jobs, with little money, and found in Sunrise a place to live, plenty to eat, and a school for their kids. We had a very fine doctor—Dr. Schiffrin—who used to work with us in the sawmill, cutting trees, and at other jobs when not tending to patients. Two of the hardest workers were Italians, Angelo Di Vitto and Paul Boattin, who later became a red-hot Communist at the Ford auto works. Angelo was very nice and very dedicated. He really believed! To him anarchism, the colony, was a religion. We had a nice social life, built a stage, had a dramatic group that put on one-acters. We also had a choral group and musicales and other kinds of entertainment.

When we came back to New York, I drifted away from the anarchist movement. By then there wasn't much of a movement left to be active in! Since the Roosevelt era began, much had changed in the American radical movement. He took the steam away from the social democrats. And anarchism, to me, was no longer an active movement but only a tradition. Besides, my ideas mellowed as I grew older. When I was young the "new world" was quite a reality. But now I would rather do partial, practical work in cooperatives and labor organizations than try to achieve a total solution all at once, which is impossible in any case.

Yet I still retain my fundamental anarchism. I don't belong to any party, though I do vote (which I never did when younger), though for an individual rather than a party. I believe in cooperatives, in trade unions; my whole ideology is that I'm a part of society, not an isolated individual, so I want to teach workers skills they don't now have (I'm a plumber by trade), to pass my knowledge down to the next generation. I want to apply my knowledge not in the future but now, in the practical world.

• LOUIS SLATER •

Long Beach, New York, October 27, 1972

Louis Slater, born in 1910, helped found the Friends of Freedom, an anarchist youth group, which held weekly forums in the Bronx. In 1931 he was a delegate to the Midwest Anarchist Conference in Chicago, which sought a measure of coordination among the diverse anarchist groups in the United States. The following year the Friends of Freedom evolved into the Vanguard Group, of which Slater was the secretary as well as a contributor to its journal, *Vanguard* (1932–1939). He and other members of Vanguard met Emma Goldman when she came to New York in 1934 (she was allowed a three-month visit to the U.S.), and he became friendly with Carlo Tresca, the Italian anarchist, who gave Vanguard a place to work in the offices of his journal *Il Martello*. In 1938 and 1939 Slater was active in the Challenge Group, an offshoot of Vanguard, and contributed to its weekly paper, *Challenge*. With the coming of the Second World War, he dropped out of the anarchist movement, although retaining his libertarian convictions throughout his life. He was shot to death in a holdup at his Brooklyn print shop on November 1, 1973. When the gunman ordered him and his partner to face the wall, Slater said, "Why don't you work for a living?" The gunman opened fire, killing Slater and wounding his partner.[608]

I WAS ABOUT seventeen or eighteen when the Road to Freedom Group was on Broadway and Fourteenth Street. I had been attending YPSL [Young People's Socialist League] meetings, but for me they were too wishy-washy, too reformist in attitude, lacking in thrust, in the dramatic drive toward a better world. I was then a high school senior in the Bronx. I and Tommy Dolgoff (my closest friend and Sam's younger brother) and a few others, including Sid Solomon [q.v.] and Whitey Genin [q.v.] were dissatisfied with socialism and formed a small anarchist group. Sam Dolgoff [q.v.] had been traveling around the country, riding the rails, soapboxing, organizing, and came to speak to us. He gave us a romantic feeling, and we were very much attracted to anarchism and the IWW.

Sam made a very strong impression on us and helped crystalize our new group, which met at first in my apartment in the Bronx. We took the name Friends of Freedom (1930), and Sam advised us what to read, especially Kropotkin. We started going to the weekly Road to Freedom meetings downtown, then launched our own weekly forums in the Bronx, inviting Sam and other Road to Freedom people (Dr. Globus, etc.) as speakers. The English-language youth page of the *Fraye Arbeter Shtime* didn't interest us much, as it was not really a youth organ but old-fashioned and outdated, almost a translation of the Yiddish into English.

A Chinese comrade named Yat Tone was active in the Road to Freedom Group. He came to every meeting. There was a Modern School in China during the late 1920s and early 1930s, and he regularly sent them money. He was a very sincere and devoted comrade. Every year he gave a party, a Chinese dinner, in the Jade Mountain restaurant to raise money for *The Road to Freedom*. He was a waiter in another, more expensive restaurant, but lost his job when someone—probably a Communist—informed on him. He went to Spain en route to China, but we never heard from him again.

The Midwest Anarchist Conference in Chicago in 1931 was held to organize more anarchist groups and achieve a measure of coordination among existing groups. I was there with Sam Dolgoff and others. I proposed organizing an anarchist youth paper, but nothing came of it. The older anarchists were of two minds about us youth: they wanted to draw the younger generation into the movement, but at the same time they resented us. They never cooperated with us, and very often opposed us, despite all their claims to attract a younger following. I returned to New York very disappointed. At Chicago I met Maximiliano Olay, a very fine man, as well as Yelensky [q.v.], Hippolyte Havel, and Krupnick, who was later at Sunrise Colony.

In New York we young people decided to publish a paper of our own. Mark Schmidt [q.v.] somehow heard about us and came to see us. We became very good friends. He was twenty or twenty-five years older, a short, stubby man with deep-set eyes and a big forehead, self-educated. When someone made a mistake, he laughed mockingly; it was almost ludicrous to see a man of his intellectual caliber behave that way. He was a disappointed man. He had gone back to Russia in 1917 but became disillusioned with the Bolsheviks and returned to the U.S. He worked on barges in New York harbor. He was extremely studious, with tremendous powers of concentration. He became a sort of mentor of our group and encouraged us with our journal.

We started *Vanguard* in 1932. Marc Epstein of Mohegan Colony had a printing press in New York—Marstin Press, it was called—and he printed it. He did a beautiful typographical job—he was very artistic at the time. Schmidt was the leading intellect and writer, and I, Sid, Sam, and Abe Bluestein [q.v.] contributed articles and put it together.

During her visit to the U.S. in 1934, Emma Goldman came to talk to us at her niece Stella Ballantine's apartment in Greenwich Village. She was a terrific egoist—everything revolved around her—and yet a very dedicated anarchist. The older anarchists were mainly interested in maintaining themselves as a social group; it gave them something to do. They were, with a few exceptions, hangers-on, using the movement as a social hangout, a way of meeting friends, a nice group to belong to for idealists who didn't like Communism. They were not active; they were not readers. They got nothing done. We, by contrast, were young intellectuals, active, enthusiastic. I devoted most of my time and energy to the movement, and most of my thinking to it. I organized the group, donated most of the money for it, and saw that it ran more or less smoothly.

Carlo Tresca was one of the exceptions. He became our good friend, gave us space in his *Il Martello* during a period when *Vanguard* was suspended, and his wife Margaret De Silver contributed money that helped keep us going. Walter Starrett of *The Road to Freedom* was another. He remained militant nearly to the end. During fights with the Communists he was knocked off the speakers' platform in Union Square. He lost his job and drank himself to death.

Joseph Cohen set up a Sunday School on Second Avenue around 1930, an anarchist school on Ferrer lines. Abba Gordin of the Clarion Group tried very hard to attract us, but his emerging Jewish-mystical-religious outlook put us off. Roman Weinrebe's father [B. Rivkin] had edited *Burevestnik* in Paris after the 1905 Revolution and was also a prolific writer for Yiddish publications. Roman inherited his father's intellect and ability but never fulfilled his potential. The Rebel Youth were younger members affiliated with the Vanguard Group—Vanguard Juniors, as they were called.

The Challenge Group was formed after the Vanguard Group split. Schmidt was living with me and my girlfriend [Elsie Milstein] and stole her away. He then embarked on a campaign of character assassination against me, typical of the tactics he was beginning to use as he drew closer to Stalinism. Sam Dolgoff, always drunk in those days, sided with Schmidt, and I have never spoken to him since. The group split, and *Vanguard* suspended publication. Schmidt said we should defend Soviet Russia no matter what, because of the rise of fascism, but we felt that Stalin was a monster and strongly opposed both totalitarian forms.

Challenge started with Abe Bluestein as editor. I wrote as "David Lawrence" and Genin as "Gike Mold." Simon Farber joined us later, and Bek-Gran too. He had been at the Mohegan school, a very intelligent fellow who fled Germany as an antifascist, well-educated, originally an engineer who claimed to have worked on the Berlin-to-Baghdad Railroad before the First World War. He married a Vassar graduate named Mary, came to our group, and became friendly with us. He introduced us to Anita Brenner, Paul Mattick, Ruth Fischer, and Dwight Macdonald [q.v.], all close friends of his who were antifascist and anti-Stalinist and leaned toward council communism.

As with *Vanguard*, I was chief administrator, money-raiser, and the like, and again I threw all my energies into it. I loved it! I thought it was an exceptionally good piece of work by a group of young people who worked hard, after our regular jobs, put our all into it, wrote the paper, edited it, distributed it, and so on. But it was a great strain for part-time young men to put out a weekly paper while working full-time during the day.

We had wonderful evenings in those days, wonderful evenings of enlightenment and education and comradeship. I don't think any group can find that now. Philosophically, I still feel that anarchism is the only political theory that can live, because power corrupts people, even the best of people. So basically I remain an anarchist, even though no longer active. I am neither an anarchist-communist nor an anarcho-syndicalist to the exclusion of the other. There must be a close relationship between the two, for both have an important place in the good society.

• CLARA SOLOMON •

Forest Hills, New York, June 2, 1973

Clara Solomon is the daughter of Samuel Freedman, a disciple of Peter Kropotkin and Rudolf Rocker in London and afterwards secretary of the Jewish Anarchist Federation in New York. During the 1930s, Clara and her husband Sidney (q.v.) were members of the Vanguard Group, of which Clara was the secretary and Sidney a writer for its journal, usually under the pen name "S. Morrison." They also helped with the distribution of *Spanish Revolution*, another anarchist journal of the period. In 1941, as Clara Fredricks and S. Morrison, they published two numbers of a mimeographed paper called *Libertarian Views*, in which, despite criticism from their pacifist comrades, they defended the war against fascism. "We cannot hope to solve our problems by turning our eyes away from this gigantic, all-consuming monster and piously repeating time-worn slogans," wrote Sid. "The issue must be faced squarely—either the fascist stranglehold is broken or we can put off all thought of being able to struggle for the realization of our aspirations for many generations."[609] After the war, Sid and Clara collaborated with Alexander Schapiro on his journal *New Trends*, to which Sid was a frequent contributor. They were also active in the Libertarian Book Club, participating in its forums and assisting in other ways. Sid, a professional book designer, was especially helpful in the publication and distribution of anarchist literature, while Clara, a concert pianist, gave recitals for the benefit of the club.

I WAS RAISED as a child at Stelton. I loved it there. For me it was an escape from the pressures of home. Economically, our family had been insecure. It was a very unhappy time in New York before we came to Stelton. When I got there it seemed wonderful from the start, when Minnie Bluestein took me by the hand and led me off to school. No one ever beat me up, as in the city. It was a relief from the pressures and dangers of city life. Also, the teachers made you feel accepted. I never got close to Aunty Ferm, though. I was always a little frightened of her. There was something of a disciplinarian about her. She had her favorites, too, mostly in the Living House. The kids living in the colony itself, with their families or others, always felt a little out of it, that the Living House kids were being given preferential treatment. The Ferms, after all, were in fact surrogate parents to these children, and the rest of us wanted more than anything to "leave home" and go to live in the Living House.

Aunty was not as yielding, as flexible, as the other teachers. She had strong ideas and stuck to them. She once chased me away from the piano in the school, saying that I had a piano at home. It was so unfair! I liked to draw and weave. Anna Koch-Riedel taught us weaving, gardening, and took us on nature walks. I also liked the carpentry shop. Anna Riedel was a remarkable woman and a good influence on the children. Hans Koch, though interesting to talk to, full of German culture, was something of a ne'er-do-well. He was a distinguished-looking man, but he never worked and was basically a phoney.

There were a lot of fantasy games at Stelton—"Fairy Land" and so on—and a great deal of protecting us from the cruel city, with its evils and hardships, an attempt to keep us isolated, exclusive. I think the Ferms were unrealistic in trying to keep us pure peaches who did not have to live in this world. They also discouraged reading. And their feelings were so strong about these things that the children at times suffered as a result. Of the other teachers, I loved Paul Scott, Joseph Ishill, and Jimmy Dick the best.

I was fourteen years old when the Sacco-Vanzetti case reached its tragic climax. Meetings were held regularly at Stelton for Sacco and Vanzetti. Someone gave me Kropotkin's *Appeal to the Young*, and it made quite an impression in the midst of the Sacco-Vanzetti affair. At Stelton we had a different culture from that of the outside world. Our assumptions about life and society were different, and quite distinctive. We all saw the Sacco and Vanzetti case as a frame-up; there was no question that the State of Massachusetts could be right.

After the Kropotkin pamphlet I read Alexander Berkman's *Prison Memoirs of an Anarchist* and other books and ate it up, including Felix Frankfurter's book on Sacco and Vanzetti. I attended school in Stelton from 1921 to 1927. On Sunday mornings my father would tell me about his earlier life, in London and so on. Then we moved back to Manhattan, and I went to Juilliard. In 1930 Father became manager of the *Fraye Arbeter Shtime*, succeeding Benjamin Axler.

In 1931, when I was eighteen, I went to a dance at 219 Second Avenue. I met Lou Slater [q.v.], Sid (who was playing the drums in the band), and others who were to form the Vanguard Group. I was invited to a meeting at Daniliuk's house on the Lower East Side. I met Mark Schmidt there [q.v.]—I never liked that man. The following week, on a Sunday afternoon, we had a meeting at my house on East Twelfth Street. At that meeting—it was at the end of 1931—the Vanguard Group was started. Present were Lou Slater, Sid Solomon, Tommy Dolgoff, Albert Weiss, and others. Tommy Dolgoff was active only a short while, then dropped out of the movement. Our purpose was to work out a positive program, to deal with anarchism in less amorphous and more concrete terms, to show it was a viable social philosophy.

Mark Schmidt came to us through the Russian comrades, such as Daniliuk and Samusin. He had been in Russia during the Revolution, he told us. He had a way of being very mysterious about his past, and I didn't like that. He also had contempt for the older comrades. He was always *ungeblozn* [puffed up], to use a Yiddish expression, unapproachable. He would work on one person at a time and gain control of him; he captured a whole group that way, à la the Bolsheviks. He took a dislike to certain people, and he had contempt for women, whom he considered inferior. His scholarship attracted us because we knew so little ourselves. His idea was of a close-knit, trained cadre of thinking revolutionaries, an intellectual anarchist elite, a Vanguard—it was he, I think, who suggested the name. He disliked the older anarchists, and how they tolerated some of our Schmidt-inspired antics I'll never know!

The Vanguard Group started a journal in 1932, organized lectures, established an anarchist library. We also distributed *Spanish Revolution*. I took it around to newsstands in New York City. I sold the *Vanguard* outside labor and radical meetings. We began to have an impact. We began to attract some young people from Brownsville: Morris Shuman (married later to Rose Sterling's sister), Sylvia Shuman, Milton Horn, Yetta and Lou Hoenig, David Koven [q.v.], Douglas Stern, Gilbert Connolly (grandson of the Irish revolutionist James Connolly), who went to Spain, and others, about two or three dozen in all, a very able group. I traveled to Boston, Framingham, and other cities to help organize youth groups.

During the summer of 1932, I was music counselor at Joseph and Sophie Cohen's camp on Lake Mohegan, opposite the colony. In the late 1930s, when I was twenty-five, I hitchhiked with Audrey Goodfriend [q.v.] to visit Emma Goldman in Toronto. We stayed with comrades, Jack and Sylvia Fitzgerald (he was a New Zealander, she a Russian Jew), who took us to Emma's house. We got a marvelous reception. We saw her every day that we were there. She was extremely interested in the *Vanguard* and in what we were doing. We told her about our activities in New York, and she told us about her activities in Toronto, in particular raising money for Ferrero [q.v.] and Sallitto [q.v.] to prevent their deportation to Italy. Ferrero was in Toronto at the time.

Emma wanted us to have a good time and arranged for us to go to a beach in the Georgian Bay. She prepared all the food—she was an excellent cook—and it was delicious. We had a great time. We then went to Detroit and stayed with comrades of the Fraye Arbeter Shtime Group. Emma was a major figure of this century, a woman who was a real genius, active and versed in almost everything. She wrote and spoke very well, despite a meager formal education. I feel very privileged that I at least got a glimpse of her.

• SIDNEY SOLOMON •

Forest Hills, New York, June 2, 1973

A book designer by profession and a talented painter, Sidney Solomon was a member of the Vanguard Group in the 1930s, the New Trends Group in the 1940s, and the Libertarian Book Club from the 1940s through the 1980s (see interview with Clara Solomon).

I WAS BORN in the town of Pogost on the Berezina River in Minsk province on December 8, 1911. Pogost had a beautiful wooden synagogue, one of the most famous in Russia. My father was a barber and had a sort of underground railroad for Jewish boys escaping from service in the tsar's army. Because of this, he himself fled to the United States in 1911, a couple of steps ahead of the police. We followed two years later: my mother, two older brothers, and myself, then one and a half years old. (A sister was born afterwards in America.)

We settled in the Bronx, near Charlotte Street, and I attended Public School 50 and Junior High School 61, where I was chosen to take part in an experimental group, headed by a teacher named Louis Klein, a socialist, with the encouragement of the principal, Edward McGuire ("Baldy" McGuire, he was called), himself a closet socialist. The group had a Painting Club—we went to Bronx Park and painted scenery—and a Science Club—the kids acted as protons, neutrons, and electrons, jumping about the room. On graduation, I and Tommy Dolgoff, also a member of the special group, were selected to go to Townsend Harris High School for gifted students.

I was a kind of black sheep in the family, which was mostly Communist. At a very early age I rebelled against their authoritarian ideas. We lived in a radical Bronx neighborhood, with intense Communist and socialist activity. As a high school senior I joined Circle One of YPSL [Young People's Socialist League] in the Bronx, a very influential group. I had gone to a YCL [Young Communist League] meeting but was horrified at how it was stage-managed and controlled. There was no free discussion—like *1984*. Downright revolting! And the Trotskyites in YCL were no different. They steam-rolled everything through. I was disgusted, turned off, so I joined YPSL.

There the older people did teach us, and there were real discussions, and I really learned something. But they too relied on authority. Marx was still there. I read Marx and was repelled by his authoritarianism. I also disliked their gradualist approach. I wanted action. So I turned toward anarchism. I talked to Sam

Dolgoff [q.v.] and Lou Slater [q.v.], who really brought me over to anarchism. I attended the founding meeting of the Vanguard Group at Clara's house. I felt there was a serious flaw in economic determinism. I believed that ideas played a big part in social change, as big a part as economics or anything else.

Vanguard became my dream, my hope. I felt it would grow to something important. Our paper had a good response. The older comrades saw us as an errant child, but they were proud of us. Clara did five times as much work as anybody else: correspondence, selling papers, organizing meetings, debates, and lectures. We debated with socialists, Trotskyists, and Communists, and attracted disaffected socialists and Communists to our group.

Our relations with the socialists were always friendly, in contrast to those with the Communists. Abe Bluestein [q.v.], Roman Weinrebe, and I carried on propaganda at City College, in the alcoves and even in the classrooms. We wanted to organize the workers and rally them to our movement. I went to the steel mills at Youngstown, I went to Boston, Philadelphia, and other cities, speaking to workers and organizing anarchist groups. I was hoping to attract really big groups among the workers. Many of them were very sympathetic to the anarchists and the IWW, especially the steel workers. You can't imagine the response I had. Louis Genin [q.v.] also went on speaking tours, before going out to Sunrise.

At its height, *Vanguard* had a circulation of about three thousand. That was in 1936, with the outbreak of the Spanish Civil War. When *Spanish Revolution* was established, Mark Schmidt [q.v.], I, Roman, and Jack White were active in it. We had close contact with foreign anarchist groups in the U.S.—the *Fraye Arbeter Shtime*, *Il Martello*, *Cultura Proletaria*, even *L'Adunata*. They were mostly workers who wanted theoreticians.

I and Roman were very close to Carlo Tresca. He was a man of action who got things done, not a purist or puritan anarchist like the *L'Adunata* crowd, but practical. I liked that. The *Fraye Arbeter Shtime* people were also for the most part practical and down-to-earth. We had an English-language page in *Il Martello*, which I edited. We wanted to get them, the other anarchists, to be less isolated within their own language groups. Tresca was a great inspiration to us. He told me quite a few times before his murder that he was gathering information on large-scale collaboration between the Communists and the fascists. I think it was the Communists who shot him.

We did a lot of work in connection with anti-fascist activity—the Terzani case,[610] for instance—especially Tresca and Roman Weinrebe. When Terzani was freed we all ate a huge Italian meal that lasted eight hours in celebration. Tresca was in the middle of everything, a man with guts. Contrast the anarchists of *L'Adunata*, who lived in a world of their own. There was an element of paranoia in their hostility toward Tresca.

The Vanguard Group was largely composed of children of Russian Jewish immigrants. But it was quite a varied group. We had a Chinese (Eddie Wong), a Negro (Glenn Carrington), a few Italians (including Bruno "Americano," who went to Spain with guns that we supplied and was imprisoned there by the

Communists), and a few Irishmen, including Gilbert Connolly, John Pinkman (a former member of the Irish Republican Army), and Albert Mullady from Brooklyn.

We were among the first to criticize Hitler, as anarchists were always alert to authoritarianism, demagogy, and bigotry. The anarchists had a great feeling for literature and were wider-ranging, less narrow and doctrinaire than other radical groups. In Vanguard we made no hard and fast distinction between anarchist-communism and anarcho-syndicalism, but we were not anarchist-individualists. Dwight Macdonald [q.v.], Edward Dahlberg,[611] and Arturo Giovannitti spoke for us, as well as Mark Schmidt and Harry Kelly. We had no contact with Abba Gordin and his *Clarion*. But we were in touch with Maximiliano Olay, who had an office on Fifth Avenue and put out an information bulletin on Spain for the CNT. We also had some contact with Robert Bek-Gran, who was more of a council communist than an anarchist.

Three issues arose almost simultaneously that caused the group to split. First, our association with *Il Martello* was opposed by a few who preferred *L'Adunata*. Then there was a personal issue that was not really crucial but became a rallying point: Lou Slater felt he owned his girlfriends. When Clara drifted toward me and Elsie Milstein toward Schmidt, Lou was greatly upset and accused us of stealing them. The whole thing was later taken to a *Fraye Arbeter Shtime* committee when Lou demanded justice. Lou was deeply hurt and resentful and made personal relations an issue in the group, and that was very disruptive. He didn't own the girls, after all. But he was especially grieved that his own mentor should steal his girlfriend. Abe Bluestein refused to stand for all this bullshit and eventually left the group and established *Challenge*.

The third and underlying issue was Schmidt himself. He was conspiratorial, devious, mysterious, while we were a fresh, open, marvelous group of youngsters. We were vigorous and wanted to do things. I think he was a paranoid schizophrenic, however well read and brilliant. He never actually did anything. More than that, he prevented us from doing anything. He felt we were theoretically unprepared for action, such as labor-organizing or forming cooperatives. He stopped us from organizing for the ILGWU. We might have had a great impact but for his negativism.

In the ILGWU the anarchists and socialists were always united against the Communists. They needed young organizers whom they could trust, and they called on Vanguard and YPSL for help. We were called to a meeting with the top brass of the union. But Schmidt got us to decline. The YPSL accepted—Gus Tyler[612] and the others—and did useful work; hence their big reputation today. It was this failure to act that led to the collapse of our group and of the anarchist movement in New York. We had so many good young people that we could reach, and now we lost them. Schmidt claimed that we weren't ready theoretically; actually, he was personally a coward, fearful of taking concrete action, a man who talked revolution but refused to mount the barricades.

Schmidt was a contradiction: he spouted anarchist ideas, while his own behavior, what he personally did, was deeply authoritarian. I too felt that leaders and activists were necessary. Even the word "government" didn't frighten me. When the Spanish Revolution came, I was not at all troubled that anarchists accepted ministries in the government. Yet I knew what the Communists were—from my family, my reading, my personal experience. In 1936, during a debate with a black Communist named Robert Moore on "The Infallibility of the Comintern," I was pulled off the platform by Communist henchmen. I saw Communist strong-arm men break up Socialist Party meetings. Clara and I were ousted from a Communist-controlled summer camp in upstate New York during the Spanish Civil War.

In this country the trend toward anarchism and socialism was not very strong. Yet there could have been an anarchist movement here, even after the defeat of the Spanish Revolution. We made the mistake of following Schmidt and keeping ourselves a small, isolated group of intellectuals. I feel that we really attracted the better element among the workers, with a sense of ethics and devotion. We did not, as the Communists did, attract the conspiratorial element. But we isolated ourselves, and I felt very bitter about it.

During the early 1940s, when the Second World War came, Clara contracted rheumatic fever, we had a new baby, and we were drawn away from the movement. Many of our group were older and had responsibilities to face. Some went back to school and became professionals. A bunch—Audrey Goodfriend [q.v.], Dave Koven [q.v.], Melvin Greig—went out to settle in California. At the end of the war, *New Trends* was for me a new attempt to try again. It was a more sophisticated journal than *Vanguard*. But Schapiro was a very sick man, and the paper died with him.

Anarchism as an ideal is still very meaningful, in some ways more meaningful than ever. Many anarchist ideas have been incorporated into the activities of other groups—rent strikes, free schools, women's liberation. All you can hope for is the right direction, rather than absolute solutions, for libertarian cultural and educational ideals, whatever label you give them. There are many ways of getting things done that are still relevant and very much alive. This is true also in the field of ecology—that man is part of nature, rather than above nature or exploiting nature. In other parts of the world too, including the Iron Curtain countries, there are signs of increasing liberation. We must advance along nonauthoritarian lines, and in that sense we both, Clara and I, remain anarchists. There are grass-roots sentiments everywhere that indicate that a libertarian movement can catch fire. People are getting tired of rigid bureaucracies and social formulas. In anarchism there is an underlying idea that relates to virtually every aspect of life. We have no regrets about those early years. We threw ourselves heart and soul into the cause. It was writing and working, it was personal involvement, it was hitchhiking and travel, it was organizing and demonstrating—it was all the energies of our youth.

• MARK SCHMIDT •

San Francisco, California, June 16, 1974 (telephone)

While visiting San Francisco in 1974, I telephoned Mark Schmidt to arrange an interview. Schmidt, born in Russia, had been the mentor of the Vanguard Group in New York during the 1930s and, under the pen name "Senex," a regular contributor to its journal, *Vanguard*. At first he did not want to talk to me, saying that his affiliation with the anarchists was "ancient history." After a few minutes of conversation, however, he began to loosen up and revealed an interesting mind. I could see how, forty years before, he had become the guru of the anarchist youth in New York. Although we spoke for more than half an hour, Schmidt refused in the end to see me. Concluding the conversation, he asked me to give his regards to Sam (q.v.) and Esther Dolgoff, whom he had not seen in thirty-five years. He died in 1978.

VANGUARD was not an important group because there was no real anarchist movement left. It had no influence and made not even a splash. I broke with it long ago, long ago. I am now almost eighty, so leave me out of your book.[613] Anarchism was fairly important during the *Mother Earth* years, but afterwards it didn't amount to anything. The anarchists idealized Makhno and Kronstadt and exaggerated their importance. The Vanguard Group was childish. They were too young and hadn't lived through the tragedy of the revolution. They were still naive and idealistic, whereas I did live through it. Their version of events is vulgarized history, an oversimplification of events and therefore antihistorical. That includes Max Nomad[614] and his "new class" theories. Socialism cannot be achieved overnight. Russian socialism will work its way out. I still believe in socialism. There is no other way. But it will take a long time, with a great deal of struggle. It is a gradual process, with periods of revolution, and depends upon historical conditions.

We all opposed Stalinism. It was not a must, but due to the existing circumstances, a dictatorship of some kind was inevitable. Without the rapid industrialization of the thirties, and even without collectivization, Russia could not have defeated fascism. It was a heroic period too, with collectivization a revolution of its own kind. It was Russia's struggle against Hitler and fascism that led me to support it.

I support the Cuban and Chinese Revolutions too. Mao, you know, was influenced by Bakunin and Kropotkin, a mixture of utopianism and chauvinism. But you cannot realize a stateless society all at once. It must take time and struggle and suffering. Some of Kropotkin's ideas are still alive and can be integrated into a broader movement, in fact are being so, without being recognized as anarchist. Socialism is in the process of being realized, not in its ideal form but within limitations imposed by historical circumstances. The quest for a pure and immediate socialism was anarchism's fatal weakness. In Spain, I think, anarchism will play some kind of role, but within an authoritarian framework.

In the nineteenth and early twentieth centuries anarchism was legitimate as a reaction against despotism and even against certain forms of Marxism of the pre-Leninist period. But societies must go through an authoritarian phase. Though Emma Goldman's ideas were quite primitive, they were in the mainstream of American history in the sense that they helped awaken American intellectuals and professionals to the libertarian tradition, for example sexual liberation, which has become a part of reality today. But she is not in the same class as Kropotkin as a thinker. Berkman was a tragic person. He wasted his life in prison and even afterwards. He never found himself.

I'm now studying philosophy, especially Hegel. I'm out of politics and certainly of anarchism. That's all behind me. I've got my own ideas. Marxism has changed a good deal too. The libertarian ideal will be realized, but maybe in a hundred years and after a lot of struggle. The relationship of the individual to authority must be worked out during this struggle. But extreme individualism is not in the cards. The state cannot be "abolished." It will be discarded only after a hundred or more years.

• FRANZ FLEIGLER •

Bronx, New York, December 29, 1972

Franz Fleigler, an Austrian-born mariner and member of the IWW, became an anarchist during the 1930s after attending meetings of the Vanguard Group in New York. During the Second World War, rejecting the pacifism of some of his comrades, he sailed as a helmsman on merchant-marine vessels carrying goods to Murmansk to assist the Soviets in their struggle against the Nazis; and after the war, in 1946, he served as captain of the *Josiah Wedgwood*, which transported Jewish concentration-camp survivors to Haifa, in defiance of a British blockade. Between 1942 and 1947, Fleigler, using the pen name "Lead Line," conducted a column entitled "On the Waterfront" in the anarchist journal *Why?*, consisting of the salty, sardonic aphorisms of a Wobbly sailor. Afterwards he wrote a similar column, "Notes of a Mariner," for *Why?*'s successor, *Resistance*, and contributed articles to *Freedom*, *The Match!*, and the *Fraye Arbeter Shtime*, of which he served on the executive board. He was also active in the Libertarian Book Club, of which his wife, Augusta Fleigler, was secretary until her untimely death in 1971.

I WAS BORN in Linz, Austria, in 1912, and came to the United States as a boy of thirteen or fourteen. My wife Gussie and I were active in the Libertarian Book Club. She served as recording secretary until her death from leukemia in 1971.

I came to anarchism through the Industrial Workers of the World. I never liked the Communists because I felt they were trying to buy me. The Wobblies seemed to have no political designs and their preamble wasn't burdened with philosophies or theories, so they attracted me more. I attended their meetings in the Wobbly hall on Cuentes Slip near South Street.

It was the Spanish Civil War that drew me to the Vanguard Group and the anarchists. There had been hardly a rumble against Hitler by the great organized working class in Germany. But when the civil war broke out in Spain, which was supposed to have a very "backward" working class, at least according to the intellectuals, the workers fought against fascism. That was what stumped me. Why? I thought about that a lot. They weren't bogged down by leaders, elites, theorists. They didn't want orders from above. And the reason they lost was no reflection on themselves but on the "democratic allies."

So I started going to the Vanguard Group forums, where Walter Starrett, Sam Weiner [Dolgoff, q.v.], and others spoke. Starrett had the native flavor of American sharpness and a good manner of talking and of making sense at the same time. But besides Starrett and Sam and Roman Weinrebe, there were only a few good ones. Irving Sterling [q.v.] was a brave young lad who used to take the floor at Rand School forums and tell the Commies off. With many other so-called anarchists you scratched them and you found the same damn cockroach as on the Wall Street market. Mark Schmidt [q.v.] was a nut, a psycho. Throughout his writings he used the word "libido," which was a reflection of his sexual impotence (his girlfriend Elsie Milstein told me this years later). Abba Gordin had his own little band of followers—another *nudnik*.

Challenge broke off from *Vanguard* and included Abe Bluestein [q.v.], Louis Slater [q.v.], Simon Farber, Bill and Sarah Taback [q.v.], and others. Robert Bek-Gran was a printer from Bavaria, who had known Ernst Toller, Erich Mühsam, and Gustav Landauer. He was a stormy petrel. Once, in 1935 I think, a group of us, including Bek-Gran, boarded the *Bremen* in New York harbor and tore down the swastika flag. But I was at sea a good deal of the time—a helmsman (*Steuermann*)—so I wasn't at anarchist meetings all that often. Gussie wrote poems for Wobbly papers. I've always hated labels: "What are you, a Communist, socialist, anarchist?" "I am I." I never did like the name Vanguard. Who are we to call ourselves a Vanguard?

When I came back from Murmansk in 1943—I was third mate on the *Israel Putnam* in the first convoy to Russia through to the White Sea—there was no paper coming out. I got in touch with Audrey Goodfriend [q.v.], who lived with Dorothy Rogers, an Englishwoman from Toronto who worshipped Emma Goldman, and we called a meeting in my apartment on Water Street on the Lower East Side. Audrey and Dave Koven [q.v.], Sam and Esther Weiner, Gussie and myself and Dorothy Rogers were there. We started *Why?*. I was "Lead Line," Gussie wrote poems, and Bek-Gran helped with the printing. Sam wrote occasionally, as "Ivan," I think. "Michael Grieg" was Melvin Greig, who is now a newspaperman in San Francisco, where Dave and Audrey also live. I was the one who suggested the name. I looked back on the rise of fascism, on workers sitting on their ass, on the war, on Soviet Russia, where I had just been, and asked, "Why? Why did all this happen?"

I went to sea again, and when I came back [after smuggling Holocaust refugees into Palestine] Dave Wieck and Diva Agostinelli were in the group. They were pacifists and opposed the war effort, while our original group thought it necessary to fight against fascism. At one meeting I remember defending Rudolf Rocker against criticisms of Diva and Dave. That's why *Resistance* was established after the war. It represented their brand of anarcho-pacifism. Paul Goodman, Jackson MacLow (a pseudonym), and others joined them.

All these newcomers, in my opinion, are the parents of the screwball New Left that you have today. They were a different breed, many of them disappointed Communists or Trotskyites, like Paul Goodman and David Wieck. It took them a long time to shed the mystique of Lenin and Trotsky and come over to the libertarian camp. In fact they never did shed it entirely—some now defend Castro and Mao. There was a certain selfishness or self-centeredness about them, a lack of true compassion and broad humanity. In their crackpot group a new deity emerged—Wilhelm Reich and his orgone box! Paul Goodman became a leading Reichian disciple and analyst. They were seeking adventure, I think. Maybe I had had my adventure by pounding the seas and they had it in other ways.

A lot of us were seekers. There was so much activity, so much searching in those days. But the main lesson is the one that Kropotkin had taught in his final years: that any movement to be worth its salt must have an ethical foundation. The trade union movement is now dead because it has no goddam ethics or morals. That was what began to bug Kropotkin in his old age: If there are no ethics, the cause isn't worth bothering about.

I'm strictly a seafaring or spittoon philosopher. I've lost my eulogizing of the masses—that's completely out! Ortega y Gasset's *Revolt of the Masses* influenced my thinking along these lines. The anarchist ideal will remain till eternity, but the masses will never reach it. Malthus was right that begetting children is not the result of love but rather for sexual gratification. The masses reproduce themselves like bloody maggots, without a thought for their offspring's future. You watch the news and see little kids with swollen heads and swollen bellies in bombed-out places. Is this the result of love? Emma Goldman and Alexander Berkman had no children, Kropotkin had only one, and Rocker two. Did you ever notice that?

• IRVING STERLING •

Piscataway, New Jersey, October 29, 1972

Irving Sterling was a leading figure in the Rebel Youth Group, a teenage affiliate of the Vanguard Group that was also known as the "Vanguard Juniors." Notwithstanding his antimilitarist convictions, Irving served in the American army during the Second World War, regarding fascism as the epitome of evil. Afterwards he was graduated from City College and became the office manager of a trucking firm in New Jersey, where he lived with his wife, Rose Geller, also an erstwhile member of the Rebel Youth. Rose, who was present at the interview, attended Hunter College and Rutgers University and taught high school English until her recent retirement. Irving died of Parkinson's disease in 1993.

MY FATHER came from Russia to New York in 1915, fleeing from conscription into the tsarist army. He soon married. Both my parents became staunch anarchists and even planned to return to Russia during the 1917 Revolution but for some reason remained. I was born in 1917 and was raised in an anarchist and working-class atmosphere. I attended a Workmen's Circle school as a child, amid growing hostility between anarchists and Communists. While still a child, I went to anarchist lectures and meetings in Harlem Center, took part in May Day parades, attended *Fraye Arbeter Shtime* dinners, and so on. ["Irving was in the movement from the minute he was born," his wife Rose interjected.]

The debates of the 1920s were not only between the anarchists and the Communists but also among the anarchists themselves. Were elected union officials to be their own men or subject to the decisions of the anarchists? This was one of the questions that they debated. Morris Sigman, an anarcho-syndicalist, argued for responsibility to the movement, while purer anarchists like Nicholas Kritzman and Mendel Bluestein wanted to be their own bosses, subject to no external authority. At the age of eight or nine I was just becoming aware of these issues. The Sacco-Vanzetti case was also very strong at that time. When I was ten I had my parents make me a red shirt as an emblem of my blossoming radicalism.

While a student in Abraham Lincoln High School in Brooklyn, I and a few friends started a discussion group, but we needed older, more experienced people to advise us. I began attending Vanguard Group meetings and lectures on Second Avenue and invited Abe Bluestein [q.v.] to lead a few of our discussions. (Our group met at the Second Avenue center and at the Wobbly hall on lower Fifth Avenue.) We called ourselves The Rebel Youth (1932) and put out a mimeographed journal of that name during 1933 and 1934.

Rose was also a member—her mother, like my parents, was an anarchist, first in Chicago and then in New York in the ILGWU. We had regular weekly discussions and forums, with about twenty members, a junior wing of the

Vanguard Group, and we renamed ourselves the Vanguard Juniors. The group broke up in 1934, some of us, including myself and Jack White, remaining with the Vanguard Seniors. In 1934 or 1935 I tried to organize an Anarchist Youth Federation and held a conference of young anarchists from various cities— New York, Boston, Philadelphia, Washington—but nothing came of it.

Some of the oldtimers branded the Vanguard Group "anarcho-Bolsheviks" because of Mark Schmidt's [q.v.] unsavory influence and because of our emphasis on organization and militancy. Around 1935 or 1936 Vanguard split into the Vanguard and Challenge Groups. It was a strictly personal quarrel, with no ideological differences. Sid Solomon [q.v.] took Clara Freedman [Solomon, q.v.] from Lou Slater [q.v.], then Schmidt took Elsie Milstein from Slater. Then the two *ganefs* [thieves] lined up and attacked the victim!

Schmidt had a good mind but pictured himself as another Lenin, a leader who would form a vanguard to lead the masses. That's how the group got its name. He was a scholar who knew history and was good in discussion groups. But he had an authoritarian personality. Any potential threat—such as Slater or Bluestein or Weinrebe—had to be eliminated. I was terribly upset; to me the only thing that mattered was the movement. Dr. Cohn was going to give us a building as a center, but we couldn't carry the ball and nothing came of it.

We had little contact with the Italian and Spanish youth, but we did have some with older Italians and Spaniards, and especially with Carlo Tresca, who helped us a lot, gave us a meeting room at 94 Fifth Avenue, where he had his offices, and a page in *Il Martello*. Tresca and Roman Weinrebe were good friends. The Spaniards were all caught up in the Civil War, and we held joint picnics and entertainments to raise funds for Spain and for our paper.

Spanish Revolution united all the principal groups—Vanguard and Challenge, individualists and syndicalists, even L'Adunata and Il Martello. An ad hoc group from these various organizations edited and distributed the paper. The Vanguard Group during this period had a library and good lectures—often drawing 150 people or more—in its hall on Fourteenth Street, next to Lüchow's restaurant. I worked very hard for that center. It was the Depression era, yet we had good times and threw our youthful energies wholeheartedly into our cause. And we've retained many friendships over the years. It was a source of richness for us.

During the Spanish Civil War, most of us young people were opposed to collaboration with the Communists. Some of the anarchists went there and were killed, or returned with terrible stories of the betrayals by the Communists. But the anarchists had no organized groups going over there, no way of getting over there. The Spanish anarchists themselves discouraged us from coming; they said they didn't need men but money and moral support. Yet some tried to get into the Lincoln Brigade in order to fight the fascists.

My active participation in the anarchist movement ended with the outbreak of the Second World War. The younger anarchists were divided once again over the antimilitarism issue. Though the Jews opposed Hitler, the Italians opposed Mussolini, and the Spaniards opposed Franco, many were restrained by their antimilitarist and pacifist traditions from supporting the war effort. Some refused to speak to me when I joined the army. The Why? Group—Audrey Goodfriend [q.v.] and the others—is a good case in point. There was so much bitterness over the war issue. We saw the Why? Group as a kind of lunatic fringe: one member defecated on the floor of the Metropolitan Museum and said, "That's what we think of your system!" They were the new youth group: David Wieck, Diva Agostinelli, Dorothy Rogers (they met in her apartment), and Audrey (she lived with Dorothy).

When I came back from the war, I began to have doubts about anarchism—not the *Weltanschauung* but some of its practical applications. Can one have true individual liberty without private property? I became more impressed with Proudhon and less with collectivism. Communes in Russia, Spain, and China had become authoritarian. But I have not become an individualist. Tucker would have fractionalized things rather than merely decentralizing the economy. I'm still sympathetic toward Kropotkin's *Fields, Factories and Workshops*, mixed with Proudhon. To make use of modern technology you need a bureaucracy, but how to control it? Anarchism has no answer. Anarchism is too vague to utilize as a practical program. The "creative spirit of the masses" is not enough. We must deal with specific problems.

Yet to me anarchism is still the fundamental answer, though it must be presented in more concrete form to attract larger numbers of people. From a historical perspective the First International (in its early period, at least), the Paris Commune, Kronstadt, the Spanish collectives can provide a living model of a decentralized society, organized and administered by workers of all categories.

A few other points are worth mentioning. During her three-month visit to the United States in 1934, Emma Goldman met with us young anarchists in her niece Stella Ballantine's apartment in Greenwich Village. We had already gone to hear her lecture; she was still a great speaker, with a clear, ringing voice and an excellent command of English and knew how to handle a crowd. Glenn Carrington, the black member of the Vanguard Group (he used the pen name "George Creighton"), was a parole officer who had an excellent collection of books on the Negro problem. At Stelton there was a bitter split between the Communists and the anarchists, and even divisions within the anarchist camp. *Looking Forward!* was put out by the Rebel Youth of Stelton, as it were. Despite our differences with the older generation, though, there was not the sharp division between fathers and sons visible today. I was raised as an anarchist, and I accepted it wholeheartedly and will always feel at once that anybody who has a dictatorial attitude is no good.

• AUDREY GOODFRIEND •

Berkeley, California, June 11, 1974

Audrey Goodfriend is the daughter of Morris Goodfriend (died 1962), a veteran anarchist of the *Fraye Arbeter Shtime* school and secretary of the Ferrer-Rocker Branch of the Workmen's Circle in the Bronx, where Audrey was born and raised. Her mother was also an anarchist, and Audrey followed her parents' example, joining a youth group of Jewish anarchist children. In 1934 Audrey met Emma Goldman in New York, and in 1939 Audrey went with Clara Solomon (q.v.) to see Goldman in Toronto. During the 1940s Audrey was active in the Why? Group in New York. In 1946, with her companion David Koven (q.v.), she moved to California and in 1958 started the Walden School in Berkeley, an experiment in libertarian education, which I visited with Audrey in 1989.

I WAS BORN in 1920 in the Bronx. My parents were both anarchists. They took us to anarchist affairs, and anarchist books were in the house. I read Berkman's *ABC* when I was eleven. It was simply written and appealed very directly to me. I remember thinking then, "I'm an anarchist." As a child I always felt deeply sorry for the poor and oppressed. When it was cold in winter, I was always wondering and worrying about where the poor people would stay. A group of us in the Bronx—including Sally Genn,[615] who was also born in 1920—our birthdays are three days apart—formed Di Yunge Odler [The Young Eagles] (you can find the name in the *Fraye Arbeter Shtime* of that period), which evolved into the Bronx chapter of the Vanguard Juniors. (I later went to Hunter College with Sally Genn.)

I met Emma Goldman when she came to New York in 1934. She was my idol. I wanted to be like her. Father hid her autobiography from me because of all the sex stories, but I sneaked it down and read it. It was very exciting to see her and to hear her speak (in the Unitarian Church in Greenwich Village). In 1939 I hitchhiked to Toronto with Clara Freedman [Solomon, q.v.] to see her. She was living with a Dutch anarchist family. She answered the door wearing a shawl. She impressed me as an old woman, but when she started to speak the years dropped off. She was one of the liveliest people I ever met. Dorothy Rogers was there, and Attilio Bortolotti [q.v.], who acted as a kind of chauffeur, driving her everywhere.

On Saturday afternoons the Vanguard Juniors of the Bronx and Brooklyn met with the parent Vanguard Group on Fifteenth Street. It was all very exciting. We cooked a meal together, and often went afterwards to a concert or to the Museum of Modern Art. It was a teenage revolutionary commune.

In 1946 Dave Koven [q.v.] and I went on a cross-country anarchist organizing tour, from New York to California. We spoke to groups and classes in a number of cities. We had been pacifists during the war, and so we spoke also for the peace movement. There was very little left of a movement, anarchist or pacifist. The war had shattered everything. People were trying to put their lives back together. We had good contacts with the Italians, who had supported us all through the war, and with the Spaniards through Frank González.

In Los Angeles we stayed with Angelo Penia and Ruth Dickstein (she was formerly with Brand [q.v.]). Once we went with Jules Scarceriaux to the Rogats for dinner. Aaron Rogat is a raw-food vegetarian who uses no spices, while Scarceriaux was a robust Frenchman who loved food and wine. While driving home he turned to his wife and said, "Sabina, how many times have I told you never to allow me to eat at the Rogats?" He gave us a hundred dollars for our organizing tour. When we got back to New York we used the money to publish Kropotkin's *Appeal to the Young*. Scarceriaux worked on Cecil B. DeMille's ornamental plaster sets for extravaganza films. He had been born in Paris and left as a child after the Commune.

When I was young I believed that anarchism was imminent. Now I see that unless you have most people in agreement, a revolution will only introduce a new dictatorship, a new imposed social system. From there I realized that education was necessary first, so I went back to school to get teaching credentials, and we organized the Walden School in Berkeley. I also see anarchism as more pluralistic than the old anarchist-communism, that even religious people can live anarchistic lives, alongside several other varieties of anarchism, that money can still exist, and so on. I can see all kinds of possibilities, so long as men do not exploit or oppress each other.

• DAVID KOVEN •

Berkeley, California, June 11, 1974

During the 1930s and 1940s, David Koven, an electrician by trade, was active in the Vanguard and Why? Groups in New York before moving to California with his companion Audrey Goodfriend (q.v.) and establishing the Walden School in Berkeley. In 1956 Koven edited *The Needle*, an anarchist journal in San Francisco.

I WAS BORN in Brownsville, Brooklyn, in 1918. I came to anarchism through the Depression and radical politics of the 1930s. I was a member of the Young Communist League but was inclined towards pacifism and broke with it in 1936 over the Oxford Pledge. Wandering around Brownsville, I bumped into a bunch of young anarchists affiliated with the Vanguard Group, including Moysh Shuman and Harry Stein. They gave me literature, which never meant much to me, but I was attracted to their outlook and basic ideas and so became an anarchist. My grandfather, by the way, had been a refugee of the 1905 Revolution and had to flee the country to escape arrest.

The anarchists became extremely active during the Spanish Revolution of 1936–1939. Life in those years was very exciting. There were demonstrations, parties, street fights. I was attracted to the Wobblies, many of whom had gone to Spain. We carried on a struggle against the Communists and a struggle against the Nazis in New York. Anarchists and Wobblies demonstrated outside a Nazi rally in Madison Square Garden in 1939 or 1940 and beat up the Nazis as they came out.

The social milieu in Brownsville was also exciting—the opening up of quasi-romantic revolutionary life, the first experiments with sex. Brownsville was one of the only places in the world where you had to reserve a copy of Turgenev or Tolstoy in the public library. Everybody was reading, and everybody was interested in political and social events and movements.

During the early 1940s I became a railroad worker, then joined the merchant marine. Towards the end of the war, when called for the draft, I was excused as a conscientious objector. As a result of the war the Vanguard Group dissolved. Fewer and fewer members came to the meetings. Dorothy Rogers had just come to New York from Toronto, after Emma Goldman's death. Dorothy, I, Audrey Goodfriend [q.v.], Sam Dolgoff [q.v.], and Franz Fleigler [q.v.] founded *Why?*. As the paper became increasingly antiwar, those who were for the war (like Fleigler and Sam) or who were ambivalent dropped out. Like *L'Adunata*, we opposed the war and were anarchist-communist rather than anarcho-syndicalist. David Wieck and Diva Agostinelli joined us and became our closest friends. Audrey wrote as "A. G." or "G. A." "Casey" or "D. K." was me, David Koven. "Wat O'Connell" was Melvin (Mike) Greig.

Following the war there was the antidraft struggle, Peacemakers, the picketing of Danbury prison, and the growing influence of Paul Goodman. He was the ferment within the Resistance Group that made our meetings—in the S.I.A. hall at 813 Broadway—the most vital and exciting in New York. He introduced us to all the nineteenth-century anarchists—our whole background was rooted in the nineteenth century—and to the contemporary world of psychology and sociology. Apart from its journal, *Resistance*, the Resistance Group published a few pamphlets: Kropotkin's *Appeal to the Young*; *War or Revolution?* by Max Sartin [Raffaele Schiavina], after the debate on the war in 1944 or 1945 between Rudolf Rocker and Armando Borghi at Mohegan Colony; and Randolph Bourne's essay on war as "the health of the state"—what a telling phrase that is!

But Audrey and I had reached a point where publishing a paper was not enough. Anarchism had to be implemented in more tangible form. We made a trip out here in 1946–1947. Radicalism was very much alive on the West Coast, with poets like Kenneth Rexroth and his group and the Italian group in San Francisco still going strong. Rexroth's group met in the Workmen's Circle Center. We continued that group when he left.

We had come out with the Greigs to found a cooperative community, and we pooled all our money for a communal house in San Francisco. The house broke up when the Greigs had their first child and wanted to live as a family unit. We helped found the Walden School on libertarian principles. For a couple of years I published *The Needle*.

For me the main changes over the years were the coming of pacifism to my life and the recognition of the need to implement anarchism in as many relationships as possible—to live an anarchist life. In our case that meant starting a libertarian school in 1958, the Walden School in Berkeley, which is still going strong today. It also meant supporting station KPFA, Pacifica Radio, founded by anarchists and pacifists (including Rexroth) who had been in jail as conscientious objectors. I became their resident anarchist spokesman, who gave the anarchist viewpoint on different issues. It meant a cooperative nursery school, cooperative food programs, and so on.

As for the school, four families simply took our own children and started it. That is anarchism: people meeting their own needs. That is the essence of anarchism, and that is how anarchism will come about. We influenced the Vietnam Day Committee by keeping it libertarian and nonauthoritarian, and many young people responded to our position and held similar views. In previous generations the trouble was that most of the anarchists led petty-bourgeois lives, and the ambitions for their children were middle-class. And nearly all of their children became middle class. They never applied their ideals to their own personal lives.

• BRONKA GREENBERG •

Bronx, New York, June 11, 1982

Bronka Greenberg was a young Jewish anarchist in Warsaw during the 1930s, a time of antiradical repression in Poland. Arrested for disseminating anarchist propaganda, she spent a year in prison and thereafter remained under surveillance. When the Germans invaded in 1939, Bronka sought refuge in the Soviet Union, where she was sent to a labor camp in Siberia. Liberated after the war, she returned to Poland, from which she emigrated to Australia and then the United States.

I WAS BORN in Warsaw in 1914 of a prosperous middle-class family. My father was a businessman, an importer and exporter, and my mother a housewife. My younger sister and I were raised in comfortable surroundings and went to an excellent school, a girls' school called Poznarowa, one of the oldest Jewish gymnasiums in Warsaw. It was there that I first encountered anarchism. When I was sixteen or seventeen, a girl in my school who belonged to an anarchist group invited me to a lecture. That was in 1931, when Poland was under a repressive right-wing government. The lecture was about Kropotkin—it was the tenth anniversary of his death—but since the anarchist movement was illegal, more persecuted even than the Communists, it was announced as being about the German writer Lessing. There were about 150 people in the audience. But just as the lecture was about to begin, the police rushed in and arrested the whole crowd. Someone had given us away, an *agent provocateur*. That was the beginning of my anarchist history. Most of those arrested, myself included, spent only three or four days in jail, but some, including the speaker, Michal Wolman, a talented young man from a prominent Warsaw Jewish family, were locked up for several months.

After my release from jail I joined the anarchist circle. I found the idea extremely attractive and wanted to learn more about it. Our group had about forty members, all of them Jewish and nearly all students. It had no name. We usually met in rented rooms in different parts of town and engaged in discussions—heated discussions. We read Kropotkin, our favorite writer. We loved his books: *Mutual Aid, Memoirs of a Revolutionist*, and the others. We also read Bakunin, but not as much. Michal Wolman was one of the most active and capable members of the circle. Halina Lew was another, a remarkable young woman who had contacts with the PPS, the Polish Socialist Party. We sometimes met at her apartment. We were completely isolated from other anarchist groups and had no contact whatever with the non-Jewish anarchists, most of whom were workers. The main reason for this was the repressive conditions in the country. The anarchists were considered dangerous and were constantly being hunted by the police.

In addition to our discussions, the group took part in demonstrations, especially on the First of May, when we distributed anarchist literature and marched with placards and banners until the police arrived. We also published a newspaper called *Walka* (Struggle), a monthly of around ten pages. The articles were written by members of the group. We wrote mostly about the future—how things were going to be, how we would carry out the revolution, how we would change the nature of society and its whole structure. We were mostly anarcho-syndicalists who wanted to build a new world around trade unions and cooperatives. We also wrote about the situation in Russia and Spain, but it was the future that dominated our thoughts. We were going to change everything. We were very optimistic and painted a very rosy picture. We had faith in the goodness of human beings. We believed in our ideal. It was good to believe in it, very good. I was deeply motivated by it. My life had a purpose. It may have been naive, but it was lovely. It was wonderful.

I was assigned to work on the newspaper. We rented a room with a family, and a member of the group, Janka Weisberg, moved in there and kept our small press, a kind of stencil on rollers worked by hand. I worked with Janka, another girl named Rachela Rubinstein, and a young man, Henek Kaliski. We had to work fast to escape detection. We got out each issue in a single day. We printed a few hundred copies, stapled them, and distributed them immediately. It was hard work. We sang all day to drown out the noise of the press. And it was hard to get paper. Each month we would go to a different store in a different part of the city in order to avoid suspicion. The storekeepers sometimes asked questions: Why did we need so much paper? What did we use it for? And so on. We had to be careful. The press was our most treasured possession. It must be kept safe at all costs. We could not socialize with anybody. But nobody! Why? Because they might be a spy, or a Communist, or might be followed by the police. So it was just the four of us, three girls and a boy. We lived like monks. We worked hard. It wasn't easy. We did not take part in the demonstrations or distribution of leaflets or pasting up of posters. The others did that. We did the printing. It was sacred work.

One time—it was in 1934 or 1935—we printed up a large batch of literature in preparation for a May First demonstration. We planned a big action, a march with leaflets and posters. We were very busy. When we finished the printing, I took a large parcel of leaflets and left for home. It was evening. On the way I met a comrade and gave him the parcel. It was done very quickly. But I felt that someone was following me. When I got to my house, Rachela was waiting to make sure I was safe—and we were both arrested. She put up a fierce struggle before being subdued. We were brought to the police station. About forty people were there already. Our whole group! All arrested. Marie Kantorowicz was among them—you know her, I believe. Our homes were searched. But nothing was found. We never left anything there. There must have been a spy in our group who gave us away.

I spent seven or eight months in prison before being let out on bail. There was a big trial, with twenty-five or thirty defendants. It was reported in the daily papers. I was sentenced to three years, others to much more, but after some months there was an amnesty and we were all freed. They took away our citizenship and passport and deprived us of our civil rights. That was a big setback for us. Afterwards we were constantly under surveillance. But they never found our printing press.

For the first few weeks in prison I was kept in solitary, and then in a cell with two other women, Marie Kantorowicz and a Communist. Soon after, I was transferred to a cell with twelve people, all of the others Communists. Some of them were very nice, some quite awful; some were well-read, some completely illiterate—and I taught them to read and write. On May First we all sang the *Internationale* in our cell and were punished by being denied packages for two months. That was terrible. You have no idea what that meant. The food they gave us in prison was meager and very poor. We relied on those parcels. We were desperately hungry.

The Communists had organized a "commune" in the prison and had a representative in each cell. They arranged to leave food for us in the toilet, with lookouts to watch for the guards. Once they left us a big sausage. It was delicious! We sent messages from one cell to another in tiny writing on pieces of cigarette paper. We were regarded as political prisoners. There were no common criminals with us. We wore civilian clothing. We could not write letters or have books. We did not have to work—no forced labor.

After our release from prison there was a period of quiet. We were happy to be free. But it was not long before we resumed our activities. The Spanish Civil

War gave a strong impetus to our movement. It was a great inspiration. We began to publish *Walka* again. One of our members, a girl named Franka, went to Spain to work for a radio station, and we got information from her and from the newspapers. The Moscow trials also made a deep impression on us but from a negative point of view. Many Communists in Poland left the party as a result.

Then came the war. When the Warsaw ghetto was established by the Germans, my sister and I fled to the east, to Soviet Russia. We lived in the town of Baranovich, west of Minsk. When the war spread to our area my sister went back to Poland and was killed. I was sent to Siberia, but that saved my life. Siberia was not easy. The trip took five weeks. My husband and I—I was married by then—were packed in a cattle car filled with people. There was very little to eat, occasionally a thin soup. There was no place to go to the bathroom. Once a day they stopped and let us out in the middle of nowhere to relieve ourselves on the tracks, while men in uniform stood over us and hurried us up. It was extremely humiliating and I hated it.

We traveled to the end of the railway line, to the banks of the Tavda River. Then we sailed on a barge for three days. The mosquitoes ate us up alive. We were put ashore and walked through a thick forest for a long time until we reached a clearing with barracks. There we lived for a year and a half. We had an NKVD commandant and a director of labor. Our work was cutting down trees, winter and summer. We walked a great distance to and from work, with swarms of mosquitoes in summer and deep snow in winter, through which we cleared a path and walked in single file. We began work very early, while it was still dark, and worked all day with little food. We were constantly hungry.

With the signing of the Sikorski agreement in 1943,[616] we were told that we were free. But they gave us no food or transportation to leave the camp. We staged a sit-in in the commandant's office, saying they could kill us but we would not leave. Finally they gave us horses. We got to the river, but no ship would pick us up. They were under orders not to. Finally a woman jumped into the water with her child, and a barge stopped for them. We all scrambled aboard. But the ship became grounded, and we didn't move for two weeks. Eventually, though, we managed to reach the railroad, only to wait weeks for a train. We spent three months on the train. Our aim was to go to Tashkent, but there was a typhus epidemic there, and we ended up in Kazakhstan.

There we worked in a factory for over a year. Then we moved to Samarkand in Uzbekistan. In 1946 we were repatriated and found ourselves back in Poland. My whole family—parents, uncles, aunts, everybody but one cousin and myself—had been annihilated by the Germans. After a short time in Poland we crossed the border illegally into Germany and lived in a D.P. camp. From there we went to Paris for four years, before emigrating to Australia. We lived there for twelve years—hard years—and came to the United States. We worked in garment factories and have lived in the Amalgamated cooperatives till we retired.

What happened to the others? Rachela Rubinstein died in Russia. Halina Lew died in the Warsaw ghetto. Henek Kaliski and Janka Weisberg were killed at the front during the war. Michal Wolman went to Palestine on the eve of the war and later taught at Hebrew University in Jerusalem. Marie Kantorowicz emigrated to Canada and lives in Montreal.

They were a marvelous group. I have never regretted joining them. It was a wonderful experience. It opened my mind to so many problems, so many questions. It made me think. I always look back in my memory to those years. I loved them. But I realize that I was not always right, that the whole idea was based on human goodness, that people are willing to help each other and work together—Kropotkin's mutual aid. But events taught us otherwise. Some people are not so good; some are selfish, some lazy, some want to take advantage of others, some are downright evil. It's a complicated world.

• DANIEL GUÉRIN •

New York City, October 27, 1973[617]

Daniel Guérin, the noted writer and historian, played an important role in the Paris uprising of May 1968 as a spokesman for *autogestion*, or workers' self-management. He is the author of numerous books on a wide range of subjects, from the Popular Front, fascism and imperialism, and the Algerian revolution, to the American labor movement, blacks in America, and the Kinsey report on sexual behavior. But he is best known, perhaps, for his study of the French Revolution, *La lutte de classes sous la Première République (1793–1797)* (1946) and for his widely read *Anarchism* (1965) and his anthology of anarchist writings, *Ni Dieu Ni Maître* (1966). He died in Paris on April 14, 1988, at the age of eighty-three.

I WAS BORN in Paris on May 19, 1904, in a liberal upper-middle-class family, which had sided with Dreyfus during his notorious persecution. My father, Marcel Guérin, was an art historian and an authority on Gauguin. I began writing poetry and fiction as a young man, and in 1928 I went to the Middle East, spending two years as the head of a large bookstore in Beirut. It was there that I learned at first hand about the evils of colonialism, and I have been a convinced anticolonialist and anti-imperialist ever since. Though my great-grandfather was a Jew, I totally support the cause of the Arabs against Israeli and American imperialism. In 1930 I went to Indo-China, and what I saw there reinforced my revulsion against colonialism of every sort.

When I returned to France, I began to write for radical newspapers about the crimes of the French in southeast Asia. I also entered the revolutionary syndicalist movement led by Pierre Monatte and contributed to his well-known journals *La Révolution Prolétarienne* and *Le Cri du Peuple*. At the same time, under the influence of Marceau Pivert, whose integrity and moral qualities I admired, I joined the left wing of the Socialist Party, but soon became disgusted by its political and electoral deals.

In 1932 and 1933 I made two trips to Germany and wrote a series of articles about the rise of Hitler that were published in book form as *La Peste Brune*. At the advice of Simone Weil, I then embarked on a long essay on fascism, which was to become a well-known book, *Fascism and Big Business*, published in 1936. In 1938 I was expelled from the Socialist Party, and I helped to found the Parti Socialiste Ouvrier et Paysan (Socialist Party of Workers and Peasants—PSOP). The following year I went to Norway to help unite left-wing European parties, and when the war broke out I was briefly interned by the Germans but allowed to return to France in 1942. My name, however, was placed on a list of banned authors, and I went into hiding in the mountains of Savoy until I was able to return in 1944 with the liberation of Paris.

After completing my book on the French Revolution, I left for the United States in December 1946, on a fellowship from the cultural department of the French foreign office, and I remained here until January 1949. When I returned to France I published a two-volume study, *Où va le peuple américain?*, which severely denounced American monopolism and imperialism.

During the 1950s I engaged in three important activities: the anticolonial movement in North Africa (Tunisia, Morocco, Algeria), an attempt to create a New Left socialist movement in France, and research on anarchism, which had lain in the back of my mind since my association with Pierre Monatte but which I had never before explored in depth. My discovery of a whole libertarian world led me to publish my little book on anarchism and my anthology *Ni Dieu Ni Maître*, as well as an autobiography of my youth, a biography of Rosa Luxemburg, and a book on the Popular Front.

I took an active part in the uprising of May 1968, when the students of the Sorbonne adopted me as their spokesman for workers' self-management. I am a believer in militant revolutionary anarchism, though I prefer the term "libertarian communism" to "anarchism"—a libertarian communism combining the best elements of Marxist and anarchist ideas. The outstanding anarchist thinkers were Proudhon and Bakunin. I have little regard for Kropotkin, who was too utopian in his writings and did not understand the class struggle, which is necessary for any successful revolution.

In my opinion, ethics must take a back place to revolutionary struggle. The main task is to seize power; we must seize power in order to destroy it. For this reason I do not much care for the anarchism of Gaston Leval[618] or of the French Anarchist Federation, who are merely Freemasons and "humanitarians" of the Kropotkin type and do not understand the need for organization, class struggle, and revolution. A practical brand of anarchism is the purpose of my own group, the Organisation Communiste Libertaire (OCL) and of the

Organisation Révolutionnaire Anarchiste (ORA), and I hope that they can merge in the near future, so that we can have an effective network of groups in every major city of France which one day will build a new society on libertarian and communist lines.

• DWIGHT MACDONALD •

New York City, March 22, 1974

Dwight Macdonald was a Marxist and Trotskyist in the 1930s. He was still a Marxist when he began his journal *Politics* in 1944, but the paper gradually veered toward anarchism, with contributions from Paul Goodman, George Woodcock, and Victor Serge, articles on Proudhon by Nicola Chiaromonte, a review of Volin's *Unknown Revolution*, etc. *Politics* was an odd name for an anarchist journal, but it was never really more than semi-anarchist or libertarian Marxist. Macdonald, like Paul Goodman, later called himself a "conservative anarchist." He lectured at the Libertarian Book Club, and the title of his book *Memoirs of a Revolutionary* echoes both Kropotkin and Victor Serge. Macdonald died of a heart attack on December 19, 1982. His papers are at Yale, from which he was graduated in 1928.

HOLLEY CANTINE, JR.,[619] was a haunter of our offices at *Politics*, a Dostoevskian character with long hair and beard. He would sit there for hours and say nothing, a sort of catatonic. Nancy [Macdonald's wife] got awfully upset. He actually had more than that to him. He later wrote a very interesting science fiction spoof of Indians taking over America. He printed it himself. It was a kind of futuristic fantasy, ironical and quite good. He used to set type for *Retort* himself, by hand, so he couldn't go for too much bullshit; that kind of cut down on the rhetoric.

Robert Bek-Gran was a familiar character. Nancy and I knew him when we lived on Tenth Street. He lived across the street from us, a fascinating fellow, always ready with a quip. He seemed an authoritarian personality, though maybe an anarchist in the intellectual sense. He was open to ideas. Yet his manner was often extremely abrupt and sharp. He would put down fools and sometimes not fools. He was not a bad painter, either.

Peacemakers was an offshoot of the War Resisters League. I broke with them and with pacifism right after the Berlin airlift. I didn't want Britain and France to withdraw from Berlin and see the Russians take over. That was the period between 1948 and 1960, when everyone was worried by the prospect of nuclear annihilation. Now it seems to me that conventional war, like the Vietnam War, is utterly wrong. I can't imagine any war that we would be involved in that

I would be in favor of, except perhaps a war to prevent Israel from being annihilated.

Paul Goodman? I never knew him very well. In fact, I would say that nobody knew him well (see his *Five Years*).[620] He was a poor writer but had many valuable ideas, which were often aborted because he didn't write well. He told me he doesn't revise. He writes it all out in first draft. But a craftsman must rewrite. He couldn't have close relations with his intellectual equals. He saw himself as a messiah, a guru, which he was! He functioned personally with younger people who were his admirers, disciples, or potential disciples. I used to meet him every year at his brother Percival's place. He would say "Hello, Dwight," but always looking off to the side or down. He just wasn't there. He had no interest in talking to me at all. He evaporated! It was a credit to him, a sign of his genius, that he could make such an impact without taking pains with his writing.

Abbie Hoffman is an anarchist. Jerry Rubin is a dope and a sidekick.[621] Abbie opposes respect for institutions and paying homage to leadership at the top. Who is that Veysey who wrote on communes?[622] I looked at his picture on the cover and didn't recognize it. If I ever met him it was very briefly and in a group. Yet he wanted to put me down. In that footnote he says I never heard of Voltairine de Cleyre, an obscure figure. Yet in fact her name does ring a bell, if vaguely. His book isn't very good, rather disjointed. The Stelton chapter is the best and much of the rest is boring.

I am not an anarchist in the way that Kropotkin was, but I am in the sense that I believe in the decentralization of authority and the ability of people to decide their own destinies. If politics begins at the bottom, people can decide much better for themselves than well-intentioned liberal bureaucrats or badly intentioned Nixonian bureaucrats. I believe in local groups and individuals deciding their own affairs. I see, though, that there are dangers to anarchism, if you think of it as just busting up things. I was appalled by the view of some student rebels that libraries were not sacred and that they could fuck up the file cards.

• ROBERT S. CALESE •

New York City, November 9, 1990

Robert Calese, a former trombonist and combat infantryman, became an anarchist after the Second World War and wrote for *Freedom, Anarchy, Views and Comments*, the *Industrial Worker*, and other anarchist and labor papers. He and his wife Phyllis—both headed branch libraries in the New York Public Library system—were close friends of Sam (q.v.) and Esther Dolgoff, founders of the Libertarian League, of which the Caleses were active members. Notable among

Calese's writings are "John Nicholas Beffel, Radical Journalist: 1887–1973," *Industrial Worker*, October 1973, and (under the pen name H. L. Morton) *Blackout: Electronic Attentat* (Chicago: Solidarity Bookshop, n.d. [1966]).

I WAS BORN in Medford, Massachusetts, on June 12, 1926, and grew up in Somerville. My father was born in Piacenza, Italy, and became a lawyer in America. Mother was born of Italian immigrant parents in Boston. I had a friend named Harry Faunce, who was a year ahead of me in high school. He was a dedicated Marxist and a member of the Workers' Socialist Party in Boston. We hung around together after the war (I served in the 87th Infantry Division in Germany and saw a good deal of combat as an eighteen-year-old kid). I had no interest in radicalism or politics. I had just gotten out of the army and wanted to get an education. I enrolled in Tufts University on the G.I. Bill and got a B.A. in 1950. Harry and Stan Perry (also a year ahead of me in high school—he had the quickest mind I ever saw) argued constantly. I listened to them open-mouthed. Harry gave me some of Marx to read, but I found it the most boring piece of shit I ever read in my life. Harry advised me to go to library school. I thought that a good idea. I got an M.S. in Library Science from Simmons College in 1951.

One day—in 1952, I think—Harry gave me Bertrand Russell's *Proposed Roads to Freedom*.[623] I liked what the anarchists said more than the socialists or Communists. I worked in a library in Boston for a couple of years, then in the Stoughton Public Library until 1953. But what I really wanted was to play music (the trombone). So I went to New York to take trombone lessons and worked in a library in Brooklyn. From there I went to Philadelphia to study with Don Reinhart for a year (1955–1956). Meanwhile I had met my wife Phyllis, who worked in the Boston Public Library. She had also graduated from Simmons. We were married by Donald Lothrop in the Community Church of Boston on February 11, 1956, and we went to live in Philadelphia so I could continue my trombone lessons. I hoped to make a career of it. Phyllis went to work in the Philadelphia public library system.

We came to New York to stay in December 1956, renting a loft in Little Italy. By now I considered myself an anarchist, though not active. I was playing on the road with bands. After a while we gave up the loft and went up to Boston, where Harry gave me a few copies of *Views and Comments*, published by the Libertarian League in New York. A subscription cost a dollar a year. Soon after, when I was playing in Washington, D.C., I wrote to the Libertarian League for back issues and got a nice letter from Russell Blackwell telling me to look him up in New York. Blackwell had been an oldtime radical. He had been a Communist till 1929 and went to Spain as an Oehlerite.[624] By the time he left Spain he was an anarchist. He had a small apartment on the Lower East Side (Thirteenth Street between Avenue A and B) and lived from hand to mouth.

When we came back to New York I called the League. At that time—it was 1957—they had a hall at 813 Broadway (near Twelfth Street, I think), which they shared with the Spaniards and Italians, splitting the rent three ways. Phyllis and I went there and met Sheldon Derechin and Blackwell. On our next visit we met Sam and Esther Dolgoff during one of the League's forums. Sam looked like he combed his hair with an eggbeater. His eyeglasses were covered with paint. His teeth were rotten, and he mispronounced every other word. But he made the other speakers look like junior high school students. He spoke well and knew what he was talking about.

Sam and Esther lived in Brooklyn at that time—they moved into the cooperatives on East Broadway a few years later. Phyllis and I lived on 100th Street near Central Park West. I played with bands and Phyllis worked at the Cornell Medical Library. [Both eventually entered the New York Public Library system and became heads of library branches.] Sam and Esther had us over to dinner. They wanted us to join the League. We talked it over later and decided to become members. They made Phyllis treasurer right off the bat. She didn't fit in at all because she could add and subtract! She kept good records and insisted on paying the bills. She approached Igal Roodenko, the printer of *Views and Comments*, and asked, "What do we owe you?" He said, "Why bother? You're not going to pay me anyway!" "Oh, yes we are," she said. And we did. I was made the literature secretary. I took care of the orders and the mailing of *Views and Comments* and our books and pamphlets. Phyllis and I made the League more efficient and put it on a responsible basis. We sold a great quantity of literature.

The League had about twenty members in New York and some branches out of town but without much coordination. Together with the Spaniards and Italians we had meanwhile moved our hall to 12 St. Mark's Place, where we held our forums. The Beatnik element in the League drove the Spaniards and Italians crazy, so they walked out and moved to John Street. The League had to pay all the rent and eventually had to leave.

There were only about a dozen Spaniards left by then. At John Street they had a chicken and rice dinner once a month; the Italians also had a dinner once a month, but the Spanish dinners were better. The Spaniards and Italians also had picnics at Van Cortlandt Park till about 1960. A couple of years later—around 1962—Phyllis and I left the League. But we remained friendly with Sam and Esther. When I read Paul Berman's eulogy to Sam in the *Village Voice*[625] I cried like a baby.

• RICHARD ELLINGTON •

Oakland, California, June 10, 1974

Richard Ellington, a free-lance printer and book designer, began his anarchist career in the Libertarian League of New York, founded by Sam (q.v.) and Esther Dolgoff in 1955. In 1960 Dick and his wife Pat moved to California with their daughter, Marie Louise, named after the Italian-British anarchist Marie Louise Berneri (1918–1949). Ellington, who had suffered from rheumatoid arthritis for many years, died of cancer in Oakland in 1991. His friend David Koven (q.v.) called him "one of the most reliable, helpful, good humored and bravest men I've ever known."[626]

I WAS RAISED in a middle-class family in Seattle. I had never heard of anarchism, but while serving in the army during the Second World War I realized that I was different from everybody else. When I came to New York after the war, I was thrilled to find that there were other people like me, that they had a name and a movement. I joined it immediately. During the 1950s I was active in the Libertarian League, mailing out literature and helping to print *Views and Comments*.

At one May First celebration, in 1955 I think, Holley Cantine walked in. He wore a green alpine hat and a soft jacket with leather elbow pads and comfortable slacks cut off at the bottom. He had a well-trimmed beard and carried a trombone case. He asked whether we would be singing *Solidarity Forever*, and we said yes. So he sat down in front and didn't say another word. When we started to sing *Solidarity Forever* he opened his case, took out the trombone, and played along with us, though he couldn't play a single note correctly, as if he had never played a trombone before. Then he left without talking to anyone.

Pat and I went to California in 1960. I became assistant manager of the Oakland Symphony Orchestra, but quit two years ago when the old conductor, a fine, decent man, was replaced by a new, unethical fellow. I've been working as a printer ever since. Pat is also an anarchist, and we have a sixteen-year-old daughter, Marie Louise, named after Marie Louise Berneri. She went to the Walden School, a libertarian school in Berkeley founded by David Koven and Audrey Goodfriend [q.v.]. My ideas on anarchism haven't changed one whit. Whether or not we ever reach it, anarchism is the finest thing there is, so why not work for it?

• FRED WOODWORTH •

New York City, October 11, 1972

Fred Woodworth, an anarchist of the younger generation, has edited *The Match!* in Tucson for more than twenty years, the longest lived and one of the best anarchist periodicals of recent decades. In October 1972 Woodworth came to New York to take part in an anarchist conference at Hunter College. He told the audience that he had once appeared at a political rally in Tucson dressed as the stereotypical anarchist terrorist, wearing a black hat and cape and carrying a black-painted glass ball with a wick, "a sort of one-man guerrilla theater," he explained.

While in New York, Woodworth stayed at the apartment of Robert Calese (q.v.) on Morningside Heights, and it was there that I went to interview him. Small, dark, intense, he had come to anarchism by way of atheism and harbored a powerful aversion to the Mormon church. He himself, however, evinced a strong authoritarian streak, being intolerant, dogmatic, and righteous in his views. "He who is not with me is against me" was his general attitude. "Why do you want to interview me?" he demanded when I arrived at the apartment. "Is all this [my work on anarchism] a game with you, or what?" The interview, however, went smoothly. Woodworth proved himself as interesting a talker as he was a writer. Apart from editing *The Match!*, an accomplishment of which he was inordinately proud ("I am *The Match!*, he declared, echoing Louis XIV on the state), he has published a steady stream of articles and pamphlets—*Selected Blasphemy* (1970), *Beast and Monster* (1973), *Anarchism* (1974), *The Atheist Cult* (1991)—as well as an autobiographical novel, *Dream World* (1988), under the pen name of Kent Winslow.

I WAS BORN in Miami in 1946. My father was an itinerant radio announcer, and after moving around a great deal we finally settled in Arizona, in Mormon country, where Father now manages a station in Tucson. I was an anarchist, but without the label, since about the age of ten. In the fourth grade I was already arguing against compulsory education. I asked my father how the government got its power, and he mentioned that there were people called anarchists who opposed the state. I've been interested in them ever since.

As a child I rejected religion and was particularly opposed to the Mormons, with their strong authoritarianism and racial prejudice. My attitude toward religion was the most important factor in my hostility to government and to authority in general. During my senior year in high school I opposed the Vietnam War. I continued as a student at the University of Arizona, where I was involved in civil rights protests, some directed against the Mormon church. By now I was not just an atheist but antireligious and antiracist.

At the University of Arizona there was a small anarchist group, established in 1969, called SLAM, Student Libertarian Action Movement. It was already publishing *The Match!*, with Conrad Goeringer as editor and the most active member of the group. I joined the group, distributed *The Match!*, and participated in demonstrations against the war, the draft, and racism, especially in the Mormon church. SLAM started out as rightist, with members coming from Goldwater supporters and Rothbardites.[627] Goeringer had even supported George Wallace before turning to anarchism! By the time I joined, though, it had shed its right-wing orientation. I married Cheryl in 1969, and she also joined SLAM.

I started writing articles for *The Match!* and typeset all the issues from volume one, number eleven. I also wrote leaflets and typeset all the leaflets. I now earn some money as a typesetter on occasional odd jobs. Cheryl and I began to read the anarchist classics—Bakunin and Kropotkin, Emma Goldman and Alexander Berkman. Berkman's *Prison Memoirs of an Anarchist* moved me more than any other book I've ever read. But I was less interested in the theories of the anarchists than in how they lived their lives, how they acted in different situations. These writings cemented my adherence to the anarchist cause.

I got my B.A. in 1969 in Spanish language and literature. I went on to graduate school in Spanish, also at the University of Arizona, but didn't finish the M.A. program. I'm not a student any more and never want to be! One day, Elizabeth Baskette, widow of Ewing Baskette, came to one of our newsstands and gave us a few copies of *Man!* Goeringer hated it as outdated and antipathetic. But I liked it at once and started printing selections in *The Match!* Goeringer wanted an "underground" paper, while I wanted a "classical" anarchist paper.

Meanwhile, Marcus Graham saw an announcement of *The Match!* in the London *Freedom* and wrote us for a copy. He used the pseudonym F. Smith, so I didn't know it was Graham. By coincidence I happened to send him the July 1971 issue with *Man!* stuff. He was delighted, wrote to me, and we started a correspondence. Cheryl and I were elated to find that he was still alive! I was influenced not only by his writings in *Man!* but by its typography and layout, as well as by Graham's dedication after years of harassment, jail, and oppression. Despite all this he never gave up!

I went to see Graham in California, and we became good friends. I urged him to write his memoirs, but lately he's become annoyed with me because of my opposition to terrorism. He hates Nicolas Walter[628] for his *Freedom* article against terrorism, which I agreed with. I can't condemn terrorism but cannot practice it. You can't make a revolution without people. You have to have the mass of people with you, and not just a small band of terrorists. I had a falling-out with Graham over this. I'm for *real* propaganda, not for "propaganda by deed," which is only a euphemism for terrorism, and one ought to come out and say so.

I have no prefix or adjective to my anarchism. I think syndicalism can work, as can free-market anarcho-capitalism, anarcho-communism, even anarcho-hermits, depending on the situation. But I do have a strong individualist streak. Just plain anarchism—against government and authority—is what I'm for. I don't like Murray Bookchin at all. I'm afraid of him. He seems to want to form a cult, and I'm always suspicious of cults. I didn't like anything about his book, either style or content, and there wasn't an antiauthoritarian idea in it.[629]

The Match! right now is just me and Cheryl. There is no more group. There's no more SLAM at the university. But we have about two thousand subscribers. Our mails are being tampered with. We have been arrested and beaten by city and campus police. Goeringer and I split. He published two issues of *Sunburst* and is now affiliated with SRAF (Social Revolutionary Anarchist Faction), but Paul Roasberry continues to write for *The Match!*

• ANNE MCVEY •

New York City, March 29, 1980

During the 1960s and 1970s, Anne McVey, a member of the War Resisters League and the Committee for Nonviolent Action, took part in the protest movement against the Vietnam War.

I WAS BORN on August 25, 1887, in Centerview, Missouri, a little wee town. My father, James Absalom McVey, was a beautiful man. He was an anarchist and a socialist packed into one, a real radical. I remember I was combing my hair, preparing for school, and Father was talking to me about socialism. He was a great admirer of Emma Goldman. He really had her on a pedestal, way up high. Where he heard about all these things I'll never know. He subscribed to the *Kansas City Star*, about as radical a paper as you could find out there. He was a farmer and did other manual work.

Mother died as I was being born, the last of five children. The neighbors and relatives all wanted to adopt us, but Father said he could never give away any of his children. So he brought us up himself. I attended an old one-room schoolhouse. I remember most vividly the history book we read. It was so thick, and I had to work hard to be able to digest it. My father talked to us about our education, how important it was. I had a brother and three sisters. I was the baby.

Father refused to join the army. He always talked against war. I first became interested in socialism through my dad. He was a real socialist, and he meant it! When I was a kid, about ten or twelve years old, I listened intently to every word he used to say because it sounded so profound to me.

When I grew up I took a loft in New York City. Theater was my love. I directed a good many plays. My husband, Theodore Upshure, was a black man, a musician. I was arrested in Washington, D.C., in 1971 and spent four days in jail. I was protesting against the Vietnam War. I was against that war with all my might, and how I fought that war! I loved the people in Vietnam. It still makes me cry to think of it, how they were made to suffer. I was in the War Resisters League and the Committee for Nonviolent Action at Voluntown, Connecticut. Walt Whitman is my favorite poet. Government? I'm against it!

Notes

PART ONE

1. Paul Avrich, *The Haymarket Tragedy* (Princeton: Princeton University Press, 1984), p. 436.

2. Emma Goldman, *Living My Life* (New York: Knopf, 1931), p. 509.

3. Paul Avrich, *An American Anarchist: The Life of Voltairine de Cleyre* (Princeton: Princeton University Press, 1978), p. 57.

4. Ibid., p. 174; James J. Martin, *Men Against the State: The Expositors of Individualist Anarchism in America, 1827–1908* (revised ed., Colorado Springs: Ralph Myles, 1970), p. 220; Paul Avrich, *Anarchist Portraits* (Princeton: Princeton University Press, 1988), p. 28.

5. Benjamin R. Tucker to C. L. Swartz, July 22, 1930, in *Free Vistas: An Anthology of Life and Letters*, ed. Joseph Ishill, 2 vols. (Berkeley Heights, N.J.: The Oriole Press, 1933–1937), II, pp. 300–301.

6. Rudolf Rocker, *Pioneers of American Freedom* (Los Angeles: Rocker Publications Committee, 1949), pp. 160–61.

7. Rudolf Rocker, *The London Years* (London: Robert Anscombe, 1956), p. 90.

8. Alexander Berkman to Michael A. Cohn, February 13, 1933, Berkman Archive, International Institute of Social History, Amsterdam.

9. *Testament to Rudolf Rocker, 1873–1943* (Los Angeles: Rocker Publications Committee, 1944), pp. 43–46.

10. Paul Avrich, "An Interview with Oriole Tucker," in *Benjamin R. Tucker and the Champions of Liberty*, ed. Michael E. Coughlin, Charles H. Hamilton, and Mark A. Sullivan (St. Paul and New York: Michael E. Coughlin and Mark A. Sullivan Publishers, 1987), pp. 20–27. Reprinted in Avrich, *Anarchist Portraits*, pp. 144–52.

11. Ralph Borsodi (1888–1977), American economist and single-taxer. He founded the School of Living in New York City in 1936 to advance the cause of self-sufficient farming and to educate people to live on the land. Viewing homesteads as islands of "intelligence and beauty amidst the chaotic seas of human stupidity and ugliness," he launched the Bayard Lane Colony in Suffern, New York, in 1936, and Stillwater in Ossining three years later. His books include *This Ugly Civilization* (1928) and *Flight from the City* (1933).

12. Edward Bond Foote (1854–1912), New York physician and reformer. He was a member of the Free Speech League and treasurer of the Francisco Ferrer Association and of the Thomas Paine National Historical Association. Together with his father, Edward Bliss Foote (1829–1906), he was a pioneer in the movement for birth control.

13. J. William Lloyd (1857–1940) was a prolific anarchist writer and poet who contributed to Tucker's *Liberty* and many other periodicals. In 1895 he broke with Tucker and began to call himself a "free socialist." He edited *The Free Comrade* from 1900 to 1902 and again (with his friend Leonard D. Abbott) from 1910–1912, and was an enthusiast of American Indian legends and myths.

14. In January 1908 a fire destroyed Tucker's Manhattan warehouse, ending his publishing venture of thirty years.

15. On George Schumm see interview with his daughter, Beatrice Fetz.

16. Fred Schulder (1874–1961), a single-tax anarchist, was Tucker's chief associate in Cleveland, where he lived with his companion Adeline Champney, a contributor to *Liberty* and *Mother Earth*. As Tucker's sales representative, Schulder traveled about the country taking subscriptions for *Liberty* and selling books and pamphlets published by Tucker. He is the author of the pamphlet *The Relation of Anarchism to Organization* (1899).

17. Henry Bool (d. 1922) was a British-born furniture dealer in Ithaca, New York, who supported Tucker's publishing ventures. He returned to his boyhood home in Montecute, Somerset, where he died at about seventy-five.

18. Georges Clemenceau (1841–1929), French premier (1906–1909 and 1917–1920) and opponent of Germany, who vigorously pressed the cause of World War I.

19. John Henry Mackay (1864–1933), half-Scottish, half-German anarchist and biographer of Max Stirner. He was a frequent contributor to *Liberty* and a friend of Tucker's until his death (he dedicated his book *Der Freiheitsucher* to Tucker "with all the friendship of a lifetime"). An English translation of his novel *Die Anarchisten* was published by Tucker in 1891. Mackay, who first met Tucker in 1889, when the latter was traveling in Europe, visited him in the United States in 1893 and saw him several times in Europe after the turn of the century. Tucker's chief disciple in Germany, he was one of the principal writers of the individualist anarchist movement.

20. George Bernard Shaw (1856–1950), the noted Irish playwright and critic, visited Tucker in Monaco in 1928 and found him as "fresh as a daisy in spite of his advanced years." Tucker had early recognized the greatness of Shaw and appears to have been the first to publish him in the United States ("What's in a Name?", *Liberty*, April 11, 1885). One of the last works published by Tucker before he moved to Europe was Shaw's *The Sanity of Art* (1908). Shaw, for his part, praised Tucker's *Liberty* as "a lively paper in which the usual proportions of a halfpenny-worth of discussion to an intolerable deal of balderdash are reversed."

21. Henry Cohen (1864–1942), a lawyer by profession, was a disciple of Tucker in Denver and afterwards Los Angeles. He contributed articles to *Liberty* and edited *Proudhon's Solution of the Social Problem* (1927).

22. Pryns Hopkins (1885–1972), a libertarian socialist and pacifist, conducted an experimental school, Boy Land, in Santa Barbara, California, from 1912 to 1918. After the First World War, which he opposed, he took a Ph.D. in psychology at the University of London. In 1926 he started another experimental school near Paris, which Emma Goldman, whom he had known in America, visited in 1931 and saw the children perform Shaw's *Androcles and the Lion*. Returning to the United States, he taught at Clairmont College in California and served on the advisory board of Amnesty International.

23. *Instead of a Book: By a Man Too Busy to Write One* (1893), a collection of Tucker's writings in *Liberty*.

24. Victor S. Yarros, "Philosophical Anarchism: Its Rise, Decline, and Eclipse," *The American Journal of Sociology* 41 (January 1936). Yarros, during the late 1880s and early 1890s, had been associate editor of Tucker's *Liberty* and one of its most prolific contributors.

25. George E. H. Macdonald (1857–1944), a contributor to Tucker's *Liberty* and longtime editor of *The Truth Seeker*, a leading free-thought publication. Macdonald was the author of *Fifty Years of Freethought* (2 vols., 1929–1931).

26. Robert M. La Follette (1855–1925) was Governor of Wisconsin from 1901 to 1906 and U.S. Senator from 1906 until his death. In 1924 he ran unsuccessfully for the presidency on the Progressive Party ticket.

27. Karl Heinzen (1809–1880), German "Forty-Eighter" and freethinker. He was the editor of *Der Pionier*, which championed the abolition of slavery, workers' and women's rights, penal reform, and other advanced causes. According to Schumm, who became his literary heir, Heinzen, though he never adopted the anarchist label, defended individualism to a point where it "bordered on anarchism."

28. William Mackintire Salter (1853–1931) was speaker of the Society for Ethical Culture of Chicago at the time of the Haymarket affair and a champion of amnesty for the defendants.

29. Sarah E. Holmes (1847–1929), contributor to *Liberty* and Tucker's sometime lover. She translated Bakunin's *The Political Theology of Mazzini and the International* (serialized in *Liberty* in 1886 and 1887) and assisted George Schumm in the translation of John Henry Mackay's *The Anarchists* (1891).

30. August Spies (1855–1887), a leading German anarchist in Chicago and editor of the *Arbeiter-Zeitung*. He was convicted in the Haymarket trial and hanged with Albert Parsons, George Engel, and Adolph Fischer on November 11, 1887.

31. "Annie Laurie," a popular Scottish ballad of the period, was sung by Albert Parsons (not Spies) on the night before his execution ("And for bonnie Annie Laurie, I'd lay me doon and dee").

32. Rachelle Slobodinsky, Russian-born physician and contributor to *Liberty*, of which her husband, Victor Yarros, was associate editor (see n. 24). Breaking with Tucker over his acceptance of Stirner's egoism, they moved to Chicago in 1895 and lived for several years at Hull House.

33. Jane Addams (1860–1935), American social reformer and founder of Hull House in Chicago in 1889. One of the first and most famous settlement houses in the United States, it served as a community center for the neighborhood poor, many of them recent immigrants. Addams, a leader in the women's suffrage and pacifist movements, was awarded the Nobel Peace Prize in 1931.

34. Leonard D. Abbott (1878–1953), associate editor of *Current Literature* and active in the socialist movement until converted to anarchism around 1910, under the influence of Emma Goldman. A freethinker and civil libertarian, Abbott was a charter member of the Francisco Ferrer Association (1910) and served as its first president. He was a frequent contributor to *Mother Earth*, *The Road to Freedom*, and other anarchist publications. From 1935 to 1939 he worked as an editor at the Federal Writers' Project in Washington.

35. Max Baginski (1864–1943), German-born anarchist and associate of Emma Goldman. A dissident socialist in Germany, where he was imprisoned for radical agitation, he emigrated to America in 1893 and joined the anarchist movement. A talented and erudite writer, he assumed the editorship of the Chicago *Arbeiter-Zeitung*, formerly edited by August Spies, and of the short-lived journal *Sturmglocken* (1896). On Johann Most's death in 1906, Baginski became the editor of *Freiheit* and was a coworker of Alexander Berkman and Emma Goldman (who had briefly been his lover) on *Mother Earth*. His wife Emilie (Millie) was a sister of George Schumm, Tucker's associate on *Liberty*. The farm in Pennsylvania where Baginski spent his last years was owned by Milly Rocker's sister, Fanny Pokrass.

36. Robert Reitzel (1849–1898), a leading anarchist in Detroit, where he published *Der Arme Teufel*, one of the foremost German anarchist papers in America. In Novem-

ber 1887, together with the American anarchist Dyer Lum, he organized a plot—never carried out—to liberate the Haymarket defendants. During the 1890s he was befriended by Emma Goldman, who visited him in Detroit.

37. Voltairine de Cleyre (1866–1912), anarchist, freethinker, and feminist. Born in rural Michigan and educated in a Catholic convent, she converted to anarchism after the hanging of the Haymarket martyrs in 1887. Most of her adult life was spent in Philadelphia, where she was a founder of the Ladies' Liberal League and a teacher among the Jewish immigrant poor. An inspired speaker and writer, she published hundreds of poems, essays, and stories in *Mother Earth* and other journals of the day. Wounded by an assassin in 1902, she refused to press charges, returning good for evil in the spirit of Tolstoy. During her last years, she was arrested in a free-speech demonstration in Philadelphia, supported the Mexican anarchist movement led by Ricardo Flores Magón, and taught in the Modern School of Chicago, where she spent the last two years of her life. She was buried in the Waldheim Cemetery beside the graves of the Haymarket anarchists, whose martyrdom had inspired her life. Emma Goldman called her "the poet-rebel, the liberty-loving artist, the greatest woman Anarchist of America."

38. Bolton Hall (1854–1938), New York attorney and single-taxer. He gave the house to Emma Goldman as a place of retreat following the assassination of President McKinley in 1901. Hall, himself a philosophical anarchist and admirer of Kropotkin, contributed to such journals as *Free Society* and *Mother Earth*. He was also the author of numerous books on the land question, most notably *Three Acres and Liberty* (1907). In 1910 he founded Free Acres, a single-tax colony in New Jersey, and in 1917 he appeared as a defense witness for Emma Goldman at her trial with Alexander Berkman for obstructing the draft.

39. William Bailie, *Josiah Warren: The First American Anarchist* (Boston: Small, Maynard & Co., 1906).

40. William Morris (1834–1896), British writer, designer, printer, and antiauthoritarian socialist, "our one acknowledged Great Man," as Bernard Shaw described him. Morris was a friend of many anarchists, among them William Bailie and especially Peter Kropotkin, whom he met in 1886 at a Paris Commune memorial. That same year he spoke out vehemently in behalf of the Haymarket anarchists, protesting against what he called their impending "political murder." His *News from Nowhere* (1891) is perhaps the greatest libertarian utopia ever written.

41. Edward Carpenter (1844–1929), English writer, sex reformer, and libertarian socialist. He was a friend of William Morris and Peter Kropotkin and an admirer of Walt Whitman, whom he visited in America in 1877. A self-confessed homosexual and author of *Love's Coming of Age* (1896), Carpenter stood at the forefront of the movement for sexual emancipation; and his essay on "Non-Governmental Society" exerted a strong influence on anarchists and socialists alike. He appealed for clemency for the Haymarket anarchists and wrote a preface to the British edition of Alexander Berkman's *Prison Memoirs of an Anarchist* (1925). Emma Goldman visited him in England not long before his death. Thomas Bell wrote a pamphlet about him (*Edward Carpenter: The English Tolstoi*, 1932), and Leonard Abbott thought him "great as a sex radical, and great in the simplicity and beauty of his personality."

42. Daughters of the American Revolution, a patriotic society organized in Washington, D.C., in 1890. It was open to women having one or more ancestors who aided the cause of the American Revolution.

43. Method of education for the preschool child originated by Maria Montessori (1870–1952), Italian pedagogue and physician. According to Montessori, children will

learn naturally if placed in an environment suited to their abilities and interests and in which the teacher intervenes only when necessary. Montessori stressed physical as well as mental education, with "learning games" and toys, as well as plants and animals cared for by the children.

44. Laurance Labadie to Joseph Ishill, May 7, 1935, Ishill Papers, Harvard.

45. See also Laurance Labadie, *Selected Essays*, ed. James J. Martin (Colorado Springs: Ralph Myles, 1978).

46. Elisée Reclus (1830–1905), like Kropotkin both an anarchist and noted geographer. A friend of Bakunin as well as Kropotkin, he took part, with his brother Elie (1827–1904), in the Paris Commune of 1871 and was one of the most respected anarchist writers and theorists. He wrote prefaces to Bakunin's *God and the State* (with the Italian anarchist Carlo Cafiero) and Kropotkin's *Words of a Rebel* and *The Conquest of Bread*, of which he also suggested the titles; and his pamphlets *Evolution and Revolution* (1880) and *An Anarchist on Anarchy* (1884) were translated into many languages. A geographer of international renown, he published, among many other works, the nineteen-volume *Nouvelle géographie universelle* (1876–1894) and the six-volume *L'Homme et la terre* (1905–1908).

47. Martin, *Men Against the State* (see n. 4).

48. Agnes Inglis (1870–1952), curator of the Labadie Collection at the University of Michigan, founded by Joseph A. Labadie in 1911. The daughter of a wealthy Michigan family, Inglis was attracted to anarchism after reading the works of Emma Goldman. In 1916 she arranged for Goldman to speak at the University of Michigan, and in 1918 she visited Goldman in Jefferson City, Missouri, where she was imprisoned for interfering with conscription. Goldman, in return, visited Inglis at the Labadie Collection in 1934, while on a ninety-day lecture tour of the United States, from which she had been banished in 1919. Inglis, who devoted the better part of her life to the collection, must be credited, along with Labadie himself, with preserving the records of anarchism for posterity.

49. On John Scott (1879–1953) see interviews with Lallah Blanpied and Jo Ann Burbank, Part Four.

50. Steven T. Byington (1868–1957), American teacher, proofreader, and frequent contributor to Tucker's *Liberty*. As a student of classics at the University of Vermont, he was elected to Phi Beta Kappa and was graduated summa cum laude in 1891. The master of ten languages, he translated Max Stirner's *The Ego and His Own* (1907) and Paul Eltzbacher's *Anarchism* (1908), both published by Tucker, who considered Byington "a living encyclopedia."

51. V. N. Cherkezov (1846–1925), Georgian anarchist of princely blood and close associate of Kropotkin in London. In 1914 Cherkezov joined Kropotkin in espousing the Allied cause in World War I. With the collapse of the Russian monarchy in 1917, he returned to his native Georgia, but went back to London after the Bolshevik consolidation of power and died there in his eightieth year. His works include *Pages of Socialist History* (1902).

52. Booker T. Washington (1856–1915), African-American educator and public figure, founder of the Tuskegee Institute in Alabama. His autobiography, *Up From Slavery*, appeared in 1901, the year of Kropotkin's second visit to America.

53. Alexander Kerensky (1881–1970), Russian lawyer and Socialist Revolutionary. He served as minister of justice, minister of war, and finally prime minister in the Provisional Government of 1917, formed after the abdication of the tsar. Kerensky took refuge in the West following the overthrow of his government by the Bolsheviks.

54. Vladimir Bonch-Bruevich (1873–1955), Bolshevik associate of Lenin who special-ized in the publication of revolutionary literature. After the October Revolution he became secretary of the Council of People's Commissars and in later years was director of the Museum of the History of Religion and Atheism. Kropotkin met Lenin at Bonch-Bruevich's Moscow apartment in May 1919.

55. In the summer of 1918 Kropotkin and his wife were compelled to leave Moscow and move to a house in Dmitrov, a town some forty miles to the north. There, until his death in 1921, he received a stream of visitors, including Emma Goldman, and worked on his book on ethics.

56. In March 1921 the sailors of the Kronstadt naval base near Petrograd rose against the Bolshevik government, which they themselves had helped into power. Under the slogans of "free soviets" and an end to "commissarocracy," they established a revolution-ary commune that survived for sixteen days before an army was sent to crush it. Meyer Rubinchik was in fact a Russian anarchist, but there is no evidence that he took part in the rising, much less organized it.

57. Barry Goldwater, the Republican candidate for President of the United States, was defeated by Lyndon B. Johnson in the 1964 general elections.

58. Fanny Schapiro was the widow of Alexander Schapiro, a well-known Russian an-archist (see n. 111), who died in 1946. Fanny felt too ill to see me. She died not long afterwards, and the papers in her possession were thrown out.

59. Justus Schwab (1847–1900), German anarchist in New York and proprietor of a saloon on the Lower East Side, where revolutionaries (including Emma Goldman) con-gregated. He broke with Most, whom he had helped bring to the U.S. in 1882, for encouraging such methods as committing arson to collect the insurance.

60. August Lott (d. 1934), a disciple of Most in New York.

61. Johnny Most (1923–1993), the anarchist's grandson and namesake, was a well-known sports announcer in Boston, where he broadcast the Celtics' basketball games.

62. C.E.S. Wood (1852–1944), single-taxer and philosophical anarchist. After gradu-ating from West Point and serving in the Indian wars (he rose to the rank of colonel), he became a lawyer in Portland and was elected to the Oregon state senate. A prolific essayist and poet, he contributed to Benjamin Tucker's *Liberty* and Emma Goldman's *Mother Earth*, among many other publications. In a letter to Wood (whose wife Sara Bard Field was also a poet) Thomas Bell said: "I put you among our Anarchist poets, such as Burns, Shelley, Whitman, Wilde, Carpenter."

63. Lucy E. Parsons (1849?–1942), American anarchist and widow of Albert Parsons, the Haymarket martyr. An important figure in her own right, she was a powerful speaker, a contributor to *The Alarm* and other journals, and editor of *Freedom* (Chicago, 1890–1892).

64. Frank Harris (1856–1931), British editor and writer, friend of Emma Goldman, Thomas Bell, and other anarchists. He published *The Bomb* in 1908, a novel based on the Haymarket case, in which he erroneously portrays Rudolph Schnaubelt as the bombthrower.

65. Alexander Horr (1871–1947), Hungarian-born anarchist and friend of Emma Goldman. A member of the Freeland League, he joined the Equality Colony on Puget Sound in 1904 and distributed *Mother Earth* in Seattle. Moving to San Francisco, he operated a bookstore and ran a jitney service for several years. In 1922, having aban-doned anarchism, he ran for Governor of California on the Socialist ticket. He published a pamphlet, *The Freeland Movement* (1904), and a journal, *Freeland* (1904, 1909).

66. On July 22, 1916, a bomb exploded during a "preparedness" parade in San Francisco, killing ten bystanders and injuring forty more. The crime was pinned on two labor militants, Thomas J. Mooney (1892–1942) and Warren K. Billings (1893–1972), who were convicted on the basis of perjured testimony and fabricated evidence. As in the Haymarket case of the 1880s, the actual bomber was never discovered, yet Billings was sentenced to life imprisonment and Mooney to death by hanging (afterwards commuted to life). The men were not released until 1939, having spent more than two decades behind bars for a crime they did not commit.

67. National Association for the Advancement of Colored People, founded in 1910 with the aim of ending racial discrimination and securing civil rights for blacks.

68. The editors of *The Firebrand*, Abe Isaak, Henry Addis, and Abner J. Pope, were arrested in 1897 for sending obscene material through the mail. The poem in question was Whitman's "A Woman Waits for Me." All three were tried and convicted. Pope, seventy-four, served four months in prison, while Isaak and Addis were released on appeal. Addis and Pope went to Home Colony near Tacoma, Washington, and Isaak and his family moved to San Francisco, where they resumed publication of the paper as *Free Society*.

69. Clarence S. Darrow (1857–1938), the celebrated American lawyer, was also a socialist, freethinker, single-taxer, and Tolstoyan pacifist. His links with the anarchist movement dated from the 1880s and 1890s, when he addressed Haymarket memorial meetings, contributed to a fund to erect a monument for the defendants in Waldheim Cemetery, and served on the amnesty committee that petitioned Governor Altgeld for the release of Samuel Fielden, Oscar Neebe, and Michael Schwab. In 1901 Darrow chaired a lecture by Peter Kropotkin in Chicago and obtained the release of Abe Isaak and other anarchists arrested after President McKinley's assassination. In 1903–1904 he served (with the poet Edgar Lee Masters) as counsel for John Turner, a British anarchist threatened with deportation under an exclusion law resulting from McKinley's killing, and in 1905 he defended Moses Harman, the anarchist sex reformer and editor of *Lucifer*. In after years Darrow took part in many similar cases, involving anarchists, IWWs, and socialists. He contributed to *The Firebrand* and other anarchist papers, was a member of the Francisco Ferrer Association, and lectured at the Ferrer Center in New York. In 1931, it might be added, he addressed a memorial meeting for Kropotkin on the tenth anniversary of his death.

70. President William McKinley was shot to death on September 6, 1901, in Buffalo, New York. His assassin, Leon F. Czolgosz, was a self-proclaimed anarchist, although he belonged to no anarchist group and was not known within the movement.

71. *Report on the President's Commission on the Assassination of President John F. Kennedy* (Washington, D.C.: Government Printing Office, 1964).

72. Max N. Maisel (1872–1959), Jewish anarchist and bibliophile. His bookstore on New York's Lower East Side carried an immense stock of radical works, some of which— by Kropotkin, Thoreau, and Oscar Wilde—he published himself. Maisel, in addition, distributed *Free Society*, *Mother Earth*, and other anarchist periodicals, sold tickets to Emma Goldman's lectures, and was a charter member of the Kropotkin Literary Society, founded in 1912.

73. Saul Yanovsky (1864–1939), editor of the *Fraye Arbeter Shtime*, the foremost anarchist paper in Yiddish, over which he presided from 1899 to 1919, the heyday of Jewish anarchism in America. Before that, he had been a member of the Pioneers of Liberty, the first Jewish anarchist group in the U.S., founded in 1886 in response to the

Haymarket trial. In 1889 he was appointed editor of *Der Arbeter Fraynd* in London, where, an eloquent speaker, he often shared the platform with Peter Kropotkin, Errico Malatesta, and Louise Michel. His pamphlet *Vos viln di anarkhistn?* (1890) was among the first expositions of anarchism in Yiddish. According to Rudolf Rocker, he was "the ablest propagandist in speech and print" among the Whitechapel Jews at that time. After five years in England, Yanovsky returned to the U.S., where he edited *Di Abend Tsaytung* (1906) and *Di Fraye Gezelshaft* (1910–1911), in addition to the *Fraye Arbeter Shtime*. During the 1920s and 1930s he remained a prominent figure, lecturing from coast to coast for the benefit of the movement.

74. David Edelstadt (1866–1892), Jewish anarchist poet, member of the Pioneers of Liberty, and an early editor of the *Fraye Arbeter Shtime*. A buttonhole maker by trade, he experienced firsthand the miseries of sweatshop life that he so hauntingly evokes in his poems, which won widespread popularity among the Yiddish-speaking workers of the day. Stricken with tuberculosis, then endemic among the toilers in the shops, he vainly sought a cure in Denver, where he died at the age of twenty-six. Emma Goldman thought him "a great poet and one of the *finest* types of Anarchists that ever lived."

75. "Fitzi" was the nickname of M. Eleanor Fitzgerald (1877–1955), Alexander Berkman's companion until his deportation in 1919 and associate editor of his paper *The Blast* (1916–1917). She was a member of the No-Conscription League in 1917 and of the League for the Amnesty of Political Prisoners from 1918 to 1920. From 1918 to 1929, when the group disbanded, she served as business manager and executive director of the Provincetown Players, becoming friends with Eugene O'Neill, Djuna Barnes, Hart Crane, and other literary figures.

76. At Thomas Mooney's trial (see n. 66) the defense produced a photograph purporting to show Mooney and his wife Rena watching the parade from the roof of a building on Market Street. A clock across the street showed the time as 2:01 P.M., five minutes before the explosion occurred more than a mile away.

77. During a bitter labor dispute in 1910 a dynamite explosion occurred in the Los Angeles Times Building, killing twenty-one people. The brothers James B. and John J. McNamara, labor militants but not anarchists, were brought to trial, defended by Clarence Darrow. In the midst of the proceedings the McNamaras suddenly changed their plea to guilty, to the dismay of all who felt they had been framed or unfairly prosecuted. James was sentenced to life imprisonment and John to fifteen years at hard labor.

78. Eric B. Morton, Scandinavian-born anarchist, known as "Ibsen" after the Norwegian playwright and as "Eric the Red," the hero of an old Icelandic saga. A practitioner of direct action, Morton was involved in an abortive attempt in 1900 to liberate Alexander Berkman from prison, and he smuggled dynamite into Russia during the Revolution of 1905. In 1910 and 1911 he edited an anarchist paper called *Freedom* in San Francisco and in 1916 worked on Berkman's *The Blast*.

79. Henry George (1839–1897), American writer and founder of the single-tax movement, who advocated an annual tax on the rental value of land and the imposition of no other taxes. His book *Progress and Poverty* (1879) became the bible of the single-tax movement, selling millions of copies around the world and influencing such diverse figures as Leo Tolstoy, George Bernard Shaw, and Sun Yat-sen. His disciples in the United States included many anarchists, among them Bolton Hall, Fred Schulder, George S. Seldes, and Alexis C. Ferm.

80. Goldman, *Living My Life*, pp. 263–64; letter of Peter Kropotkin, March 5, 1900, Bell Papers, Huntington Library, San Marino, California.

81. John Turner (1864–1934), English anarchist, member of the Freedom Group in London, and general secretary of the Shop Assistants' Union. Turner made two extended lecture tours of the United States, in 1896 and in 1903–1904, when he became the first person to be deported under the anarchist exclusion law enacted after the assassination of President McKinley. George Bernard Shaw offered Turner "many personal congratulations on having terrified the greatest democratic republic in the world into laying violent hands on him, not because of anything he said, but because of what the Americans feared he might say."

82. Louise Michel (1830–1905), a veteran of the Paris Commune and the most famous woman anarchist in France. In 1888 she was shot by a deranged individual while addressing a meeting in Le Havre, but like Voltairine de Cleyre in a similar incident she refused to press charges against her assailant. In 1891 she organized an International School in London where, according to a hostile source, the pupils were taught "to disrespect their Gods and Laws and masters." More than a few anarchists named their daughters after her, including two interviewees in this volume, Jack Frager and Louis Raymond.

83. Errico Malatesta (1853–1932), the most famous and widely admired of the Italian anarchists, converted by Bakunin in his youth. Pursued by the authorities, he lived a life of wandering and exile, suffered numerous imprisonments, and died under house arrest during Mussolini's dictatorship. Like Louise Michel and Voltairine de Cleyre, he was the victim of a shooting but refrained from pressing charges against his assailant.

84. Nicholas Chaikovsky (1850–1926), Russian populist during the 1870s, a founder (with Mark Natanson) of the Chaikovsky circle in St. Petersburg, of which Kropotkin was an active member. In the late 1870s he helped organize an experimental community in Kansas and afterwards settled in London, where he resumed his friendship with Kropotkin and collected funds for the Russian revolutionary movement. Returning to Russia during the 1905 Revolution, he joined the Popular Socialist Party and took part in the cooperative movement. After the October 1917 seizure of power, he became, like Kropotkin, an outspoken critic of Lenin. During the civil war that followed he headed an anti-Bolshevik government in northern Russia.

85. Stepniak, pseudonym of S. M. Kravchinsky (1851–1895), Russian populist and member of the Chaikovsky circle with Kropotkin. In 1877 he took part, with Malatesta, in the Benevento rising in Italy. The following year, having returned to Russia, he assassinated General N. V. Mezentsev, the chief of the tsarist police. Escaping abroad, Stepniak lived in Switzerland and then England, where he once again associated with Kropotkin. His life was cut short when he was struck by a railway locomotive. He was the author, among other works, of two widely read books, *Underground Russia* (1883) and *The Career of a Nihilist* (1889).

86. Max Nettlau (1865–1944), the foremost historian of anarchism. He was the author of innumerable articles and books on the subject, including *Bibliographie de l'anarchie* (1897) as well as a multivolume history and biographies of Bakunin, Malatesta, and Reclus. His immense collection of anarchist literature, housed in the International Institute of Social History in Amsterdam, is the most valuable in the world.

87. Whiteway Colony, started in 1898, was an anarchist community in the Cotswolds, the British equivalent of Stelton, Mohegan, and Home.

88. Rachelle Edelmann (née Krimont) was one of three daughters and a son of East European immigrants, all four of whom were anarchists (her younger sister Mary was the wife of the well-known anarchist Harry Kelly). Rachelle's husband, John H. Edelmann

(1852–1900), was himself an anarchist, as well as a respected architect, and it was at their New York apartment that Kropotkin was a guest during his first visit to America (1897). Edelmann contributed widely to anarchist periodicals, in addition to editing his own journal *Solidarity* (1892–1898). After his death at the age of forty-eight, Rachelle went to England to live at Whiteway Colony, where she raised their two children, John and Sonia (see n. 426).

89. Harry Kelly (1871–1953), prominent American anarchist, coeditor of *The Rebel* (Boston, 1895–1896) and contributor to *Mother Earth, The Road to Freedom*, and other anarchist periodicals. At the turn of the century Kelly lived for several years in England, where he became a friend of Kropotkin, Malatesta, Louise Michel, and Rudolf Rocker. After returning to the United States, he was a charter member of the Francisco Ferrer Association (1910) and a leading figure in the Modern School movement. In 1920, together with Roger Baldwin and Elizabeth Gurley Flynn, he was a founder of the League for Mutual Aid—the name derives from Kropotkin's *Mutual Aid*—which provided loans to individuals affiliated with labor and libertarian causes (see n. 165).

90. William C. Owen (1854–1929), British-American anarchist. He was born in India of an aristocratic family, studied law in London, and came to the United States in 1884, ultimately settling in California, where he was active in the labor and anarchist movements as well as campaigning for prison reform. During the years before the First World War, Owen threw himself into the movement in southern California led by Ricardo Flores Magón (1873–1922), the foremost Mexican anarchist of the twentieth century. He edited the English page of Magón's *Regeneración* and published a pamphlet on *The Mexican Revolution* (1912). In 1914 and 1915 he edited his own periodical, *Land and Liberty* (the battle cry of the Magón movement), which got him into trouble with the authorities. Threatened with deportation, he returned to England, supported Kropotkin's stand on the war, and contributed to the London *Freedom*. He severely condemned the Bolshevik dictatorship, calling Lenin the "high priest" of a new ruling oligarchy.

91. Charles B. Cooper (1852–1930), British-born anarchist, friend of W. C. Owen and Thomas Bell, like whom he spent his later years in California. He wrote for such journals as *Lucifer, Solidarity*, and *Free Society*, and published Cherkezov's *Pages of Socialist History* (1902).

92. Cassius V. Cook (1879–1950), Charles T. Sprading, Clarence Lee Swartz (1868–1936), Henry Cohen (see n. 21), and Hans F. Rossner (d. 1937) were Tuckerite anarchists who, along with Walter Holloway, Thomas Bell, and others, organized the Libertarian League in Los Angeles, which was active between the world wars. Jules Scarceriaux (1873–1963), born in Belgium, had been an anarchist in Trenton, New Jersey, where he arranged Emma Goldman's lectures. He taught pottery at the Stelton Modern School before moving to California and working as a skilled craftsman at Hollywood movie studios. Over the years he made ceramic plaques of famous anarchists, wrote for *Mother Earth, The Road to Freedom*, and *Man!*, and did translations for these and other periodicals from half a dozen foreign languages. Alfred G. Sanftleben (1871–1952) had been a socialist in Zurich and a friend of Rudolf Rocker, Max Baginski, and Gustav Landauer (he wrote for Landauer's journal *Der Sozialist*) before emigrating to the United States. Under the pen name "Slovak," he wrote articles for Most's *Freiheit* and contributed "International Notes" to other publications, including *Mother Earth* and *The Road to Freedom*. Like W. C. Owen, moreover, he edited the English page of *Regeneración*, edited by Ricardo Flores Magón.

93. Sadakichi Hartmann (1867–1944), son of a German father and a Japanese

mother, was a man of diverse artistic talents: "poet, writer, painter, and a marvelous reader of the poems and stories of Whitman and Poe," as Emma Goldman describes him. Alfred Stieglitz, proprietor of the 291 Gallery, considered him one of the best critics of photography in America (he was a frequent contributor to Stieglitz's *Camera Work*, as well as to Goldman's *Mother Earth*). Apart from criticism and poetry (he was among the first to write English haiku), he wrote fiction, drama, and sketches, as well as half a dozen books and hundreds of articles, including important studies of American and Japanese art. At the New York Ferrer Center he put on "finger dances," "shadow pictures," "perfume concerts," and pantomimes. Moving to California in the 1920s, he attached himself to John Barrymore's Hollywood circle and acted in Douglas Fairbanks's 1927 film *The Thief of Baghdad*, playing the Chinese magician.

94. Thomas H. Bell, "Oscar Wilde Without Whitewash," manuscript, 477 pages, written during the 1930s. A Spanish translation was published in 1946 under the title *Oscar Wilde: sus amigos, sus adversarios, sus ideas*. See also Bell's "Oscar Wilde's Unwritten Play," *The Bookman*, April–May 1930. Bell had met Wilde in London while employed as secretary to the writer Frank Harris.

95. Lillian Harman (1870–1929), daughter of Moses Harman (1830–1910), the sex reformer and editor of *Lucifer*, on which Lillian assisted him over the years. She herself edited *Our New Humanity* (1895–1897) and, with her husband Edwin C. Walker, *Fair Play* (1888–1908). In 1898 she went to England to assume the presidency of the Legitimation League, founded the previous year. Her son, George Harman O'Brien, became a federal judge in California.

96. Members of the Industrial Workers of the World, a militant anticapitalist labor organization, founded in Chicago in 1905. Its chief weapon, apart from oral and written propaganda, was "direct action," including strikes, demonstrations, the boycott, and free-speech fights. Among its best-known personalities were William D. (Big Bill) Haywood (see n. 296) and Joe Hill.

97. The Walt Whitman School, affiliated with the Francisco Ferrer Association, was a Modern School started in Los Angeles in 1919 under the directorship of William Thurston Brown, formerly the principal at Stelton (see Part Four). It closed in 1924.

98. William Thurston Brown (1861–1938), a socialist and former clergyman, one of the most active figures in the Modern School movement. Between 1910 and 1919 he started Ferrer Schools in Salt Lake City (1910), Portland (1911), and Los Angeles (1919), as well as directing the Modern School of Stelton from 1916 to 1919, when he left for Los Angeles. He was also an editor of *The Modern School*, which he described as "the most artistic magazine in the entire radical movement."

99. Martin Buber, the philosopher and theologian, Richard Dehmel, the poet, and Julius Bab, the drama critic, were all friends of Landauer's. Buber (1878–1965) included a chapter on Landauer in his *Paths in Utopia* (1958).

100. Erich Mühsam (1878–1934), writer and poet, editor of *Kain* and *Fanal*, and one of Germany's leading anarchists, along with Landauer and Rocker. A member of the Revolutionary Workers' Council during the Bavarian Revolution of 1918–1919, he was afterwards murdered in a Nazi concentration camp.

101. Wilhelm Spohr, a German writer and translator, was a longtime friend of Landauer's and a collaborator on *Der Sozialist*.

102. Kurt Eisner (1867–1919), German socialist and participant with Landauer and Mühsam in the Bavarian Revolution, becoming the first republican premier of Bavaria. He was assassinated on his way to present his resignation to the Bavarian parliament.

103. Fermin Rocker, "33 Dunstan Houses," manuscript, Avrich Collection, Library of Congress.

104. Robert Bek-Gran (1893–1965), Munich-born anarcho-syndicalist and anti-Nazi, author of *Vom Wesen der Anarchie* (1920) and *Apologia pro Vita Mia* (1926), and friend of Paul Mattick and the Council Communists (see n. 595). He came to the United States during the 1920s and taught at the Mohegan Modern School. During the 1930s he wrote for *Vanguard* and *Challenge*, anarchist journals in New York. He afterwards operated a print shop where he printed *Why?* and *Resistance*, of which he was also a contributor.

105. Lydia Gordon (born Landau) was a veteran anarchist and friend of Emma Goldman and Lucy Parsons. She was the wife of Harry Gordon (1866–1941), a Pittsburgh anarchist who visited Alexander Berkman in prison, and the mother of Sophie Bannister and Eva Brandes, who lived at Stelton and Mohegan. In 1915 she served as custodian of the Ferrer Center in New York.

106. Wilhelm Reich (1897–1957), Austrian psychiatrist and associate at Freud's Psychoanalytic Clinic in Vienna before moving to Berlin in 1930. Forced to leave by the Nazis, he settled in New York, where he taught at the New School for Social Research and, in 1942, founded the Orgone Institute. His invention, the "orgone box," a device that he claimed would revive sexual energy, was declared a fraud by the Food and Drug Administration in 1956. He was sentenced to two years in prison, where he died.

107. Hippolyte Havel (1871–1950), Czech-born anarchist, friend and onetime lover of Emma Goldman and contributor to her journal *Mother Earth*. He was a conspicuous figure at the New York Ferrer Center, where he was a drinking companion of Sadakichi Hartmann and edited *The Revolutionary Almanac* (1914) and a short-lived but important journal called *Revolt* (1916). At the same time he became a friend of Alfred Stieglitz, Robert Henri, Man Ray, and Eugene O'Neill, who included him as a character (Hugo Kalmar) in *The Iceman Cometh*. During the 1920s Havel edited *The Road to Freedom* at the Stelton Colony, where he lived for many years and wrote a pamphlet *What's Anarchism?* (1932).

108. Thomas E. Dewey (1902–1971), American political figure. He was Manhattan district attorney (1937 ff.), Governor of New York (1943–1955), and unsuccessful Republican candidate for President of the United States in 1944 (against Franklin Delano Roosevelt) and in 1948 (against Harry S Truman).

109. Augustin Souchy (1892–1984), well-known German anarchist. He wrote books on both the Russian and Spanish Revolutions, both of which he witnessed firsthand. In 1936, as secretary of the anarcho-syndicalist committee in Barcelona, he invited Emma Goldman to come to Spain to join in the struggle against Franco. After the Second World War he traveled to many countries, visiting anarchist comrades and groups. His memoirs, *"Vorsicht: Anarchist!" Ein Leben für die Freiheit* appeared in 1977 (English translation, 1992).

110. Marcus Graham (1893–1985), Rumanian-born anarchist and proponent of propaganda by the deed, including acts of terrorism and assassination. Nature, remarked his comrade Joseph Cohen, endowed him with "stubbornness, pride, and a hot revolutionary temperament." During the Red Scare of 1919–1920, he edited *The Anarchist Soviet Bulletin*, an illegal publication in New York, succeeded by *Free Society* (with Hippolyte Havel as coeditor). Graham was active in the Radical Library Group in Philadelphia and afterwards lived at Stelton. Cantankerous and quarrelsome, he was, said Emma Goldman, a "poison in the movement." Yet he also had positive qualities. In 1929 he published *An Anthology of Revolutionary Poetry*, a valuable compendium. Mov-

ing to California, he edited *Man!* in San Francisco, one of the principal anarchist journals of the 1930s. Throughout his radical career he was subjected to government persecution, but efforts to deport him failed since the authorities were unable to ascertain his country of origin. Graham was finally driven into hiding and lived under an assumed name for nearly five decades. His last major publication was *Man! An Anthology of Anarchist Ideas, Essays, Poetry and Commentaries* (1974).

111. Alexander Schapiro (1882–1946), prominent Russian-born anarchist, whose father, also an anarchist, was a friend of Kropotkin. Until the First World War Schapiro was active in the London movement, alongside Kropotkin, Malatesta, and Rocker. A true internationalist, with an extraordinary equipment of languages (including Bulgarian, Turkish, and Spanish, as well as English, French, German, Russian, and Yiddish), he represented the Jewish Anarchist Federation of London at the 1907 anarchist congress in Amsterdam. He was interned like Rocker during the war for his opposition to conscription. In 1917 he returned to Russia to take part in the revolution, only to leave in 1921 together with Emma Goldman and Alexander Berkman. Schapiro spent the interwar years in Berlin and then Paris, where he edited the anarcho-syndicalist journal *La Voix du Travail* with Pierre Besnard. In 1941 he arrived in New York, a refugee from Nazi oppression, and edited *New Trends* until his death (see also n. 58).

112. Ferdinand Domela Nieuwenhuis (1846–1919), former Protestant minister and leading Dutch pacifist and libertarian socialist, who edited the journal *Recht voor Allen*. He attended the Amsterdam anarchist congress of 1907 and strongly opposed the First World War.

113. Solo Linder (1888–1961), Joseph J. Cohen (1878–1953), and Michael A. Cohn (1867–1939) were important figures in the Jewish anarchist movement. Linder was a member of the Arbeter Fraynd Group in London before emigrating to New York, where he edited the *Fraye Arbeter Shtime* after World War II. Cohen, too, served as editor of the paper, succeeding Saul Yanovsky in the 1920s. A cigarmaker in Philadelphia, where he was converted to anarchism by Voltairine de Cleyre, he became a founder of the Radical Library Group as well as of the Stelton and Sunrise Colonies (see Part Four). Cohn, a physician and friend of Emma Goldman since the 1890s, wrote for *Mother Earth* and the *Fraye Arbeter Shtime* and contributed generously to anarchist groups and publications.

114. The well-known Spanish anarchists Buenaventura Durruti (1896–1936) and Francisco Ascaso (1901–1936) visited the Rockers in Berlin in 1928. See Rudolf Rocker, *Revolutsie un regresie*, 2 vols. (Buenos Aires: Jewish Rationalist Society, 1963–1964), I, pp. 275–90.

115. James Joll wrote of Durruti: "He was a man who stopped at nothing; he had robbed and murdered in the anarchist cause, and the 'innocent expression' which Gerald Brenan noted is perhaps offset in his photographs by a cruel mouth, and was certainly belied by his deeds. With his friend Francisco Ascaso, he became a symbol of anarchist cruelty and ruthlessness towards his opponents." Joll, *The Anarchists* (London: Eyre & Spottiswoode, 1964), p. 248.

PART TWO

116. Rudolf Rocker to Richard Drinnon, August 29, 1954, Rocker Archive, International Institute of Social History, Amsterdam.

117. Floyd Dell, *Women as World Builders* (Chicago: Forbes, 1913), p. 60.

118. Richard Drinnon, *Rebel in Paradise: A Biography of Emma Goldman* (Chicago: University of Chicago Press, 1961), pp. 171–72.

119. Goldman, *Living My Life*, p. 986; Frank Harris, *Contemporary Portraits: Fourth Series* (New York: Brentano, 1923), pp. 223–24.

120. Emma Goldman, *My Disillusionment in Russia* (London: C. W. Daniel, 1925), pp. xii–xiii; Goldman to Dora Stoller [Keyser], July 29, 1939, Avrich Collection, Library of Congress.

121. Goldman, *Living My Life*, p. 35.

122. Van Wyck Brooks, *The Confident Years* (New York: Dutton, 1952), p. 375.

123. Emma Goldman, *The Truth About the Boylsheviki* [sic] (New York: Mother Earth Publishing Association, 1918), pp. 5, 10.

124. Alexander Berkman to Hudson Hawley, June 12, 1932, Berkman Archive, International Institute of Social History, Amsterdam.

125. Emma Goldman, preface to Berkman's *Now and After: The ABC of Communist Anarchism*, 2d ed. (New York: Fraye Arbeter Shtime, 1937).

126. See Martin B. Duberman, *Paul Robeson* (New York: Knopf, 1988).

127. Ben L. Reitman (1879–1942), Chicago physician and Emma Goldman's longtime lover. He managed her lecture tours for several years, wrote for her journal *Mother Earth*, and in 1940 spoke at her funeral in Waldheim Cemetery, where he himself was later buried. He is the author of two books: *The Second Oldest Profession* (1931) and *Sister of the Road* (1937).

128. The bird was actually killed by another prisoner. See Alexander Berkman, *Prison Memoirs of an Anarchist* (New York: Mother Earth Publishing Association, 1912), p. 363.

129. Michael Hambourg, Jan's father, had known Kropotkin in London. See Goldman, *Living My Life*, p. 262.

130. The violinist Yehudi Menuhin was born in 1916.

131. Mrs. Jan Hambourg was the daughter of Samuel McClung of Pittsburgh, the judge who presided at Berkman's trial (September 19, 1892).

132. Goldman's copy of *Prison Memoirs of an Anarchist* remained in her possession until her death. It is now in the hands of Audrey Goodfriend (q.v.). The inscription reads: "*First Copy* off the press Oct. 14. 1912 4 P.M. To you dear Em, who helped me to live this book and to write it. Sasha."

133. Saxe Commins (1891–1958), born Isidore Cominsky, Emma Goldman's nephew. He wrote for *Mother Earth* as a young man. He later abandoned his dental practice in Rochester, New York, to become a well-known editor, first at Liveright and then at Random House, where he rose to the position of editor-in-chief. He counted Eugene O'Neill, William Faulkner, and Sinclair Lewis among his authors.

134. Eugene O'Neill (1888–1953), leading American playwright, winner of the Nobel Prize in literature. He was strongly influenced by anarchism and had many ties with the anarchists. As a young Princeton dropout he haunted Benjamin Tucker's Manhattan book store, browsing in Tolstoy, Kropotkin, and Stirner. He came to know Emma Goldman and Alexander Berkman, and his first published poem appeared in *Mother Earth*. Among his other anarchist friends were Hippolyte Havel (see n. 107) and Terry Carlin (see n. 442), whom he immortalized as Hugo Kalmar and Larry Slade in *The Iceman Cometh*, a play partly based on the McNamara case, in which several anarchists were implicated (see nn. 77 and 142). Christine Ell, an anarchist cook in Greenwich Village, was the original of Anna Christie in O'Neill's play of that name, and one of his

last works was an unfinished play about the Italian anarchist Malatesta. It might be added that O'Neill's editors at Liveright and Random House were Manuel Komroff, an anarchist at the New York Ferrer Center, and Emma Goldman's nephew Saxe Commins. Moreover his lawyer was Harry Weinberger, attorney for Goldman and Berkman. Berkman, incidentally, translated O'Neill's *Lazarus Laughed* into Russian for the Moscow Art Theater.

135. Bennett Cerf (1898–1971), American publisher and anthologist. He was vice president of Boni & Liveright and afterwards a founder and chairman of Random House, publisher of the Modern Library series.

136. See interview with Ora Robbins.

137. Claus Timmermann (1866–1941), German-American anarchist and comrade of Emma Goldman, Alexander Berkman, and Modest Stein, whom he joined in a plot against Henry Clay Frick during the Homestead strike of 1892. The following year he and Goldman were sent to prison for inciting to riot during an unemployed rally in Union Square. Timmermann edited three journals: *Der Anarchist* (1889–1891), *Die Brandfackel* (1893–1894), and *Sturmvogel* (1897–1899).

138. Actually, the sculptor Jo Davidson, not Modest Stein, executed the relief on Emma Goldman's tombstone.

139. Americans for Democratic Action, a liberal organization founded in 1946 in Washington, D.C., by a group of former advisors to President Franklin Roosevelt, including Leon Henderson, Elmer Davis, and Chester Bowles. It called for an extension of New Deal welfare programs and the expansion of civil rights.

140. I have found no evidence to support this assertion. It seems highly unlikely, though Robeson and Goldman met on several occasions during the 1920s and 1930s.

141. Ben Capes (d. 1964), anarchist in Chicago and St. Louis, friend of Emma Goldman and Alexander Berkman. He contributed to *The Road to Freedom* and ended his days at Home Colony in Washington.

142. David Caplan and Matthew Schmidt, comrades of Alexander Berkman and Emma Goldman, took part with the McNamara brothers in the dynamiting of the Los Angeles Times Building in 1910 (see n. 77). Betrayed by Donald Vose, the son of a Home Colony anarchist, Caplan was condemned to ten years and Schmidt to life in San Quentin prison in California.

143. Gregory Maximoff (1893–1950), prominent figure in the anarchist movement both in Russia and abroad. During the Revolution of 1917 he joined the staff of *Golos Truda* in Petrograd and the following year edited *Vol'nyi Golos Truda* in Moscow, where he served as secretary of the Anarcho-Syndicalist Confederation. He visited Kropotkin in Dmitrov and spoke at his funeral in 1921. In 1922 he left Russia for Berlin, where he was a founder, with Rudolf Rocker and Alexander Schapiro, of the Anarcho-Syndicalist International (the International Working Men's Association) and edited *Rabochii Put'* (1923). In 1925, after a sojourn in Paris, he emigrated to the United States. He settled in Chicago, where he worked as a paperhanger and edited *Golos Truzhenika* and *Delo Truda* (later *Delo Truda-Probuzhdenie*). He is the author of (among other books) *The Guillotine at Work: Twenty Years of Terror in Russia* (1940) and the editor of *The Political Philosophy of Bakunin* (1953). He is buried in the Waldheim Cemetery near the graves of Emma Goldman and the Chicago martyrs.

144. Goldman, *Living My Life*, pp. 699, 950, 960.

145. Lucy Robins Lang, *Tomorrow Is Beautiful* (New York: Macmillan, 1948), pp. 121–22.

146. Emmy Eckstein, Alexander Berkman's companion until his death in Nice in 1936. She herself died three years later, aged thirty-nine, after a series of stomach operations.

147. Djuna Barnes (1892–1982), American writer, best known for her novel *Nightwood* (1936). She wrote several one-act plays for the Provincetown Players in 1919 and 1920.

148. Hart Crane (1899–1932), American poet, best known for *The Bridge* (1930), a set of long poems on America in which the Brooklyn Bridge is the unifying symbol.

149. Michael Gold (real name Irwin Granich, 1893–1967), American writer and apostle of proletarian literature, best known for his novel *Jews Without Money* (1935). He was one of a number of American Communists—Robert Minor was another—who began their radical careers as anarchists. He frequented the New York Ferrer Center, where he read from the poetry of Blake and Shelley and contributed to Hippolyte Havel's *Revolt* (1916). He also contributed to *The Modern School* magazine, wrote one-acters for the Provincetown Players, and lived for several months at the Stelton Colony. During the 1920s, now a convert to Communism, he wrote powerful articles and poems on Sacco and Vanzetti and picketed in Boston to protest their execution. He afterwards wrote for the *Daily Worker*, the *New Masses*, and other Communist publications.

150. Robert Minor (1884–1952), American illustrator and writer. A comrade of Emma Goldman and Alexander Berkman, he served with them on the Mooney-Billings Defense Committee and drew covers for *Mother Earth* and Berkman's *The Blast*. In 1920, however, he abandoned anarchism for Communism, becoming a member of the party's central committee and its representative in the Communist International. During the 1930s he went to Spain as correspondent for the *Daily Worker*, of which he was an editor.

151. The reference is to the explosion for which Mooney and Billings were imprisoned. There is no convincing evidence that Mexican revolutionaries were responsible.

152. Becky Edelsohn, a New York anarchist and sometime lover of Alexander Berkman, actually died of emphysema in 1973.

153. Goldman, *Living My Life*, p. 699.

154. Harry Weinberger (1886–1944), American attorney, single-taxer, and anarchist sympathizer. Apart from Eugene O'Neill, his clients included Emma Goldman, Alexander Berkman, Ricardo Flores Magón, Jacob Abrams, and Mollie Steimer. He was also counsel for the Provincetown Players and a trustee of the Mohegan Colony Association.

155. What Goldman said, by her own account, was: "I want to thank you for your leniency and kindness in refusing us a stay for two days, a stay you would have accorded to the most heinous criminal. I thank you once more." *Living My Life*, pp. 622–23.

156. For a comprehensive history of the Abrams case, see Richard Polenberg, *Fighting Faiths: The Abrams Case, the Supreme Court, and Free Speech* (New York: Viking, 1987).

157. George S. Seldes (1860–1931), American anarchist and single-taxer. He emigrated from Russia after the assassination of Tsar Alexander II and was a founding member of the Alliance Colony in New Jersey (1882). He afterwards operated a pharmacy in Philadelphia and in Pittsburgh, corresponded with Kropotkin and Tolstoy, and became a friend of Emma Goldman and Alexander Berkman, among others. Scholarly and erudite, he was the principal intellectual figure at Mohegan Colony during the 1920s. His older son, George, became a well-known political journalist, and his younger son, Gilbert, managing editor of *The Dial* and a specialist in the popular arts. Gilbert's daughter is the actress Marian Seldes.

158. Drinnon, *Rebel in Paradise*, p. 140.

159. Roger N. Baldwin, ed., *Kropotkin's Revolutionary Pamphlets* (New York: Vanguard, 1927).

160. *New York Times*, August 27, 1981.

161. C.O.'s, abbreviation for conscientious objectors, who refused to serve in the army or assist the war effort in any way. During 1918 and 1919 Baldwin himself spent nine months in an American prison for opposing conscription.

162. Alexis C. Ferm (1870–1971) and Elizabeth Byrne Ferm (1857–1944), principals of the Stelton Modern School (see Part Four).

163. John Dewey (1859–1952), famous American philosopher and exponent of progressive education. He visited the Modern School at Stelton and the Organic School at Fairhope, Alabama. A friend of Emma Goldman, he petitioned for her readmission to the United States and spoke at a reception in New York's Town Hall during her visit in 1934. In addition, he supported the cause of Sacco and Vanzetti, protested (with Albert Einstein, Bertrand Russell, and others) Alexander Berkman's threatened expulsion from France, and served on a memorial committee organized after the murder of Carlo Tresca (1943).

164. John Haynes Holmes (1879–1964), American clergyman, civil libertarian, and social reformer, pastor of the Community Church in New York. He was a friend of Roger Baldwin and cofounder of the American Civil Liberties Union, as well as a supporter of Sacco and Vanzetti. In 1934 (together with John Dewey and others) he addressed the reception for Emma Goldman in Town Hall.

165. League for Mutual Aid, founded in 1920 by Harry Kelly, Roger Baldwin, and Elizabeth Gurley Flynn. Its name was adopted from *Mutual Aid* (1902), one of Kropotkin's most influential books. It provided interest-free loans to American political prisoners and victims of the Red Scare, later extended to those affiliated with libertarian and labor causes. The League dissolved in 1971 after fifty years of activity.

166. I interviewed Roger Baldwin at the home of his daughter at 282 West Eleventh Street in Greenwich Village.

167. Carlo Tresca (1879–1943), Italian-American anarcho-syndicalist and antifascist, eloquent speaker, and editor of *Il Martello* in New York. Together with his companion Elizabeth Gurley Flynn, he played an important role in the Lawrence and Paterson strikes of 1912 and 1913. After Luigi Galleani's deportation in 1919, Tresca became the leading Italian anarchist in the United States. In 1937 he served with John Dewey and others on the investigating commission that cleared Trotsky of alleged crimes against Stalin and the Soviet Union. He was shot to death at Fifth Avenue and Fifteenth Street by a Mafia hit man named Carmine Galante.

168. The Ferrer Center was an anarchist meeting place and school on East 107th Street in New York (see Part Four).

169. Henry G. Alsberg (1881–1970), correspondent for the New York *World*, *The Nation*, and other publications. He went to Soviet Russia to report on the civil war and met Alexander Berkman and Emma Goldman in 1920. In 1934 he attended a reception for Goldman during her visit to the United States. He served as director of the Federal Writers' Project under Franklin D. Roosevelt's New Deal.

170. Free Acres, a single-tax colony in Berkeley Heights, New Jersey, founded in 1910 on land donated by Bolton Hall (see n. 38). The residents at various times included such anarchists as Mollie Albert, Benzion Liber, Konrad Bercovici, and Alexis and Elizabeth Ferm.

171. Joseph Ishill (1888–1966), Rumanian-born anarchist and printer. He frequented

the New York Ferrer Center, printed *The Modern School* magazine, and taught printing to the pupils at Stelton. Most important, he published artistic hand-printed books on Kropotkin, Benjamin Tucker, and Elisée and Elie Reclus, to mention only a few—books, as Leonard Abbott described them, "of the rarest beauty and inspiration." The Ishill Collection of anarchist literature at Harvard University is among the richest in the United States.

172. Kurt Tucholsky (1890–1935), German political satirist and antifascist. He was the author, among other works, of *Deutschland, Deutschland, über Alles* (1929).

173. Rebecca West (1892–1983), English novelist and critic. Her novels include *The Return of the Soldier* (1918), *The Judge* (1922), *The Thinking Reed* (1939), *The Fountain Overflows* (1956), and *Birds Fall Down* (1966). Her most famous works of nonfiction are *Black Lamb, Grey Falcon* (1942), a combination of travel book and political study of Yugoslavia, and *The Meaning of Treason* (1947), based on the treason trials at the end of World War II. West met Emma Goldman shortly after her arrival in London in 1924 and supported her right to criticize Bolshevik tyranny. She wrote a preface to the British edition of *My Disillusionment in Russia* 1925), in which she calls Goldman "a mountain of integrity."

174. Colonel Josiah Wedgwood, member of the Independent Labour Party and descendant of the famous English potters. Together with Rebecca West, Edward Carpenter, and Havelock Ellis, among others, he welcomed Emma Goldman to London. She arrived in September 1924, two months before Javsicas. Doris Zhook, it might be noted, was an old comrade of Emma's, as was Zhook's brother, William Wess.

175. Gregory Zinoviev (1883–1936), Bolshevik leader in Petrograd at the time of the Kronstadt rebellion (March 1921) and head of the Communist International (1919–1926). He was afterwards purged by Stalin.

176. On December 2, 1919, shortly before Berkman and Goldman were deported to Russia, news came of the death of Henry Clay Frick, whom Berkman had tried to assassinate in 1892. According to Goldman's account, a reporter asked Berkman for his reaction. "Deported by God," was his reply. *Living My Life*, p. 709.

177. Juan Montseny (1864–1942), who wrote under the name of Federico Urales, was a highly esteemed anarchist in Barcelona. His daughter Federica (1905–1994) was a leading figure in the civil war of 1936–1939, serving as minister of health in the Popular Front government.

178. *Nowhere at Home: Letters from Exile of Emma Goldman and Alexander Berkman*, ed. Richard and Anna Maria Drinnon (New York: Schocken Books, 1975), p. 86.

179. Emma Goldman and Alexander Berkman were deported to Russia on the *Buford* on December 22, 1919.

180. Emily Holmes Coleman, *The Shutter of Snow* (New York: Viking, 1930).

181. Goldman, *Living My Life*, pp. vii, 960.

182. In 1934 Frances Perkins, Secretary of Labor in the Roosevelt administration, granted Goldman a ninety-day visa to lecture in the United States.

183. Walter Starrett, pseudonym of Warren Starr Van Valkenburgh (1884–1938). He was called "Van" by his anarchist comrades, among them Emma Goldman, whom he met in 1911 in Schenectady, New York, where he arranged for her to lecture on anarchism. He contributed to Goldman's *Mother Earth* and Berkman's *The Blast*, as well as to Hippolyte Havel's *Revolt*, and he campaigned against the execution of Sacco and Vanzetti and the deportation of Armando Borghi, serving as treasurer of the Borghi Defense Committee. From 1928 to 1932 he edited *The Road to Freedom*, a leading anarchist journal of the time.

184. William J. Durant (1885–1981), American writer and historian. In 1912 and 1913 he was the principal and teacher of the Modern School in New York, as well as lecturing to adults in the evening (see Part Four). He also lectured at the Modern School in Philadelphia and published a pamphlet on *The Ferrer Modern School* (1912). His marriage to a fifteen-year-old pupil (Ida Kaufman, later known as Ariel) created a sensation and led to his departure from the school. He enrolled at Columbia University (Ph.D., 1917) and went on to become a successful writer. *The Story of Philosophy* (1926) brought him fame and fortune. Later, in collaboration with Ariel, he published *The Story of Civilization* in eleven volumes, a project that took nearly fifty years to complete (the last volume appeared in 1975).

185. Sherwood Trask (1890–1973), one of the most notable teachers at the Stelton Modern School during the 1920s. He taught basketry as well as history and geography and took the children hiking and camping. A graduate of Dartmouth, he also taught at the Manumit School in Pawling, New York, and the Organic School in Fairhope, Alabama, ending his career as a celebrated social science teacher at the Walden School in New York City. He published a book of poems, *The Interweaving Poetry of American History* (1967).

186. Mary Hansen (d. 1952), Danish-born anarchist and poet. A contributor to *Free Society* and *Mother Earth*, she was Voltairine de Cleyre's closest friend in Philadelphia and assisted Joseph Cohen at the Radical Library Sunday School, where her daughter Heloise and Cohen's daughter Emma were pupils. Her companion George Brown, an English-born shoemaker, was a popular anarchist orator. They had a cottage at the single-tax colony in Arden, Delaware, where they spent their summers. After Brown's death in 1915, Mary took Heloise to the Ferrer School in New York and afterwards to the Stelton Colony. A sweet and loveable personality, she is remembered with affection by those who knew her.

187. In 1925 Emma Goldman entered into a Platonic marriage with James Colton, a retired Welsh anarchist coal miner, in order to acquire a British passport.

188. Senya Fleshin (1894–1981) and Mollie Steimer (1897–1980), Russian-born anarchists, closely associated with Emma Goldman and Alexander Berkman. In 1918 Mollie, Jacob Abrams, and other members of the Frayhayt Group in New York distributed leaflets opposing American intervention in Soviet Russia, for which they were arrested on charges of sedition. The Abrams case, as it became known, was a landmark in the repression of civil liberties during the Red Scare hysteria following World War I. Mollie was sentenced to fifteen years in prison plus a five-hundred-dollar fine, and in November 1921 she was deported to Russia. It was in Petrograd that she met Senya, who, before returning to Russia in 1917, had worked at the office of *Mother Earth*. The two became devoted companions. Evicted in 1923 for criticizing the Bolshevik dictatorship, they spent two decades in Berlin and Paris, where Senya operated a photography studio. In 1942 they found refuge in Mexico, where they lived out the rest of their lives.

189. Goldman, *Living My Life*, p. 991.

190. Isadora Duncan (1878–1927), the pioneer modern dancer, was a friend of Emma Goldman in France during the 1920s. She died when her scarf caught in the wheel of her car while she was motoring in Nice.

191. The Workmen's Circle (Arbeter-Ring), a Jewish fraternal society in the United States and Canada, founded in 1900. It provided life insurance, sickness and accident benefits, and educational and cultural programs for its members. Although predominantly socialist in orientation, it had a number of anarchist branches, including the

Radical Library Group in Philadelphia, the Kropotkin Group in Los Angeles, the Ferrer-Rocker Branch in New York, and the Fraye Gezelshaft Branch in Toronto.

192. Dorothy Rogers (real name Giesecke, d. 1966), was Emma Goldman's comrade and helper during her last years in Toronto. On May 31, 1940, she spoke at a Goldman memorial meeting in New York, together with Rudolf Rocker, Harry Kelly, and others. Remaining in New York, she was active from the 1940s until her death in the Why? and Resistance Groups and the Libertarian League (see Part Six).

193. Carl Newlander (b. 1893), Swedish-born anarchist in New York, associated with Emma Goldman and *Mother Earth*. He was deported to Sweden in 1919 and afterwards settled in Canada, where he resumed his friendship with Goldman.

194. See also Ahrne Thorne, "La muerte de Emma Goldman," *La Protesta* (Buenos Aires), May 1960; and Thorne, "Tsu Emma Goldmans 45-er yortsayt," *Problemen* (Tel Aviv), July 1985.

195. J. L. Cohen, Toronto attorney specializing in labor and civil liberties cases.

196. Cf. interview with Valerio Isca, Part Three.

197. J. Edgar Hoover (1895–1972), director of the Federal Bureau of Investigation from 1924 until his death. As a Justice Department official in 1919 he had played a key role in securing Goldman's deportation.

PART THREE

198. *The Sacco-Vanzetti Case: Transcript of the Record of the Trial of Nicola Sacco and Bartolomeo Vanzetti in the Courts of Massachusetts and Subsequent Proceedings, 1920–7,* 6 vols. (New York: Henry Holt, 1928–1929), V, 5378l.

199. *The Nation*, November 23, 1921.

200. Edmund Wilson, *Letters on Literature and Politics* (New York: Farrar, Straus & Giroux, 1977), p. 154.

201. Dukakis's proclamation is reproduced in Upton Sinclair, *Boston: A Documentary Novel of the Sacco-Vanzetti Case* (Cambridge, Mass.: Robert Bentley, 1978), pp. 797–99.

202. Bartolomeo Vanzetti, *Non piangete la mia morte: Lettere ai familiari*, ed. Cesare Pillon and Vincenzina Vanzetti (Rome: Riuniti, 1962), p. 49.

203. Nicola Sacco and Bartolomeo Vanzetti, *The Letters of Sacco and Vanzetti*, ed. Marion Denman Frankfurter and Gardner Jackson (New York: Viking, 1928), p. 274.

204. Nicola (Ferdinando) Sacco and Rosina Zambelli were married in 1912 in Milford, Massachusetts, where their son Dante was born in 1913.

205. Carlo Valdinoci (1895–1919), Italian anarchist militant, follower of Luigi Galleani and contributor to *Cronaca Sovversiva*. He was a comrade of Sacco and Vanzetti, with whom he went to Mexico in 1917 to avoid registering for the draft. Returning to the United States, he was a key figure in a dynamite conspiracy in which Sacco and Vanzetti also took part. He accidentally blew himself up on June 2, 1919, while planting a bomb at the Washington, D.C., home of Attorney General A. Mitchell Palmer.

206. The name of Valdinoci's brother was Ercole, and he had no connection with the Wall Street bombing (September 16, 1920), which occurred after his return to Italy (see n. 273).

207. Parents and Teachers Association.

208. Caryl Chessman (1921–1960) was executed for rape and murder in a highly publicized case in California.

209. Torremaggiore, in Foggia province, region of Puglia, was Sacco's birthplace. Vanzetti was born in Villafalletto, Cuneo province, Piedmont. His sister Vincenzina, still alive, resides in the city of Cuneo.

210. The names of Edward Holton James's daughters were Mary and Louisa. Louisa married Alexander Calder.

211. Filene's is a well-known Boston department store.

212. Aldino Felicani (1891–1967), Italian anarchist printer in Boston. He was the founder and treasurer of the Sacco-Vanzetti Defense Committee, the defendants' main source of financial and moral support during their seven-year ordeal. He edited L'Agitazione (1920–1925), the defense committee's Italian-language organ, and Controcorrente (1938–1967).

213. Robert D'Attilio, a leading authority on the Sacco-Vanzetti case and the Italian anarchist movement in America.

214. Upton Sinclair visited Massachusetts after the executions of Sacco and Vanzetti in 1927 to conduct research for his novel Boston (1928).

215. Luciano Pavarotti (b. 1935), the great Italian lyric tenor.

216. Ines was Sacco's daughter, born after his arrest in 1920.

217. Michael F. Kelley was a superintendent in the Milford Shoe Factory, where Sacco worked as an edge-trimmer. Kelley later employed Sacco in his own Three-K Shoe Factory in Stoughton (see interview with George T. Kelley).

218. Luigi Galleani (1861–1931), editor of Cronaca Sovversiva (1903–1920) and the foremost Italian anarchist in the United States during the first two decades of the century. He advocated armed resistance to oppression, including the use of explosives (he published a bomb manual in 1905). An outspoken opponent of World War I, he was harassed by the authorities, arrested in 1917, and his newspaper soon afterwards suppressed. In 1919 he was deported to Italy, where he was persecuted and imprisoned after Mussolini's rise to power.

219. In the spring of 1913 a bitter strike occurred at the Draper Company in Hopedale, Massachusetts, a manufacturer of textile machinery. Sacco, who had worked at Draper in 1908 and 1909, took an active part on the picket line. Joseph Ettor and Arturo Giovannitti (see n. 303), who had been arrested in Lawrence the previous year, came to agitate in favor of the strike.

220. Riccardo Orciani (b. 1893), disciple of Galleani and comrade of Sacco and Vanzetti. An iron molder by trade, he was arrested on suspicion of taking part in the South Braintree holdup but soon released for lack of evidence. In 1921 he acted as chauffeur for Fred H. Moore, chief defense counsel at the Dedham trial. The following year he quit the United States and returned to his hometown (Fano) in Italy.

221. Gemma Mello was a silk worker in Paterson, New Jersey, and a member of Gli Insorti (The Insurgents), a militant anarchist group. In 1920 she was held for deportation but ultimately released. She died in New York City in the 1950s.

222. On February 28, 1919, four Italian anarchists blew themselves up while planting a bomb at a textile mill in Franklin, Massachusetts, where a strike was in progress. All were disciples of Galleani and supporters of Cronaca Sovversiva.

223. Gabriella Antolini (1899–1984), Italian anarchist of the Galleani school, imprisoned for illegally transporting dynamite (see interview with Febo Pomilia).

224. Nicola Piesco (d. 1990), Italian anarchist in Milford, Massachusetts, supporter of Cronaca Sovversiva and comrade of Sacco and Vanzetti.

225. Giovanni (John) Scussel (1882–1947), Italian anarchist and bricklayer. He went to Mexico in 1917 and was involved in the dynamite conspiracy of 1917–1919. In 1920

he went back to Italy and opposed the fascist dictatorship. Returning to the United States, he settled in Needham, Massachusetts, and worked for the release of Sacco and Vanzetti. He died of tuberculosis at the age of sixty-five.

226. Emilio Coda (1881–1946), coal miner and militant anarchist, a friend and disciple of Galleani. Like Giovanni Scussel, with whom he was in Mexican exile, he took part in the bomb plot against government officials. In 1924 he served as secretary of the Sacco-Vanzetti Defense Committee and afterwards lived in Needham next to Scussel and Ella Antolini. He was struck and killed by an automobile while walking to work.

227. Luigi Falsini (b. 1888), a marble setter from Carrara and follower of Galleani. He too was involved in the dynamite plot of 1917–1919. He was a member of the Gruppo Autonomo of East Boston and later of the Gruppo Libertà of Needham.

228. Adelfo Sanchioni, a shoe worker in Massachusetts, who in 1917 went to Mexico with his brother Renato and other Italian anarchists. He afterwards took part in the campaign to free Sacco and Vanzetti.

229. *Rasputin* was written by Saverio Piesco and *Tempeste Sociali* by Pietro Gori (1865–1911), the most popular Italian anarchist dramatist and poet. Gori, who conducted an evangelical tour of the United States in 1895 and 1896, wrote many plays that were performed by anarchist theatrical groups, *Senza Patria* and *Primo Maggio* being among the favorites.

230. William J. Callahan, a lawyer in Brockton, Massachusetts, served as a defense attorney for Sacco and Vanzetti.

231. Elizabeth Glendower Evans, *Outstanding Features of the Sacco-Vanzetti Case* (Boston: New England Civil Liberties Committee, 1924), p. 26.

232. In 1917 Sacco and Vanzetti, along with other disciples of Galleani, went to Mexico to avoid registration for the draft and to prepare for the revolution in Italy, which they expected to break out at any moment.

233. Felix Frankfurter, "The Case of Sacco and Vanzetti," *The Atlantic Monthly*, March 1927, reprinted in book form as *The Case of Sacco and Vanzetti: A Critical Analysis for Lawyers and Laymen* (Boston: Little, Brown, 1927).

234. John Dos Passos (1896–1970), the well-known American novelist, worked as a publicist for the Sacco-Vanzetti Defense Committee, for which he wrote *Facing the Chair: Story of the Americanization of Two Foreignborn Workmen* (1927). He also picketed the Massachusetts State House in August 1927 on the eve of the executions.

235. Elizabeth Glendower Evans (1856–1937), social reformer of old American lineage, friend of William James and Louis Brandeis. A "woman of wealth and great humanity," as Gardner Jackson described her, she worked indefatigably to secure clemency for Sacco and Vanzetti and wrote a valuable booklet on the case (see n. 231).

236. At the Dedham trial in 1921 Joseph Rosen, a peddler from Dorchester, testified that he sold Vanzetti a piece of cloth in Plymouth on the day of the South Braintree holdup.

237. Assunta Valdinoci (known as Susie) was the younger sister of Carlo Valdinoci, a key figure in the bombings of 1917–1919 (see n. 205). After her brother's death, she lived for many years with the Sacco family before returning to Italy.

238. Andrea Salsedo (1881–1920) and Roberto Elia (1871–1924), Italian anarchist printers, were arrested by the Bureau of Investigation in connection with the 1919 bomb plot directed against Attorney General Palmer and other officials. They were held without warrant at the Justice Department offices in New York, from which Salsedo plunged to his death after undergoing interrogation. Elia was deported to Italy three months later.

239. Grace Kelly, the American movie star, married Prince Rainier of Monaco on April 19, 1956.

240. Henry A. Wallace (1888–1965), Franklin Roosevelt's secretary of agriculture and Vice President of the United States (1941–1945), ran unsuccessfully for the presidency in 1948 as a candidate of the Progressive Party.

241. Mario Buda (1883–1963), militant Italian anarchist and disciple of Galleani. He was suspected by the authorities of taking part in the South Braintree holdup. He went to Mexico with Sacco and Vanzetti in 1917 and participated in the bomb conspiracy that followed. He was probably responsible for the Wall Street explosion of September 16, 1920 (see n. 273), after which he returned to Italy.

242. Giovanni Gambera (1889–1982), Italian anarchist in Boston and member of the Sacco-Vanzetti Defense Committee. According to his son Ideale, Gambera maintained that Sacco was indeed a participant in the holdup for which he was executed in 1927. See Francis Russell, *Sacco and Vanzetti: The Case Resolved* (New York: Harper & Row, 1986), pp. 11–18.

243. Antonio Cesarini, Eduardo Alessi, Fernando Tarabelli, Salvatore (Sam) Farulla, Felice Guadagni, Giuseppe Amari, and Amleto Fabbri were all active anarchists in the Boston area at the time of the Sacco-Vanzetti case. Alessi, Farulla, Guadagni, and Fabbri were members of the Sacco-Vanzetti Defense Committee.

244. See also Luciano Farinelli, "La Scomparsa di 'Catina,'" *L'Internazionale* (Ancona), March–April 1992.

245. Giovanni Eramo, printer of *Cronaca Sovversiva* in Lynn, Massachusetts. He was arrested with Galleani in 1917 and fined for conspiracy to obstruct the draft.

246. Bruno was a pseudonym of Raffaele Schiavina (1894–1987), also known as Max Sartin. The manager of *Cronaca Sovversiva*, he spent a year in prison for failing to register for the draft and was deported with Galleani in 1919. In 1928 he returned illegally to the United States and assumed the editorship of *L'Adunata dei Refrattari*, which ran until 1971. He is the author, among other works, of *Sacco e Vanzetti: Causi e fini di un delitto di stato* (1927).

247. Louis Bernheimer and Gardner Jackson worked as publicists for the Sacco-Vanzetti Defense Committee in Boston. Bernheimer published a pamphlet, *The Trial of Sacco and Vanzetti* (1927), while Jackson, among many other duties, edited *The Official Bulletin of the Sacco-Vanzetti Defense Committee* (1925–1930). In 1928 he edited *The Letters of Sacco and Vanzetti*, together with Marion Denman Frankfurter. During the 1930s and 1940s he was an official in Franklin Roosevelt's New Deal, serving in the Agricultural Adjustment Administration (AAA).

248. See n. 242.

249. Costantino Zonchello (1883–1967), Sardinian-born anarchist in Boston and New York. Apart from being a speaker, he contributed to *Cronaca Sovversiva* and was an editor of *Il Diritto* and of *L'Adunata dei Refrattari*.

250. Umberto Postiglione (1893–1924), Italian anarchist in Chicago, where he edited the journals *Germinal!* (1913) and *L'Allarme* (1915–1917), suppressed by the federal authorities. He also contributed to *Cronaca Sovversiva*, which he edited for several months in 1916 while Galleani was on a lecture tour. In 1917 he went to Mexico along with other opponents of the war. From there he went to South America before returning to Italy, where he died at the age of thirty-one.

251. Fred H. Moore (1882–1933), chief defense counsel for Sacco and Vanzetti from 1920 to 1924, when he was succeeded by William G. Thompson. A longtime attorney for the Industrial Workers of the World, he was involved in some of their most impor-

tant cases, including the defense of Ettor and Giovannitti in Lawrence (1912–1913) and the trial of 101 Wobblies in Chicago (1918).

252. Vanzetti lived in Youngstown for nearly a year (1917–1918) after returning to the United States from Mexico.

253. Nicola Recchi (1889–1975), militant Italian anarchist who lost a hand while making bombs. A comrade of Sacco and Vanzetti, he took part in the dynamite plots of 1917–1919. Taking refuge in Argentina, he was deported to Mussolini's Italy, where he was summarily imprisoned. After the Second World War he returned to Argentina, where he spent the last decades of his life.

254. Zechariah Chafee, Jr., of Harvard Law School, author of (among other works) *Free Speech in the United States* (1942).

255. Art Shields, *Are They Doomed? The Sacco-Vanzetti Case and the Grim Forces Behind It* (New York: Workers Defense Union, 1921). See also his *On the Battle Lines, 1919–1939* (New York: International Publishers, 1986).

256. Elizabeth Gurley Flynn (1890–1964), American feminist and syndicalist, associated with the IWW since 1906, a year after its founding in Chicago. The "rebel girl" of Joe Hill's song, she was active in the Lawrence strike of 1912, the Paterson strike of 1913, and many other labor struggles. She was a charter member of the American Civil Liberties Union and of the League for Mutual Aid, both established in 1920, and was the companion of Carlo Tresca for many years. She joined the Communist Party during the 1920s and died in Moscow.

257. See Eugene Lyons, *The Life and Death of Sacco and Vanzetti* (New York: International Publishers, 1927) and *Assignment in Utopia* (New York: Harcourt, Brace, 1937).

258. See John N. Beffel, "Eels and the Electric Chair," *The New Republic*, December 29, 1920.

259. According to the available evidence, only Ehrmann and Felicani went to search for the receipt. Michael A. Musmanno, then a young lawyer from Pittsburgh, became a justice of the Pennsylvania Supreme Court. He wrote a book about the Sacco-Vanzetti case, *After Twelve Years* (1939).

260. On the McNamara case see nn. 77 and 142.

261. Francis Russell, *Tragedy in Dedham: The Story of the Sacco-Vanzetti Case* (New York: McGraw-Hill, 1962).

262. Thomas F. O'Connor (d. 1966), Boston journalist who worked without pay for the Sacco-Vanzetti Defense Committee and defense attorney William G. Thompson. He later founded the Committee for the Vindication of Sacco and Vanzetti.

263. See also George Vaux, "Recollections of Edward Holton James," manuscript, Avrich Collection, Library of Congress.

264. Edward F. Mylius, English radical, who served a year in prison for libeling King George V. After his release, he went to the United States and frequented the Ferrer Center in New York, where he was a friend of Hippolyte Havel, among others. He was also a lover of Christine Ell, a Greenwich Village anarchist, the original of Eugene O'Neill's Anna Christie. He wrote for *The Social War* (1913) and was advertising manager for *The Liberator* (1918–1924).

265. Rosa Luxemburg (1871–1919), German revolutionary, born in Russian Poland, a founder of the Polish Socialist Party (1892). A brilliant writer and speaker, she acquired German citizenship through marriage in 1898 and was a leader of the German Social Democratic Party. With Karl Liebknecht she formed the Spartacus League and edited its journal *Rote Fahne*. She and Liebknecht were murdered by soldiers during the Spartacus rising of January 1919 while being taken to prison in Berlin.

266. James's daughter Louisa was married to the sculptor Alexander Calder (see n. 210).

267. Guy A. Aldred (1886–1963), Glasgow anarchist writer and publisher (the Bakunin Press, the Strickland Press), husband of Milly Rocker's sister Polly. He edited *The Voice of Labour* (1913), *The New Spur* (1933–1934), and *The Word* (1950–1963).

268. On September 27, 1932, five years after the execution of Sacco and Vanzetti, a bomb wrecked the Worcester home of Judge Webster Thayer, who had presided at their trial. Thayer, although uninjured, moved to his club in Boston, where he died seven months later.

269. Ferruccio Coacci (b. 1892), a militant anarchist in Massachusetts and supporter of *Cronaca Sovversiva*. According to the authorities, he took part in the South Braintree holdup together with Sacco, Vanzetti, Riccardo Orciani, and Mario Buda. He was deported to Italy in April 1920, shortly before the arrest of Sacco and Vanzetti, and later left Italy for Argentina.

270. On February 20, 1924, the young Italian anarchist Ernesto Bonomini shot and killed Nicola Bonservizi, Mussolini's chief agent in Paris, where he edited the fascist paper *L'Italie Nouvelle*. Bonomini spent six years in prison and afterwards came to the United States, where he went under the name of Dick Perry. He died in Florida in 1986.

271. See also Charles Poggi, "A Short Biography," manuscript, Avrich Collection, Library of Congress.

272. Michael E. Stewart, police chief of Bridgewater, Massachusetts, an important figure in the Sacco-Vanzetti case.

273. On September 16, 1920, a bomb planted in a wagon exploded at the corner of Wall and Broad Streets in New York City, killing thirty-three people and injuring more than two hundred. Evidence points to Mario Buda (see n. 241) as the perpetrator of the bombing, in reprisal for the indictment of Sacco and Vanzetti.

274. Andrea Ciofalo (b. 1886), a tile setter from Palermo and disciple of Galleani. He was a member of the Bresci Group in New York. In 1917 he was in Mexico with Sacco and Vanzetti and afterwards took part in the bomb conspiracy. Threatened with deportation, he returned to Sicily in 1919. Three years later, with the accession of Mussolini, he went back to the United States and served as administrator of *L'Adunata dei Refrattari*.

275. Clément Duval (1850–1935), Parisian anarchist and jewel thief, deported to French Guiana in 1886. He escaped in 1901 and found his way to New York, where he was sheltered by Italian anarchists. His memoirs, translated by Galleani, were serialized in *Cronaca Sovversiva*, and published in part in book form by Andrea Salsedo (1917). A complete edition, *Memorie autobiografiche*, appeared in 1929.

276. On Gambera see n. 242.

277. Luigi Quintiliano, secretary of the Italian Committee for Political Victims, organized by Carlo Tresca during the Red Scare. Vanzetti went to New York in April 1920 and consulted with Quintiliano about the arrest of Salsedo and Elia (see n. 238). A tailor by trade, Quintiliano became manager of Local 38 of the International Ladies' Garment Workers' Union (theatrical costume, ladies' tailors, custom dress and alterations workers).

278. Israel Shenker, *Coat of Many Colors* (Garden City, N.Y.: Doubleday, 1985), pp. 240–41. For an obituary of Alberico Pirani see *L'Internazionale* (Ancona), April 1985.

279. In Milan in May 1898 nearly one hundred civilians were killed and some five hundred wounded by government troops. In reprisal, Gaetano Bresci (1869–1901), an

anarchist from Paterson, New Jersey, assassinated King Umberto at Monza (July 29, 1900). Bresci died in prison the following year.

280. At a banquet in February 1916 to honor Archbishop Mundelein, Jean Crones (real name Nestore Dondoglio), a chef at the University Club in Chicago, laced the soup with arsenic. Two hundred guests fell ill, though none fatally. Crones, an Italian anarchist, was never apprehended. He was sheltered by comrades in Connecticut, where he died in 1934.

281. Armando Borghi (1882–1968), a well-known Italian anarchist, entered the United States through Canada in 1926.

282. See Alberico Pirani, *Poesie: un poco bizzarre per far pensare* (Boston: Excelsior Press, 1982).

283. The Communist International (Comintern), founded in Moscow in 1919 to promote worldwide proletarian revolution. It was dissolved in 1943.

284. On Francesco Ghezzi see interview with Frank Brand and n. 324.

285. Ludovico Caminita (b.1879), Italian printer and draftsman, converted to anarchism from socialism after a debate with the Spanish anarchist Pedro Esteve. Caminita followed Esteve to Paterson and worked with him on *La Questione Sociale*. This journal was succeeded in 1908 by *L'Era Nuova*, edited by Caminita and Franz Widmer until its suppression in 1917. In 1919 Caminita edited an illegal anarchist paper, *La Jacquerie*. Threatened with deportation, he supplied information to J. Edgar Hoover about the 1919 bomb conspiracy.

286. On Pedro Esteve see interviews with Marcelino García and Sirio Esteve, Part Five.

287. On April 6, 1930, Armando Borghi was arrested by an immigration officer while speaking at an antifascist meeting in Cooper Union. He jumped from the platform and escaped, but a detective shot and killed an Italian anarchist and wounded two others. Borghi's book was *Mussolini in camicia* (1927), published in English as *Mussolini Red and Black* (1938).

288. Simon Radowitzky (1889–1956), Russian-Jewish anarchist in Argentina. On November 13, 1909, he blew up the police chief of Buenos Aires, Colonel Ramón Falcón, a notorious persecutor of radicals. He was imprisoned until 1930 and lived in Mexico from 1939 until his death.

289. See Valerio Isca, *Ida Pilat Isca: Translator, Writer, Activist, Friend* (St. Paul: Michael Coughlin, 1984).

290. Frank Mandese (1887–c.1960), Italian anarchist militant, disciple of Galleani, and member of the Bresci Group in East Harlem.

291. Virgilia D'Andrea (1890–1933), Italian anarchist poet and speaker, companion of Armando Borghi, and secretary of the Unione Sindacale Italiana, in which Borghi was the principal figure. After Mussolini's rise to power, she found refuge in Paris, where she campaigned for Sacco and Vanzetti. In 1928 she came to the United States, traveling across the country on lecture tours and publishing poems in the anarchist press.

292. Rose Pesotta (1896–1965), Russian-Jewish anarchist and shirtwaist maker. She was a friend of Emma Goldman, secretary of the Road to Freedom Group, and worked for the release of Sacco and Vanzetti. She became a national organizer and vice-president of the International Ladies' Garment Workers' Union. With Morris Sigman, Anna Sosnovsky, and other anarchists, she opposed the efforts of the Communists to win control of the union. She wrote two autobiographical works (both with the aid of John Beffel): *Bread Upon the Waters* (1944) and *Days of Our Lives* (1958).

293. William Taback (1902–1976), New York anarchist, president of the Libertarian Book Club from 1971 to 1975 (see interview with Sarah Taback, Part Six).

294. Arden Colony, a single-tax community in Delaware of which Frank Stephens of Philadelphia was the principal founder and Upton Sinclair a sometime member. As in the other single-tax colonies (at Free Acres, New Jersey, and Fairhope, Alabama), anarchists were among the residents and visitors, including George Brown, Mary Hansen, Nathan Navro, and Alexis and Elizabeth Ferm.

295. Tony Martocchia and Osvaldo Maraviglia, Galleanists in San Francisco, formerly of Chicago and Newark, respectively.

296. William D. Haywood (1869–1928), American labor militant, known as "Big Bill" Haywood. A coal miner as a youth, he became a socialist and head of the Western Federation of Miners. In 1905 he was the keynote speaker in Chicago at the founding convention of the Industrial Workers of the World, which he called "the Continental Congress of the working class." In 1907 he was acquitted with Charles Moyer and George Pettibone of the bomb murder of former Idaho governor Frank Steunenberg. As an IWW leader he took part in the Lawrence and Paterson strikes of 1912 and 1913. In 1918 he was convicted in the sedition trial of the 101 Wobblies and sentenced to twenty years' imprisonment and a twenty-thousand-dollar fine. Forfeiting bail, he fled to Soviet Russia, where he died. His ashes were buried in the Kremlin wall and in the Waldheim Cemetery near Chicago.

297. Residence of the Botto family in Haledon, New Jersey, a suburb of Paterson. It is now the American Labor Museum, a national landmark.

298. Serafino Grandi and Pietro Baldiserotto were members of the L'Era Nuova Group in Paterson, the principal anarchist organization in the city. Both were held for deportation during the Red Scare but released for insufficient evidence.

299. See *Un trentennio di attività anarchica (1914–1945)* (Cesena: Antistato, 1953), p. 151.

300. For an obituary of Guy Liberti see *L'Internazionale* (Ancona), January 20, 1976.

301. Rocker's position on World War II—he supported the Allied cause—is explained in the introduction to Part Six.

302. Letter of Hugo Rolland, August 1, 1967, Avrich Collection, Library of Congress.

303. The IWW organizers Joseph Ettor (1885–1948) and Arturo Giovannitti (1882–1959), an admired poet and playwright, were acquitted of trumped-up murder charges during the Lawrence strike of 1912.

304. In March 1915 Frank Abarno and Carmine Carbone, members of the Bresci Group in East Harlem, were imprisoned for conspiring to blow up St. Patrick's Cathedral, in spite of evidence of entrapment by an undercover police detective.

305. Giacomo Matteotti (1885–1924), a leading socialist member of parliament and critic of Mussolini, was kidnapped and murdered by fascist thugs, who received nominal prison sentences.

306. *Mother Earth*, March 1915.

307. Giuseppe Ciancabilla (1872–1904), Italian anarchist and antiorganizationist. He edited several journals in the United States, among them *La Questione Sociale* in Paterson (1899), *L'Aurora* in West Hoboken (1899–1901), and *La Protesta Umana* in Chicago and San Francisco (1903–1904). A capable editor and writer, he died of consumption at the age of thirty-two.

308. Harvey O'Connor (1897–1987), West Coast radical writer, author of *Revolution in Seattle* (1964) and other books.

309. Angelo Luca (1895–1972), anarchist and antifascist, lost a leg in 1927 while trying to blow up the Italian consulate in San Francisco.

310. *Vanguard*, May–June 1935. See also *Fight Against Deportation: Free Ferrero and Sallitto* (New York: The Ferrero-Sallitto Defense Conference, 1936). A. Mitchell Palmer was the U.S. Attorney General at the time of the Red Scare, during which many Italian anarchists were deported.

311. On the Ferrero-Sallitto case see interview with Valerio Isca. An obituary of Ferrero appeared in *L'Internazionale* (Ancona) in May 1985.

312. In 1923 Carlo Tresca was arrested for publishing a birth control advertisement in his journal *Il Martello*. He was sentenced to one year in the federal penitentiary at Atlanta, but Congressman Fiorello La Guardia persuaded President Coolidge to commute the term to four months. On his way back to New York, Tresca stopped in Washington and shook hands with Coolidge at the White House, an act for which the Galleanists never forgave him. According to his supporters, Tresca had merely been among a group of tourists when the President appeared and shook hands all around.

313. Shenker, *Coat of Many Colors*, p. 241.

314. Ibid. On Brand see also *Black Rose* (Boston), Winter 1986–1987.

315. The first Italian edition was Max Stirner, *L'Unico*, trans. Ettore Zoccoli (Turin: Fratelli Bocca, 1902). Another edition—the one to which Brand probably refers—appeared in Milan in 1911.

316. On September 10, 1898, Luigi Lucheni, a young Italian anarchist, assassinated Empress Elizabeth of Austria in Geneva.

317. Luigi Bertoni (1872–1947), editor of *Le Réveil/Il Risveglio*, an anarchist journal in Geneva.

318. See n. 265 on the Spartacus revolt and the murder of Liebknecht and Luxemburg. Gustav Noske, a socialist, was the German prime minister at the time.

319. Angelica Balabanoff (1878–1965), Russian Bolshevik and secretary of the Communist International. In 1921 she arranged for Emma Goldman and Alexander Berkman to meet with Lenin in the Kremlin. Turning against Lenin's dictatorship, she emigrated to the West, spending a number of years in the United States, where she was a member of the League for Mutual Aid and a visitor to Mohegan Colony.

320. Béla Kun (1886–1939), Hungarian Communist, head of a short-lived revolutionary government in 1919. He was active in the Communist International until purged by Stalin.

321. Diego Abad de Santillán (1897–1983), Spanish anarchist and member of the CNT-FAI, prominent during the civil war. He wrote on economic reconstruction in Spain.

322. Kurt Wilckens (1886–1923), German-born anarchist and Wobbly, deported from the U.S. in 1920. In 1923 he killed Lieutenant-Colonel Varela in Buenos Aires and was himself afterwards murdered in prison.

323. Fritz Kater (1863–1946), German anarcho-syndicalist printer and comrade of Rudolf Rocker. He published *Der Syndikalist* in Berlin.

324. Francesco Ghezzi, after being detained for sixteen months in Switzerland, returned to Italy and was implicated in a bomb plot in Milan (the "Diana" affair of 1921). He took refuge in Soviet Russia but was arrested in 1929, during Stalin's consolidation of power. In spite of an international campaign for his release, he died in 1941 in a Siberian labor camp, a victim of the Great Purge.

325. E. Armand, pseudonym of Ernest-Lucien Juin (1872–1962), editor of *L'Endehors* and the leading individualist in France.

326. Emma Goldman to Nick Di Domenico, November 20, 1939, Avrich Collection, Library of Congress. See also A. Bortolotti, "My Memories of Emma Goldman," *The Libertarian*, May 1968.

327. Sébastien Faure (1856–1942), the foremost anarchist orator in France. He wrote a number of widely distributed pamphlets—including *Autorité ou liberté* (1891), *La question sociale* (1906), and *Douze preuves de l'existence de Dieu* (1914)—and edited the journal *Le Libertaire* as well as the four-volume *Encyclopédie anarchiste* (1934). During the early years of the century he conducted an anarchist school, La Ruche (The Beehive), in Rambouillet (near Paris), which Emma Goldman visited in 1907.

328. See *Un trentennio di attività anarchica*, p. 163.

329. Ibid, pp. 160–61.

330. Jacob Margolis, anarchist lawyer in Pittsburgh and friend of Emma Goldman and Alexander Berkman.

331. Luigi (Gigi) Damiani, Italian anarchist writer, editor of *Fede!* and *Umanità Nova* in Rome.

332. Giordano Bruno (1548–1600), Italian philosopher who challenged conventional ideas. Tried for heresy, he was imprisoned in Rome and afterwards burned at the stake. His martyrdom inspired later dissenters, including freethinkers and anarchists. At the New York Ferrer Center Leonard Abbott lectured on "Giordano Bruno, the Free Thought Martyr." Moses Harman, in dating his journal *Lucifer*, calculated from the execution of Bruno rather than the birth of Jesus Christ.

PART FOUR

333. Manuel Komroff, "Homage to the Modern School," audiocassette, 1974, Avrich Collection, Library of Congress.

334. See Benzion Liber, *The Child at Home* (New York: Rational Living, 1922) and *A Doctor's Apprenticeship* (New York: Rational Living, 1956).

335. John R. (1851–1924) and Abby Hedge Coryell (1859–1957), the first teachers at the New York Modern School (1911). John, a contributor to *Mother Earth*, was the originator of the famous "Nick Carter" detective stories and "Bertha M. Clay" romances.

336. Robert Henri (1865–1929), American painter and teacher, associated with the "ash can" school of artists. He was also a philosophical anarchist who, influenced by Bakunin, Nietzsche, and Ibsen, declared that "all government is violence." At the invitation of Emma Goldman, of whom he was a keen admirer, he conducted (with George Bellows) the adult art class at the Ferrer Center, whose pupils included Man Ray, Max Weber, and other artists of distinction.

337. Goldman, *Living My Life*, p. 706; Leonard D. Abbott to Lola Ridge, March 18, 1919, Ridge Papers, Smith College.

338. James F. Morton, Jr. (1870–1941), a graduate of Harvard and a single-taxer as well as an anarchist. In the early 1900s he lived at Home Colony, edited its paper *The Demonstrator*, and taught at its school. Returning east (he hailed from Massachusetts), he taught Esperanto at the New York Ferrer School and ended his career as curator of the Paterson Museum in New Jersey.

339. Jack London (1876–1916), American writer and socialist, author of such works as *The Call of the Wild* (1903), *The Sea Wolf* (1904), and *Martin Eden* (1909). He was a friend of Emma Goldman and Alexander Berkman and a supporter of the Magón

movement in California. He was also a member of the Francisco Ferrer Association and lectured at the New York Modern School.

340. Margaret H. Sanger (1879–1966), American nurse and birth control activist. She became an anarchist under the influence of Emma Goldman, a major source of her ideas on "family limitation," as she called it. Her journal *The Woman Rebel* (1914), which bore the slogan "No Gods, No Masters," carried articles by Goldman and Voltairine de Cleyre. Sanger took part in the Paterson strike of 1913, about which she wrote in Hippolyte Havel's *Revolutionary Almanac*. She also contributed to Havel's *Revolt*, Goldman's *Mother Earth*, Berkman's *The Blast*, and *The Modern School* magazine. She sent her children to the Modern Schools of New York and Stelton, where her daughter contracted pneumonia from which she died. Sanger soon after abandoned anarchism and refrained from acknowledging Goldman's role in the birth control movement or in her own intellectual development.

341. See also Komroff's obituary in the *New York Times*, December 11, 1974.

342. The Rand School of Social Science, established in New York in 1906 as an intellectual center of the socialist movement. It boasted an extensive library (now part of the Tamiment Library of New York University) and a comprehensive program of adult lectures and classes. The lecturers included such notable figures as Jack London, Clarence Darrow, and Upton Sinclair.

343. Joseph McCabe (1867–1955), British writer and freethinker. He spent twelve years in a Franciscan monastery and was the author of many biographies and books on religion, literature, history, and philosophy, including *The Martyrdom of Ferrer* (1909).

344. Theodore A. Schroeder (1864–1953), attorney, single-taxer, and champion of free speech. A friend of Emma Goldman, he lectured often at the New York Ferrer Center. He was a founder of the Free Speech League (1911), an antecedent of the American Civil Liberties Union, and the author of many books and pamphlets, including *Free Press Anthology* (1909) and *Free Speech for Radicals* (1916).

345. Stewart Kerr, Scottish-born anarchist and associate of Emma Goldman, who valued his "considerate and non-invasive nature" (*Living My Life*, p. 546). A charter member of the Francisco Ferrer Association, he edited its *News Letter* with Harry Kelly and wrote on Ferrer and Montessori in *The Modern School* magazine.

346. The Ferrer Center was located at 67 East 107th Street and *Mother Earth* at 74 West 119th Street, a dozen blocks away.

347. John Reed (1887–1920), noted American journalist, author of *Insurgent Mexico* (1914), *Ten Days That Shook the World* (1919), and other works. In 1913, with the assistance of Manuel Komroff, he staged the Paterson strike pageant in Madison Square Garden, and in 1916 he wrote one-act plays for the Provincetown Players. An opponent of America's entry into World War I, he appeared as a defense witness for Alexander Berkman and Emma Goldman in their 1917 anti-conscription trial. Soon afterwards he went to Russia and witnessed the Bolshevik seizure of power, of which he wrote a glowing account. On his return to the United States, he helped organize the Communist Labor Party and served as Soviet consul in New York. He died of typhus in Moscow at the age of thirty-two and was buried in the Kremlin wall.

348. Alfred Stieglitz (1864–1946), American photographer and art exhibitor. Like Robert Henri, he was a supporter of Emma Goldman's *Mother Earth*. He also edited his own journal *Camera Work* (1902–1917) and conducted a gallery at 291 Fifth Avenue, which was a magnet for avant-garde artists.

349. Adolf Wolff (1883–1944), Belgian-born sculptor and anarchist, who conducted an art class for children at the New York Modern School, where his daughter Esther was

a pupil. He wrote for *The Modern School* magazine, of which he was an associate editor, and for Hippolyte Havel's *Revolt*, as well as drawing for Emma Goldman's *Mother Earth*. He was a friend of Man Ray, who married his former wife. He visited Ray at the artists' colony in Ridgefield, New Jersey, and contributed to his journal *The Ridgefield Gazook* (1915). In 1919 he and Ray (together with Henry S. Reynolds) published an avant-garde journal *TNT*. Wolff abandoned anarchism in the succeeding years and shifted his allegiance to Communism.

350. Man Ray (1890–1976), avant-garde painter and photographer. He attended Robert Henri's art class at the Ferrer Center in New York, where he exhibited his early paintings. He also frequented Alfred Stieglitz's 291 Gallery, drew antiwar covers for *Mother Earth*, wrote poems for *The Modern School*, and was a resident of the Ridgefield Colony, where in 1915 he met Marcel Duchamp, with whom he was a founder of the Dada movement.

351. In fact the Lexington Avenue bomb was intended for Rockefeller's home in Tarrytown, New York, not for his office at 26 Broadway.

352. See *Benjamin Benno: A Retrospective Exhibition, September 11–November 20, 1988* (New Brunswick, N.J.: The Jane Voorhees Zimmerli Museum, 1988).

353. Cora Bennett Stephenson (b. 1872), American teacher, novelist, and socialist. She was the teacher at the New York Modern School in 1913 and 1914. She started a summer school in 1913 and introduced a kindergarten for children too young to attend the primary class.

354. Joseph O'Carroll, New York Wobbly and habitué of the Ferrer Center. An active figure in the unemployed demonstrations of 1913 and 1914, he was savagely beaten by policemen in Union Square (April 1914).

355. Frank Tannenbaum (1893–1969), Columbia University historian and authority on Latin America. As a youth he was an anarchist and Wobbly who frequented the Ferrer Center and the offices of *Mother Earth*. In 1914, at twenty-one, he organized a series of demonstrations and church sit-ins by unemployed workers, for which he was imprisoned for a year on Blackwell's Island. The sit-in at St. Alphonsus's Church on West Broadway took place on March 4, 1914.

356. On Joseph Brandes see interview with Eva Brandes, his wife.

357. Hollod is mistaken. Emma Goldman was away on a lecture tour at the time of the Lexington Avenue incident.

358. Alden Freeman (1862–1937), wealthy son of the treasurer of the Standard Oil Company. In 1909 he attended an Emma Goldman lecture on Ibsen that was broken up by the police. Outraged by the suppression of fundamental liberties, he invited her to speak at his estate in East Orange, New Jersey. Thus began a friendship which involved him with the Ferrer movement. In 1910 he became a founding member of the Francisco Ferrer Association and a member of its advisory board. He paid the rent of the New York Modern School and took its principal, Will Durant, on a tour of Europe, in addition to paying his salary. He severed his connections with the school, however, after the Lexington Avenue explosion.

359. David Sullivan was in fact a detective in the New York City Police Department (see interviews with Moritz Jagendorf and Emma Gilbert).

360. Bertram D. Wolfe (1896–1977), American teacher and writer. He was the author of *Diego Rivera* (1939), *Marxism* (1965), and *Three Who Made a Revolution* (1948), a classic study of Russian Communism. During the 1920s, he was a member of the American Communist Party and picketed the Massachusetts State House in behalf of Sacco and Vanzetti.

361. Louise Berger, Latvian-born anarchist and half-sister of Carl Hanson, who was killed in the Lexington Avenue explosion. She returned to Russia in 1917 and took part in the revolution. Like John Reed, she died in the typhus epidemic that swept the country in 1920–1921.

362. In the spring of 1914 anarchists from the Ferrer Center demonstrated at Tarrytown, New York, near the Rockefeller family estate, in protest against the Ludlow, Colorado, massacre. Apart from Berkman and the Goldblatt sisters, the demonstrators included Adolf Wolff, Charles Plunkett, Arthur Caron, Jack Isaacson, and Becky Edelsohn. The suppression of the demonstrations and arrest of the participants precipitated the Lexington Avenue conspiracy.

363. Commonwealth College in Mena, Arkansas, founded in 1923 by Kate Richards O'Hare and other socialists. Its director, Dr. William E. Zeuch, had been a principal of the Organic School in Fairhope, Alabama, a single-tax colony. Under Franklin D. Roosevelt's New Deal he served as an advisor on agricultural cooperatives in the Federal Emergency Relief Administration.

364. Hillel Solotaroff (1865–1921), Jewish physician and anarchist on the Lower East Side. He contributed to the *Fraye Arbeter Shtime* and other Yiddish papers. In 1889 he introduced Emma Goldman to Alexander Berkman, and in 1897 he hosted a gathering for Kropotkin on his first visit to the United States. He was a member of the executive committee of the Kropotkin Literary Society, founded in 1912. Note that he died in 1921, not "around 1917," as Gussie Denenberg states.

365. De Cleyre herself criticized Goldman's book as "an incoherent collection of badly written lectures." Avrich, *An American Anarchist*, p. 88.

366. Sidney (1859–1947) and Beatrice Webb (1858–1943), English socialists and reformers who wrote extensively on labor questions. They were leading members of the Fabian Society and instrumental in the creation of the Labour Party and of the London School of Economics.

367. Joseph J. Cohen, *Di yidish-anarkhistishe bavegung in Amerike* (Philadelphia: Radical Library, 1945); Saul Yanovsky, *Ershte yorn fun yidishn frayhaytlekhen sotsializm* (New York: Fraye Arbeter Shtime, 1948); *Modern School of Stelton: Twenty-Fifth Anniversary, 1915–1940* (Stelton, N.J.: The Modern School Association, 1940), pp. 11–12.

368. Donald Vose, the son of Gertie Vose, an anarchist at Home Colony. As an informer for the Burns Detective Agency he came to New York and wormed his way into the Ferrer Center and the *Mother Earth* office and betrayed David Caplan and Matthew Schmidt, who had taken part in the 1910 bombing of the Los Angeles Times Building (see nn. 77 and 142). Vose appears as "Don Parritt" (i.e., stool pigeon) in Eugene O'Neill's *The Iceman Cometh*, a guilt-racked soul who had informed on his own mother.

369. Minna Lowensohn, an anarchist at the Ferrer Center and friend of Alexander Berkman and Emma Goldman. Her younger sister Leah became Harry Kelly's second wife.

370. Morris Becker, a Ferrer Center anarchist who took part in the anti-conscription movement, for which he served twenty months in Atlanta penitentiary. In December 1919 he was deported to Russia on the *Buford* together with Alexander Berkman and Emma Goldman.

371. Anna Edelstein Olay, Jewish anarchist in Chicago and member of the Free Society Group. She was the wife of the Spanish anarchist Maximiliano Olay (see n. 469), who acted as liaison with the CNT during the Civil War of 1936–1939.

372. Gray Wu, Chinese anarchist from Canton. He wrote for *The Modern School* magazine and worked as a handyman and cook at Stelton. While studying philosophy at Columbia with John Dewey, he organized a union of cooks and waiters in Chinatown,

which cost him his job in a restaurant and got him into trouble with the authorities. He returned to China during the 1920s.

373. *Principia Mathematica*, by Bertrand Russell and Alfred North Whitehead (3 vols., 1910–1913).

374. Thomas Hunt Morgan (1866–1945), biologist and specialist in genetics, winner of the 1933 Nobel Prize in physiology and medicine. From 1904 to 1928 he was Professor of Zoology at Columbia University and from 1928 director of the laboratory of biological science at the California Institute of Technology.

375. Berkman did in fact go to Tarrytown to take part in the protests against Rockefeller but was driven out of town by the police.

376. "Frank" was probably Frank Mandese (see n. 290).

377. Ridgefield Colony, an artists' enclave in Ridgefield, New Jersey, begun in 1913. Among its inhabitants were Manuel Komroff and Man Ray, who issued *The Ridgefield Gazook* in March 1915, the only number to appear. That summer Ray met Marcel Duchamp, who was visiting the colony, beginning a friendship that lasted until Duchamp's death in 1968. Ray, Duchamp, and Francis Picabia comprised the nucleus of a Dada school in New York before the label was invented and the movement officially launched in Zurich in 1916.

378. On July 11, 1914, at a memorial meeting for Caron, Hanson, and Berg, Plunkett quoted the Haymarket anarchist Louis Lingg: "If you attack us with cannon, we will attack you with dynamite." *Mother Earth*, July 1914.

379. Trofim Lysenko (1898–1976), Soviet agronomist and biologist. He rejected the chromosome theory of heredity in favor of the discredited Lamarckian view that hereditable changes can be brought about by environmental influences. Claiming that his ideas corresponded to Marxist theory, he succeeded in winning the support of Stalin. He became a member of the Supreme Soviet and director of the Academy of Agricultural Sciences (1938), instituting a reign of terror against his colleagues. His best-known opponent, N. I. Vavilov, the leading geneticist in the Soviet Union, died in a Siberian labor camp.

380. See M. Jagendorf, "Drama in the Ferrer School," in *Modern School of Stelton*, pp. 19–20.

381. On Christine Ell see nn. 134 and 264.

382. André Tridon (1877–1922), French-born anarcho-syndicalist, secretary of *The Masses*, and frequent visitor to the Ferrer Center, where he took part in Jagendorf's Free Theatre and lectured on literature and art. In 1913 he published *The New Unionism*, one of the first American books on revolutionary syndicalism. By 1920 he had become a lay psychoanalyst. That year he published an unauthorized edition of Freud's *General Introduction to Psychoanalysis* as well as a book on *Psychoanalysis and Behavior*.

383. Benjamin De Casseres (1873–1945), American essayist and critic. A descendant of Spinoza, he mingled with the intelligentsia in Greenwich Village and frequented the Ferrer Center in Harlem, where he contributed to Hippolyte Havel's *Revolt*. He also contributed to *Camera Work*, being a friend of Alfred Stieglitz, as well as of Sadakichi Hartmann, Benjamin Tucker, and Eugene O'Neill.

384. See also Paul Avrich, "Tsvey anarkhisten," *Fraye Arbeter Shtime*, June 1973; and Boris Yelensky, "Morris Beresin," *The Match!*, April 1974.

385. Isaac Altman, Moisei Mets, and Olga Taratuta took part in the bombing of the Café Libman in Odessa in December 1905. Mets went to the gallows the following year. See Paul Avrich, *The Russian Anarchists* (Princeton: Princeton University Press, 1967), pp. 49, 68, 105, 207.

386. Samuel Gordon, Nathan Navro, Joseph Kucera, and Natasha Notkin were all anarchist comrades of Voltairine de Cleyre (Gordon and Kucera were also her lovers).

387. See Emma [Cohen Gilbert], "In the Days Before Stelton," in *Modern School of Stelton*, pp. 22–24.

388. The reference is to the Broad Street Riot, February 20, 1908, when anarchists in Philadelphia marched on city hall to protest against unemployment. Voltairine de Cleyre was arrested and charged with incitement. See Avrich, *An American Anarchist*, pp. 200–201.

389. Will Durant, *Transition: A Sentimental Story of One Mind and One Era* (New York: Simon & Schuster, 1927), p. 201.

390. In September 1914 Robert and Delia Hutchinson succeeded Cora Bennett Stephenson as directors of the New York Modern School. They moved with the school to Stelton in May 1915 but left after two months to start their own school at Stony Ford, New York, which closed in 1918.

391. Laurence Veysey, *The Communal Experience: Anarchism and Mystical Counter-Culture in America* (New York: Harper, 1973).

392. Henry T. Schnittkind (b. 1888), teacher at the Stelton Modern School in 1915. A Harvard Ph.D., socialist, and author of children's books, he soon returned to Boston to work as an editor and writer. Under the name of Henry Thomas he compiled a series of "Living Biographies" of famous writers, painters, philosophers, and the like, as well as anthologies of stories and poems.

393. Harry L. Hopkins (1890–1946), head of the Works Progress Administration (WPA) and later Secretary of Commerce under Franklin Roosevelt's New Deal. As special assistant to the President during World War II he administered the lend-lease program and went on missions to London and Moscow.

394. Fred Dunn (d. 1925), British anarchist in London, where he edited *The Voice of Labour* (1914–1916). An opponent of World War I (he was a signatory of the International Manifesto on the War in 1915), he took refuge in the U.S. and taught at the Stelton Modern School. With James Dick he organized a cooperative jitney service at the colony. He worked as an organizer for the Consumer Cooperative Housing Association until his untimely death.

395. Henrietta Rodman (d. 1923), teacher, feminist, and disciple of Charlotte Perkins Gilman (1860–1935). As a teacher in the New York City school system, she fought the Board of Education on many fronts, but especially for discrimination against the hiring of married women teachers and for denying women the right to their jobs after having children. For these criticisms she was suspended from her post at Wadleigh High School in 1914. She was a charter member of the Francisco Ferrer Association and spoke at its first annual dinner (1911). In 1914, while serving on the advisory board of the association, she organized the Feminist Alliance to fight for women's rights.

396. See Ray Porter Miller, "My Teachers at Stelton," in *Modern School of Stelton*, pp. 27–28.

397. Scott Nearing (1883–1983), socialist economist. He taught at the Wharton School of Finance of the University of Pennsylvania, from which he was dismissed in 1915 because of his radical views. In 1918 he was tried but acquitted for opposing the war effort. After the Bolshevik Revolution he supported the Soviet experiment. He joined the American Communist Party in 1927, only to quit two years later after being denounced for heretical opinions. With his wife Helen he advocated and practiced organic farming, described in their widely read *Living the Good Life* (1954). He was also

the author of *Dollar Diplomacy* (1925), *The Making of a Radical* (1972), and other books.

398. Eugene Victor Debs (1855–1926), America's preeminent socialist leader. He was a founder of the IWW in 1905 and four times a candidate for President of the United States. Despite their political differences, he was an admirer of Emma Goldman and a supporter of Sacco and Vanzetti. In 1918 he was sentenced to ten years in prison for making an antiwar speech but was released in 1921 by President Harding.

399. Henry Wadsworth Longfellow Dana was dismissed from the Columbia faculty for opposing America's entry into World War I. He was later active in behalf of Sacco and Vanzetti.

400. Friedrich Froebel (1782–1852), German educational innovator and founder of the kindergarten system. Education, he said, must be adapted to each pupil's "nature and needs." He called for a method that was "not directive and interfering" but that "would have each human being develop from within, self-active and free." He sought to bring out the creative potential of the pupils by exposing them to play materials, or "gifts" (balls, blocks, cubes, cylinders, prisms), all in primary colors to stimulate interest in harmony and form.

401. Carl Jung (1875–1961), Swiss psychiatrist and founder of analytical psychology, president of the International Psychoanalytical Society (1911).

402. Martha Gruening, American progressive educator. She attended Robert Henri's art class at the New York Ferrer Center, wrote for *The Modern School* magazine, and took part in Alexander Berkman's No-Conscription League in 1917. Her brother Ernest Gruening (1897–1974) was Governor of Alaska from 1939 to 1953 and U.S. Senator from 1959 to 1969.

403. John and Evelyn Dewey, *Schools of Tomorrow* (New York: Dutton, 1915).

404. In 1907 Marietta Johnson founded the School of Organic Education at the single-tax colony of Fairhope, Alabama. See her *Thirty Years with an Idea* (Fairhope: The Organic School/University of Alabama Press, 1974).

405. For example, Lillian Rifkin, *When I Grow Up I'll Be a Doctor* (New York: Lothrop, Lee & Shepard, 1943).

406. Charles Garland (1899–1974), millionaire from Boston who during the 1920s founded utopian communities in Massachusetts and Pennsylvania (see interview with Esther Walters). On the advice of Roger Baldwin, he created the American Fund for Public Service (known as the Garland Fund) to assist liberal and radical causes. The fund, for example, supported Vanguard Press, publisher of books on socialism and anarchism.

407. Hans Koch, anarchist editor, poet, and master builder. He supervised the construction of the Stelton Modern School, where he taught woodworking and metal crafts and where his wife Anna Riedel taught basketry, sewing, and weaving. Koch left Stelton during the 1920s to work for Frank Lloyd Wright in Arizona. In the early years of the century he had edited *Das Freie Wort* (1907), *Der Anti-Autoritär* (1911), and *Der Strom* (1910–1912), which included an article on education by Elizabeth Ferm.

408. Ernest Howard Crosby (1856–1907), a leading American Tolstoyan and single-taxer. He was an admirer of William Morris, Edward Carpenter, and Peter Kropotkin, and chaired a lecture by Kropotkin in New York in 1897. A lawyer by profession, Crosby served as a judge on the International Court in Alexandria, Egypt. Converted to Tolstoyan pacifism, he resigned his post, visited Tolstoy at Yasnaya Polyana, and became Tolstoy's principal disciple in the United States. His poems appeared in such anarchist

periodicals as *Liberty*, *Lucifer*, and *Free Society*. He worked for Alexander Berkman's pardon in the 1890s and for the release of John Turner in 1903–1904.

409. The crisis was the departure in 1925 of Alexis and Elizabeth Ferm, codirectors of the Stelton school, followed by years of decline.

410. Dr. Bertha F. Johnson was the sister-in-law of Benjamin Tucker.

411. In December 1910 a band of alleged anarchists shot three policemen during the holdup of a jewelry shop in the Houndsditch section of London. Troops called out by Winston Churchill, the then Home Secretary, killed two of the robbers after a siege in Sidney Street. Luba Milstein was the lover of Fritz Svaars, a Latvian revolutionary who took part in the holdup.

412. Alexander Berkman, *Now and After: The ABC of Communist Anarchism* (New York: Vanguard, 1929), also published as *What Is Communist Anarchism?*

413. Abraham J. Muste (1885–1967), Dutch-born minister, pacifist, and labor activist. A participant in the movement for workers' education between the world wars, he was the head of Brookwood Labor College in Katonah, New York, and chairman of the board of directors of Manumit, an experimental school for workers' children in Pawling, New York. After the Second World War he was executive director of the Fellowship of Reconciliation, a pacifist organization, and strongly opposed nuclear armament and the Vietnam War.

414. Leonard Abbott's wife, Rose Yuster Abbott, was paralyzed for many years with multiple sclerosis, from which she died in 1930.

415. Bern Dibner (1897–1988), engineer and bibliophile, founder of the Burndy Engineering Company in Norwalk, Connecticut. He amassed a major collection of books and manuscripts on the history of science and technology, which he donated to the Smithsonian Institution.

416. Tennessee Valley Authority, U.S. agency created in 1933 at the beginning of Franklin Roosevelt's New Deal. Encompassing a vast scheme of regional planning, it was responsible for the development of the Tennessee River valley, including flood control, electric power, and economic growth.

417. Johann Pestalozzi (1746–1827), Swiss educational reformer, director of the experimental institute at Yverdon. To Pestalozzi, as to Froebel, the individuality of each child was paramount. Emphasizing learning by doing and observation, he opposed the traditional system of memorization and discipline and sought to replace it with love and understanding.

418. The L'Endehors Group was a circle of individualist anarchists in Paris associated with E. Armand's journal of that name (see n. 325).

419. Thomas H. Keell (1866–1938), prominent British anarchist. He attended the International Anarchist Congress in Amsterdam (1907), contributed to the *Voice of Labour*, and was compositor and editor of *Freedom* for many years. An opponent of World War I, he signed the International Manifesto on the War (1915). In 1916 the offices of *Freedom* were raided and Keell and his companion Lilian Wolfe were imprisoned. From the 1920s until Keell's death, they lived at Whiteway Colony in Gloucestershire.

420. In 1911 Kotoku Shusui, an anarchist, was executed for conspiring to assassinate the Japanese emperor.

421. Bella Abzug (b. 1920), Democratic Congresswoman from New York during the 1970s, involved primarily with labor and civil rights issues. In 1961 she helped found the Women's Strike for Peace. She was a vigorous proponent of women's rights and critic of the Vietnam War.

422. Isidore Wisotsky, Jewish anarcho-syndicalist and member of the IWW in New York. He took part in the unemployed demonstrations led by Frank Tannenbaum in 1913 and 1914. Towards the end of his life, during the 1960s, he was an editor of the *Fraye Arbeter Shtime*. His unpublished autobiography, "Such a Life" (with a preface by Norman Thomas), is housed in the Labadie Collection in Ann Arbor.

423. Sally Axelrod was a resident of the Stelton Colony, in charge of the children's dormitory for many years.

424. See also Jo Ann Wheeler, "From a 'Tough' School to the Modern School," in *Modern School of Stelton*, p. 20.

425. John Cowper Powys (1872–1963), Welsh novelist, essayist, and poet, a friend and correspondent of Emma Goldman.

426. John W. Edelman (1893–1971) was the son of John H. Edelmann and Rachelle Krimont (see n. 88). He and his sister Sonia grew up at Whiteway Colony, the English equivalent of Stelton. He joined the Independent Labour Party and attended the London School of Economics, becoming a journalist and labor organizer. He returned to the U.S. in 1916 and settled at Stelton, where he directed the children's theater group with the artist Hugo Gellert. In 1919 and 1920, until the arrival of the Ferms, he served (with the aid of his wife Kate Van Eaton) as acting principal of the Stelton school. In the succeeding years he resumed his labor activities, organizing hosiery workers and editing trade-union publications. He headed the CIO Regional Division in Philadelphia and afterwards directed the Washington office of the Textile Workers' Union of America until his retirement in 1963. After this he served on the Task Force on the Aging Poor under the Kennedy and Johnson administrations and as president of the National Council of Senior Citizens.

427. Warren E. Brokaw (b. 1860), a single-tax anarchist, like Bolton Hall, Alexis Ferm, and George Seldes, and a member of the Fairhope Colony in Alabama. He edited *The Equitist* (1923–1933) and contributed to Abba Gordin's *The Clarion* and John Scott and Jo Ann Wheeler's *Mother Earth*. He was the author of *The Equitist Plan* (1922) and *Equitable Society and How to Create It* (1927).

428. Ewing C. Baskette, American lawyer, librarian, and correspondent of Benjamin Tucker. He established the Baskette Collection at the University of Illinois, Urbana.

429. Ammon A. Hennacy (1893–1970), American anarchist and pacifist. In 1918 and 1919 he was a prison mate of Alexander Berkman in Atlanta and afterwards was a leading figure in the Catholic Worker movement, along with Dorothy Day and Peter Maurin. He was the author, among other works, of *The Book of Ammon* (1965) and *The One-Man Revolution in America* (1970).

430. Social Credit was an economic plan popular in Canada (and to a lesser extent in the United States) during the Depression era. Based on the theories of Clifford H. Douglas, an English engineer, it aimed to reduce the unequal distribution of income by issuing dividends to every citizen in an amount determined by an estimate of the nation's real wealth.

431. Protocols of the Elders of Zion, a fraudulent document that recorded the purported proceedings of a conference of Jews in the late nineteenth century at which plans were laid to overthrow Christianity and establish control of the world. The Protocols, first published in their entirety in 1905, were widely distributed during the 1920s and 1930s, fanning the flames of anti-Semitism. Subsequent investigation showed the document to be a forgery perpetrated by the tsarist secret police.

432. Jacob Coxey (1854–1951), American social reformer, was bent on alleviating the plight of the unemployed. He acquired a measure of fame as leader of "Coxey's army,"

a band of jobless men who marched on Washington in 1894 to petition Congress for relief.

433. Edgar Tafel (b. 1912), a pupil at the Stelton Modern School who later studied with Frank Lloyd Wright at Taliesin, Wisconsin. He assisted Wright in designing the famous Johnson Building in Racine and became a leading architect in New York. He is the author of *Apprentice to Genius: Years with Frank Lloyd Wright* (1979).

434. In 1949 a riot occurred when the black actor and singer Paul Robeson (1898–1976) gave a concert at Mohegan Lake, near Peekskill, New York. A crowd of vigilantes, assisted by the police, attacked and beat members of the departing audience.

435. Popular Front, a coalition of Communists, socialists, and other radicals during the 1930s to resist the rise of fascism in Europe.

436. Pierre Martin (1856–1916), veteran French anarchist, contributor to *Le Libertaire* and other journals.

437. Jay Fox (1870–1961), Irish-born anarchist and labor activist, first in Chicago and afterwards at Home Colony, where he edited *The Agitator* (1910–1912). Fox attended the Haymarket meeting in 1886 and in 1905 was a delegate to the founding convention of the IWW. He was a frequent contributor to *Free Society*, *Mother Earth*, and other anarchist publications.

438. The Dukhobors were a Russian religious sect founded in the eighteenth century. Its adherents, mostly peasants, preached Christian love and rejected military conscription, for which they were persecuted by the tsarist government. In the 1890s, with the help of Tolstoy and Kropotkin, many of them emigrated to Canada.

439. See n. 105 and Berkman's *Prison Memoirs of an Anarchist*, p. 411.

440. Emanuel Haldeman-Julius (1889–1951), socialist editor and publisher in Girard, Kansas. In addition to *The Appeal to Reason*, a socialist journal, he published his widely read "little blue books," a collection of blue-covered social and literary booklets.

441. Harry Kemp (1883–1960), the "hobo poet" from Mornington, Ohio. He lectured and read his poems at the Ferrer Center and published them in *Mother Earth*, *Revolt*, and *The Modern School*.

442. Terry Carlin (real name Terence O'Carolan, 1855–1934), Irish-born anarchist and Tuckerite, secretary of the Liberty Group in Chicago. Later, while living in New York, he became a friend of Eugene O'Neill (see n. 134). He wrote on Ibsen in Tucker's *Liberty* and contributed to Hippolyte Havel's *Revolt*. His lover Marie was the subject of Hutchins Hapgood's *An Anarchist Woman* (New York: Duffield, 1909).

443. David Isakovitz (d. 1949), Jewish anarchist in London and later New York. He was a friend of Rudolf Rocker and Peter Kropotkin and contributed to the *Fraye Arbeter Shtime*. His son, Henry David, wrote a history of the Haymarket affair.

444. William MacQueen (1875–1908), British anarchist. He contributed to the London *Freedom*, edited *The Free Commune* (1898–1899), and published an English translation of Johann Most's *Communist Anarchism* (1901). Emigrating to the United States, he edited *Liberty* in Paterson and New York (1902–1903). Together with Luigi Galleani, he was involved in the Paterson silk strike of 1902 and was arrested for inciting to riot. Jumping bail, he went back to England but soon returned to face trial, which brought him a five-year prison term. He was released after three years on condition that he quit the U.S. and never return. Broken in health, he died at the age of thirty-three.

445. Rudolf Grossmann (1882–1942), Austrian anarchist and sexual reformer, known as "Pierre Ramus." He emigrated to New York, where he edited *Der Zeitgeist* (1901). Arrested during the Paterson strike, along with MacQueen and Galleani, he fled the country to England. He afterwards established a vasectomy clinic in Vienna, wrote a

number of books and pamphlets, and edited the *Freie Generation* and *Erkenntnis und Befreiung*. During World War I he served three months at hard labor for antimilitarist agitation. He translated several anarchist works into German, including Kropotkin's *Words of a Rebel*.

446. Cf. Fritz Brupbacher, "A Visit to Kropotkin in 1905," in Joseph Ishill, ed., *Peter Kropotkin: The Rebel, Thinker and Humanitarian* (Berkeley Heights, N.J.: The Free Spirit Press, 1923), p. 93: "Guillaume played dances on the piano and Kropotkin danced with the young girls and did all sorts of nonsense and playful tricks."

447. *Chants of Labour: A Song Book of the People*, ed. Edward Carpenter (London, 1888).

448. Andrew Bonar Law (1858–1923), Conservative member of parliament and spokesman for tariff reform. In 1911 he succeeded Arthur Balfour as leader of the Conservative Party. He served as colonial secretary in Herbert Asquith's cabinet, and in 1916 became chancellor of the exchequer under David Lloyd George. He became prime minister in 1922 but had to resign because of ill health.

449. The maid was probably Julia, employed by Emma Goldman's niece Stella Ballantine (who lived in Greenwich Village) as a nanny for her baby son Ian (see Goldman, *Living My Life*, p. 650).

450. Marsh House, founded in 1915 as a gathering place for London anarchists. It was named in memory of Alfred Marsh (1858–1914), an editor of *Freedom* and of *The Voice of Labour*.

451. Lilian Wolfe (1875–1974), British anarchist and longtime member of the Freedom Group. She was the companion of Thomas Keell (see n. 419), with whom she was imprisoned for opposition to the war.

452. Joseph Freeman (1897–1965), American Communist writer, associate of Mike Gold and Robert Minor. He was the author of *Voices of October* (1930), *The Soviet Worker* (1932), and *An American Testament* (1936).

453. Alexander Sutherland Neill (1884–1973), Scottish teacher and founder of Summerhill, an experimental school at Leiston, Suffolk. He was the author, in addition to the "Dominie" books, of *Summerhill: A Radical Approach to Child-Rearing* (1960).

454. In 1950 Julius and Ethel Rosenberg were arrested on charges of spying for the Soviet Union. In spite of worldwide appeals for clemency, they were executed on June 19, 1953, the first American civilians to suffer the death penalty in an espionage case.

455. Joan Baez refers to Stelton in her book *Daybreak* (New York: Dial, 1968), p. 26.

456. James F. Morton, Jr., who lived at Home from 1901 to 1905 (see n. 338).

457. Charles P. LeWarne, "The Anarchist Colony at Home," *Arizona and the West* 14 (Summer 1972), pp. 155–68.

458. Radium was discovered in 1898 by Pierre and Marie Curie.

459. William J. Burns, head of the well-known detective agency and future director of the Bureau of Investigation. Caplan was wanted in connection with the Los Angeles Times Building explosion (see nn. 77 and 142).

460. Andrew Klemencic, Slovenian-born anarchist tailor. He was a delegate to the founding convention of the IWW, held in Chicago in 1905. Fluent in several languages, he wrote widely for the anarchist press.

461. Samuel T. Hammersmark, Scandinavian-born anarchist and Chicago bookseller, who afterwards lived in Seattle. He was a friend of Jay Fox and William Z. Foster and a member of the Syndicalist League of North America.

462. William Z. Foster (1881–1961), American Communist leader. He was a socialist and Wobbly before becoming a Communist. In 1912 he founded in Chicago the Syndi-

calist League of North America and wrote a pamphlet (with Earl C. Ford) on *Syndicalism*. In 1913, with Jay Fox, he edited *The Syndicalist*, an "Exponent of Revolutionary Unionism, Direct Action and Sabotage." Foster played a role in the great steel strike of 1919, during the labor ferment following the war. After visiting Soviet Russia in 1921 he joined the American Communist Party. He was its candidate for the American presidency in 1924, 1928, and 1932, and served as party chairman from 1932 to 1957. He died in Moscow, and his ashes were buried in Waldheim Cemetery near Chicago.

463. Joseph J. Cohen, *In Quest of Heaven: The Story of the Sunrise Co-operative Farm Community* (New York: Sunrise History Publishing Committee, 1957), p. 137.

464. See M. Stein, "The Sunrise Colony," *Man!*, June 1935.

465. Camillo Berneri (1897-1937), a leading Italian anarchist, was murdered by Communist gunmen in Barcelona.

466. See also Paul Avrich, "Geshtorbn Sheyndl Bluestein-Ostroff," *Problemen* (Tel Aviv), January 1986.

467. This occurred at a meeting to protest the execution of Francisco Ferrer on October 13, 1909.

468. Abba Gordin (1887-1964), Russian anarchist during the Revolution of 1917. He was a member of the Moscow Soviet and editor of *Burevestnik* (Petrograd) and *Anarkhiia* (Moscow). In 1920 he founded the Universalists, a pro-Bolshevik group that endorsed a temporary dictatorship of the proletariat. He emigrated to the U.S. in 1924 and edited *The Clarion* in New York (1932-1934). During the 1950s he moved to Israel, where he spent his remaining years.

469. Maximiliano Olay (1893-1941), Spanish anarchist from Asturias who, as "Juan Escoto," emigrated in 1914 from Havana to Tampa and worked as a cigarmaker. Deported to Cuba as a "dangerous anarchist," he later returned to the U.S. and settled in Chicago, where he operated a translation bureau and was active with his wife Anna (see n. 371) in the Free Society Group. Under the pen name "Onofre Dallas" he wrote for *Vanguard* and other anarchistic periodicals. With the outbreak of the Spanish Civil War he became the CNT-FAI representative in New York. He died in Chicago in 1941, and his wife afterward committed suicide.

PART FIVE

470. *Sacco and Vanzetti: Developments and Reconsiderations* (Boston: Boston Public Library, 1982), p. 4.

471. Errico Malatesta, *A Talk Between Two Workers* (Oakland, Calif.: Man!, 1933), p. iii.

472. *New York Times*, June 5, 1977.

473. William J. Fishman, *East End Jewish Radicals, 1875-1914* (London: Duckworth, 1975), p. 254. See also Nicolas Walter, "Sam Dreen," *Freedom* (London), February 24, 1979.

474. The Jewish Bund was the principal Jewish socialist organization in Russia and Poland. Founded in Vilna in 1897, it took part a year later in the formation of the Russian Social Democratic Workers' Party. The Bund was suppressed in Russia during the 1920s but continued in Poland until the Second World War. A remnant survives in New York, along with the organization's library and archives.

475. Two London groups, the tailors and dock workers, went out on strike in 1912.

Rocker and his wife Milly played a prominent role in organizational and propaganda work.

476. Arthur Balfour, the British foreign secretary, declared in November 1917 that "His Majesty's Government view with favour the establishment in Palestine of a national home for the Jewish people."

477. Poale Zion was a major Labor Zionist party in Russia and other countries.

478. Chaim Weizmann (1874–1952) and Nahum Sokolow (1859–1936), prominent Zionist leaders. The Russian-born Weizmann, a well-known chemist, was president of the World Zionist Organization from 1920 to 1931 and 1935 to 1946 and President of Israel from 1948 to 1952. Sokolow, born in Poland, served as secretary of the Zionist Organization and editor of its publications. With Weizmann he participated in the London meetings during World War I that led to the Balfour Declaration and the Palestinian mandate. He was the author of a two-volume history of Zionism (1919) and served as president of the World Zionist Organization (1931–1935).

479. Ravachol (real name François-Claudius Koenigstein, 1859–1892), French anarchist and terrorist. Condemned to death after a chain of burglaries, bombings, and murders, he shouted *Vive l'anarchie* and walked to the guillotine singing an anarchist song.

480. Nestor Makhno (1889–1934), anarchist guerrilla chieftain during the Russian Civil War. Under the black flag of anarchy, he led the Insurgent Army of the Ukraine against Whites and Reds alike. Driven out of the country in 1921, he ultimately found refuge in Paris, where he died of tuberculosis.

481. Volin (pseudonym of V. M. Eikhenbaum, 1882–1945), prominent Russian anarchist during the 1917 Revolution. He was the editor of *Golos Truda*, an anarcho-syndicalist journal in Petrograd and Moscow, and afterwards of *Nabat* in the Ukraine. He took part in Makhno's insurgent army as a cultural and educational advisor, for which he was arrested by the Bolsheviks and imprisoned in Moscow. Allowed to leave the country, he went to Berlin, where he edited *Anarkhicheskii Vestnik* (1923–1924) and published a catalogue of Bolshevik repressions against the anarchists. Volin moved to Paris in 1924 and embarked on his most ambitious work, *La révolution inconnue*, a history of the revolution from the anarchist point of view. It was published posthumously in 1947.

482. Sholem Schwartzbard, Russian-Jewish anarchist. In Paris in 1926 Schwartzbard assassinated the Ukrainian nationalist leader Semyon Petliura, whom he held responsible for the massacre of Jews during the Civil War.

483. Paul Avrich, "Memoirs of an Anarchist: An Interview with Lena Shlakman (1872–1975)," *Freedom* (London), December 6, 1975. Yiddish translation in the *Fraye Arbeter Shtime*, January and February 1976.

484. Emma Goldman (*Living My Life*, p. 992) calls Lena Shlakman one of the truly "hard workers" in Montreal.

485. *Narodniki*, the Russian populist revolutionaries of the 1870s and 1880s.

486. Eleanor Marx (1855–1898), Karl Marx's youngest daughter, a capable speaker, writer, and translator (of Flaubert and Ibsen, among others). On a lecture tour of the U.S. in 1886 she visited the Haymarket anarchists in prison, together with her husband Edward Aveling.

487. Vera Zasulich (1849–1919), Russian revolutionary populist, born of a gentry family. In 1878 she shot and wounded the governor of St. Petersburg, who had ordered the flogging of a political prisoner. Though acquitted, she was driven into hiding and in 1880 fled to Geneva, where she was a founder of the Liberation of Labor (1883), an early

Russian Marxist group. She published a history of the First International and translated the works of Marx and Engels. Returning to Russia during the 1905 Revolution, she remained there until her death, a staunch opponent of the Bolsheviks.

488. Isidore Rudashevsky (shortened to Rudash, 1862–1938), who immigrated from Russia in 1885, was a pioneer Jewish anarchist on the Lower East Side of New York. He was the manager of *Varhayt* (1889), the first Yiddish anarchist paper, and a distributor of *Di Fraye Gezelshaft, The Rebel,* and *Free Society.*

489. J. A. Maryson (1866–1941), Jewish anarchist and physician. He was a member of the Pioneers of Liberty in New York and of the editorial board of its paper *Varhayt.* He also served briefly as editor of the *Fraye Arbeter Shtime,* to which he was a frequent contributor. In addition, he wrote for *Di Fraye Gezelshaft, Solidarity* (as "F. A. Frank"), and other anarchist publications, edited *Dos Fraye Vort* (1911), and translated into Yiddish works ranging from Marx's *Capital* to Stirner's *The Ego and His Own* and Thoreau's *Civil Disobedience.* His book *The Principles of Anarchism* appeared in 1935.

490. Goldman, *Living My Life,* p. 990.

491. I. N. Steinberg (1888–1957), Left Socialist Revolutionary, People's Commissar of Justice in the Soviet government from December 1917 to March 1918. Breaking with the Bolsheviks, he emigrated to the West, living in Berlin (where he collaborated with Alexander Berkman on the *Bulletin of the Joint Committee for the Defense of Revolutionists Imprisoned in Russia*), London, Toronto, and finally New York. He was close in spirit to the anarchists, being a friend of Rudolf Rocker and an admirer of Gustav Landauer. He is the author of *Als ich Volkskommissar war* (1929) and *In the Workshop of the Revolution* (1953).

492. See also Paul Avrich, "An Anarchist Life," *Freedom* (London), February 12, 1972. French translation in *Le Monde Libertaire* (Paris), April 1972.

493. Thomas H. Bell to Joseph Spivak, November 17, 1927, Avrich Collection, Library of Congress.

494. See also Rebecca August, "My Autobiography," manuscript, 1955, Avrich Collection, Library of Congress.

495. Louise Olivereau, anarchist and feminist poet. She was the assistant of William Thurston Brown at the Portland Modern School (1911–1912). She later worked at the IWW office in Seattle and lectured to women's groups (on Ibsen among other subjects). She was arrested in 1917 for agitating against conscription, having published leaflets which, quoting Tolstoy and Thoreau, advised young men to resist the draft. She spent two and a half years in a Colorado prison, where she taught her fellow inmates English. She died in San Francisco in 1963.

496. On Zalman Deanin see also the *Fraye Arbeter Shtime,* July–August 1976.

497. See also Ahrne Thorne, "Geshtorbn di umfargeslekhe Sonya Deanin," *Fraye Arbeter Shtime,* March 1977.

498. Sam Margolis, a shoe-cutter from Vitebsk, Russia, was an ardent anarchist, atheist, and anti-Zionist, who would not attend his own grandson's bar-mitzvah. During the First World War he was a member of the executive committee of the Kropotkin Literary Society and operated a little anarchist bookstore in Harlem. He later ran a hotel in Lakewood, New Jersey, where he died in 1964.

499. Everett massacre (November 5, 1916). During a free-speech struggle in Everett, Washington, on Puget Sound, a party of IWWs who arrived from Seattle by ferry were met with gunfire from policemen and vigilantes. More than thirty people were killed and wounded, including five Wobblies and a deputy sheriff.

500. Charles Ashleigh, English-born IWW poet and agitator. A defendant in the

IWW trial in Chicago (1918), he was imprisoned at Leavenworth for five years and deported in 1923. Back in England he quit the IWW for the Communist Party. His poems appeared in *The Masses, The Liberator,* and *The Little Review.*

501. George Plekhanov (1856–1918), Russian socialist thinker, known as "the father of Russian Marxism." As a youth during the 1870s he was a follower of Bakunin and a member of Land and Liberty, a populist organization. He left Russia as a political refugee and, turning to Marxism, was a founder of the Liberation of Labor Group in Geneva (1883). An opponent of the Bolsheviks, he became an independent figure in the Russian Marxist movement. He supported Russia's participation in the First World War. Returning from exile in 1917, he died the following year.

502. Adolf Schnabel, a Russian anarchist in New York, was an active figure in the Union of Russian Workers in the United States and Canada and managing editor of its journal *Nabat* (1918). In December 1919 he was deported on the *Buford* together with Emma Goldman and Alexander Berkman.

503. On March 25, 1911, a tragic fire occurred at the Triangle Shirtwaist Factory in New York City. One hundred fifty-four employees, mostly young women, lost their lives, alerting the public to hazardous factory conditions. An investigation followed which led to safety laws in New York and other states.

504. David Dubinsky (1892–1982) and Charles ("Sasha") Zimmerman (1896–1983) were president and vice-president, respectively, of the International Ladies' Garment Workers' Union.

505. Ethel Bernstein was a Jewish anarchist in New York and a member of the Frayhayt Group, together with Jacob Abrams and Mollie Steimer. She was deported to Russia in December 1919 with Emma Goldman, Alexander Berkman, and other anarchists.

506. Nadezhda Krupskaya (1869–1939), wife of Lenin and member of the Bolshevik central committee. She was an active figure in the People's Commissariat of Education.

507. Morris Hillquit (1869–1933), American lawyer and socialist leader. He emigrated to America from Russia in 1886 and was active in the Jewish labor movement. He twice ran for Mayor of New York City on the Socialist ticket and five times for U.S. Congressman, unsuccessfully in all cases. His most notable writings are a *History of Socialism in the United States* (1903, revised 1910) and *Leaves from a Busy Life* (1933).

508. Kate Richards O'Hare (1876–1948), American socialist leader and colleague of Eugene Victor Debs. She was a popular orator, advocate of birth control and prison reform, and opponent of the First World War. Convicted under the Espionage Act after delivering an antiwar speech, she was sentenced to five years in Jefferson City penitentiary, where Emma Goldman was a fellow inmate. She served fourteen months (1919–1920) before her term was commuted by President Wilson.

509. Covington Hall (1871–1951), Wobbly poet and songwriter, editor of *The Lumberjack* and *Rebellion.* His poems are collected in *Battle Hymns of Toil* (1946) and *Dreams and Dynamite* (1985).

510. Actually Victor Bondarenko was still alive at the time of the interview (1974), residing in Los Angeles.

511. A Yiddish translation of this interview, by Ahrne Thorne, appeared in the *Fraye Arbeter Shtime,* June 1977.

512. See Paul Avrich, ed., "Prison Letters of Ricardo Flores Magón to Lilly Sarnoff," *International Review of Social History* 22 (1977), p. 421.

513. Earl R. Browder (1891–1973), American Communist leader. A socialist during the First World War, he was imprisoned for opposing the draft. He afterwards joined the Communist Party, serving as general secretary from 1930 to 1944 and running for

President of the United States in 1936 and 1940. He was editor-in-chief of the *Daily Worker* in 1944 and 1945 but was expelled from the party for dissident views in 1946.

514. James P. Cannon (1890–1974), leader of the Trotskyist movement in the United States. A socialist and Wobbly during his earlier years, he joined the Communist Party after the Bolshevik seizure of power and served as American delegate to the Comintern. He later became a Trotskyist and was national secretary of the Socialist Workers' Party from 1938 to 1953. He was the author of *The History of American Trotskyism* (1944), *The First Ten Years of American Communism* (1962), and *Letters from Prison* (1968), among other works.

515. Ricardo Flores Magón (see n. 90) was repeatedly imprisoned by the U.S. government, the last time in 1918. He apparently died of natural causes. There is no reliable evidence of foul play, though his imprisonment may have hastened his death.

516. Golda Meir (1898–1978), Israeli political leader. Born in Russia, she emigrated to the United States in 1906 and settled in Milwaukee, where she became a schoolteacher and involved herself in the Zionist movement. She left the U.S. for Palestine in 1921. After Israel became an independent state in 1948, she served as ambassador to Moscow, minister of labor, and foreign minister, before becoming prime minister in 1969.

517. Sonya Farber describes her experiences as an anarchist and garment worker in the film *The Free Voice of Labor: The Jewish Anarchists* (Pacific Street Films, 1980). See also Paul Avrich, "Oyfn frishn keyver fun Sonya Farber," *Problemen* (Tel Aviv), March 1984.

518. Morris Sigman (1880–1931), an anarcho-syndicalist from Bessarabia, was president of the ILGWU from 1923 to 1928. He waged an all-out campaign to prevent a Communist takeover of the union.

519. For an obituary of Israel Ostroff see the *Fraye Arbeter Shtime*, June 1974. See also Paul Avrich, "In undenk fun Israel Ostroff (1892–1974)," *Dos Fraye Vort* (Buenos Aires), May 1974.

520. "And they shall beat their swords into plowshares, and their spears into pruning hooks: nation shall not lift up sword against nation, neither shall they learn war any more" (Isaiah 2:4). "In those days there was no king in Israel: every man did that which was right in his own eyes" (Judges 21:25).

521. Herman Frank (1892–1952), Jewish anarchist and devotee of Gustav Landauer. He was editor of the *Fraye Arbeter Shtime* from 1940 to 1952.

522. Max Shachtman (1903–1972), American radical and translator of Trotsky. He joined the Communist Party during the early 1920s, edited *The Labor Defender*, and campaigned for the release of Sacco and Vanzetti, about whom he published a book, *Sacco and Vanzetti: Labor's Martyrs* (1927). In 1928 he became a Trotskyist and edited *The Militant* and *The New International*. He broke with Trotskyism after World War II and subsequently drifted to the right, opposing U.S. withdrawal from Vietnam.

523. Paul Avrich, "The Last Maximalist: An Interview with Klara Klebanova," *The Russian Review* 32 (October 1973), pp. 413–20. Reprinted in *Freedom* (London), March 9 and 16, 1974.

524. Dora Lazurkina, speech at the Twenty-Second Congress of the Soviet Communist Party in 1961.

525. P. L. Lavrov (1823–1900), Russian populist leader and theorist. He edited the journal *Vpered* and was the author of *Historical Letters* (1868–1869).

526. N. K. Mikhailovsky (1842–1904), Russian populist writer, author of *What Is*

Progress? (1869–1870). In contrast to the Marxists, he put his faith in the village commune as the model of Russia's future society.

527. Yevno Azef (1869–1918), a founder of the Socialist Revolutionary Party and head of its "fighting organization." He engineered a number of terrorist acts, including the assassination of Minister of the Interior V. K. Plehve (1904) and Grand Duke Sergei Aleksandrovich (1905). At the same time he was an informer for the tsarist police. Unmasked as a spy, he fled to Germany, where he lived out the rest of his life.

528. Mikhail Ivanovich Sokolov. See his *Sushchnost' maksimalizma* (St. Petersburg, 1906).

529. P. A. Stolypin (1862–1911), Russian minister of the interior in 1906. He carried out a dual policy of firm repression of revolutionary activity and social reform to remove the causes of discontent. He served as prime minister from 1907 until his death by an assassin's bullet.

530. The Maximalists met at Abo from October 25 to November 3, 1906.

531. Paul Avrich, "An Interview with Meishka Schulmeister," *Freedom* (London), July 22, 1978.

532. Halper Leivick (1888–1962), noted Yiddish poet. He contributed to the *Fraye Arbeter Shtime* and was the author, most famously, of *Der Goylem*.

533. Ahad Ha-am (Asher Zvi Ginsberg, 1856–1927), theoretician of "spiritual" Zionism.

534. Archduke Franz Ferdinand, nephew of Emperor Franz Josef of Austria, was assassinated in Sarajevo, Bosnia, on June 28, 1914, precipitating the First World War.

535. The Lusk Committee was established by the New York State legislature in 1919 to investigate subversive activities.

536. Russkoe Ob'edinennoe Obshchestvo Vzaimopomoshchi v Amerike (Russian United Society of Mutual Aid in America).

537. See M. Weitzman [Ganberg], "Der Anarkhistisher Royter Krayts," *Fraye Arbeter Shtime*, January 15, 1966.

538. *Al'manakh: sbornik po istorii anarkhicheskogo dvizheniia v Rossii*, ed. N. Rogdaev (Paris, 1909).

539. In June 1905 the sailors of the battleship *Potemkin* mutinied in Odessa harbor. The crew, unable to win support from other ships, found asylum in Rumania. A major incident in the 1905 Revolution, it was the subject of a celebrated film by Sergei Eisenstein (1925).

540. Isaac A. Hourwich (1860–1924), prominent Jewish socialist in New York. He was the author of *The Economics of the Russian Village* (1892) and *Immigration and Labor* (1912). In 1915 he debated with Emma Goldman on the question of "social revolution or social reform."

541. B. Charney Vladeck (1886–1938), Jewish socialist and trade unionist. He took part in the 1905 Revolution and emigrated to the U.S. in 1908. He was a member of the Jewish Labor Committee and general manager of the *Jewish Daily Forward*.

542. Daniel De Leon (1852–1914), socialist writer, lecturer, and debater. He was an instructor at Columbia University and author of works on trade unionism, industrial unionism, and Marxism. A leading figure in the Socialist Labor Party and editor of its journal *The People*, he was a sharp critic of the anarchists, including Kropotkin and Emma Goldman. He was a founding member of the IWW in 1905.

543. Dmitri Bogrov, a double agent, assassinated Prime Minister Stolypin at the Kiev opera house in 1911 (see n. 529).

544. *Petliurovtsy* and *Denikintsy*: the forces of the Ukrainian leader S. V. Petliura (1877–1926) and of General A. I. Denikin (1872–1947), who carried out ferocious attacks on the Jews during the Civil War of 1918–1921.

545. Mary Heaton Vorse (1874–1966), American journalist. She covered strikes and labor struggles for the radical press, took part in the unemployed and Ludlow protests in 1914, and wrote on Sacco and Vanzetti, whom she visited in prison. She was the author of *Footnote to Folly* (1935) and *Labor's New Millions* (1938).

546. See also Paul Avrich, "Geshtorbn an alter anarkhist," *Problemen* (Tel Aviv), September 1985 ff.

547. David Shub (b. 1887), Jewish socialist writer. A member of the Russian Social Democratic Workers' Party, he took part in the 1905 Revolution and afterwards escaped from Siberia, reaching the United States in 1908. He is best known for his biography of Lenin, published in 1948.

548. Efim Yarchuk and Anatoli Zhelezniakov were anarchists in Kronstadt during the 1917 Revolution. In January 1918 Zhelezniakov dispersed the popularly elected Constituent Assembly. He died in combat against the Whites during the Russian Civil War.

549. *Barimte redes fun di Shikagoer Martirer*, trans. Abraham Frumkin, with a foreword by Alexander Berkman (New York: Amshol-Kropotkin Group, 1933).

550. Salvador Allende (1908–1973), Marxist physician and President of Chile from 1970 to 1973. In September 1973 he was overthrown by a military coup, during which he was murdered or committed suicide.

551. Goldman, *Living My Life*, p. 927.

552. See also P. Constan [Ahrne Thorne], "Tsu di shloyshim nokh unzer guter khaver Mark Mratchny," *Fraye Arbeter Shtime*, May–June 1975; and Paul Avrich, "Di tsente yortsayt nokh Mark Mratchny," *Problemen* (Tel Aviv), July 1985.

553. On September 25, 1919, a group of anarchists and SRs bombed the Moscow Communist Party headquarters on Leontievsky Street, killing twelve members of the party committee and wounding fifty-five others, among them Nikolai Bukharin, the eminent Bolshevik theorist. A number of anarchists, including Fanny Baron and Lev Chorny, were executed for complicity in the attack.

554. Boris Nicolaevsky (1887–1966), Menshevik historian of the Russian revolutionary movement. Under Nicholas II he twice escaped from Siberian exile and once from prison. After the October 1917 Revolution he served as director of the Marx-Engels Institute in Moscow. Deported in 1922, he worked at the Marx-Engels Institute in Berlin and at the International Institute of Social History in Amsterdam, coming to the United States in 1942. He is the author of *Azef, the Spy* (1934) and *Power and the Soviet Elite* (1965). His extensive archival collection is housed in the Hoover Institution at Stanford.

555. Carl Nold (1869–1934), German-born anarchist. He served five years in prison following the Homestead strike of 1892. He later taught at the Detroit Modern School and wrote for *Free Society*, *Mother Earth*, and other anarchist periodicals.

556. P. N. Miliukov (1859–1943), Russian historian and political leader. He was a founder of the Constitutional Democratic Party in 1905 and a member of the State Duma from 1907 to 1917. After the abdication of the tsar in March 1917, he became foreign minister in the Provisional Government. He supported the Russian war effort and sided with the Whites against the Bolsheviks. He fled to Western Europe, settling eventually in Paris. During the Second World War he advocated support for the Soviet Union against Germany.

557. Boris Yelensky, *In sotsialn shturem* (Buenos Aires: Jewish Rationalist Society, 1967). An unpublished English translation, "In the Social Storm: Memoirs of the Russian Revolution," is to be found in the Avrich Collection, Library of Congress.

558. See Boris Yelensky, "25 Years of 'Free Society' Activity in Chicago," *The World Scene from the Libertarian Point of View* (Chicago: Free Society Group, 1951), pp. 90–94; and Yelensky, *In the Struggle for Equality* (Chicago: Alexander Berkman Aid Fund, 1958).

559. See also *Venceremos: B. Yelensky 60th Anniversary* (Chicago: International Printing Co., 1949); and Irving Abrams, "Boris Yelensky: A Personal Remembrance," *Equality* (Evansville, Ind.), May 1977.

560. See also Paul Avrich, "Marcelino García (1893–1977)," *Freedom* (London), June 11, 1977, and *España Libre* (New York), May–June 1977.

561. Michele Angiolillo, an Italian anarchist, assassinated the Spanish prime minister, Antonio Cánovas del Castillo, on August 8, 1897.

562. Sirio Esteve to Paul Avrich, April 4, 1973, Avrich Collection, Library of Congress.

563. Sirio Esteve, *The Experience: A Celebration of Being* (New York: Random House, 1974).

564. See Manuel Rey, "Thoughts of a Dead-Living Soul" (poem), *One Big Union Monthly*, August 1919, reprinted in *Rebel Voices: An IWW Anthology*, ed. Joyce L. Kornbluh (2d ed., Chicago: Charles H. Kerr Publishing Co., 1988), pp. 339–40; M. R. [Manuel Rey] poem in *The American Political Prisoner* (New York, 1922); and Lilly Raymond, *Miscellaneous Poems* (Stelton, N.J.: The Author, 1971).

565. On November 12, 1912, José Canalejas, the prime minister of Spain, was shot to death in Madrid by the anarchist Manuel Pardinas.

566. Emma Goldman, *The Crushing of the Russian Revolution* (London: Freedom Press, 1922).

567. See Marcelo Salinas, *Anarquía y anarquismo* (Havana, n.d.); *Marcelo Salinas: un ideal sublime y elevado* (Miami: Ediciones del Movimiento Libertario Cubano en el Exilio, n.d.); *Guángara Libertaria* (Miami), Summer 1989.

568. Valentine Rogin-Levine (1907–1982) attended the Modern School at Stelton and the Stony Ford School conducted by Robert and Delia Hutchinson. His father, Louis Levine, was an anarchist scholar who lectured at the Ferrer Center and whose Columbia doctoral thesis, *Syndicalism in France*, was published in 1914. As Val R. Lorwin, the son became a distinguished economic historian, an authority, like his father, on the French labor movement.

569. Li Pei-kan (b. 1904), an anarchist known as Pa Chin, was one of China's most popular novelists during the 1930s and 1940s. He is still alive at eighty-nine, a resident of Shanghai.

570. Ricardo Mella (1861–1925), Spanish anarchist theorist and proponent of "anarchism without adjectives."

571. See also F. A. [Federico Arcos], "Germinal Gracia: The Marco Polo of Anarchism," *Fifth Estate* (Detroit), Winter 1992.

572. Durruti (see n. 114) was shot to death during the siege of Madrid in November 1936.

573. R. Lone (real name Jésus Louzara de Andres, 1883–1973), Spanish anarchist in Steubenville, Ohio, a patriarchal figure in the movement.

574. Volume one of Rocker's memoirs (Buenos Aires: Editorial Americalee, 1947).

575. See Olga Lang, *Pa Chin and His Writings: Chinese Youth Between the Two Revolutions* (Cambridge, Mass.: Harvard University Press, 1967), pp. 113–16.

576. In 1913 the Chinese anarchist Liu Shi-fu began to publish a journal whose first two numbers were entitled *Hui-ming lu* (Crying in the Darkness Notes). In succeeding issues the name appeared as *Ming-sheng* (People's Voice). Lang, *Pa Chin and His Writings*, pp. 51–52; and Robert A. Scalapino and George T. Yu, *The Chinese Anarchist Movement* (Berkeley: Center for Chinese Studies, University of California, 1961), p. 39.

577. Pierre Besnard, French anarcho-syndicalist, coeditor (with Alexander Schapiro) of *La Voix du Travail* (1926–1927) and author of *Les syndicats ouvriers et la révolution sociale* (1930).

578. Jean Grave (1854–1939), prominent French anarchist. He edited *Le Révolté* (later *La Révolte* and *Les Temps Nouveaux*), the leading anarchist paper in France, and published numerous pamphlets and books, including *La société mourante et l'anarchie* (1893), *Le mouvement libertaire sous la 3e république* (1930), and *Quarante ans de propagande anarchiste* (1973).

579. Paul Reclus (1858–1941), French anarchist, son of Elie Reclus and nephew of Elisé (see n. 46), author of *Les frères Elie et Elisée Reclus* (1964).

580. Yat Tone, Chinese anarchist in New York, where he worked in a Chinese restaurant. A teacher in a Ferrer School in China before coming to the United States, he visited the Stelton Colony and attended meetings of the Road to Freedom Group. He went to Spain in 1933 and from there returned to China.

581. Bao Puo was one of a group of young Chinese who attended the Communist University of the Toilers of the East in Moscow, where he met Emma Goldman and Alexander Berkman in 1921. By translating Berkman's writings on the Russian Revolution, he alerted his comrades in China to the dangers of Bolshevism. He returned to China in 1923. See Bao-Puo, "The Anarchist Movement in China," *Freedom* (London), January 1925.

582. Emma Goldman, *Anarchism and Other Essays* (New York: Mother Earth Publishing Association, 1910), p. 191.

583. Lang, *Pa Chin and His Writings*, p. 345.

584. The full quotation is: "I am free only when all human beings surrounding me— men and women alike—are equally free. The freedom of others, far from limiting or negating my liberty, is on the contrary its necessary condition and confirmation." G. P. Maximoff, ed., *The Political Philosophy of Bakunin: Scientific Anarchism* (Glencoe, Ill.: The Free Press, 1953), pp. 267–68.

585. See interview with Dominick Sallitto, Part Three.

PART SIX

586. Alexander Berkman to Max Nettlau, June 28, 1927, Berkman Archive, International Institute of Social History, Amsterdam.

587. *Freedom* (New York), February 25, 1933.

588. *The Road to Freedom*, December 1927.

589. W. S. Van Valkenburgh to Emma Goldman, May 23, 1929, Goldman Archive, International Institute of Social History, Amsterdam.

590. "Declaration of Policy," *Vanguard*, April 1932.

591. Marcus Graham, *The Issues of the Present War* (London: Freedom Press, 1943),

pp. 29–30; Rudolf Rocker to Ben Capes, April 16, 1941, Joseph Cohen Papers, Bund Archives, New York.

592. Dwight Macdonald, *Politics Past: Essays in Political Criticism* (New York: Viking, 1970), pp. 27–28.

593. *The Libertarian League: Provisional Statement of Plans* (New York, n.d. [1955]).

594. See also Paul Berman, "Death of a Wobbly," *The Village Voice*, November 13, 1990; and Paul Avrich, "Sam Dolgoff (1902–1990)," *CIRA Bulletin* (Lausanne), no. 47 (January 1991), pp. 4–6.

595. Paul Mattick (b. 1904), leading Council Communist in the United States. The Council Communists, originating in Germany and Holland after the Bolshevik seizure of power, spread to North America after Mattick's arrival in 1926. Rejecting the Soviet model as authoritarian and bureaucratic, they advocated a decentralist form of communism based on workers' self-organization and initiative. Mattick, who edited the journal *New Essays* (1934–1943), wrote widely on Marxism and economics.

596. Norman Thomas (1884–1968), American socialist leader. Ordained a Presbyterian minister in 1911, he became a socialist and pacifist during World War I and was afterwards active in such groups as the League for Industrial Democracy, the Fellowship of Reconciliation, and the American Civil Liberties Union. Following the death in 1926 of Eugene Victor Debs, Thomas assumed the leadership of the Socialist Party and was its candidate for the U.S. presidency from 1928 until 1948, polling his highest vote in 1932. Like Debs, he had friendly relations with the anarchists, visiting Mohegan Colony and speaking at a memorial meeting for Emma Goldman, along with Rudolf Rocker, Harry Kelly, and others. After World War II he was a founder of the Committee for a Sane Nuclear Policy (SANE) and an opponent of the Vietnam War.

597. William Green (1872–1952), president of the American Federation of Labor from 1924 to 1952, succeeding Samuel Gompers.

598. Ellington was in fact the assistant manager of the Oakland Symphony Orchestra.

599. Jules Bonnot (d. 1912), leader of a gang of French anarchist holdup men in Paris on the eve of World War I. Bonnot was killed in a shootout with the police, and several of his confederates went to the guillotine.

600. For an obituary of William Taback see the *Fraye Arbeter Shtime*, July–August 1976.

601. V. G. Korolenko (1853–1921), Russian novelist and story writer, who spent five years in Siberian exile. His writings were particularly influential among populist and anarchist groups. An opponent of the Bolshevik dictatorship, he died during the famine that followed the civil war.

602. Sergei Nechaev (1847–1882), Russian revolutionist and disciple of Bakunin. He was the author (possibly with Bakunin's collaboration) of *The Catechism of a Revolutionary* (1869), which justified all means—theft, treachery, blackmail, murder—that might advance the revolution and bring about the destruction of the existing order. In a letter to Nechaev, dated June 2, 1870, Bakunin rejected this "false Jesuitical system" as potentially fatal to the cause of freedom.

603. See also Jack Frager, "Emma Goldman as I Knew Her" and "My Experiences in the Russian Revolution," videocassette by Robert Palmer, New York, May 31, 1986, Avrich Collection, Library of Congress.

604. Gustav Landauer, *Di Revolutsie* (Warsaw, 1933).

605. Hippolyte Havel, *What's Anarchism?* (Chicago: Free Society Group, 1932).

606. *Burevestnik* (The Stormy Petrel), a Russian anarchist journal published in Paris from 1906 to 1910, edited by Maksim Raevsky and Nikolai Rogdaev, with B. Rivkin (1883–1945) as a contributor. Rivkin emigrated to the United States in 1911 and wrote for the *Fraye Arbeter Shtime* and other publications.

607. Lincoln Steffens (1866–1936), American journalist and muckraker, author of *The Shame of the Cities* (1904) and other books. *The Autobiography of Lincoln Steffens* was published in 1931.

608. See also *Louis Slater: Libertarian—Humanitarian, 1912–1973* (New York: Tamiment Library, 1973).

609. S. Morrison, "Hitler Must Be Stopped," *Libertarian Views*, February 1941.

610. In 1933 Athos Terzani, a young antifascist, was accused of shooting Anthony Fierro to death at a fascist rally in Astoria, New York. Tried the following year, Terzani was acquitted. Frank Moffer, an avowed fascist, confessed to the crime and was sentenced to five to ten years' imprisonment for first-degree manslaughter.

611. Edward Dahlberg (1900–1977), American novelist and critic. His books include *Bottom Dogs* (1929), *Those Who Perish* (1934), and two autobiographical works, *Because I Was Flesh* (1963) and *The Confessions of Edward Dahlberg* (1971).

612. Gus Tyler (b. 1911), labor educator and trade-unionist, assistant president of the ILGWU. He edited *Free Youth* and the *Socialist Call* and was labor editor for the *Jewish Daily Forward*. His books include *The Labor Revolution* (1967), *The Political Imperative* (1968), and *Scarcity* 1976).

613. I was working on a history of American anarchism.

614. Max Nomad (1881–1973), Austrian-born radical writer. He was a follower of the Polish revolutionary Jan Wacław Machajski and publicized his theory that the Marxists constituted a "new class" of rulers and exploiters. His books include *Rebels and Renegades* (1932), *Aspects of Revolt* (1959), and *Political Heretics* (1963).

615. Sally Genn (1920–1985), daughter of Jewish anarchists in the Bronx and secretary of the Libertarian Book Club during the late 1970s and early 1980s. For many years she edited the *Labor Chronicle*, organ of the New York Central Labor Council.

616. During the Second World War General Władysław Sikorski (1881–1943) was premier of the Polish government in exile and commander-in-chief of its army. In 1941 he restored diplomatic relations with the Soviet Union, allowing Polish citizens to leave Russia.

617. Paul Avrich, "Anarchists: Daniel Guérin," *The Match!*, January 1974. Yiddish translation in the *Fraye Arbeter Shtime*, January 1974; reprinted in *Problemen* (Tel Aviv), January 1980.

618. Gaston Leval (real name Pierre Robert Piller, 1895–1978), French anarchist. An opponent of World War I, he took refuge in Spain and was a Spanish delegate to the congress of the Profintern (Red International of Trade Unions) held in Moscow in 1921. He was the editor of *Cahiers de l'Humanisme Libertaire*, and his books include *L'indispensable révolution* (1948), *Espagne libertaire, 1936–1939* (1971), and *La pensée constructive de Bakounine* (1976).

619. Holley Cantine, Jr. (1917–1977), American anarchist and pacifist, follower of Kropotkin and Tolstoy. With his companion Dachine Rainer he edited *Retort* (1942–1951), a quarterly anarchist journal, as well as *Prison Etiquette* (1950), a collection of writings by conscientious objectors during World War II. His translation of Volin's *La révolution inconnue* was published by the Libertarian Book Club and Freedom Press (2 vols., 1954–1955). He died in a fire at his home in Woodstock, New York.

620. Paul Goodman, *Five Years: Thoughts of a Useless Time* (New York: Random House, 1966).

621. Abbie Hoffman (1936–1989) and Jerry Rubin were active anarchists during the New Left era of the 1960s and 1970s. They were founders of the Youth International Party (Yippies), an anticapitalist, antiwar, and antigovernment group, whose chief weapons were mockery and ridicule. In 1968 the Yippies nominated a pig for President of the United States. Their aim, declared Hoffman, was to "win the election, declare victory, and eat the candidate." Hoffman's books include *Revolution for the Hell of It* (1967), *Woodstock Nation* (1969), and *Steal This Book* (1971). Rubin, who abandoned anarchism and became a stock broker, is the author of *Do It* (1970), *We Are Everywhere* (1971), and *Growing Up at Thirty-Seven* (1976).

622. See n. 391.

623. Bertrand Russell, *Proposed Roads to Freedom: Socialism, Anarchism and Syndicalism* (New York: Holt, 1919).

624. A follower of Hugo Oehler (1903–1983), an American Communist who played an important role in the Trotskyist movement. Expelled as a dissident, he founded the Revolutionary Workers League (known as "Oehlerites") and went to Spain in 1937.

625. See n. 594.

626. David Koven, "Richard (Dick) Ellington, 1930–1991," *Freedom* (London), August 24–September 7, 1991.

627. Followers of Murray N. Rothbard (b. 1926), American economist, historian, and individualist anarchist. He edited *Left & Right* during the 1960s. His books include *The Panic of 1819* (1962), *Man, Economy, and State* (1962), *America's Great Depression* (1963), *Power and Market* (1970), *For a New Liberty* (1973), and *Conceived in Liberty* (3 vols., 1975–1976).

628. Nicolas Walter (b. 1934), British anarchist and freethinker. A prolific contributor to *Freedom, Anarchy*, and other periodicals and editor of works by Peter Kropotkin, Joseph Lane, and Charlotte Wilson, he is managing director of the Rationalist Press Association and author of *About Anarchism* (1969) and *Blasphemy: Ancient and Modern* (1990).

629. Murray Bookchin (b. 1921), a leading American anarchist theorist since the 1960s, with an emphasis on ecological concerns. He taught at Goddard College in Vermont, where he founded the Institute of Social Ecology (1974), and at Ramapo College in New Jersey, where he was Professor of Social Theory. He is the author of many books, including *Post-Scarcity Anarchism* (1971—the book to which Woodworth refers in his interview), *The Limits of the City* (1974), *The Spanish Anarchists* 1977), and *The Ecology of Freedom* (1982).

7. International Anarchist Press, 1975 (Paul Avrich Collection)

List of Periodicals

L'Adunata dei Refrattari. New York, 1922–1971. Ed. Max Sartin (Raffaele Schiavina).

The Agitator. Home, Wash., 1910–1912. Ed. Jay Fox. "A Semi-Monthly Advocate of Syndicalism, the Modern School, Individual Freedom."

L'Agitazione. Boston, 1920–1925. Ed. Aldino Felicani.

The Alarm. Chicago; New York, 1884–1889. Ed. Albert R. Parsons and Dyer D. Lum.

L'Allarme. Chicago, 1915–1917. Ed. Umberto Postiglione. "Contro ogni forma di autorità e di sfruttamento."

The American Political Prisoner. New York, 1921–1922. Published by the Political Prisoners Defense and Relief Committee. "Voices from Behind the Bars."

Amerikanskie Izvestiia. New York, 1920–1924. Organ of the Russian Workers' Organizations of the United States and Canada. "Ot kazhdogo po sposobnosti—kazhdym po potrebnostiam."

Anarchist News. New York, 1980–1982. Ed. Abe Bluestein, Sam Dolgoff, and Gabriel Javsicas.

Anarkhicheskii Vestnik. Berlin, 1923–1924. Ed. V. M. Eikhenbaum (Volin).

Der Anarchist. St. Louis; New York, 1889–1895. Ed. Claus Timmermann and Josef Peukert.

The Anarchist Soviet Bulletin. New York, 1919–1920. Ed. Marcus Graham.

Anarchos. New York, 1968–1972. Ed. Murray Bookchin.

Der Arbeter Fraynd. London, 1885–1914. Ed. Rudolf Rocker et al. Organ of the Jewish Federation of Anarchists.

The Ark. San Francisco, 1947–1957.

Der Arme Teufel. Detroit, 1884–1900. Ed. Robert Reitzel.

Aurora. New York, 1919. Ed. R. Delgado.

Behind the Bars. New York, 1924. "The Voice of the Imprisoned."

The Blast. San Francisco; New York, 1916–1917. Ed. Alexander Berkman. "Revolutionary Labor Weekly."

Die Brandfackel. New York, 1893–1894. Ed. Claus Timmermann.

Broyt un frayhayt. Philadelphia, 1906. Ed. Joseph J. Cohen.

Bulletin of the Anarchist Red Cross. New York, 1924.

Bulletin of the Joint Committee for the Defense of Revolutionists Imprisoned in Russia. Berlin, 1923–1926. Ed. Alexander Berkman.

Bulletin of the Relief Fund of the International Working Men's Association for Anarchists and Anarcho-Syndicalists Imprisoned or Exiled in Russia. Berlin; Paris, 1926–1932. Ed. Alexander Berkman.

Bulletin of the Seattle Group. Seattle, 1965–1969. Ed. George and Louise Crowley.

Burevestnik. Paris, 1906–1910. Ed. Maksim Raevsky and Nikolai Rogdaev.

Burevestnik. New York, 1921–1922. Ed. Victor Bondarenko et al. Publication of the Group of Anarchist-Communists. "Pust' sil'nee grianet buria!" "Ot kazhdogo po sposobnosti—kazhdym po potrebnostiam."

Challenge. New York, 1938–1939. Ed. Abe Bluestein. "A Libertarian Weekly."

Chicagoer Arbeiter-Zeitung. Chicago, 1876 ff. Ed. August Spies et al.

The Clarion. New York, 1932–1934. Ed. Abba Gordin.

Cogito, Ergo Sum. San Francisco, 1908.

La Comune. Philadelphia, 1910–1915. Ed. Erasmo Abate et al. "Organo di difesa prole-taria." "L'Emancipazione dei lavoratori sarà opera dei lavoratori stessi."

Controcorrente. Boston, 1938–1967. Ed. Aldino Felicani. "Organo d'agitazione e di bat-taglia contro il fascismo."

Il Contro-pelo. Barre, Vt., 1911–1912. "Periodico mensile di critica, polemica e propa-ganda anarchica."

Cronaca Sovversiva. Barre, Vt.; Lynn, Mass.; 1903–1919. Ed. Luigi Galleani. "Ebdoma-dario anarchico di propaganda rivoluzionaria."

Cultura Obrera. New York, 1911–1927. Ed. Pedro Esteve. "Periodico obrero, de doctrina y de combate."

Cultura Proletaria. New York, 1927–1953. Ed. Marcelino García. "Periodico de ideas, doctrina y combate."

The Dawn. Seattle, 1922. Ed. Eugene Travaglio. "A Journal of Free Expression."

Delo Truda. Paris; Chicago; New York, 1925–1939. Ed. Gregory Maximoff et al. Organ of the Federation of Russian Workers' Organizations of the United States and Canada.

Delo Truda-Probuzhdenie. New York, 1940–1963. Ed. Gregory Maximoff et al. Organ of the United Federation of Russian Workers' Organizations of the United States and Canada.

The Demonstrator. Home, Wash., 1903–1908. Ed. James F. Morton, Jr. "A Weekly Peri-odical of Fact, Thought and Comment."

El Despertar. New York, 1891–1902. Ed. Pedro Esteve. "Periodico quincenal dedicado a la defensa de los trabajadores."

Discontent. Home, Wash., 1898–1902. Ed. Charles L. Govan et al. "Mother of Progress."

Discussion. Detroit, 1937–1938. Ed. Laurance Labadie. "A Journal for Free Spirits."

L'Emancipazione. San Francisco, 1927–1932. Ed. Vincenzo Ferrero. "Mensile libertario del West."

L'Era Nuova. Paterson, N.J., 1908–1917. Ed. Ludovico Caminita et al. "Periodico setti-manale anarchico."

Eresia. New York, 1928–1932. Ed. Enrico Arrigoni (Brand). "Per l'affrancamento dell'idividuo."

The Fifth Estate. Detroit, 1976–present. "Non Serviam."

The Firebrand. Portland, Ore., 1895–1897. Ed. Henry Addis, Abe Isaak, and A. J. Pope. "For the Burning Away of the Cobwebs of Ignorance and Superstition."

Fraye Arbeter Shtime. New York, 1890–1977. Ed. Saul Yanovsky, Joseph Cohen, Ahrne Thorne et al. "Let the Voice of the People Be Heard!"

Di Fraye Gezelshaft. New York, 1895–1900, 1910–1911. Ed. Saul Yanovsky et al.

Di Frayhayt. New York, 1913–1914. Ed. L. Barone. Organ of the Federated Anarchist Groups.

Frayhayt. New York, 1918. Ed. Jacob Abrams et al. "Monthly Journal of Revolutionary Propaganda." "That Government is Best Which Governs Not at All." "The Only Just War is the Social Revolution."

The Free Commune. Manchester; Leeds, 1898–1899. Ed. William MacQueen.

Free Society. San Francisco; Chicago; New York, 1897–1904. Ed. Abe Isaak. "An Advo-cate of Communal Life and Individual Sovereignty."

Freedom. London, 1886–present. Founded by Peter Kropotkin et al.

Freedom. San Francisco, 1910–1911. Ed. Eric B. Morton. "A Monthly Journal Devoted to the Destruction of Superstition and the Uplift of the Under Dog."

Freedom. New York; Stelton, N.J., 1919. Ed. Harry Kelly et al. "A Journal of Constructive Anarchism."

Freedom. New York, 1933–1934. Ed. Harry Kelly, Moritz Jagendorf, and Louis Raymond. "An Anarchist Weekly."

Freeland. New York; Bow, Wash.; San Francisco, 1904, 1909. Ed. Alexander Horr.

Freiheit. New York, 1882–1910. Ed. Johann Most. "Internationales Organ der communistischen Anarchisten deutsche Sprache."

Germinal. Chicago, 1926–1930. Ed. Hugo Rolland, Silvestro Spada et al.

Golgota. San Francisco, 1927. Ed. Vincenzo Ferrero.

Golos Ssyl'nykh i Zakliuchennykh Russkikh Anarkhistov. New York, 1913–1914. Organ of the Anarchist Red Cross.

Golos Truda. New York, 1911–1917. Ed. Avgust Rode-Chervinsky, Maksim Raevsky et al. Organ of the Federation of Unions of Russian Workers of the United States and Canada.

Golos Truzhenika. Chicago, 1918–1927. Ed. Yakov Sanzhur, Gregory Maximoff et al.

L'Internazionale. Ancona, 1966–present. Ed. Luciano Farinelli et al.

Intesa Libertaria. New York, 1939–1940. Ed. Virgilio Gozzoli. "Organ dei gruppi del Nord America."

Khleb i Volia. Geneva, 1903–1905; Paris, 1909.

Khleb i Volia. New York, 1919. Ed. L. Lipotkin (Lazarev). Organ of the Union of Russian Workers of the United States and Canada.

Kolokol. New York, 1918. Ed. Adolf Schnabel. Organ of the Group of Russian Anarchists in America. "Dukh razrushchaiushchii—dukh sozidaiushchii."

Land and Liberty. Hayward, Calif.; San Francisco, 1914–1915. Ed. W. C. Owen. "An Anti-Slavery Journal."

Left and Right. New York, 1965–1967. Ed. Murray N. Rothbard et al. "A Journal of Libertarian Thought."

Le Libertaire. Paris, 1895–1956. Ed. Sébastien Faure, Pierre Martin et al.

The Libertarian. Toronto, 1968–1969. Ed. Attilio Bortolotti. Published by the Toronto Libertarian Group.

Libertarian Views. New York, 1941. Ed. Sidney and Clara Solomon. "A Libertarian Communist Publication."

Il Libertario. Toronto, 1933–1935. Ed. Attilio Bortolotti. Published by the Gruppo Libertario di Toronto.

Liberty. Boston; New York, 1881–1908. Ed. Benjamin R. Tucker. "Liberty, Not the Daughter but the Mother of Order."

Looking Forward! Stelton, N.J., 1937–1938. Published by the Stelton Anarchist Youth Group.

Lucifer. Valley Falls, Kans; Topeka, Kans.; Chicago, 1883–1907. Ed. Moses Harman. "Devoted to the Emancipation of Women from Sex Slavery."

Man! San Francisco, 1933–1940. Ed. Marcus Graham. "A Journal of the Anarchist Ideal and Movement."

Il Martello. New York, 1916–1946. Ed. Carlo Tresca. "Settimanale di battaglia."

The Match! Tucson, 1969–present. Ed. Fred Woodworth.

The Modern School. New York; Stelton, N.J., 1912–1922. Ed. Carl Zigrosser et al. "A Monthly Magazine Devoted to Advanced Ideas in Education." "To Retain the World for the Masters They Cripple the Souls of the Children."

Mother Earth. New York, 1906–1917. Ed. Emma Goldman and Alexander Berkman. "Monthly Magazine Devoted to Social Science and Literature."

Mother Earth. Craryville, N.Y.; Stelton, N.J., 1933–1934. Ed. John G. Scott and Jo Ann Wheeler. "A Libertarian Farm Paper Devoted to the Life of Thoreauvian Anarchy." "Proclaim Liberty Throughout the Land!"

Nabat. Kharkov, 1917–1920. Organ of the Nabat Confederation in the Ukraine.

Nabat. New York, 1918. Ed. Adolf Schnabel. Organ of the Federation of Unions of Russian Workers in America. "Dukh razrushchaiushchii—dukh sozidaiushchii."

The Needle. San Francisco, 1956. Ed. David Koven.

The New Era. Home, Wash., 1897. Ed. Oliver A. Verity.

New Trends. New York, 1945–1946. Ed. Alexander Schapiro. "A Magazine of Modern Thought and Action."

News from Libertarian Spain. New York, 1977–1980. Ed. Abe Bluestein, Murray Bookchin, Sam Dolgoff, and Gabriel Javsicas. Sponsored by the Libertarian Labor Fund.

Nihil. San Francisco, 1908–1909. Ed. Adolfo Antonelli. "Individualista-anarchico."

The Official Bulletin of the Sacco-Vanzetti Defense Committee. Boston, 1925–1928. Ed. Gardner Jackson et al.

Open Vistas. Stelton, N.J., 1925. Ed. Hippolyte Havel and Joseph Ishill. "A Bi-Monthly of Life and Letters."

Out at Sunrise. Alicia, Mich., 1936.

The Petrel. San Francisco, 1904. Ed. Samuel Mintz and Eugene Travaglio. "An Anarchist-Communist Periodical."

P'ing-teng. San Francisco, 1927–1929. Published by the Equality Group.

La Plebe. New Kensington, Pa., 1906–1909. Ed. Carlo Tresca.

Politics. New York, 1944–1949. Ed. Dwight Macdonald.

Pravda. Brooklyn, N.Y., 1917. Ed. Mikhail Raiva. "Antireligioznyi ezhemesiachnik."

Probuzhdenie. Detroit, 1927–1939. Ed. E. Z. Moravsky and M. I. Rubezhanin. Publication of Russian Trade Organizations of the United States and Canada. "Organ svobodnoi mysli."

Il Proletario. New York, 1905–1942. Ed. Arturo Giovannitti et al. An edition was published in Somerville, Mass., in 1935.

La Protesta Umana. Chicago; San Francisco, 1900–1905. Ed. Giuseppe Ciancabilla and Eugene Travaglio. "Periodico settimanale dell'anarchismo."

La Questione Sociale. Paterson, N.J., 1895–1908. Ed. Giuseppe Ciancabilla, Luigi Galleani et al. "Periodico socialista-anarchico."

El Quixote. Barcelona, 1937. Ed. Federico Arcos, Diego Camacho, Germinal Gracia, and Liberto Sarrau.

Rabochaia Mysl'. New York, 1916–1917. Ed. Adolf Schnabel. "Organ Vol'nykh Rabochikh Ameriki."

Rabochii i Krest'ianin. New York, 1918–1919. Ed. Alexander Brailovsky et al. Organ of the Soviet of Workers' Deputies.

Rabochii Put'. Berlin, 1923. Ed. Gregory Maximoff.

Rassvet. New York; Chicago, 1924–1937.

The Rebel. Boston, 1895–1896. Ed. C. W. Mowbray, Harry Kelly, and N. H. Berman. "A Monthly Journal Devoted to the Exposition of Anarchist Communism."

Rebel Youth. New York, 1934. Ed. Irving Sterling. Published by the Vanguard Juniors.

Regeneración. Los Angeles, 1910–1918. Ed. Ricardo Flores Magón. "Periodico revolucionario."

Resistance. New York, 1947–1954. Ed. David Thoreau Wieck et al. "Against Oppression—For Freedom!"

Retort. Bearsville, New York, 1942–1951. Ed. Holley Cantine, Jr., and Dachine Rainer. "A Quarterly of Social Philosophy and the Arts." "An Anarchist Review."

Le Réveil. Geneva, 1900–1947. Ed. Luigi Bertoni.

Revolt. New York, 1916. Ed. Hippolyte Havel.

The Rising Youth. New York, 1928–1929. Ed. Sara and Elizabeth Goodman. Published by the Rising Youth Group. "A Voice of Youth without the Authority of Age."

The Road to Freedom. Stelton, N.J.; New York, 1924–1932. Ed. Hippolyte Havel and Walter Starrett (W. S. Van Valkenburgh). "A Periodical of Anarchist Thought, Work, and Literature."

La Scolta. San Francisco, 1926. Ed. Vincenzo Ferrero. "Publicazione anarchica di difesa e avanzamento sociale."

Di Shtime fun di rusishe gefangene. New York, 1912–1916. Organ of the Anarchist Red Cross.

Der Shturm. New York, 1917–1918. Ed. Jacob Abrams et al.

Social Anarchism. Baltimore, 1980–present. Ed. Howard J. Ehrlich. "A Journal of Practice and Theory."

The Social War. New York, 1913. Ed. Robert Warwick and Charles Plunkett. "A Revolutionary Weekly Advocate of Free Communism."

Solidarity. New York, 1892–1898. Ed. F. S. Merlino and J. H. Edelmann. "An International Review of Anarchist Communism."

Di Sonrayz Shtime. Alicia, Mich., 1934.

Der Sozialist. Berlin, 1891–1899, 1909–1915. Ed. Gustav Landauer.

Spanish Revolution. New York, 1936–1937. Published by the United Libertarian Organizations.

The Storm! New York, 1976–1988. Ed. Mark A. Sullivan. "A Journal for Free Spirits."

Sturmvogel. New York, 1897–1899. Ed. Claus Timmermann.

Sunrise News. Alicia, Mich., 1934–1935.

Svobodnoe Obshchestvo. Toronto, 1920–1921. Ed. V. I. Dodokin. Organ of Anarchist Associations. "Ot kazhdogo po sposobnosti—kazhdym po potrebnostiam." "Dukh razrushchaiushchii—dukh sozidaiushchii."

The Syndicalist. Chicago, 1913. Ed. Jay Fox.

Truth. San Francisco, 1882–1884. Ed. Burnette G. Haskell. "A Journal for the Poor."

Umanità Nova. Rome, 1946–present. Organ of the Italian Anarchist Federation.

Vanguard. New York, 1932–1939. Ed. Abe Bluestein et al. Published by the Vanguard Group.

Varhayt. New York, 1889. Published by the Pioneers of Liberty Group.

Views & Comments. New York, 1955–1965. Ed. Sam Weiner (Dolgoff). The last number (Summer 1965) is titled *Towards Anarchism.*

The Voice of the Children. Stelton, N.J., 1929–1935. Edited by the Children of the Modern School.

The Voice of Labour. Liverpool, 1913.

The Voice of Labour. London, 1914–1916. Ed. Fred Dunn.

Volna. New York, 1920–1924. Ed. V. I. Dodokin and L. Lipotkin (Lazarev). Organ of Anarcho-Communists. "Ot kazhdogo po sposobnosti—kazhdym po potrebnostiam." "Dukh razrushchaiushchii—dukh sozidaiushchii."

Vostochnaia Zaria. Pittsburgh, 1916. Ed. Petr Rybin (Zonov) et al.

Walka. Warsaw, 1930s.

Why? Tacoma, Wash., 1913–1914. Ed. Eugene Travaglio et al.

Why? New York, 1942–1947. "A Bulletin of Free Enquiry." "An Anarchist Bulletin."

The Woman Rebel. New York, 1914. Ed. Margaret H. Sanger. "No Gods, No Masters."

The Word. Glasgow, 1938–1965. Ed. Guy A. Aldred.

Wu-cheng-fu kung-ch'an yüeh-k'an. San Francisco, 1934. Ed. R. Jones. Published by the Anarchist Communist Alliance. "Anarchist Communist Socialist Revolution! Revolution!"

Der Yunyon Arbeter. New York, 1925–1927. Ed. Simon Farber. Published by the Anarchist Group, I.L.G.W.U.

Zherminal. London, 1900–1912. Ed. Rudolf Rocker.

Zherminal. Brooklyn, N.Y., 1913–1916? Ed. Zalman Deanin. Published by the Germinal Group.

8. Peter Kropotkin, Michael Bakunin, and Emma Goldman, Libertarian Book Club Catalog, Summer 1988 (Paul Avrich Collection)

Further Reading

THE LITERATURE on anarchism is so immense that a comprehensive list of sources would fill several large volumes. The present bibliography makes no attempt at completeness. It includes, rather, only works that are of basic importance or that shed valuable light on the topics and personalities dealt with in the interviews. Although the emphasis is on books in English, key works in other languages are included. Additional sources, both printed and manuscript, are cited in the notes.

In addition to general works on anarchism, this bibliography contains sections on specific topics, including pioneers, Emma Goldman, Sacco and Vanzetti, schools and colonies, and ethnic anarchists.

GENERAL WORKS ON ANARCHISM

Avrich, Paul. *Anarchist Portraits*. Princeton: Princeton University Press, 1988.

Berman, Paul, ed. *Quotations from the Anarchists*. New York: Praeger, 1972.

Creagh, Ronald. *Histoire de l'anarchisme aux États-Unis d'Amérique*. Grenoble: Éditions La Pensée Sauvage, 1981.

Dubovsky, Melvyn. *We Shall Be All: A History of the Industrial Workers of the World*. Chicago: Quadrangle Books, 1969.

Dulles, John W. F. *Anarchists and Communists in Brazil, 1900–1935*. Austin: University of Texas Press, 1973.

Edwards, Stewart. *The Paris Commune, 1871*. London: Eyre & Spottiswoode, 1971.

Eltzbacher, Paul. *Anarchism: Exponents of the Anarchist Philosophy*. New York: Libertarian Book Club, 1960.

Frost, Richard H. *The Mooney Case*. Stanford: Stanford University Press, 1968.

Graham, Marcus, ed. *Man! An Anthology of Anarchist Ideas, Essays, Poetry and Commentaries*. London: Cienfuegos Press, 1974.

Guérin, Daniel. *Anarchism: From Theory to Practice*. New York: Monthly Review Press, 1970.

———, ed. *Ni dieu, ni maître: Anthologie historique du mouvement anarchiste*. Lausanne: La Cité, 1969.

Hart, John M. *Anarchism and the Mexican Working Class, 1860–1931*. Austin: University of Texas Press, 1978.

Horowitz, Irving L., ed. *The Anarchists*. New York: Dell, 1964.

Joll, James. *The Anarchists*. London: Eyre & Spottiswoode, 1964.

Kedward, Roderick. *The Anarchists: The Men Who Shocked an Era*. New York: American Heritage Press, 1971.

Kornbluh, Joyce L., ed. *Rebel Voices: An IWW Anthology*. Expanded ed., Chicago: Charles H. Kerr Publishing Company, 1988.

Krimerman, Leonard I., and Lewis Perry, eds. *Patterns of Anarchy*. Garden City, N.Y.: Anchor Books, 1966.

Lang, Lucy Robins. *Tomorrow Is Beautiful*. New York: Macmillan, 1948.

Maitron, Jean. *Le mouvement anarchiste en France.* 2 vols., Paris: Maspero, 1975.

Marsh, Margaret S. *Anarchist Women, 1870–1920.* Philadelphia: Temple University Press, 1981.

Marshall, Peter. *Demanding the Impossible: A History of Anarchism.* London: Harper Collins, 1992.

Nettlau, Max. *Bibliographie de l'anarchie.* Paris: Les Temps Nouveaux, 1897.

———. *Geschichte der Anarchie.* 5 vols., Glashütten im Taunus: Verlag Detlev Auvermann; Vaduz: Topos Verlag, 1972–1984.

Reichert, William O. *Partisans of Freedom: A Study in American Anarchism.* Bowling Green, Ohio: Bowling Green University Popular Press, 1976.

Renshaw, Patrick. *The Wobblies: The Story of Syndicalism in the United States.* Garden City, N.Y.: Anchor Books, 1967.

Rocker, Rudolf. *Anarcho-Syndicalism: Theory and Practice.* Enlarged ed., London: Pluto Press, 1989.

Shatz, Marshall S., ed. *The Essential Works of Anarchism.* New York: Bantam Books, 1971.

Silverman, Henry J., ed. *American Radical Thought: The Libertarian Tradition.* Lexington, Mass.: D.C. Heath, 1970.

Walter, Nicolas. *About Anarchism.* London: Freedom Press, 1969.

Woodcock, George. *Anarchism: A History of Libertarian Ideas and Movements.* Cleveland: World Publishing Company, 1962.

———, ed. *The Anarchist Reader.* London: Fontana, 1977.

Zoccoli, Ettore. *L'Anarchia: gli agitatori, le idee, i fatti.* Turin: Bocca Editori, 1907.

PIONEERS

Avrich, Paul. *The Haymarket Tragedy.* Princeton: Princeton University Press, 1984.

Cahm, Caroline. *Kropotkin and the Rise of Revolutionary Anarchism, 1872–1886.* Cambridge: Cambridge University Press, 1989.

Carr, E. H. *Michael Bakunin.* New York: Vintage Books, 1961.

Confino, Michael, ed. *Daughter of a Revolutionary: Natalie Herzen and the Bakunin/ Nechayev Circle.* La Salle, Ill.: Open Court, 1974.

David, Henry. *The History of the Haymarket Affair.* New York: Farrar & Rinehart, 1936.

Dolgoff, Sam, ed. *Bakunin on Anarchy.* New York: Knopf, 1972.

Dunbar, Gary S. *Élisée Reclus: Historian of Nature.* Hamden, Conn.: Archon Books, 1978.

Godwin, William. *The Anarchist Writings of William Godwin.* Ed. Peter Marshall. London: Freedom Press, 1986.

———. *Enquiry Concerning Political Justice.* New York: Penguin Books, 1976.

The Haymarket Scrapbook. Ed. Dave Roediger and Franklin Rosemont. Chicago: Charles H. Kerr Publishing Company, 1986.

Hoffman, Robert L. *Revolutionary Justice: The Social and Political Theory of P.-J. Proudhon.* Urbana: University of Illinois Press, 1972.

Ishill, Joseph, ed. *Élisée and Elie Reclus: In Memoriam.* Berkeley Heights, N.J.: The Oriole Press, 1927.

———, ed. *Peter Kropotkin: The Rebel, Thinker and Humanitarian.* Berkeley Heights, N.J.: Free Spirit Press, 1923.

Kropotkin, Peter. *The Conquest of Bread.* London: Chapman & Hall, 1906.

———. *The Essential Kropotkin*. Ed. Emile Capouya and Keitha Tompkins. New York: Liveright, 1975.

———. *Fields, Factories and Workshops*. Revised ed., London: Nelson, 1913.

———. *Kropotkin's Revolutionary Pamphlets*. Ed. Roger N. Baldwin. New York: Vanguard Press, 1927.

———. *Memoirs of a Revolutionist*. Boston: Houghton Mifflin, 1899.

———. *Mutual Aid: A Factor of Evolution*. London: Heinemann, 1902.

———. *Selected Writings on Anarchism and Revolution*. Ed. Martin A. Miller. Cambridge, Mass.: MIT Press, 1970.

Lehning, Arthur, ed. *Michael Bakunin: Selected Writings*. London: Jonathan Cape, 1973.

Link-Salinger, Ruth. *Gustav Landauer: Philosopher of Utopia*. Indianapolis: Hackett Publishing Company, 1977.

Lunn, Eugene. *Prophet of Community: The Romantic Socialism of Gustav Landauer*. Berkeley: University of California Press, 1973.

Marshall, Peter. *William Godwin*. New Haven: Yale University Press, 1984.

Martin, James J. *Men Against the State: The Expositors of Individualist Anarchism in America, 1827–1908*. Revised ed., Colorado Springs: Ralph Myles, 1970.

Maurer, Charles B. *Call to Revolution: The Mystical Anarchism of Gustav Landauer*. Detroit: Wayne State University Press, 1971.

Maximoff, G. P., ed. *The Political Philosophy of Bakunin: Scientific Anarchism*. Glencoe, Ill.: The Free Press, 1953.

Miller, Martin A. *Kropotkin*. Chicago: University of Chicago Press, 1976.

Proudhon, Pierre-Joseph. *Selected Writings of Pierre-Joseph Proudhon*. Ed. Stewart Edwards. Garden City, N.Y.: Anchor Books, 1969.

Pyziur, Eugene. *The Doctrine of Anarchism of Michael A. Bakunin*. Milwaukee: Marquette University Press, 1955.

Rocker, Rudolf. *Johann Most: das Leben eines Rebellen*. Berlin: Der Syndikalist, 1924.

———. *The London Years*. London: Robert Anscombe, 1956.

———. *Nationalism and Culture*. Los Angeles: Rocker Publications Committee, 1937.

———. *Pioneers of American Freedom*. Los Angeles: Rocker Publications Committee, 1949.

Schuster, Eunice M. *Native American Anarchism: A Study of Left-Wing American Individualism*. Northampton, Mass.: Smith College, 1932.

Sears, Hal D. *The Sex Radicals: Free Love in High Victorian America*. Lawrence: The Regents Press of Kansas, 1977.

Stirner, Max. *The Ego and His Own*. New York: Benjamin R. Tucker, 1907.

Tucker, Benjamin R. *Instead of a Book: By a Man Too Busy to Write One*. New York: Benjamin R. Tucker, 1893.

Woodcock, George, and Ivan Avakumović. *The Anarchist Prince: A Biographical Study of Peter Kropotkin*. London: T. V. Boardman, 1950.

EMMA GOLDMAN

Avrich, Paul. *An American Anarchist: The Life of Voltairine de Cleyre*. Princeton: Princeton University Press, 1978.

Berkman, Alexander. *The Bolshevik Myth (Diary 1920–1922)*. Enlarged ed., London: Pluto Press, 1989.

Berkman, Alexander. *Now and After: The ABC of Communist Anarchism*. New York: Vanguard Press, 1929. Also published as *What Is Communist Anarchism?*
_____. *Prison Memoirs of an Anarchist*. New York: Mother Earth Publishing Association, 1912.
Bruns, Roger A. *The Damndest Radical: The Life and World of Ben Reitman*. Urbana: University of Illinois Press, 1987.
Drinnon, Richard. *Rebel in Paradise: A Biography of Emma Goldman*. Chicago: University of Chicago Press, 1961.
De Cleyre, Voltairine. *Selected Works of Voltairine de Cleyre*. Ed. Alexander Berkman. New York: Mother Earth Publishing Association, 1914.
Falk, Candace. *Love, Anarchy, and Emma Goldman*. New York: Holt, Rinehart and Winston, 1984.
Goldman, Emma. *Anarchism and Other Essays*. New York: Mother Earth Publishing Association, 1910.
_____. *Living My Life*. New York: Knopf, 1931.
_____. *My Disillusionment in Russia*. London: C. W. Daniel, 1925.
_____. *The Social Significance of the Modern Drama*. Boston: R. G. Badger, 1914.
Goldman, Emma, and Alexander Berkman. *Nowhere at Home: Letters from Exile of Emma Goldman and Alexander Berkman*. Ed. Richard and Anna Maria Drinnon. New York: Schocken Books, 1975.
Peirats, José. *Emma Goldman: Anarquista de ambos mundos*. Madrid: Campo Abierto Ediciones, 1978.
Porter, David, ed. *Vision on Fire: Emma Goldman on the Spanish Revolution*. New Paltz, N.Y.: Commonground Press, 1983.
Shulman, Alix Kates, ed. *Red Emma Speaks: An Emma Goldman Reader*. New York: Schocken Books, 1983.
_____. *To the Barricades: The Anarchist Life of Emma Goldman*. New York: Crowell, 1971.
Wexler, Alice. *Emma Goldman: An Intimate Life*. New York: Pantheon Books, 1984.
_____. *Emma Goldman in Exile: From the Russian Revolution to the Spanish Civil War*. Boston: Beacon Press, 1989.

SACCO AND VANZETTI

Avrich, Paul. *Sacco and Vanzetti: The Anarchist Background*. Princeton: Princeton University Press, 1991.
Creagh, Ronald. *Sacco et Vanzetti*. Paris: Editions La Découverte, 1984.
Ehrmann, Herbert B. *The Case That Will Not Die: Commonwealth vs. Sacco and Vanzetti*. Boston: Little, Brown, 1969.
Felix, David. *Protest: Sacco-Vanzetti and the Intellectuals*. Bloomington: Indiana University Press, 1965.
Feuerlicht, Roberta S. *Justice Crucified: The Story of Sacco and Vanzetti*. New York: McGraw-Hill, 1977.
Fraenkel, Osmond K. *The Sacco-Vanzetti Case*. New York: Knopf, 1931.
Frankfurter, Felix. *The Case of Sacco and Vanzetti: A Critical Analysis for Lawyers and Laymen*. Boston: Little, Brown, 1927.
Gallagher, Dorothy. *All the Right Enemies: The Life and Murder of Carlo Tresca*. New Brunswick, N.J.: Rutgers University Press, 1988.

Joughin, G. Louis, and Edmund M. Morgan. *The Legacy of Sacco and Vanzetti*. New York: Harcourt, Brace, 1948.

Lyons, Eugene. *The Life and Death of Sacco and Vanzetti*. New York: International Publishers, 1927.

Montgomery, Robert H. *Sacco-Vanzetti: The Murder and the Myth*. New York: Devin-Adair, 1960.

Pernicone, Nunzio. *Italian Anarchism, 1864–1892*. Princeton: Princeton University Press, 1993.

Richards, Vernon, ed. *Errico Malatesta: His Life and Ideas*. London: Freedom Press, 1965.

Russell, Francis. *Sacco and Vanzetti: The Case Resolved*. New York: Harper & Row, 1986.

————. *Tragedy in Dedham: The Story of the Sacco-Vanzetti Case*. New York: McGraw-Hill, 1962.

Sacco, Nicola, and Bartolomeo Vanzetti. *The Letters of Sacco and Vanzetti*. Ed. Marion Denman Frankfurter and Gardner Jackson. New York: Viking, 1928.

Sacco-Vanzetti: Developments and Reconsiderations—1979. Boston: Boston Public Library, 1982.

Sinclair, Upton. *Boston: A Documentary Novel of the Sacco-Vanzetti Case*. 2 vols., New York: Albert and Charles Boni, 1928.

Un trentennio di attività anarchica (1914–1945). Cesena: Antistato, 1953.

Vanzetti, Bartolomeo. *The Story of a Proletarian Life*. Boston: Sacco-Vanzetti Defense Committee, 1923.

Young, William, and David E. Kaiser. *Postmortem: New Evidence in the Case of Sacco and Vanzetti*. Amherst: University of Massachusetts Press, 1985.

SCHOOLS AND COLONIES

Avrich, Paul. *The Modern School Movement: Anarchism and Education in the United States*. Princeton: Princeton University Press, 1980.

Cohen, Joseph J. *In Quest of Heaven: The Story of the Sunrise Co-operative Farm Community*. New York: Sunrise History Publishing Committee, 1957.

Cohen, Joseph J., and Alexis C. Ferm. *The Modern School of Stelton*. Stelton, N.J.: The Modern School Association of North America, 1925.

Ferm, Elizabeth B. *Freedom in Education*. New York: Lear Publishers, 1949.

Ferrer y Guardia, Francisco. *The Origin and Ideals of the Modern School*. London: Watts, 1913.

LeWarne, Charles P. *Utopias on Puget Sound, 1885–1915*. Seattle: University of Washington Press, 1975.

Modern School of Stelton: Twenty-Fifth Anniversary, 1915–1940. Stelton, N.J.: The Modern School Association, 1940.

Spring, Joel H. *A Primer of Libertarian Education*. New York: Free Life Editions, 1975.

Veysey, Laurence. *The Communal Experience: Anarchist and Mystical Counter-Cultures in America*. New York: Harper, 1973.

ETHNIC ANARCHISTS

Arshinov, P. A. *History of the Makhnovist Movement (1918–1921)*. Detroit and Chicago: Black & Red, 1974.

Avrich, Paul, ed. *The Anarchists in the Russian Revolution.* Ithaca, N.Y.: Cornell University Press, 1973.

———. *Kronstadt 1921.* Princeton: Princeton University Press, 1970.

———. *The Russian Anarchists.* Princeton: Princeton University Press, 1967.

Bolleten, Burnett. *The Spanish Civil War: Revolution and Counterrevolution.* Chapel Hill: University of North Carolina Press, 1991.

Bookchin, Murray. *The Spanish Anarchists: The Heroic Years, 1868–1936.* New York: Free Life Editions, 1977.

Brenan, Gerald. *The Spanish Labyrinth.* London: Cambridge University Press, 1943.

Cohen, Joseph J. *Di yidish-anarkhistishe bavegung in Amerike.* Philadelphia: Radical Library, 1945.

D'Agostino, Anthony. *Marxism and the Russian Anarchists.* San Francisco: Germinal Press, 1977.

Esenwein, George R. *Anarchist Ideology and the Working-Class Movement in Spain, 1868–1898.* Berkeley: University of California Press, 1989.

Fishman, William J. *East End Jewish Radicals, 1875–1914.* London: Duckworth, 1975.

Kaplan, Temma. *Anarchists of Andalusia, 1868–1903.* Princeton: Princeton University Press, 1977.

Lang, Olga. *Pa Chin and His Writings.* Cambridge, Mass.: Harvard University Press, 1967.

Maximoff, G. P. *The Guillotine at Work: Twenty Years of Terror in Russia.* Chicago: Alexander Berkman Aid Fund, 1940.

Mintz, Jerome P. *The Anarchists of Casas Viejas.* Chicago: University of Chicago Press, 1982.

Polenberg, Richard. *Fighting Faiths: The Abrams Case, the Supreme Court, and Free Speech.* New York: Viking, 1987.

Scalapino, Robert A., and George T. Yu. *The Chinese Anarchist Movement.* Berkeley: Center for Chinese Studies, University of California, 1961.

Volin [V. M. Eikhenbaum]. *The Unknown Revolution, 1917–1921.* Revised ed., Detroit and Chicago: Black & Red, 1974.

Index

Page numbers in boldface refer to interviews. Page numbers in italics refer to figures.

Ciancabilla, Giuseppe, 161, 164
Ciminieri, Antonio, 152
Ciofalo, Andrea, 133, 137–38, 152
Ciofalo, Ottavio, 138
Circolo Volontà, 111, 146, 173
City of Hope, 310, 312
Clarion, The (journal), 425, 451, 516n.468
Clarion Group, 445
Clemenceau, Georges, 10
Clua, Pedro, 396
Coacci, Ferruccio, 130
Cocchio (anarchist from Toronto), 185
Coda, Emilio, 97, 118, 124, 130, 131, 135, 138, 152
Cogito, Ergo Sum (newspaper), 164
Cohen, Henry, 10, 32
Cohen, Henry D., 337
Cohen, J. L., 81, 186
Cohen, Joseph J.: anarchist philosophy of, 249; deference to, 304; as editor of Fraye Arbeter Shtime, 61, 317, 352, 376, 423; and education reform, 195, 445; at Ferrer Center, 201, 212, 220, 240, 278; financial position of, 41; at Mohegan Colony, 263; opinion of Marcus Graham, 488n.110; personality of, 75, 230, 233, 240, 305, 308, 336, 352, 376, 380, 386, 389, 430, 441; publications by, 223; at Radical Library, 224, 306; reputation as a speaker, 74; at Stelton Colony, 229, 257, 263, 279, 287, 307, 338, 347, 423, 438; summer camp run by, 448; at Sunrise colony, 196, 229, 241, 255, 297–300, 302–9 passim, 310, 311–12, 349, 380, 435, 438, 441, 442
Cohen, Sam, 165, 167
Cohen, Shprintse, 429–30, 431
Cohen, Sophie, 224, 311, 448
Cohn, Dr. Michael A., 41, 211, 329, 350, 351, 433, 458
Colarossi, Umberto, 110
Colarossi, Vincenzo, 110, 121
Cole, A. L., 161
Coleman, Emily Holmes ("Demi"), 71
collectivist anarchism: of Bakunin, 3, 4; condemned by Kropotkin, 4; description of, 3; disdained by individualist anarchists, 5; of Most, 3–4
Colton, James, 495n.187
Colum, Padraic, 288
Cominsky, Lena Goldman, 53
Commins, Louis ("Beenie"), 53
Commins, Ruth ("Ruthie"), 53
Commins, Saxe (Isidore Cominsky), 53, 54, 69, 71

Committee for Nonviolent Action, 476
Committee for the Protection of the Foreign-Born, 148
Committee for the Vindication of Sacco and Vanzetti, 500n.262
Committee of Non-Violent Revolution, 425
Committee to Aid Political Prisoners, 390
Commonwealth College, 211
Communal Experience, The (Veysey), 227
communism: anarchists converted to, 210, 239, 242, 250, 279, 290, 348, 369, 415, 424; opposition to, 38, 162, 210, 252, 270, 298, 318; principles of, 64–65; as a workable system, 39
communist anarchism: in America, 5; of Berkman, 250; of Charles Plunkett, 215; description of, 4; Frank Brand's comments on, 174; of Goldman, 15; Helen Tuft Bailie's sympathies for, 15; of Kropotkin, 4, 16, 215, 428–29; of Most, 4; published in Eresia, 174
Communist International (Comintern), 143, 172
Communist Labor Party, 506n.347
Communist Manifesto, The, 214
Communist Party, 23, 38, 250, 500n.256, 507n.360, 510–11n.397
Communist Youth League, 387
community control, 428
companionate marriage, 76
Comune, La (journal), 159
Conason, Emanuel Voltaire ("Red"), 224, 308–9
Confederación Nacional del Trabajo-Federación Anarquista Iberica (CNT-FAI), 48, 66, 82, 148, 400, 402–4, 422, 439, 451, 504n.321, 516n.469
Coniglio, Alfonso, 158, 398
Connolly, Gilbert, 448, 451
Connolly, James, 448
Conquest of Bread (Kropotkin), 146, 359, 436
conscientious objectors: Charles Plunkett as, 218; in Mexico (1917), 102, 105–6, 110, 117, 129, 139, 156, 254, 496n.205, 497–98n.225, 498nn.228, 232, 499nn.241, 250, 501n.274; Russian, 63
Conti, Joe, 174
Controcorrente (journal), 140, 150, 174–75, 316, 320, 497n.212
Contro-pelo, Il (journal), 158
Cook, Cassius V., 32, 160, 333, 370
Cook, Evadna, 32
Cook, Fred J., 126–27
Cook, Johanna, 198
Coolidge, Calvin, 94, 504n.312

Tedeschi, Adele Zambelli, 93, 96
Tedeschi, Joseph, 93
Tempeste Sociali (Gori), 98, 109
Tennessee Valley Authority (TVA), 258
Teplov (a Socialist Revolutionary), 322
Terentieva, Nadya, 358
Terra (journal), 161
terrorism: and anarchism, 330, 427; Berkman's
    views on, 218, 226, 335; of Ferrer Center an-
    archists, 202; of Galleani, 91, 146, 159; of
    Johann Most, 4; of Maximalists, 355, 357;
    and revolution, 272, 350; of Rocker, 324;
    Woodworth's views on, 475; Yanovsky's
    views on, 350
Terzani, Athos, 450
Textile Workers' Union of America, 513n.426
Thayer, Webster, 87, 88, 103–4, 106, 114, 118,
    122–23, 130
theater: avant-garde theater, 7; Spanish, 400.
    See also Gori, Pietro; O'Neill, Eugene;
    Provincetown Players/Playhouse
Third International. *See* Communist Interna-
    tional (Comintern)
Thomas, Norman, 426
Thompson, Big, 344
Thompson, William G., 114, 115, 122, 123,
    133, 499–500n.251
Thoreau, Henry David, 62, 63, 144, 203, 248,
    258, 266, 267, 396, 440, 483n.72
Thorne (Thorenberg), Ahrne, 50, 51, 79, 80–
    83, 185, 186, 187, 299, 318, 359, 364
Thorne, Paula, 80, 81, 82
Thorpe, Johanna Altgeld Schwab ("Jennie"),
    23
Thorpe, Dr. Milton W., 23
Tiempos Nuevos, Los (journal), 397
Tierra! (journal), 402
Tilden, Dr., 336
Tillman, Jim, 293
Timmermann, Claus, 56
TNT (journal), 506–7n.349
Tobia, Galileo, 137–38, 433
Tog, Der, 211
Toller, Ernst, 7, 455
Tolstoy, Leo, 6, 63, 161, 162, 170, 218, 231,
    275, 335, 353, 369, 370, 430, 452, 480n.37,
    484n.79, 511–12n.408; nephew of, 10
Tone, Yat, 267, 408, 410, 411, 424, 444
Towards Anarchism (journal), 425, 427
Toynbee Hall settlement house, 285
Tragedy in Dedham (Russell), 126
Transition (Durant), 226
Trask, Sherwood, 75, 230, 245, 437
Trauner (a Jewish anarchist), 210

Travaglio, Esther Hartz, 160–62
Travaglio, Eugene, 160–62, 164, 167, 168
Travis, Marie, 231
Tresca, Carlo: accusation against Ludovico
    Caminita, 159; and cooperation among all
    anarchists, 174; and defense of Sacco and
    Vanzetti, 122; Flynn as companion of,
    500n.256; as friend of Van Valkenburgh,
    421; influence among Italian anarchists,
    315; interaction with young anarchists,
    439, 445, 450, 458; and Italian Commit-
    tee for Political Victims, 501n.277; murder
    of, 64, 160, 493nn.163, 167; not in IWW,
    217; and Paterson strike (1913), 155; person-
    ality of, 143, 434; political philosophy of,
    146, 147, 165, 168; reputation as a speaker,
    319; and Sacco's guilt, 152; as a socialist,
    157
Trial of the Forty-Four Maximalists (1908),
    358
Triangle Shirtwaist Factory fire (1911), 339
Tridon, André, 221
Trotsky, Leon, 63, 311, 340, 353, 362, 384,
    442, 456, 493n.167
Truman, Harry S, 345
Trupin, Eva, 297
Trupin, Joel Sunrise, 297
Trupin, Philip, 296–99, 305
Truth (journal), 16
Truth Seeker, The (journal), 478n.25
Tsereteli, I. G., 387
Tucholsky, Kurt, 67
Tucker, Benjamin R.: admiration for the
    French, 9–10; as an atheist, 11; anti-
    German sentiments of, 9; attitude toward
    communism, 11; Bailie as associate of,
    14, 15; death of, 3, 6, 10; and individualist
    anarchism, 5–6, 63, 158, 459; influence of
    Stirner on, 5, 16; influence on Italian and
    Spanish anarchists, 158, 396; Labadie as as-
    sociate of, 15; laugh of, 12; move to France,
    9; opposition to collectivists and commu-
    nists, 5; pessimism of, 6, 11; as publisher of
    Liberty, 3, 5, 6; Schumm as associate of, 11,
    12, 37; as a translator, 5–6
Tucker, Oriole. *See* Riché, Oriole Tucker
Tucker, Pearl Johnson. *See* Johnson, Pearl
Tucker, Sonya, 333–34
Tufts, Anne Adams, 14
Turgenev, Ivan S., 154, 353, 462
Turkel, Pauline H., 50, 58–59, 261
Turner, Albert, 30–31
Turner, Archie, 421, 433
Turner, Charles, 31